Kirk Cameron Ray Comfort

The School of Biblical Evangelism

101 lessons

How to share your faith
simply, effectively, biblically...
the way Jesus did

BRIDGE LOGOS
FOUNDATION

Alachua, Florida 32615 USA

Bridge-Logos
Alachua, FL 32615, USA

The School of Biblical Evangelism
Ray Comfort and Kirk Cameron

Edited by Lynn Copeland

Design and production by Genesis Group, Inc. (www.genesis-group.net)

Cover by Joe Potter Design (joepotter.com)

Printed in the United States of America

ISBN 978-0-88270-968-0

Library of Congress Catalog Card Number: 2008940872

While every effort has been made to ensure the accuracy of this publication, if you feel you've found an error, please send a notice to lynncopeland@genesis-group.net.

G218.321.B.m910.35240

Dedicated to:
Darrel & Tammy Rundus

Special thanks to:
our good friend Mark Spence
(Dean of the online School of Biblical Evangelism)
for his invaluable contributions to this publication,
and Lynn Copeland
for her dedication and wonderful editorial work

Contents

Contents

PREFACE 9

HOW TO USE THESE LESSONS .10

1. The Forgotten Key to Biblical Evangelism 11
2. Making Grace Amazing 18
3. The Problem with the Modern Gospel 25
4. How to Confront Sinners 32
5. The Ten Commandments, Part 1 39
6. The Ten Commandments, Part 2 45
7. The Ten Commandments, Part 3 52
8. The Ten Commandments, Part 4 59
9. The Ten Commandments, Part 5 65
10. The Ten Commandments, Part 6 70
11. The Ten Commandments, Part 7 76
12. The Ten Commandments, Part 8 84
13. The Ten Commandments, Part 9 90
14. The Ten Commandments, Part 10 96
15. Our Ally: The Conscience 103
16. The Necessity of Repentance 110
17. Personal Witnessing: How Jesus Did It 116
18. The Sinner's Prayer .123
19. True and False Conversions 129
20. Hypocrisy 134

21. The Certainty of Judgment 139
22. Judgment Day 146
23. The Reality of Hell 154
24. Man's Sinful Condition 161
25. Our Primary Task 168
26. Fear of Man 173
27. The Empowering of the Holy Spirit 179
28. How to Capture the World's Attention 184
29. Gospel Tracts, Part 1 190
30. Gospel Tracts, Part 2 197
31. Personal Testimony 203
32. Creative Ways to Share Your Faith 209
33. How to Witness to Hurting People 215
34. Open-Air Preaching, Part 1 221
35. Open-Air Preaching, Part 2 228
36. Open-Air Preaching, Part 3 235
37. Faith, Part 1 242
38. Faith, Part 2 247
39. The Enemy, Part 1 253
40. The Enemy, Part 2 259
41. The Enemy, Part 3 265
42. The Enemy, Part 4 271
43. Prayer 278
44. The Survivor's Guide 285
45. Holiness 291
46. Water Baptism, Part 1 297
47. Water Baptism, Part 2 303
48. The Trinity 309
49. The Deity of Christ 317
50. The Holy Spirit 325
51. The Resurrection 332

52. The Bible, Part 1 339

53. The Bible, Part 2 345

54. The Bible, Part 3 352

55. The Bible, Part 4 358

56. Contradictions in the Bible 365

57. Prophecy 372

58. Messianic Prophecies, Part 1 378

59. Messianic Prophecies, Part 2 385

60. Non-Messianic Prophecies 392

61. Scientific Facts in the Bible, Part 1 399

62. Scientific Facts in the Bible, Part 2 405

63. Scientific Facts in the Bible, Part 3 411

64. Evolution, Part 1 418

65. Evolution, Part 2 426

66. Evolution, Part 3 433

67. Evolution, Part 4 442

68. Evolution, Part 5 450

69. Atheism 458

70. How to Prove the Existence of God 464

71. Atheist Obstacles 471

72. Atheists' Questions, Part 1 477

73. Atheists' Questions, Part 2 485

74. Relativism, Part 1 491

75. Relativism, Part 2 498

76. Reincarnation 510

77. Islam, Part 1 516

78. Islam, Part 2 526

79. Hinduism 532

80. Buddhism, Part 1 540

81. Buddhism, Part 2 549

82. What Makes a Group Non-Christian? 557

83. Unitarianism 564
84. Mormonism, Part 1 571
85. Mormonism, Part 2 580
86. Jehovah's Witnesses, Part 1 587
87. Jehovah's Witnesses, Part 2 594
88. Catholicism 602
89. Oneness Pentecostals 612
90. International Church of Christ 620
91. Seventh-Day Adventists 630
92. New Age Movement 638
93. The Will of God 647
94. Our Most Valuable Commodity 653
95. Consolation for the Average Christian 658
96. When You've Been Wronged 664
97. The Source of Revival .671
98. Hindrances to Revival .678
99. How to Maintain Zeal .684
100. Ten Ways to Raise Laborers in Your Church . . .690
101. The Christian's Prayer .699

ANSWERS 707
RECOMMENDED RESOURCES 759
MEMORIZING AND REMEMBERING SCRIPTURE 765

Preface Preface

In 2001, we decided to create an online Bible school called "The School of Biblical Evangelism," in which we would systematically equip Christians to share their faith. It would have a total of 120 lessons. We couldn't wait to get it underway, so we placed the first ten lessons online, thinking we could write the others before students caught up with us. We were wrong. Almost immediately students were banging on our door asking, "Where is the next lesson?"

The experience of trying to outrun hungry students was a taste of what was to come. Within a short time we were delighted to find that over 2,000 students from 18 countries had enrolled in the school.

It was because of this response that we decide to publish the "School of Biblical Evangelism" in a printed format for those who don't have Internet access, or who prefer to work directly from the printed page. It was a huge task, and it was one that we delegated to our brilliant editor, Lynn Copeland. We are very appreciative of her talents, not only for revising and refining the lessons, but for making them so pleasing to the eye. The School has been streamlined and now consists of 101 enhanced lessons focusing on how to share your faith biblically.

It is our deepest hope that you not only will enjoy each lesson, but will be motivated by them to fulfill the Great Commission, while there is still time.

Yours faithfully,
Kirk Cameron & Ray Comfort

How to Use These Lessons

This study course is designed for you to proceed at your own pace. Don't hurry through; take all the time you need to digest the content. The goal isn't simply to complete the course but to truly learn the way of the Master in sharing the gospel.

Each of the 101 lessons begins with a thought-provoking quote, followed by a comment from Kirk Cameron sharing his thoughts on the subject. In the "Questions & Objections" is a common question or objection to the Christian faith along with a response.

At the end of each lesson are various features to enhance the lesson content. The "Preacher's Progress" sections, written in the style of John Bunyan's classic *Pilgrim's Progress*, are sample witnessing conversations intended to help convey biblical concepts.

You will also see "Feathers for Arrows." Just as feathers help arrows to find their target, these paragraphs will help you to drive home certain truths when you are witnessing or preaching. The occasional "Words of Comfort" we hope will put a smile on your face and console you if you sometimes do dumb things.

Each lesson concludes with the "Last Words" of a famous person, as well as a "Memory Verse." (The back of the book includes a suggestion on how to commit these verses to memory.)

The "Questions" following each lesson are designed to help you better recall the lesson content. Please think through the questions and come up with your own responses. Possible answers are provided in the back of the book.

May God bless you as you study His Word.

The Forgotten Key to Biblical Evangelism

"'I was alive without the law once: but when the commandment came, sin revived' (Romans 7:9). So it is with the work-righteous and the proud unbelievers. Because they do not know the Law of God, which is directed against them, it is impossible for them to know their sin. Therefore also they are not amenable to instruction. If they would know the Law, they would also know their sin; and sin to which they are now dead would become alive in them."

MARTIN LUTHER

Kirk's Comment This teaching is critically important. To be properly instructed in how to effectively reach the lost with the gospel, you must begin with the *biblical* foundation for evangelism. Read this lesson very thoughtfully. Don't let anything distract you as you discover what Charles Spurgeon called "our ablest auxiliary"—that is, our most powerful weapon.

QUESTIONS & OBJECTIONS

"I'm as good as any Christian!"

A Christian, by himself, isn't good. Jesus said that God alone is good. The only "goodness," or righteousness, that the believer has comes from Jesus Christ (2 Corinthians 5:21; Philippians 3:9). The Bible tells us that, without Christ, man is corrupt and filthy; "there is none that does good, no, not one" (Psalm 14:3).

wotmwotmwotmwotmwotmwotmwotmwotmwotmwotmwotm

Have you ever thought, "There must be a key to reaching the lost"? There is—and it's rusty through lack of use. The Bible does actually call it "the key," and its purpose is to bring us to Christ, to unlock the Door of the Savior (John 10:9). Not only is it biblical, but it was used throughout church history to unlock the doors of revival. Much of the church today doesn't even know it exists. The problem is that it was lost around the turn of the twentieth century. Keys have a way of getting lost.

Jesus used it. So did Paul (Romans 3:19,20) and James (James 2:10). Stephen used it when he preached (Acts 7:53). Peter found that it had been used to open the door to release 3,000 imprisoned souls on the Day of Pentecost. Jesus said that the lawyers had "taken away" the key, and had even refused to use it to let people enter into the kingdom of God (Luke 11:52). The Pharisees didn't take it away; instead, they bent it out of shape so that it wouldn't do its work (Mark 7:8). Jesus returned it to its true shape, just as the Scriptures prophesied that He would do (Isaiah 42:21). Satan has tried to prejudice the modern church against the key. He has maligned it, misused it, twisted it, and, of course, hidden it—he hates it because of what it does. Perhaps you are wondering what this key is. I will tell you. All I ask is that you set aside your traditions and prejudices and look at what God's Word says on the subject.

In Acts 28:23 the Bible tells us that Paul sought to persuade his hearers "concerning Jesus, both out of the law of Moses, and out of the prophets." Here are two effective means of persuading the unsaved "concerning Jesus."

Let's first look at how the prophets can help persuade sinners concerning Jesus. Fulfilled prophecy *proves* the inspiration of Scripture. The predictions of the prophets present a powerful case for the inspiration of the Bible. Any skeptic who reads the prophetic words of Isaiah, Ezekiel, Joel, etc., or the words of Jesus in Matthew 24 cannot help but be challenged that this is no ordinary book.

The other means by which Paul persuaded sinners concerning Jesus was "out of the law of Moses." The Bible tells us that the Law of Moses is good if it is used lawfully (1 Timothy 1:8). For what purpose was God's Law designed? The following verses tell us: "The Law is not made for a righteous person, but . . . for sinners" (1 Timothy 1:9,10). It even lists the sinners for us: the disobedient, the ungodly, murderers, fornicators, homosexuals, kidnappers, liars, etc. The Law was designed primarily as an evangelistic tool. Paul wrote that he "had not known sin, but by the law" (Romans 7:7). The Law of God (the Ten Commandments) is evidently the "key of knowledge" that Jesus mentioned in Luke 11:52. He was speaking to lawyers—those who should have been teaching God's Law so that sinners would receive the "knowledge of sin," and thus recognize their need of the Savior.

Prophecy speaks to the *intellect* of the sinner, while the Law speaks to the *conscience*. One produces *faith* in the Word of God; the other brings *knowledge* of sin in the heart of the sinner. The Law is the God-given "key" to unlock the Door of salvation.

The Bible says in Psalm 19:7, "The law of the Lord is perfect converting the soul." Scripture makes it very clear that it is the Law that actually converts the soul. To illustrate the function of God's Law, let's look for a moment at civil law. Imagine if I said to you, "I've got some good news for you: someone has just paid a $25,000 speeding fine on your behalf." You'd probably react by saying, "What are you talking about? That's not good news—it doesn't make sense. I don't have a $25,000 speeding fine." My good news wouldn't be good news to you; it would seem foolishness. But more than that, it would be offensive to you, because I'm insinuating you've broken the law when you don't think you have.

However, if I put it this way, it may make more sense: "While you were out today, the law clocked you going 55 miles an hour through an area set aside for a blind children's convention. There were ten clear warning signs stating that fifteen miles an hour was the maximum speed, but you went straight through at 55 miles an hour. What you did was extremely dangerous; there's a $25,000 fine. The law was about to take its course, when someone you don't even know stepped in and paid the fine for you. You are very fortunate."

Can you see that telling you precisely what you've done wrong first actually enables the good news to make sense? If I don't clearly bring understanding that you've violated the law, then the good news will seem foolishness and offensive. But once you understand that you've broken the law, then that good news will become good news indeed.

In the same way, if I approach an impenitent sinner and say, "Jesus Christ died on the cross for your sins," it will be foolishness and offensive to him. It will be foolishness because it won't make sense. The Bible says that "the preaching of the cross is to them that perish foolishness" (1 Corinthians 1:18). And it will be offensive because I'm insinuating he's a sinner when he doesn't think he is. As far as he's concerned, there are a lot of people far worse than him. But if I take the time to follow in the footsteps of Jesus, it may make more sense. If I open up the divine Law, the Ten Commandments, and show the sinner precisely what he's done wrong —that he has offended God by violating His Law—then when he becomes "convinced of the law as a transgressor" (James 2:9), the good news of the fine being paid will not be foolishness. It will not be offensive. It will be "the power of God unto salvation" (Romans 1:16).

With that in mind, let's look at some of the functions of God's Law for humanity. Romans 3:19 says, "Now we know that whatsoever things the law says, it says to them who are under the law that every mouth may be stopped and all the world may become guilty before God." So one function of God's Law is to stop the mouth, to keep sinners from justifying themselves by saying, "There are plenty of people worse than me. I'm not a bad person, really." No, the law stops the mouth of justification and leaves, not just the Jews, but the whole world guilty before God.

In Romans 3:20 we read, "Therefore by the deeds of the law there shall no flesh be justified in his sight: for by the law is the knowledge of sin." So God's Law tells us what sin is. First John 3:4 says, "Sin is transgression of the law." In Galatians 3:24 we learn that God's Law acts as a schoolmaster to bring us to Jesus Christ that we might be justified through faith in His blood. The Law doesn't help us; it just leaves us helpless. It doesn't justify us; it just leaves us guilty before the judgment bar of a holy God.

Charles Spurgeon, called the Prince of Preachers, stated, "I do not believe that any man can preach the gospel who does not preach the Law. The Law is the needle, and you cannot draw the silken thread of the gospel through a man's heart unless you first send the needle of the Law to make way for it."

QUESTIONS

1. How did Paul seek to persuade his hearers concerning Jesus? Why did he do this?

2. What is it that actually converts the soul? (See Psalm 19:7.)

3. Why do you think the preaching of the cross seems foolish and offensive to an unregenerate sinner?

4. Therefore, what should someone be told first, before he hears the good news of his fine being paid?

5. What does it mean that the Law "stops every mouth"? (See Romans 3:19.)

6. What are four functions of the Law? (See Romans 3:19,20; 7:7; Galatians 3:24.)

7. What is the biblical definition of sin? (See 1 John 3:4.)

PREACHER'S PROGRESS

I, Christian, am waiting at the bus stop when *Stan Doffish* approaches; apparently he too is waiting for the bus to arrive. My heart begins to pound, as I know this is my opportunity to witness to him. The bus is in sight; I have about two minutes until it picks him up. The dialogue begins with me starting in the natural and quickly swinging over to the spiritual.

Christian: "How's it going?"

Stan Doffish: "Okay."

Christian: "Nice day."

Stan Doffish: "It's all right."

Christian: "Do you live around here?"

Stan Doffish: "No."

Christian: "Did you get one of these?"

Stan Doffish: "No. What is it?"

Christian: "It's a gospel tract. Do you have a Christian background?"

Stan Doffish: "Sort of. I went to church when I was a kid, but drifted away from it."

Christian: "Do you know what it was that got me thinking seriously about the things of God?"

Stan Doffish: "No. What?"

Christian: "It was the Ten Commandments. Jesus said that if you as much as look at a woman with lust, you have committed adultery with her already in your heart."

Stan Doffish: "Wow…"

Christian: "And that's just one Commandment. It leaves us all guilty, huh?"

Stan Doffish: "Yeah."

Christian: "So you've broken that Commandment too?"

Stan Doffish: "*Many* times."

Christian: "God doesn't want you to go to hell. That's why you must repent and trust Jesus. He took the punishment for your sins on the cross. Do you have a Bible at home?"

Stan Doffish: "Yes, I do actually."

Christian: "I encourage you to read it. Here comes your bus. Thanks for listening to me."

Stan Doffish: "Thank you."

Memory Verse

"Wherefore the law was our schoolmaster to bring us to Christ, that we might be justified by faith."

GALATIANS 3:24

Last Words

Martin Luther, the monk God used to shake the world, was spared the agony of a torturous death. When he came to die, his lips were laden with Scripture. As he breathed his last, Luther repeated John 3:16 and this verse from Psalm 68:

> **"Our God is the God of whom cometh salvation. God is the Lord by whom we escape death."**

With his hands clasped together, and without a finger or a feature being disturbed, this mighty man of God ended his pilgrimage.

Making Grace Amazing

"All heaven is interested in the cross of Christ, all hell terribly afraid of it, while men are the only beings who more or less ignore its meaning."

OSWALD CHAMBERS

Kirk's Comment Grace never made more sense to me, or became so beautiful, as when I saw it in the light of God's Holy Law. The Law illuminates a sinner's understanding and shows that God's grace is amazing.

QUESTIONS & OBJECTIONS

"Mother Nature sure blew it..."

Hurricanes, tornadoes, floods, droughts, and earthquakes kill tens of thousands of people each year. Multitudes endure crippling diseases, endless suffering, and unspeakable pain. Many non-Christians credit a heartless Mother Nature for giving us all this grief. They fail to consider that "Mother Nature" has a Senior Partner—Father God.

However, if God is responsible for all this heartache, that presents an interesting dilemma. If God is an "all-loving" Father figure, as we are told, we seem to have three choices: 1) God blew it when He made everything (He's creative but incompetent); 2) God is a tyrant, who gets His kicks from seeing kids die of leukemia; 3) something between God and man is radically wrong. These are our choices...and those who take time to consider the evidence will lean toward number three. Something between man and God is radically wrong, and the Bible tells us what it is.

There is a war going on. We are told that mankind is an enemy of God in his mind through wicked works (Colossians 1:21). That's not too hard to see. Man is continually committing violent acts such as murder and rape, lying, stealing, etc., as the daily news confirms. He uses God's name as a curse word, while Mother Nature gets the glory for His creation—unless there's a horrible disaster; then man calls that "an act of God."

An applicable acronym for WAR is We Are Right. Any country going to war does so because it has the conviction that it is in the right. However, a quick look at God's Law shows us who is right and who is wrong. We, not God, are the guilty party. If we want His blessing back on our nation and in our lives, we must make peace with Him, and that is possible only through faith in Jesus Christ.

wotmwotmwotmwotmwotmwotmwotmwotmwotmwotmwotm

The good news of the gospel is that, in the cross of Calvary, God extended grace toward humanity. Words cannot express the wonders of His grace so graphically illustrated in that bloody cross. Grace can be defined as "unmerited favor to the infinitely ill-deserving," or, in other words, "God's Riches At Christ's Expense."

The question that should be on the heart of every Christian is how we may best show God's amazing grace to this lost world. We tell sinners God loved them so much that He gave His only Son to die in their place, and yet it seems to have less relevance than the day's weather forecast. To them, the forecast is at least applicable to them here and now.

The solution to this dilemma can be found in Romans 5:20. Here we are informed why God gave His Law to us: "Moreover the law entered, that the offense might abound. But where sin abounded, grace did much more abound."

When sin abounds, grace "much more" abounds, and according to Scripture, the thing that makes sin abound is the Law.

We can see the work of God's Law illustrated in civil law. For example, when there is no visible sign of the law on a freeway, motorists often transgress the speed limit. Apparently each speedster says to himself that the law has forgotten to patrol his part of the freeway. He is transgressing the law by only 15 mph, and besides, he isn't the only one doing it.

Notice what happens when the law enters the fast lane, with red lights flashing. The speedster's heart misses a beat. He is no longer secure in the fact that other motorists are also speeding. He knows that he is *personally* as guilty as the next guy, and *he* could be the one the law pulls over. The fact that there are other people doing it is irrelevant. Suddenly, his "mere" 15 mph transgression doesn't seem such a small thing after all; it seems to abound.

Look at the freeway of sin. The whole world naturally goes with the flow. Who hasn't had an "affair" (or desired to) at one time or another? Who in today's society doesn't tell the occasional "white" lie? Who doesn't take something that belongs to someone else, even if it's just a little "white-collar" crime? Sinners know they are doing wrong, but their security is in the fact that so many others are just as guilty, if not more so. It seems God has forgotten all about sin and the Ten Commandments; the sinner says in his heart, "God has forgotten; He hides His face; He will never see it" (Psalm 10:11).

Now watch the Law enter with red lights flashing. The sinner's heart skips a beat. He lays his hand upon his mouth. He examines the speedometer of his conscience. Suddenly, it shows him the measure of his guilt in a new light—the light of the Law. His sense of security in the fact that there are multitudes doing the same thing becomes irrelevant, because every man will give an account of *himself* to God. Sin not only becomes personal, it seems to "abound." His mere lust becomes *adultery of the heart* (Matthew 5:27,28); his white lie, *false witness* (Revelation 21:8); his own way becomes *rebellion*; his hatred, *murder* (1 John 3:15); his "sticky" fingers make him a thief—"Moreover the law entered, that the offense might abound." Without the Law entering, sin is neither personal, nor is it evident: "For without the Law, sin is dead [the sense of it is inactive...]" (Romans 7:8, Amplified).

It was the "Commandment" that showed Paul sin in its true light—that it is "exceedingly sinful" (Romans 7:13). Paul spoke from his own experience because he had sat at the feet of Gamaliel, the great "teacher of the law," and therefore saw sin in its vivid colors.

According to the Scriptures, "[the real function of] the law is to make men recognize and be conscious of sin [not mere perception, but an acquaintance with sin which works toward repentance...]" (Romans 3:20, Amplified).

Charles Spurgeon said that "the Law serves a most necessary purpose." How true are his words regarding sinners: "They will *never* accept grace, until they tremble before a just and holy Law." Those who see the role of the Law will be Sons of Thunder *before* they are the Sons of Consolation. They know that the shoes of human pride must be removed before sinners can approach the burning bush of the gospel.

It is important to realize that we *can* evoke a tearful response from sinners by saying that God loves them. The message is more appealing to both the Christian and the sinner. It certainly is easier to speak of love than of sin. Many years ago, before I understood the function of God's Law, I told a prostitute of God's love and was delighted that she immediately began weeping. Unbeknown to me, her tears were not tears of godly sorrow for sin, but merely an emotional response to the need of a father's love. In my ignorance, I joyfully led her in a sinner's prayer. However, I was disappointed sometime later when she fell away, and her tender heart became very callous toward the things of God.

Paradoxically, the Law makes grace abound, in the same way that darkness makes light shine. It was John Newton, the writer of "Amazing Grace," who said that a wrong understanding of the harmony between Law and grace would produce "error on the left and the right hand." I don't know if any of us could claim to have a better understanding of grace than the one who penned such a hymn.

To help sinners understand that grace is truly amazing, use the Moral Law of God. As John Wesley advised a young evangelist, for effective evangelism, preach 90 percent Law and 10 percent grace.

QUESTIONS

1. What is a definition of grace?

2. Why should the Christian be concerned about how to make grace amazing to the world?

3. What is it that makes grace abound?

4. What caused the speedster to see the seriousness of his transgression?

5. What did Charles Spurgeon say about the Law?

6. Why did the prostitute weep at the mention of God's love?

7.   What did John Newton say about the harmony between Law and grace?

FEATHERS FOR ARROWS

Imagine going back in time two hundred years and trying to describe a jumbo jet. You say, "Where I come from, we have these huge tin cans, weighing hundreds of thousands of tons, that float across the sky filled with hundreds of people." Someone says, "Do you think we are stupid? That's impossible. There is such a thing as the law of gravity. Not even a feather can float across the sky unaided, without descending."

However, we now have discovered that when an object of a particular shape travels at a certain speed, it moves out of the law of gravity into another law, the law of aerodynamics. The law of gravity remains, but the object supercedes it.

We have also discovered that when a person becomes a Christian, he moves out of one law into another. The law of life in Christ Jesus supercedes the law of sin and death. The Christian lives in a higher plane: "For the law of the Spirit of life in Christ Jesus has made me free from the law of sin and death" (Romans 8:2).

WORDS OF COMFORT

As I stood at the checkout counter in a well-known hardware chain, a woman gasped and pointed to the floor. There was a pile of white sand pouring from a 50-pound bag I had placed into my shopping cart. I had accidentally made a hole in it when I lifted it a few minutes earlier. I looked behind me and saw a 180-foot trail of white sand going back to where I had begun my journey. The sand was thin when I had sped up and thick when I had slowed down. Its trail not only revealed when I had turned to the left and to the right, but it also led directly to the guilty party.

Last Words

Tony Hancock (British comedian):

"Nobody will ever know I existed. Nothing to leave behind me. Nothing to pass on. Nobody to mourn me. That's the bitterest blow of all."

Memory Verse

"Moreover the law entered, that the offense might abound. But where sin abounded, grace did much more abound."
ROMANS 5:20

The Problem with the Modern Gospel

"The trouble with people who are not seeking for a Savior, and for salvation, is that they do not understand the nature of sin. It is the peculiar function of the Law to bring such an understanding to a man's mind and conscience. That is why great evangelical preachers 300 years ago in the time of the Puritans, and 200 years ago in the time of Whitefield and others, always engaged in what they called a preliminary 'Law work.'"

MARTYN LLOYD-JONES

Kirk's Comment Give some deep thought to this lesson, because the essence of the entire School of Biblical Evangelism pivots on the illustration given in this chapter. It exposes the *motive* of the sinner and reveals the pitfalls of the modern gospel message.

QUESTIONS & OBJECTIONS

"I'm doing fine. I don't need God."

Many people feel this way because of the modern gospel message. It says that Jesus will help their marriage, remove their drug problem, fill the emptiness in their heart, give them peace and joy, etc. In doing so, it restricts the gospel's field of influence. If the message of the cross is for people who have bad marriages, are lonely, and have problems, then those who are happy won't see their need for the Savior.

In truth, the forgiveness of God in Jesus Christ is for people with bad marriages and people with good marriages. It is for the happy and the sad. It is for people with problems and those without problems. It is for those who are miserable in their sins, as well as those who are enjoying the pleasures of sin for a season. Those who think they are doing fine need to be confronted with a holy Law that they have violated a multitude of times. Then they will see themselves through the eyes of the Judge of the Universe and will flee to the Savior.

wotmwotmwotmwotmwotmwotmwotmwotmwotmwotmwotm

As I began to look at church growth records from around the country, I found to my horror that 80 to 90 percent of those making a decision for Christ were falling away from the faith. That is, modern evangelism was creating 80 to 90 of what we commonly call backsliders for every hundred decisions for Christ.

For example, in 1991, a major U.S. denomination was able to obtain 294,000 decisions for Christ. Unfortunately, they could find only 14,000 in fellowship, which means they couldn't account for 280,000 of their decisions—and this is a normal, modern evangelical result.

The tragedy of modern evangelism is that, around the turn of the twentieth century, the church forsook the Law in its capacity to convert the soul and drive sinners to Christ. Modern evangelism therefore had to find another reason for sinners to respond to the gospel, and the reason it chose was the issue of "life enhancement." The gospel degenerated into "Jesus Christ will give you peace, joy, love, fulfillment, and lasting happiness." Something like this is usually said, "You will never find true happiness until you come to the Lord. You have a 'God-shaped vacuum' in your heart that only He can fill. God will heal your marriage and take away that addiction problem. He'll get you out of financial difficulty and be your best friend." The following anecdote will illustrate the unscriptural nature of this very popular teaching.

Two men are seated on a plane. The first is given a parachute and told to put it on, as it would improve his flight. He's a little skeptical at first, since he can't see how wearing a parachute on a plane could possibly improve his flight. He decides to experiment and see if the claims are true. As he puts it on, he notices the weight of it upon his shoulders and he finds he has difficulty in sitting upright. However, he consoles himself with the fact he was told that the parachute would improve his flight. So he decides to give it a little time.

As he waits he notices that some of the other passengers are laughing at him for wearing a parachute on a plane. He begins to feel somewhat humiliated. As they continue to point and laugh at him, he can stand it no longer. He slinks in his seat, unstraps the parachute, and throws it to the floor. Disillusionment and bitterness fill his heart, because as far as he was concerned he was told an outright lie.

The second man is given a parachute, *but listen to what he is told.* He's told to put it on because at any moment he'll be jumping 25,000 feet out of the plane. He gratefully puts the parachute on. He doesn't notice the weight of it upon his shoulders, nor that he can't sit upright. His mind is consumed with the thought of what would happen to him if he jumped without the parachute.

Let's now analyze the motive and the result of each passenger's experience. The first man's motive for putting the parachute on was solely to improve his flight. The result of his experience was that he was humiliated by the passengers, disillusioned, and somewhat embittered against those who gave him the parachute. As far as he's concerned, it will be a long time before anyone gets one of those things on his back again.

The second man put the parachute on solely to escape the jump to come. And because of his knowledge of what would happen to him if he jumped without it, he has a deep-rooted joy and peace in his heart knowing that he's saved from sure death. This knowledge gives him the ability to withstand the mockery of the other passengers. His attitude toward those who gave him the parachute is one of heartfelt gratitude.

Now listen to what the modern gospel says: "Put on the Lord Jesus Christ. He'll give you love, joy, peace, fulfillment, and lasting happiness." In other words, Jesus will improve your flight. The sinner responds, and in an experimental fashion puts on the Savior to see if the claims are true.

And what does he get? The promised temptation, tribulation, and persecution—the other "passengers" mock him. So what does he do? He takes off the Lord Jesus Christ; he's offended for the Word's sake; he's disillusioned and somewhat embittered... and quite rightly so. He was promised peace, joy, love, and fulfillment, and all he got were trials and humiliation. His bitterness is directed at those who gave him the so-called "good news." His latter end becomes worse than the first, and he's another inoculated and bitter "backslider."

Instead of preaching that Jesus improves the flight, we should be warning sinners that they have to jump out of the plane—that it's appointed for man to die once and then face judgment (Hebrews 9:27). When a sinner understands the horrific consequences of breaking the Law of God, he will flee to the Savior, solely to escape the wrath that is to come. If we are true and faithful witnesses, that's what we'll be preaching —that there is wrath to come—that God "commands all men every where to repent: *because* he has appointed a day, in which he will judge the world in righteousness" (Acts 17:30,31).

The issue isn't one of life enhancement, but one of righteousness. It doesn't matter how happy a sinner is, or how much he is enjoying the pleasures of sin for a season; without the righteousness of Christ, he will perish on the day of wrath. Proverbs 11:4 says, "Riches profit not in the day of wrath: but righteousness delivers from death."

Peace and joy are legitimate *fruits* of salvation, but it's not legitimate to use these fruits as a drawing card *for* salvation. If we continue to do so, the sinner will respond with an impure motive, lacking repentance.

Can you remember why the *second* passenger had joy and peace in his heart? It was because he knew that the parachute was going to save him from sure death. In the same way, as believers we have "joy and peace in believing" (Romans 15:13) because we know that the righteousness of Christ is going to deliver us from the wrath to come.

With that thought in mind, let's take a close look at an incident aboard the plane.

We have a brand-new flight attendant. It's her first day. She's carrying a tray of boiling hot coffee. She wants to leave an impression on the passengers, and she certainly does! As she's walking down the aisle, she trips over someone's foot and slops the hot coffee all over the lap of our second passenger.

What's his reaction as that boiling liquid hits his tender flesh? Does he say, "Man, that hurt!"? Yes, he does. But then does he rip the parachute from his shoulders, throw it to the floor, and say, "The stupid parachute!"? No; why should he? He didn't put the parachute on for a better flight. He put it on to save him from the jump to come. If anything, the hot coffee incident causes him to cling tighter to the parachute and even look forward to the jump.

If we have put on the Lord Jesus Christ for the right motive—to flee from the wrath to come—then when tribulation strikes, when the flight gets bumpy, we won't get angry at God, and we won't lose our joy and peace. Why should we? We didn't come to Christ for a better lifestyle, but to flee from the wrath to come. If anything, tribulation drives the true believer *closer* to the Savior. Sadly, we have multitudes of professing Christians who lose their joy and peace when the flight gets bumpy. Why? They are the product of a man-centered gospel. They came lacking repentance, without which they cannot be saved.

QUESTIONS

1. **What percentage of those making decisions fall away from the faith?**

2. **What is the tragedy of modern evangelism?**

3. **What was the result of the first passenger's experience?**

4. **What was the result of the second passenger's experience?**

5. **What should we be telling the other "passengers"?**

6. **What is it that the Bible says "delivers from death"?**

7. **Why should a Christian have joy and peace?**

8. **As Christians, what should tribulation do to us?**

PREACHER'S PROGRESS

Christian Loveless: "Hi, Mrs. Smith. How are you doing? Is Erik in yet?"

Mrs. Smith: "Lunch again, huh? I haven't seen him come through the lobby today. He came into work last week with a bad hangover. Probably the same thing has happened today. How was church?"

Christian Loveless: "It was really good. We had Brother Don Waterdowns come in and do a series of healing meetings. Hundreds gave their hearts to the Lord. I'm in charge of the follow-up program. Man, I didn't realize how easy it is to get people saved. Lots were getting healed and people were coming to the altar without even being preached to."

Mrs. Smith: "What a blessing. We had him at our church too. He advocates 'friendship evangelism,' doesn't he?"

Christian Loveless: "Yes. I like that. It's what I've been using on Erik. We've become good buddies over the years."

Mrs. Smith: "I like that approach. It's so much better than shoving the gospel down people's throats."

Christian Loveless: "True. That can alienate them. I'm waiting for the right time to mention the things of God to Erik; I don't want to make him feel uncomfortable. Erik came to one of the meetings, and he really seemed to enjoy it. That's the good thing about non-confrontational evangelism. He didn't give his heart to the Lord, though. Maybe today he will bring up the subject. I never do, because I don't want to offend him. I'm just a good friend, and I think that's the right approach."

Mrs. Smith: "I agree. I'll call the Third Floor and speak to his secretary. Perhaps she will know why he's late."

Christian Loveless: "Okay."

Mrs. Smith: "Jeannie, Rose Smith. Is Erik Tuday in yet? Christian Loveless is here to see..."

Christian Loveless: "What's wrong? Your face has gone pale!"

Mrs. Smith: "I'm afraid Erik died during the night. He had an aneurysm in his sleep and was pronounced dead at 8:17 this morning..."

Memory Verse

"Riches profit not in the day of wrath: but righteousness delivers from death."
PROVERBS 11:4

Last Words

Daniel Webster stated shortly before his death, "The great mystery is Jesus Christ—the gospel. What would the condition of any of us be if we had not the hope of immortality?... Thank God, the gospel of Jesus Christ brought life and immortality to light." His last words were:

"I still live."

How to Confront Sinners

"Scratching people where they itch and addressing their 'felt needs' is a stratagem of the poor steward of the oracles of God. This was the recipe for success for the false prophets of the Old Testament."

R. C. SPROUL

Kirk's Comment In this lesson, we will look at how the prophet Nathan confronted King David about his sin with Bathsheba. It would be a good idea to first review this incident in 2 Samuel 12:1–9 in your Bible, and become familiar with the story.

QUESTIONS & OBJECTIONS

"I am doing the best I can and I'm sincere."

Even if you could do far better than you are doing now, you still can't do well enough because you don't please God by being good (Galatians 2:21), but by trusting Jesus (John 1:12).

Also, sincerity is not the way to heaven. What if you are sincerely wrong? (Remember John 14:6?) If you are relying on your sincerity, then you are saying that because you are sincere, you are good enough on your own to be with God. To appeal to your sincerity is to appeal to pride, because you are appealing to something that is in you, and not to God, for your reason to go to heaven. You must have faith in Jesus.

God's Love: The Biblical Presentation

The modern message of the gospel is "God loves you and has a wonderful plan for your life." However, our idea of "wonderful" and the world's may be a little different. Take a sinner through the pages of the Book of Acts and show him the terrifying scene of rocks breaking the bones of Stephen. Then smile and whisper, "Wonderful..." Listen together to the sound of a cat-o'-nine-tails as it rips the flesh off the back of the apostle Paul. Follow together the word "suffering" through the Epistles, and see if you can get the world to whisper, "Wonderful!" Tell them that "we must through much tribulation enter into the kingdom of God" (Acts 14:22). After such a ride down Honesty Road, they may think the pleasures of sin are a little more attractive than the call to "suffer affliction with the people of God" (Hebrews 11:25).

Who in the world is going to listen to our message if we are so blatantly honest about the Christian life? Perhaps not as many as are attracted by the talk of a wonderful plan. The answer to our dilemma is to make the issue one of righteousness, rather than happiness. This is what Jesus did. He used the Ten Commandments to show sinners the righteous standard of God (Luke 10:25,26; 18:18–20). Once the world sees the perfect standard by which they will be judged, they will begin to fear God, and it is through the fear of the Lord that men depart from sin (Proverbs 16:6). They will begin to hunger and thirst after the righteousness that is in Jesus Christ alone.

If you study the New Testament, you will see that God's love is almost always given in direct correlation to the cross: herein is love, for God so loved, God commended His love, etc. (See John 3:16; Romans 5:5,6,8; Galatians 2:20; Ephesians 2:4,5; 5:2,25; 1 John 3:16; 4:10; and Revelation 1:5, among others.) The cross is the focal point of God's love for the world. How can we point to the cross without making reference to sin? How can we refer to sin without using the Law (Romans 7:7)? The biblical way to express God's love to a sinner is to show him how great his sin is (using the Law—see Romans 7:13; Galatians 3:24), and then give him the incredible grace of God in Christ. This was the key to reaching so many on the Day of Pentecost. They were "devout" Jews who knew the Law and its holy demands, and therefore readily accepted the mercy of God in Christ to escape its fearful wrath.

When you use the Law to show the world their true state, get ready for sinners to thank you. For the first time in their lives, they will see the Christian message as an expression of love and concern for their eternal welfare, rather than of merely proselytizing for a better lifestyle while on this earth.

Ponder this quote by John MacArthur until it is written in the corridors of your mind: "We need to adjust our presentation of the gospel. We cannot dismiss the fact that God hates sin and punishes sinners with eternal torment. How can we begin a gospel presentation by telling people on their way to hell that God has a wonderful plan for their lives?" It is true that God has a wonderful plan for their lives—but it is that they would repent and trust the Savior, and receive the righteousness of Christ.

Making Sinners Tremble

For a biblical illustration of how to confront sinners using the issue of righteousness, let's look to the life of King David. When David sinned with Bathsheba, he broke *all* of the Ten Commandments. He coveted his neighbor's wife, lived a lie, stole her, committed adultery, murdered her husband, dishonored his parents, and thus broke the remaining four Commandments by dishonoring God. Therefore, the Lord sent Nathan the prophet to reprove him (2 Samuel 12:1–14).

There is great significance in the order in which the reproof came. Nathan gave David, the shepherd of Israel, a parable about something he could understand—sheep. He began with the natural realm, rather than immediately exposing the king's sin. He told a story about a rich man who, instead of taking a sheep from his own flock, killed a poor man's pet lamb to feed a stranger.

David was indignant, and sat up on his high throne of self-righteousness. He revealed his knowledge of the Law by declaring that the guilty party must restore fourfold and must die for his crime. Nathan then exposed the king's sin of taking another man's "lamb," saying, "You are the man . . . Why have you despised the commandment of the Lord, to do evil in his sight?" When David cried, "I have sinned against the Lord," the prophet *then* gave him grace and said, "The Lord also has put away your sin; you shall not die."

Imagine if Nathan, fearful of rejection, changed things around a little, and instead told David, "God loves you and has a wonderful plan for your life. However, there is something that is keeping you from enjoying this wonderful plan; it is called 'sin.'" Imagine if he had glossed over the *personal nature* of David's sin, with a general reference to *all* men having sinned and fallen short of the glory of God (Romans 3:23). David's reaction might have been, "What *sin* are you talking about?" rather than to admit his terrible transgression.

Think of it—why should he cry, "I have sinned against the Lord" at the sound of *that* message? Instead, he may have, in a sincere desire to experience this "wonderful plan," admitted that he, like all men, had sinned and fallen short of the glory of God. If David had not been made to *tremble* under the wrath of the Law, the prophet would have removed the very means of producing godly sorrow, which is necessary for repentance (2 Corinthians 7:10).

It was the weight of David's guilt that caused him to cry out, "I have sinned against the Lord." The Law caused him to labor and become heavy laden; it made him hunger and thirst for righteousness. It enlightened him as to the *serious* nature of sin as far as God was concerned.

Here, then, is how we can get sinners to cry out, according to Paris Reidhead:

> If I had my way, I would declare a moratorium on public preaching of "the plan of salvation" in America for one to two years. Then I would call on everyone who has use of the airwaves and the pulpits to preach the holiness of God, the righteousness of God, and the Law of God, until sinners would cry out, "What must we do to be saved?" Then I would take them off in a corner and whisper the gospel to them. Don't use John 3:16. Such drastic action is needed because we have gospel-hardened a generation of sinners by telling them how to be saved before they have any understanding why they need to be saved.

QUESTIONS

1. Why should we not tell sinners that God has a wonderful plan for their lives?

2. Give an example where Jesus used the Ten Commandments to show sinners God's righteous standard.

3. If we mention God's love to a lost person, in what context should it be?

4. How did David come to realize his sin? (See 2 Samuel 12:1–13.)

5. Why is citing Romans 3:23 to a sinner not sufficient for bringing about repentance?

PREACHER'S PROGRESS

Christian: "How are you doing?"

Al Cohol: "Awful!"

Christian: "Why's that?"

Al Cohol: "I've got troubles."

Christian: "What sort of troubles?"

Al Cohol: "My wife left me."

Christian: "Why's that?"

Al Cohol: "I've got a small problem with alcohol…and a bit of a gambling problem. Mind if I smoke?"

Christian: "Go ahead."

Al Cohol: "Can you lend me a couple of dollars? I smashed my car up the other day and need to get it fixed."

Christian: "How did that happen?"

Al Cohol: "I'd had a couple of beers and was on my way to the courts to pay a speeding fine—third DUI this month. What a pain!"

Christian: "Do you ever pray?"

Al Cohol: "All the time. I told you; I have problems."

Christian: "Do you see your need of God's forgiveness?"

Al Cohol: "No."

Christian: "The Ten Commandments will help you…" (Christian goes through the Commandments, then into the gospel.)

Al Cohol: "I know I'm guilty, and I know that if I died tonight I would go to hell, but I've got all these problems I've got to work out before I get into that stuff."

Christian: "Listen to me, Al. All these problems combined a thousand times over won't be anything like the problem you will have on Judgment Day if you refuse to repent. You may not see this now, but I care enough about you to tell you the truth. I don't want you to go to hell—neither does God. Don't put off your eternal salvation. There is nothing more important."

Feathers for Arrows

Memory Verse

"For godly sorrow works repentance to salvation not to be repented of: but the sorrow of the world works death."

2 Corinthians 7:10

A pastor was once approached by his six-year-old son who said he wanted to "ask Jesus into his heart." The father, suspecting that the child lacked the knowledge of sin, told him that he could do so when he was older, then sent him off to bed.

A short time later, the boy got out of bed and asked his father if he could give his life to the Savior. The father still wasn't persuaded of the son's understanding, so, not wanting the child's salvation to be spurious, he sent him back to his room.

A third time the son returned. This time the father questioned him about whether he had broken any of the Ten Commandments. The young boy didn't think he had. When asked if he was a liar, the child said he wasn't. The father thought for a moment, then asked him how many lies he had to tell to be a liar. When it was established that one lie made a person a liar, the child realized he had lied, and broke down in uncontrollable tears. When the father then inquired whether he wanted to "ask Jesus into his heart," the child cringed and shook his head. He was fearful because now he knew that he had sinned against God. At this point, he could do more than experimentally "ask Jesus into his heart." He could find a place of godly sorrow, repentance toward God, and faith toward our Lord Jesus Christ (Acts 20:21).

Last Words

William Shakespeare (1564–1616), the world's outstanding figure in literature, lived near his Bible, as shown by the numerous quotations from it in his plays and dramas. His end came when he was only 52 years of age. His last will and testament revealed his faith in God:

> **"I commend my soul into the hands of God my Creator, hoping and assuredly believing, through the only merits of Jesus Christ my Saviour, to be made partaker of life everlasting; and my body to the earth, whereof it is made."**

The Ten Commandments, Part 1

"You cannot say, 'No, Lord,' and mean both words; one annuls the other. If you say no to Him, then He is not your Lord."

D. JAMES KENNEDY

Kirk's Comment   Now we're going to look at the Law of God to see how it serves as a schoolmaster to lead sinners to Christ. Any soldier who wants to be effective in warfare will become intimately familiar with his weapons. Think of the Commandments as ten great cannons given to you by God, each with tremendous power to destroy self-righteousness. If we want to be effective in reaching the lost, we must be intimately familiar with these great weapons that God has given us. As we follow in the footsteps of Jesus, who opened up the spiritual nature of the Law when dealing with sinners, we will discover the key to genuine repentance.

QUESTIONS & OBJECTIONS

"The First Commandment says, 'You shall have no other gods before Me.' That proves He isn't the only God!"

That's true. Man has always made false gods. An old adage says, "God created man in His own image, and man has been returning the favor ever since." Hindus have millions of gods. Sometimes gods are made of wood or stone; other times man makes up a god in his mind. Whatever the case, making a god to suit yourself is called "idolatry," and it is a transgression of both the First and Second Commandments.

wotmwotmwotmwotmwotmwotmwotmwotmwotmwotmwotm

In this lesson we will look at the First Commandment: "I am the LORD your God, which has brought you out of the land of Egypt, out of the house of bondage. **You shall have no other gods before me**" (Exodus 20:2,3).

We are to have no other gods before (or "besides") the one true God. He is to be preeminent in our hearts. Jesus said that "the first of all the commandments is, Hear, O Israel; The Lord our God is one Lord: And you shall love the Lord your God with all your heart, and with all your soul, and with all your mind, and with all your strength: this is the first commandment" (Mark 12:29,30).

There is only One who can stand uncondemned regarding this Commandment. Jesus of Nazareth lived a life without sin; He was perfect in thought, word, and deed (see Hebrews 4:15). *Everything* He did pleased the Father absolutely. The cross not only revealed that He loved His Father with all of His heart, soul, mind, and strength, but it proved that He loved His neighbor as much as He loved Himself.

Those who profess to keep this Commandment would do well to run their eyes over the Westminster Confession of Faith. This was penned by godly men in 1646, and expressed their thoughts (based on Scripture) about the essence of this Commandment:

> The duties required in the First Commandment are, the knowing and acknowledging of God to be the only true God and our God; and to worship and glorify Him accordingly, by thinking, meditating, remembering, highly esteeming, honoring, adoring, choosing, loving, desiring, fearing of Him, believing Him, trusting, hoping, delighting, rejoicing in Him, being zealous for Him, calling upon Him, giving all praise and thanks, and yielding all obedience and submission to Him with the whole man; being careful in all things to please Him, and sorrowful when in anything He is offended; and walking humbly with Him.

Someone once said, "It is agreeable to reason that men who have their beings from God, and are upheld in them by him, and are followed with the bounties of Providence; and especially who are made new creatures, and are blessed by him with all spiritual blessings in Christ, that they should give up themselves to him, and cheerfully serve him in their day and generation."

Sinful humans, however, don't love God. They don't delight to do His will. Instead, the Law of sin and death has written its bloody signature across the godless human breast (Romans 7:21–24). Our inborn cry is, "Not Your will, but mine be done!" The devil is our father and his will we gladly do. The carnal mind is not subject to the Law or God, nor indeed can it be (Romans 8:7). See how the Law condemns us. We fail to love the God who gave us life.

The inevitable result is that sinful man will think that he himself is God. His pride takes over his brain, as shown in this quote by Jeremy Rifkin in his book *Algeny:*

> We no longer feel ourselves to be guests in someone else's home and therefore obliged to make our behavior conform with a set of preexisting cosmic rules. It is our creation now. We make the rules. We establish the parameters of reality. We create the world, and because we do, we no longer feel beholden to outside forces. We no longer have to justify our behavior, for we are now the architects of the universe. We are responsible to nothing outside ourselves, for we are the kingdom, the power, and the glory forever and ever.

QUESTIONS

1. Name the First of the Ten Commandments.

2. Why do you think humanity has such a shallow understanding about what God requires of them? (See 2 Corinthians 4:3,4.)

3. What do you think could be the greatest sin of humanity?

4. In what ways have you transgressed this Commandment?

5. Using Psalm 14 and Romans 3:10–18, list the characteristics of human nature.

6. How did Jesus demonstrate that He kept this Commandment?

7. Why should we put God first?

PREACHER'S PROGRESS

Alec Smart: "Hey, Christian. I want you to give me the 'good' test."

Christian: "Are you sure?"

Alec Smart: "Yep."

Christian: "Okay, then. Have you ever told a lie?"

Alec Smart: "Never."

Christian: "Not once? Not a fib, white lie, half-truth, or an exaggeration?"

Alec Smart: "Never!"

Christian: "You have always spoken the truth, the whole truth, and nothing but the truth, so help you God?"

Alec Smart: "Yep."

Christian: "Have you ever stolen anything?"

Alec Smart: "Never."

Christian: "Not even a ballpoint pen?"

Alec Smart: "Never!"

Christian: "Okay. Have you kept the First of the Ten Commandments?"

Alec Smart: "Yep."

Christian: "What is it?"

Alec Smart: "I don't know."

Christian: "It is to put God first in your life. Have you loved God with all of your heart, soul, mind, and strength?"

Alec Smart: "Yep."

Christian: "The Bible says that there are none who seek after God. So one of you is lying—either you or God, and the Bible says that it's impossible for God to lie. So you've broken the First of the Ten Commandments, and you've broken the Ninth by lying. You will be in big trouble on Judgment Day."

FEATHERS FOR ARROWS

Memory Verse

"You shall love the Lord your God with all your heart, and with all your soul, and with all your mind, and with all your strength: this is the first commandment."

MARK 12:30

A father once purchased a TV for his kids to watch cartoons in the afternoon. When he arrived home that night, his kids didn't come to greet him; they were busy watching TV. His homecoming had become a non-event. He walked over to the TV and turned it off, explaining to the children that he had purchased it for their pleasure, but if it came between him and their love for him, it was going. They were setting their affection on the gift, rather than on the giver. If we love anything more than God —our spouse, child, car, sport, or even our own life—we are setting our affection on the gift, rather than on the Giver. Placing anything above God is a transgression of the First of the Ten Commandments.

Last Words

Kurt Cobain (in his suicide note):

> "Frances and Courtney, I'll be at your altar. Please keep going, Courtney, for Frances. For her life will be so much happier without me. I love you. I love you."

6 The Ten Commandments, Part 2

"If the giving of the Law, while it was yet unbroken, was attended with such a display of awe-inspiring power, what will that day be when the Lord shall, with flaming fire, take vengeance on those who have willfully broken that Law?"

CHARLES SPURGEON

Kirk's Comment In this lesson we will study the meaning of the Second of the Ten Commandments. This is one that many don't think about today, but creating false gods is much more common than you may believe.

QUESTIONS & OBJECTIONS

"Jesus taught hatred by saying that a Christian should 'hate' his father and mother."

This is called "hyperbole"—a statement of extremes, contrasting love with hate for emphasis' sake. The Bible often does this (Proverbs 13:24; 29:24). Jesus tells us that the first and greatest Commandment is to love God with all of our heart, soul, and mind (Matthew 22:37,38). As much as we treasure our spouse and family, and even our own life, there should be no one whom we love and value more than God, no one who takes precedence in our life. To place love for another (including ourself) above God is idolatry.

I n this lesson we will look at the Second Commandment: "**You shall not make for yourself any graven image**...You shall not bow down yourself to them, nor serve them: for I the LORD your God am a jealous God, visiting the iniquity of the fathers upon the children to the third and fourth generation of them that hate me; and showing mercy to thousands of them that love me and keep my commandments" (Exodus 20:4–6).

Idolatry is perhaps the greatest of all sins because it opens the door to unrestrained evil. It gives sinners license not only to tolerate sin, but to sanction it, fanned by demonic influence. If you make a god in your image, one you feel comfortable with, you can then create your own moral standards to go along with him...or her.

For example, feminists bristle at the Bible's statement that God made man in *His* image. This doesn't mean that God is a man, or that He looks like man (John 4:24). It means that when God made man and woman, He endowed them with a mind, emotions, and a will. Humans are rational, moral beings with an inherent God-consciousness. However, in revealing Himself to mankind, God describes Himself in the male gender using terms such as Father, Son, Bridegroom, etc. Those who consider God to be female and call Him "Mother" are engaging in idolatry. To change who God has revealed Himself to be is to create a god in their own image.

Some like to make a god that believes in a woman's right to kill her children in the womb. Others prefer to create a god that rewards the killing of innocent people by granting immortality. The following letter to the editor, printed in *Time* magazine, epitomizes idolatry (the oldest sin in the Book):

> Excellent topic! I truly enjoyed reading "Does Heaven Exist?" I am a devout Christian, and I don't give much thought to heaven. My spirituality isn't based on an anthropomorphic, kick-butt God who will throw four generations of children into eternal damnation because some distant forefather ticked him off [see Proverbs 28:5]. Heaven is the flip side of the absolutely barbaric notion of hell that evolved under that kick-butt mindset...To me, God is a symbol for something unfathomable, an utter mystery that fills my heart with joy and my spirit with song.

Notice the use of the words "To me..." That is the key. To be an idolater, you make a god to suit yourself, one devoid of reference to sin, righteousness, and judgment. Make sure he or she likes the things you like and hates the things you hate. If you like lust, so will your god. If your god doesn't mind lying and stealing, then you can lie, steal, and lust to your heart's content. Your god will fill your heart with joy and your spirit with song...right up until Judgment Day.

Take the time to study 1 Corinthians 10:1–14 and see how idolatry leads to sexual sin. So do yourself a big favor: destroy your idols. An idol doesn't have to be something tangible; anything that takes the place of God in our life serves as an idol, whether it be our job, a person, possessions, etc. Cultivate an understanding of what God is like, as revealed in Scripture. That will put the fear of God in you and cause you to keep your heart free from sin, and at the same time you will have strong motivation to do what He says regarding the Great Commission.

Bear in mind, when you speak with Roman Catholics, that this Commandment doesn't exist in their catechism. When you mention the Second Commandment, don't be surprised if they think it is "You shall not take the name of the LORD your God in vain." It's therefore understandable why many sincere Roman Catholics bow down to statues, even though the Bible makes it clear that this is a great sin in God's eyes. Worshiping images or paying divine honor to *any* created object (including people) is a violation of this Commandment. Unbelievably, those who formulated the official Roman Catholic catechism took the liberty of deleting the Second of the Ten Commandments, and then splitting the Tenth into two, thus keeping the total at ten. Below is the Catholic version of the Ten Commandments:

1. I am the Lord thy God. Thou shalt not have strange gods before me.

2. Thou shalt not take the name of the Lord thy God in vain.

3. Remember to keep the Sabbath Day.

4. Honor thy Father and thy Mother.

5. Thou shalt not kill.

6. Thou shalt not commit adultery.

7. Thou shalt not steal.

8. Thou shalt not bear false witness against thy neighbor.

9. Thou shalt not covet thy neighbor's wife.

10. Thou shalt not covet thy neighbor's goods.

Here is their justification for removing the Second Commandment (from "The Commandments of God," *The Catholic Encyclopedia, Volume IV* (www.newadvent.org/cathen/04153a.htm):

> ...the Tenth embraces both the Ninth and Tenth of the Catholic division. It seems, however, as logical to separate at the end as to group at the beginning, for while one single object is aimed at under worship, two specifically different sins are forbidden under covetousness; if adultery and theft belong to two distinct species of moral wrong, the same must be said of the desire to commit these evils.

Yet, notice the explicit wording of the Second Commandment (the deleted one): "You shall not make for yourself any graven image, or any likeness of any thing that is in heaven above, or that is in the earth beneath, or that is in the water under the earth. You shall not bow down yourself to them, nor serve them" (Exodus 20:4,5).

First Corinthians 10:19,20 warns us that things offered to idols are actually offered to demons, rather than to God, and we are not to have fellowship with demons.

QUESTIONS

1. Why is idolatry perhaps the greatest sin?

2. **Why do you think idolatry appeals to the secular mind?**

3. **Before you were saved, what was your concept of God like?**

4. **Think of someone you know who is an idolater. What is his god like?**

5. **How does the Catholic version of the Ten Commandments sidestep this prohibition?**

PREACHER'S PROGRESS

Christian: "Hi, Sally. Good to see you. Have you thought much about what we spoke of last time—that the Day is coming in which God will judge the world in righteousness?"

Sal Frighteous: "Yes, I have … and it doesn't concern me because my god would never send anyone to hell."

Christian: "Do you realize that you are breaking the Second of the Ten Commandments by saying that?"

Sal Frighteous: "What do you mean?"

Christian: "You have made a god to suit yourself. Your god would never send anyone to hell, because he couldn't—he doesn't exist. He's a figment of your imagination. You have made a god you feel comfortable with. That's called idolatry, and it's the oldest sin in the Book. I did the same for many years before I became a Christian."

Sal Frighteous: "Well, I still believe that I am a good person. I believe in God and I go to church. I think God will let me into heaven because I am a good person."

Christian: "Sal, you believe that because the god you have conceived in your mind has a low standard of morality. Did you know that the God of the Bible—the God you will have to face on the Day of Judgment—commands you to be perfect? He is perfect, and He will judge you with a perfect Law that demands perfection."

FEATHERS FOR ARROWS

A preacher was once given free tickets to the rock musical *Jesus Christ Superstar*. The cast had extended the invitation, insisting that he attend, so for their sake he went. After the show he was invited to meet the cast. He told the talented singers that he enjoyed their performance, but that the Jesus they portrayed was not the Jesus of the Bible. The woman who played Mary Magdalene replied, "But we are making Jesus acceptable to the twentieth century."

Her statement was true. Man has always tried to make God acceptable to himself. He prefers to try to change God rather than change his own sinful ways. It is called "idolatry"—making a god in your own image.

WORDS OF COMFORT

I was making a cup of tea early one morning. As I reached over a gas burner on the stove, I suddenly heard a *woof* noise, and looked down to see that the sleeve of my bathrobe was on fire. Then I heard another *woof* as the fire spread around to the back of the robe, and another little *woof* as it spread to the sleeve on the other side. At that moment I remembered that I had purchased a fire extinguisher for such a time as this. What was I supposed to do now: "Stand six feet from the flame and aim the extinguisher at the base of the fire"? This wasn't going to be easy. I took the robe off and threw it to the floor, and heard another *woof* as the whole thing caught fire. The manufacturers of the robe had obviously soaked it in gasoline to make life more exciting for the wearer.

It was then that my daughter walked back into the room and said, "Dad! I can't believe this. I leave the room for two minutes and while I'm away, you manage to catch on fire."

I learned two valuable lessons from the incident. First, don't lean over on open flame in a bathrobe, and second, a man on fire moves rather quickly.

Last Words

Elizabeth the First:

"All my possessions for one moment of time."

Memory Verse

"You adulterers and adulteresses, do you not know that the friendship of the world is enmity with God? whosoever therefore will be a friend of the world is the enemy of God."

JAMES 4:4

LESSON 7

The Ten Commandments, Part 3

"Does it grieve you my friends, that the name of God is being taken in vain and desecrated? Does it grieve you that we are living in a godless age? . . . But, we are living in such an age and the main reason we should be praying about revival is that we are anxious to see God's name vindicated and His glory manifested. We should be anxious to see something happening that will arrest the nations, all the peoples, and cause them to stop and to think again."

MARTYN LLOYD-JONES

Kirk's Comment   As we look at the Third Commandment, consider how you would feel if someone demonstrated enough disrespect for your mother to use her name as a curse word. No doubt you would be offended. How much more respect does Almighty God deserve from us, to whom He has given life.

QUESTIONS & OBJECTIONS

"Isn't it blasphemous to call the Bible 'God's Word' when it makes Him look so bad?"

I am going to tell you some things about my father that will make him look bad. He regularly left my mother to fend for herself. I was once horrified to hear that he deliberately killed a helpless animal. Not only that, but he hit me (often).

Here's the information that's missing: The reason he left my mom during the day was to work to earn money to take care of her and their children. He killed the animal because it had been run over by a car and was suffering. He regularly chastened me because he loved me enough to teach me right from wrong (I was a brat).

Portions of the Bible that "make God look bad" merely reveal that we lack understanding. I never once questioned my dad's integrity, because I trusted him (see Mark 10:15).

w o t m w o t m w o t m w o t m w o t m w o t m w o t m w o t m w o t m w o t m w o t m

In this lesson we will look at the Third Commandment: "**You shall not take the name of the LORD your God in vain**; for the LORD your God will not hold him guiltless that takes his name in vain" (Exodus 20:7).

Transgression of the Third Commandment reinforces the biblical case that the mind of unregenerate man is hostile to God and His Law, that they "hate God without cause." This thought is offensive to idolaters, who strongly contest that they don't hate God. This is because they don't hate their own concept of God; they are on congenial terms with the idol they have created.

Using God's name in profanity is perhaps the simplest, most effective way for man to show his contempt toward his Creator. Godly Jews won't even speak God's name because it is so holy, yet unregenerate man uses it to express revulsion.

To slur someone's name is to insult the very person. Even a foul-mouthed, tattooed, hardhearted biker has a soft spot for his mother. He may have a tattoo of the devil on one arm and "Mom" on the other. If you want to get a free facial, insult his mother.

When Moses asked to see the glory of God, notice how God responded: "I will make all my goodness pass before you, and I will proclaim the name of the LORD before you . . ." (Exodus 33:19).

God's glory, His name, and His goodness are synonymous. Moses was told that if he saw God face to face in all of His glory, he would die (Exodus 33:20). How fearful it will be for blasphemous humanity to stand before the unspeakable glory of God, in all of His goodness, and give an account for every idle word. God's goodness will ensure that His justice is carried out.

It is also interesting to note that when a blasphemer is questioned about why he would do such a thing, his reaction will often confirm the words of Scripture that he is taking God's name "in vain." He will say, "I wasn't really using God's name as a cuss word. It's just a word." In essence, God's name isn't anything special and isn't worthy of any respect. His attempt at justification merely adds to his sin. It is hard to understand how the world can hold the names of God and Jesus Christ in such disdain that they can be used to express disgust. Hitler's name wasn't despised enough to be used as a cuss word.

If you hear God's name taken in vain, don't tell the person it's offensive; use it as an opening for the gospel. While the Bible instructs us to "reprove and rebuke," it says to do so with "all longsuffering [patience] and doctrine." It is therefore important that we don't alienate the person we are trying to reach with the gospel. Our objective isn't to reprove someone because he has offended us with blasphemy, but to reach him for Christ. It is wise to try to engage the person in a conversation about natural things with the objective of witnessing to him. Because you know that he has openly transgressed the Third Commandment, when you ask if he has ever used God's name in vain, you can gently remind him that you heard him do so.

QUESTIONS

1. **What does blasphemy reveal?**

2. **Why will some people claim that they don't truly hate God?**

3. **With what is God's name synonymous? Why is this fearful?**

4. **How do blasphemers often compound their sin?**

5. **How should you react if you hear someone using God's name in vain?**

PREACHER'S PROGRESS

Lucy Mouth: "I heard what you said to Sal. I haven't made a #!*$ god to suit myself. And I don't believe in heaven or hell."

Christian: "May I ask you a few questions?"

Lucy Mouth: "Sure."

Christian: "Have you ever used God's name in vain?"

Lucy Mouth: "What do you mean?"

Christian: "Have you ever used God's name as a cuss word? You know… when something goes wrong, you say, 'Oh, G-d!'"

Lucy Mouth: "Yeah, I've done that, plenty of times. So what?"

Christian: "Do you know what you are doing when you do that?"

Lucy Mouth: "No. And I don't *!#+$ care."

Christian: "Let me tell you what you are doing. Instead of saying a filth word beginning with 's' to express disgust, you are taking the holy name of the God who gave you life and using it as a substitute to express your disgust."

Lucy Mouth: "I don't believe in !@$!* God."

Christian: "That doesn't matter. You still have to face Him on Judgment Day whether you believe in Him or not. What you've done is called blasphemy, and the Bible says, 'The Lord will not hold him guiltless who takes His name in vain.' God gave you a conscience. You know right from wrong...and I wouldn't be in your shoes on Judgment Day for all the tea in China. But thanks for listening to me. Bye."

Never be afraid to be (lovingly) confrontational. You will be amazed at what you can say to someone if your tone is in the right spirit of gentleness. And don't be afraid to use fear as a motivator. Any fear a person has now because of your words of warning will be nothing compared to the fear he will have if he "falls into the hands of the living God." The Lake of Fire should motivate the Christian to cast aside his own fear of rejection that can come in the guise of not wanting to offend the unbeliever.

FEATHERS FOR ARROWS

The Parable of the Fishless Fishermen Fellowship: The fishermen were surrounded by streams and lakes full of hungry fish. They met regularly to discuss the call to fish, the abundance of fish, and the thrill of catching fish. They got excited about fishing!

Someone suggested that they needed a philosophy of fishing, so they carefully defined and redefined fishing, and the purpose of fishing. They developed fishing strategies and tactics. Then they realized that they had been going at it backwards. They had approached fishing from the point of view of the fisherman, and not from the point of view of the fish. How do fish view the world? How does the fisherman appear to the fish? What do fish eat, and when? These are all good things to know. So they began research studies, and attended conferences on fishing. Some traveled to faraway places to study different kinds of fish with different habits. Some got doctorates in fishology. But no one had yet gone fishing.

So a committee was formed to send out fishermen. As prospective fishing places outnumbered fishermen, the committee needed to determine priorities. A priority list of fishing places was posted on bulletin boards in all of the fellowship halls. But still, no one was fishing. A survey was launched to find out why. Most did not answer the survey, but from those who did, it was discovered that some felt called to study fish, a few to furnish fishing equipment, and several to go around encouraging the fishermen. What with meetings, conferences, and seminars, they just simply didn't have time to fish.

Now, Jake was a newcomer to the Fisherman's Fellowship. After one stirring meeting of the Fellowship, he went fishing and caught a large fish. At the next meeting, he told his story and was honored for his catch. He was told that he had a special "gift of fishing." He was then scheduled to speak at all the Fellowship chapters and tell how he did it.

With all the speaking invitations and his election to the board of directors of the Fisherman's Fellowship, Jake no longer had time to go fishing. But soon he began to feel restless and empty. He longed to feel the tug on the line once again. So he canceled the speaking, he resigned from the board, and he said to a friend, "Let's go fishing." They did, just the two of them, and they caught fish.

The members of the Fisherman's Fellowship were many, the fish were plentiful, but the fishers were few! —*Anonymous*

WORDS OF COMFORT

I have found an excellent way to inoffensively and effectively share my faith. All I do is carry in my pocket a few pennies that are pressed with the Ten Commandments. I take one out and give it to a stranger and say, "Here, I have a gift for you." As I hand people the glistening penny, they ask, "What is it?" I reply, "It's a penny with the Ten Commandments on it. How many have you kept?" They predictably say, "Pretty much all of them. I've broken one or two here and there, but I've never killed anybody." Then I gently go through each Commandment. It never fails to work.

On one occasion, I had only thirty seconds to speak to someone who was in an elevator with me. I pulled a penny out of my pocket, handed it to him and said, "Here, I have a gift for you." He predictably asked, "What is it?" I said, "It's a penny with the Ten Commandments on it. How many have you kept?" I waited for the usual response. Instead, he looked down at the penny and said, "This is the first one I've been given." He walked out before I could say another word.

Memory Verse

"But as many as received him, to them gave he power to become the sons of God, even to them that believe on his name."

JOHN 1:12

Last Words

The Duke of Buckingham, a professed atheist, confessed as he died:

"I sported with the holy name of heaven. Now I am haunted by remorse, and, I fear, forsaken by God."

LESSON 8

The Ten Commandments, Part 4

"I am no preacher of the old legal Sabbath. I am a preacher of the gospel. The Sabbath of the Jew is to him a task; the Lord's Day of the Christian, the first day of the week, is to him a joy, a day of rest, of peace, and of thanksgiving. And if you Christian men can earnestly drive away all distractions, so that you can really rest today, it will be good for your bodies, good for your souls, good mentally, good spiritually, good temporally, and good eternally."

CHARLES SPURGEON

Kirk's Comment Although the Christian is not required to keep the Sabbath, the Commandment does reveal our self-centered nature. How often do we wish there were eight days in a week to spend pursuing our own agenda, and rarely set aside one day for God's?

QUESTIONS & OBJECTIONS

"I believe I will go to heaven because I live by the Golden Rule."

Much of the world knows the Golden Rule simply as "do unto others as you would have them do unto you" (see Luke 6:31). According to this verse, if we can live by this rule and love our neighbor as much as we love ourselves, we fulfill the Law. Ask those who claim to do this if they have ever lied, stolen, hated, or looked with lust. If they have broken any of these Commandments, then they haven't loved those they have lied to, stolen from, etc. This will show them that they have violated the Golden Rule. They are under God's wrath (John 3:36), desperately needing the Savior's cleansing blood.

w o t m w o t m w o t m w o t m w o t m w o t m w o t m w o t m w o t m w o t m w o t m

In this lesson we are going to look at the Fourth Commandment: "**Remember the sabbath day, to keep it holy**" (Exodus 20:8).

Some today insist that Christians must keep the Sabbath day, and that those who worship on the first day of the week (Sunday) are in great error. They reason that "Sun-day" originates from the pagan worship of the Sun god, that Jesus and Paul kept the Sabbath day as an example for us to follow, and that the Roman Catholic church is responsible for the change in the day of worship. Those who continue to worship on Sunday, they believe, will receive the mark of the beast. Let's look briefly at these arguments.

First, nowhere does the Fourth Commandment say to *worship* on the Sabbath. It commands *rest* on that day: "Remember the sabbath day, to keep it holy. Six days shall you labor, and do all your work: But the seventh day is the sabbath of the LORD your God: in it you shall not do any work...For in six days the LORD made heaven and earth, the sea, and all that in them is, and rested the seventh day: therefore the LORD blessed the sabbath day, and hallowed it" (Exodus 20:8–11).

Sabbath-keepers worship on Saturday. However, the word "Satur-day" comes from the Latin for "Saturn's day," a pagan day of worship of the planet Saturn (astrology).

If a Christian's salvation depends upon his keeping a certain day, surely God would have told us. At one point, the apostles gathered specifically to discuss the relationship of believers to the Law of Moses. Acts 15:5–11,24–29 was God's opportunity to make His will clear to His children. All He had to do to save millions from damnation was say, "Remember to keep the Sabbath holy," and millions of Christ-centered, God-loving, Bible-believing Christians would have gladly kept it. Instead, the only commands the apostles gave were to "abstain from meats offered to idols, and from blood, and from things strangled, and from fornication."

There isn't even one command in the New Testament for Christians to keep the Sabbath holy. In fact, we are told not to let others judge us regarding Sabbaths (Colossians 2:16), and that man was not made for the Sabbath, but the Sabbath for man (Mark 2:27). The Sabbath was given as a sign to Israel (Exodus 31:13–17); nowhere is it given as a sign to the church. Thousands of years after the Commandment was given, we can still see the sign that separates Israel from the world—they continue to keep the Sabbath holy.

The apostles came together on the first day of the week to break bread (Acts 20:7). The collection was taken on the first day of the week (1 Corinthians 16:2). When do Sabbath-keepers gather together to break bread or take up the collection? It's not on the same day as the early church. They tell us that the Roman Catholic church changed their day of worship from Saturday to Sunday, but what has that got to do with the disciples keeping the first day of the week? That was the Roman Catholic church in the early centuries, not the church in the Book of Acts.

Romans 14:5–10 tells us that one man esteems one day of the week above another; another esteems every day alike. Then Scripture tells us that everyone should be fully persuaded in his own mind. We are not to judge each other regarding the day on which we worship.

Jesus did keep the Sabbath. He had to keep the whole Law to be the perfect sacrifice. The Bible makes it clear that the Law has been satisfied in Christ. The reason Paul went to the synagogue each Sabbath wasn't to keep the Law; that would have been contrary to everything he taught about being saved by grace alone (Ephesians 2:8,9). Instead, it was so he could preach the gospel to the Jews, as evident in the Book of Acts. Paul had an incredible evangelistic zeal for Israel to be saved (Romans 10:1). To the Jew he became as a Jew, that he might win the Jews (1 Corinthians 9:19,20). That meant he went to where they gathered on the day they gathered—"he reasoned in the synagogue every sabbath" (Acts 18:4). D. L. Moody said, "The Law can only chase a man to Calvary, no further." Christ redeemed us from the curse of the Law so we are no longer in bondage to it. If we try to keep one part of the Law (even out of love for

God), we are obligated to keep the whole Law (Galatians 3:10)—all 613 precepts. If those who insist on keeping the Sabbath were as zealous about the salvation of the lost as they are about other Christians keeping the Sabbath, we would see revival.

QUESTIONS

1. **What does the Bible say to do on the Sabbath?**

2. **According to Exodus 31, to whom was the Sabbath given?**

3. **Did Paul worship on the Sabbath? Why or why not?**

4. **Why is the Christian free from the Law?**

PREACHER'S PROGRESS

Dan Druff: "I think Christians are flakes!"

Christian: "Why's that?"

Dan Druff: "They are weak-minded people who need a crutch in life."

Christian: "You are right, if you define a parachute as a 'crutch' for someone jumping out of a plane."

Dan Druff: "Huh?"

Christian: "Don't you realize that you will have to someday pass through death? That's when you will need a Savior, or the 'crutch' you spoke about. When you die you will have to face a Moral Law that is far harsher than the law of gravity."

Dan Druff: "I don't believe in the 'Law.'"

Christian: "That doesn't matter. If a man jumped off a ten-story building not believing in the law of gravity, he still has to face the consequences of his action, despite the fact that he doesn't believe in it…Have you kept God's Law, the Ten Commandments? Have you ever told a lie?"

Dan Druff: "You're starting to get under my skin."

Christian: "I'm only telling you this because I care about you. God is going to judge with a fine-toothed comb on Judgment Day. He will judge right down to the thoughts and intents of your heart. In fact, the Bible says in Psalm 68:21 that 'God shall wound the head of his enemies, and the hairy scalp of such an one as goes on still in his trespasses.' You need to repent today and put your faith in Jesus Christ."

FEATHERS FOR ARROWS

In 1969, twenty-four people decided to ignore warnings that Hurricane Camille was heading for Mississippi. They instead made up their minds that they were going to ride it out. Twenty-three of them died in the hurricane. The cross is a warning of the fierce hurricane of God's wrath, which no one will "ride out" on Judgment Day. The only way to flee the coming wrath is to "kiss the Son"—to yield to the Lordship of the Savior, Jesus Christ. Those who put their trust in Him are blessed with forgiveness and eternal life.

WORDS OF COMFORT

I felt an earthquake the other night. I am amazed at the sensitivity the human body has to detect not only the moment an earthquake begins, but even the size of the shaker. Living in California has given me acuteness to a point where I can accurately guess the size of the quake (within a few points). The one I felt must have been a 5.5 at least. It was strong enough to wake me out of a deep sleep and say to Sue, "Wow! That was a big one..." She was already awake at the time, and said that she hadn't felt it. Strange. She also said that she had just turned over in bed.

Last Words

Ludwig van Beethoven (1770-1827), German composer:

"Too bad, too bad! It's too late!"

The Ten Commandments, Part 5

*"How many observe Christ's birthday! How few, his precepts!
O! 'tis easier to keep holidays than commandments."*

BENJAMIN FRANKLIN

Kirk's Comment The Fifth Commandment has to do with honoring your father and mother. As a teenager, I was guilty of breaking this Commandment on a daily basis.

QUESTIONS & OBJECTIONS

"God is unfair in that Hitler and a dear old lady (who never accepted Jesus) will both go to hell."

Sinners often accuse God of being unjust, because they assume that everyone will receive the same punishment in hell regardless of whether their sins are menial or heinous. God's judgment, however, will be according to righteousness (Acts 17:31). In Matthew 11:24, Jesus said, "It shall be more tolerable for the land of Sodom in the day of judgment, than for you." And in Luke 10:14, we see that the more sinful cities of Chorazin and Bethsaida will receive a more harsh judgment than Tyre and Sidon. These verses show that there will be degrees of punishment. (See also Luke 12:47,48; Hebrews 10:29.)

I n this lesson we are going to look at the Fifth Commandment: "**Honor your father and your mother**: that your days may be long upon the land which the Lord your God gives you" (Exodus 20:12).

This Commandment is unique, because it is "the first commandment with promise" (Ephesians 6:2). To honor our parents is to esteem them, show them respect, and obey them. The New Testament instructs children to "obey your parents in the Lord: for this is right" (Ephesians 6:1) and "obey your parents in all things: for this is well pleasing to the Lord" (Colossians 3:20). Are children to obey only the things they want to, or that sound reasonable to them? No; in order to please the Lord, they are to obey "in all things." That doesn't mean their parents will always make wise decisions or treat their children as they should, but God will hold the parents accountable for their own actions. Regardless of the parents' parenting skills, the children are to obey—that is their role for which God will hold them accountable.

Why is this so important? Since children are naturally sinful, they need to be instructed in the ways of the Lord; parents must "train up a child in the way he should go" (Proverbs 22:6). Proverbs 29:15,17 warns, "The rod and reproof give wisdom: but a child left to himself brings his mother to shame...Correct your son, and he shall give you rest; yes, he shall give delight unto your soul." One who will not submit to the authority of his parents, who are God's agents to train and discipline him, is very unlikely to submit to God's authority and obey God's Laws.

In essence, this commandment promises that, if children do not honor their parents, all will not go well with them and their days will not be long upon the earth. This is the reason all isn't well with this generation. It has been left in the dark about the requirements of the Law and is suffering the consequences of its transgression. It is plagued with drug and alcohol addiction, promiscuity, sexually transmitted diseases, broken families, and a massive suicide rate (go to www.1000deaths.com, click on the photos, and weep).

The Bible says that the Messiah would magnify the Law and make it honorable (Isaiah 42:21). Jesus did this many times, particularly in the Sermon on the Mount. Mark 7:5–13 tells us that the Pharisees had dishonored the Law by merely giving God lip service. They made this Commandment void through their tradition, teaching for doctrines the commandments of men. The Savior brought honor back to the Law by teaching that the Law was spiritual in nature, and that outward observance was not enough. God required truth in the inward parts (the thought-life, intent, and motives).

Again, the lawful use of the Law is to show us how far we have fallen short of God's perfect standard. The Law brings the knowledge of sin. The best of us haven't honored our parents as we should. However, in witnessing, you will encounter some who will contend that they have kept this Commandment and have perfectly honored their parents. They therefore need to be confronted with the sins of the flesh first before they are confronted with this Commandment. Have they lied? Have they stolen? Almost everyone will admit to lying and stealing; therefore, they have dishonored their parents' name by being a lying thief.

QUESTIONS

1. What does it mean to "honor" your mother and father?

2. Should someone always have to honor his mother, even if, for example, she's a prostitute?

3. Why is it so important for children to obey this Commandment?

4. **When witnessing, why is it important to go through the Commandments that deal with the sins of the flesh before mentioning this one?**

PREACHER'S PROGRESS

Miss Informed: "I don't think that the Bible can be trusted because there are so many versions. Which one is right?"

Christian: "There are versions in Chinese for the Chinese. There are versions in Russian for the Russian people. There are actually thousands of versions of the Bible—some are in modern languages, some in foreign languages, and some are in old English. Few, in the printing age, can claim that they don't have access to the Scriptures in their own language."

Miss Informed: "The Bible is open to interpretation. I mean, so many people think that one verse means one thing and someone else thinks it means something completely different. It's so totally confusing."

Christian: "Try deciphering this: Jesus said, 'Unless you repent, you shall perish.'"

Miss Informed: "Um..."

Christian: "How would you interpret that?"

Miss Informed: "Hasn't the Bible changed down through the ages?"

Christian: "No, it hasn't. God has preserved His Word. Anyone can now obtain access to computer programs that give the original Hebrew and Greek words, and the only 'changes' are ones that have been made for clarity. Take for example the verse we just looked at. The old English says, 'Except ye repent, ye shall all likewise perish,' while a contemporary version may say something like, 'Unless you repent, you too will all perish.'"

Miss Informed: "Okay. I'm getting the message."

FEATHERS FOR ARROWS

Back in the Old West, a number of men were upstairs in a boarding house amusing themselves with a game of cards when they heard a cry from the street below: "Fire! Fire!" The men looked at one another in disbelief. One of the windows grew orange with the flames. "Wait!" said the dealer. "Let's just finish this hand; we've got plenty of time—I have a key to the back door." The men nodded in approval, then quickly picked up the dealt cards. Precious minutes passed. One of the men became nervous as the flames licked through the now broken window. With darting eyes and a sweat-filled brow, he asked for the key. "Coward!" muttered the dealer as he tossed across the key. Each of them then rushed to the door and waited with bated breath as the key was placed into the lock. "It won't turn!" the man cried. "Let me have it!" said the dealer. As he tried in vain to turn the key, he whispered in horror, "It's the wrong key!"

WORDS OF COMFORT

I have an uncanny knack of getting stuck in places. When I was a small boy, I got stuck on a high cliff and someone had to rescue me. When I was in my thirties I stayed off cliffs, but still managed to get stuck. I forgot to take a key to use a restroom that was shared by a number of shopkeepers. Fortunately, the door wasn't locked. I went inside and shut the door. However, I discovered that I couldn't get *out* without a key. I had to put my head through a small gap, and humbly ask a passerby to go to a store and ask for a key to let me out.

Memory Verse

"Depart from evil, and do good; seek peace, and pursue it. The eyes of the LORD are upon the righteous, and his ears are open unto their cry."
PSALM 34:14,15

Last Words

St. Francis of Assisi (1182–1226), founder of the Franciscan order of monks:

"Farewell, my children; remain always in the fear of the Lord. That temptation and tribulation which is to come is now at hand and happy shall they be who persevere in the good they have begun. I hasten to go to our Lord, to whose grace I recommend you."

10

The Ten Commandments, Part 6

"If you will not have death unto sin, you shall have sin unto death.
There is no alternative. If you do not die to sin, you shall die for sin.
If you do not slay sin, sin will slay you."
CHARLES SPURGEON

Kirk's Comment   We can all agree that murder is a very serious sin. Most of us think we're safe with this Commandment. But from God's point of view, you and I are not so innocent. This is a sobering lesson.

QUESTIONS & OBJECTIONS

"If abortion wasn't legal, we'd have all those poor girls slipping off to see back-alley butchers. At least this way they'll get counseling."

You're right. Think of all those poor murderers who are consigned to slip around and kill in secret. We ought to legalize murder too! Then they can kill in a nice, clean, safe environment. They will be protected from getting splashed with blood that might contain diseases, and we can offer counseling so they won't have any post-murder trauma from the choices they have made.

n this lesson we will look at the Sixth Commandment, and what it means in light of New Testament revelation: "**You shall not kill**" (Exodus 20:13).

In the dim light of their ignorance, the world looks at the Sixth Commandment and proclaims itself "not guilty." However, God requires truth in the inward parts (Psalm 51:6). In other words, He sees the thought-life—the intent, the innermost motive of every human being. If civil law can prove that you are planning to assassinate the President, you can be prosecuted and severely punished. That law, however, is limited in its search for evidence—it can't see what a man *thinks*. Not so with the all-seeing eye of our Creator. His Law searches the heart, and He sees "evil thoughts." To even *think* hatred is to transgress the Sixth Commandment.

Jesus said, "You have heard that it was said by them of old time, You shall not kill; and whosoever shall kill shall be in danger of the judgment: But I say to you, That whosoever is angry with his brother without a cause shall be in danger of the judgment" (Matthew 5:21,22). The Bible further adds that if we hate someone, we are murderers (1 John 3:15). There are many who would like to kill, but refrain because of fear of punishment. God counts them guilty of murder.

Even if we don't have thoughts of physically murdering someone we hate, there is another sense in which we desire their death. John 8:44 says of the devil that "he was a murderer from the beginning." While Satan didn't go around physically killing men and women, by tempting Adam and Eve he did bring about the spiritual death of all mankind through sin (see Romans 5:12). If we hate someone, the last thought in our minds will be sharing the gospel with them out of concern for their salvation. In that sense, we too become a murderer, desiring the person's eternal death, by not giving them the words of life.

Some states have laws that declare a bystander guilty for standing by and failing to prevent a crime. In the same way, God declares us guilty of murder if we stand by and do nothing to prevent someone's eternal death. Their blood is our on hands (see Ezekiel 3:18).

Sixty people are murdered each day in the United States (FBI statistics reveal an average of around 20,000 murders per year). Homicide has become so common that it hardly merits a mention on the news.

Some time ago, Thomas Lyndon Jr. of Rocky Point, Long Island, confessed to the murder of a woman during a robbery. He admitted that he held the point of a four-inch hunting knife to her throat, and then "dug it in a little deeper" after she awoke and began to struggle. He said that after Lea Greene stopped moving, "I counted her heartbeats out of curiosity to see how long it'd take her to die...I knew exactly what I was doing...I knew it was against the law...I felt powerful—invincible, sort of, you know?" How true are the words of Charles Spurgeon, the Prince of Preachers: "Look at fallen human nature. Whitefield used to say that it was half beast and half devil. I question whether both beast and devil are not slandered by being compared with man when he is left to his own."

In our day, abortion is another common occurrence. Many people try to convince themselves that the unborn child is nothing but a "blob of tissue," making it acceptable to destroy. But at 21 days gestation, the child's heart is beating, and at 40 days brain waves can be measured. If by our medical criteria a life is ended when there is no heartbeat or brain activity, then surely by their presence we can assert that life has begun. The Bible tells us that taking the life of the unborn is clearly murder: "He slew me not from the womb; or that my mother might have been my grave" (Jeremiah 20:17), and God vowed to punish those who "ripped up the women with child" (Amos 1:13). God, the Creator of life, commanded us, "Do not shed innocent blood" (Jeremiah 7:6).

Some equate capital punishment with murder, and cite Jesus' command to love our enemies (Matthew 5:44) as evidence that He did not endorse capital punishment. However, just because we have love for an enemy doesn't give us the right to allow him to escape punishment for murder. The Bible says, "Let every soul be subject to the higher powers. For there is no power but of God: the powers that be are ordained of God. Whosoever therefore resists the power, resists the ordinance of God: and they that resist shall receive to themselves damnation...But if you do that which is evil, be afraid; for he bears not the sword in vain: for he is the minister of God, a revenger to execute wrath upon him that does evil" (Romans 13:1–4).

The Bible says that anyone who deliberately takes a life should lose his own: "Whoso kills any person, the murderer shall be put to death by the mouth of witnesses: but one witness shall not testify against any person to cause him to die. Moreover you shall take no satisfaction for the life of a murderer, which is guilty of death: but he shall be surely put to death" (Numbers 35:30,31). Genesis 9:6 says, "Whoso sheds man's blood, by man shall his blood be shed: for in the image of God made he man." This shows the value God places on human life. The seriousness of a crime is revealed in the punishment dealt to the criminal. It is interesting to note that when Oklahoma City bomber Timothy McVeigh requested the death penalty, 250 relatives of the victims he killed asked to watch his execution. Their desire to actually see justice done testifies to the value they place on the loved one they lost. Despite claims to the contrary, capital punishment does deter crime. The person executed will not do it again.

Still, there are respected Christian leaders whose conscience will not allow them to advocate capital punishment, out of concern that innocent people may fall through the cracks of a godless justice system. That is why such extensive effort is expended to ascertain the guilt of the accused in a capital murder case. However, despite civil law's imperfections, we are told to be subject to the governing authorities.

It was God who instituted the death penalty in the beginning. The Judge of the Universe pronounced the death sentence upon all humanity when He said, "The soul that sins, it shall die" (Ezekiel 18:20).

QUESTIONS

1. **Why is civil law limited when it comes to prosecuting criminals?**

2. **Most people will claim to be not guilty of violating the Sixth Commandment. How can you explain God's perspective?**

3. Why does God consider hatred to be murder?

4. Is there someone you dislike strongly enough to not want to see the person in heaven? Do you think God considers you a murderer for this?

5. Do you think God views abortion as murder? Why or why not?

6. Does the Bible equate capital punishment with murder? Why or why not?

PREACHER'S PROGRESS

Ben Gay: "Hey, Christian, I'm gay, and science has proved that I was born like this."

Christian: "True. I was born with homosexual tendencies."

Ben Gay: "Huh?"

Christian: "I was also born with a tendency to lie, steal, commit adultery, and fornicate. It's called 'sin' and it's in every one of us."

Ben Gay: "So are you saying that I'm going to hell just because I'm homosexual?"

Christian: "I didn't even mention hell. Where do you think you will go when you die?"

Ben Gay: "Heaven."

Christian: "Why?"

Ben Gay: "Because I'm a good person."

Christian: "Do you want to do a short test to see if you are?"

Ben Gay: "Okay."

Christian: "Have you ever told a lie? Stolen? Used God's name in vain?"

The Bible tells us that the Moral Law was made for homosexuals (see 1 Timothy 1:8–10). If you use the Law when witnessing, you won't even have to mention their "sexual preference," and thus be accused of "hate." The Law will show the homosexual that he is damned despite his sexual preference. When he finds a place of true repentance and faith in Jesus, God will take away his unclean spirit and give him a new heart with new desires.

WORDS OF COMFORT

In Lakewood, California, a man who sent four golf balls into the lake at the local golf club decided that he wasn't a gifted golfer. He was so upset at his effort that he threw his golf bag into the lake and stormed off to his car. Onlookers thought that he had had a change of heart when he went back down to the lake and waded out into the water. He then grabbed the bag, searched the pockets until he found his car keys, returned to his car bagless, and drove away.

Memory Verse

"Whosoever hates his brother is a murderer: and you know that no murderer has eternal life abiding in him."

1 JOHN 3:15

Last Words

Edith Louisa Cavell (1865–1915) was a British nurse martyred by the Germans for harboring British refugees. About to die, she said:

"Standing, as I do, in view of God and eternity...I realize that patriotism is not enough. I must have no hatred or bitterness against anyone."

The Ten Commandments, Part 7

"In my preaching of the Word, I took special notice of this one thing, namely, that the Lord did lead me to begin where His Word begins with sinners; that is, to condemn all flesh, and to open and allege that the curse of God, by the Law, doth belong to and lay hold on all men as they come into the world, because of sin."

JOHN BUNYAN

Kirk's Comment Although Jesus issued a very serious warning about breaking the Seventh Commandment, it is perhaps the one that is broken with the most enthusiasm and excitement.

QUESTIONS & OBJECTIONS

"God made me to be a homosexual, so He doesn't want me to change."

Homosexuals argue that they did not make a conscious decision to be that way, so it must be natural. They *are* born that way—just as all of us are born with a sin nature and sinful desires (Ephesians 2:1–3). Tell them that it is natural for them, and for all of us, to be tempted to do things that God says are wrong. In the same way, pedophiles, adulterers, alcoholics, drug addicts, etc., don't make a conscious decision to "choose" that self-destructive lifestyle; they simply give in to their sinful desires. However, although sin is natural for unbelievers, that doesn't mean God wants them to remain that way. God can set them free from their sinful nature (Romans 7:23–8:2), give them new desires (Ephesians 4:22–24), and help them withstand temptations (1 Corinthians 10:13).

wotmwotmwotmwotmwotmwotmwotmwotmwotmwotmwotm

In this lesson we will look at the Seventh Commandment and what it means in light of New Testament revelation: "**You shall not commit adultery**" (Exodus 20:14).

The Bible said that the Messiah would magnify the Law and make it honorable (Isaiah 42:21). The Pharisees had dishonored the Law by teaching that God required only an outward show of piety. However, Jesus explained that God judges even the thought-life. He said, "You have heard that it was said by them of old time, You shall not commit adultery: But I say to you, that whosoever looks on a woman to lust after her has committed adultery with her already in his heart" (Matthew 5:27,28). In doing so He touched the apple of the eye of humanity. Men live for and will die because of lust. For them it is life's greatest pleasure, and they would rather be damned than let it go. If salvation were the work of man, no one would be saved. The evangelistic endeavor would be hopeless. But thank God it is He who gives us repentance leading us to the knowledge of the truth (2 Timothy 2:25). It is God who brings us to our senses and shows us the end of our transgressions. This Commandment is perhaps the most powerful of the mighty cannons of God and therefore must be used often to awaken sinners to their plight.

Lust is especially dangerous because it rarely lies alone. Its bedfellows are fornication, adultery, perversion, rape, and even murder. It burns in the heart of man, and like acid reflux, it forces its way through his flesh in a great all-consuming wave with a mind of its own. Lust caused Herod to murder John the Baptist, the greatest man born of women. It doesn't want a mere half of your kingdom, it wants your head on a plate. It brings forth sin, and sin when it's conceived brings forth death. Proverbs 6:32 warns us, "But whoso commits adultery with a woman lacks understanding: he that does it destroys his own soul."

The gift of sex was given by God for procreation and pleasure. Scripture says that the only time a husband and wife should refrain from the joys of sex is when they are praying and fasting; otherwise, they set themselves up for temptation (1 Corinthians 7:5). The Bible also says that a man should be ravished (enraptured) always with her love (Proverbs 5:18–20). The only stipulation is that it is his wife he is to be enraptured with—not the woman down the street.

Men will often deceive themselves by believing that the Ten Commandments condemn only adultery, leaving them free to have sex outside of marriage. However, the Law condemns all unlawful sex. First Timothy 1:8–10 tells us that the Law was also made for fornicators (whoremongers). Galatians 5:19 lists adultery and fornication at the top of the list of works of the flesh.

Those who forsake marriage thinking that they can enjoy sex outside the bonds of the institution risk getting AIDS and numerous other sexually transmitted diseases—several of which are incurable. It is interesting to note that a man and a woman can engage in sex ten thousand times within marriage and never even once risk contracting any sexually transmitted disease.

One who commits fornication (from the Greek *Porneia*, "illicit sexual intercourse") takes what could lawfully be his as a gift from God, and corrupts it. He is like a child who one night steals a crisp, new twenty-dollar bill from his father's wallet, not realizing that his father intended to give it to him as a gift in the morning.

The fornicator not only sins against God and incurs the wrath of eternal justice, but he sins against his conscience, and his own body (1 Corinthians 6:18). Fornicators will not inherit the kingdom of God (1 Corinthians 6:9). Scripture warns us to "abstain from fleshly lusts which war against the soul" (1 Peter 2:11).

Don't be discouraged if you have a battle with lust. If you are struggling, then at least you are fighting it. If you have no problem with it, then you have given your heart to demons and they will drag you to hell. These are fearful words—but they are needed to awaken us to what is at stake.

Would you ever take pornography to church and look at it during worship? You may as well, because God is just as present in your bedroom as He is in the church building. If you are given to pornography, face the fact that you may not be saved. Examine yourself to ensure that Christ is living in you (2 Corinthians 13:5). See Romans 6:11–22; 8:1–14; Ephesians 5:3–8.

Realize that when you give yourself to pornography, you are committing adultery (Matthew 5:27,28). Grasp the serious nature of your sin. Jesus said that it would be better for you to be blind and go to heaven than for your eye to cause you to sin and end up in hell (Matthew 5:29). Those who profess to be Christians yet drool over pornographic material evidently lack the fear of God (Proverbs 16:6). Cultivate the fear of the Lord by reading Proverbs 2:1–5. Think of where lust led King David. He opened himself to many other sins, including murder, and brought misery and shame to his family name. Read Psalm 51 and make it your own prayer.

Memorize James 1:14,15 and 1 Corinthians 10:13. Follow Jesus' example (Matthew 4:3–11) and quote the Word of God when you are tempted (see Ephesians 6:12–20).

Make no provision for your flesh (Romans 13:14; 1 Peter 2:11). Get rid of every access to pornographic material—the Internet, printed literature, TV, videos, and movies. Stop feeding the fire. Instead, guard your heart with all diligence (Proverbs 4:23). Don't let the demonic realm have access to your thought-life. If you give yourself to it, you will become its slave (Romans 6:16).

Read the Bible daily, without fail. As you submit to God, the devil will flee (James 4:7,8). The next time temptation comes, do fifty push-ups, then fifty sit-ups. If you are still burning, repeat the process (see 1 Corinthians 9:27).

Take confidence that even though sinners may shake off your words when you talk to them about lust, they will find it more difficult to shake off the conviction of the Holy Spirit. Plant the seed of truth in the soil of the heart. Tell them what Jesus said about this sin, and then pray that the Holy Spirit makes the word grow in their hearts.

QUESTIONS

1. How did the Messiah make the Law "honorable"?

2. What are some of the sins that accompany lust?

3. What does lust want from you? (See John 10:10 and James 1:14,15.)

4. How would you answer someone who said that the Ten Commandments do not condemn sex outside of marriage?

5. Why shouldn't you be discouraged if you have a problem with lust?

6. What does the Bible say to those who consider viewing pornography to be a harmless activity?

7. What can we learn from Proverbs 2:1–5?

PREACHER'S PROGRESS

Christian: "Hey, Larry. Good to see you again."

Larry Lovelust: "Hey, Christian. What's up?"

Christian: "Heaven. Do you think you will be going there?"

Larry Lovelust: "Sure. I'm as good as any Christian."

Christian: "That wasn't the case the last time we spoke. Are you still lusting after women?"

Larry Lovelust: "Absolutely. I love it. What you see as lust, I see as pleasure. There's nothing wrong with looking at a woman and saying, 'She's pretty.'"

Christian: "That's right. There's nothing wrong with that. But God says that there is something wrong with lusting after her. He calls it adultery."

Larry Lovelust: "How do you know the difference?"

Christian: "Your conscience. It will tell you when it changes from 'look' to 'lust,' if you have a mind to listen."

Larry Lovelust: "Well, like I said, it sure gives me pleasure."

Christian: "Just because it gives pleasure doesn't mean that it's right. Rape can give pleasure. So can an exciting bank robbery. Jesus said that if your eye causes you to sin, you should pluck it out rather than let that sin take you to hell."

Larry Lovelust: "I don't think God will send me to hell for just looking at a woman."

Christian: "He won't, but He will send you to hell for committing adultery in your heart. I appreciate your listening to me. Let me know if you want to talk further, Larry."

FEATHERS FOR ARROWS

So much of the world's misery is self-inflicted: AIDS, alcoholism, obesity, guilt, drug addiction, nicotine addiction and its related diseases, etc. Look at the repercussions of adultery, revealed in this unsigned letter: "Eleven years ago, I walked out on a twelve-year marriage. My wife was a good person, but for a long time she was under a lot of stress. Instead of helping her, I began an affair with her best friend. It was a disaster. This is what I gave up: 1) seeing my daughter grow up; 2) the respect of many long-time friends; 3) the enjoyment of living as a family; 4) a wife who was loyal, was appreciative and tried to make me happy. This is what I got: 1) two stepchildren who treated me like dirt; 2) a wife who didn't know how to make anything for dinner but reservations; 3) a wife whose only interest in me was how much money she could get; 4) a wife who made disparaging remarks about my family and ruined all my existing friendships; 5) finally, the best thing I got was a bitter, expensive divorce."

WORDS OF COMFORT

A lady named Peggy stepped into the lobby of our ministry and asked if she could park her 18-wheeler cab in front of our building. I said that it was fine, and then gave her one of our Elvis "collectible" tracts. She looked at the picture and said, "That looks like my first husband." I asked how many she had had. She said that she was now with her fourth husband.

I held back from saying "...and he whom you have now is not your husband," and instead gave her a penny with the Ten Commandments pressed into it. I told her what it was, and then asked, "Do you think you have kept the Ten Commandments?" When she admitted that she had lied and stolen, I gently said, "By your own admission, you are a lying thief. If God judges you by the Ten Commandments on Judgment Day, will you be innocent or guilty?" She said that she would be guilty and end up in hell. I told her that it wasn't God's will that she go there, and asked if she knew what God had done so that she wouldn't go to hell. She widened her eyes and sincerely said, "He gave His only forgotten Son."

Most of America knows John 3:16, even if they don't get it quite right.

Last Words

Zuniger was a Professor of Medicine at Basel who, although renowned for his skill, was a simple-hearted believer who lived in the light of eternity. His last words were:

> "I rejoice, yea, my spirit leaps within me for joy, that now the time at last is come when I shall see the glorious God face to face; whom I have by faith longed after, and after whom my soul has panted."

Memory Verse

"You have heard that it was said by them of old time, You shall not commit adultery: But I say to you, That whosoever looks on a woman to lust after her has committed adultery with her already in his heart."
MATTHEW 5:27,28

12

The Ten Commandments, Part 8

"Grace means nothing to a person who does not know he is sinful and that such sinfulness means he is separated from God and damned. It is therefore pointless to preach grace until the impossible demands of the Law and the reality of guilt before God are preached."

JOHN MACARTHUR

Kirk's Comment This Commandment really serves to wake up the conscience. It is wonderfully effective in alerting individuals to the serious condition of their hearts. Remember, petty theft is still theft.

QUESTIONS & OBJECTIONS

"Aren't there some circumstances when violating God's Law is justified?"

A man's wife is dying. She needs medicine that is available at only one store, and it's currently closed. They're too far from any hospital, and the man doesn't have enough money to buy the medicine even if the store were open. So he breaks in that night, steals the medicine (and doesn't touch anything else), and saves his wife's life. Is this morally incorrect? Is this a sin?

The Bible says, "Men do not despise a thief, if he steals to satisfy his soul when he is hungry; but if he be found, he shall restore sevenfold; he shall give all the substance of his house" (Proverbs 6:30,31).

If a man steals to save the life of his wife, he "steals." He is therefore guilty of breaking both man's law and God's Law. However, any reasonable judge would take into account the motive for his transgression and be merciful. Obviously, God will do the same on Judgment Day with those who have found themselves in such a predicament. God will do what is right. However, if you dig a little into the motive of the person who is asking whether breaking the law is ever justifiable, you will likely find that neither he nor a loved one is in a life-or-death predicament; he is merely creating imaginary scenarios to try to justify his love of sin.

wotmwotmwotmwotmwotmwotmwotmwotmwotmwotmwotm

In this lesson we will look at the Eighth Commandment: "**You shall not steal**" (Exodus 20:15).

Most people don't think that God considers theft to be theft until the value of what is taken impresses Him. However, if I open your wallet and take just one dollar, I'm a thief, and the Bible says that thieves will not enter the kingdom of God. What would be worth stealing for the loss of your soul? Jesus asked, "What is a man profited if he shall gain the whole world, and lose his own soul?" (Matthew 16:26).

It is a sad testimony to the wickedness of the human heart when the world honors an honest person. Someone finds a wallet filled with money and returns it to the owner—and that makes national news. It is rare when a human being does what he should. Theft comes easily to us because our spiritual father is a thief. He came to steal, kill, and destroy, and his will we willingly do…and love it. As a child I would use an eel spear connected to a piece of rope to spear apples in my neighbor's yard and pull them through the hedge onto our property. We had apples at home, but the stolen apples tasted sweeter.

We don't realize how sin crouches at the door of the human heart. Many would never consider theft until temptation arises. Take for instance the situation on May 14, 1993, in Chicago, when $600,000 fell out of an armored truck onto the interstate. Panic-stricken motorists screeched their vehicles to a halt and stuffed bills into their pockets. Motorcyclists were seen cramming their helmets with cash, and speeding off into the distance. Two paramedics handed police $120,000. They returned the cash only because they suspected it was drug money and therefore "marked." Around $450,000 is still missing.

Sinners will often dig deep into the realm of fantasy to try to justify theft. They will say, "Are you telling me that if a man steals a loaf of bread to feed his starving children that God calls that theft?" The answer is yes. It is theft and the Bible says that he should make restitution for his crime. If a man is hungry, he should beg before he steals. A sinner will often admit to stealing but say that it was just a bar of candy when he was young. Or he will say that he has stolen once, but has since reformed. He must be told that time doesn't forgive sin, and that God still sees the sins of yesterday as if they were committed today. Stop his mouth using the Law (Romans 3:19). Show him that the only way to escape the terrible consequences of his sin is the Door of the Savior. Let the hurricane of the wrath of the Law of God blow far from him the scanty leaves of self-righteousness. Have him admit his transgression by name—that he is a thief. Then point to (and have him read) 1 Corinthians 6:9,10.

Charles Finney said, "This Law, then, should be arrayed in all its majesty against selfishness and enmity of the sinner. All men know that they have sinned, but all are not convicted of the guilt and ill dessert of sin. But without this they cannot understand or appreciate the gospel method of salvation. Away with this milk-and-water preaching of a love of Christ that has no holiness or moral discrimination in it. Away with preaching a love of God that is not angry with sinners every day."

QUESTIONS

1. **Why is the value of a stolen item irrelevant?**

2. What does a news item about someone returning a lost wallet reveal about human nature?

3. Is it wrong for a man to steal when he is hungry?

4. How would you react if you saw $600,000 fluttering along a freeway?

5. What would keep you from stealing the money?

6. Why isn't it enough for a thief to reform his ways?

PREACHER'S PROGRESS

Christian: "How are you doing?"

Robin Banks: "Fine. How are you?"

Christian: "Good. Do you know of any good churches in this area?"

Robin Banks: "I don't know. I haven't been to church for years."

Christian: "Do you have a Christian background?"

Robin Banks: "Yes. I went to Sunday school, but grew out of it when I got older."

Christian: "By the way, my name's Christian. What's yours?"

Robin Banks: "Robin Banks."

Christian: "Nice to meet you. Do you consider yourself to be a good person... I mean, have you kept the Ten Commandments?"

Robin Banks: "Pretty much."

Christian: "Have you ever told a lie?"

Robin Banks: "Yes."

Christian: "What does that make you?"

Robin Banks: "A liar."

Christian: "Have you ever stolen something?"

Robin Banks: "You are laying a guilt trip on me."

Christian: "Really? Which Commandment makes you feel guilty—You shall not lie?"

Robin Banks: "No."

Christian: "You shall not steal?"

Robin Banks: "I really don't want to talk about this anymore."

Christian: "I'm sorry. I didn't mean to offend you. What do you do for a living?"

Robin Banks: "I... um... I work in a bank. I've got to go now..."

WORDS OF COMFORT

I once made a 15-foot-long wooden seat for the inside of a bus I had purchased. I was thrilled that, for a change, everything worked out fine. Then I turned my energy to the seating to go along the wall on the *other* side of the bus. I determined that I wasn't going to blow it, so I did everything *identical* to the first one. I made an exact replica, knowing that I couldn't go wrong if I did so. It was only when I picked it up to turn it around to fit against the other wall that I realized my little error. There was a *clunk!* as it hit the wall of the bus. The seat was 15 feet long, but the bus was only about 10 feet wide—I couldn't turn the seat around to put it against the wall.

I loved that bus. We put Bible verses around the outside and painted a large picture of a man in a coffin on the back of the bus. Piled around him were masses of money, and underneath were the words, "What shall it profit a man if he gains the whole world and loses his own soul?" For some reason we didn't get too many tailgaters.

It was a big bus. In fact, it was so big that I steered the thing while Sue worked the pedals. One day I was driving through the city and found that it was too big to make it around a corner. I carefully checked the rearview mirrors and backed up. Then I heard a sound I will never forget: a high-pitched *Ne-ne-ne-ne-ne-ne!* followed by a *scrrrraaaaape*. I checked my mirrors again—nothing there. I drove forward. Again I heard the mystifying *scrrrraaaaape*, so I pulled in around the corner to check what I thought was something dragging under the bus. Suddenly, there was a feverish knock at the door. I opened it and saw a young man with a pale face. He had been stopped directly behind the bus in a very small car, when a coffin with "What shall it profit a man if he gains the whole world and loses his soul?" began heading toward him. He honked his car horn *Ne-ne-ne-ne-ne-ne!* as the bus scraped across the hood of his car—taking the corpse, the coffin, and the Scripture right up to his windshield. Poor man.

Memory Verse

"For what shall it profit a man, if he shall gain the whole world, and lose his own soul? Or what shall a man give in exchange for his soul?"
MARK 8:36,37

Last Words

Socrates (470–309 B.C.), Greek philosopher of whom Plato was so proud:

"All of the wisdom of this world is but a tiny raft upon which we must set sail when we leave this earth. If only there was a firmer foundation upon which to sail, perhaps some divine word."

13 The Ten Commandments, Part 9

> *"I do not believe that any man can preach the gospel who does not preach the Law."*
>
> **CHARLES SPURGEON**

Kirk's Comment   Is a white lie still a lie? Is half of the truth only half of a lie? If you tell a lie for a "good reason," is it still a sin? What qualifies us as a liar? By whose standards will we be judged?

QUESTIONS & OBJECTIONS

"What if someone says they've never lied, stolen, lusted, blasphemed—if they deny having any sin at all?"

Ask the person if he has kept the First of the Ten Commandments. Has he always loved God above all else—with all of his heart, soul, mind, and strength (Mark 12:30)? If he says that he has, gently say, "The Bible says that 'there is none that seeks after God' (Romans 3:11). *Nobody* (except Jesus Christ) has kept the First of the Ten Commandments. One of you is lying—either you or God—and the Bible says that it is impossible for God to lie" (Hebrews 6:18; Titus 1:2).

In this lesson we will look at the Ninth Commandment: "**You shall not bear false witness** against your neighbor" (Exodus 20:16).

It is common when mentioning this Commandment to hear the response, "You mean that if some lady asks you if you think she is ugly, you have to tell her the truth—that she is?" Let the person know that there is a big difference between discretion (wise self-restraint in speech) and lying (a false statement intended to deceive), and that God knows the difference.

Should a Christian ever tell a lie? There are times when we may find ourselves in the difficult position of realizing that telling the truth may have dire repercussions. For example, you are asked by a Nazi if you are hiding any Jews in your home. Should you tell him there are two under your bed? To do so would result in their sure death. Your choice is to lie and save lives, or tell the truth and be a party to murder. Another example is putting "tourist" rather than "Bible smuggler" on your visa into China, or not telling the police in a persecuted country the names of other members of your underground church. Perhaps the answer is that it is the *motive* that matters. However, the issue depends on the conscience of each individual.

The Bible tells us that God doesn't lie, and the Ninth Commandment makes it clear that bearing false witness against our neighbor is wrong. Bearing false witness in order to cause harm to another, or to avoid the consequences of our own wrong behavior, is never acceptable to a holy God who knows our motive.

The dictionary defines a lie as a false statement deliberately presented as being true; a falsehood; something intended to deceive or give a wrong impression. People often claim that they have told only a "white lie." But there is *no* difference between a white lie, a half-truth, a fib, or an exaggeration. All are lies in the sight of God. How many murders does one have to commit to be a murderer? Just one. In the same way, if they have told even one lie, no matter what color or size, that makes them a liar.

The Ninth Commandment requires the truth, the whole truth, and nothing but the truth. God is a God of truth and His Law demands absolute honesty from the heart. Yet the human heart is deceitful above all things. It has been well said that taking the easy path is what makes rivers and men crooked. Look at this telling quote:

> ... 20,000 middle and high-schoolers were surveyed by the Josephson Institute of Ethics—a nonprofit organization in Marina del Rey, Calif., devoted to character education. Ninety-two percent of the teenagers admitted having lied to their parents in the previous year, and 73 percent characterized themselves as "serial liars," meaning they told lies weekly. Despite these admissions, 91 percent of all respondents said they were "satisfied with my own ethics and character." (*Reader's Digest*, November 1999)

The path of lies is often the easy path, but it leads to hell. The Bible warns that all liars will have their part in the Lake of Fire (Revelation 21:8). What a fearful thought! People may not think deceitfulness is a serious sin, but God does. It should break our hearts to even think of the fate of the ungodly.

QUESTIONS

1. **What is the dictionary definition of a lie?**

2. **What is the difference between a lie and discretion?**

3. **Do you think it is ever okay for a Christian to tell a lie in order to protect someone? Why or why not?**

4. **What is the difference between a white lie, a half-truth, a fib, and an exaggeration?**

5. **How many lies must one tell to be a liar?**

6. **What will happen to all liars?**

PREACHER'S PROGRESS

Darrell De' Seat: "Excuse me. I heard you talking to that person, and I don't think that you have the right to judge her. The Bible says, 'Judge not, lest you be judged.'"

Christian: "I wasn't judging her. She told me that she was a liar, and I believed her."

Darrell De' Seat: "Well, I still don't think you have any right to tell her what you did. You embarrassed her. I'm a Christian and what you did was wrong."

Christian: "I'm only saying what the Bible says. It warns that all liars will have their part in the Lake of Fire. Aren't you at all concerned for her salvation?"

Darrell De' Seat: "Yes. But I didn't like the way you spoke to her."

Christian: "What would you have told her?"

Darrell De' Seat: "That God loves her."

Christian: "May I ask you a question?"

Darrell De' Seat: "Sure."

Christian: "Do you consider yourself to be a good person?"

Darrell De' Seat: "Yes."

Christian: "Have you kept the Ten Commandments?"

Darrell De' Seat: "Yes."

Christian: "You've never told a white lie, fib, half-truth, or exaggeration?"

Darrell De' Seat: "Never."

Christian: "How could you say that you are a good person when the Bible says that there is none good—not one?"

Darrell De' Seat: "Now you are judging me. I think you are a !$*! idiot and you shouldn't be ramming your beliefs down people's throats."

Christian: "I'm not doing that. I'm simply warning people that God will judge the world in righteousness, and that they need the Savior."

Darrell De' Seat: "As long as these people believe in God and live a good life, they are okay."

Christian: "No, they're not. They must repent and trust Jesus Christ."

Darrell De' Seat: "That's just your belief. So what if I've told a few lies in my life? I didn't hurt anybody. God's not going to throw me in hell just for some white lie."

Christian: "Darrell, look at me. If your eyes meet mine on the Day of Judgment, and you're still in your sins...I'm free from your blood. I haven't held back from telling you the truth. You need to confess and forsake your sins. It's not enough to just believe in God."

FEATHERS FOR ARROWS

Two women from Southern California were about to cross the Mexican border to return to the U.S. when they saw what looked like a very small, sick animal in the ditch beside their car. As they examined it in the darkness of the night, they saw that it was a tiny Chihuahua. They decided to take it home with them and nurse it back to health. However, because they were afraid that they were breaking the law, they put it in the trunk of their car, and drove across the border. Once they were in the U.S., they retrieved the animal and nursed it until they arrived home.

One of the women was so concerned for the ailing dog that she actually took it to bed with her, and reached out several times during the night to touch the tiny animal and reassure it that she was still present.

The dog was so sick the next morning, she decided to take it to the veterinarian. That's when she found out that the animal wasn't a tiny, sick dog. It was a Mexican water rat, dying of rabies.

The world, in the blackness of its ignorance, thinks that sin is a puppy to be played with. It is the light of God's Law that enlightens the sinner to the fact that he is in bed with a deadly rat.

We were once "deceived, serving diverse lusts and pleasures," but now, if we are truly converted, our eyes have been opened. We see sin for the sugar-coated venom that it is.

Memory Verse

"A false witness shall not be unpunished, and he that speaks lies shall not escape."
PROVERBS 19:5

WORDS OF COMFORT

In Houston, Texas, police set out with their sirens wailing after three bank robbers, who had merged into freeway traffic. Unbeknown to the police, two burglars who had just pulled a job were also on the freeway, and took off at high speed mistakenly thinking that the law was chasing them. The police immediately did give chase...and apprehended the men after they crashed their car in a panic.

Last Words

Isaac Watts (hymn writer):

"It is a great mercy that I have no manner of fear or dread of death. I could, if God please, lay my head back and die without terror this afternoon."

The Ten Commandments, Part 10

"I would think it a greater happiness to gain one soul to Christ than mountains of silver and gold to myself."

MATTHEW HENRY

Kirk's Comment This is the final Commandment in our study. After completing this lesson, you might want to review all ten to make sure you understand the spiritual nature of each. Remember, these Commandments are the mirror that will show people their sin in its true light. Study them until you have them memorized. They will prove to be invaluable weapons as you speak with the lost.

QUESTIONS & OBJECTIONS

"I have broken the Ten Commandments, but I do good things for people."

Many people do similar things. They may steal from their employer or cheat on their taxes, then give to a charity or spend Thanksgiving helping at a soup kitchen. They think they are balancing the scales: they have done bad, and now they are doing good. However, the Bible reveals that the motive of guilty sinners is one of guilt (see Hebrews 9:14). They are attempting to bribe the Judge of the Universe. The Judge in this case will not be corrupted. He must punish all sinners. Good works cannot earn mercy; it comes purely by the grace of God. He will dismiss our iniquity only on the grounds of our faith in Jesus.

I n this lesson we will look at the Tenth Commandment: "**You shall not covet**...anything that is your neighbor's" (Exodus 20:17). Covetousness is perhaps the most subtle of sins. It seems minor compared to adultery, theft, or rape. However, before a man steals, he covets. Before he rapes or commits adultery, he covets. Covetousness is the spark that sets off the fuse of sin. It is a sin that lies close to the surface of every human being. Few children are content with ten pieces of candy when the child next to him gets eleven. Covetousness is the bedfellow of jealousy, greed, and lust. It was this quiet sin that found a place in the heart of King David, rich and blessed though he was. His covetous eye roamed toward another man's wife, and opened the door to a multitude of sins.

Who of us can stand guiltless and say that we have never jealously desired something that belongs to someone else? Whether we long for another's house, car, income, or lifestyle, our covetousness reveals a lack of gratitude for what God has already given us. That's why Scripture admonishes us to "be without covetousness; and be content with such things as you have" (Hebrews 13:5). Learn to pray along with the psalmist, "Incline my heart unto your testimonies, and not to covetousness. Turn away my eyes from beholding vanity..." (Psalm 119:36,37).

Matthew Henry said, "The Tenth Commandment strikes at the root; Thou shalt not covet. The others forbid all desire of doing what will be an injury to our neighbour; this forbids all wrong desire of having what will gratify ourselves."

Look at this incredible quote from Martin Luther. It reminds us of the function and power of the Law to reveal our "hidden" sins:

> As long as a person is not a murderer, adulterer, thief, he would swear that he is righteous. How is God going to humble such a person except by the Law? The Law is the hammer of death, the thunder of hell and the thunder of God's wrath to bring down the proud and shameless hypocrites. When the Law was instituted on Mount Sinai it was accompanied by lightning, by storms, by the sounds of trumpets, to tear to pieces that monster called self-righteousness. As long as a person thinks he is right he is going to be incomprehensibly proud and presumptuous. He is going to hate God, despise His grace

and mercy, and ignore the promises in Christ. The gospel of free forgiveness of sins though Christ will never appeal to the self-righteous. This monster of self-righteousness, this stiff-necked beast, needs an axe. And that is what the Law is, a big axe. Accordingly the proper use and function of the Law is to threaten until the conscience is scared stiff.

It's important to warn those who are guilty of this "harmless" sin that according to Scripture, "No covetous man, who is an idolater, has any inheritance in the kingdom of Christ and of God" (Ephesians 5:3,5). In coveting, a person transgresses not only the Tenth, but also the First and Second Commandments. When he loves material things more than he loves God, he is setting his affections on the gift, rather than on the Giver. What father wouldn't be grieved if his beloved child loved his toys more than the father who gave him the toys? A child should love his father first and foremost. He should love the giver more than the gift, and be content with what he has.

QUESTIONS

1. **What does it mean to covet?**

2. **Why is the quiet sin of covetousness so harmful?**

3. **What is the opposite of covetousness? (See Hebrews 13:5.)**

4. **What can we learn from Psalm 23 about this sin?**

5. **Are there some areas in which you are guilty of this sin?**

6. **Why do you think covetousness is so prevalent?**

PREACHER'S PROGRESS

Phil Osiffer: "I understand that you are the religious person who has been giving out this literature."

Christian: "Yes, sir."

Phil Osiffer: "You don't believe this stuff do you?"

Christian: "Sure."

Phil Osiffer: "It has been proven that the Bible is full of mistakes."

Christian: "Name one."

Phil Osiffer: "I can't think of any at the moment, but it is well known that the manuscripts have been changed down through the ages."

Christian: "No, they haven't. The Dead Sea Scrolls proved that."

Phil Osiffer: "Whatever. I prefer to put my faith in proven science rather than in an ancient book filled with myths."

Christian: "Did you know that that Bible is packed with scientific and medical facts that were written thousands of years before man discovered them?"

Phil Osiffer: "No, I didn't."

Christian: "The fact that they are in the Bible proves that it is supernatural in origin. Not only that, but the Bible is also filled with prophecies that are 100% accurate."

Phil Osiffer: "What about Nostradamus and his prophecies?"

Christian: "Nostradamus read the Bible in secret, stole its prophecies, and made them his own. Anyone who is ignorant of Bible prophecy will be impressed with the 'prophecies' of Nostradamus."

Phil Osiffer: "My life's philosophy is that we should do to others as we would have them do to us."

Christian: "Those are the words of Jesus. Have you done that?"

Phil Osiffer: "What?"

Christian: "Treated others as you would like to be treated?"

Phil Osiffer: "Pretty much."

Christian: "Have you ever lied to someone?"

Phil Osiffer: "Yes."

Christian: "Have you ever stolen anything from someone?"

Phil Osiffer: "Yes."

Christian: "You have lied to and stolen from others, and therefore haven't treated others as you would like them to treat you. You haven't lived up to your life's philosophy. Do you know what that's called?"

Phil Osiffer: "What?"

Christian: "Hypocrisy. If God judges you by the Ten Commandments on the Day of Judgment—bearing in mind that you are a lying thief who is guilty of hypocrisy, and no hypocrite will enter heaven—do you think you will be innocent or guilty?"

FEATHERS FOR ARROWS

Years ago, Southern California police carried out an interesting sting operation. They had a list of thousands of wanted criminals who had somehow evaded jail. Instead of risking their lives by attempting to arrest each one, they sent all the criminals a letter telling them they had won a large amount of money in a drawing.

The police put signs and banners on a building, and placed balloons and even a clown on the outside to create a festive atmosphere in order to welcome the "winners." As each criminal entered the building, he heard music and other sounds of celebration. He was then ushered into a room where he smiled as his hand was shaken. The facial expression changed from joy to unbelief as each was told, "Congratulations, you have just won time in prison!" Dozens of criminals made their way through the main doors, were arrested and ushered out the back door.

It was interesting to note that many of the lawbreakers admitted as they were apprehended, "I *thought* it was a sting operation!" but they couldn't stay away because of their greed. Their love of money blinded them to reason. Don't be like them. Think deeply about the issue of eternity, asking yourself, "What shall it profit a man if he shall gain the whole world and lose his own soul?"

WORDS OF COMFORT

Some years ago I felt sorry for one of our neighbors. The poor man spent a great deal of time and money pouring concrete, hour after hour, night after night, week after week, for a long driveway in front of his new home. The finished product looked superb—until it rained. Puddles formed every two or three yards.

So he took a sledgehammer and spent hour after hour, night after night, week after week, smashing it into small pieces, which he loaded onto his trailer and made *many* trips to the dump. Then he splashed out, bought some more cement, and spent hour after hour, night after night, week after week laboriously pouring concrete. For many days we heard the sound of a concrete mixer, mixing concrete as our neighbor tried to rectify his mistake.

Finally, the job was completed. This driveway looked even better than the first. One could even say that it looked as if a professional had done it...until it rained and revealed puddles slightly shallower than the first effort.

He moved.

Last Words

Anne Boleyn (1507–1536), second wife of Henry VIII:

> **"O God, have pity on my soul. O God, have pity on my soul."**

Our Ally:
The Conscience

"Conscience is the internal perception of God's Moral Law."
OSWALD CHAMBERS

Kirk's Comment I have seen in my personal experience how the Law can awaken a person's conscience—even when it has been dead for many years due to sinful living. The Law is like a jolt of electricity powered by the Holy Spirit that shocks the conscience back into life, causing it to shine its light upon the sinner's heart.

QUESTIONS & OBJECTIONS

"You are trying to make me feel guilty by quoting the Ten Commandments."

Ask the person which one of the Ten Commandments makes him feel guilty. Simply state, "The Bible says, 'You shall not steal.' If you feel guilty when you hear that, why do you think that is? Could it be because you *are* guilty?" God gave us our conscience so we would know when we break His Law; the guilt we feel when we do something wrong tells us that we need to repent.

We live in a hostile world that is at war with God and with those who represent Him. It is therefore a great consolation to the soldier of Christ to know that he has a faithful ally right in the heart of the enemy. That ally is the sinner's conscience. The dictionary defines the conscience as "the human faculty that enables one to decide between right and wrong acts or behavior, especially in regard to one's own conduct." This is what the Bible is speaking of when it says that God has given "light" to every man. The word "conscience" (*con* + *science*) means "with knowledge." Whenever we sin, we do so "with knowledge" that what we're doing is wrong.

The problem is that sin is so enticing to the lost that they prefer to live in darkness rather than remain in the light of the conscience. To the lost, the conscience is a "party pooper." Many people snuff out the light and abandon themselves to the dark world of sin, not realizing the terrible consequences of their actions. As A. W. Tozer wrote, idolatry (making a god to suit ourselves) leads to a dulled conscience:

> God's justice stands forever against the sinner in utter severity. The vague and tenuous hope that God is too kind to punish the ungodly has become a deadly opiate for the consciences of millions. It hushes their fears and allows them to practice all pleasant forms of iniquity while death draws every day nearer and the command to repent goes unregarded. As responsible moral beings, we dare not so trifle with our eternal future. (*The Knowledge of the Holy*)

How true are his words. As long as the voice of the sinner's conscience is silenced, he will readily embrace iniquity and will not flee from the wrath to come. We must therefore do all we can to awaken this ally so that it can do its intended work. Thank God that He has given us something to do the job—it is the rousing sound of the ten cannons of His Law that stirs the sleeping conscience. Charles Spurgeon said, "The conscience of a man, when he is really quickened and awakened by the Holy Spirit, speaks the truth. It rings the great alarm bell. And if he turns over in his bed, that great alarm bell rings out again and again, 'The wrath to come! The wrath to come! The wrath to come.'"

Walter Chantry wrote, "The absence of God's holy Law from modern preaching is perhaps as responsible as any other factor for the evangelistic impotence of our churches and missions. Only by the light of the Law can the vermin of sin in the heart be exposed. Satan has effectively used a very clever device to silence the Law, which is needed as an instrument to bring perishing men to Christ. It is imperative that preachers of today learn how to declare the spiritual Law of God; for, until we learn how to wound consciences, we shall have no wounds to bind with gospel bandages" (*Today's Gospel: Authentic or Synthetic?*).

It's been said that the conscience is the headline warning of sin, while the Law is the fine print. The spiritual nature of the Law gives the details to what the conscience already knows. When the Law is preached, the conscience affirms its truth. You can see this verified when using the Law, as the sinner's head nods in affirmation of each Commandment.

Unfortunately, in modern evangelism, few believers address the sinner's conscience as we should. Spurgeon said, "In many ministries, there is not enough of probing the heart and arousing the conscience by the revelation of man's alienation from God, and by the declaration of the selfishness and the wickedness of such a state."

It was the use of God's Law, when applied to the conscience, that was the key to great revivals of the past. Martyn Lloyd-Jones noted this fact:

> The trouble with people who are not seeking for a Savior, and for salvation, is that they do not understand the nature of sin. It is the peculiar function of the Law to bring such an understanding to a man's mind and conscience. That is why great evangelical preachers 300 years ago in the time of the Puritans, and 200 years ago in the time of Whitefield and others, always engaged in what they called a preliminary "Law work."

The preaching of the Law was also the great key used by John Wesley to open the hearts of men and women to the gospel. He said,

> It is the ordinary method of the Spirit of God to convict sinners by the Law. It is this which, being set home on the conscience, generally breaks the rocks in pieces. It is more especially this part of the

Word of God which is quick and powerful, full of life and energy and sharper than any two-edged sword.

Consider these wise words from Charles Spurgeon:

> When once God the Holy Spirit applies the Law to the conscience, secret sins are dragged to light, little sins are magnified to their true size, and things apparently harmless become exceedingly sinful. Before that dread searcher of the hearts and trier of the reins makes His entrance into the soul, it appears righteous, just, lovely, and holy; but when He reveals the hidden evils, the scene is changed. Offenses which were once styled peccadilloes, trifles, freaks of youth, follies, indulgences, little slips, etc., then appear in their true color, as breaches of the Law of God, deserving condign punishment.

Never forget that the sinner's conscience is your ally. Rather than fight against you, it will work with you. It is independent of his sin-loving will. Sin, however, has the conscience tied hand and foot and its voice gagged. You must cut the ropes with the sharp edge of the sword of God's Law and untie the gag. Don't be afraid to appeal directly to the sinner's conscience: "God gave you a conscience; you know right from wrong. Listen to the voice of your conscience. It will remind you of sins that you have committed." You will be encouraged in battle when you hear the voice of conscience coming through. It is the work of the Law written on the sinner's heart, and it will bear witness with the Law of God (Romans 2:15).

QUESTIONS

1. What does the word "conscience" mean?

2. What is the function of the conscience?

3. **How do sinners dull the voice of their conscience?**

4. **How can you (with God's help) awaken a conscience?**

5. **According to John Wesley, what is "the ordinary method of the Spirit"?**

6. **What are some phrases you can use in addressing the conscience?**

PREACHER'S PROGRESS

Larry Lustburger: "I heard you say that pornography is wrong. I disagree."

Christian: "Why's that?"

Larry Lustburger: "There's nothing wrong with it."

Christian: "Do you think child pornography is right or wrong?"

Larry Lustburger: "It's wrong."

Christian: "So you have drawn a moral line between what you think is right and what you think is wrong. At what age then does child pornography become respectable pornography? Is it when the child turns 14, 15, 16,…17 years old?"

Larry Lustburger: "16."

Christian: "Can't you see what you are doing? You are judging whether something is morally acceptable by when it gives you pleasure."

Larry Lustburger: "But . . ."

Christian: "God gave you a conscience. You know right from wrong. Isn't that true?"

Larry Lustburger: "No."

Christian: "So if someone steals your wallet, you don't mind because you have no idea what's right and what's wrong?"

Larry Lustburger: "Okay. So I know right from wrong."

Christian: "You are like a man who has removed the batteries from his smoke detector because he doesn't want it to alarm him. Listen to your conscience. It is trying to warn you of danger. Jesus said, 'Whoever looks upon a woman to lust after her has committed adultery already with her in his heart.' You are in big trouble. If you don't repent and trust the Savior, you will end up in hell. On Judgment Day you will be without excuse."

FEATHERS FOR ARROWS

An old drunk once stumbled along a sidewalk heading for his home. His faithful dog saw him approaching and watched his every move. As he entered his home, his dog joyfully followed him. When the drunken man collapsed on the floor in his living room, the dog snuggled up to him, waiting for his master to wake up.

Suddenly, in the middle of the night, the old drunk was roused by the dog's barking. The last thing he wanted was a barking dog! He staggered to his feet, grabbed a chair and threw it at the dog, then collapsed again.

It the morning he awoke to a shocking sight. Thieves had broken into the house in the night and stolen everything he owned—everything, that is, except a broken chair and a dead dog. His faithful friend had been trying to warn him of danger and he had killed the best friend he had.

WORDS OF COMFORT

For some time, I was a regular guest on an interesting radio talk show called "Religion on the Line." The two-hour program had a Catholic priest, a Protestant minister, and a rabbi as guests each week.

One day, as Sue and I arrived at the studio and were signing in, the security guard asked, "How was church today?" I told him it was good, and asked if he was a Christian. He said he was one once, but had fallen away from his faith. I suggested that what would get him back to the faith was a look at the Ten Commandments. I asked him if he had lied. He had, so I asked, "What does that make you?"

He hedged by saying, "A storyteller."

I smiled and said, "Come on ... what does that make you?"

He said, "A liar."

He had also stolen, and was therefore a thief. But when I asked him if he had ever broken the Seventh Commandment by lusting after a woman, he said that he never had. I didn't believe him, so when his eyes looked down in conviction, I put my hand on his to get back his eye contact and said, "Now, be honest."

His eyes then sparkled as he said, "I'm gay."

It was then that I lost eye contact. I was holding his hand! Sometimes things don't go the way we plan.

Memory Verse

"Which show the work of the law written in their hearts, their conscience also bearing witness, and their thoughts the mean while accusing or else excusing one another."

ROMANS 2:15

Last Words

John Wilhot, the second Earl of Rochester, lived a life of sin and infidelity. But God saved him from his sin and skepticism. Just before he died in 1680, he laid his hand on the Bible and said solemnly and earnestly:

"The only objection against this Book is a bad life! I shall die now, but oh what unspeakable glories do I see! What joys beyond thought or expression am I sensible of! I am assured of God's mercy to me through Jesus Christ. Oh, how I long to die!"

The Necessity of Repentance

"There are many who speak only of the forgiveness of sin, but who say little or nothing about repentance. If there is nevertheless no forgiveness of sins without repentance, so also forgiveness of sins cannot be understood without repentance. Therefore, if forgiveness of sins is preached without repentance, it follows that the people imagine they have already received the forgiveness of sins, and thereby they become cocksure and fearless, which is then greater error and sin than all the error that preceded our time."

MELANCHTHON

Kirk's Comment Sometimes, in our attempt to be theologians, we make simple things complicated. Repentance simply means to turn away from sin and turn to God.

QUESTIONS & OBJECTIONS

"What should I say to someone who acknowledges his sins, but says, 'I just hope God is forgiving'?"

This person could be referred to as "awakened, but not alarmed." Explain that God *is* forgiving—but only to those who repent of their sins. Ask him, "If you died right now, where would you go?" If he says, "Hell," ask if that concerns him. If it does concern him, ask, "What are you going to do?" Then tell him that God *commands* him to repent and trust the Savior. If it doesn't concern him, speak of the value of his life, the threat of *eternal* damnation, and the biblical description of hell. Caution him that he doesn't have the promise of tomorrow, and plead with him to come to his senses.

w o t m w o t m w o t m w o t m w o t m w o t m w o t m w o t m w o t m w o t m w o t m

Some people insist "repentance" is an old-fashioned word that the world cannot understand. "Sin" is another word that falls into that category. However, we must carefully check our motives for avoiding their use. Do we want to substitute different words to help the world understand, or do we simply want to shake off the reproach that comes with their use? If the world cannot comprehend spiritual words, then we should explain their meanings. Sin is transgression of the Law (1 John 3:4), and repentance means to turn from sin. It is more than contrition (sorrow for sin); to repent means to confess sin and forsake it—to agree with God that it is wrong and to turn and go in the opposite direction. An old soldier once summed up repentance this way: "God said, 'Attention! About turn! Quick march!'"

It is true that numerous Bible verses speak of the promise of salvation with no mention of repentance. These verses merely tell us to "believe" on Jesus Christ and we shall be saved (Acts 16:31; Romans 10:9). However, the Bible makes it clear that God is holy and man is sinful, and that sin makes a separation between the two (Isaiah 59:1,2). Without repentance from sin, wicked men cannot have fellowship with a holy God. We are dead in our trespasses and sins (Ephesians 2:1) and until we forsake them through repentance, we cannot be made alive in Christ. The Scriptures speak of "repentance unto life" (Acts 11:18). We must turn from sin to the Savior. This is why Paul preached "repentance toward God, and faith toward our Lord Jesus Christ" (Acts 20:21).

Jesus said that He came to call "sinners to repentance" (Matthew 9:13). The first public word He preached was "repent" (Matthew 4:17). John the Baptist began his ministry the same way (Matthew 3:2). Jesus told His hearers twice that without repentance, they would perish (Luke 13:3,5).

If belief is all that is necessary for salvation, then the logical conclusion is that one need never repent. However, the Bible tells us that a false convert "believes" and yet is not saved (Luke 8:13); he remains a "worker of iniquity."

In his book *One Thing You Can't Do in Heaven*, Mark Cahill notes that, when witnessing to the lost, "if there is no desire to walk away from sin, the person is not really making a true heart commitment to the Savior. In John 6:44 Jesus says, 'No one can come to Me unless the Father who sent Me draws him.' If God is drawing someone to Him, He would also be drawing the person away from his sin."

Look at the warning of Scripture: "If we say that we have fellowship with him, and walk in darkness, we lie, and do not the truth" (1 John 1:6). The Scriptures also say, "He that covers his sins shall not prosper, but whoso confesses and forsakes them [repents] shall have mercy" (Proverbs 28:13). Jesus said that there was joy in heaven over one sinner who "repents" (Luke 15:10). If there is no repentance, there is no joy because there is no salvation.

As Peter preached on the Day of Pentecost, he commanded his hearers to repent "for the remission of sins" (Acts 2:38). Without repentance, there is no remission of sins; we are still under God's wrath. Peter further said, "Repent...and be converted, that your sins may be blotted out" (Acts 3:19). We cannot be converted, or have our sins blotted out, unless we repent. God Himself "commands *all* men *everywhere* [leaving no exceptions] to repent" (Acts 17:30). Peter said a similar thing at Pentecost: "Repent, and be baptized *every one* of you" (Acts 2:38). Scripture says that the Lord is "not willing that any should perish, but that *all* should come to repentance" (2 Peter 3:9). Clearly, those who do not repent will perish.

If repentance wasn't necessary for salvation, why then did Jesus command that *repentance* be preached to all nations (Luke 24:47)? When He sent out His disciples two by two, they "preached that men should repent" (Mark 6:12).

The necessity of repentance underscores the importance of going through the Law with a sinner. If a man doesn't know what sin is, how can he repent? Any "repentance" would be merely "horizontal repentance." He's responding to the Savior because he's lied to men, he's stolen from men, etc. But when David sinned with Bathsheba, he didn't say, "I've sinned against man." He said to God, "Against you, and you only, have I sinned, and done this evil in your sight" (Psalm 51:4). When Joseph was tempted sexually, he said, "How can I do this thing and sin against God?" (Genesis 39:9). The prodigal son said, "I've sinned against heaven" (Luke 15:21). That's why Paul preached "repentance toward God" (Acts 20:21). When a man doesn't understand that his sin is primarily vertical, he'll merely exercise superficial, experimental, horizontal repentance, and fall away when tribulation, temptation, and persecution come.

QUESTIONS

1. Why do you think it would be easier to tell sinners to "believe" than to tell them they need to repent?

2. How did the old soldier sum up repentance?

3. Explain why salvation entails more than merely "believing in Jesus."

4. Who does God command to repent? (See Acts 17:30.)

5. **According to Scripture, what should we be preaching?**

PREACHER'S PROGRESS

Tele Marketer: "Hello, Mr. Christian. How are you? I wonder if I could have just one moment of your time. We want to offer you a subscription to *Sports Ill-Lust-rated* with the special 'Swimsuit Issue.' If you subscribe, we will give you a chance to win a free trip for two to Hawaii, beer for a year, or a new car. We will also give you, absolutely free of charge, a brand new duffel bag with your favorite sports hero's picture on it. How would you like to pay for your subscription—with a Visa or MasterCard?"

Christian: "May I ask you a question?"

Tele Marketer: "Certainly, Mr. Christian. I would be happy to answer any questions you may have."

Christian: "Have you kept the Ten Commandments?"

Tele Marketer: "Huh?"

Christian: "Have you kept the Ten Commandments? Have you ever told a lie?"

Tele Marketer: "Yes, Mr. Christian. I have to admit that I have told a few fibs and white lies, but they were in the past."

Christian: "What does that make you?"

Tele Marketer: "It doesn't make me anything."

Christian: "If I told a lie, what would I be called?"

Tele Marketer: "A liar."

Christian: "So what are you?"

Tele Marketer: "A liar. But that was in the past."

Christian: "Everything was in the past. Have you ever stolen something, even if it's small?"

Tele Marketer: "Yes, sir."

Christian: "What does that make you?"

Tele Marketer: "A thief."

Christian: "Jesus said that if you look with lust, you commit adultery in your heart. Have you ever looked with lust?"

Tele Marketer: "Many times…"

Christian: "If God were to judge you by the Ten Commandments on Judgment Day, would you be innocent or guilty?"

Tele Marketer: "Guilty."

Christian: "Would you go to heaven or hell?"

Tele Marketer: "Hell…"

Telemarketers are a good way for you to practice what you preach. You don't have to look them in the eye. You can't be injured by them. The worst thing they can do is hang up in your ear. If that happens, you can rejoice that they were convicted enough to do so. You not only had the privilege of planting the seed of God's Word in the heart of a stranger, but you proved yourself to be faithful to the Lord, you conquered the fear of man, and now you can rejoice that you were rejected for the sake of righteousness. If they hang up, spend a moment in prayer for them.

If they are open to hearing more, take them through the cross, repentance, and faith. Ask if they have a Bible at home, encourage them to read it daily, and then thank them for listening to you.

Memory Verse

"Repent therefore, and be converted, that your sins may be blotted out, when the times of refreshing shall come from the presence of the Lord."

ACTS 3:19

Last Words

Phillip III, King of France:

"What an account I shall have to give to God! How I should like to live otherwise than I have lived."

17

Personal Witnessing: How Jesus Did It

"Before I can preach love, mercy, and grace, I must preach sin, Law, and judgment."

JOHN WESLEY

Kirk's Comment In this lesson we will look at the story of the woman at the well from a very different perspective than perhaps you ever have before. Here we see Jesus in action, witnessing to a stranger in an everyday situation. It is so instructive that we've called it "The Way of the Master."

QUESTIONS & OBJECTIONS

"I've made my peace with 'the Man upstairs.'"

When people refer to God as "the Man upstairs," they reveal that they have no concept of (nor living relationship with) Him. They will use such words because they feel uncomfortable saying His name. Often they will have a measure of reverence for God, but not enough to obey Him. Ask if the person thinks he will go to heaven when he dies. He'll almost certainly say he will, and a little probing will reveal that he's trusting in his own goodness to save him. However, the only way sinners can have peace with the God they have offended is through the shed blood of the Savior.

Therefore, it's important to take the person through the Ten Commandments to strip him of his self-righteousness and his false sense of assurance of salvation. As you do so, you may feel bad that you are making him uncomfortable, but if you care about his eternal salvation, you must ask yourself, "Which is worse: a few moments of conviction under the sound of God's Law, or eternity in the Lake of Fire?" Unless there is a knowledge of sin (which comes by the Law—Romans 7:7), there will be no repentance.

wotmwotmwotmwotmwotmwotmwotmwotmwotmwotmwotm

In John 4:7–26, the Bible gives us the Master's example of how to share the gospel. Notice that Jesus spoke to the woman at the well when she was alone. When witnessing, we will often find that people are more open and honest when they are alone. So, if possible, pick a person who is sitting by himself.

From these verses, we can see four clear principles to follow. I call this the RCCR method of evangelism, which consists of Relate, Create, Convict, and Reveal. Let's see how Jesus put these into practice.

Relate: Jesus began by relating to her in the natural realm (v. 7). This woman was unregenerate, and the Bible tells us "the natural man receives not the things of the Spirit of God" (1 Corinthians 2:14). He therefore spoke of something she could relate to—water. Most of us can strike up a conversation with a stranger in the natural realm. It may be a friendly "How are you doing?" or a sincere "Good morning!" If the person responds with a sense of warmth, we may then ask, "Do you live around here?" and from there develop a conversation.

Create: Jesus created an opportunity to talk about the spiritual realm (v. 10). He simply mentioned the things of God. This will take courage. We may say something like, "Did you go to church on Sunday?" or "Did you see that Christian TV program last week?" If the person responds positively, the question "Do you have a Christian background?" will probe his background. He may answer, "I went to church when I was a child, but I drifted away from it."

Another simple way to swing to the spiritual is to offer the person a gospel tract and ask, "Did you get one of these?" When he takes it, simply say, "It's a gospel tract. Do you come from a Christian background?"

Convict: Jesus brought conviction using the Law of God (vv. 16–18). Jesus gently spoke to her conscience by alluding to the fact that she had transgressed the Seventh Commandment. He used the Law to bring "the knowledge of sin" (Romans 3:19,20). We can do the same by asking, "Do you think you have kept the Ten Commandments?" Most people think they have, so quickly follow with, "Have you ever told a lie?" This *is* confrontational, but if it's asked in a spirit of love and gentleness, there won't be any offense. This is because the "work of the Law [is] written in their hearts" and their conscience will also bear "witness" (Romans 2:15).

Jesus confronted the rich young ruler in Luke 18:18–21 with five of the Ten Commandments and there was no offense. Have confidence that the conscience will do its work and affirm the truth of each Commandment. Don't be afraid to gently ask, "Have you ever stolen something, even if it's small?"

Learn how to open up the spirituality of the Law and show how God considers lust to be the same as adultery (Matthew 5:27,28) and hatred the same as murder (1 John 3:15). Make sure you get an admission of guilt. Then ask the person, "If God judges you by the Ten Commandments on Judgment Day, do you think you will be innocent or guilty?" If he says he will be innocent, ask, "Why is that?" If he admits his guilt, ask, "Do you think you will go to heaven or hell?"

From there the conversation may go one of three ways:

- *He may confidently say, "I don't believe in hell."* Gently respond, "That doesn't matter. You still have to face God on Judgment Day *whether you believe in it or not.* If I step onto the freeway when a massive truck is heading for me and I say, 'I don't believe in trucks,' my lack of belief isn't going to change reality." Then tenderly tell him he has *already* admitted to you that he has lied, stolen, and committed adultery in his heart, and that God gave him a conscience so he would know right from wrong. His conscience and the conviction of the Holy Spirit will do the rest. That's why it is essential to draw out an admission of guilt *before* you mention Judgment Day or the existence of hell.

- *He may say that he's guilty, but that he will go to heaven.* This is usually because he thinks that God is "good," and that He will, therefore, overlook sin in his case. Point out that if a judge in a criminal case has a guilty murderer standing before him, the judge, if he is a good man, can't just let him go. He must ensure that the guilty man is punished. If God is good, He must (by nature) punish murderers, rapists, thieves, liars, adulterers, fornicators, and those who have lived in rebellion to the inner light that God has given to every man.

- *He may admit that he is guilty and therefore going to hell.* Ask him if that concerns him. Speak to him about how much he values his eyes and how much more he should value the salvation of his soul.

Reveal: Jesus revealed Himself to her (v. 26). Once the Law has humbled the person, he is ready for grace. The Bible says that God resists the proud and gives grace to the humble (James 4:6). The gospel is for the humble. Only the sick need a physician, and only those who will admit that they have the disease of sin will truly embrace the cure of the gospel. Learn how to present the work of the cross—that God sent His Son to suffer and die in our place, and that Jesus rose from the dead and defeated death. Take the person back to civil law and say, "It's as simple as this: We broke God's Law, and Jesus paid our fine. If you will repent and trust in the Savior, God will forgive your sins and dismiss your case."

Ask him if he understands what you have told him. If he is willing to confess and forsake his sins, and trust the Savior with his eternal salvation, have him pray and ask God to forgive him. Then pray for him. Get him a Bible. Instruct him to read it daily and obey what he reads, and encourage him to get into a Bible-believing, Christ-preaching church.

QUESTIONS

1. **What are the four principles of evangelism that Jesus demonstrated with the woman at the well?**

2. List some different ways to relate in the natural realm to sinners.

3. Why can you ask if someone has kept the Ten Commandments without it seeming confrontational?

4. Why doesn't our unbelief negate reality?

5. Why can the sinner not rely on God's "goodness" to save him?

6. At what point in the evangelism process should you talk about the Savior? Why?

PREACHER'S PROGRESS

Christian: "Hi. Do you know of any good churches around here?"

Abby Thetic: "No."

Christian: "Do you have a Christian background?"

Abby Thetic: "No. I don't bother with that stuff."

Christian: "So, you never think about life and death?"

Abby Thetic: "Never."

Christian: "Do you think that you have kept the Ten Commandments?"

Abby Thetic: "Most of them."

Christian: "Have you ever told a lie?"

Abby Thetic: "Sure, who hasn't?"

Christian: "What does that make you?"

Abby Thetic: "A liar?"

Christian: "That's right. Have you ever stolen anything, even if it's small?"

Abby Thetic: "Maybe one or two things when I was younger."

Christian: "What does that make you?"

Abby Thetic: "A thief."

Christian: "Then, by your own admission, you are a lying thief, and we have only looked at two of the Ten Commandments. Have you ever used God's name in vain?"

Abby Thetic: "Yes. It's a bit of a habit that I've been trying to break."

Christian: "Do you realize what you have done?"

Abby Thetic: "No, what?"

Christian: "You have taken the name of your Creator—the One who has given you life—and brought it down to the same level as a four-letter curse word to express disgust. The Bible says that God will not hold him guiltless who uses His name in vain."

Abby Thetic: "Uh..."

Christian: "If God were to judge you by this standard, the Ten Commandments, would you be innocent or guilty on the Day of Judgment?"

Abby Thetic: "By that standard, I would be guilty."

Christian: "Would you go to heaven or hell?"

Abby Thetic: "I think I would go to heaven."

Christian: "Why is that? Are you hoping that God will overlook your sins because He is full of love?"

Abby Thetic: "Yeah, that's it."

WORDS OF COMFORT

Memory Verse

"Jesus answered and said to her, Whosoever drinks of this water shall thirst again: But whosoever drinks of the water that I shall give him shall never thirst; but the water that I shall give him shall be in him a well of water springing up into everlasting life."

JOHN 4:13,14

The *Ouachita Mountain Neighbor* newspaper in Arkansas reported the following incident on September 26, 1995:

A local woman in a small town came out of a Wal-Mart store, placed her groceries in the back of her car, and sat in the driver's seat.

Suddenly, she heard what sounded like a loud gunshot crashing through her back window, and in the same instant something impacted the back of her head. Terrified, she put her hand on the back of her head and felt the horrific sensation of her warm brains oozing onto her hand. She screamed in terror and went into a fit of uncontrollable hysterics.

A number of frantic shoppers immediately called 911 on their cell phones, and within minutes police arrived and rushed to the aid of the screaming woman.

After hearing that the woman was literally holding her brains in, an officer gently pried away her hand and found some gooey, warm biscuit dough. The woman had purchased a can of the mixture with her groceries, and it had expanded in the hot sun and exploded with a bang, sending warm dough onto the back of her head.

Last Words

Thomas Hobbes (1588–1674) was a noted English political philosopher whose most famous work was *Leviathan*. This cultured, clever skeptic corrupted many of the great men of his time. But what hopelessness permeated his last words:

"If I had the whole world, I would give it to live one day. I shall be glad to find a hole to creep out of the world at. About to take a leap in the dark!"

 **LESSON 18**

The Sinner's Prayer

"The chief danger of the 20th century will be religion without the Holy Spirit, Christianity without Christ, forgiveness without repentance, salvation without regeneration, politics without God, and heaven without hell."

WILLIAM BOOTH

Kirk's Comment We often become so familiar with church evangelism methods and traditions that we often just assume they are biblical, without checking into them. This lesson takes a close look at the value of one very common and well-intentioned evangelistic tradition.

QUESTIONS & OBJECTIONS

"What if someone says, 'I've broken every one of the Ten Commandments'?"

Do not take this statement to mean that the person has seen the gravity of his sinful state before God. He may say something like, "I'm a really bad person!" It is often used as a way of shrugging off conviction. Pharaoh admitted that he had sinned, but his repentance was superficial. Say to the person, "Well, let's take the time to go through the Ten Commandments one by one and see if you have." As the person is confronted with the righteous standard of God's Moral Law, pray that the Holy Spirit brings conviction of sin.

Perhaps by now you feel reasonably comfortable about witnessing using the Law to bring the knowledge of sin. You know how to present the cross and the necessity of repentance toward God and faith in Jesus—but then what? Is it valid to "close the sale" (as modern evangelism often puts it)? Should you suddenly revert back to the old, "Would you like me to lead you in a sinner's prayer right now?" Or should we just leave the person in the hands of a faithful Creator?

Perhaps the answer comes by looking at the natural realm. As long as there are no complications when a child is born, all the doctor needs to do is *guide the head.* The same applies spiritually. When someone is "born of God," all we need to do is guide the head—make sure that the person *understands* what he is doing. Philip the evangelist did this with the Ethiopian eunuch when he asked, "Do you understand what you read?" (Acts 8:30).

In the Parable of the Sower, the true convert (the "good soil" hearer) is the one who hears "and understands." This understanding comes by the Law (Romans 7:7) in the hand of the Spirit, who will "convict the world of sin, and of righteousness, and of judgment" (John 16:8). If a sinner is ready for the Savior, it is because he has been drawn by the Holy Spirit (John 6:44). This is why we must be careful to allow the Holy Spirit to do His work and not rush in where angels fear to tread. Praying a sinner's prayer with someone who isn't genuinely repentant may leave you with a stillborn on your hands. Therefore, rather than lead him in a prayer of repentance, it is wise to encourage him to pray himself.

When Nathan confronted David about his sin, he didn't lead the king in a prayer of repentance. If a man committed adultery, and his wife is willing to take him back, should you have to write out an apology for him to read to her? No; sorrow for his betrayal of her trust should spill from his lips. She doesn't want eloquent words, but simply sorrow of heart. The essence of his apology should be something like this: "Please forgive me. I have betrayed your trust. I am so sorry." The same applies to a prayer of repentance. If a person is genuinely repentant (he has sorrow of heart and his mouth is stopped from self-justification), he should pray himself; his words aren't as important as the presence of "godly sorrow."

The sinner should be told to repent—to confess and forsake his sins. He could do this as a whispered prayer, then you could pray for him. Tell him, "Quietly confess your sins to God, asking Him to forgive you, then put your trust in Jesus in the same way you would put on a parachute to save you. You wouldn't just *believe* in it; you would put it on—entrusting your life to it. After you have done that, I will pray for you and give you some literature to help you." If he's not sure what to say, perhaps David's prayer of repentance (Psalm 51) could be used as a model, but his own words are more desirable.

If you study the ministry of Charles Spurgeon, you will find that he invited men and women to come to *Christ*, not to an altar. Listen to him invite sinners to come to the Savior:

Before you leave this place, breathe an earnest prayer to God, saying, "God, be merciful to me a sinner. Lord, I need to be saved. Save me. I call upon Thy name . . . Lord, I am guilty, I deserve Thy wrath. Lord, I cannot save myself. Lord, I would have a new heart and a right spirit, but what can I do? Lord, I can do nothing, come and work in me to do of Thy good pleasure.

Thou alone hast power, I know
To save a wretch like me;
To whom, or whither should I go
If I should run from Thee?

But I now do from my very soul call upon Thy name. Trembling, yet believing, I cast myself wholly upon Thee, O Lord. I trust the blood and righteousness of Thy dear Son . . . Lord, save me tonight, for Jesus' sake."

Go home alone trusting in Jesus. "I should like to go into the enquiry-room." I dare say you would, but we are not willing to pander to popular superstition. We fear that in those rooms men are warmed into a fictitious confidence. Very few of the supposed converts of enquiry-rooms turn out well. Go to your God at once, even where you now are. Cast yourself on Christ, at once, ere you stir an inch!

QUESTIONS

1. **How can we "guide the head" in a spiritual birth?**

2. **Why is this understanding important?**

3. **Where does this understanding come from?**

4. **Why are the sinner's words not important?**

5. **Does your church invite sinners to the altar, or to the Savior?**

PREACHER'S PROGRESS

Ree Peterson: "I know that I am a sinner, but I confess my sins to God each night. I tell Him that I am sorry and that I won't sin again. The trouble is that I repeat the sin."

Christian: "If you find yourself in court with a $50,000 fine, will a judge let you go simply because you say that you are sorry and that you won't commit the crime again?"

Ree Peterson: "No, he won't. I'd still have the fine to pay."

Christian: "That's right. Besides, you should be sorry for breaking the law, and of course you shouldn't commit the crime again. However, if someone stepped in and paid the $50,000 fine, then you would be free from the demands of the law. God will not forgive a sinner on the basis that he is sorry. Of course we should be sorry for sin—we have a conscience to tell us that adultery, rape, lust, murder, hatred, lying, stealing, etc., are wrong. And of course we shouldn't sin again. God will, however, release us from the demands of eternal justice on the basis that someone else paid our fine. Two thousand years ago, Jesus Christ died on the cross to pay for the sins of the world. His words on the cross were, "It is finished!" In other words, the debt has been paid in full. All who repent and trust in Him receive forgiveness of sins. Their case is dismissed on the basis of His suffering death. Does that make sense to you?"

Ree Peterson: "It does, actually."

Christian: "Can you see that sorrow for your sin, and even repentance, isn't enough to save you from hell? You must trust in the Savior. If you are born again, God will give you a new heart with new desires, so that you won't continue to repeat the sins that you did before your conversion."

FEATHERS FOR ARROWS

Many years ago we had in our home a stubborn spider that kept building a web against our house. No matter how many times we swept it away, the spider and its web would reappear the next morning. One day I enlisted the help of one of my sons, as well as a small stick and a can of insect spray. I had my son gently tap the stick on the web while I made the sound of a fly in distress. The hungry spider came out of his hiding place, and that's when I killed him with the insect spray.

There is a stubborn web of sin that continually plagues mankind. It is the web of violence, corruption, rape, greed, wars, theft, etc. We try to sweep it away through political means. Yet these crimes remain, and few seem to identify the root cause of the problem. That remains in hiding.

We must use the stick of God's Law to gently tap on the human heart. Suddenly, the cause of sin appears. And that's when sin can be put to death with the power of the gospel. It is God's Law that reveals the human heart as desperately wicked, and it is the gospel that delivers us from the power of sin. In Christ we are born again (John 3:3) and become new creatures.

Memory Verse

"No man can come to me, except the Father which has sent me draw him: and I will raise him up at the last day."

JOHN 6:44

WORDS OF COMFORT

I walked confidently onto a plane, followed by my daughter and her friend. As a seasoned traveler, I was leading the way. Not only was I an example of travel in action for my daughter and her friend, Rebekah, but I was on the cutting edge in contemporary travel gear. Before it became trendy for travelers to pull black bags with wheels on them, I had purchased a big blue travel bag with wheels. The only difference was that mine wasn't as slick as those used by flight crews. I didn't pull it along with an adjustable steel handle; I pulled it with a strap that was four feet long.

However, this day I was amazed at how quickly family and friends disowned me, merely because the bag caught on the armrest of an aisle seat near the front of the plane, ripped it off, and I dragged it unknowingly for half the length of the aircraft.

They also disowned me merely because, earlier on the same trip, one of my bags fell down an escalator, scattering people behind me.

Last Words

Captain John Lee, who was executed for forgery, sought to do away with God, yet in death longed for the assurance and hope of faith:

"I leave to the world this mournful memento, that however much a man may be favored by personal qualifications or distinguished mental endowments, genius will be useless, and abilities avail little, unless accompanied by religion and attended by virtue. Oh, that I had possession of the meanest place in heaven, and could but creep into one corner of it."

True and False Conversions

"That is the reason we have so many 'mushroom' converts, because their stony ground is not plowed up; they have not got a conviction of the Law; they are stony-ground hearers."

GEORGE WHITEFIELD

Kirk's Comment I thought "backsliding" was a common, normal occurrence in Christianity until I understood the reality of false conversions and their prevalence in our churches today. This lesson is a real eye-opener.

QUESTIONS & OBJECTIONS

"I was once a born-again Christian. Now I believe it's all rubbish!"

When a person maintains that he was once a Christian, but came to his senses, he is saying that he once knew the Lord (see John 17:3). Ask him, "Did you know the Lord?" If he answers yes, gently say, "So you admit that He is real and that you are in rebellion to His will." If he says, "I *thought* I did!" this gives you license to gently say, "If you don't *know* so, then you probably didn't." If he didn't know the Lord, he was therefore never a Christian (1 John 5:11–13,20). Explain to him that the Bible speaks of false conversion, in which a "stony ground" hearer receives the Word with joy and gladness. Then, in a time of tribulation, temptation, and persecution, falls away. If he is open to reason, take him through the Ten Commandments, into the message of the cross, and the necessity of repentance and faith in the Savior.

w o t m w o t m w o t m w o t m w o t m w o t m w o t m w o t m w o t m w o t m w o t m

Perhaps one of the most neglected concepts in the contemporary Body of Christ is that of true and false conversion. Why it is neglected is a mystery because the New Testament is filled with teachings about the subject and gives many examples of false converts. The Scriptures speak of false prophets, false teachers, false apostles, and false brethren.

A clear understanding of the subject will help ensure that we are not guilty of preaching a gospel that reaps false converts.

When Jesus gave His disciples the Parable of the Sower, it seems that they lacked understanding of its meaning: "He said to them, 'Do you not know [understand] this parable? and how then will you know [understand] all parables?'" (Mark 4:13). In other words, the Parable of the Sower is the key to unlocking the mysteries of all the other parables. If any message comes from the parable, it is the fact that when the gospel is preached, there are true and false conversions. This parable speaks of the thorny ground, the stony ground, and the good-soil hearers—the false and the genuine converts.

Once that premise has been established, the light of perception begins to dawn on Jesus' other parables about the kingdom of God. If one grasps the principle of the true and false being *alongside each other*, then the other parabolic teachings make sense: the Wheat and Tares (true and false), the Good Fish and Bad Fish (true and false), the Wise Virgins and the Foolish (true and false), and the Sheep and Goats (true and false).

After telling about the Wheat and Tares, Jesus gave the Parable of the Dragnet:

Again, the kingdom of heaven is like to a net, that was cast into the sea, and gathered of every kind: which, when it was full, they drew to shore, and sat down, and gathered the good into vessels, but cast the bad away. So shall it be at the end of the world: the angels shall come forth, and sever the wicked from among the just, and shall cast them into the furnace of fire: there shall be wailing and gnashing of teeth. Jesus said to them, Have you understood all these things? They said to Him, Yes, Lord (Matthew 13:47–51).

Notice that the good fish and the bad fish were in the net together. The *world* is not caught in the dragnet of the kingdom of heaven; they remain in the world. The "fish" that are caught are those who respond to the gospel—the evangelistic "catch." They remain together until the Day of Judgment.

False converts lack genuine contrition for sin. They make a profession of faith but are deficient in biblical repentance—"They profess that they know God; but in works they deny him, being abominable, and disobedient, and to every good work reprobate" (Titus 1:16). A true convert, however, has a knowledge of sin and has godly sorrow, truly repents, and produces the "things that accompany salvation" (Hebrews 6:9). This is evident by the fruit of the Spirit, the fruit of righteousness, etc.

Judas was a false convert. It would seem that he was an example of the thorny ground. The Bible says of the thorny-ground hearer: "The cares of this world, and the deceitfulness of riches, and the lusts of other things entering in, choke the word, and it becomes unfruitful" (Mark 4:19). Some of these professing Christians stay within the church, and they are the ones who often discredit the name of Jesus Christ.

Although false converts fail to repent of their sins, they *do* have a measure of spirituality. Judas did. He convinced some of the disciples that he did truly care for the poor. He *seemed* so trustworthy that he was the one who looked after the finances. When Jesus said, "One of you will betray me," the disciples didn't point the finger at the faithful treasurer, but instead suspected themselves, saying, "Is it I, Lord?" So it's not surprising that few within the Body of Christ would ever suspect that we are surrounded by those who fall into the "Judas" category. However, alarm bells should go off when the church, which ought to have massive clout in society, sadly lacks it when push comes to shove. With our 142 million professed believers, we can't even outlaw the killing of unborn children.

As William Iverson wrote in *Christianity Today*, "A pound of meat would surely be affected by a quarter pound of salt. If this is real Christianity, the 'salt of the earth,' where is the effect of which Jesus spoke?"

God knows the genuine from the false, and He will separate them on the Day of Judgment.

QUESTIONS

1. **What did Jesus tell His disciples when they questioned Him about the Parable of the Sower?**

2. **Name some of the parables Jesus told that speak of true and false conversions.**

3. **When will false converts be exposed?**

4. **What damage can be done by a Christian who doesn't understand that there is such a thing as a false conversion?**

5. **How can we make sure we are not responsible for bringing false converts into the church?**

FEATHERS FOR ARROWS

The Bible tells us in Luke 22:47 that Judas led a "multitude" to Jesus. His motive, however, wasn't to bring them to the Savior for salvation. Modern evangelism is also bringing "multitudes" to Jesus. Their motive may be different from Judas's, but the end result is the same. Just as the multitudes that Judas directed to Christ fell back from the Son of God, statistics show that up to 90 percent of those coming to Christ under the methods of modern evangelism fall away from the faith. Their latter end becomes worse than the first. They openly crucify the Son of God afresh.

In their zeal without knowledge, those who prefer the ease of modern evangelism to biblical evangelism betray the cause of the gospel with a kiss. What may look like love for the sinner's welfare is in truth eternally detrimental to him.

Like Peter (Luke 22:51), our zeal without knowledge is actually cutting off the ears of sinners. Those we erroneously call "backsliders" won't listen to our reasonings. As far as they are concerned, they have tried it once, and it didn't work. What a victory for the prince of darkness, and what an unspeakable tragedy for the church!

Last Words

William McKinley (1843–1901), twenty-fifth President of the U.S., was assassinated six months after his inauguration. Shot by an anarchist at an Exposition in Buffalo, New York, he lingered for eight days. His farewell words were:

> **"Nearer, my God to Thee, nearer to Thee. It is the Lord's way. Goodbye all!"**

Memory Verse

"Whosoever therefore shall confess me before men, him will I confess also before my Father which is in heaven. But whosoever shall deny me before men, him will I also deny before my Father which is in heaven."
MATTHEW 10:32,33

LESSON 20

Hypocrisy

"I am told that Christians do not love each other. I am very sorry if that be true, but I rather doubt it, for I suspect that those who do not love each other are not Christians."

CHARLES SPURGEON

Kirk's Comment As a teenager, religious hypocrites on TV were a major reason why I thought Christianity was a joke. Then I learned that there will be no hypocrites in heaven.

QUESTIONS & OBJECTIONS

"You shouldn't talk about sin because Jesus didn't condemn anyone. He was always loving and kind."

Jesus is loving, and that's why He had harsh words of warning for sinners. In Matthew 23, Jesus called the religious leaders "hypocrites" seven times. He told them that they were "blind fools," children of hell, full of hypocrisy and sin. He climaxed His sermon by saying, "You serpents, you generation of vipers, how shall you escape the damnation of hell?" He then warned that He would say to the wicked, "Depart from Me, you cursed, into everlasting fire, prepared for the devil and his angels" (Matthew 25:41).

It seems that no one likes any kind of hypocrite. However, there is something particularly distasteful about those who profess to love God, but whose lives don't match their claims. A great preacher once said that if a man's life didn't correspond with what he professed, and he wanted to preach the gospel, he should go a great distance from his home, and when he stands up to preach he should say nothing.

One of the greatest hindrances to people coming to Christ is the view that the church is "full of hypocrites." Some maintain that it is full to the brim; others will admit that there are genuine Christians in the church among the false. Whatever the case, those who present this argument usually do so because they themselves love the darkness and hate the light. While they may have a genuine grievance about the issue, the hypocrisy of others will not be a legitimate excuse for them on the Day of Judgment.

Hypocrite comes from the Greek word for "actor," or pretender. Hypocrisy is "the practice of professing beliefs, feelings, or virtues that one does not hold." Hypocrites may show up at a church building, but in reality there are no hypocrites in the Church. In its ignorance, the world thinks that the Church is the building, and that those who sit within its confines are Christians. However, the Church is the Body of Christ, which consists only of true believers; hypocrites are "pretenders" who sit among God's people. They dwell as goats among the Lord's sheep, bad fish among the good, tares among wheat until the day God separates them.

It is interesting to note that the human body will reject any foreign transplant—even down to the single root of a transplanted hair. The false convert (the hypocrite) is not part of the Body of Christ. He has never truly repented, and because of his sin he is therefore rejected as part of the Body. God knows those who love Him, and the Bible warns that all hypocrites—those merely pretending to be Christians—will end up in hell (Matthew 24:51).

The root of hypocrisy is idolatry, which easily takes root in the soil of a sinful heart. The false convert has created a god that he doesn't fear. The tree that grows from the root bears fruit that is visible for all to see. That's why we are cautioned to examine ourselves to ensure that we are in the faith, that Jesus Christ lives in us (2 Corinthians 13:5). Jesus said, "Every good tree brings forth good fruit" (Matthew 7:17). We must follow Paul's example and strive to be devout, just, and blameless in the sight of a sinful world (1 Thessalonians 2:10). God forbid that any soul should stumble because he sees what he perceives to be hypocrisy in our lives. Do our coworkers ever hear us laughing at a smutty joke? Have we been seen going into an "adult" movie? Is there anger or bitterness, or any bad fruit in our lives for the world to see? Then we must lay the axe to the root.

If there is any pretense in anything we do, we evidently don't fear God. Our concept of His character is erroneous, and we must therefore cultivate a biblical understanding from which we will acquire a proper fear of God.

Judas Iscariot was a hypocrite, a pretender. He had no idea who Jesus was. He complained that an act of sacrificial worship was a waste of money; the expensive ointment with which a woman anointed Jesus should have been sold and the money given to the poor. Jesus of Nazareth just wasn't worth such extravagance. In his estimation, He was worth only thirty pieces of silver.

The Bible tells us that Judas was lying when he said that he cared for the poor. He was actually a thief, and so lacked a healthy fear of God that he was stealing money from the collection bag (see John 12:6).

It's interesting to note that the world hates hypocrisy in the church. They detest the "pretender." Does that mean that they want the Christian to be genuine? Do they *want* us to be true and faithful in our witness and therefore speak of sin, righteousness, and judgment? Do they *want* us to live in holiness rather than in compromise? Does the world really want us to speak up against pornography, greed, adultery, abortion, homosexuality, fornication, and other sins they so love? In their eyes we are damned if we do, and damned if we don't.

QUESTIONS

1. **Why do unbelievers argue that the church is full of hypocrites?**

2. What is "hypocrisy"?

3. Why are there no hypocrites in the Church?

4. What will be the final end of hypocrites?

5. What is the root of hypocrisy? Explain.

6. Why should we examine ourselves?

FEATHERS FOR ARROWS

The way bank officials train tellers to recognize counterfeit bills is to have them study the genuine article. When they see the false, they can spot it because their eye is trained to know the real thing. The real thing in Christianity is someone who is faithful, kind, loving, good, without hypocrisy, gentle, humble, patient, self-controlled, and who speaks the truth in love.

So the next time you're watching TV and see a black-hatted, Abraham Lincoln–style bearded, booze-sodden, Old-English-speaking, Bible-quoting hypocrite plunge a pitchfork into his neighbor's back "in the name of the Lord," ask yourself, "Is this a genuine Christian? Does he love his neighbor as himself? Is he kind, gentle, good, generous, self-controlled? Does he love his enemies? Does he do good to those who spitefully use him?" If not, then what you see is another non-Christian who is pretending to be a Christian.

Last Words

James Buchanan (1791–1868), fifteenth President of the U.S., retired from office and lived in quiet obscurity until his death. His last words were:

"O Lord Almighty, as Thou wilt."

Memory Verse

"You hypocrites, well did Isaiah prophesy of you, saying, This people draws near to me with their mouth, and honors me with their lips; but their heart is far from me."

MATTHEW 15:7,8

 **LESSON**

The Certainty of Judgment

"When we merely say that we are bad, the 'wrath' of God seems a barbarous doctrine; as soon as we perceive our badness, it appears inevitable, a mere corollary from God's goodness..."

C. S. LEWIS

Kirk's Comment Just as human beings value the virtue of justice and demand that justice be served when someone has been wronged, so does God value justice and promise to execute judgment upon mankind according to His perfect standards. All of creation will rejoice when the Judge of the Universe comes to bring truth and justice upon a sin-loving world.

QUESTIONS & OBJECTIONS

"Why does the Old Testament show a God of wrath and the New Testament a God of mercy?"

The God of the New Testament is the same as the God of the Old Testament. The Bible says that He *never* changes. He is just as merciful in the Old Testament as He is in the New Testament. Read Nehemiah 9 for a summary of how God mercifully forgave Israel, again and again, after they repeatedly sinned and turned their backs on Him. The psalms often speak of God's mercy poured out on sinners.

He is also just as wrath-filled in the New Testament as He is in the Old. The Book of Acts records that He killed a husband and wife simply because they told one lie. Jesus warned that He was to be feared because He has the power to cast the body and soul into hell. The apostle Paul said that he persuaded men to come to the Savior because he knew the "terror of the Lord." Read the dreadful judgments of the New Testament's Book of Revelation. That will put the "fear of God" in you, which incidentally is "the beginning of wisdom."

Perhaps the most fearful display of God's wrath is seen in the cross of Jesus Christ. His fury so came upon the Messiah that it seems God enshrouded the face of Jesus in darkness so that creation couldn't gaze upon His unspeakable agony. Whether we like it or not, our God is a consuming fire of holiness (Hebrews 12:29). He isn't going to change, so we had better—before the Day of Judgment. If we repent, God, in His mercy, will forgive us and grant us eternal life in heaven with Him.

w o t m w o t m w o t m w o t m w o t m w o t m w o t m w o t m w o t m w o t m

The prophet Jeremiah warned King Zedekiah repeatedly of the coming judgment of God upon the tribe of Judah. At times the king appeared to actually believe the prophet, then in the next moment he had him shut up in prison.

The world at times seems to believe the gospel. They enjoy gospel music, they will listen to popular prosperity and positive-principle preachers—but they seek to shut us up the moment we speak of a coming judgment. John the Baptist preached judgment for sin. He told Herod that he had transgressed God's Law in taking his brother's wife, and that cost John his life (Mark 6:18). In the eyes of the world, there is nothing popular or positive about preaching the reality of Judgment Day.

Jeremiah's message also put his life in jeopardy. He openly preached that Judah had strayed from the Moral Law. He even expounded the Law to reveal their specific sins (Jeremiah 7:9). They had transgressed the First and Second Commandments by going after other gods. They broke the Sixth, Seventh, Eighth, and Ninth Commandments, and then walked in hypocrisy (v. 10). And still they continued in sin by following after their own counsels and the imagination of their hearts.

The prophet also had to contend with those who preached a life-improvement message rather than one of judgment (Jeremiah 28:1–17). The Bible tells us that such a message was in truth "rebellion against the LORD" (v. 16). It still is. When the preaching of Judgment Day is neglected, people don't see a need to repent. Why should they, if they are not warned that there is a fearful consequence for sin? (See Jeremiah 23:14.)

When Jeremiah spoke of God's judgment upon the nation, he described it as total and absolute. His message left no room for doubt:

> For thus says the LORD, Behold, I will make you a terror to yourself, and to all your friends: and they shall fall by the sword of their enemies, and your eyes shall behold it: and I will give all Judah into the hand of the king of Babylon, and he shall carry them captive into Babylon, and shall slay them with the sword. Moreover I will deliver all the strength of this city, and all the labors thereof, and all the precious things thereof, and all the treasures of the kings of Judah will I give into the hand of their enemies, which shall spoil them, and take them, and carry them to Babylon (Jeremiah 20:4,5).

In these two verses, the word "all" is mentioned six times, "will" four times, and "shall" five times. *This was going to happen.*

So this is the setting in which the king of Judah questions Jeremiah about why he preaches the judgment of God:

> For Zedekiah king of Judah had shut him up, saying, Why do you prophesy, and say, Thus says the LORD, Behold, I will give this city into the hand of the king of Babylon, and he shall take it; and Zedekiah king of Judah shall not escape out of the hand of the Chaldeans, but shall surely be delivered into the hand of the king of Babylon, and shall speak with him mouth to mouth, and his eyes shall behold his eyes; and he shall lead Zedekiah to Babylon, and there shall he be until I visit him, says the LORD: though you fight with the Chaldeans, you shall not prosper (Jeremiah 32:3–5).

Jeremiah's answer to the king's question about why he so adamantly preached judgment is a strange one. He gives a parable that seems totally unrelated to the question. This is what he says:

> The word of the LORD came to me, saying, Behold, Hanameel the son of Shallum your uncle shall come to you saying, Buy my field that is in Anathoth: for the right of redemption is yours to buy it. So Hanameel my uncle's son came to me in the court of the prison according to the word of the LORD, and said to me, Buy my field, I pray you, that is in Anathoth, which is in the country of Benjamin: for the right of inheritance is yours, and the redemption is yours; buy it for yourself. Then I knew that this was the word of the LORD (Jeremiah 32:6–8).

The story seems unrelated to the question, until one understands the meanings of the names he used. The name Hanameel means "God has compassion." Shallum means "retribution." Hanameel and Shallum were father and son; they were related to each other. The compassion of God should never be separated from the retribution of God; they are related. Because He is a just God of retribution and must punish sin, God was in Christ reconciling the world to Himself because of His great compassion. There would be no cross unless there was wrath against sin.

When the world asks us why we preach that there will be a fearful Day of Judgment, we could simply say that it will come to pass because the Bible says so. While this is true, that isn't the only reason we are sure Judgment Day will take place. Our assurance comes from the fact that God has revealed His retribution and His compassion in the gospel, and now offers humanity forgiveness in the Savior. It is through the power of the gospel that we gain assurance that Judgment Day will surely happen.

Those who are seeking safety will find it in the Savior. One who repents and trusts the Savior becomes a new creature; he is born again. Nothing can convince a sinner of the reality of Holy Scripture and its great warning of the coming wrath like a new life with a new heart and new desires.

How then do we best drive men to the Savior? By preaching that the God of compassion is also the God of retribution. It is by opening up the spirituality of the Moral Law that men are made to realize their guilt and see their need of refuge from the coming wrath.

Scripture then gives us additional details of what happened after the purchase of the field:

> Thus says the LORD of hosts, the God of Israel; Take these evidences, this evidence of the purchase, both which is sealed, and this evidence which is open; and put them in an earthen vessel, that they may continue many days.

We are "evidence of the purchase." We stand as a testimony of a transaction of Almighty God. We have been purchased by the blood of Jesus Christ (Acts 20:28), have been sealed by the Holy Spirit of promise unto the day of redemption (Ephesians 1:13; 4:30), and now have the unspeakable riches of this treasure in earthen vessels (2 Corinthians 4:7).

If we are faithful witnesses, our testimony will consist of both God's compassion and His retribution, and we will warn others of the coming Day of Judgment.

QUESTIONS

1. **Why was John the Baptist imprisoned?**

2. **According to Jeremiah 28:1–9, what did the false prophet say?**

3. Why do those who neglect to preach future punishment teach "rebellion against the Lord"?

4. How would you compare this false message to the modern gospel?

5. Why did God judge Judah?

6. Do you think the United States is under judgment? If so, why?

7. Explain how God's retribution and compassion are related.

FEATHERS FOR ARROWS

A man thought of a unique way to paint the eaves of his A-frame house. He threw a rope over the roof and tied it in a secure knot to the bumper of his car. No doubt he also made sure the emergency brake was on so the vehicle wouldn't roll back with his weight. He then went around to the back of the house, climbed onto the roof, and tied the rope tightly around his waist. Then he leaned back, impressed by his ingenuity.

A short time later his wife, not knowing what her inventive husband had done, came out of the house with her car keys in hand. She got into the vehicle and drove off, pulling her husband over the roof and down the other side. The man was seriously injured.

The moral of this true story is that you are only as secure as that to which you secure yourself. If you entrust yourself to the belief that good works will save you on Judgment Day, it will bring about your tragic and eternal downfall.

Last Words

Cardinal Cesare Borgia (1476–1507):

"I have provided in the course of my life for everything except death, and now, alas, I am to die unprepared."

Memory Verse

"Jesus answered, Verily, verily, I say to you, Except a man be born of water and of the Spirit, he cannot enter into the kingdom of God."
JOHN 3:5

22

Judgment Day

> *"Give me one hundred preachers who fear nothing but sin and desire nothing but God, and I care not a straw whether they be clergymen or laymen, such alone will shake the gates of hell and set up the kingdom of God upon earth."*
>
> **JOHN WESLEY**

Kirk's Comment A friend once asked me, "What's Judgment Day?" If sinners are not aware of the Day in which they will give an account of their lives to God, they will not see a need to heed God's command to repent: "[God] commands all men everywhere to repent: because he has appointed a day, in which he will judge the world in righteousness" (Acts 17:30,31).

QUESTIONS & OBJECTIONS

"Jesus didn't condemn the woman caught in the act of adultery, but condemned those who judged her. Therefore you shouldn't judge others."

The Christian is not "judging others" but simply telling the world of God's judgment—that God (not the Christian) has judged all the world as being guilty before Him (Romans 3:19,23). Jesus was able to offer that woman forgiveness for her sin, because He was on His way to die on the cross for her. She acknowledged Him as "Lord," but still He told her, "Go, and sin no more." If she didn't repent, she would perish.

magine a town in the Old West in which there is no justice. Its citizens are robbed, raped, and murdered. The townspeople meet and decide to bring to town a famous marshal who has the reputation of bringing justice wherever he goes. All the good citizens would rejoice to see the guilty brought to justice.

During the 1990s in the U.S., there were 200,000 murders. Amazingly, half of those murders were unsolved. That means 100,000 murderers were never brought to justice. Therefore, 100,000 people were shot, stabbed, strangled, pushed off buildings, bludgeoned to death, etc., and no one was punished for the crimes. Humanity may be unable to right such terrible injustice, but God isn't. He will ensure that every murderer gets his just dessert. On the Day of Judgment, all murderers, as well as rapists, thieves, liars, adulterers, fornicators, etc., will finally be brought to justice.

Judgment Day is the climax of the ages. It is a day that the whole of creation eagerly awaits, an event for which the very ground cries out. It has done so from the blood of Abel and will continue to the last injustice of this age. God loves justice—and He will have it:

> Let the heavens rejoice, and let the earth be glad; let the sea roar, and the fullness thereof. Let the field be joyful, and all that is therein: then shall all the trees of the wood rejoice before the LORD: for he comes, *for he comes to judge the earth*: he shall judge the world with righteousness, and the people with his truth (Psalm 96:11–13, emphasis added).

Don't be concerned that, by referring to the Judgment, you are causing sinners to fear. They have sinned against God and His wrath abides on them. In fact, the Bible calls them "children of wrath." Shouldn't they then fear Him? Look at these words from Isaac Watts:

> I never knew but one person in the whole course of my ministry who acknowledged that the first motions of religion in his own heart arose from a sense of the goodness of God, "What shall I render to the Lord, who has dealt so bountifully with me?" But I think all besides who have come within my notice have rather been first awakened to fly from the wrath to come by the passion of fear.

The Day of Judgment is the reason men are commanded to repent (Acts 17:30,31). If we don't preach that God will judge the world in righteousness, we shouldn't be surprised that men and women are passive about responding to the Savior. If we tell them that they need only believe, then neither should we be surprised when the church fills up with false converts who believe but don't even have enough fear of God to obey.

Therefore, we must remember that it isn't enough to preach the Moral Law. It must be preached in conjunction with future punishment. It has been well said that Law without consequence is nothing but good advice. We must instead preach that those who commit adultery, those who lie and steal, etc., will be punished on the Day of Wrath. It is the preaching of future punishment that produces fear, and it is through the fear of the Lord that men depart from sin (Proverbs 16:6). The Bible tells us that "the Law works wrath" (Romans 4:15). Martin Luther stated, "The proper effect of the Law is to lead us out of our tents and tabernacles, that is to say, from the quietness and security wherein we dwell, and from trusting in ourselves, and to bring us before the presence of God, to reveal his wrath to us, and to set us before our sins."

No man will let go of his darling sins unless he sees a reason to. Hell is a good reason. However, it is difficult for any Christian to preach judgment and the reality of hell without using the Law. Imagine if the police burst into your home, arrested you, and angrily said, "You are going away for a long time!" Such conduct would leave you bewildered and angry. What they have done seems *unreasonable*.

However, imagine if the law burst into your home and instead told you specifically what you had done wrong: "We have discovered 10,000 marijuana plants growing in your back yard. You are going away for a long time!" You would then understand *why* you are in trouble. Knowledge of the law you have transgressed furnishes you with that understanding. It makes judgment *reasonable*.

Hell-fire preaching without the use of the Law to show sinners why God is angry with them will more than likely leave them bewildered and angry—for what they consider unreasonable punishment. A sinner cannot conceive of the thought that God would send anyone to hell, as long as he is deceived into thinking that God's standard of righteousness is the same as his. R. C. Sproul rightly said, "There's probably no concept in theology more repugnant to modern America than the idea of divine wrath." This is because America has been left in the dark about the spiritual nature of God's Law, and therefore has no understanding of God's absolute and uncompromising holiness.

However, when we use the Law lawfully, it appeals to the "reason" of sinners. Paul *reasoned* with Felix about his sins and the judgment to come so that the governor "trembled" (Acts 24:25). He suddenly understood that he was a guilty sinner in the sight of a holy God, and hell became reasonable. No doubt the "righteousness" Paul spoke of was the righteousness which is of the Law, with the result that the fear of God fell upon the heart of his hearer.

Therefore, never underestimate the power of reasoning with a sinner (using the Law) about the reality of hell. Learn how to give extreme scenarios that stretch him into a moral dilemma. Say, "Imagine if someone raped your mother or sister, then strangled her to death. Do you think God should punish him?" If the person is reasonable, he will say, "Yes, of course. That makes sense." Then ask, "Do you think He should punish thieves?" Then follow with liars, etc. Tell him that God is perfect, holy, just, and righteous, and that His "prison" is a place called "hell."

Always take the sinner back to his personal sins. Remember to speak to his conscience: "You know right from wrong. God gave you a conscience." Some people believe in a temporary hell (purgatory), or in "annihilation" (that the soul ceases to exist after death). The Bible, however, speaks of conscious, eternal punishment. If he thinks that is harsh, tell him that it is. If we think eternal punishment is horrific, what should we do about it—shake our fists at God? When such foolish thoughts enter our minds, we must go to the foot of the cross and meditate on the great love God had for us—that He was in Christ reconciling the world to Himself. Then we must turn any horror into concern, and plead with sinners to flee from the wrath to come.

Charles Spurgeon said, "God [has] appointed a day in which He will judge the world, and we sigh and cry until it shall end the reign of wickedness, and give rest to the oppressed. Brethren, we must preach the coming of the Lord, and preach it somewhat more than we have done, *because it is the driving power of the gospel.* Too many have kept back these truths, and thus the bone has been taken out of the arm of the gospel. Its point has been broken; its edge has been blunted. The doctrine of judgment to come is the power by which men are to be aroused. There is another life; the Lord will come a second time; judgment will arrive; the wrath of God will be revealed. *Where this is not preached, I am bold to say the gospel is not preached.*

"It is absolutely necessary to the preaching of the gospel of Christ that men be warned as to what will happen if they continue in their sins. Ho, ho sir surgeon, you are too delicate to tell the man that he is ill! You hope to heal the sick without their knowing it. You therefore flatter them; and what happens? They laugh at you; they dance upon their own graves. At last they die! Your delicacy is cruelty; your flatteries are poisons; *you are a murderer.* Shall we keep men in a fool's paradise? Shall we lull them into soft slumbers from which they will awake in hell? Are we to become helpers of their damnation by our smooth speeches? In the name of God we will not."

QUESTIONS

1. Why should we not be concerned that speaking of judgment causes sinners to fear?

2. If we don't preach about the coming judgment, what will result?

3. **Why is it difficult for Christians to preach about judgment and hell without making reference to the Law?**

4. **What does the Law do to judgment?**

5. **According to R. C. Sproul, what do most people think of God's wrath?**

6. **What does eternal punishment for sin show us about God?**

PREACHER'S PROGRESS

Candice B. Fureal: "Christian, I want to ask you a question."

Christian: "Sure. What is it?"

Candice B. Fureal: "I admit that I have told fibs and white lies in the past. But will God send me to hell for telling one lie?"

Christian: "Are you saying that your sins are 'petty' sins, so you don't think they should take you to hell?"

Candice B. Fureal: "I guess that's what I'm saying."

Christian: "Let's put it this way. How many lies have you told in your life: one or two, or more?

Candice B. Fureal: "I think it would be in the 'more' category."

Christian: "So what does that make you?"

Candice B. Fureal: "Not a 'liar'—the word sounds too harsh."

Christian: "Candice, you have told many lies, and even if you told one lie, it makes you a liar."

Candice B. Fureal: "I can't see that."

Christian: "If I commit one murder, it makes me a murderer. If I rob one bank, it makes me a bank robber. If I commit adultery once, it makes me an adulterer. It's the same with lies."

Candice B. Fureal: "Okay. That makes sense."

Christian: "Your sins may seem petty to you, but to God they are many and are very serious. If a judge gave a sentence of a $5 fine, you may conclude that the criminal's crime was petty. The punishment reflects the crime. However, if you read that a judge has given a criminal five life sentences, you may conclude that the crime was heinous. God's punishment for sin is everlasting damnation in hell. That shows how our 'petty' sins are unspeakably serious in the sight of a holy God."

Candice B. Fureal: "Okay."

Christian: "So can you see that you have a multitude of sins, all of which God is aware of, and that you are in danger of being damned forever?"

Candice B. Fureal: "Yes. I can see that now."

Christian: "Candice, God loved you so much that He became a human being in Jesus Christ to take the punishment for your sins. If you repent and trust in Jesus, because of His death and resurrection, God can now grant you everlasting life."

Candice B. Fureal: "Can this be for real? What you are saying sounds too good to be true."

Christian: "If it were the mere word of man, it would be too good to be true. But this is the promise of Almighty God to all who obey Him."

FEATHERS FOR ARROWS

Years ago, a television advertisement had a deep-voiced commentator ask the sobering question, "What goes through the mind of a driver at the moment of impact in a head-on collision if he's not wearing a seat belt?" As he spoke, the commercial showed a dummy without a safety belt, reacting in slow motion to a head-on collision. As the dummy moved forward on impact, the steering wheel went right through its skull. Then the commentator somberly continued, "...the steering wheel. You can learn a lot from a dummy. Buckle up!"

How could the censors allow such fear tactics? This advertisement struck trepidation in the hearts of motorists. The reason is clear: they were speaking the truth. It is a fearful thing to be in a head-on collision when you're not wearing a seat belt.

What you are sharing with people is the gospel truth. The Bible warns, "It is a fearful thing to fall into the hands of the living God." It is right that sinners should fear, because they are in danger of eternal damnation. They are going to collide head-on with God's Law. Let Judgment Day play out before their eyes in slow motion.

Memory Verse

"If we say that we have no sin, we deceive ourselves, and the truth is not in us. If we confess our sins, he is faithful and just to forgive us our sins, and to cleanse us from all unrighteousness."

1 JOHN 1:8,9

Last Words

Karl Marx, revolutionary, died in 1883. To his housekeeper, who urged him to tell her his last words so she could write them down for posterity, he answered:

"Go on, get out—last words are for fools who haven't said enough."

23 The Reality of Hell

"Save some, O Christians! By all means, save some. From yonder flames and outer darkness, and the weeping, wailing, and gnashing of teeth, seek to save some! Let this, as in the case of the apostle, be your great, ruling object in life, that by all means you might save some."

CHARLES SPURGEON

Kirk's Comment Hell is an unthinkable place for my loved ones—or for anyone else. I can't make it go away, so I will do everything I can to point sinners to the Savior, who alone can save them from going there.

QUESTIONS & OBJECTIONS

"Could you be wrong in your claims about Judgment Day and hell?"

The existence of hell and the surety of the judgment are not the claims of fallible man. The Bible is the source of the claim, and it is utterly infallible. When someone becomes a Christian, he is admitting that he was in the wrong, and that God is justified in His declarations that we have sinned against Him. However, let's surmise for a moment that there is no Judgment Day and no hell. That would mean that the Bible is a huge hoax, in which more than forty authors collaborated (over a period of 1,500 years) to produce a document revealing God's character as "just." They portrayed Him as a righteous judge, who warned that He would eventually punish murderers, rapists, liars, thieves, adulterers, etc. Each of those writers (who professed to be godly) therefore bore false witness, transgressing the very Commandments they claimed were true. It would mean that Jesus Christ was a liar, and that all the claims He made about the reality of judgment were therefore false. It would also mean that He gave His life in vain, as did multitudes of martyrs who have given their lives for the cause of Christ. In addition, if there is no ultimate justice, then the Creator of all things is unjust—He sees murder and rape and couldn't care less, making Him worse than a corrupt human judge who refuses to bring criminals to justice.

Here's the good news, though, if there is no hell: You won't know a thing after you die. It will be the end. No heaven, no hell. Just nothing. You won't even realize that it's good news.

Here's the bad news if the Bible is right and there is eternal justice: You will find yourself standing before the judgment throne of a holy God. Think of it. A holy and perfect Creator has seen your thought-life and every secret sin you have ever committed. You have a multitude of sins, and God must by nature carry out justice. Ask Him to remind you of the sins of your youth. Ask Him to bring to remembrance your secret sexual sins, the lies, the gossip, and other idle words. You may have forgotten your past sins, but God hasn't. Hell will be your just dessert (exactly what you deserve), and you will have no one to blame but yourself. This is the claim of the Bible. If you don't believe it, it is still true. It will still happen.

Yet, there is good news—incredibly good news. We deserve judgment, but God offers us mercy through the cross. He paid our fine so that we could leave the courtroom. He destroyed the power of the grave for all who obey Him. Simply obey the gospel, and live. By doing that you will find out for yourself that the gospel is indeed the "gospel truth." Jesus said that if you obey Him, you will know the truth, and the truth will make you free (see John 8:31,32). Get on your knees today, confess and forsake (turn from) your sins. Tell God you are truly sorry, then trust the Savior as you would trust yourself to a parachute. Then you will find yourself in a terrible dilemma. You will know for certain that hell is a reality. When you get up the courage to warn people you care about, they will smile passively and say, "Could you be wrong in your claims about Judgment Day and the existence of hell?"

w o t m w o t m w o t m w o t m w o t m w o t m w o t m w o t m w o t m w o t m w o t m w o t m

Some who are enjoying the pleasures of sin for a season will brush off thoughts of God's eternal justice by joking, "I don't mind going to hell. All my friends will be there." Obviously, those who flippantly say such things don't believe in the biblical concept of hell. They are like a slow-witted criminal who thinks that the electric chair is a place to put up his feet for a while and relax. Their understanding of the nature of God is erroneous, so it may be wise to speak for a few moments about the reasonableness of hell. Explain that the Bible tells us that God will punish murderers and rapists, and the place of punishment—the "prison" God will send them to—is a place called "hell." However, God is so good, He will also punish thieves, liars, adulterers, fornicators, and blasphemers. He will even punish those who desired to murder and rape but never took the opportunity. He warns that if we hate someone, we commit murder in our hearts. If we lust, we commit adultery in the heart, etc. All are sins that will send us to hell.

C. S. Lewis summed up all the terrors of hell when he said, "There is no doctrine which I would more willingly remove from Christianity than the doctrine of hell, if it lay in my power. But it has the full support of Scripture and, especially, of our Lord's own words; it has always been held by the Christian Church, and it has the support of reason."

Take the time to tell people of the reality of hell and its biblical description. Some sinners like to picture hell as a fun, hedonistic, pleasure-filled place where they can engage in all the sensual sins that are forbidden here. Others accept that hell is a place of punishment, but believe that the punishment is to be annihilated—to cease conscious existence. Because they can't conceive that a loving God would punish people in eternal torment, they believe hell is just a metaphor for the grave. If they are correct, then a man like Adolph Hitler, who was responsible for the death of millions, is being "punished" merely with eternal sleep. His fate is simply to return to the non-existent state he was in before he was born, where he doesn't even know that he is being punished.

While it is true that God is love (1 John 4:8), He is also just (Nehemiah 9:32,33; 2 Thessalonians 1:6) and eternal (Psalm 90:2; 1 Timothy 1:17). God will therefore punish the evil doer (Isaiah 13:11) and this punishment will be eternal. It will also be conscious. Scripture tells us of the rich man who found himself in hell (Luke 16:19–31). He was conscious and was able to feel pain, to thirst, and to experience remorse. He wasn't asleep in the grave; he was in a place of "torment."

We tend to forget what pain is like when we don't have it. Can you imagine how terrible it would be to be in agony, with no hope of relief? Many human beings go insane if they are merely isolated for a long time from other people. Imagine how terrible it would be if God simply withdrew all the things we hold so dear—friendship, love, color, light, peace, joy, laughter. Hell isn't just a place with an absence of God's blessings; it is punishment for sin. It is literal torment, forever. That's why the Bible warns that it is a fearful thing to fall into the hands of the living God. The fate of the unsaved is described with such fearful words as the following:

- "Shame and everlasting contempt" (Daniel 12:2)
- "Everlasting punishment" (Matthew 25:46)
- "Weeping and gnashing of teeth" (Matthew 24:51)
- "Fire unquenchable" (Luke 3:17)
- "Indignation and wrath, tribulation and anguish" (Romans 2:8,9)
- "Everlasting destruction from the presence of the Lord" (2 Thessalonians 1:9)
- "Eternal fire . . . the blackness of darkness for ever" (Jude 7,13)

Revelation 14:10,11 tells us the final, eternal destiny of the sinner: "He shall be tormented with fire and brimstone . . . the smoke of their torment ascended up for ever and ever: and they have no rest day or night."

Scripture is quite clear: hell is a real place. It is not mere unconsciousness. It is not temporal. It is eternal torment. If hell is a place of knowing nothing or a reference to the grave into which we go at death, Jesus' statements about hell make no sense. He said that if your hand, foot, or eye causes you to sin, it would be better to remove it than to "go into hell, into the fire that never shall be quenched: where their worm dies not, and the fire is not quenched" (Mark 9:43–48). Jesus spoke more of hell than of heaven and spent much time warning people not to go there. After all, if people just stopped existing, why warn them? If hell were temporal, they'd get out in a while. But because it is eternal and conscious, we must do everything we can to warn them.

However, a sinner won't see that hell is his eternal destiny unless he is convinced by the Law that he has sinned against God. He may consider hell a fit place for others, but not for himself. That's why we must not hesitate to open up the Law and show that each individual is personally responsible for his sin, and that God's wrath abides on him because of it.

QUESTIONS

1. What would be the implications if hell were not real?

2. What are some of the ways that people picture hell?

3. What are some of the ways that the Bible describes hell?

4. Why does the concept of annihilation go against our desire for justice?

5. What will help convince sinners of the reality of hell?

Words of Comfort

You can probably understand how careful I am when it comes to touching something like Super Glue. One drop can immediately stick the fingers together, so with great care I tried to tear open a plastic packet that contained a tube of Super Glue. I stopped at the thought, "I'm not stupid. I'm not going to tear it open and accidentally pull the top off." So with the skill of a brain surgeon, I cut the cardboard backing off the packet with a sharp knife, and carefully took out the tube of glue. Then I cautiously removed the cap and gently squeezed the tube, keeping my flesh back from the nozzle, knowing that just one drop on my fingers could mean surgery to separate them. Successful operation. I had the top off and there wasn't a drop on my fingers.

There was, however, a strange feeling in my left hand. The sharp knife I had used to cut into the packet had penetrated the soft steel of the tube, and the palm of my hand was filled with Super Glue!

Feathers for Arrows

When surfing first began, surfboards were much longer. Surfers would kneel on their boards and paddle in that position, rather than lying down. In large surfs this had a great advantage, enabling the surfer to stand on his board to see if any large sets of waves were on the horizon.

One would often hear a surfer call out, "Big set coming!" Other surfers would quickly begin paddling toward the horizon, because they didn't want to get caught "inside," and have gigantic waves break on them.

If a surfer found himself caught within the breaking area, he had a choice. He could either hold onto his board and allow tons of water to break upon him, or he could get off his board, thrust it away from his body, and dive deep into the water to escape the crushing power of the waves. If he choose to stay with his board, he took his life into his hands. If the board was ripped from his hands and hit his head, he could drown —so it was wise to push it as far away as possible.

For thousands of years the prophets have called, "Big set coming!" The coming of the great and terrible day of the Lord is closer than when we first believed. All human beings have a choice. They can either cling to their sins, or thrust them far from them and dive deep into the mercy of God, which is available only in Jesus Christ. Those who choose to hold onto their sins will find that what they love will turn against them, become evidence of their guilt, and be the death of them.

Memory Verse

"If your eye offends you, pluck it out: it is better for you to enter into the kingdom of God with one eye, than having two eyes to be cast into hell fire: where their worm dies not, and the fire is not quenched."

MARK 9:47,48

Last Words

Robert Green Ingersoll (1833–1899), famous American lawyer and prominent agnostic, lectured on biblical inaccuracies and contradictions. His famed lecture "The Mistakes of Moses" led one defender of the Bible to say that he would like to hear Moses speak for five minutes on "The Mistakes of Ingersoll." Standing by his graveside, his brother exclaimed:

> **"Life is a narrow vale between the narrow peaks of two eternities. We strive in vain to look beyond the heights. We cry aloud, and the only echo is the echo of our wailings."**

LESSON 24

Man's Sinful Condition

"The evangelist who preaches for eternity is never great on numbers. He is not apt to count hundreds of converts where there is no restitution, no confession, and no glad cry which proclaims, 'The lost is found, the dead is made alive again!'"

E. M. BOUNDS

Kirk's Comment Unless a man sees himself as "not good," as truly filthy and sinful, he will never thirst for the righteousness that is in Christ. A man who is content with his own filthy rags will not see the infinite value of the robe of righteousness God extends to him. It is not until we see ourselves as God sees us that we can recognize our need for the Savior and come to Him in repentance and faith.

QUESTIONS & OBJECTIONS

"Adam didn't die the day God said he would!"

He certainly did—he died spiritually. The moment he sinned, he became "dead in trespasses and sins" (Ephesians 2:1). Ezekiel 18:4 says, "The soul that sins, it shall die." Ian Thomas explained it this way: "We are born dead in trespasses and sins, alienated, cut off, detached from the life of God. The day that man believed the devil's lie (which is sin), he forfeited

161

the life that distinguished him from the animal kingdom—the life of God. When sin came in, the life went out."

It is because we are born spiritually dead that Jesus came to give us spiritual life (John 5:40; 10:10; 14:6; etc.). This is why Jesus told us that we must be born again (John 3:3). When we repent of our sins and place our trust in the Savior, the Bible tells us that we "pass from death to life" (John 5:24; Romans 6:13; 1 John 3:14).

wotmwotmwotmwotmwotmwotmwotmwotmwotmwotmwotm

The majority of humanity believes that some amount of good works is sufficient to gain them entrance into heaven. This belief is due to a faulty concept of man's true condition. Helping people understand the concept of "original sin" will enable them to see their need for the Savior.

Two things are meant by the expression "original sin": the first sin of Adam, and the sinful nature possessed by every person since Adam, due to Adam's first transgression. This sinful nature is called "depravity." Depravity consists of four things, which are true of every individual when he is born:

1. *He is completely void of original righteousness.* "Behold, I was shaped in iniquity, and in sin did my mother conceive me" (Psalm 51:5).

2. *He does not possess any holy affection toward God.* "They changed the truth of God into a lie, and worshiped and served the creature more than the Creator, who is blessed for ever" (Romans 1:25). "There is none righteous, no, not one; there is none who understands; there is none who seeks after God" (Romans 3:10,11). "For men shall be lovers of their own selves,...lovers of pleasures more than lovers of God" (2 Timothy 3:2–4).

3. *There is nothing from without a man, that can defile him; but the things which come out of him, these are they that defile the man.* "For from within, out of the heart of men, proceed evil thoughts, adulteries, fornications, murders, thefts, covetousness, wickedness, deceit, lasciviousness, an evil eye, blasphemy, pride, foolishness: all these evil things come from within, and defile the man" (Mark 7:15,21–23).

4. *He has a continual bias toward evil.* "And God saw that the wickedness of man was great in the earth, and that every imagining of the thoughts of his heart was only evil continually" (Genesis 6:5).

Lest the term "depravity" be misunderstood, it is well to note the following, quoted from *Lectures in Systematic Theology* by Henry C. Thiessen:

> From the negative standpoint, it does not mean that every sinner is devoid of all qualities pleasing to men; that he commits, or is prone to commit every form of sin; that he is as bitterly opposed to God as it is possible for him to be... Jesus recognized the existence of pleasing qualities in some individuals (Mark 10:21; Matt. 23:23).
>
> ... From the positive standpoint, it does mean that every sinner is totally destitute of that love to God which is the fundamental requirement of the law: "Hear, O Israel: The LORD our God is one LORD. And thou shalt love the LORD thy God with all thine heart, and with all thy soul, and with all thy might" (Dt. 6:4,5). See Matt. 22:35–38; that he is supremely given to a preference of himself to God (2 Tim. 3:2–4); that he has an aversion to God which on occasion becomes active enmity to Him: "because the carnal mind is enmity against God, for it is not subject to the law of God, neither indeed can be" (Rom. 8:7); that his every faculty is disordered and corrupted: "having the understanding darkened, being alienated from the life of God through the ignorance that is in them because of the blindness of their heart" (Eph. 4:18); that he has no thought, feeling, or deed of which God can fully approve: "For I know that in me (that is, in my flesh) dwelleth no good thing; for to will is present with me; but how to perform that which is good, I find not" (Rom. 7:18); and that he has entered upon a line of constant progress in depravity from which he can in no wise turn away in his own strength.

The result of man's depravity, or sin nature, is his willful rebellion against God. Such an attitude cannot but bring forth evil results. The awful results of sin are obvious. It is not possible for men to continue sinning and receive anything but a harvest of sorrows of the worst kind. Paul states in Galatians 6:8, "For he that sows to his flesh shall of the flesh reap corruption." Hosea said concerning Israel, "For they have sown the wind, and they shall reap the whirlwind" (Hosea 8:7). He also declared, "You have plowed wickedness, you have reaped iniquity; you have eaten the fruit of lies" (Hosea 10:13).

One would have to be blind not to see the result of sinful depravity in the minds and bodies of the human race today. Superstition, barbarity, and the grossest iniquity are seen in every land where the gospel has not yet gone. Where the message of salvation from sin has been preached and rejected, the condition is almost worse, for here is added the condemnation of light that has been rejected. In the United States, probably the richest Christian nation in the world, every institution of correction, every prison of punishment, every sanitarium and asylum is bulging with the results of sin. Every policeman in the country is a silent tribute to the reality of sin.

So devastating is its influence upon the human consciousness that now sin is glamorized until it is being recognized in society as the thing to do. A great man once said, "Our greatest defense against sin is to be shocked at it"; and when this attitude ceases, sin has accomplished its direst results. Paul, in that terrible list of gross iniquities in Romans 1:24–32, climaxed the whole dread situation when he said, "Who knowing the judgment of God, that they which commit such things are worthy of death, not only do the same, but have pleasure in them that do them" (v. 32). When sin loses its sinfulness, and men take pleasure in the grossest of sinful practices, there is little hope left . . . but for the grace of God.

QUESTIONS

1. **What two things are meant by the expression "original sin"?**

2. What is the sinful nature called?

3. In what four ways are all individuals "depraved" when they are born?

4. Some individuals claim that people are basically good. How does that fit with the concept of depravity?

5. What is the greatest defense against sin?

6. Based on that, how do you think the U.S. is faring?

FEATHERS FOR ARROWS

A true story was told of a young soldier in the Civil War. After an explosion left him seriously injured, he lay on the battlefield covered in blood. A male nurse sat beside the helpless trooper, holding his thumb on the man's neck to stop the bleeding.

In the heat of battle, a doctor came alongside the two men. He looked closely at the wound and told the soldier that he was very fortunate. The damage was very close to a main artery, and if that had been severed he would have died almost immediately.

The doctor carefully stitched the small veins over which the nurse had applied pressure.

A few minutes later, he was called back. The terrified nurse was holding his thumb over a main artery, which had suddenly burst. The good doctor explained that he could now do nothing for the soldier. As soon as the nurse removed his thumb, blood would gush out rapidly, and there was no way he could contain its flow.

Over the next three hours, the brave young soldier thanked the nurse for what he had done for him, wrote farewells to his loved ones, put his affairs in order, then told the nurse to remove his thumb. The horrified nurse turned his face away from the young warrior as he removed his thumb; the soldier was dead within minutes.

Whether we are enlightened to understand it or not, the eternal God of creation holds our life in His hands. When the preserving presence of His hand is removed, we die. We are but mortal human beings, and "in Him we live and move and have our being." Every breath we take, and every heartbeat that follows, comes only because He keeps His gracious hand upon our lives.

He alone is the origin of human life, the One who sustains our very existence.

WORDS OF COMFORT

My lovely wife is very conservative in nature. After a meal at a mall, she bought an ice cream, held it out, and said, "Here you are...handsome." My heart skipped a beat. I was about to blush when I realized that I had misheard what she had said. She actually said, "Here you are...have some." A similar thing happened about two weeks later. I was speaking to her long-distance when she said, "I will see you tomorrow morning...baby." Baby! Wow! I was excited, until I asked her to repeat what she had said. She said, "I will see you tomorrow morning...maybe."

Last Words

Andrew Jackson (1767–1845), the seventh President of the U.S., loved to read the Bible, and heaven was near and dear to him. Shortly before he died, he gathered his family and servants to his bedside and told them:

> "I have suffered much bodily pain, but my sufferings are but as nothing compared with that which our blessed Redeemer endured upon the accursed cross, that all might be saved who put their trust in Him."

Memory Verse

"As it is written, There is none righteous, no, not one: there is none that understands, there is none that seeks after God. They are all gone out of the way, they are together become unprofitable; there is none that does good, no, not one."

ROMANS 3:10–12

LESSON 25

Our Primary Task

"You have nothing to do but to save souls. Therefore spend and be spent in this work. And go not only to those that need you, but to those that need you most... It is not your business to preach so many times, and to take care of this or that society; but to save as many souls as you can; to bring as many sinners as you possibly can to repentance."

JOHN WESLEY

Kirk's Comment   While prayer and worship are vital elements of the Christian life, I believe that if God wanted us to spend the majority of our time in conversation with Him, He'd take us to heaven right now so we could do that without distraction. Jesus came to this world for one reason: to seek and save the lost. If we are going to live as He lived, pray as He prayed, and obey His Great Commission, then that's what we should be doing: seeking and saving the lost. To love and honor Jesus is to obey Him, and He has commanded us to preach the gospel to every creature, in season and out of season. For believers still on earth, evangelism is our primary task.

QUESTIONS & OBJECTIONS

"Do you think that Christians are better than non-Christians?"

The Christian is no better than a non-Christian, but he is infinitely better *off*. It is like two men on a plane, one of whom is wearing a parachute while the other is not. Neither is better than the other, but the man with the parachute is certainly better off than the man who is not wearing a parachute. The difference will be seen when they jump from the plane at 20,000 feet. Jesus warned that if we "jump" into death without Him, we would perish.

Even harsher than the law of gravity is the Law of an infinitely holy and just Creator. Scripture states that sinners are God's enemy (Romans 5:10) and that "it is a fearful thing to fall into the hands of the living God" (Hebrews 10:31).

wotmwotmwotmwotmwotmwotmwotmwotmwotmwotmwotm

A lighthouse keeper gained a reputation of being a very kind man. He would give free fuel to ships that miscalculated the amount of fuel needed to reach their destination port. One night during a storm, lightning struck his lighthouse and put out the light. He immediately turned on his generator, but it soon ran out of fuel—and he had given his reserves to passing ships. During the dark night, a ship struck the rocks and many lives were lost.

At the lighthouse keeper's trial, the judge knew of his reputation as a kind man and wept as he passed sentence. He charged the lighthouse keeper with neglecting his primary responsibility: to keep the light shining.

The church can so often get caught up in legitimate acts of kindness —standing for political righteousness, feeding the hungry, etc.—but our primary task is to warn sinners of danger. We are to keep the light of the gospel shining so that sinners can avoid the jagged-edged rocks of wrath and escape being eternally damned.

Imagine seeing a group of firefighters polishing their engine outside a burning building with people trapped at a top floor window. Obviously, there is nothing wrong with cleaning a fire engine—*but not while people are trapped in a burning building!* Instead of ignoring their cries, the firefighters should have an overwhelming sense of urgency to rescue them. That's the spirit that should be behind the task of evangelism. Yet according to Bill Bright of Campus Crusade for Christ, "Only two percent of believers in America regularly share their faith in Christ with others." That means 98 percent of the professing Body of Christ is "lukewarm" when it comes to obeying the Great Commission.

Oswald J. Smith said, "Oh my friends, we are loaded down with countless church activities, while the *real* work of the Church, that of evangelizing and winning the lost, is almost entirely neglected." We have polished the engines of worship, prayer, and praise and neglected the sober task given to us by God. A firefighter who ignores his responsibilities and allows people to perish in the flames is not a firefighter; he is an impostor. How could we ignore our responsibility and allow the world to walk blindly into the fires of hell? If God's love dwells within us, we must warn the lost. The Bible tells us to "have compassion...save with fear, pulling them out of the fire; hating even the garment spotted by the flesh" (Jude 22,23). If we don't have love and compassion, then we don't know God—we are impostors (see 1 John 4:8). Charles Spurgeon said, "Have you no wish for others to be saved? Then you are not saved yourself. Be sure of that." Each of us should examine ourselves in light of these sobering thoughts (2 Corinthians 13:5) so that we won't be part of the great multitude who called Jesus "Lord," but refused to obey Him. It will be professing *believers* who will hear those fearful words, "I never knew you: depart from me" (Matthew 7:21–23).

A popular episode of the "Andy Griffith Show" is called "Man in a Hurry." It tells the story of a businessman who rushes through the quiet town of Mayberry. He is uptight and very hyper and finds the laid-back lifestyle of the locals to be extremely frustrating. However, in time he begins to enjoy the take-it-easy way of life. While it's a wonderful lesson on the importance of not rushing through life, the "man in a hurry" should be the Christian's hero. We are in a hurry. We should work while it is yet day with a sense of extreme urgency. We must preach the Word in season and out of season, always abounding in the work of the Lord.

Take to heart these words from Billy Sunday: "I believe that lack of efficient personal work is one of the failures of the Church today. The people of the Church are like squirrels in a cage. Lots of activity, but accomplishing nothing. It doesn't require a Christian life to sell oyster soup or run a bazaar or a rummage sale. Many churches report no new members on confession of faith. Why these meager results with this tremendous expenditure of energy and money? Why are so few people coming into the Kingdom? I will tell you—there is not a definite effort put forth to persuade a definite person to receive a definite Savior at a definite time, and that definite time is now."

May God give us a renewed sense of urgency and such love for sinners that we will be convicted by our conscience if we walk past any person without a deep concern for his salvation. May He also work in our hearts so that our prayers will be permeated with a cry for laborers, so that this world may be reached with the message of eternal salvation.

QUESTIONS

1. **What was the crime of the lighthouse keeper?**

2. **Did the judge do the right thing in punishing him? If so, why?**

3. **What is the primary responsibility of the Church?**

4. **What did Oswald J. Smith say about our wrong priorities?**

5. **What tasks is your own church involved in, while it neglects evangelism?**

6. **What does it indicate if we have no concern for the lost?**

FEATHERS FOR ARROWS

Memory Verse

"Preach the word; be instant in season, out of season; reprove, rebuke, exhort with all longsuffering and doctrine."

2 TIMOTHY 4:2

A true story is told of a millionaire who had a portrait painted of his beloved son before the son went to war. He was tragically killed in battle, and shortly afterward, the heartbroken millionaire died. His will stated that all his riches were to be auctioned, specifying that the painting must sell first.

Many showed up at the auction, where a mass of the rich man's wealth was displayed. When the painting was held up for sale, no bids were offered. It was an unknown painting by an unknown painter of the rich man's uncelebrated son, so, sadly, there was no interest. After a few moments, a butler who worked for the man recalled how much the millionaire loved his son, so he made a bid and purchased the portrait for a very low price.

Suddenly, to everyone's surprise, the auctioneer brought down his gavel and declared the auction closed. The rich man's will had specified that the person who cared enough to purchase the painting of his beloved son was also to be given all the riches of his will.

This is precisely what God has done through the gospel. He who accepts the beloved Son of God also receives all the riches of His will—the gift of eternal life and "pleasures for evermore." They become "joint heirs" with the Son (Romans 8:16,17).

Last Words

Henry Wadsworth Longfellow (1807–1882) is the most famous of American Puritan poets. Having the Christian outlook on life both here and hereafter, Longfellow left us this testimony on the continuity of life beyond the grave:

"There is no death; what seems so is transition."

The Fear of Man

"We fear men so much, because we fear God so little. One fear causes another. When man's terror scares you, turn your thoughts to the wrath of God."

WILLIAM GURNALL

Kirk's Comment If you're like me, you care about what others think of you, and the last thing you want is for people to think you're a religious fruit-cake. While it's good to be concerned about having a reputation of integrity, the "fear of man" is from Satan, and will constantly attempt to discourage you and destroy your enthusiasm to talk with people about Jesus Christ.

QUESTIONS & OBJECTIONS

"Christianity is boring."

Then you haven't experienced it. No one who is a Christian will ever say that it is boring; it is an adventure. There are millions of people who have a lot of fun being Christian. What do you think we do all day, sit around fireplaces and read Bibles? We ski, swim, play sports, read, and spend time with friends like anybody else. We just do it with a lot less sin, and therefore a lot less problems. Maybe it's only your problems that keep you from getting bored.

Someone once said, "Keep your fears to yourself. Share your courage with others." While that is true when it comes to specific fears, it is a consolation to know that heroes do heroic deeds *despite* their fears. Courage isn't the absence of fear, but the conquering of it. If a hero didn't have fear to overcome, then his act of courage wouldn't truly be an act of courage.

It is a consolation to know that almost every Christian has a battle with the "fear of man" when it comes to reaching out to the lost. Take the time to look at the fears of the apostle Paul (1 Corinthians 2:1–4). He said that when he reached out to the Corinthians with the gospel, he did so not with "excellency of speech or of wisdom." He confided that he had "weakness" (he was not trusting in his own strength or ability) and "fear" (in Greek, *phobos*, "that which is caused by being scared"), resulting in "much trembling" (awareness of his insufficiency). Paul battled the fear of man.

There are certain keys that can help to bring our fears into perspective. One is to meditate on what God is *not* asking us to do. Here's the scenario. You are outside a shopping mall and see a man standing by himself. You feel a strong conviction that God wants you to give the man a tract. Your heart begins to pound. Thoughts flood your mind: *What if he gets angry? He is going to think I'm a religious nut who is trying to ram religion down his throat.* Here is what to say to yourself to make the task easier. God is not asking you to stand on a soapbox and preach to a crowd. You are not being asked to do this in a country where you could be jailed for handing out Christian literature. All God is asking you to do is hand one tract to one man.

When the U.S. Navy trains rescue pilots, they place so much psychological pressure on recruits that half of them drop out. Because the Navy wants the best, those who enlist are pushed to the limits by being dropped out of helicopters into freezing water. In the water, a man simulates a drowning, and when his rescuer reaches him, he deliberately panics, grabbing the would-be rescuer and pulling him under. The trainee must take charge of the situation or be disqualified from the course. He must take control, not only of the circumstances, but also of his own fears.

If we want to rescue humanity from the fires of hell, we must take control of our own fears and reject the fears the enemy whispers to our hearts. Don't let the lies of the enemy penetrate your mind any longer. Remember the command, "Fear not; for I am with you: be not dismayed; for I am your God: I will strengthen you; yes, I will help you; yes, I will uphold you with the right hand of my righteousness" (Isaiah 41:10).

To be dismayed or discouraged is to dishonor God. Since He is always with us, we must never lose courage. Remember that Satan is just a creation of Almighty God. A blind, anemic, weak-kneed flea on crutches would have a greater chance of defeating a herd of a thousand wild, stampeding elephants than the enemy has of defeating God!

The Book of Revelation says of the glorified Jesus, "out of his mouth went a sharp two-edged sword" (1:16). Soldier of Christ, throw away your sheath; it is not part of your armor. Your sword, the Word of God, should always be at the ready.

There is power in the Word of God. When the light of the Word is spoken, the darkness of the enemy must vanish. Make it a habit to quote God's Word at fear: "He that dwells in the secret place of the Most High shall abide under the shadow of the Almighty. I will say of the LORD, He is my refuge and my fortress: my God; in him will I trust" (Psalm 91:1,2).

We are not to fear man, but to fear God—the one who has power to cast into hell (Luke 12:5). This thought may help you get rid of the fear of man and replace it with the fear of God: *He executes cowards, deserters, and traitors* (see Hebrews 10:26,27; Revelation 21:8). His army is for men and women of faith. Our courage is fueled by our faith in God. If we lack courage, it's only because we lack faith. If we lack faith, we insult the integrity of Almighty God.

A number of years ago at a church in Minneapolis, the pastor of evangelism took hold of the microphone. He was an ex-cop, and his voice cracked with emotion as he spoke of an accident victim he once held in his arms. The critically injured man thrashed back and forth for a moment, sighed deeply, and then passed into eternity. The pastor's voice was filled with emotion because his own church had over a thousand members, yet only five attended his evangelism class.

It was obvious that the army's hive of activity was in the barracks of everything but evangelism. He pleaded, "What's wrong with you? *Don't you care that people in our city are going to hell?* I can teach you to rid yourself of fear..." His was no proud boast. The prison doors of fear can be opened with very simple keys: a knowledge of God's will, ordered priorities, love that is not passive, gratitude for the cross, and the use of the Law before grace—just to name a few.

What is wrong with us? How can we not care that sinners are being swallowed by death? Why are we worried about petty fears when people are going to hell? We should grieve if our eyes are dry when we pray for the unsaved and when we speak to them.

QUESTIONS

1. **How did Paul describe his feelings when evangelizing?**

2. **Can anything positive come from a fear to reach out to the lost?**

3. **How can we put our fears in perspective?**

4. **What was the lesson the U.S. Navy wanted their recruits to learn?**

5. **Why should we quote God's Word in the face of fear?**

6. **According to William Gurnall, why do we experience fear and how should we overcome it?**

FEATHERS FOR ARROWS

"Mr. Thorpe was a member of an 'infidel' club. Among their amusements was that of holding imitations of religious services, and exhibiting mimicries of popular ministers. Thorpe went to hear George Whitefield preach, that he might caricature him before his profane associates. He listened to Whitefield so carefully that he caught his tones and his manner, and somewhat of his doctrines.

"When the club met to see his caricature of Whitefield, Thorpe opened the Bible that he might take a text to preach from it after the manner of Whitefield. His eye fell on the passage, "Except you repent, you shall all likewise perish." As he spoke upon that text he was carried beyond himself, lost all thought of mockery, spoke as one in earnest, and was the means of his own conversion! He was carried by the force of truth beyond his own intention, like one who would play in a river, and is swept away by its current.

"Even the scoffer may be reached by the arrows of truth! Scripture has often been the sole means in the hands of its divine Author of converting the soul."

Excerpted from Charles Spurgeon's sermon #950, "Means for Restoring the Banished."

WORDS OF COMFORT

I have a way with children. It was obvious as a couple's eight-year-old was wide-eyed as he cuddled into me. The little fellow called me "Uncle Ray" and was extremely mature for an eight-year-old. I had stayed with these friends many times when traveling to their city, and so I felt I had the liberty with their boy to share my knowledge with him. He was eating a hard-boiled egg. While his parents were watching, I put my arms on his shoulders and lovingly said, "Jeremy, did you know that the number one thing people choke to death on in the U.S. is a hard-boiled egg? So you be very careful when you eat that. Just take little bites, one at a time." Then I left the room feeling pleased that I had given a little of my wisdom to the child.

Thirty seconds later, I heard a commotion and returned to the kitchen. My dumb advice had so scared the poor kid that he became hysterical and threw up egg all over the kitchen floor.

Last Words

David Hume (1711–1776), Scottish philosopher and historian, who on being told by his doctor that he was a little better, said:

"Doctor, as I believe you would not choose to tell anything but the truth, you had better say that I am dying as fast as my enemies, if I have any, could wish, and as easily and cheerfully as my best friends could desire."

27

The Empowering of the Holy Spirit

"You don't have to be perfect to share the love of Christ with someone. But you do have to be pursuing a right relationship with God. If you are not, your witnessing will be ineffective."

SCOTT HINKLE

Kirk's Comment Where is the source of power, boldness, and courage to witness that filled Peter, Paul, and the early church? I have only tapped the beginning of the power of the Holy Spirit who longs to fill each believer to overflowing.

QUESTIONS & OBJECTIONS

"God made me like this. Sin is His fault!"

If this won't work in a civil court, it certainly won't work on Judgment Day. Even with an expert defense lawyer, it would take a pretty inept judge to fall for the old "God made me do it" defense. We are responsible moral agents. The "buck" stopped at Adam. He tried to blame both God and Eve for his sin; Eve blamed the serpent. It is human nature to try, but it doesn't work with God.

Jesus told His disciples that when the Holy Spirit came upon them, they would receive "power," and the result would be that they would be His witnesses. These are His words:

> But you shall receive power, after that the Holy Spirit is come upon you: and you shall be witnesses to me both in Jerusalem, and in all Judea, and in Samaria, and to the uttermost part of the earth (Acts 1:8).

Notice that they were not told they would be *Jehovah's* witnesses. If we have received the Holy Spirit, we will be witnesses of Jesus Christ. We speak of him, think of Him, love Him, and want to obey His words because He is our Lord. Jesus told His disciples that the Holy Spirit would speak of Him:

> But when the Comforter is come, whom I will send to you from the Father, even the Spirit of truth, which proceeds from the Father, he shall testify of me (John 15:26).

Therefore, someone who has received the Holy Spirit should be "Christ-centered." In fact, the Bible has a sober warning for us if we are not: "If any man love not the Lord Jesus Christ, let him be Anathema Maranatha [accursed]" (1 Corinthians 16:22).

After Jesus returned to heaven, He sent the Holy Spirit to indwell believers, just as He said He would. God kept His promise to rescue humanity from death—Pentecost was the giving of the life of the Spirit to humanity. The Messiah had suffered and died, and His body was placed in the grave. Three days later, in the deathly coldness of the darkened tomb, a faint sound was heard. It was the sound of a human heartbeat within the frigid and lifeless corpse of Jesus of Nazareth. That one tiny sound brought with it implications that resounded in thunder throughout the universe. The Father had accepted the Son's sacrifice. Death had lost its sting! Jesus Christ burst from the grave holding the keys to death and hell. All that was necessary now was for the disciples to take the message of eternal life to those who were sitting in the shadow of death.

However, there was a problem. The chosen disciples were frozen with fear. Despite three years of intense training, they ran in the face of danger.

They had been given the keys of the kingdom, but they hid behind locked doors. They needed power from on high.

When the Holy Spirit was poured out at Pentecost (see Acts 2), the *immediate* result was that the fearful disciples became fearless. They were empowered *to be witnesses*. They didn't remain inside and have a time of worship. Nor did they stay for a time of fellowship, or carpet the room and invite the world in. *They went out.* The gas was in the tank, the spark had ignited the flame, the power was there, so they put their foot down and headed in the direction of the unsaved. In James 3:6 we are told that the tongue is set on fire by hell. At Pentecost, God gave man a new tongue —set on fire by heaven.

It is evident in contemporary Christendom that many who profess to have the power of the Holy Spirit have not had the same experience as the disciples. They shake and quiver, rattle and roll...but they are still hiding inside. As Bill Bright found, only two percent of believers in America regularly share their faith in Christ with others. How could anyone who claims to possess the power to witness not be a witness of Christ?

If you are a Christian, you have the Holy Spirit living in you, but are you *filled* with the Spirit? Are you filled to overflowing? Are you like the fearful disciples before Pentecost, or are you like the faith-filled disciples *after* that day? Are you warning sinners about the wrath that is to come, which is the only thing that will matter on Judgment Day? Evangelistic zeal is evidence of the Holy Spirit's presence and power. If fear is prevalent when it comes to sharing your faith, then perhaps you need to be *filled* with the Spirit, something you and I are commanded to be (see Ephesians 5:18).

How do you do that? In order to be filled with God's Holy Spirit, you must be emptied of self. It's said that we don't need more of the Holy Spirit, but He needs more of us. Get on your knees in a quiet place and invite the Spirit to reveal any hidden sins to you. Confess all known sin and submit your entire being—your mind, emotions, and will—to God. Give Him complete control of your daily life. Seek His face, until you are so filled with the Holy Spirit that your love for Jesus will overflow to others as you go out into the world with the gospel of salvation.

Let these words of Bill Bright encourage you to be a bold, obedient witness for Christ:

> When you represent the Lord Jesus Christ as His disciple, you can be assured that you are representing the One who possesses all power, wisdom, and authority. You have everything when you have Him. Jesus said: "I tell you the truth, anyone who has faith in me will do what I have been doing. He will do even greater things than these, because I am going to the Father" (John 14:12). You have the promise, "The one who is in you is greater than the one who is in the world" (1 John 4:4). And you are assured that even the gates of hell will not prevail against you (Matthew 16:18).

QUESTIONS

1. Why did God give His Holy Spirit to the Church?

2. What did the disciples do when they received the Spirit?

3. What did Bill Bright say about the contemporary church?

4. Why do you think so many don't share their faith?

5. How can you be "filled" with the Spirit?

FEATHERS FOR ARROWS

In the epic movie *Ben Hur*, Judah was a galley slave. He had been unjustly doomed and sent to die as a slave of Rome. However, because he reminded the new commander of his son who had been killed in battle, the commander took pity on him.

As they headed into a battle, the commander gave instructions that a chain was not to be threaded through Ben Hur's ankle ring. The practice of securing the slaves to the ship ensured there would be a commitment to rowing during the battle, because if the ship went down, so did they.

During the ferocious encounter, the ship was rammed and began to sink. The slaves cried out in panic and tried to rip the chain from their ankle rings, cutting into their bloodied flesh.

The unchained Ben Hur was the only slave who could leave the ship. However, instead of saving himself, he overpowered the guard who held the keys, and released the condemned and helpless prisoners.

There was only One who was free from the chains of sin and death—Jesus. But instead of saving Himself, he went for the one with the keys, and said, "I am he that lives, and was dead; and, behold, I am alive for ever-more, Amen; and have the keys of hell and of death" (Revelation 1:18).

Through His death and resurrection, He removed the chains of sin and death from the human race. Now all we need to do is tell the lost to get up and save themselves from the sinking ship.

Memory Verse

"But the Comforter, which is the Holy Spirit, whom the Father will send in my name, he shall teach you all things, and bring all things to your remembrance, whatsoever I have said to you."
JOHN 14:26

Last Words

Sir Walter Raleigh (1552–1618), sentenced to death by James I, said to the executioner:

"Show me the axe. Show me the axe. This gives me no fear. It is a sharp medicine to cure me of all my diseases."

LESSON 28
How to Capture the World's Attention

"Surely God would not have created such a being as man,
with an ability to grasp the infinite, to exist only for a day.
No, no, man was made for immortality."

ABRAHAM LINCOLN

Kirk's Comment This lesson will teach you a great way to appeal to someone who doesn't seem to be interested in Christianity or God. All people share certain thoughts and reactions—and even have a common fear.

QUESTIONS & OBJECTIONS

"I'll take my chances."

With what, eternity? Eternity is a long time to be wrong. Why would you want to take a gamble on something as important as your eternal destiny? It takes only a moment to trust Christ for your salvation. There will be an eternity of pain and regret if you don't.

You don't take chances with guns, do you? You don't take chances and run red lights, do you? Why would you take a chance on something that is far more important than these? Don't take a chance on something eternal. It isn't worth it.

Jesus said He was the only way to God. He forgave sins, walked on water, calmed a storm with a command, raised people from the dead, and rose from the dead Himself. No one else in all of history has done that. If He can do all that, don't you think you should listen to Him?

wotmwotmwotmwotmwotmwotmwotmwotmwotmwotmwotm

Millions of people spend dozens of hours each week watching dead people on TV. From Elvis to Lucy to Jimmy Stewart, the faces of folks who no longer exist entertain us. Time not only snatched their looks, it snatched their lives. Today, good-looking Hollywood stars are making movies so that tomorrow's generation can also pass the time by watching dead people on TV.

Time makes today tomorrow's memory. Weeks seem to pass us by like blurred telephone poles flashing past the window of this speeding train called life.

Before my conversion, I had thoughts that I was compelled to keep to myself. I would think, "It makes no sense that the whole of humanity is heading for death, and instead of seeking a cure to the aging process, we are searching for intelligent life in space or for a cure to the common cold. No one seems concerned about our big problem. No one even talks about death." But now that I have found that God has provided a cure, salvation through Jesus Christ, for man's greatest disease, death, I cannot and will not stop talking about it.

If I purchased a new car and saw in the owner's manual that it had a certain type of engine, I shouldn't be surprised to lift the hood and find the engine to be exactly as the manual said it would be. The maker's handbook gives me insight into the unseen workings of the vehicle. This is also true with human beings. The Maker's Manual explains how we think and why we react the way we do. It lifts the hood and reveals the inner workings of *homo sapiens.*

In doing so, the Bible discloses an often-overlooked tool that we can use to reach the lost. That tool is the "fear of death." For the Christian who may find such an approach to be negative, it may be viewed in a *positive* light by calling it "the will to live." Every human being in his right mind has a fear of death (Hebrews 2:15). *He doesn't want to die.* He sits wide-eyed, staring out the window of the speeding train, watching life pass him by.

Here is how to use the fear of death as a tool when speaking to an unsaved person: "Let's assume that the average person dies at 70 years old. Then if you are 20 years old, you have just 2,500 weekends left to live. If you have turned 30, you have 2,000 weekends left until the day you die. If you are 40 years old, you have only 1,500 weekends left. If you are 50 years old, then you have just 1,000 weekends, and if you are 60 years old, you have a mere 500 weekends left until the day death comes to you."

We can better relate to "weekends," while "years" put death into the distance. It should shake us enough to ask, *What I am doing with my life?* What are we doing to reach the lost? It should concern us if we have dry eyes when we pray. The Christian's "train" will take him into the presence of God. For those trusting in Jesus Christ, death has been defeated. But the train of the unregenerate will take them to horrific disaster. Their end will be eternal torment in hell. In light of such terrible thoughts, all of our activities are trivial compared to warning the lost of their destination.

It has been wisely stated that every one of us is unique...*just like everyone else.* In truth, each unique individual is uniquely predictable. Every sinner has a fear of death. He can't deny that he naturally has a will to live. Therefore, it makes sense to confront him with reality by reminding him that he has an "appointment" to keep. Bluntly tell him how many weekends he has remaining. Then appeal to his reason by saying, "If there was one chance in a million that Jesus Christ 'has abolished death and brought life and immortality to light through the gospel,' then you owe it to your good sense to look into it." As Charles Spurgeon said, "Men have been helped to live by remembering that they must die."

QUESTIONS

1. What is an often-overlooked tool for reaching the lost?

2. **What Bible verse tells us that every human being fears death?**

3. **Why should we not speak of the remaining life in terms of years?**

4. **How should the awareness of our own mortality affect us as Christians?**

5. **Why should we be concerned for the ungodly?**

6. **What did Charles Spurgeon say about this subject?**

PREACHER'S PROGRESS

Libby Manhater: "Christianity oppresses women by making them submit to their husbands!"

Christian: "The Bible does say, 'Wives, submit yourselves to your own husbands, as to the Lord. Husbands, love your wives, even as Christ also loved the Church, and gave himself for it.'"

Libby Manhater: "See, I am right, you chauvinistic, Bible-thumping, narrow-minded fundamentalist! People like you should be locked up."

Christian: "You missed what I was saying."

Libby Manhater: "What are you saying?"

Christian: "A man who understands that Jesus gave His life for the Church will likewise love his wife sacrificially and passionately. He will honor, respect, protect, love, and cherish her as much as he does his own body. He will never say or do anything to harm or demean her. It is in this atmosphere of love and security that a godly wife willingly submits to the protective arms of her husband. She does this not because he is better than she is, but simply because this is God's order for His creation.

"A lion rests while his mate prepares his food. He lies in the shade and now and then roars to let everyone know he is king of the jungle. The world stands in awe at this order in nature, but refuses to acknowledge that the same One who ordered nature orders mankind. A godless world rejects the God-given formula to make marriage work. It thinks it knows best, and suffers the heartbreaking consequences of destroyed marriages and ruined lives. The Christian ideal of marriage is not one of an authoritarian and chauvinist male holding his cringing wife in submission like an obedient dog. It's the very opposite. While most of the great religions treat women as inferior to men, the Bible gives them a place of dignity, honor, and unspeakable worth. Do you believe in women's liberation?"

Libby Manhater: "Absolutely."

Christian: "Have you found liberation from death?"

Libby Manhater: "Are you serious?"

Christian: "I am deadly serious. If you will repent and trust Jesus Christ, God will free you from your greatest oppressor. Do you ever think about death?"

Libby Manhater: "Yes."

Christian: "Are you afraid of dying?"

Libby Manhater: "No."

Christian: "Are you telling me that you have no will to live?"

Libby Manhater: "Yes. I love life."

Christian: "So you don't want to die."

Libby Manhater: "No, I don't."

Christian: "Well, why don't you set aside your grievances against men, and listen for a few minutes to the claims of the Bible. Would you do that?"

Libby Manhater: "Sure."

Christian: "Do you consider yourself to be a good person?" Etc.

FEATHERS FOR ARROWS

A teenage boy once took his younger brother to a movie called *The Scarlet Pimpernel*. The seven-year-old watched in horror as, during the height of the French Revolution, aristocrats were executed by guillotine. The guillotine was surrounded by old hags, who shrieked for joy as each head rolled into the basket and was then held high for the crowds to see.

The young boy began thinking how horrific it must have been to be waiting on death row, and then taken to the town square and put to death in such a manner. However, as life progressed, he realized that this was the plight of every human being. All of humanity has a large holding cell, with bright lighting, good ventilation, and a big blue roof. We can travel around this great world and enjoy its pleasures, but we are still in a holding cell, waiting for the moment when the great chopper of death falls upon us. We are all part of the ultimate statistic: ten out of ten die.

> ### Memory Verse
>
> *"Forasmuch then as the children are partakers of flesh and blood, he also himself likewise took part of the same; that through death he might destroy him that had the power of death, that is, the devil; and deliver them who through fear of death were all their lifetime subject to bondage."*
> **HEBREW 2:14,15**

Last Words

George Washington (1732–1799) was the first President of the United States. Over the door of his tomb at Mount Vernon are the words of his Savior: "I am the resurrection and the life. He that believeth in Me, though he were dead, yet shall he live." At the end he said to his physician:

"Doctor, I have been dying a long time; my breath cannot last long— but I am not afraid to die."

LESSON 29 Gospel Tracts, Part 1

"When we share our faith, it is a win/win situation. If people accept what we say, we win. If we plant the seed of God's Word, we win; and even if we are rejected, we win. The Bible says that when that happens, the Spirit of glory and of God rests upon us (see 1 Peter 4:14). When we contend for the faith and are rejected, we are to rejoice and leap for joy, for great is our reward in heaven (see Luke 6:22,23). It is a winning situation every single time that we share our faith!"

MARK CAHILL

Kirk's Comment I used to cringe at the thought of giving someone a gospel tract. I didn't want to appear as a religious fruitcake. But the sobering thought that every unsaved person will be spending eternity in hell compels me to do *something*. If I don't have the opportunity to speak with someone about the Lord, a well-written tract can do the speaking for me. A tract may not be as good as a personal conversation, but a sincere gospel tract is better than no gospel at all.

QUESTIONS & OBJECTIONS

"I hope I'm going to heaven when I die."

Of all the things that you should be sure of, it's your eternal destiny. To say "I hope I'm going to heaven" is like standing at the open door of a plane 25,000 feet in the air and, when asked "If you have your parachute on, answering with "I hope so." You want to *know* so—and you can, simply by obeying the gospel. If you repent and place your faith in Jesus Christ, He will give you eternal life and you can know that your eternity is secure. In 1 John 5:12,13, the Bible also makes clear that those who refuse to trust in the Son of God can likewise know that they do not have eternal life—they will remain dead in their sins.

wotmwotmwotmwotmwotmwotmwotmwotmwotmwotmwotm

In writing to the Corinthian believers, Paul explains the lengths to which he would go to share the gospel: "To the weak became I as weak, that I might gain the weak: I am made all things to all men, that I might by all means save some" (1 Corinthians 9:22). If Paul meant "by all means," he no doubt would have used gospel tracts as one means to reach the lost.

Never underestimate the power of a gospel tract. After George Whitefield read one called "The Life of God in the Soul of a Man," he said, "God showed me I must be born again or be damned." He went on to pray, "Lord, if I am not a Christian, or if I am not a real one, for Jesus Christ's sake show me what Christianity is, that I may not be damned at last!" Then his journal tells us "from that moment...did I know that I must become a new creature."

A Christian book relates the true story of a diver who saw a piece of paper clutched in the shell of an oyster. The man grabbed it, found that it was a gospel tract and said, "I can't hold out any longer. His mercy is so great that He has caused His Word to follow me even to the bottom of the ocean." God used a tract to save the man. He also used a tract to save the great missionary Hudson Taylor, as well as innumerable others.

Why should Christians use tracts? Simply because *God* uses them. That fact alone should be enough incentive for a Christian to always use tracts to reach the lost, but there are even more reasons why we should use them. Here are a few:

- Tracts can provide an opening for us to share our faith. We can watch people's reaction as we give them a tract, and see if they are open to listening to spiritual things.

- They can do the witnessing for us. If we are too timid to speak to others about the things of God, we can at least give them a tract, or leave one lying around so that someone will pick it up.

- They speak to the individuals when they are ready; people don't read it until they want to.

- They can find their way into people's homes when we can't.

- They don't get into arguments; they just state their case.

Oswald J. Smith said, "The only way to carry out the Great Commission will be by the means of the printed page." Charles Spurgeon stated, "When preaching and private talk are not available, you need to have a tract ready...Get good striking tracts, or none at all. But a touching gospel tract may be the seed of eternal life. Therefore, do not go out without your tracts."

If you want people to accept your literature, try to greet them before offering them a tract. If you can get them to respond to a warm "Good morning," or "How are you doing?" that will almost always break the ice and they will take it. After the greeting, don't ask, "Would you like this?" They will probably respond, "What is it?" Instead, say, "Did you get one of these?" That question has a twofold effect. You stir their curiosity and make them ask, "One of what?" That's when you hand them a tract. It also makes them feel as though they are missing out on something. So they are.

Perhaps you almost pass out at the thought of passing out a tract. Don't worry; you are not alone. We *all* battle fear. The answer to fear is found in the prayer closet. Ask God to give you a compassion that will swallow your fears. Meditate on the fate of the ungodly. Give hell some deep thought. Confront what it is that makes you fearful.

Do you like roller coasters? Some Christians want to try skydiving or bungee-jumping. Isn't it strange? We are prepared to risk our lives for the love of fear—and yet we are willing to let a sinner go to hell for fear of giving out a tract. Ask yourself how many piles of bloodied stones you can find where Christians have been stoned to death for preaching the gospel. How much singed soil can you find where they have been burned at the stake? Part of our fear is a fear of rejection. We are fearful of looking foolish. That's a subtle form of pride. The other part of our battle with fear comes directly from the enemy. He knows that fear paralyzes. We must resist the devil and his lies. If God is with us, nothing can be against us.

If you have never given out tracts, why not begin today? If you are fearful when it comes to witnessing, here's something you can do that doesn't take much courage. Go into a phone booth. Open the phone book to the Yellow Pages; find "Abortion" and slip a tract between the pages. Then look for the category "Escorts" and slip a tract in there. Many phone booths have a door, so you can close the door behind you and do this without fear of being seen. You are not breaking the law, and simply leaving a gospel tract in those two places may not only keep someone from making a terrible life-changing decision, but it may bring them to faith in the Savior.

Then each night as you shut your eyes to go to sleep, you will have something very special to pray about—that God will use the tracts you put somewhere. You will also have a deep sense of satisfaction that you played a small part in carrying out the Great Commission to reach this dying world with the gospel of everlasting life. Don't waste your life. Do something for the kingdom of God while you are able to. Always remember: treat every day as though it were your last—one day you will be right.

QUESTIONS

1. **Name some individuals who were saved through a gospel tract.**

2. **List five advantages of using gospel tracts.**

3. **What is an effective way to get people to take a tract?**

4. **If you are fearful of passing out tracts, what are the sources of that fear?**

5. **How can we conquer our fears?**

6. **What was Charles Spurgeon's advice on gospel tracts?**

PREACHER'S PROGRESS

Stan Dup: "I'm a Christian, but I feel that it would be better for me just to live the life, rather than talk to people about Christ."

Christian: "Why is that?"

Stan Dup: "I don't have the gift of evangelism. I don't know what to say."

Christian: "There's no such thing as the 'gift of evangelism.' That's like saying someone has the 'gift' of feeding starving children. It's not a gift— it's love in action. Another word for 'evangelism' is 'love.'"

Stan Dup: "I've never thought of it like that. Perhaps I should go to Bible college and study first."

Christian: "Take the time to see how long the woman at the well (in John chapter 4) spent at Bible school before she shared her faith."

Stan Dup: "But…"

Christian: "No 'buts.' Just stand up for Christ. You can do it."

Stan Dup: "Do you think so?"

Christian: "Yes. Say, 'I can do all things through Christ who strengthens me.'"

Stan Dup: "What should I do?"

Christian: "Start by placing a few tracts here and there."

Stan Dup: "Where?"

Christian: "Anywhere. How about leaving one in a shopping cart, or in the phone book at a pay phone?"

Stan Dup: "I could do that."

Christian: "Just think—as you lay your head on your pillow at night, you can have the satisfaction that you stood up for the kingdom of God."

FEATHER FOR ARROWS

Consider the way dogs cross the road. A dog will wander onto a freeway oblivious to the danger. His tail wags as he steps between cars without a second thought. Cars swerve. Tires squeal. The noise is deafening as vehicles smash into each other. The sleepy dog stops wagging his tail for a moment and looks at the pile of smoldering, broken cars on the freeway. His expression betrays his thoughts. His bone-burying brain doesn't realize for one moment that he is responsible for the disaster.

When man wanders onto the freeway of sin, his tail wags with delight. He thinks that this is what he was made for. His thoughts of any repercussions for his actions are shallow. His mind wanders into lust, then predictably he wanders onto the path of adultery. Suddenly a disaster sits before him. His marriage is shattered, his name is slurred, and his children are twisted and scarred. But like the dumb dog, he doesn't realize for one moment that he is solely responsible for his sin. This is why the perfect Law of God needs to be arrayed before his darkened eyes—to show him that his way is not right in the eyes of a perfect God.

Memory Verse

"To the weak became I as weak, that I might gain the weak: I am made all things to all men, that I might by all means save some."

1 CORINTHIANS 9:22

Last Words

Alexander Hamilton (1757–1804), who was mortally wounded in a duel with Aaron Burr, stated:

"I have a tender reliance on the mercy of the Almighty, through the merits of the Lord Jesus Christ. I am a sinner. I look to Him for mercy."

30 Gospel Tracts, Part 2

"Nothing surpasses a tract for sowing the seed of the Good News."

BILLY GRAHAM

Kirk's Comment   A woman I know wants to give her unsaved friends a tract, but can't find one she feels fits her personality. So she's going to collect her thoughts and write her own. You might want to do the same.

QUESTIONS & OBJECTIONS

"Will people who have never heard the gospel go to hell because they haven't heard about Jesus Christ?"

No one will go to hell because they haven't heard of Jesus Christ. The heathen will go to hell for murder, rape, adultery, lust, theft, lying, etc. Sin is not failing to hear the gospel. Rather, "sin is the transgression of the Law" (1 John 3:4). In John 16:8,9, Jesus said that when the Holy Spirit comes, "He will convict the world of guilt in regard to . . . sin, because men do not believe in me." The verse can be understood this way: If a man jumps out of a plane without a parachute, he will perish because he transgressed the law of gravity. Had he put on a parachute, he would have been saved. In one sense, he perished because he didn't put on the parachute. But the primary reason he died was because he broke the law of gravity.

If a sinner refuses to trust in Jesus Christ when he passes through the door of death, he will perish. This isn't because he refused to trust the Savior, but because he transgressed the Law of God. Had he "put on the Lord Jesus Christ" (Romans 13:14), he would have been saved; but because he refused to repent, he will suffer the full consequences of his sin. If we really care about the lost, we will become missionaries and take the good news of God's forgiveness in Christ to them.

w o t m w o t m w o t m w o t m w o t m w o t m w o t m w o t m w o t m w o t m w o t m

I find it hard to understand why *every* Christian doesn't carry gospel tracts. Joey Hancock of the American Tract Society said, "Fifty-three percent of all who come to Christ worldwide come through the use of printed gospel literature." If we really care about the eternal salvation of those around us, how could we not carry tracts everywhere we go?

Look at these words from Charles Spurgeon on the use of tracts:

> I well remember distributing them in a town in England where tracts had never been distributed before, and going from house to house, and telling in humble language the things of the kingdom of God. I might have done nothing, if I had not been encouraged by finding myself able to do something... [Tracts are] adapted to those persons who have but little power and little ability, but nevertheless, wish to do something for Christ. They may not have the tongue of the eloquent, but they may have the hand of the diligent. They cannot stand and preach, but they can stand and distribute here and there these silent preachers... They may buy their thousand tracts, and these they can distribute broadcast.
>
> I look upon the giving away of a religious tract as only the first step for action not to be compared with many another deed done for Christ; but were it not for the first step we might never reach to the second, but that first attained, we are encouraged to take another, and so at the last... There is a real service of Christ in the distribution of the gospel in its printed form, a service the result of which heaven alone shall disclose, and the judgment day alone discover. How many thousands have been carried to heaven instrumentally upon the wings of these tracts, none can tell.

I might say, if it were right to quote such a Scripture, "The leaves were for the healing of the nations"—verily they are so. Scattered where the whole tree could scarcely be carried, the very leaves have had a medicinal and a healing virtue in them and the real word of truth, the simple statement of a Savior crucified and of a sinner who shall be saved by simply trusting in the Savior, has been greatly blessed, and many thousand souls have been led into the kingdom of heaven by this simple means. *Let each one of us, if we have done nothing for Christ, begin to do something now. The distribution of tracts is the first thing.*

If you are wondering where you could leave tracts, here are several suggestions:

- At pay phones
- In shopping carts
- In clothes pockets in stores
- In letters to loved ones
- With a generous tip
- On seats in restaurant lobbies
- With fast-food employees, cashiers, and gas station workers
- In restrooms
- At rest areas
- On ATM machines and bank counters
- In envelopes with bill payments
- In elevators
- On hotel dressers for the maid
- On ice machines
- On newspaper racks
- In waiting rooms of doctors' offices and hospitals
- On seats at airports, subways, and bus stations

- With flight attendants and cab drivers
- In plane seat pockets
- Inside magazines
- In cabs
- In laundromats

Many Christians also give gospel tracts and candy to children who knock on their door during Halloween. What other day do scores of young people come to your door for gospel tracts?

To take advantage of another great opportunity to sow seeds for the gospel, you may want to use our unique "Court Tract." Over the past four years we have given out more than 40,000 tracts outside the courthouse, about 60 feet from our office. This tract is designed especially for those who line up outside the courtrooms each morning to pay misdemeanor fines. The front, back, and first pages explain courtroom etiquette (the do's and don'ts when in court); then when the tract is unfolded, the inside explains the gospel (that each of us will face a Judge on Judgment Day). As you go along the line and hand out tracts, you may like to tell people, "Make sure all cell phones and pagers are turned off." This is true, so you are doing both them and the courts a favor.

Perhaps you might like to consider preaching the gospel outside the court buildings in your area. I did this recently with the forty to sixty people waiting to enter the courthouse. I began by saying, "You are here because you have allegedly violated civil law. The Bible says that each of us have violated God's Law, the Ten Commandments. I would like to put you on the stand and examine you for a moment to see if you are guilty."

I went through the Law and the reality of hell, then preached the cross, repentance, and faith. They all seemed to be listening, and no one was offended. It's an incredible opportunity. The line is made up of different people every day, from all walks of life. As they are waiting to go to court they are no doubt praying for mercy...and they can't get out of line because they will lose their place.

Another tract that is easy to give away is our "Giant Money tract." When you go to pay in a store or restaurant, ask if the cashier can "break a large bill" as you hand the person this tract. People who have tried this have been practically swarmed by others wanting to have one. One individual said, "These tracts almost give themselves away and they put a smile on the face of the person receiving them!"

If, in Spurgeon's words, you feel you "have but little power and little ability, but nevertheless, wish to do something for Christ," then begin today to give out tracts. May God give you the zeal of Mark Cahill, our all-time biggest tract customer (6'6"). Just since January 2001, he has ordered 368,500 tracts. You can likewise "distribute here and there these silent preachers."

If you have Internet access: Please go to the address below and listen to a brief message entitled "Just One Person: George Street." This incredible true story of how God worked in a little place called George Street will show what "just one person" can do. This nine-minute testimony will be a real blessing: www.livingwaters.com/listenwatch/georgestreet.m3u

QUESTIONS

1. **According to the American Tract Society, what percentage of conversions to Jesus Christ comes through the use of printed gospel literature?**

2. **For what kind of people did Charles Spurgeon say tracts were adapted?**

3. **What did Spurgeon call gospel tracts?**

4. What are some of the places where you will commit today to begin giving out tracts?

5. What encouragement did you receive from the "George Street" message?

Memory Verse

"The fruit of the righteous is a tree of life; and he that wins souls is wise."

PROVERBS 11:30

FEATHERS FOR ARROWS

Although the prophet Jeremiah was assured that God formed him, knew him, sanctified and ordained him, he still was paralyzed by the fear of man (Jeremiah 1:5,6). When fear of man seeks to paralyze us, we must stop saying, "I cannot speak," and instead say, "I can do all things through Christ who strengthens me" (Philippians 4:13). This verse obliterates our every excuse for not preaching the gospel to every creature. It counters the fear of man, the fear of rejection, the fear of public speaking, and the fear of offering a stranger a gospel tract. Remember the words of Hudson Taylor: "All God's giants have been weak men, who did great things for God because they believed that God would be with them."

Last Words

Jean Claude (1619–1687) was among the Protestants driven out of France during the reign of Louis XIV. As leader of the French Protestants he vigorously defended the tenets of the faith. Stricken with a fatal illness, Claude gathered his family around his bed. To his wife kneeling at his side, he said:

"I have always tenderly loved you. Be not afflicted at my death. The death of the saints is precious in the sight of God. In you I perceive a sincere piety; I bless God for it. Be constant in serving Him with all your heart, and He will bless you."

31

Personal Testimony

"So long as there is a human being who does not know Jesus Christ, I am his debtor to serve him until he does."

OSWALD CHAMBERS

Kirk's Comment For years I unknowingly mislead people into a false conversion experience with a man-centered personal testimony. I was missing the true target until I learned how to present the gospel biblically. If you want to effectively share your faith with someone, this lesson is critical for you—and for them, because you are dealing with their eternal future. Study until you really understand it.

QUESTIONS & OBJECTIONS

"How do I witness to someone I know?"

For most of us, it is far easier to witness to a stranger than to someone we know and respect. An effective way to soften the message without compromise is to speak in the "first person" or in testimonial form. Say something like, "I didn't realize that the Bible warns that for every idle word I have spoken, I will have to give an account on Judgment Day. I thought that as long as I believed in God and tried to live a good life, I would go to heaven when I died. I was so wrong. Jesus said that if I as much as looked with lust, I had committed adultery in my heart, and that there was nothing I could do to wash away my sins. I knew that if God judged me by the Ten Commandments on Judgment Day, I would end up guilty, and go to hell.

"It was when I acknowledged my sins that I began to understand why Jesus died. It was to take the punishment for my sins, and the sins of the world." Then, depending on the person's openness, you may ask, "How do you think you will do on Judgment Day, if God judges you by the Ten Commandments?"

w o t m w o t m w o t m w o t m w o t m w o t m w o t m w o t m w o t m w o t m w o t m

A friend once related that she didn't like her husband giving out tracts, because she felt they had a hidden agenda. The tracts were about the things of God, but didn't look like they were. Her contention was that it was deceitful. She thought he should be upfront and just say, "I want to talk to you about God."

Shortly afterwards, she admitted the truth: she was embarrassed when her husband gave out tracts, and she realized her fears were spiritual in origin.

What may seem like deceit to some is in truth "discretion." When Jesus spoke to the woman at the well, He didn't say, "I want to talk to you about God. You are living in adultery." That was His agenda, but such an abrupt approach may have created a closed door. Instead, Jesus spoke to her about water, something she could relate to, and then He gently swung to the subject of the things of God. He used the essence of the Seventh Commandment to convict her that she was living an adulterous life.

The result was that the woman became a believer in Jesus, and she immediately gave her testimony to the unsaved in her village. She simply said, "Come, see a man, which told me all things that ever I did: is not this the Christ?" (John 4:29). We are called to say the same thing. We are to tell people that God is omniscient; He sees everything we do. Nothing is hidden from His holy eyes. He hears every word, and He demands an account of every idle word we speak. This holy Judge of the universe has set aside a Day in which He will judge the world in righteousness. Then we are to point to Jesus Christ, the awaited Messiah, as the woman did.

It is wise to have our testimony prepared and memorized. We should know the reason we became Christians, and how we were converted. It is important that we learn how to share our testimony in a way that is effective. Our salvation centers on the cross, so that's where we should be heading. The cross was the evidence of God's love for humanity, and is the essence of the gospel. Paul said he "gloried" only in the cross (Galatians 6:14). He preached "Jesus Christ, and him crucified."

Three times in Scripture, Paul gave his testimony. That speaks volumes. You may not have had a Road to Damascus experience, but you have experienced the same risen Lord Paul experienced. You were on the Road of Sin. You saw the light and the Lord opened your blinded eyes. You came to know the One who is life eternal. You had a Road to the Cross experience.

Why do we need to be able to share the experience of being converted? Because the man with an experience is not at the mercy of a man with an argument. A skeptic may disagree with what we say, but he cannot truly deny what we have experienced. The Christian knows the Lord.

The question that may come to mind is, "How do I *know* that I know the Lord?" The answer is in God's Word: "We do know that we know him, *if we keep his commandments*" (1 John 2:3). That's the backbone of our testimony. God gives us a new heart with new desires. We are made new creatures in Christ. We have been born again with God's Spirit living within us. Where we once had no interest in the things of God, now we love Him and yearn to please Him. We want to keep His commandments. (See Ezekiel 36:26,27.)

Sadly, many modern converts miss the evangelistic target when they share their testimony. They say things like, "I was into drugs, etc., but Jesus filled my heart with joy." Rather, structure your testimony to preach sin, righteousness, and judgment.

Here is a suggested way to compose your testimony:

1. Learn how to include the spiritual nature of the Ten Commandments in your testimony. ("I never understood what sin was until I looked at the Ten Commandments...")

2. State that nothing is hidden from God—He sees even the thought-life.

3. Stress the reality of the Day of Judgment.

4. Preach the cross, repentance, and faith. ("Then I understood why He died. He was bruised for my iniquities," etc.)

5. Explain that you weren't "converted by the Bible" but by the power of the gospel. Emphasize that you now *know* the Bible is true, because when you obeyed the gospel you were transformed—taken from darkness into light, born again, a new creature with a new heart and new desires. The Bible came alive because you now have God's Holy Spirit living in you, who leads you into all truth.

QUESTIONS

1. Why is it wise to speak in the natural realm first when witnessing?

2. Why was the woman at the well able to persuade others to come to Christ, despite the fact that she wasn't well versed?

3. What was the essence of the woman's testimony?

4. What should we include in our testimony?

5. On what should our testimony center?

6. Why should we have our testimony prepared and memorized?

7. How do we know that we know the Lord?

PREACHER'S PROGRESS

Ron Number: "Hi. Is Eric there, please?"

Christian: "There's no Eric here. What number did you want?"

Ron Number: "(555) 920-8431."

Christian: "You've dialed a wrong number."

Ron Number: "Sorry…"

Christian: "That's okay. Don't go. May I ask you a question?"

Ron Number: "Um, sure."

Christian: "Would you consider yourself to be a good person?"

Ron Number: "Yes."

Christian: "Do you think that you've kept the Ten Commandments?"

Ron Number: "Probably."

Christian: "Do you have a minute to check?"

Ron Number: "I suppose."

Christian: "Have you ever told a lie? (etc.)...Thanks for listening to me."

Ron Number: "Thank you."

Memory Verse

"But sanctify the Lord God in your hearts: and be ready always to give an answer to every man that asks you a reason of the hope that is in you with meekness and fear."

1 PETER 3:15

Last Words

Christian F. Gellert (1715–1769), a German philosopher and author, wrote many hymns including "Jesus Lives, and I with Him." His *Fables* was one of the most popular books in Germany during the 17th century. Triumph in Christ was his when he died at Leipzig, where he had been professor of theology at the university. In his last moments Gellert requested:

> "Only repeat to me the name of Jesus. Whenever I hear it or pronounce it myself I feel myself refreshed with fresh joy. God be praised, only one hour more."

Creative Ways to Share Your Faith

"I think a good rule of thumb to follow would be to presume the Lord wants you to share the gospel with everyone unless He leads you not to."

DANNY LEHMANN

Kirk's Comment This lesson is where the rubber meets the road. Study this carefully, and then put what you've learned into practice. Nothing in all my years of being a Christian has been as thrilling and humbling as verbally sharing the whole gospel (sin, Law, righteousness, future judgment, and grace) with a complete stranger, and seeing how effectively God brings genuine repentance and faith. It's truly amazing.

QUESTIONS & OBJECTIONS

"How do I reach my neighbors with the gospel?"

Neighbors are like family. We don't want to offend them unnecessarily, because we have to live with them. We need to be rich in good works toward all men, but especially our neighbors. The Bible reveals that this is a legitimate means of evangelism. Jesus said, "Let your light so shine before men, that they may see your good works, and glorify your Father who is in heaven" (Matthew 5:16). It is God's will that "with well doing you may put to silence the ignorance of foolish men" (1 Peter 2:15). Sinners may disagree with what you believe, but seeing your good works makes them think, "I don't believe what he believes, but he sure does. He certainly is sincere in his faith."

A friendly wave, a gift for no reason, fresh-baked goods, etc., can pave the way for evangelism. Offer to mow your neighbors' lawn or help do some painting. Volunteer to pick up their mail and newspapers while they are on vacation. Compliment them on their landscaping and ask for gardening tips. Invite them over for a barbecue or dessert. Pray for an opportunity to share the gospel, and be prepared for it when it comes.

wotmwotmwotmwotmwotmwotmwotmwotmwotmwotmwotm

How deep is your love? Here's the way to measure it. I'm sure you are concerned about your immediate family's salvation, but what about your other relatives? How about your neighbors? What about strangers? Are you concerned for the salvation of people you don't know? How about your enemies? Are you deeply worried about the salvation of people who have crossed you? Do you love your enemies enough to be troubled by the fact that they will go to hell forever if they die in their sins? If you have measured up to all of the above, congratulations—you are a normal biblical Christian, who has been commanded to love your enemies and your neighbor as much as you love yourself.

Here's one way to demonstrate the depth of your love. Do you say "hello" to strangers? It may not come naturally to you, but for the sake of the gospel, I would like you to try this experiment. The next time you are leaving a restaurant, or anyplace where someone is standing—maybe at a counter waiting to pay for something—study the person's facial expression for a moment. It will probably look a little grumpy. We don't like to admit to it, but we all look a little grumpy while we are waiting for something; the burdens of the day tend to find expression through our face. Here now is the experiment: Forget about your fears, and with a warm and enthusiastic tone to your voice, smile and say, "Hello." Then watch the person's expression change from grumpy to happy. The individual will almost certainly smile.

If by chance the person doesn't respond, you have lost nothing (you will just feel very slightly silly). However, if there is a smile, there's your opportunity for the gospel. Reach into your pocket, and say (as if you had just thought of it), "Oh…did you get one of these?" I like to use our tract "101 of the World's Funniest One-Liners." With this tract, instead of the person seeing you as a religious nut who is trying to ram religion down the throat of a complete stranger, you will be seen as someone who is trying to brighten the person's day.

Here is something else that I have found to be very effective. An excellent way to gain instant credibility with young people, particularly teenagers, is to approach a group of two or three and ask, "Did you guys see this?" Then show them our pink and blue "Curved Illusion" tracts. That will get their attention. For credibility, have about ten one-dollar bills in your pocket, and ask (while holding the bills in your hand), "What's the capital of England?" When someone responds, "London," give him or her a dollar bill. (They will often say things like, "Can I keep this? Do you really mean it?") If they don't know the answer, ask for the capital of France, or the capital of your state. After two simple questions (and after giving another dollar bill), say, "Which of you folks think that you are a good person?" Usually someone will say, "I'm a good person!" Then ask, "Do you want to go for $20? I will ask you three questions. If you prove to be a good person, I will give you $20. Do you want to give it a try?" If one is interested in trying, ask the person's name and say, "Okay, John. I'm going to give you three questions to see if you are a good person. Here goes. Have you ever told a lie?"

Most people will say that they have. If John says that he hasn't, press him with, "You've never told a fib, a white lie, or a half-truth?" When he says that he has, ask what that makes him. Most will say, "Liar," while others may say, "Not a good person." If John doesn't want to call himself a liar, ask him what *you* would be called if you lied. That usually gets the person to admit that someone who has lied is called a liar. Once he has admitted that he is a liar, ask him if he has ever stolen something. If he says he hasn't, smile as you tell him that you don't believe him because he has just admitted that he is a liar. Then say, "Come on, be honest. Have you ever stolen anything…in your whole life…*even if it's small*?" When he says yes, ask what that makes him. He will more than likely say, "A thief."

Third question: "Jesus said, 'Whoever looks upon a woman to lust after her has already committed adultery with her in his heart.' Have you ever looked at a woman with lust?" Males usually laugh when they say that they have, so soberly say, "John, by your own admission, you are a lying, thieving, adulterer-at-heart, and you have to face God on Judgment Day. If God judges you by the Ten Commandments on the Day of Judgment, do you think you would be innocent or guilty?" If he says, "Guilty," ask him if he would go to heaven or hell. If he responds, "Hell," ask if that concerns him. If he says, "Heaven," ask why. Then follow it with this verse: "All liars will have their part in the Lake of Fire" (Revelation 21:8, paraphrased). This verse may sound harsh, but quote it anyway. It's God's Word and it is quick and powerful. Also quote 1 Corinthians 6:9,10: "Do not be deceived. Neither fornicators, nor idolaters, nor adulterers, nor homosexuals, nor sodomites, nor thieves, nor covetous, nor drunkards ...will inherit the kingdom of God." This covers the First, Second, Seventh, Eighth, and Tenth Commandments. It also covers the Fifth; someone who proves to be a lying thief has dishonored his parents' name. Your goal at this point is to awaken people to the standard of God's Law and to their desperate state before the Judge of the Universe.

Show genuine concern for their plight. Try to ensure that all your hearers (the other teenagers) are listening and let them know that they too have to face God. Say, "I don't want you to go to hell. You don't want to go to hell, and God doesn't want you to go to hell. Do you know what He did so that you wouldn't have to go there?" Then take them to the cross of Calvary, stressing their urgent need to repent, and inform them that they may not be here tomorrow.

Take great confidence that you don't have to convince a sinner of the reality of Judgment Day. That is the work of the Holy Spirit. John 16:8 says that the Holy Spirit will convict the world of sin, righteousness, and judgment. The mind of the unsaved cannot understand the judgment of God: "The wicked in his proud countenance does not seek God; God is not in all his thoughts. His ways are always grievous; *your judgments are far above out of his sight*" (Psalm 10:4,5, emphasis added). The Greek word used for "convict" in John 16:8 is *elegcho,* which also means "to convince." The same word is used in Jude 15: "To execute judgment upon all, and to *convince* all that are ungodly among them of all their ungodly deeds..." Only the Holy Spirit can *convict* a sinner about his sin and *con-*

vince him of judgment. We can't do that. All we can do is plant the seed of truth. When the sinner repents and trusts the Savior, the Holy Spirit then dwells within him and seals him (John 14:17; Ephesians 1:13).

QUESTIONS

1. Why do you think giving a dollar bill would establish credibility with young people?

2. Why ask your listeners questions?

3. Why should you quote Scripture when witnessing?

4. What is the responsibility of the Holy Spirit in witnessing?

5. What is our responsibility as Christians?

FEATHERS FOR ARROWS

Christians often find themselves in a dilemma when it comes to explaining the things of God to a sinner. It is like trying to explain color to a man who has been born blind. Think of such a situation. You say to a blind man, "What a lovely blue sky," to which he asks, "What is 'blue' like?" What can you tell him? Nothing can explain what color is like to a man who has never seen light.

The same applies to those who are blind to the things of God. The Bible says that the god of this world has blinded their minds (2 Corinthians 4:4). If they are not born of the Spirit, they cannot receive the things of the Spirit of God (1 Corinthians 2:14). Scripture also tells us that unless they are born again, they cannot see the kingdom of God (John 3:3). This is why we must be both gentle and prayerful.

WORDS OF COMFORT

A young pastor in Costa Mesa, California, was officiating at the wedding of a Mr. Bill Henry and Miss Talia Crooks, his lovely bride. In a cool, clear voice he said, "We are gathered here today to celebrate the wedding of Bill and Henry."

Last Words

John Milton (1608–1674) ranks with Shakespeare and Wordsworth as one of the three greatest poets of England. His famous *Paradise Lost* enshrines in stately verse the general scheme of Puritan theology. Because of the God-ward aspect of his life, we can appreciate his farewell saying:

"Death is the great key that opens the palace of Eternity."

33

How to Witness to Hurting People

> *"Do all the good you can, by all the means you can,*
> *in all the places you can, at all the times you can,*
> *to all the people you can, as long as you ever can."*
> **JOHN WESLEY**

Kirk's Comment This is a very important and beneficial lesson. It helped me tremendously with a concern I had about how to share Christ with someone who is really hurting. I recommend reading it twice.

QUESTIONS & OBJECTIONS

"What should I say to someone who has lost a loved one through cancer?"

Be very careful not to give the impression that God was punishing the person for his sins. Instead, speak about the fact that all around us we can see the evidence of a "fallen creation." Explain how in the beginning there was no disease, pain, suffering, or death. But when sin entered the world, it brought suffering with it. Then gently turn the conversation away from the person who died to the person who is still living. Ask if he has been thinking about God, and if he has kept the Ten Commandments. Then take the opportunity to go through the spiritual nature of God's Law. Someone who has lost a loved one often begins to ask soul-searching questions about God, death, and eternity. Many people are so hardhearted that it takes a tragedy to make them receptive to God.

w o t m w o t m w o t m w o t m w o t m w o t m w o t m w o t m w o t m w o t m w o t m

An unsaved woman recently confided in a preacher that she harbored bitterness toward God, because both her father and her brother were victims of murder. The question then arises, how do we witness to a person in such a state? Do we blatantly talk about sin, righteousness, and judgment? The answer can be seen in the story of a little boy who was running through some woods. He suddenly tripped over a log and cut his jugular vein on a stick. His father quickly picked him up and held his finger tightly on the vein to stop the blood flow as they rushed the child to a hospital.

As they entered the operating room, the distressed child held out his thumb to the surgeon. When he had fallen, a splinter of wood had entered his thumb. Of course the good doctor ignored the boy's plea to remove the splinter, and immediately set to work on stopping the blood flow from his jugular vein.

There are not many in the world who escape suffering. Two hundred thousand people were murdered in the U.S. during the 1990s, leaving perhaps a million loved ones to fight bitterness and ask why God allowed the murder to happen. No doubt each unsaved person held up a pained thumb to God, when He is more interested in stopping the blood flowing from the jugular vein. We expect God to immediately fix what we consider the most serious wound, when God wants to first deal with the "sin" issue—that which will be the death and eternal damnation of us. So, if we as Christians care about the will of God and the eternal welfare of the person to whom we are speaking, we will go for the jugular; we will speak about the sin issue.

However, it goes without saying that we need to show a deep empathy for the person who is suffering as we gently take him through the Law. This may require a little practice, but it is something in which each of us must become proficient, if we want to see the lost come to Christ.

This is how best to handle the sensitive issue of witnessing to someone who is hurting. Tell him that you are sorry about his loss. Again, make sure that you show genuine sensitivity, then do what a surgeon would do with a severed jugular vein. Turn immediately to the serious issue at hand: the person's salvation. Unless you know that the deceased was a Christian, stay clear of any talk about whether or not the loved one went to heaven or hell, by saying that God is good and that He will do what is right on Judgment Day.

Say something like, "When we are confronted with the issue of death, it can often make us think about God and about our own eternal salvation. Do you ever think about God? Do you consider yourself to be a good person?" Then gently take him through the Law.

If there is any offense, apologize and change the subject. But more than likely you will find that by talking about his personal salvation, it will be like a complete subject change, and therefore won't be offensive.

If he has any bitterness toward God that is hindering him from opening his heart, gently let him know that many people have suffered terrible losses in this life, and they have let that suffering bring them to the cross, and consequently to everlasting life. An analogy that may be helpful is to say that if someone offers to lift you out of quicksand, don't let the fact that you don't like the color of their skin, or you can't understand why they are wearing certain clothes, etc., stop you from giving your hand to your rescuer. God offers to lift us out of the quicksand of death itself. Tell the person: "Let God pull you out, and once you are saved, ask your questions. If you don't get an answer in this life, you are guaranteed to get one in the next."

QUESTIONS

1. **Why do you think tragedy makes some people look to God, while others become bitter?**

2. Would you consider a surgeon who dealt with a splinter, rather than a severed jugular vein, to be a good surgeon?

3. Why must we "go for the jugular" when speaking with someone who is suffering?

4. What must you remember when speaking with someone who has lost a loved one?

5. Why should you avoid any talk about the salvation of a deceased loved one?

PREACHER'S PROGRESS

Christian: "Hi. How are you doing?"

Helen Back: "Okay."

Christian: "Do you see this?"

Helen Back: "What is it?"

Christian: "It's an optical illusion."

Helen Back: "Wow!"

Christian: "You can have that if you want. It's a gospel tract."

Helen Back: "Thanks."

Christian: "Do you have a Christian background?"

Helen Back: "I went to church when I was a child, but my stepfather stopped me from going."

Christian: "That's awful."

Helen Back: "He used to beat up my mother. He raped me when I was fourteen."

Christian: "You must be carrying a lot of scars."

Helen Back: "I ran off with the first boyfriend I had. Then I became pregnant by him. Then I lost my job, got into drugs—I already had a problem with alcohol. That's one of the reasons my boyfriend left me. My child was taken from me by the courts. That threw me into depression, and I tried to commit suicide twice—see these scars? The doctors gave me some drugs to help my depression."

Christian: "I suppose the drugs had side-effects."

Helen Back: "Yes. They were terrible. I thought I was going insane, so I checked myself into a mental hospital. I just got out today."

Christian: "Are you hungry?"

Helen Back: "Yes, I am."

Christian: "Let me buy you something to eat . . . So, do you think you will get back to church?" *

Helen Back: "I haven't thought about it."

Christian: "Do you see yourself as being a good person?"

Helen Back: "Yes, I do."

Christian: "Do you think that you have kept the Ten Commandments?"

Helen Back: "Pretty much."

Christian: "Let's go through a few of them to see how you will do on Judgment Day…"

* *The question arises, should Christian tell this poor woman that God loves her and can help her with all of her problems, or should he speak to her about sin? The answer is that, even though he may be tempted to console this woman, if she doesn't come to the Savior with a knowledge of sin, she will not find a place of repentance and will end up in hell. Imagine you are on a plane. The man next to you has a broken leg. He has to jump out of the plane at any minute. Do you fail to warn him about the jump because he is in pain? No. You just hope that his pain doesn't distract him from the sober message you have for him.*

FEATHERS FOR ARROWS

Khrushchev, the Soviet leader in the sixties, said, "The chief failure with communism is its inability to create a new man." He was right. Communism said, "A new coat for every man," while Jesus Christ says, "A new man in every coat."

If we didn't like the way pigs lived, we could take a pig and scrub it clean, put deodorant under its pig-pits, and place it in a clean, thickly carpeted room. In a few days, however, the place would become a pig-sty. The only way to change a pig is to change its nature. The same applies to man. Politics cannot change the heart of man. History proves that. The only one who can change the human heart is Almighty God. When an item breaks down, take a look at the Instruction Book. The Bible says sin is the cause of all human suffering. Jesus Christ is the only cure.

Last Words

William of Normandy (943 A.D.), in a farewell word, ordered that his body be placed in a stone coffin and not buried, but placed under the eaves outside the chapel for this reason:

> **"That the drippings of the rain from the roof may wash my bones as I lie, and cleanse them from the impurity contracted in my sinful and neglected life."**

Memory Verse

"Every one that has forsaken houses, or brethren, or sisters, or father, or mother, or wife, or children, or lands, for my name's sake, shall receive an hundredfold, and shall inherit everlasting life."

MATTHEW 19:29

LESSON 34 Open-Air Preaching, Part 1

Kirk's Comment Open-air preaching gave me a whole new perspective on what it was like when Jesus, Paul, Peter, and the others preached the gospel to the unsaved. Hearing a well-done open-air is like watching Paul preach on Mars Hill in Acts chapter 17. What a rush!

QUESTIONS & OBJECTIONS

"Do you sin, as a Christian?"

If a Christian sins, it is against his will. One who is regenerate *falls* rather than *dives* into sin; he resists rather than embraces it. Any dead fish can float downstream. It takes a live one to swim against the flow. Christians still experience temptations and can sometimes fall into sin, but they are no longer slaves to sin (Romans 6:6). They have God's Holy Spirit within them to help them say no to temptation, and to convict their conscience of wrongdoing when they do sin.

Perhaps the topic of open-air preaching seems irrelevant to you. You could never see yourself standing up among strangers and preaching the gospel to them. However, John the Baptist was an open-air preacher. Jesus was an open-air preacher. He preached the greatest sermon of all time, the Sermon on the Mount, in the open air. Peter preached in the open air at Pentecost and Paul chose to stand on Mars Hill and preach open-air to the Athenians.

If we are serious about reaching this world, let us follow in the footsteps of Jesus and the apostles and preach where sinners gather. In thirty minutes, a good open-air preacher can reach more sinners than the average church does in twelve months.

Thank God that the disciples didn't stay in the upper room. They didn't carpet the building, pad the pews, then put a notice on the front door saying, "Tonight: Gospel outreach service, 7 p.m.—all welcome." They went into the open air.

The gospel is for the world, not the church. That's why we are commanded to "go into all the world, and preach the gospel to every creature" (Mark 16:15). One-third of the word "gospel" is "go." Two-thirds of "God" is "go"; but like King Og, we seem to have it backwards. We take sinners to meetings rather than meetings to sinners. The church prefers to fish on dry land rather than get its feet wet. Charles Finney put his finger on the reason why: "It is the great business of every Christian to save souls. People complain that they do not know how to take hold of this matter. Why, the reason is plain enough; they have never studied it. They have never taken the proper pains to qualify themselves for the work. If you do not make it a matter of study, how you may successfully act in building up the kingdom of Christ, you are acting a very wicked and absurd part as a Christian."

He who loves his neighbor as himself will be concerned for his eternal welfare. He who couldn't care less that every day multitudes of living people are being swallowed by the jaws of hell has a heart of stone indeed.

Perhaps you lack the courage to preach open-air. Congratulations—you have just qualified for the job. If you consider yourself to be a "nobody" with nothing to offer God, you are His material. When you submit yourself to Him for His use, He promises to do "exceedingly abundantly above all that we ask or think, according to the power that works in us" (Ephesians 3:20). Now all you need is a compassion that will swallow your fear and a conscience that will give you no rest until you break the sound barrier.

Open-air preaching is not without its difficulties, however. The first is how to draw a crowd to hear the gospel. Today's society has been programmed to want immediate action, and open-air preaching isn't too attractive to guilty sinners. Therefore we have to be as wise as serpents and as gentle as doves. A serpent gets its heart's desire subtly. Our desire is for sinners to gather under the sound of the gospel.

Here is one way to get attention: Ask people passing by what they think is the greatest killer of drivers in the U.S. This stirs their curiosity. Some begin calling out, "Alcohol!" or, "Falling asleep at the wheel!" Tell them it's not and repeat the question a few more times, saying that you will give a dollar to the person who gets the answer. Tell them that they will never guess what it is that kills more drivers than anything else in America. A few more shouts emit from the crowd. People are now waiting around for the answer. What is it that kills more drivers than anything else in the United States? What is it that could be the death of you and me? You won't believe this, but it is "trees." Millions of them line our highways. When one is struck, the tree stays still, sending the driver into eternity.

Then tell the crowd that you have another question for them. Ask what they think is the most common food on which people choke to death in U.S. restaurants. Over the next few minutes, go through the same scenario. People may call out, "Steak!" "Chicken bones!" Believe it or not, the answer is "hard-boiled egg yoke."

By now you have a crowd that is enjoying what is going on. Ask them what they think is the most dangerous job in America. Someone calls out, "Cop." It's not. Someone else may name another dangerous profession like, "Firefighter." Say, "Good one...but wrong." Give a suggestion by saying, "Why doesn't someone say 'electrician'?" Someone takes the suggestion and says, "Electrician!" Say, "Sorry, it's not electrician." The most dangerous job in the United States...is to be the president. Out of forty or so, four have been murdered while on the job.

Here are some additional questions to use for crowd drawing:

- Who wrote, "Ask not what your country can do for you. Ask what you can do for your country"? *(President Kennedy's speechwriter)*

- What is the only fish that can blink with both eyes? *(A shark)*

- Who was John Lennon's first girlfriend? *(Thelma Pickles)*

- How long does it take the average person to fall asleep: 2 minutes, 7 minutes, or 4 hours? *(7 minutes)*

- How long is a goldfish's memory span: 3 seconds, 3 minutes, or 3 hours? *(3 seconds)*

- How many muscles does a cat have in each ear: 2, 32, or 426? *(32)*

Once you've asked three or four questions and captured the crowd's attention, tell them you have another question. "Does anyone in the crowd consider himself to be a 'good person'?" By now you will have noted who in the crowd has the self-confidence to speak out. Point to one or two and ask, "Sir, do you consider yourself to be a good person?" The Bible tells us that "every man will proclaim his own goodness" (Proverbs 20:6), and he does. He smiles and says, "Yes, I do consider myself to be a good person." Ask him if he has ever told a lie. Has he stolen, lusted, blasphemed, etc.? That's when all heaven breaks loose. There is conviction of sin, sinners hear the gospel, and angels rejoice.

Crowd Etiquette

If other Christians are with you, have them form an audience and look as though they are listening to your preaching. This will encourage others to stop and listen. Tell the Christians to never stand with their back to the preacher. I have seen open-air meetings when a fellow laborer is preaching for the first time, and what are the Christians doing? They are talking among themselves. Why then should anyone stop and listen if those in front of the speaker aren't even attentive? It is so easy to chat with friends when you've heard the gospel a million times before. I have found myself doing it, but it is so disheartening for the preacher to speak to the backs of a crowd.

Also, instruct Christians not to argue with hecklers. That will ruin an open-air meeting. I have seen an old lady hit a heckler with her umbrella and turn the crowd from listening to the gospel to watching the fight she has just started. Who can blame them? Remember, the enemy will do everything he can to distract your listeners. Don't let him.

Give Yourself a Lift

If you are going to preach in the open air, elevate yourself. For eighteen months, I preached without any elevation and hardly attracted any listeners. As soon as I got a "soapbox" to stand on, people stopped to listen. Their attitude was, "What has this guy got to say?" They had an excuse to stop.

Also, elevation will give you protection. I was once almost eaten by an angry 6'6" gentleman who kept fuming, "God is love!" We were eye to eye...while I was elevated. On another occasion, a very heavy gentleman who had a mean countenance placed it about 6" from mine and whispered, "Jesus said to love your enemies." I nodded in agreement. Then he asked in a deep voice, "Who is your enemy?" I shrugged. His voice deepened and spilled forth in a chilling tone, *"Lucifer!"* I was standing beside my stepladder at the time so he pushed me backwards with his stomach. He kept doing so until I was moved back about 20 feet. I prayed for wisdom, then said, "You are either going to hit me or hug me." He hugged me and walked off. That wouldn't have happened if I had been elevated.

Elevation will also give you added authority. Often hecklers will walk right up to you and ask questions quietly. This is an attempt to stifle the preaching, and it will work if you are not higher than your heckler. If they come too close to me, I talk over their heads and tell them to go back to the heckler's gallery. They actually obey me because they get the impression I am bigger than they are.

When Ezra preached the Law, he was elevated (Nehemiah 8:4,5). John Wesley used elevation to preach. Jesus preached the greatest sermon in history on a mount (Matthew 5–7), and Paul went up Mars Hill to preach (Acts 17:22). So if you can't find a hilltop to preach from, use a soapbox or a stepladder.

QUESTIONS

1. What are some reasons why you should preach the gospel open-air?

2. What is the solution if you lack the courage to preach open-air?

3. What are some ways you can draw a crowd to hear the gospel?

4. If other Christians are with you, what should you have them do?

5. Why should you elevate yourself to preach?

FEATHERS FOR ARROWS

"One night when [Dwight L.] Moody was going home, it suddenly occurred to him that he had not spoken to a single person that day about accepting Christ. *A day lost*, he thought to himself. But as he walked up the street he saw a man by a lamppost. He promptly walked up to the man and asked, 'Are you a Christian?'

"Nor did Moody find soul-winning easy. In fact, even Christians often criticized him for having 'zeal without knowledge.' Others called him 'Crazy Moody.' Once when he spoke to a perfect stranger about Christ, the man said, 'That is none of your business…If you were not a sort of a preacher I would knock you into the gutter for your impertinence.'

"The next day, a businessman friend sent for Moody. The businessman told Moody that the stranger he had spoken to was a friend of his. 'Moody, you've got zeal without knowledge: you insulted a friend of mine on the street last night. You went up to him, a perfect stranger, and asked him if he were a Christian.'

"Moody went out of his friend's office almost brokenhearted. For some time he worried about this. Then late one night a man pounded on the door of his home. It was the stranger he had supposedly insulted. The stranger said, 'Mr. Moody, I have not had a good night's sleep since that night you spoke to me under the lamppost, and I have come around at this unearthly hour of the night for you to tell me what I have to do to be saved.'" —*Harry Albus*

WORDS OF COMFORT

When I was in my late teens, my younger sister asked me to change the tire on her car. It was good that she asked me to do it, because every sister needs a big brother to take care of her. It gives them a "safe" feeling. This was a unique opportunity to cultivate the protective big brother image.

Two weeks later, as she was going around a corner, the wheel fell off!

Last Words

Lew Wallace (1827–1905), author of the remarkable book *Ben Hur*, had a sentence from "The Lord's Prayer" on his lips as he died:

"Thy will be done."

Memory Verse

"If you shall confess with your mouth the Lord Jesus, and shall believe in your heart that God has raised him from the dead, you shall be saved. For with the heart man believes to righteousness; and with the mouth confession is made to salvation."
ROMANS 10:9,10

35 Open-Air Preaching, Part 2

"The open-air speaker's calling is as honorable as it is arduous,
as useful as it is laborious. God alone can sustain you in it,
but with Him at your side you will have nothing to fear."

CHARLES SPURGEON

Kirk's Comment   The first time I saw the videos *Open-Air Preaching in New York* and *In Season, Out of Season* (available on our website), I was inspired beyond words. My heart was crying out, "Yes, that's it! That's what I want to do!"—except I couldn't imagine me ever having the courage to do it. But God had no plans of leaving me as an evangelistic chicken. Within months, not only was I compelled to stand up and speak to a crowd, even my own mother felt led to climb up on a box and say a few words!

QUESTIONS & OBJECTIONS

"What should I say if someone asks, 'Have you ever lusted?'"

An individual may challenge you on this issue while you're going through the Ten Commandments with him. Take care when answering. There is such a thing as being too candid. A U.S. president became synonymous with the word "lust" because he lacked discretion in answering this question. Soften your answer with, "I have broken all of the Ten Commandments in spirit, if not in letter." That will not only defuse the issue, but will give you an opportunity to explain that we all have a sin nature and need God's forgiveness.

wotmwotmwotmwotmwotmwotmwotmwotmwotmwotmwotm

You may have a few concerns about open-air preaching. Perhaps one of them is the thought of hecklers—people verbally disagreeing with what you say. However, the best thing that can happen to an open-air meeting is to have a good heckler. Jesus gave us some of the greatest gems of Scripture because someone either made a statement or asked a question in an open-air setting. A good heckler can increase a crowd of 20 people to 200 in a matter of minutes. The air becomes electric. Suddenly, you have 200 people listening intently to how you will answer a heckler. All you have to do is remember the attributes of 2 Timothy 2:23–26: be patient, gentle, humble, etc. Don't worry if you can't answer a question. Just say, "I can't answer that, but I'll try to get the answer for you if you really want to know." With Bible "difficulties," I regularly fall back on the powerful statement of Mark Twain: "Most people are bothered by those passages of Scripture they don't understand, but for me I have always noticed that the passages that bother me are those I do understand."

A "good" heckler is one who will provoke your thoughts. He will stand up, speak up, and then shut up so that you can preach. Occasionally, you will get hecklers who have the first two qualifications, but they just won't be quiet. If they will not let you get a word in, move your location. Most of the crowd will follow. Better to have 10 listeners who can hear than 200 who can't. If the heckler follows, move again...then the crowd will usually turn on him.

One ploy that often works with a heckler who is out solely to hinder the gospel is to wait until he is quiet and say to the crowd (making sure the heckler is listening also), "I want to show you how people are like sheep. When I move, watch this man follow me because he can't get a crowd by himself." His pride usually keeps him from following.

If you have a "mumbling heckler" who won't speak up, ignore him and talk over the top of him. This will usually get him angry enough to speak up and draw hearers. There is a fine line between him getting angry enough to draw a crowd, and hitting you; you will find it in time.

If you are fortunate enough to get a heckler, don't panic. Show him genuine respect, not only because he can double your crowd, but because the Bible says to honor all men, so you don't want to offend him unnecessarily. Ask the heckler his name, so that if you want to ask him a question and he is talking to someone, you don't have to say, "Hey, you!"

Often, people will walk through the crowd so they can get close to you and whisper something like, "I think you are a #@*!$!" Answer loud enough for the crowd to hear, "God bless you." Do it with a smile so that it looks as though the person has just whispered a word of encouragement to you. This will stop him from doing it again. The Bible says to bless those who curse you, and to do good to those who hate you.

Remember that you are not fighting against flesh and blood. Hecklers will stoop very low and be cutting and cruel in their remarks. If you have some physical disability, they will play on it. Try to smile back at them. Look past the words. If you are reviled for the name of Jesus, "rejoice, and be exceeding glad." Read Matthew 5:10–12 until it is written on the corridors of your mind.

The angriest hecklers are usually what we call "backsliders." These are actually false converts who never slid forward in the first place. They "asked Jesus into their heart" but never truly repented. Ask him, "Did you know the Lord?" If he answers, "Yes," then he is admitting that he is willfully denying Him. If he answers, "No," then he was never a Christian in the first place—"This is eternal life, that they might know you, the only true God, and Jesus Christ, whom you have sent" (John 17:3).

Make the Bullet Hit the Target

It is obvious from Scripture that God requires us not only to preach to sinners, but also to teach them. The servant of the Lord must be "able to teach, patient, in meekness instructing" those who oppose them (2 Timothy 2:24,25). For a long while I thought I was to leap among sinners, scatter the seed, then leave. But our responsibility goes further. We are to bring the sinner to a point of understanding his need before God. Psalm 25:8 says, "Good and upright is the LORD: therefore will he teach sinners in the way." Psalm 51:13 adds, "Then will I teach transgressors your ways; and sinners shall be converted to you." The Great Commission is to teach sinners: "teach all nations…teaching them to observe all things" (Matthew 28:19,20). The disciples obeyed the command: "daily in the temple, and in every house, they ceased not to *teach* and preach Jesus Christ" (Acts 5:42, emphasis added).

The "good-soil" hearer is he who "hears…and *understands*" (Matthew 13:23). Philip the evangelist saw fit to ask his potential convert, the Ethiopian, "Do you understand what you are reading?" Some preachers are like a loud gun that misses the target. It may sound effective, but if the bullet misses the target, the exercise is in vain. He may be the largest-lunged, chandelier-swinging, pulpit-pounding preacher this side of the Book of Acts. He may have great teaching on faith, and everyone he touches may fall over, but if the sinner leaves the meeting failing to understand his desperate need of God's forgiveness, then the preacher has failed. He has missed the target, which is the understanding of the sinner. Sinners will not flee from the wrath to come until they understand that they are guilty and under condemnation.

This is why the Law of God must be used in preaching. It brings "the knowledge of sin" and serves as a "schoolmaster" leading sinners to the Savior. It teaches and instructs. A sinner will come to "know His will, and approve the things that are more excellent," if he is "instructed out of the Law" (Romans 2:18).

QUESTIONS

1. **Why is it beneficial to have a heckler when you're preaching open-air?**

2. **How should you respond to a heckler?**

3. How can you deal with a "mumbling heckler"?

4. What should you do if you are "reviled" for the name of Jesus?

5. Why is it important to bring "understanding" to your hearers?

6. How does the Law bring understanding?

Preacher's Progress

Miss Communication: "God is all-loving."

Christian: "No, He's not."

Miss Communication: "Yes, He is. The Bible says so."

Christian: "No, it doesn't. It says that God is love."

Miss Communication: "See."

Christian: "But that doesn't say He's all-loving. He's not a slave to love. The Bible reveals that He's also just, holy, and righteous."

Miss Communication: "So... what does that mean?"

Christian: "When people say God is all-loving, they are implying God is so loving that He wouldn't send people to hell."

Miss Communication: "Well, if He was loving, He wouldn't send anyone to hell."

Christian: "I have a question for you. If a man sexually abused children, tortured them, cut their throats, and said he would do it again if he had half a chance, should a judge punish him?"

Miss Communication: "Of course."

Christian: "What if the judge is a loving man?"

Miss Communication: "He should still punish that wicked person."

Christian: "Right...and God will punish all wicked men, even though He is 'love.' Does that make sense?"

Miss Communication: "Now it does."

FEATHERS FOR ARROWS

Ira Sankey, before he became D. L. Moody's famous song leader (and a powerful preacher himself), was assigned to night duty in the American Civil War. While he was on duty, he lifted his eyes toward heaven and began to sing, praising the Lord while he was alone. At least, he thought he was alone.

Years later, after the war had ended, Sankey was on a ship traveling across the Atlantic Ocean. Since he was now a famous singer, a crowd of people approached him and asked him to sing. He lifted his eyes toward heaven and sang a beautiful hymn.

After his song, a man from the crowd asked him if, on a certain night during the Civil War, he had performed night duty for a certain infantry unit. "Yes, I did," was his reply.

The man continued, "I was on the opposite side of the war, and I was hiding in a bush near your camp. With my rifle aimed at your head, I was about to shoot you when you looked toward heaven and began to sing. I thought, 'Well, I like music, and this guy has a nice voice. I'll sit here, let him sing the song,...and then shoot him. He's not going anywhere.' But then I realized what you were singing. It was the same hymn my mother used to sing at my bedside when I was a child. And it's the same hymn you sang tonight! I tried, but that night during the Civil War, I was powerless to shoot you."

Ira Sankey pointed that man to Christ. He and thousands of others were saved under Sankey's ministry. All this stemmed from the fact that Sankey praised the Lord at all times.

Last Words

Horace Greeley, journalist and founder of the *New York Tribune*, uttered these words when dying:

"I know that my Redeemer liveth."

Open-Air Preaching, Part 3

"The great benefit of open-air preaching is that we get so many newcomers to hear the gospel who otherwise would never hear it."

CHARLES SPURGEON

Kirk's Comment If you're feeling the Spirit's tug in your heart about open-air preaching, watch the open-air videos mentioned in the previous lesson. They'll show you that it's not about being a crazy-eyed lunatic; it's about powerful and effective evangelism, following in the footsteps of Jesus, Paul, and the other normal, biblical Christians. They will stir you and light a fire in your soul to reach out to the unsaved. The "Open-Air" page of the Living Waters website is full of additional information and instructions on how to get your feet wet.

QUESTIONS & OBJECTIONS

"It's intolerant to say that Jesus is the only way to God!"

Jesus is the One who said that He is the only way to the Father. For Christians to say that there are other ways to find peace with God is to bear false testimony. In one sweeping statement, Jesus discards all other religions as a means of finding forgiveness of sins. In John 14:6 He says, "I am the way, the truth, and the life: no man comes to the Father, but by me." This agrees with other Scriptures: "Neither is there salvation in any other: for there is no other name under heaven given among men, whereby we must be saved" (Acts 4:12), and, "For there is one God, and one mediator between God and men, the man Christ Jesus" (1 Timothy 2:5).

w o t m w o t m w o t m w o t m w o t m w o t m w o t m w o t m w o t m w o t m w o t m

When you're preaching the gospel, don't let angry reactions from your listeners concern you. A dentist knows where to work on a patient when he touches a raw nerve. When you touch a raw nerve in the heart of the sinner, it means that you are in business. Anger is a thousand times better than apathy. Anger is a sign of conviction. If I have an argument with my wife and suddenly realize that I am in the wrong, I can come to her in a repentant attitude and apologize, or I can save face by lashing out in anger.

Read Acts 19 and see how Paul was a dentist with an eye for decay. He probed raw nerves wherever he went. At one point, he had to be carried shoulder height by soldiers because of the "violence of the people" (Acts 21:36). Now *that* is a successful preacher! He didn't seek the praise of men. John Wesley told his evangelist trainees that when they preached, people should either get angry or get converted. No doubt, he wasn't speaking about the "Jesus loves you" gospel, but about sin, Law, righteousness, judgment, and hell.

Always follow the wisdom of Solomon: "A soft answer turns away wrath: but grievous words stir up anger" (Proverbs 15:1). This verse needs to be written on the hearts of all who preach the gospel, whether they share their faith with sinners one-on-one or preach open-air. If sinners become angry when you witness to them, speak softly. If you think you are about to be hit, ask the person his name to help diffuse the situation. Don't be afraid to gently change the subject, and don't wait to be a martyr. Jesus said to flee from a city that persecutes you (Matthew 10:23). Paul left one city in a basket (2 Corinthians 11:33).

The Bible warns us to avoid foolish questions because they start arguments (2 Timothy 2:23). Most of us have fallen into the trap of jumping at every objection to the gospel. However, these questions can often be arguments in disguise to sidetrack you from the "weightier matters of the

Law." While apologetics (arguments for God's existence, creation vs. evolution, etc.) are legitimate in evangelism, they should merely be "bait," with the Law of God being the "hook" that brings the conviction of sin. Those who witness solely in the realm of apologetical argument may just get an intellectual decision rather than a repentant conversion. The sinner may come to a point of acknowledging that the Bible is the Word of God and Jesus is Lord—but even the devil knows that. Always pull the sinner back to his responsibility before God on Judgment Day, as Jesus did in Luke 13:1–5.

Whenever you are in an open-air situation, be suspicious of so-called Christians who are intent on distracting workers from witnessing. They argue about prophecy, of how much water one should baptize with, or in whose name they should be baptized. It is grievous to see five or six Christians standing around arguing with some sectarian nitpicker, while sinners are sinking into hell.

There may also be occasions when a non-Christian appears to be "helping" you, like the demon-possessed woman who followed Paul (Acts 16:16–18). The woman (or the demon) was speaking the truth: Paul and his companions were servants of the Most High God, and they were showing the way of salvation. Why then was Paul grieved? Satan is very subtle. Rather than openly oppose the truth, he will often attempt to conceal it by implying that the occult and God are compatible. If you are open-air preaching, don't be surprised to have someone who is apparently demonically controlled loudly agree with you, so that it looks to the crowd that you are both preaching the same message. This is very frustrating.

For two years I was heckled almost daily by a woman named Petra. She dressed in black, carried a wooden staff, and said she was a prophet to the nation. As in the days of Noah, only eight would be saved. She maintained that she was one of them, and that she determined who the other seven would be. She also claimed that my spirit visited her spirit in the night (it did not!). My problem was that she would "Amen" much of what I preached, adding her thoughts at the points I made. She would do this at the top of her very loud voice. It must have appeared to newcomers to the crowd that we were a team, preaching the same thing. This was why I was delighted when (every now and then) she would get angry with something I said and let out a string of cuss words, revealing to the crowd that we were *not* on the same side.

As you share the gospel, divorce yourself from the thought that you are merely seeking "decisions for Christ." What we should be seeking is repentance within the heart. This is the purpose of the Law, to bring the knowledge of sin. How can sinners repent if they don't know what sin is? If there is no repentance, there is no salvation. Jesus said, "Unless you repent, you shall all likewise perish" (Luke 13:3). God is not willing that any should perish, but that all should come to repentance (2 Peter 3:9).

Many don't understand that the salvation of a soul is not a resolution to change a way of life, but "repentance toward God, and faith toward our Lord Jesus Christ" (Acts 20:21). Billy Graham said, "If you have not repented, you will not see the inside of the kingdom of God." The modern concept of success in evangelism is to relate how many people were "saved" (that is, how many prayed the "sinner's prayer"). This produces a "no decisions, no success" mentality. This shouldn't be, because Christians who seek decisions in evangelism become discouraged after a time of witnessing if "no one came to the Lord." The Bible tells us that as we sow the good seed of the gospel, one sows and another reaps. If you faithfully sow the seed, someone will reap. If you reap, it is because someone has sown in the past, but it is God who causes the seed to grow. If His hand is not on the person you are leading in a prayer of committal, if there is not *God-given* repentance, then you will end up with a stillbirth on your hands, and that is nothing to rejoice about. We should measure our success by how faithfully we sowed the seed. In that way, we will avoid becoming discouraged.

There is one passage in Scripture to which I point for all those who want to witness or preach in the open-air. It is 2 Timothy 2:24–26. Memorize it. Scripture tells us that sinners are blind; they *cannot* see. What would you think if I were to stomp up to a blind man who had just stumbled, and say, "Watch where you're going, blind man!"? Such an attitude is completely unreasonable. The man *cannot* see.

The same applies to the lost—spiritual sight is beyond their ability. Look at the words used in Scripture: "Except a man be born again, he *cannot* see the kingdom of God...The god of this world has *blinded* the minds of them which believe not... But the natural man receives not the things of the Spirit of God: for they are foolishness to him: neither *can* he know them... Having the understanding *darkened*... because of the *blindness* of their heart... Ever learning, and *never able* to come to the knowledge of the truth."

With these thoughts in mind, read 2 Timothy 2:24–26 again and look at the adjectives used by Paul to describe the attitude we are to have with sinners: "must not strive... be gentle... patient... in meekness." Just as it is unreasonable to be impatient with a blind man, so it is with the sinner.

QUESTIONS

1. **Why should we not be discouraged by an angry reaction to our message?**

2. **What did John Wesley say about angry reactions?**

3. **Why should we be careful not to witness and preach solely in the realm of apologetics?**

4. **Why should we aim at obtaining more than just "decisions for Christ"?**

5. **How should we gauge evangelistic success?**

6. **According to 2 Timothy 2:24–26, what should be our attitude toward sinners?**

FEATHERS FOR ARROWS

When Jesus went to the temple, He found it to be filled with those buying and selling merchandise. According to the Jewish historian Josephus, at each Passover, over 250,000 animals were sacrificed. The priests sold licenses to the dealers and therefore would have had a great source of income from the Passover. When the Bible called them "changers of money," it was an appropriate term.

There is, however, another theft going on in another temple. Mankind was made as a dwelling place for his Creator. God made man a little lower than the angels, crowned him with glory and honor, and set him over the works of His hands (Hebrews 2:7), yet sin has given the dwelling place to the devil. The thief, who came to steal, kill, and destroy, is making merchandise out of mankind. Instead of the heart of man being a temple of the living God (2 Corinthians 6:16)—a house of prayer—iniquity has made it a den of thieves.

When someone repents and calls upon the name of Jesus Christ, He turns the tables on the devil. The ten stinging cords of the Ten Commandments in the hand of the Savior cleanse the temple of sin. Charles Spurgeon had a resolute grasp of the Law. In preaching to sinners, he said, "I would that this whip would fall upon your backs, that you might be flogged out of your self-righteousness and made to fly to Jesus Christ and find shelter there."

WORDS OF COMFORT

When I was in school, during a music class with our partly deaf music teacher, I noticed that a boy had crawled under the seats. He was pulling another boy by his leg under the seat. Filled with indignation, I crawled under the seats, grabbed his foot, and began pulling. Suddenly, some clown with a firm grip grabbed my foot and began pulling, so I used my free foot to kick him loose.

It was then that I looked around and saw that it was the principal who was pulling my leg! That incident left two lasting impressions upon the seat of my learning.

Last Words

Blaise Pascal (1623–1662), French mathematician and philosopher:

> **"My God, forsake me not."**

Memory Verse

"The servant of the Lord must not strive; but be gentle to all men, able to teach, patient, in meekness instructing those that oppose themselves; if God peradventure will give them repentance to the acknowledging of the truth; and that they may recover themselves out of the snare of the devil, who are taken captive by him at his will."
2 TIMOTHY 2:24–26

LESSON 37

Faith, Part 1

> *"The beginning of anxiety is the end of faith, and the*
> *beginning of true faith is the end of anxiety."*
> **GEORGE MUELLER**

Kirk's Comment   Faith levels the playing field. Again, let's keep the simple things simple. Jesus said, "Except you be converted, and become as little children, you shall not enter into the kingdom of heaven" (Matthew 18:3). It seems that one of the greatest virtues of children is their ability to trust. If I tell my three-year-old daughter that the earth is round, she believes me simply because she trusts my word. Because God is always faithful and does not lie, we can trust Him completely and have faith in His Word.

QUESTIONS & OBJECTIONS

"If God gives me some 'sign,' then I will believe."

The unsaved often want a "sign" from God. This is in spite of the testimony of creation, their conscience, the Bible, and the Christian. The cross is the only thing that can truly convince sinners of the reality of who Jesus is. Once they understand that the holes in His hands and His feet are there because of their own sin, they will fall at His feet and cry, "My Lord and my God!"

When a young man once told me, "I find it hard to believe some of the things in the Bible," I smiled and asked, "What's your name?" When he said, "Paul," I casually answered, "I don't believe you." He looked at me questioningly. I repeated, "What's your name?" Again he said, "Paul," and again I answered, "*I don't believe you.*" Then I asked, "Where do you live?" When he told me, I said, "I don't believe *that* either." His reaction was to become (understandably) angry. I said, "You look a little upset. Do you know why? You're upset because I didn't believe what you told me. If you say your name is Paul and I reply, 'I don't believe you,' it means that I think you are a liar. You are trying to deceive me by telling me your name is Paul, when it's not."

Then I pointed out that if he, a mere man, felt insulted by my lack of faith in his word, how much more does he insult Almighty God by refusing to believe His Word. In doing so, he was saying that God isn't worth trusting—that He is a liar and a deceiver. The Bible says, "He that believes not God has made him a liar" (1 John 5:10). It also warns, "Take heed, brethren, least there be in any of you *an evil heart of unbelief*" (Hebrews 3:12, emphasis added). Martin Luther stated, "What greater insult . . . can there be to God than not to believe His promises."

I have heard people say, "I just find it hard to have faith in God," not realizing the implications of their words. These are the same people who often believe the weather forecast, accept what the newspapers say as true, and trust their lives to a pilot they have never seen whenever they board a plane. We exercise faith every day. We rely on our car's brakes. We trust history books, medical journals, and elevators. Yet elevators can let us down; history books can be wrong; planes can crash. How much more, then, should we trust the sure and true promises of Almighty God? He will *never* let us down . . . if we trust Him.

The Scriptures tell us that we should "above all, [take] the shield of faith" (Ephesians 6:16). This part of our armor is essential because it extinguishes all the "fiery darts of the wicked." If you don't have faith as your shield, you will be wounded, perhaps fatally, by the enemy.

Faith is spiritually what oxygen is physically. Without faith, the unbeliever gasps, writhes, and then dies. We know that without faith it is impossible to please God (Hebrews 11:6). Without faith, the sharks will devour us. With faith, it is possible not only to please Him, but to float above the infested waters of this world. It is also possible to move mountains, subdue kingdoms, work righteousness, obtain promises, and stop the mouths of lions.

God has even given us an honor roll of soldiers who have gone before us in battle. Hebrews 11 lists those who through faith obeyed their Commander and were afterward promoted to Headquarters. Many, like Paul, carried in their bodies the scars of the Lord Jesus. We are told that they "were tortured, not accepting deliverance; that they might obtain a better resurrection: and others had trial of cruel mockings and scourgings...of bonds and imprisonment: they were stoned...sawn asunder...slain with the sword" (Hebrews 11:35–37). They exercised faith throughout the battle, proving its worth. It's now up to us to follow their example. These soldiers of the cross found that faith in God gave them the ability to be "strong in the Lord and in the power of His might," to be "more than conquerors," because they knew that God was for them, that He always caused them to triumph—through faith.

QUESTIONS

1. **What is the biblical definition of "faith"? (See Hebrews 11:1.)**

2. **In layman's terms, what is faith?**

3. **Why was the young man offended because I didn't believe him?**

4. What are some of the things in which people have faith?

5. What is implied when someone finds it hard to have faith in God?

6. What does the Bible mean when it says that it is "impossible" for God to lie?

7. On a scale of one to ten, how much faith do you have in God?

FEATHERS FOR ARROWS

I have often heard cynics say, "You can't trust the Bible—it's full of mistakes." It is. The first mistake was when man rejected God, and the Scriptures show men and women making the same tragic mistake again and again. It's also full of what *seem to be* contradictions. For example, the Scriptures tell us that "with God, nothing shall be impossible" (Luke 1:37). We are told that there is nothing Almighty God can't do. Yet we are also told that it is "impossible for God to lie" (Hebrews 6:18). So there is something God cannot do! Isn't that an obvious "mistake" in the Bible? No, it isn't. The answer to this dilemma is found in the lowly worm.

Memory Verse

"But without faith it is impossible to please him: for he that comes to God must believe that he is, and that he is a rewarder of them that diligently seek him."

HEBREWS 11:6

I can safely say that it would be impossible for me to eat worms, although I have seen it done. I once saw a man on TV butter his toast, then pour on a can of live, fat, wriggling, dirt-filled worms. He carefully took a knife and fork, cut into his moving meal, and ate it. *It made me feel sick.* It was disgusting. The thought of chewing cold, live worms is so repulsive, so distasteful, that it would be *impossible* for me to eat them. It is so abhorrent, I draw on the strength of the word "impossible" to substantiate my claim.

Lying, deception, bearing false witness, etc., are so repulsive to God, so disgusting to Him, so against His holy character, that the Scriptures draw on the strength of the word "impossible" to substantiate the claim. He cannot, could not, and would not lie.

That means that in a world where we are frequently let down, we can totally rely on, trust in, and count on His promises. They are sure, certain, indisputable, true, trustworthy, reliable, faithful, unfailing, dependable, steadfast, and an anchor for the soul. In other words, you can truly believe them, and because of that, you can throw yourself blindfolded and without reserve into His mighty hands. He will *never, ever* let you down. Do you believe that?

Last Words

Casanova, renowned for his self-indulgence, probably ended his life in self-deception. On his deathbed at the age of 73, he said:

"I have lived as a philosopher and die as a Christian."

LESSON 38

Faith, Part 2

"Never be afraid to trust an unknown future to a known God."

CORRIE TEN BOOM

Kirk's Comment It's amazing to me that the people who say they cannot have faith in God because they cannot see Him will still fly in airplanes. Flying requires that you trust your life to two pilots you've never met, who are flying over 500 miles an hour in a tin can with wings, built by people you don't know, and inspected by people you've never seen. Even an atheist has enough "faith" to fly in an airplane and trust in the things he wants to trust in.

QUESTIONS & OBJECTIONS

"I made a commitment, but nothing happened."

Some people don't get past "square one" because they trust in their feelings rather than in God. His promises are true, despite our feelings. If I make a promise to my wife, that promise is true whether she is feeling happy or sad. If she doubts my word, then she brings a slur to my integrity.

Anyone who genuinely repents and trusts in Christ will be saved. The Bible makes this promise: "He that has my commandments, and keeps them, he it is that loves me: and he that loves me shall be loved of my Father, and I will love him, and will manifest myself to him" (John 14:21).

There's the promise, and there's the condition. Any person who loves and obeys Jesus will begin a supernatural relationship with Him and the Father. He said, "And this is life eternal, that they might know you the only true God, and Jesus Christ, whom you have sent" (John 17:3). That doesn't mean you will hear voices or see visions. God will instead make you a new person from within. He will send His Spirit to live within you. You will have a new heart with new desires. You will suddenly become conscious of God and His creation. The Bible will open up to you and become a living Word, and you will have an inner witness that you are saved, that your name is written in heaven, and that death has lost its sting (1 John 5:10–12).

w o t m w o t m w o t m w o t m w o t m w o t m w o t m w o t m w o t m w o t m w o t m

Every Christian should be familiar with the faith experiences of "Christian" and "Hopeful," so richly illustrated in the great classic, *Pilgrim's Progress*. Both Christian and Hopeful left the King's Highway and fell asleep on the grounds of Doubting Castle. Giant Despair woke them and asked what they were doing on his grounds. They replied that they were pilgrims who had lost their way. Giant Despair, being stronger than both of them, drove them into Doubting Castle and threw them into a dungeon that was "very dark, nasty and stinking."

For four long days and nights they lay there until Giant Despair's wife, Diffidence (lack of self-confidence), counseled her husband to beat them without mercy. Giant Despair obeyed his sweet wife and beat them, then advised them to kill themselves (nice guy).

Christian and Hopeful actually considered the suggestion, but the fear of God stopped them.

The next evening, the big fellow returned, furious that they hadn't taken his advice. Mrs. Despair suggested he show Christian and Hopeful a few skeletons they had in their closet. The hen-pecked hulk then took them down to the castle-yard, showed them the bones and skulls of those he had already dispatched, and explained, "These were pilgrims who trespassed on my grounds and I tore them to pieces." The giant made no bones about the fact that he would do the same to them within ten days. Hopeful and Christian decided to pray. Good idea.

After about six hours of prayer, Christian cried, "What a fool I am, thus to live in this stinking dungeon when I may as well walk out in liberty. I have a key in my bosom called 'promise.' That will, I am persuaded, open any lock in Doubting Castle." Christian then pulled out the key, unlocked the door, and they escaped—no doubt the wiser.

What a wonderful allegory of those who doubt the promises of God. How perfectly it describes our own experience. The second our minds doubt the promises of God, Giant Despair appears and begins to beat us without mercy. What fools we are to lie in such a dark, nasty, and stinking dungeon! The moment we take out the key of promise, we find release.

The way to measure the depth of our faith is to see how much joy we retain in tribulation. This fact was illustrated by what appeared to be a life-threatening situation in which Jesus and His disciples found themselves. They were in a boat during a violent storm. While the disciples panicked in fear, Jesus slept. That's the peace that faith produces. The Bible said He also had an "oil of gladness above [His] fellows" (Hebrews 1:9). That's because He lived in absolute faith in His Father. May God help us to have that level of faith.

Imagine that we told you that you would receive a million dollars when you finished this course. Think of it: if you simply complete these lessons, you would get ten thousand $100 bills—all yours. If you truly believed the promise, you would have immediate joy. If you didn't believe it, you would have no joy at all.

If you have faith in the exceedingly great and precious promises of God, you should have instant and exceeding joy—and the joy of the Lord will be your strength. If you have no joy, then you don't believe God's promises—in essence, it means you think God is a liar. So if you are joyless, repent from the grievous sin of having "an evil heart of unbelief." You should be able to say with the apostle Paul, "I am exceedingly joyful in all our tribulation" (2 Corinthians 7:4). The promises of God are still true no matter what the situation in which you find yourself.

QUESTIONS

1. What is the name of the giant in Doubting Castle, and why is his name applicable for those who enter his territory?

2. What is it that tests our faith in God and what is the measure of faith?

3. Why would any of us lose faith in the promises of God?

4. What is the source of our strength to endure any circumstance? (See Nehemiah 8:10.)

5. Name someone in Scripture who slept when others would have been fearful.

FEATHERS FOR ARROWS

Roman prisoners were usually chained with one end fastened around the wrist of their fighting hand, and the other end attached to the wrist of a soldier's left hand. This left the soldier's right arm free in case the prisoner attempted to escape. For greater security the prisoner was sometimes chained to two soldiers, one on each side, as Peter was in Acts 12:6. Meanwhile, "Peter was sleeping"! In a few hours he expected a sting-less death. Like Paul, he didn't count his life dear to himself, so that he might finish his course with joy, and the ministry he has received from the Lord Jesus (see Acts 20:24). In this frame of mind he had fallen asleep, and he slept in perfect peace. Truly this is an example of someone who was eternally minded. Psalm 4:8 says, "I will both lay me down in peace, and sleep: for you, LORD, only make me dwell in safety."

WORDS OF COMFORT

Sue mentioned that an overzealous clock on the kitchen stove was ticking too loudly, so (much to her dismay) I volunteered to fix it. When I pulled it to bits, I noticed that it was run by electricity. All I had to do to stop the ticking was to simply pull out one of the wires.

When I pulled on it, it bent and exposed a small piece of live wire. This was the same stupid stove that had set me on fire, so I decided not to proceed any further. I'm a wise man. The clock had stopped . . . time was standing still. That's all that mattered.

I carefully put the glass back on, which wasn't easy (this was because I had accidentally broken the clips off when I removed it). The face was a little loose, but I had succeeded as a handyman. Job well done.

About two months later, I draped a dish towel over the oven handle and it caught the face of the clock. The towel pulled it back, causing the tiny piece of bare wire to touch some metal. That caused a small explosion with a flash of flame that frightened the living daylights out of me and blew out some of the household appliances. The stove had joined the clock. Now it didn't work. That wouldn't have been too bad, if Sue hadn't been right in the middle of baking chocolate chip squares.

The incident also caused a gas leak bad enough for the gas company to have to come out and shut the gas off.

Memory Verse

"I am crucified with Christ: nevertheless I live; yet not I, but Christ lives in me: and the life which I now live in the flesh I live by the faith of the Son of God, who loved me, and gave himself for me."

GALATIANS 2:20

Last Words

Chrysostom, being led out to exile and death, could triumphantly say:

"Glory to God for all events."

LESSON 39

The Enemy, Part 1

"There was a day when I died, utterly died—died to George Mueller, his opinions, preferences, tastes, and will; died to the world, its approval or censure; died to the approval or blame even of my brethren and friends—and since then I have only to show myself approved to God."

GEORGE MUELLER

Kirk's Comment   Often I fail to see how subtle and crafty the enemy is. A fear of looking like a freak is often the jab he gives me when I want to preach or share my faith with someone. Overcoming fear is a discipline we can learn.

QUESTIONS & OBJECTIONS

"I will wait until I am old, then I will get right with God."

You may not get the chance. God may just lose patience with you and end your life. Perhaps you don't think He would do such a thing. Then read Genesis 38:7 to see how God killed a man because He didn't like something he did. Jesus told of a man who boasted that he had so many goods that he would have to build bigger barns. God called the man a fool and took his life that night.

Those who say they will repent in their own time lack the fear of God. Their understanding of His nature is erroneous. If they caught a glimpse of His holiness, His righteousness, and His consuming justice, they would not trifle with His mercy.

Such arrogance needs to be confronted with the thunders of Mount Sinai. He is not wise who thinks he can outwit his Creator, enjoy a lifetime of sin, and repent at the last minute. Deathbed repentance is very rare. God killed a husband and wife because they told one lie (Acts 5:1–10). He lost patience with them. Most people think that God's patience is eternal. It evidently is not. The Bible says that it is through the fear of the Lord that men depart from sin (Proverbs 16:6). If they don't fear God, they will be complacent about their eternal salvation (Matthew 10:28).

wotm wotm wotm wotm wotm wotm wotm wotm wotm wotm wotm

The moment we exercise repentance toward God and put our faith in the Savior, we step right into the middle of a threefold battle. We find that we are torn by the world, the flesh, and the devil. Let's look at these three resistant enemies.

Our first enemy is the world, which refers to the sinful, rebellious world system. The world loves the darkness and hates the light (John 3:20), and is governed by the "prince of the power of the air" (Ephesians 2:2). The Bible says the Christian has escaped the corruption that is in the world through lust. "Lust" is unlawful desire, and is the life's blood of the world—whether it be the lust for sexual sin, for power, for money, or for material things. Lust is a monster that will never be gratified, so don't feed it. It will grow bigger and bigger until it weighs heavy upon your back, and will be the death of you (James 1:15).

There is nothing wrong with sex, power, money, or material things, but when desire for these becomes predominant, it becomes idolatry. We are told, "Love not the world, neither the things that are in the world. If any man love the world, the love of the Father is not in him"; whoever is "a friend of the world is the enemy of God" (1 John 2:15; James 4:4).

The second enemy is the devil, who is the "god of this world" (2 Corinthians 4:4). He was your spiritual father before you joined the family of God (John 8:44; Ephesians 2:2). Jesus called the devil a thief who came to steal, kill, and destroy (John 10:10).

To overcome him and his demons, make sure you are outfitted with the spiritual armor of God (Ephesians 6:10–20). Become intimately familiar with it. Sleep in it. Never take it off. Bind the sword to your hand so you never lose its grip. The reason for this brings us to the third enemy.

The third enemy is what the Bible calls the "flesh." This is your sinful nature. The only access the enemy has to cause you to sin is through the flesh. Before your conversion, the appetite of the flesh was fully satisfied with the pleasures of sin. Suddenly it is starved to the point of gnawing at the mind for want of food. It causes what the Scriptures call a "war in your members." Thoughts that once were acceptable now stir the alarm of conscience. This battle of the mind is fought against the powerful and corrupt Adamic nature.

The fleshly nature continually wants to sin. If you allow it to do so, it will take the "edge" off your prayer life. No longer will you come before the throne of God with confidence. You will be like Adam, who hid from God because of sin. None of us can afford to let that happen, not only for the sake of our own salvation, but for the sake of the world around us.

You will also see "Adam" pushing through if you have ever been gripped by fear when it comes to personal witnessing, or even handing someone a tract. The Adamic nature wants the approval of men, preferring the praise of men to the praise of God. It is proud and concerned about self rather than the eternal welfare of sinners. Crucified Christians don't care what people think and are not ashamed of the gospel. They care only about the will of God and therefore the salvation of the lost.

Just after a young couple's first child began to walk, he picked up a blanket and adopted it as his "cuddly." He would take that blanket wherever he went. In the usual childlike manner, he would put his thumb and part of his blanket into his mouth and make sucking noises. When his blanket was washed and hung on the clothesline, he would stand beneath it and jump up to try to grab it. The parents felt that they had better try to break his habit before his wedding day, so they cut it in half and gave it to him. The next day, they secretly cut it in half again. Every few days, they would cut it in half, until it became so small it just disappeared.

This is what we are to do with the flesh. It is forever running around like a turkey with its head chopped off. It is dead, but it won't lie down without a little help from the whetted blade of the two-edged sword. The witless creature needs to be gutted, plucked, and its soft flesh carved on the wooden plate of Calvary's cross. That will put thanksgiving in our hearts.

If we deal with our flesh once and for all, the world will have no attraction for us, and the devil will have no foothold in us. It is vital to identify this Judas in our heart. Our old nature is nothing more than a cowardly traitor who will cry "Master, Master," and then betray the Son of God with a kiss. We must hang Judas by the neck until he has "burst asunder in the midst, and all his bowels gushed out" (Acts 1:18). If we do not deal with this enemy, he will quietly steal from us until he betrays us and the cause for which we stand.

To defeat this enemy, we must consider ourselves to be dead to sin, and alive to God. We do this by not allowing sin to reign in our bodies. Rather than obeying its lusts, we must yield ourselves fully to God and offer our bodies to Him as instruments of righteousness (Romans 6:11–13).

QUESTIONS

1. What happens the moment we repent and trust the Savior?

2. How can we overcome our enemy the devil?

3. What is the door of access for sin?

4. **How does sin affect our prayer life?**

5. **What is the source of most fear when it comes to witnessing?**

6. **What must we do to stop the enemy's access?**

PREACHER'S PROGRESS

Homer Sexual: "Why do Christians single out gay people and condemn them?"

Christian: "If they do, they shouldn't."

Homer Sexual: "That's a change. I thought you believed that homosexuals will go to hell."

Christian: "They will, if they refuse to repent and trust Jesus."

Homer Sexual: "So now you're saying that homosexuals will go to hell just because they don't accept Jesus."

Christian: "I didn't say that."

Homer Sexual: "Then what did you say?"

Christian: "I said that, according to the Bible, homosexuals will not enter the kingdom of God; but they are not 'singled out.' Neither will fornicators, adulterers, thieves, or liars. Have you ever lied?"

Homer Sexual: "Yes."

Christian: "Have you ever stolen anything?"

Homer Sexual: "No."

Christian: "I don't believe you, because you just told me that you are a liar. Have you ever stolen anything, in your whole life—even if it was small?"

Homer Sexual: "Yes...I have."

Christian: "So you are a lying thief. If God judges you by the Ten Commandments on the Day of Judgment, will you be innocent or guilty?"

Homer Sexual: "I'd be guilty."

Christian: "Would you go to heaven or hell?"

Homer Sexual: "I guess I would go to hell."

Christian: "Homer, you don't need to guess. The Bible makes it clear that all liars will have their part in the Lake of Fire. Does it concern you that if you died tonight in your sleep, or a drunk driver killed you on the way home, that you would go to hell...forever, with no escape?"

Homer Sexual: "Absolutely."

Last Words

Oscar Wilde (1854–1900), writer:

"My wallpaper and I are fighting a duel to the death. One or the other of us has to go ..."

40 The Enemy, Part 2

"A barracks is meant to be a place where real soldiers were to be fed and equipped for war, not a place to settle down in or as a comfortable snuggery in which to enjoy ourselves. I hope that if ever they, our soldiers, do settle down God will burn their barracks over their heads!"

CATHERINE BOOTH

Kirk's Comment Lust is a favorite and effective tool for the enemy, and the entertainment industry is eager to be a partner in the devil's attacks.

QUESTIONS & OBJECTIONS

"Was it Herod or his wife, Herodias, who wanted to kill John the Baptist?"

Both Matthew 14:1–11 and Mark 6:14–29 state that Herod had John imprisoned because of his wife, Herodias. Although Herod would have liked John dead, he did not want to kill him; Herod was afraid of John because he was righteous and holy and had influence over the people. But, swayed by the enticing dancing of Herodias's daughter, Herod foolishly promised her anything. It was only when the girl (prompted by her mother) asked for John's death that Herod felt compelled to oblige. Therefore it was the underlying influence of Herodias that is the important factor in John's beheading.

Do you have a problem with lust? Hopefully you do. When a Christian doesn't have a battle with it, it may be because he isn't fighting. Maybe he has surrendered to the enemy. If you are fighting daily, know that you are not alone in the battle against the "lust of the flesh, the lust of the eyes, and the pride of life" (1 John 2:16).

Our sex-drive is God-given, and can find satisfaction in marriage. But lust is more than a "drive." It is a vehicle that overtakes the driver. It straps him in, locks the doors, and takes over the wheel. It steers him onto a fatal collision course with the Law of God. Lust is a spark in the eye that will start a fire in the heart if we don't put it out as soon as we detect its presence. In almost every case where Scripture details specific sins, sexual sin is at the top of the list. Sin, especially sexual sin, draws us as a moth to a flame. Scripture speaks of being "hardened through the *deceitfulness* of sin" (Hebrews 3:13). The Amplified Bible puts the same verse this way: "hardened through the trickery which the delusive glamour of his sin may play on him." Sin has a delusive glamour to it. The old saying "as miserable as sin" just isn't true. The person who said it probably also said, "Crime doesn't pay." Moses chose to suffer affliction with the people of God, rather than *enjoy* the pleasures of sin for a season. Sin is enjoyable. I have walked the streets of New York and have noticed that porn stores don't have to do too much advertising. All they need is a peephole for perverts.

The domain for the battle is your mind. *If you have a mind to*, you will be attracted to the world and all its sin. The mind is the control panel for the eyes and the ears, the center of your appetites. We think of sin before we commit it. James 1:15 warns that lust brings forth sin, and sin when it's conceived brings forth death. Impure thoughts fill the room of the mind with lethal gas, and all it takes is an ember of opportunity to create a disaster. Sin holds a deep-rooted charm for our sin-full nature, but carries the sting of death with it. Lust is a landmine hidden in the dirt of the world. Keep out of the world or you will end up maimed by it. People in the world stomp around in dirt and wonder what hits them when things blow up in their face.

Every day of life, we have a choice. To sin or not to sin—that is the question. The answer is the fear of God. If you don't fear God, you will sin to your sinful heart's delight.

Did you know that God kills people? He killed a man for what he did sexually (Genesis 38:9,10), killed another man for being greedy (Luke 12:15–21), and killed a husband and wife for lying (Acts 5:1–10). Knowledge of God's goodness—His righteous judgments against evil—should put the fear of God in us and help us not to indulge in sin.

If you have a desire to reach the lost, know that you will be a target of the enemy. So be very careful when it comes to what you look at. So much of the world's entertainment is designed to stir up lust…and it is easy to stir it up because it is pleasurable to the sinful human heart. Like Job, make a covenant with your eyes not to look with lust upon a young woman (Job 31:1).

One great tool of the devil is idle hands. Do nothing and you can be sure the enemy will do something with you…it won't be long until your mind wanders into forbidden territory. So do something with your brain. Fill it with activity. Join a club (golf or anything where you break free from the Christian environment) so that you can rub shoulders with the world. Either that, or find yourself a "fishing hole"—somewhere where sinners sit and nibble their lunch outdoors. Go there to strike up conversations with the unsaved. If you can't find a fishing hole, make a video for your church on what people don't like about the church. Perhaps you could take a video camera to a university to interview students. You are sure to get a few bites with that subject. Don't forget to take tracts with you and give them to those you meet.

A great preacher once said that we may not be able to stop birds flying over our head, but we can certainly stop them making a nest in our hair. One way to do that is to always be abounding in the labor of the Lord.

QUESTIONS

1. **What could be the case if a Christian does not have a battle with lust?**

2. How does the sex drive differ from lust?

3. What quality does the Bible say exemplifies sin?

4. Is it true that people who are sinful are usually miserable?

5. When are we a target for the enemy?

6. What is one great tool that the enemy likes to exploit?

7. How can we avoid lust?

PREACHER'S PROGRESS

Christian: "Hello, ma'am. How are you doing?"

Izzy Backyet: "Good."

Christian: "Did you get one of these?"

Izzy Backyet: "What is it?"

Christian: "It's a gospel tract.

Izzy Backyet: "Oh…"

Christian: "Do you have a Christian background?"

Izzy Backyet: "Actually, I was brought up in a Christian home. All of my family are Christians."

Christian: "How about you?"

Izzy Backyet: "I used to be…sort of."

Christian: "What do you mean?"

Izzy Backyet: "I gave my heart to Jesus, out of fear."

Christian: "Fear of God?"

Izzy Backyet: "Sort of. I am really scared of the Second Coming. Whenever I do something I know is wrong, I have this thought in my mind that He could come back at any minute."

Christian: "What's stopping you from getting right with God?"

Izzy Backyet: "My boyfriend."

Christian: "How is he's stopping you?"

Izzy Backyet: "We're living together."

Christian: "You mean you're having sex outside of marriage?"

Izzy Backyet: "Yes."

Christian: "Do you know that fornicators will not enter the kingdom of God?"

Izzy Backyet: "I know that."

Christian: "Listen to this, Izzy: A father went to the bank and purchased a brand new twenty-dollar bill to give to his son. During the night, the son crept into his dad's room and stole the money out of his dad's wallet. He took something that was going to be his—something good—and made it something bad. That's what you did with God's gift of sex. It was

263

yours anyway, in the bonds of marriage, and you turned something good into something bad. And the problem with giving your heart to Jesus was that you had fear without the knowledge of sin. This left you without any sorrow for your sin (contrition), which is necessary for true repentance. Let me ask you a question. Do you consider yourself to be a good person?"

Izzy Backyet: "Basically, I am."

Christian: "Let me give you a test to see if that's true, using the Ten Commandments. Is that okay?"

Izzy Backyet: "Okay . . ."

FEATHERS FOR ARROWS

African natives found an effective way to capture monkeys. They would hollow out a coconut, cut a small hole in one end, and drop in four or five stones. They would then secure the coconut to the ground and wait for a victim to come along.

It wasn't long until a curious monkey saw the coconut with the hole in it. He would put his hand into the hole and grab the stones. The monkey then wouldn't be able to pull his hand out as long as he held onto the stones and he wouldn't let the stones drop out of his hands because he was curious to see what they were. The natives would sneak up behind the creature and *whack!*—monkey soup.

The devil has an effective way of dragging sinners to hell. He knows that many will hold onto sin, even if it means the death of them. Encourage sinners to come to their senses—to let go of sin and escape the power of death.

Last Words

Woodrow Wilson (1856–1924), twenty-eighth President of the U.S., said when he died:

> **"I am ready."**

41

The Enemy, Part 3

"When people inquire as to the relevance of our gospel, we must not be tricked into going on the defensive. We must immediately take the offensive, for our Lord Himself has promised that the gates of hell shall not withstand the assault of His Church."

DR. LEIGHTON FORD

Kirk's Comment The enemy is extremely smart and persuasive. He knows how to find our weakness and attack us there without mercy. We must put on the full armor of God and live not by sight, but by faith.

QUESTIONS & OBJECTIONS

"Didn't Jesus pray to the Father to prevent the crucifixion?"

Matthew 26:39, Mark 14:36, and Luke 22:42 are parallel passages that take place in the Garden of Gethsemane just before Jesus' arrest. In all these passages Jesus never asks for the crucifixion to be prevented, but does express His fears of the difficulties, pain, and suffering that He will encounter over the next few hours. He will be enduring His trials, beatings, whippings, loneliness, alienation from people and from God on the cross, the ordeal of crucifixion itself, and the upcoming triumph over Satan. He does, however, more importantly ask for God's will to be carried out over the next few hours knowing that this is the means by which

He will die and rise again, and by doing so atone for all the sins of the world.

In John 12:27, which takes place before the circumstances described above, Jesus is speaking to a crowd during the Passover Festival at the Temple in Jerusalem (before the gathering of the Twelve with Jesus at the Upper Room). On this occasion, Jesus again says something very similar to the passages above: "Now my heart is troubled, and what shall I say? 'Father save me from this hour'? No it was for this very reason that I came to this hour. Father, glorify your name!"

Again we are reminded that Jesus is feeling troubled. He knows that events are fast unfolding around Him. Is it really conceivable that this Man wants to prevent the crucifixion from taking place? I think not! As He stated, this is the very reason that He came to earth—to give His life as a ransom for many.

wotmwotmwotmwotmwotmwotmwotmwotmwotmwotmwotm

God is calling each soldier in His army to become personally involved in the battle to win this world for Christ. No longer can we rely solely upon great preachers to do our fighting for us. Billy Graham said, "Mass crusades, to which I have committed my life, will never finish the job; but one to one will."

The answer to the dilemma of how to reach the unsaved is for each of us to do battle right in our workplace, to rub shoulders with those held captive by the enemy. Each of us has a unique sphere of influence.

As Christians we are called to follow Jesus and be "fishers of men." If we are not preaching the Word in season and out of season, it is probably because we are following at too great a distance. We can neither see His example nor hear His voice. Those who follow close to the Master will know His voice. They will obey it and be true and faithful witnesses.

If you are going to do anything for the kingdom of God, be ready for unexpected abuse. This may come through a Christian brother or sister —the place least expected. Satan spoke directly through Peter in an attempt to stop Jesus from doing the will of the Father. It was David's elder brother who tried to discourage him from slaying Goliath.

A zealous Christian once had a conversation with his mother that totally discouraged him from seeking the lost. She was his own flesh and blood, and he listened to her speak nothing but discouragement for over an hour. She told him of his foolishness in wanting to preach when he hadn't even been through seminary. Who was he to go around telling people about their need of Christ, when he wasn't even trained to be a minister! Words of death went right into his heart and stole his courage. He lost his zeal, his direction, and his desire to do anything for the kingdom of God. It was only when he gave himself to prayer that he realized Satan's subtlety. The enemy will stop at nothing to get you back into the barracks of your local church building. He wants you worshiping God and ignoring His will. He will use any mouthpiece available, and there are plenty of willing lips. Jesus told us to watch out for this: "What I say to you I say to all, Watch" (Mark 13:37).

Satan will often withhold an attack until you are in a place of vulnerability. He will not strike when you are full of faith and power, but when you are tired, fasting, or carrying a problem on your shoulders. If you witness or preach open-air, you may be approached by a Christian brother or sister who will say things like, "You're doing a fine job, but do you think you are really doing any good?" They will tell you that you should just be living the Christian life rather than confronting people about their sin.

Satan has no mercy. He will stomp on you when you are down and dig his grimy heel into the back of your neck. *Don't listen to his lies!* Satan hates you and has a rotten plan for your life. Your downfall is his delight. So, keep your shield of faith held high and "watch."

We should love the word en*courage*ment. Robert Louis Stevenson said, "Keep your fears to yourself but share your courage with others." This was clearly illustrated in the lives of Joshua and Caleb, who had positive, hopeful, valiant, courageous, optimistic spirits. This is also called "faith."

If we can't say something positive, we shouldn't say anything. The children of Israel were told not to speak as they walked around the walls of Jericho. What they were doing was foolish. They were opening themselves to the ridicule of the enemy. It would have been hard to say anything positive, but when they did say something, it brought the downfall of the enemy, not their brethren. Let's be the same. May we never be a vehicle of the enemy, and may each of us be ready to lift our shield high so that subtle words of discouragement are deflected from their target.

QUESTIONS

1. What is God calling each of us to do?

2. What did Billy Graham say about the means of evangelism?

3. If we are not "fishers of men," what could be the problem?

4. Through what source does Satan sometimes attack us?

5. At what point does Satan usually attack?

6. What were the children of Israel not allowed to do as they walked around Jericho?

7. How should Christians use their shield of faith?

FEATHERS FOR ARROWS

Recently two boys who were fishing tried to cross a swift stream. As they did so, a log knocked them both into deeper water. One made it to the riverbank but the other got into difficulty. A man saw him, dived in, and after a long while fighting the current, got the exhausted boy to the edge of the riverbank. With both of his arms lifting the lad, he tossed him onto the bank. A woman grabbed the boy, and then watched as the man sunk down into the water. She thought he was swimming to the shore. He came up once more, then drowned. Tragically, he gave his all in saving the boy, and had nothing left to save himself.

Imagine relating that story to someone without giving the details preceding it: "A man drowned in a river today." The truth is that the danger the boy was in, due to the swiftness of the current, led the man to give his all, showing what love he had for the boy.

WORDS OF COMFORT

Many years ago, as our family was about to start a meal at a friend's house, our five-year-old child said in a clear voice, "Dad, I don't like this food. When are we going home?"

I read of a similar incident where a mother and her young daughter were visiting their neighbor when the little girl asked if she could see her neighbor's newly painted bedroom. The woman was quite taken aback that she was interested, so the three of them went into the bedroom. When they stepped into the room, the little girl turned to her mother and said in that clear voice children reserve for such occasions, "Mom, it doesn't make *me* sick!"

Last Words

Anna M. Shurman, who passed away in 1678, was a German artist and scholar whose works were of high repute. She was likewise a humble believer and as she died bore this testimony:

> **"I have proceeded one step farther toward eternity, and if the Lord shall be pleased to increase my pains, it will be no cause of sorrow to me."**

The Enemy, Part 4

"Satan, the God of all dissension, stirreth up daily new sects, and last of all, which of all other I should never have foreseen or once suspected, he has raised up a sect such as teach . . . that men should not be terrified by the Law, but gently exhorted by the preaching of the grace of Christ."

MARTIN LUTHER

Kirk's Comment While not everyone is called to be a full-time evangelist, all genuine followers of Christ have the indwelling Holy Spirit who cannot rest while sinners are perishing. He urges every Christian to seek and save the lost, and no true believer will fail to respond in some way. Understanding the enemy's propaganda will help us faithfully complete our mission.

QUESTIONS & OBJECTIONS

"The Bible says 'an eye for an eye,' encouraging us to take the law into our own hands by avenging wrongdoing."

This verse is so often misquoted by the world. Many believe it is giving a license to take matters into our own hands and render evil for evil. In reality, it is referring to civil law concerning restitution. If someone steals your ox, he is to restore the ox. If someone steals and wrecks your car, he is to buy you another one . . . a car for a car, an eye for an eye, a tooth for a tooth.

The spirit of what Jesus is saying here is radically different from the "sue the shirt off the back of your neighbor" society in which we live.

w o t m w o t m w o t m w o t m w o t m w o t m w o t m w o t m w o t m w o t m w o t m

Our enemy has many names. The devil is called the god and prince of this world, and the ruler of darkness (2 Corinthians 4:4; John 12:31; Acts 26:18; Ephesians 6:12). He is the promoter of pride (Genesis 3:5; 1 Timothy 3:6), the stimulator of lust (Ephesians 2:2,3), and the tempter (Luke 4:1–13). Satan seeks to hinder God's work and suppress His Word (Matthew 13:38,39; 1 Thessalonians 2:18).

The Scriptures speak of the gospel as being light, and the sinner as being in darkness. Second Corinthians 4:3,4 says that "the god of this world has blinded the minds of them which believe not, lest the light of the glorious gospel of Christ, who is the image of God, should shine to them." The Bible tells us that the lost have their "understanding darkened, being alienated from the life of God through the ignorance that is in them, because of the blindness of their heart" (Ephesians 4:18).

This is why it is so vital to use the Law of God when witnessing: "For by the law is the knowledge of sin" (Romans 3:20). Remember that Paul said, "I had not known sin, but by the Law" (Romans 7:7). As the sinner begins to see himself according to the Law of God, it gives him something by which to measure himself. He begins to understand what sin is. He will only call for mercy when he understands that he *needs* to call for mercy. Satan hates for Christians to grasp the reason why God gave His Law. He knows that when they work with the Holy Spirit and use the Law to convince and convict men of sin, there will be more soldiers enlisted in the army of God. A sinner's decision to follow Jesus will then not be made in blindness, nor from an emotional response, but from a clear understanding of the issues of salvation. That why the god of this world so hates the Law and particularly its use in reaching the lost.

Those who preach judgment, but fail to use the Law to give the sinner something to measure himself by, will produce either a spurious convert or one who lacks gratitude. If hell alone is preached, those who come to a decision do so solely out of fear, and not out of repentance. They flee from the wrath to come but deep in their heart they consider God to be unjust. They don't see themselves worthy of hell because they haven't seen sin as being "exceedingly sinful," which comes only by the Commandment (see Romans 7:13). This state of deception hides from sinners the true nature of Calvary's cross. They fail to truly see it as an expression of God's love for undeserving sinners.

Our enemy, Satan, is also a counterfeiter. He has created a massive religious system that masquerades as God's representative on earth: "For such are false apostles, deceitful workers, transforming themselves into the apostles of Christ. And no marvel; for Satan himself is transformed into an angel of light. Therefore it is no great thing if his ministers also be transformed as the ministers of righteousness; whose end shall be according to their works" (2 Corinthians 11:13–15).

Because Satan can disguise himself as an angel of light, it is vital for us to exercise godly discernment. We are to judge prophecy, test the spirits, walk in wisdom, watch for wolves, mark those causing division in the ranks, and look for the fruit of genuine conversion.

The enemy is also called a devourer and our adversary (1 Peter 5:8). The Greek word for "adversary" is *antidikos*, which primarily means an opponent in a lawsuit (accuser). We are exhorted to resist him steadfast in the faith, taking consolation that other Christians are involved in the very same battle.

Satan is a liar, the father of lies, and a murderer (John 8:44). Fear is perhaps the most subtle of his lies. It is a continual hindrance to us doing what we know we should. For instance, would you find it difficult to preach in the open air? Could you give a tract to the person behind you in a supermarket line? Do you fight fear? Most of us do. The thought of front-line (or even back-line) battle paralyzes us. We are therefore going to cut away the lies so that we have a clear path to do God's will.

Here are some more questions. Would you like to try bungee jumping? Many Christians would. Ask any congregation how many would like to try skydiving. Hands will shoot up. How many like roller coasters? Most *love* them. What it is that they like? It's the fear, the adrenaline rush. There have been cases where people have bungee jumped and the bungee cord has come untied. A teenager from a youth group tried the thrill of skydiving, and her parachute twisted. *She fell to her death at the age of 17.*

She was the one in every 100,000 who fall to their deaths. You may have seen on television an incident where a 13-year-old boy tried skydiving. He became so paralyzed by fear that he didn't pull the ripcord, and for some unknown reason, his automatic emergency chute didn't open. He fell 2,000 feet to his death. Between 1973 and 1996 there were 45 deaths in the U.S. from roller-coaster-type rides, and over 6,000 injuries.

Think of it. We are prepared to put our lives on the line—*to risk death*—for the love of fear. But for the *fear* of fear, we are prepared to let sinners go the hell forever.

What then is the difference between the two fears? One we love, one we hate. One is a thrill, the other a torment. The tormenting fear that we feel is very real, yet the reason for this fear is irrational. You will experience it almost every time you give out a tract, or when you strike up a conversation with a stranger with the objective of sharing your faith. Yet when you rationalize the feeling, it is totally *unfounded* fear. There is nothing to fear, but the next time it manifests, it is just as strong.

How then do we overcome it? Simply by realizing that the fear we feel in our hearts is a barometer of the truth we hold in our hands. God has not given us the spirit of fear, so it is obvious where the "tormenting" fear is coming from. *It is enemy propaganda.* We wrestle not against flesh and blood, but against spiritual wickedness (see Ephesians 6:12). The origin of our fear is not from within our hearts, it is from the hosts of hell. So don't listen to it. Become deaf to the enemy's whispering and blind to his will. Set your thoughts on the welfare of the sinner and the will of the Father, and let love swallow your fear.

QUESTIONS

1. **Why can't unbelievers see the light of the gospel?**

2. Why is the unbeliever's understanding darkened?

3. What can Satan disguise himself as?

4. What else is Satan called?

5. Why does the enemy hate that Christians use the Law in witnessing?

6. If preaching fails to present the standard of the Law, what might happen?

7. What has Satan created as a substitute for God's true Church?

PREACHER'S PROGRESS

Christian: "How are you doing?"

Iva Lotasin: "Fine."

Christian: "Did you get one of these?"

Iva Lotasin: "What is it?"

Christian: "It's a gospel tract."

Iva Lotasin: "Oh."

Christian: "Do you have a Christian background?"

Iva Lotasin: "Yep. I used to go to church but I kind of grew out of it."

Christian: "Do you see your need of God's forgiveness?"

Iva Lotasin: "Yes, sir. I'm a really bad sinner. Really bad."

Christian: "So you've broken all of the Ten Commandments."

Iva Lotasin: "Every one of them...and probably a lot more. Yep, I'm a real bad sinner."

Christian: "Why are you smiling then? Let's go through a few of those Commandments and see if you are as bad as you say. Have you ever told a lie?"

Iva Lotasin: "One or two."

Christian: "What does that make you?"

Iva Lotasin: "A really bad person."

Christian: "No. What would you call me if I told lies?"

Iva Lotasin: "A liar."

Christian: "So what are you?"

Iva Lotasin: "A...liar."

Christian: "Have you ever stolen anything?"

Iva Lotasin: "Just small things."

Christian: "Like diamonds?"

Iva Lotasin: "No. Just things not worth much."

Christian: "So what does that make you?"

Iva Lotasin: "A thief."

Christian: "So you are a lying thief. You were right. You are in big trouble on Judgment Day. God has seen every sin you have ever committed and all that sin will come out as evidence of your guilt on what the Bible calls 'the Day of Wrath.' Do you have a Bible at home?"

Iva Lotasin: "Yes, sir."

Christian: "Please read it, starting with the Gospel of John. There's nothing more important than your eternal salvation..."

Last Words

John Bacon, the British sculptor of great ability who died in 1799, left the following self-composed inscription for his tombstone:

> **"What I was as an artist seemed to me of some importance while I lived, but what I really was as a believer in Christ Jesus is the thing of importance to me now."**

Memory Verse

"Submit yourselves therefore to God. Resist the devil, and he will flee from you. Draw near to God, and he will draw near to you. Cleanse your hands, you sinners; and purify your hearts, you double minded."

JAMES 4:7,8

LESSON 43

Prayer

"The reason why many fail in battle is because they wait until the hour of battle. The reason why others succeed is because they have gained their victory on their knees long before the battle came... Anticipate your battles; fight them on your knees before temptation comes, and you will always have victory."

R. A. TORREY

Kirk's Comment   I admit that I don't pray as much as I should. Prayer is the power behind everything we do. No prayer, no power. With prayer, God does miracles.

QUESTIONS & OBJECTIONS

"Did Simon Peter find out that Jesus was the Christ by a revelation from heaven (Matthew 16:17), or by his brother Andrew (John 1:41)?"

The emphasis of Matthew 16:17 is that Simon did not just hear it from someone else—God had made it clear to him. That does not preclude him being told by other people. Jesus' point is that Peter was not simply repeating what someone else had said. He had lived and worked with Jesus and he was now clear in his mind that Jesus was none other than the Christ (Messiah), the Son of the Living God. Jesus did not ask, "Who have you heard that I am?" but, "Who do you say I am?" There is all the difference in the world between these two questions, and Peter was no longer in any doubt.

wotmwotmwotmwotmwotmwotmwotmwotmwotmwotmwotm

Ephesians chapter 6 tells us that a great weapon of the soldier of Christ is prayer. It is the line of communication we have with Headquarters. It is by that line that we request supplies for the troops—ammunition, food, medical aid, etc. This is why it is essential to keep the communication line open, free from interference and from Satanic static. Sin interferes with earth-to-heaven communication.

For the soldier of Christ, true prayer should be a way of life, not just a call for help in the heat of battle. This is made very clear in Scripture:

- Romans 12:12: "Continuing instant [steadfast] in prayer."

- Ephesians 6:18: "Praying always..."

- Colossians 4:2: "Continue in prayer..."

- 1 Thessalonians 5:17: "Pray without ceasing."

God loves His children coming to Him in the intimate communion of prayer. The Scriptures tell us, "The prayer of the upright is his delight" (Proverbs 15:8). Since prayer is our lifeline to God, to not pray is an insult to Him. Ben Jennings wrote, "Every prayerless day is a statement by a helpless individual, 'I do not need God today.' Failing to pray reflects idolatry—a trust in substitutes for God. We rely on our money instead of God's provision. We rest on our own flawed thinking rather than on God's perfect wisdom. We take charge of our lives rather than trusting God. Prayerlessness short-circuits the working of God. Neglecting prayer, therefore, is not a weakness; it is a sinful choice."

Hardly a day goes by when I don't beseech God for wisdom. I *need* the wisdom of God. The Scriptures say, "He that gets wisdom loves his own soul" (Proverbs 19:8). If you have wisdom from above, you *will* seek to save souls. If you have wisdom, you will see the traps set by the enemy, you will encourage other Christians with insights from the Word, and you will cut sinners to the heart with the wisdom of God.

It has been said that he who is a stranger to prayer will also be a stranger to God's power. The great missionary Hudson Taylor said, "The prayer power has never been tried to its full capacity. If we want to see mighty works of Divine power and grace wrought in the place of weakness, failure and disappointment, let us answer God's standing challenge, 'Call to me, and I will answer you, and show you great and mighty things, which you do not know'" (Jeremiah 33:3).

Let us never face a day in battle until we have faced the Father in prayer. John Bunyan stated, "Prayer is a shield to the soul, a delight to God, and a scourge to Satan." Someone once said that Satan trembles when he sees the feeblest Christian on his knees. How utterly convicting are the words of Martin Luther: "I have so much to do [today] that I should spend the first three hours in prayer." Luther was a monk, and therefore had the time to spend in prayer, but we can see the principle of what he was saying: Seek first the kingdom of God.

A man was once cutting a tree stump with an obviously blunt axe. He was only bruising the bark as sweat poured from his beaded brow. Someone suggested that he stop for a moment and sharpen the axe, to which he replied, "I'm too busy chopping the tree to stop for anything." If he would only stop for a moment and sharpen the axe, he would be able to slice through the tree with far greater ease.

Stop at the beginning of each day to "sharpen the axe" through prayer. Seek first the kingdom of God and you will slice through that day with far greater ease.

How to Pray

God always answers prayer. Sometimes He says yes; sometimes He says no; and sometimes He says, "Wait for a minute." And since to the Lord a thousand years is the same as a day (2 Peter 3:8), that could mean a ten-year wait for us. So ask in faith, but rest in peace-filled patience.

Surveys show that more than 90 percent of Americans pray daily. No doubt they pray for health, wealth, happiness, etc. They also pray when grandma gets sick, and when grandma doesn't get better (or dies), many end up disillusioned or bitter. This is because they don't understand what the Bible says about prayer. It teaches, among other things, that our sin will keep God from even hearing our prayer (Psalm 66:18), and that if we pray with doubt, we will not get an answer (James 1:6,7).

Here's how to be heard:

- Pray with faith (Hebrews 11:6).

- Pray with clean hands and a pure heart (Psalm 24:3,4).

- Pray genuine heartfelt prayers, rather than vain repetitions (Matthew 6:7).

- Make sure that you are praying to the God revealed in the Scriptures (Exodus 20:3–6).

1. *How do you "pray with faith"?* Someone once told me, "Ray, you're a man of great faith in God," thinking they were paying me a compliment. They weren't. What if I said to you, "I'm a man of great faith in my doctor"? It's a compliment to the doctor. If I have great faith in him, it means that I see him as being a man of integrity, a man of great ability—that he is trustworthy. I give "glory" to the man through my faith in him. The Bible says that Abraham "staggered not at the promise of God through unbelief; but was strong in faith, giving glory to God; and being fully persuaded that, what he had promised, he was able also to perform" (Romans 4:20,21). Abraham was a man of great faith in God. Remember, that is not a compliment to Abraham. He merely caught a glimpse of God's incredible ability, His impeccable integrity, and His wonderful faithfulness to keep every promise He makes. Abraham's faith gave "glory" to a faithful God.

As far as God is concerned, if you belong to Jesus, you are a VIP. You can boldly come before the throne of grace (Hebrews 4:16). You have access to the King because you are the son or daughter of the King. When you were a child, did you have to grovel to get your needs met by your parents? I hope not.

So when you pray, don't say, "Oh God, I hope you will supply my needs." Instead, say something like, "Father, thank You that You keep every promise You make. Your Word says that You will supply all my needs according to Your riches in glory by Christ Jesus. Therefore, I thank You that You will do this thing for my family. I ask this in the wonderful name of Jesus. Amen."

2. *How do you get "clean hands and a pure heart"?* Simply by confessing your sins to God through Jesus Christ, whose blood cleanses from all sin (1 John 1:7–9). God will not only forgive your every sin, He promises to forget them (Hebrews 8:12). Based on the sacrifice of the Savior, He will justify you—just as if you had never sinned. He will make you pure in His sight—sinless. He will even "purge" your conscience, so that you will no longer have a sense of guilt that you sinned. That's what it means to be "justified by faith." That's why you need to soak yourself in Holy Scripture; read the letters to the churches and see the wonderful things God has done for us through the cross of Calvary. If you don't bother to read the "will," you won't have any idea what has been given to you.

3. *How do you pray "genuine heartfelt prayers"?* Simply by keeping yourself in the love of God. If the love of God is in you, you will never pray hypocritical or selfish prayers. Just talk to your heavenly Father as candidly and intimately as a young child, nestled on Daddy's lap, would talk to his earthly father. How would you feel if every day your child pulled out a pre-written statement to dryly recite to you, rather than pouring out the events and emotions of that day? God wants to hear from your heart. When your prayer-life is pleasing to God, He will reward you openly (Matthew 6:6).

4. *How do you know you're praying to "the God revealed in Scripture"?* Study the Word. Don't accept the image of God portrayed by the world, even though it appeals to the natural mind. A kind, gentle Santa Claus figure, dispensing good things with no sense of justice or truth, appeals to guilty sinners. Look to the thunderings and lightnings of Mount Sinai. Gaze at Jesus on the cross of Calvary—hanging in unspeakable agony because of the justice of a holy God. Such thoughts tend to banish idolatry.

To inspire you to daily go before the throne of grace, let this description of transforming prayer, by Alvin J. Vander Griend, encourage you:

> Prayer can move mountains. It can change human hearts, families, neighborhoods, cities, and nations. It's the ultimate source of power because it is, in reality, the power of Almighty God.
>
> Prayer can do what political action cannot, what education cannot, what military might cannot, and what planning committees cannot. All these are impotent by comparison.

By prayer the kingdom of God is built, and by prayer the kingdom of Satan is destroyed. Where there is no prayer, there are no great works, and there is no building of the kingdom. Where there is much prayer and fervent prayer, there are great gains for the kingdom: God's rule is established, His power is directed, His will is done, society is transformed, lost persons are saved, and saints are enabled to "stand against the devil's schemes" (Eph. 6:11). If that isn't enough to compel us to "devote [ourselves] to prayer" and "always [wrestle] in prayer" (Col. 4:2,12), I don't know what is!

QUESTIONS

1. **Why do we need to pray?**

2. **What does the Bible say about how often we should pray?**

3. **According to Ben Jennings, what does prayerlessness reflect?**

4. **How does God feel about our prayers?**

5. **How can we make sure our prayers are heard?**

6. **How much time do you spend in prayer each day?**

Memory Verse

"This is the confidence that we have in him, that, if we ask any thing according to his will, he hears us."

1 JOHN 5:14

FEATHERS FOR ARROWS

In Leviticus 26:1–13, God promises Israel many wonderful blessings if they would simply obey Him: the rain would come in due season; the land would yield its harvest and the trees would yield their fruit; their food would satisfy them; they would have peace and safety in the land (no violence); and they would prevail over their enemies. Truly, blessed is the nation whose God is the Lord.

Daniel Webster said, "If we abide by the principles taught in the Bible, our country will go on prospering and to prosper; but if we and our posterity neglect its instructions and authority, no man can tell how sudden a catastrophe may overwhelm us and bury all our glory in profound obscurity."

Last Words

Ignatius, in the arena, before the lions had reached him, said:

"I am the wheat of Christ; I am going to be ground with the teeth of wild beasts, that I may be found pure bread."

LESSON 44

The Survivor's Guide

"Suppose a nation in some distant region should take the Bible for their only law book, and every member should regulate his conduct by the precepts there exhibited! Every member would be obligated in conscience, to temperance, frugality, and industry; to justice, kindness and charity towards his fellow men; and to piety, love, and reverence toward Almighty God... What a Utopia, what a paradise would this region be."

JOHN ADAMS

Kirk's Comment I love reading the Bible. It is without a doubt my favorite book to read and my survival guide for life—both this one and the one to come.

QUESTIONS & OBJECTIONS

"God couldn't forgive my sin."

Those who think they are too sinful for God to accept them don't understand how merciful God is. The Bible says that He is "rich in mercy" (Ephesians 2:4). The Scriptures also tell us that "the mercy of the Lord is from everlasting to everlasting upon them that fear him" (Psalm 103:17). God was merciful to King David and forgave him when he committed adultery and murder. He forgave Moses when he committed murder. He also forgave Saul of Tarsus for murdering Christians (Acts 22:4). God promises to save "all" who call upon the name of Jesus (Romans 10:13). Those who think this promise isn't worth the paper it's written on are calling God a liar (see 1 John 5:10). Jesus shed His precious blood to pay for their sins. Wasn't it good enough for them? It was good enough for God. God commands them to repent. To offer any excuse is to remain in rebellion to His command—no matter how "noble" it may seem to say that they are too sinful.

wotmwotmwotmwotmwotmwotmwotmwotmwotmwotmwotm

In the well-known movie *Castaway*, a high-powered FedEx manager found himself marooned on a deserted island. Some of the packages from his crashed plane had washed up on the shore, so the lone survivor began going through each package, opening them and retrieving what he could to help him survive on the island. He found a pair of ice skates, which he made into a knife, as well as a number of other helpful items. However, he decided not to open one of the boxes, but kept it in the hope that one day he would be rescued and be able to hand-deliver it to its owner.

One of the film's climaxes was his intense battle to create fire. He rubbed sticks together for hours until finally there was smoke, followed by a small flame, and then a fire. The ecstatic castaway danced and sang for joy around his homemade bonfire.

For the next four years the poor man lived in a cave. He struggled with loneliness to the point of almost losing his mind. He caught fish with a sharpened wooden pole, and survived by eating coconuts and crabs. At one point he was so plagued with an agonizing toothache, he was driven to smash a large rock into the end of the ice skates to knock the tooth out. The pain was so great that he passed out.

He finally left the island on a homemade raft and was discovered—almost out of his mind and near death—by a passing ship.

He arrived back in the States to discover that his beloved girlfriend thought that he had died and therefore had married another. The movie ended with the heartbroken survivor hand-delivering the unopened package to its owner, the audience still not being privy to its contents.

Here's what the package may have contained: Novocain, a flare gun, a satellite cellular telephone, a blanket, a compass, a cave liner, an inflatable bed, a life preserver, waterproof matches, batteries, a first-aid kit, a solar-powered battery charger, a Swiss army knife, sunglasses, sunscreen, and a coconut- and crab-cracker.

Have you opened the package that God gave you in His Word? Or are you like the many who don't see the Bible as the ultimate Survivor's Guide? It contains all things necessary for godliness and tells us how to survive not only in this life, but also in the next. We are assured that "his divine power has given to us all things that pertain to life and godliness, through the knowledge of him that has called us to glory and virtue" (2 Peter 1:3). The Bible tells us how to hold on to faith and a good conscience, so that we don't shipwreck our faith (1 Timothy 1:19).

God's Word will also teach you how to be a fisher of men. It will even place in your hand the rod of the Law of God, to get the point across to sinners. There are two pieces of wood that two thousand years ago were joined together. They can start a fire in the coldest of hearts, and that fire will burn for eternity. The Bible tells us how to use faith to produce a joy that will carry us through life. It will teach us how to deal with the pains of everyday living, and how to have all our needs supplied in Christ. The psalmist exclaimed, "I rejoice at your word, as one that finds great spoil" (Psalm 119:162). The Scriptures are full of unspeakable riches.

The Word of God even provides us with the way to have a hotline to heaven so that if we find ourselves shipwrecked by life, there is deliverance through faith in Jesus who loved us and gave Himself for us.

Those who fail to open the wealth of God's Word are liable to fall into "many foolish and hurtful lusts" (1 Timothy 6:9). Let's feed on the Bible and heed the words of the apostle Paul, who said, "But I keep under my body, and bring it into subjection: lest that by any means, when I have preached to others, I myself should be a castaway" (1 Corinthians 9:27).

QUESTIONS

1. List three "survival" techniques that you have learned through opening the Bible.

2. What has God given us, according to 2 Peter 1:3?

3. How can the Bible help us avoid shipwrecking our faith?

4. Over what did the psalmist rejoice?

5. What did Paul bring into subjection, and why did he do so?

6. What do you think Paul meant by bringing his body into subjection?

PREACHER'S PROGRESS

Christian: "Hi. How are you doing?"

Joe King: "Fine...I heard you talking about sin. I don't think God has any right to condemn us for lust."

Christian: "Why is that?"

Joe King: "Because He made us like this."

Christian: "You've got to be joking. Even though you were made by God, He still holds you responsible for your actions."

Joe King: "That's not right. If a toy is faulty, you take it back to the manufacturer. It's his responsibility."

Christian: "That would make sense if you were a toy. But you are a moral human being. You have a conscience that tells you when you do wrong."

Joe King: "Well, I think that is wrong."

Christian: "No criminal is going to be happy when the law catches him, and no judge in his right mind will fall for the old 'God made me like this' routine."

Joe King: "I have prayed a number of times and don't feel that my prayers got past the ceiling."

Christian: "They probably didn't. The Bible says that your sins make a separation between you and God so that He will not hear."

Joe King: "Are you saying that God doesn't hear my prayers?"

Christian: "If you are in sin, the Book of Proverbs says that your prayers are an abomination to the Lord."

Joe King: "So what does that mean?"

Christian: "It means that you need Jesus Christ to wash away your sin, because you are an enemy of God in your mind. Did you know that?"

Joe King: "I didn't know that."

Memory Verse

"Your word is true from the beginning: and every one of your righteous judgments endures for ever."

PSALM 119:160

Christian: "Did you know that the Bible teaches that God's wrath abides on you?"

Joe King: "I didn't know that either."

Christian: "Joe, imagine if we had placed a microchip behind your ear a month ago, and everything you had thought about, all those unclean thoughts, had been recorded for everyone to see. Would you be ashamed?"

Joe King: "I sure would."

Christian: "That's what has happened. God made your mind. He sees what you think—all that lust that has gone on in your heart. Every word you have spoken has been heard by Him. Even the darkness is pure light to Him... and you will have to give an account for every idle word you have spoken. The Bible says that it is a fearful thing to fall into the hands of the Living God."

Joe King: "That's heavy. What should I do?"

Christian: "You need to repent and trust in Jesus as your Lord and Savior."

Last Words

Adoniram Judson (1788–1850), missionary to Burma, was privileged to see hundreds converted to Christ. Broken in health, he died while making a voyage to the Isle of Bourbon. Before he breathed his last, he said to those around him onboard the ship:

> **"I go with the gladness of a boy bounding away from school, I feel so strong in Christ."**

Holiness

"To ask that God's love should be content with us as we are is to ask that God should cease to be God: because He is what He is, His love must, in the nature of things, be impeded and repelled by certain stains in our present character, and because He already loves us He must labor to make us lovable."

C. S. LEWIS

Kirk's Comment   Before I knew the Lord, I wanted to be loved by the world and set apart for my own glory. Now, as a Christian, I want to be holy, loved by God, and set apart for Him and His glory. I think of "holiness" as living for an audience of One.

QUESTIONS & OBJECTIONS

"The Bible says 'God repented.' Doesn't that show He is capable of sin?"

"Repent" means "to have a change of mind." When the Bible tells sinners to repent, it means to change their direction, to turn from their sins. God has no sin. God's "repenting" is when He turns away from His fierce anger toward sinners. He warns men of the consequences of their disobedience. If they repent (turn from their sins), He will "repent" by not pouring out His promised wrath on them. For instance, Jonah 3:8,9 says, "Let them turn every one from his evil way...Who can tell if God will turn and repent, and turn away from his fierce anger, that we perish not?"

The word "holiness" carries with it some unwanted baggage, thanks to "religion." In the East, to be a holy man means to sit half-naked with your legs crossed, and having folks give you money in return for your blessing. Some holy men sit on poles for twenty years. Others stay off poles but they also stay away from any contact with a sinful world, in holier-than-thou legalism. Some live in monasteries and have a vow of silence.

Most of the church doesn't live on poles or have a holier-than-thou attitude. They do, however, live in a monastery—one without walls. They too have a vow of silence. Few have physical contact with the world. Their association with humanity is strictly confined to the church. Fellowship is what they have on Wednesday nights, Sunday mornings, and Sunday nights. They are salt among salt, light among light.

True holiness is the opposite of the above. It means that we cut ourselves off from sin, but not from sinners. True holiness is to be like Jesus —"separate from sinners"—and yet He was accused of being a "friend of sinners." The Scriptures admonish us with these thought-provoking words:

> I wrote to you in an epistle not to company with fornicators: yet not altogether with the fornicators of this world, or with the covetous, or extortioners, or with idolaters; for then you would need to go out of the world. But now I have written to you not to keep company, if any man that is called a brother be a fornicator, or covetous, or an idolater, or a railer, or a drunkard, or an extortioner; with such an one no not to eat (1 Corinthians 5:9–11).

Can you see what the Bible is saying? If we separate ourselves from sinners, we won't be able to reach them with the gospel of salvation. The only ones we are told to separate ourselves from are hypocrites. Look at these wonderful words from George MacLeod of Scotland:

> I simply argue that the cross should be raised at the center of the marketplace as well as on the steeple of the church. I am recovering the claim that Jesus was not crucified in a cathedral between two candles, but on a cross between two thieves; on the town's garbage heap; at a crossroad, so cosmopolitan they had to write His title in Hebrew and Latin and Greek...at the kind of a place where cynics

talk smut, and thieves curse, and soldiers gamble. Because that is where He died. And that is what He died for. And that is what He died about. That is where church-men ought to be and what church-men ought to be about.

There is nothing "spiritual" about being holy. It just means a separation from sin. God is holy—He is sinless (see Isaiah 6:3; Revelation 4:8; 15:4). We too are called to be holy: "But as he which has called you is holy, so be holy in all manner of conversation" (1 Peter 1:15). See also Romans 6:19, 22; Ephesians 1:4; Titus 1:8. If you want to be an effective witness, remember Charles Spurgeon's words: "In proportion as a church is holy, in that proportion will its testimony for Christ be powerful."

It's as simple as this—God has given us an umbrella in the Savior to shelter us from the reign of His wrath. God has given the covering, and we are told to stay under that covering of holiness. How can we best do this? We do this by reading God's Word daily, by keeping a tender conscience, by having an obedient heart, and by living in the fear of God.

The next time you are witnessing to someone you know isn't right with God, and he says, "Oh, I've been born again. I know the Lord," ask him if he is "living in holiness." More than likely he will say that he is. Then call his bluff. Ask him to define "holiness." As he is straining his brain to come up with a definition, say, "The Bible says, 'Without holiness, no man shall see the Lord.'" That means that we should be separated from sin and the world. Then ask him if he thinks he's a good person. More than likely he will, so take the time to go through the Moral Law with him.

QUESTIONS

1. **What does the word "holiness" mean to many?**

2. **Why do you think the church has become a "monastery without walls"?**

3. **What is "true holiness"?**

4. **Why do you think Jesus was a "friend of sinners"?**

5. **With whom does the Bible say that we should have no fellowship?**

6. **List four things you can do to cultivate holiness.**

PREACHER'S PROGRESS

Ian Oculated: "I know what you are saying is true."

Christian: "Good."

Ian Oculated: "I gave my heart to Jesus when I was 14 years old."

Christian: "Where was that?"

Ian Oculated: "At a Christian rock crusade. Some guy at the end said that Jesus loved us, so I went up to the front with some friends."

Christian: "Did you repent?"

Ian Oculated: "I don't know about that; but I became involved in a youth group for a while. Then I got mixed up with this girl and we...well, you know what I mean. I'm not going to any church at the moment, but I still love the Lord."

Christian: "Do you know that if you are not trusting in Jesus, you are an enemy of God in your mind through wicked works?"

Ian Oculated: "I don't believe that. I do believe that God loves me...and I have been born again, and that's all that matters."

Christian: "Are you living in holiness? The Bible says 'Without holiness, no man will see the Lord.'"

Ian Oculated: "Yes."

Christian: "What is holiness?"

Ian Oculated: "Ah...I don't really know."

Christian: "Are you reading your Bible?"

Ian Oculated: "Sometimes."

Christian: "Would you consider yourself to be a 'good' person?"

Ian Oculated: "Of course."

Christian: "Let's see. We'll look for a moment at the Ten Commandments and see how you will do on Judgment Day. Okay?"

Ian Oculated: "Okay..."

FEATHERS FOR ARROWS

In 1976 in Britain, the army was called in to do the work of firefighters during a fireman's strike. When a call came from an elderly woman whose cat was stuck up a tree, the army officers were immediately dispatched to the scene. After the cat was rescued, the grateful woman asked the officers into her home for tea and cookies. Afterwards, fond farewells were given. Then the army drove off...over the cat and killed it.

When one studies the Christian faith, there seems to be a common denominator. Many were converted after a "ran over the cat and killed it" experience. Some terrible tragedy, financial collapse, or the loss of a loved one brought them to their knees. Sadly, most of us are so rebellious that it does take some traumatic experiences to cause us to stop in our tracks and look heavenward.

Memory Verse

"But as he which has called you is holy, so be holy in all manner of conversation; because it is written, Be holy; for I am holy."

1 PETER 1:15,16

Last Words

Aldous Huxley (1894–1963), author and humanist:

"It is a bit embarrassing to have been concerned with the human problem all one's life and find at the end that one has no more to offer by way of advice than 'Try to be a little kinder.'"

Water Baptism, Part 1

> *"The greatest proof of Christianity for others is not how far a man can logically analyze his reasons for believing, but how far in practice he will stake his life on his belief."*
>
> **T. S. ELIOT**

Kirk's Comment When I got married, I wanted the whole world to know. When we become Christians, Jesus wants the whole world to know. Can you imagine if the person you were going to marry didn't want to declare his or her love for you in public, or just didn't take the time to? Your Bridegroom has called you to publicly declare your love for Him in baptism. Jesus said, "If you love me, keep my commandments."

QUESTIONS & OBJECTIONS

"Because Jesus died on the cross, we are all *forgiven of every sin."*

The forgiveness that is in Jesus Christ is conditional upon "repentance toward God, and faith toward our Lord Jesus Christ" (Acts 20:21). It is a gift that God offers to everyone, but individuals must receive it by repenting and trusting in Christ, or they will remain dead in their sins.

No one has biblical grounds to continue in sin, assuming that they are safe just because Jesus died on the cross. See 1 John 3:4–6.

Water baptism is an ordinance that Jesus established for the Church, as shown by His command in the Great Commission (Matthew 28:19; Mark 16:16). Jesus Himself set an example for His Church by submitting to baptism by His forerunner, John the Baptist (Matthew 3:13–17). Peter echoed the command to be baptized in his sermon on the Day of Pentecost (Acts 2:38,41). Throughout the Book of Acts, the apostles observed the ordinance, baptizing their converts (Acts 8:12; 8:36–38; 9:18; 10:47,48; 16:15; 16:33; 18:8; 19:5,6; 22:16). The spiritual significance of water baptism is taught in the epistles (Romans 6:3; 1 Corinthians 10:2; Galatians 3:27). There is no question about whether you *should* be baptized. The questions are how, when, and by whom?

The manner of water baptism prescribed in Scripture is by immersion. This is clearly seen in the meaning of the Greek word *baptizo*, which means to immerse. This fact is admitted even by scholars whose churches sprinkle, and is confirmed by the biblical description of Jesus' baptism in the Jordan River. It is also further established by the fact that when John was baptizing, he did so in Aenon "because there was much water there" (John 3:23). If he were merely sprinkling believers, he would have needed only a cupful of water. When Philip baptized the Ethiopian eunuch, "they both went down into the water" (Acts 8:38). Baptism by immersion pictures our death to sin, burial, and resurrection to new life in Christ: "We are buried with him by baptism into death: that like as Christ was raised up from the dead by the glory of the Father, even so we also should walk in newness of life" (Romans 6:4). Likewise, Scripture tells us that we are "buried with him in baptism, wherein also you are risen with him through the faith of the operation of God, who has raised him from the dead" (Colossians 2:12).

The following statement, a typical *Declaration of Faith* from an evangelical organization, affirms the doctrine of baptism and explains the significance of the ordinance:

> We believe that water baptism in the name of the Father and of the Son and of the Holy Spirit, according to the command of our Lord, is a blessed outward sign of an inward work, a beautiful and

solemn emblem reminding us that even as our Lord died upon the cross of Calvary so we reckon ourselves now dead indeed unto sin, and the old nature nailed to the tree with Him; and that even as He was taken from the tree and buried, so we are buried with Him by baptism into His death; that like as Christ was raised up from the dead by the glory of the Father, even so we should walk in newness of life.

It is important that an individual be baptized right away once he has placed his faith in the finished work of Christ on the cross. To put it off would be disobedient to the teachings of Scripture. The Philippian jailer and his family were baptized at midnight, the same hour they believed (Acts 16:30–33). The Ethiopian eunuch was baptized as soon as he believed (Acts 8:35–37), as was Paul (Acts 9:17,18). Baptism is a step of obedience, and God blesses our obedience.

As far as *who* should baptize you, it is clear from Scripture that other believers had the privilege, but check with your pastor; he may want the honor himself.

Some ask whether Acts 2:38 teaches that one should be baptized "in the name of Jesus Christ" only. The phrase "in the name of" in the Bible often means "by the authority of." For example, Colossians 3:17 instructs us, "Whatsoever you do in word or deed, do all in the name of the Lord Jesus, giving thanks to God the Father by him." Acts 2:38 simply indicates that people are to be baptized *according to the authority of* Jesus Christ. Jesus, who has been given all authority, instructs us to baptize "in the name of the Father, and of the Son, and of the Holy Spirit" (Matthew 28:19). This emphasizes the Christian baptism as distinct from John's baptism.

Though this description of baptism would be considered the main view of evangelical Christianity, the Body of Christ need not divide over the issue. We should major on the major issues and minor on the minor issues. Division is appropriate, however, when one teaches that a person must be baptized in order to go to heaven. This will be covered in our next lesson.

QUESTIONS

1. What are two verses where Jesus mentioned water baptism?

2. What is the meaning of the Greek baptizo, from which we get the word "baptism"?

3. According to Jesus in Matthew 28:19, in whose name (authority) should believers be baptized?

4. Is it true or false that baptism is an outward sign of an inward work?

5. Have you been obedient to follow Christ in baptism?

FEATHERS FOR ARROWS

A man was having difficulty hearing, but not to a point where it would justify the purchase of an expensive hearing device. He was tired of asking people to speak louder, so he had a simple but novel idea. He tied two small buttons to some thread, placed one button in his shirt pocket, and the other in his ear. Those who spoke to him saw the thread running from his pocket to his ear, concluded that he was having trouble hearing, and consequently spoke louder. The devise was simple, cheap, and effective. The lesson is that we should never overlook the power of simplicity.

The apostle Paul reminds those who preach the gospel not to move away from the "simplicity that is in Christ" (2 Corinthians 11:3). Thank God that He made the message of salvation so simple that all humanity can understand it.

WORDS OF COMFORT

Someone gave me a tandem bicycle, which I have always wanted. It needed a little repair work, but it was just a matter of fixing a flat in the back tire. An hour or so later and the tire was as good as new…for about two minutes. Then it went as flat as a tone-deaf teen. I abandoned the idea of fixing it, drove to the bicycle store, and bought a new tube. Two hours later, the tire was pumped up to 60 pounds per square inch, and it looked as good as new again.

Our van needed to be picked up from the repair shop, so I talked Sue into riding there on the tandem, and we rode off together on a bicycle built for two.

It was much harder to pedal than I expected, so I called from the front seat, "Are you pedaling?" She puffed that she was. A few minutes later I called the same question and she gave the same answer, but this time she could barely speak because she was so out of breath.

A short time later, it was so hard to pedal that we dismounted under a freeway overpass. While we were inspecting the back wheel, there was a deafening explosion, which was greatly amplified under the overpass, scaring the wits out of both of us.

We decided that Sue should walk on to get the van while I wheeled the bike back home, somewhat deflated.

The next day I learned a fundamental bit of knowledge one should have when repairing bike tires that are pumped up to 60 pounds per square inch. Before inflating the tube, the nozzle should be pushed in and twisted back and forth so that the tube won't be pinched when it is inflated. I hadn't done that and blew it big time.

It was only later that we wondered how the episode must have looked to the neighbors. We both begin our ride happily together on the tandem, then I yell, "Are you pedaling?" When we get around the corner, I holler the same question again, then there is what sounds like a gunshot...and I come back alone. How would that look to the neighbors? For California, normal.

Last Words

Colonel Charters, an infidel who at the end was not so blatant in his denial of an afterlife, said as he died:

"I would gladly give 30,000 Lira to have it proved to my satisfaction that there is no such place as hell."

LESSON 47

Water Baptism, Part 2

"Receive every inward and outward trouble, every disappointment, pain, uneasiness, temptation, darkness and desolation with both hands, as to a true opportunity and blessed occasion of dying to self and entering into a fuller fellowship with thy self-denying, suffering Savior."

JOHN WESLEY

Kirk's Comment   I thank God that I am saved by grace alone, because anything else I tried to add would only pollute it. Apart from His grace, all the prayers, church attendance, good works, even my baptism wouldn't save me: "Not by works of righteousness which we have done, but according to His mercy He saved us" (Titus 3:5).

QUESTIONS & OBJECTIONS

"I need to get my life cleaned up first."

Those who think that they can clean up their lives don't see their true plight. They are standing guilty before a wrath-filled God. They have been condemned by His Law (John 3:18; Romans 3:19). If a man commits rape and murder and admits to the judge that he is guilty, will the judge let him go just because the man promises to clean up his life? He is in debt to the law and must be punished. We may be able to clean up our lives in the sight of man, but not in the sight of God. The only way we can be cleansed is to repent and trust in the Savior.

wotmwotmwotmwotmwotmwotmwotmwotmwotmwotmwotm

As mentioned in the previous lesson, water baptism is an important ordinance that has been established for the purpose of our identification with Christ. Water baptism is merely an outward expression of an inward change. Baptism is a humbling act of obedience that follows salvation; by no means does it make a person a Christian, any more than sitting in a garage makes a person an automobile.

While we should preach that all men are commanded to repent and be baptized (Acts 2:38), adding any other requirement to salvation by grace becomes "works" in disguise. Although numerous Scriptures speak of the importance of baptism, adding *anything* to the work of the cross demeans the sacrifice of the Savior, implying that His finished work wasn't enough. The Bible makes clear that we are saved by grace alone (Ephesians 2:8,9). Baptism is simply a step of obedience to the Lord following our repentance and confession of sin. Our obedience regarding baptism, prayer, good works, fellowship, witnessing, etc., issues from our faith in Christ. Salvation is not what we do, but who we have: "He that has the Son has life" (1 John 5:12).

Some people believe that baptism is a requirement for salvation. Let's look at a couple of the "proof texts" that they would use when discussing water baptism. Remember that we are to never build a theology on difficult passages; the context, original language, and other passages must be taken into consideration for correct interpretation.

Mark 16:16: *"He that believes and is baptized shall be saved; but he that believes not shall be damned."*

It is clear that it is *unbelief* that brings damnation, not a lack of being baptized: "he that believes not shall be damned." When a person rejects the gospel, refusing to believe it, he is damned.

Other verses in Scripture reinforce that baptism is not necessary for salvation.

- Jesus told the repentant thief, "Today shall you be with me in paradise" (Luke 23:43). The thief was saved without baptism.

- In Acts 10 Cornelius exercised faith in Christ and was clearly saved prior to being baptized in water. The moment Cornelius believed in Christ, he received the Holy Spirit (Acts 10:45).

- Paul separates baptism from the gospel, saying, "Christ sent me not to baptize, but to preach the gospel" (1 Corinthians 1:17). It is the gospel that saves us (Romans 1:16; 1 Corinthians 15:1,2); therefore, baptism is not what saves us.

Acts 2:38: *"Then Peter said to them, Repent, and be baptized every one of you in the name of Jesus Christ for the remission of sins, and you shall receive the gift of the Holy Spirit."*

To properly understand Peter's meaning, we must consider the phrase *"for* the remission of sins" in light of its usage, its context, and the rest of Scripture.

- The word "for" (*eis*) can mean either "with a view to" or "because of." In the latter case, a person would be baptized *because* he had been saved, not *in order* to be saved.

- People are saved by receiving (not rejecting) God's Word, and Peter's audience "gladly received his word" before they were baptized (Acts 2:41).

- Verse 44 speaks of "all that believed" as constituting the early church, not all who were baptized.

- Those who believed Peter's message clearly received the Holy Spirit before they were baptized. Peter said, "Can any man forbid water, that these should not be baptized, which have received the Holy Spirit as well as we?" (Acts 10:47).

- Jesus referred to His baptism as a work of righteousness (Matthew 3:15). But the Bible declares clearly that salvation is "not by works of righteousness which we have done, but according to his mercy he saved us, by the washing of regeneration, and renewing of the Holy Spirit" (Titus 3:5).

- Not once in the entire Gospel of John, written explicitly so that people could believe and be saved (John 20:31), is baptism noted as a condition of salvation. Rather, this Gospel instructs people to "believe" to be saved (John 3:16,18,36).

It seems best, therefore, to understand Peter's statement like this: "Repent, and be baptized, *as a result of* the remission of sins." That this view looked backward to sins being forgiven at the moment of salvation is clear by the context and the rest of Scripture. Believing or repenting is often mentioned with being baptized, since baptism should follow belief. But Jesus does not say in Mark 16:16, or anywhere in Scripture, "He that is not *baptized* shall be damned," but instead states emphatically "he that *believes* not is condemned already" (John 3:18). Nowhere does Scripture make baptism a condition of salvation.

QUESTIONS

1. **What does salvation by grace become when any requirement is added to it?**

2. **What verse tells us that we are saved by grace and not by works?**

3. **What are some acts of obedience that are important but not essential to salvation?**

4. According to Mark 16:16, what is it that brings damnation?

5. Was the thief on the cross ever baptized?

6. In 1 Corinthians 1:17, what did the apostle Paul say that he was sent to do?

PREACHER'S PROGRESS

Will Fullyblind: "I think seeing is believing. If I can't see it, I don't believe it exists."

Christian: "So if there's anything you can't see, you don't believe it exists?"

Will Fullyblind: "That's right."

Christian: "Have you ever seen your brain?"

Will Fullyblind: "No."

Christian: "Doesn't that make you think?"

Will Fullyblind: "Yes."

Christian: "We believe in many things that we can't see. Have you ever seen the wind? Have you seen history? We see the effects of the wind, but the wind is invisible. We have records of history, but it is by 'faith' that we believe certain historical events happened. Television waves are invisible, but an antenna and a receiver can detect their presence. By the way, did you know that you have a receiver?"

Will Fullyblind: "No."

Christian: "Your 'receiver' (your spirit) is dead because of sin [see Ephesians 2:1]. You need to be plugged into the life of God, and then you will come alive and be aware of the invisible spiritual realm. Do you think you have kept the Ten Commandments?..."

WORDS OF COMFORT

When my 11-year-old niece wrote to me from New Zealand, I wrote back and, as an added blessing, I dropped in a few Russian rubles that someone had sent me. Russian currency wasn't worth the paper it was printed on, but I thought she would like to see how their money looked. I liked to do little things that would make her happy.

I found out later that the letter arrived on her birthday, and that she excitedly rushed to the bank to see how much I had sent her.

> **Last Words**
>
> **Vicomtesse D'Houdetot**, daughter-in-law of Rousseau's Madame D'Houdetot, left the sad lament:
>
> **"I regret my life."**

Memory Verse

"For by grace are you saved through faith; and that not of yourselves: it is the gift of God: not of works, lest any man should boast."
EPHESIANS 2:8,9

LESSON 48

The Trinity

"What comes into our minds when we think about God is the most important thing about us."

A. W. TOZER

Kirk's Comment This is a very interesting lesson. Try to fully comprehend the Trinity—that God is three in one—and you'll find that reason, logic, and faith are stretched to their limits. However, God's Word is faithful and true and can be trusted completely.

QUESTIONS & OBJECTIONS

"Why does God allow evil?"

Why does God allow evil men and women to live? Should He instead kill them before they do evil deeds? Should He punish murderers and rapists now? What about thieves and liars, adulterers, fornicators, those who lust, and those who hate? If God judged evil today, all unconverted men and women would perish under His wrath. Thank God that He is patiently waiting for them to turn to the Savior and thus be saved from His terrible wrath.

By Matthew J. Slick

The Trinity—the triune nature of God—is a basic doctrine of Christianity. Although the word "Trinity" is not found in the Bible, the elements of this doctrine are all taken directly from God's Word.

The doctrine of the Trinity states that there is one God who exists eternally as three distinct persons: the Father, the Son, and the Holy Spirit. The Bible could not be more explicit that there is only one God, which it declares about two dozen times. In Isaiah 45:5 God says, "I am the LORD, and there is no other; besides me there is no God." In Mark 12:29 Jesus states, "The first of all the commandments is, Hear, O Israel; The LORD our God is one Lord . . .'"

Jesus referred to God as His Father, and the apostles frequently spoke of "God the Father." But the New Testament also insists that Jesus is God. For example, Thomas acknowledged Jesus as "my Lord and my God" (John 20:28), and both Peter and Paul spoke of Jesus as "our God and Savior" (2 Peter 1:1; Titus 2:13). Yet the New Testament also makes the distinction between the Father and the Son as two very different persons. In fact, they tell us that they love one another, speak to each other, and seek to glorify each other (e.g., John 17:1–26).

The Old Testament refers often to the Holy Spirit as God at work in the world, without distinction from the Father. But Jesus in John 14—16 explained that the Father at Christ's request would send this Holy Spirit. The Holy Spirit would teach and guide the disciples, not speaking on His own initiative, but speaking on Christ's behalf and glorifying Christ. Thus, the Holy Spirit is revealed by Christ to be a third person distinct from the Father and from the Son.

The three persons of the Trinity—the Father, the Son, and the Holy Spirit—are distinct persons, yet they are all the one God. They are in absolute perfect harmony consisting of one substance. They are coeternal, coequal, and copowerful. If any one of the three were removed, there would be no God.

There is, though, an apparent separation of some functions among the members of the Godhead. For example, the Father chooses those in Christ to be saved (Ephesians 1:4); the Son redeems them (Ephesians 1:7); and the Holy Spirit seals them (Ephesians 1:13).

A further point of clarification is that God is not one person, the Father, with Jesus as a created being and the Holy Spirit as a force (Jehovah's Witnesses). Neither is He one person who took three consecutive forms, i.e., the Father became the Son, who became the Holy Spirit. Nor is God the divine nature of the Son, where Jesus had a human nature perceived as the Son and a divine nature perceived as the Father (United Pentecostal). Nor is the Trinity an office held by three separate Gods (Mormonism).

It has been interestingly said, "If you try to figure out the Trinity, you will lose your mind; if you deny the Trinity, you will lose your soul." In short, the doctrine of the Trinity is completely biblical, and it is essential that all Christians give assent to this doctrine.

The Trinity at Work in Redemption

In every major phase of the redemption, each person of the Godhead is directly involved. Their involvement in each successive phase can be seen in the following:

1. *Incarnation.* The Father incarnated the Son in the womb of Mary by the Holy Spirit (see Luke 1:35).

2. *Baptism in the Jordan River.* The Spirit descended on the Son, and the Father spoke His approval from heaven (see Matthew 3:14–17).

3. *Public ministry.* The Father anointed the Son with the Spirit (see Acts 10:38).

4. *The crucifixion.* Jesus offered Himself to the Father through the Spirit (see Hebrews 9:14).

5. *The resurrection.* The Father resurrected the Son by the Spirit (see Acts 2:32; Romans 1:4).

6. *Pentecost.* From the Father the Son received the Spirit, whom He then poured out on His disciples (see Acts 2:33).

The following chart should help you to see how the doctrine of the Trinity is derived from Scripture. The list is only illustrative, not exhaustive.

	Father	Son	Holy Spirit
Called God	Phil. 1:2	John 1:1,14; Col. 2:9	Acts 5:3,4
Creator	Gen. 1:1; Isaiah 64:8	John 1:3; Col. 1:16	Job 33:4; 26:13
Resurrects	Gal. 1:1; 1 Thes. 1:10	John 2:19; 10:17	Rom. 8:11
Indwells	2 Cor. 6:16	Col. 1:27; Gal. 2:20	John 14:17; Rom. 8:9,11
Everywhere	1 Kings 8:27	Matt. 28:20	Psalm 139:7–10
All-knowing	1 John 3:20	John 16:30; 21:17	1 Cor. 2:10,11
Sanctifies	1 Thes. 5:23	Heb. 13:12	1 Pet. 1:2
Life giver	Gen. 2:7; John 5:21	John 1:3; 5:21	2 Cor. 3:6; Rom. 8:11
Fellowship	1 John 1:3	1 Cor. 1:9; 1 John 1:3	2 Cor. 13:14; Phil. 2:1
Eternal	Psalm 90:2	Micah 5:2; John 8:58	Heb. 9:14
Wills	Luke 22:42	Luke 22:42	1 Cor. 12:11
Speaks	Matt. 3:17; Heb. 1:1,2	Luke 9:26	Acts 8:29; 13:2
Loves	John 3:16	Eph. 5:25	Rom. 15:30
Searches the heart	Jer. 17:10	Rev. 2:23	1 Cor. 2:10
We belong to	John 17:9	John 17:6	—
Savior	1 Tim. 1:1; 2:3	2 Tim. 1:10; Titus 3:6	—
We serve	Matt. 4:10	Col. 3:24	
Believe in	Num. 14:11; John 14:1	John 11:26; 12:44	1 John 4:1,2
Gives joy	Neh. 12:43	John 15:11	Gal. 5:22; 1 Thes. 1:6
Judges	John 8:50; Heb. 12:23	John 5:22,30	—

Additional Descriptions Applied to All Three in the Trinity

1) Who gives us words to speak?

Father—Matthew 10:19,20: "But when they deliver you up, take no thought how or what you shall speak: for it shall be given you in that same hour what you shall speak. For it is not you that speak, but the Spirit of your Father which speaks in you."

Holy Spirit—Mark 13:11: "But when they shall lead you, and deliver you up, take no thought beforehand what you shall speak, neither premeditate: but whatsoever shall be given you in that hour, that speak: for it is not you that speak, but the Holy Spirit."

Son—Luke 21:14,15: "Settle it therefore in your hearts, not to meditate before what you shall answer: For I will give you a mouth and wisdom, which all your adversaries shall not be able to gainsay nor resist."

2) Who gave the New Covenant?

Father—Jeremiah 31:33,34: "But this shall be the covenant that I will make with the house of Israel; after those days, says the LORD, I will put my law in their inward parts, and write it in their hearts; and will be their God, and they shall be my people. And they shall teach no more every man his neighbor, and every man his brother, saying, Know the LORD: for they shall all know me, from the least of them to the greatest of them, says the LORD: for I will forgive their iniquity, and I will remember their sin no more."

Holy Spirit—Hebrews 10:15–17: "Whereof the Holy Spirit also is a witness to us: for after that he had said before, This is the covenant that I will make with them after those days, said the Lord, I will put my laws into their hearts, and in their minds will I write them; and their sins and iniquities will I remember no more."

Son—Hebrews 12:24: "And to Jesus the mediator of the new covenant…"

3) Who is our helper?

Father—Hebrews 13:6: "So that we may boldly say, The Lord is my helper, and I will not fear what man shall do to me."

Holy Spirit—Romans 8:26: "Likewise the Spirit also helps our infirmities."

Son—Hebrews 4:16: "Then came she and worshipped him, saying, Lord, help me."

4) Who comforts us?

Father—2 Corinthians 1:3,4: "Blessed be God, even the Father of our Lord Jesus Christ, the Father of mercies, and the God of all comfort; who comforts us in all our tribulation..."

Holy Spirit—Acts 9:31: "Then had the churches rest throughout all Judea and Galilee and Samaria, and were edified; and walking in the fear of the Lord, and in the comfort of the Holy Spirit, were multiplied."

Son—2 Corinthians 1:5: "For as the sufferings of Christ abound in us, so our consolation also abounds by Christ."

5) Who gives us peace?

Father—1 Corinthians 14:33: "For God is not the author of confusion, but of peace, as in all churches of the saints."

Holy Spirit—Galatians 5:22: "But the fruit of the Spirit is love, joy, peace, longsuffering, gentleness, goodness, faith..."

Son—John 14:27: "Peace I leave with you, my peace I give to you: not as the world gives, give I to you. Let not your heart be troubled, neither let it be afraid."

6) Who sends out Christians?

Father—Matthew 9:38: "Pray therefore the Lord of the harvest, that he will send forth laborers into his harvest."

Holy Spirit—Acts 13:4: "So they, being sent forth by the Holy Spirit, departed to Seleucia; and from thence they sailed to Cyprus."

Son—Matthew 10:16: "Behold, I send you out as sheep in the midst of wolves. Therefore be wise as serpents and harmless as doves."

7) Who calls Christians to ministry?

Father—1 Corinthians 1:1: "Paul, called to be an apostle of Jesus Christ through the will of God..."

Holy Spirit—Acts13:2: "As they ministered to the Lord, and fasted, the Holy Spirit said, Separate me Barnabas and Saul for the work whereunto I have called them."

Son—Romans 1:6: "Among whom are you also the called of Jesus Christ."

Adapted from an article by the Christian Apologetics and Research Ministry (www.carm.org).

QUESTIONS

1. **Where in the Bible do we find the word "Trinity"?**

2. **What is the doctrine of the Trinity?**

3. **What are some of the separate functions of the Godhead according to Ephesians 1?**

4. **How does the JW's view of God differ from the Bible's description?**

5. **How can seeing each person of the Trinity intimately involved in redemption serve to strengthen your faith?**

FEATHERS FOR ARROWS

The world's has many ignorant maxims: **1.** "All good things must come to an end." This isn't true for the Christian; see Ephesians 2:4–7. **2.** "Which came first, the chicken or the egg?" The chicken; see Genesis 1:20. **3.** "There's no such thing as a free lunch." See Matthew 14:19. **4.** "You can't take it with you." The Christian's works "follow" him; see Revelation 14:13. **5.** "There are only two things in life that are sure—death and taxes." Plenty of people avoid taxes; none avoid death. See Hebrews 9:27. **6.** "Crime doesn't pay." It does...up until Judgment Day; see Romans 2:6. **7.** "As miserable as sin." Sin gives pleasure; see Hebrews 11:25. **8.** "That's impossible!" With God, nothing is impossible; see Mark 10:27. **9.** "No one will know!" God knows; see 1 John 3:20. **10.** "It's the perfect crime." Judgment Day will prove that there is no such thing as a crime that escapes justice; see Hebrews 4:13. **11.** "Seeing is believing." Any magician knows that isn't true. The eyes are easily fooled; see Proverbs 28:26. **12.** "God helps those who help themselves." God helps those who cannot help themselves; see Romans 5:6.

Last Words

Dr. Samuel Johnson (1709–1784), the lexicographer author, after being told by his doctor that he could not recover, said:

"Then I will take no more physics—not even opiates. I have prayed that I may render up my soul to God unclouded."

LESSON 49 The Deity of Christ

"I know men and I tell you that Jesus Christ is no mere man. Between Him and every other person in the world there is no possible term of comparison. Alexander, Caesar, Charlemagne, and I have founded empires. But on what did we rest the creations of our genius? Upon force. Jesus Christ founded His empire upon love; and at this hour millions of men would die for Him."

NAPOLEON BONAPARTE

Kirk's Comment So many mistakes are made in religions today because of a failure to acknowledge that Jesus Christ was God in human form—not just a good teacher, but God Himself.

QUESTIONS & OBJECTIONS

"Jesus wasn't sinless—He became 'angry' when He cleared the temple."

The temple of God was filled with that day's equivalent of money-grabbing televangelists. Jesus called it a "den of thieves" (Mark 11:17), because the moneychangers were not interested in God but in taking financial advantage of those who came to worship. Anger at hypocrisy isn't a sin—it's a virtue.

The Bible gives us a fascinating insight into the deity of Christ in Matthew 16:13–17. Jesus asked the disciples who they thought He was. Peter replied that He was the Son of God. Here Jesus made an interesting statement. He said, "Blessed are you, Simon Barjona: for flesh and blood has not revealed it to you, but my *Father* which is in heaven." In other words, the Father must be the one to reveal to humanity who Jesus truly is. We can try to correct the popular, erroneous teaching that Jesus is less than God, but unless our Father opens the eyes of the individual, our argument is in vain.

The Attributes of Christ

God has certain attributes, many of which are also attributes of man. There are, however, attributes or qualities of God that He reserves for Himself. Man is not omniscient, omnipotent, eternal, or omnipresent. These are qualities that God alone possesses. Man cannot forgive sin, create from nothing, or know the future. These are qualities that make God who He is, and that separate Him from man. We will look at some of these qualities of God, and see that Jesus Christ had these same attributes.

1) God is omniscient: God knows all things. He knows the hearts and thoughts of men. He knows the past and the future. He knows the number of grains of sand, and the number of the stars. There is nothing He does not know.

Christ is omniscient:

- "But Jesus did not commit himself to them, because he knew all men, and needed not that any should testify of man: for he knew what was in man" (John 2:24,25).
- He knew the whereabouts of Nathaniel: "Nathaniel said to him, Where do you know me from? Jesus answered and said to him, Before Philip called you, when you were under the fig tree, I saw you" (John 1:48).
- He knew the plot of Judas: "Jesus answered them, Have not I chosen you twelve, and one of you is a devil? He spoke of Judas Iscariot the son of Simon" (John 6:70,71).

- He knew the heart of the Pharisees: "And Jesus knew their thoughts" (Matthew 12:25). "But when Jesus perceived their thoughts" (Luke 5:22). "But he knew their thoughts" (Luke 6:8).

- He knew the history of the Samaritan woman (John 4:16–29).

2) God is worshiped: Only God can rightly be worshiped. "For you shall worship no other god: for the LORD, whose name is Jealous, is a jealous God" (Exodus 34:14). Whenever a man was worshiping another man, he was immediately rebuked: "And as Peter was coming in, Cornelius met him, and fell down at his feet, and worshiped him. But Peter took him up, saying, Stand up; I myself also am a man" (Acts 10:25,26). See also Acts 14:11–15 where Paul refuses worship. Even the angels refuse worship of men: "I fell down to worship before the feet of the angel which showed me these things. Then said he to me, See you do it not: for I am your fellow-servant, and of your brethren the prophets, and of them which keep the sayings of this book: worship God" (Revelation 22:8,9).

Christ is worshiped:

- He was worshiped by the wise men: "And when they were come into the house, they saw the young child with Mary his mother, and fell down, and worshiped him" (Matthew 2:11).

- He was worshiped by the leper: "And behold, there came a leper and worshiped him" (Matthew 8:2).

- He was worshiped by the ruler: "While he spoke these things to them, behold, there came a certain ruler, and worshiped him" (Matthew 9:18).

- He was worshiped by the angels: "And again, when he brought in the first begotten into the world, he said, And let all the angels of God worship him" (Hebrews 1:6).

There are many other examples of people worshiping Christ. At no time did He rebuke them. He accepted their worship.

3) God forgives sin: Only God can forgive sin, because all sin is against a holy God. No man can truly forgive sin. "Who can forgive sins but God only?" (Mark 2:7).

Christ forgives sin:

- "When Jesus saw their faith, he said unto the sick of the palsy, Son, your sins be forgiven you" (Mark 2:5).
- "And he said to her, Your sins are forgiven" (Luke 7:48).

4) God creates: Only God can truly create. To form something where before was nothing takes an act of God. Man can refashion or reform something that already exists, but only God can create.

Christ creates:

- "For by him were all things created, that are in heaven, and that are in earth, visible and invisible, whether they be thrones, or dominions, or principalities, or powers: all things were created by him, and for him" (Colossians 1:16).
- "All things were made by him; and without him was not anything made that was made" (John 1:3).

5) God saves: "Salvation belongs unto the LORD" (Psalm 3:8).

Christ saves:

- "For the Son of man is come to save that which was lost" (Matthew 18:11).
- "For the Son of man is not come to destroy men's lives, but to save them" (Luke 9:56).
- "For God sent not his Son into the world to condemn the world; but that the world through him might be saved" (John 3:17).
- "If any man hear my words, and believe not, I judge him not: for I came not to judge the world, but to save the world" (John 12:47).

Jesus Christ has the attributes of God, even the attributes reserved solely for God. There are many other attributes of God that are attributes of Christ as well. The following chart lists just a few.

Description	Father	Jesus Christ
God	Genesis 1:1 Deuteronomy 6:4 Psalm 45:6,7	Isaiah 7:14; 9:6; John 1:1,14; 20:28; Titus 2:13; Hebrews 1:8; 2 Peter 1:1; Matthew 1:23; 1 John 5:20
Yahweh, "I AM"	Exodus 3:14 Deuteronomy 32:39	John 8:24; 8:58; 18:4–6
Alpha & Omega	Isaiah 41:4; 48:12 Revelation 1:8	Revelation 1:17,18; 2:8
Lord	Isaiah 45:23	Matthew 12:8 Acts 7:59,60; 10:36 1 Corinthians 2:8; 12:3 Philippians 2:10,11
Savior	Isaiah 43:3; 43:11; 63:8 Luke 1:47 1 Timothy 4:10	Matthew 1:21; Luke 2:11; John 4:42; 2 Timothy 1:10; Titus 2:13
King	Psalm 95:3; Isaiah 43:15; 1 Timothy 6:14–16	Revelation 17:14; 19:16
Judge	Genesis 18:25 Deuteronomy 32:36 Psalm 50:4,6; 75:7; 96:13	John 5:22 2 Corinthians 5:10 2 Timothy 4:1
Light	2 Samuel 22:29; Psalm 27:1	John 1:4,9; 3:19; 8:12; 9:5
Rock	Deuteronomy 32:3,4; 2 Samuel 22:32	Romans 9:33; 1 Corinthians 10:3,4; 1 Peter 2:4–8
Redeemer	Psalm 130:7,8; Isaiah 43:1; 48:17; 49:26	Acts 20:28; Ephesians 1:7; Hebrews 9:12
Our righteousness	Isaiah 45:24	Jeremiah 23:6; Romans 3:21

Description	Father	Jesus Christ
Husband	Isaiah 54:5; Hosea 2:16	Matthew 25:1; Mark 2:18,19; 2 Corinthians 11:2; Revelation 21:2,9
Shepherd	Genesis 49:24; Psalm 23:1; 80:1; 95:7	John 10:11,16; Hebrews 13:20; 1 Peter 2:25; 5:4
Creator	Genesis 1:1; Job 33:4; Psalm 95:6; Isaiah 40:28; 43:1; Acts 4:24	John 1:2,3,10; Colossians 1:15–18; Hebrews 1:1–3
Giver of life	Genesis 2:7; Deuteronomy 32:39; 1 Samuel 2:6	John 5:21; 10:28; 11:25
Forgiver of sin	Exodus 34:6,7; Nehemiah 9:17; Daniel 9:9	Matthew 9:2; Acts 26:18; Colossians 2:13; 3:13
Omnipresent	Psalm 139:7–12; Proverbs 15:3	Matthew 18:20; 28:20; Ephesians 3:17; 4:10
Omniscient	1 Kings 8:37–39; Jeremiah 17:9,10	Matthew 9:4; 11:27; Luke 5:4–6; John 2:25; 16:30; 21:17; Acts 1:24
Omnipotent	Isaiah 40:10–31; 45:5–13; Revelation 19:6	Matthew 28:18; Mark 1:29–34; John 10:18; Jude 24
Pre-existent	Genesis 1:1	John 1:1,2; 3:13,31,32; 16:28; 17:5
Eternal	Psalm 102:26,27; Habakkuk 3:6	Isaiah 9:6; Micah 5:2; John 8:58
Immutable	Malachi 3:6; James 1:17	Hebrews 13:8
Receiver of worship	Matthew 4:10; John 4:24; Revelation 7:11; 19:4; 19:10	John 9:38; Philippians 2:10,11; Hebrews 1:6
Who gets the glory?	Isaiah 42:8; 48:11	Hebrews 13:21; John 17:5

QUESTIONS

1. How can individuals come to understand Jesus' true identity as the Son of God?

2. Cite at least one verse that shows the omniscience of Jesus.

3. What is at least one verse that tells of Jesus receiving worship?

4. How does Jesus accepting worship counter the claim that He was merely a good man?

5. Cite at least one verse that identifies Jesus as the Creator.

6. How does man's creative ability differ from God's?

FEATHER FOR ARROWS

Memory Verse

"I said therefore to you, that you shall die in your sins: for if you believe not that I am he, you shall die in your sins."

JOHN 8:24

"This Jesus of Nazareth, without money and arms, conquered more millions than Alexander, Caesar, Mohammed, and Napoleon; without science and learning, He shed more light on things human and divine than all philosophers and scholars combined; without the eloquence of schools, He spoke such words of life as were never spoken before or since, and produced effects which lie beyond the reach of orator or poet; without writing a single line, He set more pens in motion, and furnished themes for more sermons, orations, discussions, learned volumes, works of art, and songs of praise than the whole army of great men of ancient and modern times." —Philip Schaff, *The Person of Christ*

Last Words

Madame Rolland (1866–1944), French writer:

"O liberty! What crimes are committed in thy name!"

The Holy Spirit

"When 100 years ago earnest scholars decreed that the Law had no relationship to the preaching of the gospel, they deprived the Holy Spirit in the area where their influence prevailed of the only instrument with which He had ever armed Himself to prepare sinners for grace."

PARIS REIDHEAD

Kirk's Comment The Holy Spirit is the wonderful One who helped me see my need of God's forgiveness. The biblical truths in this lesson explain the Holy Spirit's identity as well as His role in salvation.

QUESTIONS & OBJECTIONS

"I have been born again many times."

Like Nicodemus, many people have no concept of what it means to be born again. He thought Jesus was speaking of a physical rebirth. Others see the experience as being a spiritual "tingle" when they think of God or a warm fuzzy feeling when they enter a church building. Or maybe they are of the impression that one is born again when one is "christened" or "confirmed." However, the new birth spoken of by Jesus is absolutely essential for sinners to enter heaven. If they are not born again, they will not enter the kingdom of God. Therefore it is necessary to establish the fact that one becomes a Christian by being born again, pointing out that Jesus Himself said the experience was crucial. The difference between believing in Jesus and being born again is like believing in a parachute, and putting one on. The difference will be seen when you jump. (See Romans 13:14.)

How is one born again? Simply through repentance toward God and faith in the Lord Jesus Christ. All who confess and forsake their sins, and trust in Jesus alone for their eternal salvation, receive spiritual life through the Holy Spirit who comes to live within them.

w o t m w o t m w o t m w o t m w o t m w o t m w o t m w o t m w o t m w o t m w o t m

The Holy Spirit's Role in Salvation

Some have wondered about the Holy Spirit's role in the salvation of sinners. The answer is clear from Scripture. We are drawn by, convicted by, born of, and kept by the Holy Spirit. Why then do we need to use the Law when witnessing? Why don't we just leave the salvation of sinners up to the Holy Spirit? Simply because, just as God has condescended to use the foolishness of preaching to save those who believe, so He has chosen the Moral Law to bring the knowledge of sin. And He has given us the privilege of being involved in the process.

Jesus Himself tells us how the Holy Spirit works in the salvation of the lost. He said that when the Holy Spirit comes, "he will reprove the world of sin [which is *transgression* of the Law—1 John 3:4], and of righteousness [which is *of* the Law—Romans 8:4], and of judgment [which is *by* the Law—Romans 2:12]. So when we use the Law to bring the knowledge of sin to the lost, we simply become instruments the Holy Spirit uses to lead sinners to the Savior.

Billy Graham stated, "The Holy Spirit convicts us . . . He shows us the Ten Commandments; the Law is the schoolmaster that leads us to Christ. We look in the mirror of the Ten Commandments, and we see ourselves in that mirror."

The Holy Spirit is a Person: 35 Personal Attributes

1) *Helps:* John 14:16,26; Romans 8:26

2) *Glorifies:* John 16:13,14

3) *Can be known:* John 14:17

4) *Gives abilities:* Acts 2:4; 1 Corinthians 12:7–11

5) *Referred to as "He":* John 15:26; 16:7,8,13

6) *Loves:* Romans 15:30

7) *Guides:* John 16:13

8) *Comforts:* John 14:26; Acts 9:31

9) *Teaches:* Luke 12:12; John 14:26

10) *Reminds:* John 14:26

11) *Bears witness:* John 15:26; Acts 5:32; Romans 8:16

12) *Hears:* John 16:13

13) *Leads:* Matthew 4:1; Acts 8:29; Romans 8:14

14) *Pleads:* Romans 8:26,27

15) *Longs (yearns):* James 4:5

16) *Wills:* 1 Corinthians 12:11

17) *Thinks:* Acts 15:28

18) *Sends:* Mark 1:12; Acts 10:20; 13:4

19) *Speaks:* John 16:13; Acts 10:19

20) *Forbids:* Acts 16:6,7

21) *Appoints:* Acts 20:28

22) *Reveals:* Luke 2:26; 1 Corinthians 2:10

23) *Calls to ministry:* Acts 13:2

24) *Can be grieved:* Isaiah 63:10; Ephesians 4:30

25) *Can be insulted:* Hebrews 10:29

26) *Can be lied to:* Acts 5:3,4

27) *Can be blasphemed:* Matthew 12:31,32

28) *Strives:* Genesis 6:3

29) *Is knowledgeable:* Isaiah 40:13; Acts 10:19; 1 Corinthians 2:10–13

30) *Judges:* John 16:8

31) *Prophesies:* Acts 21:11; 28:25; 1 Timothy 4:1

32) *Has fellowship:* 2 Corinthians 13:14

33) *Gives grace:* Hebrews 10:29

34) *Offers life:* 2 Corinthians 3:6; Revelation 22:17

35) *Is the Creator:* Job 33:4

The Holy Spirit is God: Direct Biblical Evidence

1) Job 33:4: "The Spirit of God has made me, and the breath of the Almighty has given me life." [only God is the Creator]

2) Matthew 12:31: "All manner of sin and blasphemy shall be forgiven to men: but the *blasphemy* against the Holy Spirit shall not be forgiven to men." [only God can be blasphemed]

3) John 4:24: "God is a Spirit: and they that worship him must worship him in spirit and in truth."

4) Acts 5:3,4,9: "But Peter said, Ananias, why has Satan filled your heart to *lie to the Holy Spirit*, and to keep back part of the price of the land? While it remained, was it not your own? and after it was sold, was it not in your own power? why have you conceived this thing in your heart? *You have not lied to men, but to God.*" [the Holy Spirit is unquestionably called God]

5) Acts 13:2: "As they ministered to the Lord, and fasted, the Holy Spirit said, Separate me Barnabas and Saul for the work whereunto I have called them." [only God calls]

Additionally, in the following parallelisms, the Holy Spirit is equated with God the Father twice, and with God the Son, Jesus, twice:

1) Who spoke through the prophets?

Father—Luke 1:68,70: "Blessed be the Lord God of Israel; for he has visited and redeemed his people, ... as he spoke by the mouth of his holy prophets, which have been since the world began."

Holy Spirit—Acts 28:25: "And when they agreed not among themselves, they departed, after that Paul had spoken one word, Well spoke the Holy Spirit by Isaiah the prophet to our fathers."

2) Who "works" all things?

Father—1 Corinthians 12:6: "And there are diversities of operations, but it is the same God which works all in all."

Holy Spirit—1 Corinthians 12:11: "But all these works that one and the selfsame Spirit, dividing to every man severally as he will."

3) Who is speaking to the churches in Revelation 2 and 3?

Son—Revelation 2:18: "These things says the Son of God, who has his eyes like to a flame of fire, and his feet are like fine brass."

Holy Spirit—Revelation 2:7: "He that has an ear, let him hear what the Spirit says to the churches."

4) Who intercedes for believers?

Son—Romans 8:34: "It is Christ ... who is even at the right hand of God, who also makes intercession for us."

Holy Spirit—Romans 8:26,27: "Likewise the Spirit also helps our infirmities: for we know not what we should pray for as we ought: but the Spirit itself makes intercession for us with groanings which cannot be uttered. And he that searches the hearts knows what is the mind of the Spirit, because he makes intercession for the saints according to the will of God."

QUESTIONS

1. Name four main things that the Holy Spirit does for sinners.

2. How did Billy Graham say that the Holy Spirit convicts us?

3. When the Law is not used in preaching the gospel, how is the Holy Spirit's work impacted, according to Paris Reidhead?

4. Name at least two qualities of the Holy Spirit that indicate He is God.

5. Identify two verses that equate the Holy Spirit with the Father and with the Son.

6. Are any of these characteristics of the Holy Spirit ones you were not aware of?

FEATHERS FOR ARROWS

A scientist once conducted an interesting series of experiments. He placed two people in separate studios, facing each other through a sheet of glass. Each person had a row of lights at his fingertips. As a light came on, they raced to switch it off. The person who turned the light off first won. The winner then sent an electric shock into his opponent. The interesting thing was that the winner was able to choose the degree of shock he sent, on a one-to-ten scale.

The scientist found, without exception, that when the players were in any way intoxicated by alcohol, the size of the shocks sent into the opponent were far greater. When the players were sober, they always sent less-powerful shocks. But when they were drunk, no matter whether it was male playing female, or female playing female, or male versus male, the players became very cruel, sending maximum strength shocks if alcohol was involved.

Last Words

Wentworth Dillon, who became Earl of Roscommon, was a poet whose anchor was fixed within the veil. When he died in 1684, his last words were from one of his own hymns:

"My God, my Father, and my Friend. Do not forsake me in the end."

Memory Verse

"And whosoever speaks a word against the Son of man, it shall be forgiven him: but whosoever speaks against the Holy Spirit, it shall not be forgiven him, neither in this world, neither in the world to come."

MATTHEW 12:32

The Resurrection

"About this time there lived Jesus, a wise man, if indeed one ought to call him a man... He was the Christ. When Pilate, upon hearing him accused by men of the highest standing among us, had condemned him to be crucified, those who had in the first place come to love him did not give up their affection for him. On the third day he appeared to them restored to life, for the prophets of God had prophesied these and countless other marvelous things about him."

JOSEPHUS

Kirk's Comment   If Jesus did not rise physically, then what happened to His body? Did it dissolve? Did it evaporate? Was it moved somewhere? There is *no* biblical account of what happened to Jesus' body other than that it was raised from the dead. Therefore, His body was raised from the dead.

QUESTIONS & OBJECTIONS

"Is it possible that Jesus simply fainted on the cross, and revived while He was in the tomb?"

Jesus had been whipped and beaten, and was bleeding from His head, back, hands, and feet for at least six hours. While he was on the cross, a soldier pierced His side with a spear and blood and water gushed out.

Professional soldiers would certainly have completed their assigned task and ensured his death.

"It is impossible that a being who had stolen half-dead out of the sepulcher, who crept about weak and ill, wanting medical treatment, who required bandaging, strengthening, and indulgence, and who still at last yielded to his sufferings, could have given to the disciples the impression that he was a conqueror over death and the grave, the Prince of Life: an impression which lay at the bottom of their future ministry. Such a resuscitation could only have weakened the impression which he had made upon them in life and in death, at the most could only have given it an elegiac voice, but could by no possibility have changed their sorrow into enthusiasm, have elevated their reverence into worship." —Strauss, *New Life of Jesus* (quoted in *Who Moved the Stone?* by Frank Morison)

w o t m w o t m w o t m w o t m w o t m w o t m w o t m w o t m w o t m w o t m w o t m

The Resurrection: Miracle or Myth

By Hank Hanegraaff

What was the central truth of the early apostles' preaching? What was the stimulus to the miraculous growth of the early church? What was the energizing force which spread the gospel across the face of the earth? These questions, posed by Dr. Walter Martin in his book *Essential Christianity*, all find their answer in the singular event of the resurrection of Jesus Christ. "He is risen!" was the victory cry of the early Christians, as they spread the message of Christ's bodily resurrection to the ends of the earth.

The resurrection of Jesus Christ is the very capstone in the arch of Christianity. When it is removed, all else crumbles. It is, in fact, the singular doctrine that elevated Christianity above all the pagan religions of the Mediterranean world. And it is precisely because of its strategic importance to the Christian faith that each person who takes the sacred name *Christian* upon his lips must be prepared to defend its historicity.

Thus the question must be asked, How can we know beyond any doubt that Jesus really rose from the dead—that this singular event is not some predilection on the part of the Christian but is rather *faith* founded on irrefutable *fact?*

As Christians, we must be prepared to demonstrate that Christ's resurrection was an event that occurred in time and space—that it was, in reality, *historical* and not *mythological* (cf. 2 Peter 1:16). The importance of this event cannot be minimized, for Jesus Himself proclaimed that His resurrection would prove His power over death, and thus His deity (John 2:18–22). Not only that, but Christ's resurrection is the very heart of the gospel (1 Corinthians 15:1–4).

When I first began examining the evidences for Christianity, I discovered that belief in the resurrection does not constitute a blind leap into a dark chasm but rather a step into the light. Indeed, the evidence for Christ's resurrection is so overwhelming that no one can examine it with an open mind desiring to *know* the truth without becoming *convinced* of its truth.

Of the many evidences available, none is more compelling than the fact that the resurrected Christ appeared to over five hundred individuals *at a single time* (1 Corinthians 15:6). Christ appeared to numerous other individuals as well, providing "many convincing proofs" of His resurrection (Acts 1:3). Christ in His resurrection body was even touched on two occasions (Matthew 28:9; John 20:17), and He challenged the disciples (Luke 24:39) and Thomas (John 20:27) to feel His wounds.

For those who continue to harbor doubts about the veracity of the biblical evidence, one need only point to Dr. Simon Greenleaf, the greatest authority on legal evidences in the 19th century. It is noteworthy that after examining the evidence for the resurrection of Jesus Christ, Greenleaf suggested that any cross-examination of the eyewitness testimonies recorded in Scripture would result in "an undoubting conviction of their integrity, ability, and truth."

Despite the biblical evidence, some have suggested that Jesus' body was stolen from the tomb—by either the Romans, the Jews, or the disciples. However, even as we consider such alternative explanations, reason drives us back to the conclusion that Christ rose from the dead. Consider the following: We know that the *Romans* would have no reason to steal Christ's body. After all, they wanted to keep the peace in Palestine.

The *Jewish religious leaders* would also have no motive in stealing the body since that would only stir up the very movement they had tried to crush. Besides, if the Jewish leaders had stolen the body, they could have later *openly displayed* the body to prove to the disciples and indeed the world that Jesus had not really risen from the dead.

And certainly, the *disciples* wouldn't have stolen the body, for why would they choose to suffer and die for a cause they knew to be a lie? While it is conceivable that someone might choose to die for what they know to be the truth, it is inconceivable that hundreds of Jesus' followers would be willing to die for what they knew to be a lie.

Another theory that has been resuscitated (*ad nauseam* and *ad infinitum*) in a desperate attempt to explain away the resurrection is the so-called "swoon theory." This theory says that Jesus did not really die on the cross, but merely passed out and was later revived. However, this theory is hopelessly flawed. Think about it for a minute. Can you imagine that Jesus endured several trials, a crown of thorns, a Roman scourge, a crucifixion, a spear thrust into His side, the loss of a great deal of blood, going three days without medical attention or food, pushing a two-ton stone away from His tomb's entrance, and then *physically overcoming an armed Roman guard while walking on pierced feet?* No! The swoon theory is ridiculous in the extreme. And yet, amazingly, some people continue to hang their hats on it.

After carefully examining all the evidence, one can only come to the singular conclusion that *Jesus did indeed rise from the dead and that He now lives to be our Lord and Savior* (Revelation 1:18). And let me emphasize that the resurrection of Christ is not just an Easter-time phenomenon to be celebrated in song and service. Rather, it is a truth that should daily fill us with eternal hope. Not only did the resurrection of Christ transform the disciples from cowards to lions of the faith, but His resurrection still continues to transform lives today. Because Christ lives, the Scripture says, we will live also. Indeed, in an instant, in the twinkling of an eye, we shall be transformed into physical resurrected bodies like unto His resurrected body.

Does Circumstantial Evidence Confirm It?

As Chuck Colson reported in his BreakPoint commentary (April 19, 2001), philosopher J. P. Moreland was once asked, "Can you give me five pieces of solid circumstantial evidence that convince you Jesus rose from the dead?" (Circumstantial evidence is an accumulation of facts from which one can draw intelligent conclusions.)

Certainly, Moreland responded. First, there's the evidence of the skeptics. Some of those who were most hostile to Jesus prior to his death became his most ardent supporters afterwards.

Second, the ancient Jews had a number of immensely important religious rituals. These included the offering of animal sacrifices, obeying the Mosaic law, and keeping the Sabbath. But within five weeks of Jesus' death, more than 10,000 Jews had suddenly altered or abandoned these rituals. Moreland asked: Why would they relinquish rites that had long given them their national identity? The implication is that something enormously significant had occurred.

Third, we see the emergence of new rituals: the sacraments of communion and baptism. The early Jews baptized in the name of the Father, the Son, and the Holy Spirit, "which," Moreland said, "meant they had elevated Jesus to the full status of God."

Fourth, we see the rapid rise of a new church, beginning shortly after the death of Jesus. Within twenty years, this new church—begun by the companions of a dead carpenter—had reached Caesar's palace in Rome, and eventually spread throughout the Roman Empire.

And fifth, Moreland said, there's the most convincing circumstantial evidence of all: the fact that every one of Jesus' disciples was willing to suffer and die for his beliefs. These men spent the rest of their lives witnessing about Christ. They frequently went without food; they were mocked, beaten, and thrown into prison. In the end, all but one died a painful martyr's death.

Would they have done this for a lie? Of course not. They did it because they were convinced beyond a doubt that they had seen the risen Christ.

Even if we doubted 2,000-year-old evidence, we have all the circumstantial evidence we could possibly want—right in front of us. It is, as Moreland said, "the ongoing encounter with the resurrected Christ that happens all over the world, in every culture, to people from all kinds of backgrounds and personalities. They all will testify that more than any single thing in their lives, Jesus Christ has changed them."

QUESTIONS

1. **What is the most compelling evidence that Jesus rose from the dead?**

2. **How do we know the Romans didn't steal the body of Jesus?**

3. **How do we know the Jewish religious leaders didn't steal Jesus' body?**

4. **How do we know the disciples didn't steal Jesus' body?**

5. **How would you refute the "swoon theory"?**

6. **What change took place among Jewish believers to substantiate the resurrection?**

FEATHERS FOR ARROWS

A young man once jumped from a plane for his first skydive. When he pulled his main parachute, it failed to open. As he thought on what he was supposed to do regarding the emergency chute, he hit the ground. His friends rushed up to him, thinking he was dead. They instead found that he had miraculously landed on freshly plowed ground and was still alive. As he lay there with fourteen broken bones, and a bone protruding vertically from his leg, he mumbled, "Boy, did I blow it!"

He was right; he blew it. He had listened to his instructor. He had believed. However, he hadn't obeyed. Don't blow it for eternity. Listen, believe, and obey.

Last Words

William Etty, the British painter who died in 1849, was another who believed that death was not an end but an episode in one's experience. Full of confidence of what was on the other side, he died saying:

"Wonderful, wonderful, this death!"

The Bible, Part 1

"I believe the Bible is the best gift God has given to man . . . But for this Book, we could not know right from wrong . . . Take all you can of this Book upon reason, and the balance on faith, and you will live and die a happier man."

ABRAHAM LINCOLN

Kirk's Comment   A good understanding of what makes the Bible unique is very helpful in witnessing to others. These next few lessons will help you understand the Bible better yourself.

QUESTIONS & OBJECTIONS

"The fact that there are so many versions proves that the Bible has mistakes. Which one is right?"

True, there are many different versions of the Bible. There are versions in Chinese for the Chinese. There are versions in Russian for the Russian people. There are actually thousands of versions of the Bible—some are in modern languages, some in foreign languages, and some are in old English. Few, in the printing age, can claim that they don't have access to the Scriptures in their own language. However, each translation is based on the original biblical texts.

The Bible doesn't attempt to defend its inspiration. But here is an interesting thing: Genesis opens with the words "God said" nine times in the first chapter. The statement "Thus says the Lord" appears 23 times in the last Old Testament book, Malachi. So you have "God says" from Genesis to Malachi. "The Lord spoke" appears 560 times in the first five books of the Bible and at least 3,800 times in the whole of the Old Testament! Isaiah claims at least 40 times that his message came directly from the Lord; Ezekiel, 60 times; and Jeremiah, 100 times. What could therefore be more important than discovering what God reveals to us in His Word?

In this lesson we begin a series on the authenticity of the Scriptures. What exactly is the Bible and is it reliable? The following lessons contain a brief look at these questions. Most of the content of this lesson was taken from Don Stewart's book *The Bible*.

Our English word "Bible," from the Latin *biblia* and the Greek *biblios*, simply means "book." From the second century A.D., the Christian church has used the term "Bible" to refer to the sixty-six books that they hold to be Scripture. The Bible is made up of two testaments: the Old Testament (containing 39 books) was composed from about 1400 B.C. to 400 B.C., and the New Testament (containing 27 books) was written from approximately A.D. 50 to A.D. 90.

The Bible declares that it is the Word of God, His communication to humanity. Within its pages we learn about the existence and nature of God—a personal, infinite God who created the entire universe and created man in His image. We also discover the identity and purpose of man. For centuries people have turned to the Bible for answers to the basic questions of life: Where did we come from? Why are we here on earth? What will happen to us when we die?

The Bible also gives a purpose for history. History is not merely a series of unrelated events. The Bible tells us the beginning and shows a progression to an end, and promises that the world in which we live, with all its corruption, will one day be made into a new world without sin.

The Bible served as a basis for modern scientific pursuits. Modern science was born in the seventeenth century because of a belief in an unchanging God of order, purpose, and consistency—the God portrayed in the Bible.

In addition, our modern concept of law and order are based on the Bible. The Bible says that God has set standards of right and wrong behavior. Many of our current laws are based upon biblical morality.

Some have questioned why a written record from God is important. Is it possible that man can know God apart from a revelation that was committed to writing? The answer is a resounding no. There are several reasons why a written revelation is necessary.

If we were given only an oral communication from God, then we would have a message that could be changed and misinterpreted when repeatedly told. The more a story was repeated orally, the more the story could be changed. This would not give us much confidence in the message. If the message began to differ considerably, how would anyone know what version to trust?

A written revelation therefore solves doctrinal controversies. If there is a question of Christian belief, the written Bible can be studied as an authoritative source. Once a revelation is committed to writing, it can also be translated into different languages. This allows the message to be spread and copied with the assurance that the original thoughts will stay intact. All of these factors demonstrate the necessity of a written revelation from God.

Interesting Bible Statistics

Number of books in the Bible: 66

Chapters: 1,189

Verses: 31,101

Words: 783,137

Letters: 3,566,480

Longest word (and name): Mahershalalhashbaz (Isaiah 8:1)

Longest verse: Esther 8:9 (78 words)

Shortest verse: John 11:35 (2 words: "Jesus wept")

Middle books: Micah and Nahum

Middle chapter: Psalm 118

Middle verse: Psalm 118:8

Shortest book (number of words): 3 John

Shortest chapter (number of words): Psalm 117

Longest book: Psalms (150 chapters)

Longest chapter: Psalm 119 (176 verses)

Number of times the word "God" appears: 3,358

Number of times the word "Lord" appears: 7,736

Number of different authors: Approximately 40

Number of languages the Bible has been translated into: more than 1,200

Number of new Bibles distributed (sold or given away) in the U.S.: about 168,000 per day

The Middle of the Bible

Psalm 118 is the middle chapter of the entire Bible. Psalm 117 is the shortest chapter in the Bible; Psalm 119 is the longest chapter in the Bible. The Scriptures have 594 chapters before Psalm 118, and 594 chapters after Psalm 118. If you add up all the chapters before and after Psalm 118, you get a total of 1188 chapters. Psalm 118:8 is the middle verse of the entire Bible. It goes without saying that the central verse has an important message: "It is better to trust in the Lord than to put confidence in man."

QUESTIONS

1. **What does the word "Bible" mean?**

2. **How many books are in the Bible?**

3. **When were the Old and New Testaments composed?**

4. **What are some of the topics the Bible tells us about?**

5. **What are the benefits of having a written communication from God?**

6. **What important message is contained in the central verse in the Bible?**

FEATHERS FOR ARROWS

A young man once received a letter from a lawyer stating that his grandmother had left him an inheritance. To his astonishment, it was $50,000 plus "my Bible and all it contains." The youth was delighted to receive the money. However, he knew what the Bible contained, and because he wasn't into religion he didn't bother to open it. Instead, he put it on a high shelf. He gambled the $50,000, and over the next fifty years he lived as a pauper, scraping for every meal. Finally he became so destitute, he had to move in with his relatives. When he cleaned out his room, he reached up to get the dusty old Bible from the shelf. As he took it down, his trembling hands dropped it onto the floor, flinging it open to reveal a $100 bill between every page. The man had lived as a pauper, simply because of his prejudice. He thought he knew what the Bible "contained."

Memory Verse

"All scripture is given by inspiration of God, and is profitable for doctrine, for reproof, for correction, for instruction in righteousness: that the man of God may be perfect, thoroughly furnished to all good works."
2 TIMOTHY 3:16,17

Last Words

Robert Louis Stevenson (1850–1894), Scottish novelist and poet, was one of the greatest storytellers of his day and a master of beautiful language. Stevenson died at his beloved Samoa at age 44 from his lifelong disease of consumption. Just before he breathed his last, he gathered his household together and prayed:

"Behold with favor, O Lord, the weak men and women gathered together in the peace of this roof. When the day returns God would call them with morning faces and morning hearts, eager to labor, eager to be happy if happiness should be their portion."

The Bible, Part 2

"The Bible is endorsed by the ages. Our civilization is built upon its words. In no other Book is there such a collection of inspired wisdom, reality, and hope."

DWIGHT D. EISENHOWER

Kirk's Comment The Bible is our authority on God's will. It is very important to know why we can trust it. It is also inevitable that a true seeker will ask you to answer some questions about the Bible.

QUESTIONS & OBJECTIONS

"Didn't men write the Bible?"

Absolutely. When you write a letter, do you write the letter, or does the pen? Obviously you do; the pen is merely the instrument you use. God used men as instruments to write His "letter" to humanity. They ranged from kings to common fishermen, but the 66 books of the Bible were all given by inspiration of God. Proof that this Book is supernatural can been seen with a quick study of its prophecies.

The Bible Stands Alone

Compiled by Jordan and Justin Drake

In 1889 a schoolteacher told a ten-year-old boy, "You will never amount to very much." That boy was Albert Einstein. In 1954 a music manager told a young singer, "You ought to go back to driving a truck." That singer was Elvis Presley. In 1962 a record company told a group of singers, "We don't like your sound. Groups with guitars are definitely on their way out." They said that to the Beatles. Man is prone to make mistakes. Those who reject the Bible should take the time to look at the evidence before they come to a verdict.

1. It is unique in its continuity. If today just 10 people were picked who were from the same place, born around the same time, spoke the same language, and made about the same amount of money, and were asked to write on just one controversial subject, they would have trouble agreeing with each other. But the Bible stands alone. It was written over a period of about 1,500 years by more than 40 writers from all walks of life. Some were fishermen; some were politicians. Others were generals or kings, shepherds, or historians. They were from three different continents, and wrote in three different languages. They wrote on hundreds of controversial subjects yet they wrote with agreement and harmony. They wrote in dungeons, in temples, on beaches, and on hillsides, during peacetime and during war. Yet their words sound like they came from the same source. So even though 10 people today couldn't write on one controversial subject and agree, God picked 40 different people to write the Bible—and it stands the test of time.

2. It is unique in its circulation. The invention of the printing press in 1450 made it possible to print books in large quantities. The first book printed was the Bible. Since then, the Bible has been read by more people and printed more times than any other book in history. By 1930, over one billion Bibles had been distributed by Bible societies around the world. By 1977, Bible societies alone were printing over 200 million Bibles each year, and this doesn't include the rest of the Bible publishing companies. No one who is interested in knowing the truth can ignore such an important book.

3. It is unique in its translation. The Bible has been translated into approximately 1,400 languages. No other book even comes close.

4. It is unique in its survival. In ancient times, books were copied by hand onto manuscripts which were made from parchment and would decay over time. Ancient books are available today only because someone made copies of the originals to preserve them. For example, the original writings of Julius Caesar are no longer around. We know what he wrote only by the copies we have. Only 10 copies are still in existence, and they were made 1,000 years after he died. Only 600 copies of Homer's *The Iliad* exist, made 1,300 years after the originals were written. No other book has as many copies of the ancient manuscripts as the Bible. In fact, there are over 24,000 copies of New Testament manuscripts, some made within 35 years of the writer's death.

5. It is unique in withstanding attack. No other book has been so attacked throughout history as the Bible. In A.D. 300 the Roman emperor Diocletian ordered every Bible burned because he thought that by destroying the Scriptures he could destroy Christianity. Anyone caught with a Bible would be executed. But just 25 years later, the Roman emperor Constantine ordered that 50 perfect copies of the Bible be made at government expense. The French philosopher Voltaire, a skeptic who destroyed the faith of many people, boasted that within 100 years of his death, the Bible would disappear from the face of the earth. Voltaire died in 1728, but the Bible lives on. The irony of history is that 50 years after his death, the Geneva Bible Society moved into his former house and used his printing presses to print thousands of Bibles.

The Bible has also survived criticism. No book has been more attacked for its accuracy. And yet archaeologists are providing more proof every year that the Bible's detailed descriptions of historic events are correct.

Josh McDowell, writing in *Evidence That Demands a Verdict*, puts the Bible's uniqueness into perspective for us:

> The [Bible's] authors, speaking under the inspiration of the Holy Spirit, . . . wrote on hundreds of controversial subjects with absolute harmony from the beginning to the end. There is one unfolding story from Genesis to Revelation: the redemption of mankind through the Messiah—the Old Testament through the coming Messiah, the New

Testament from the Messiah that has come. In Genesis, you have paradise lost, in Revelation you have paradise gained. You can't understand Revelation without understanding Genesis. It's all interwoven on hundreds of controversial subjects.

Now here's the picture: 1,600 years, 60 generations, 40-plus authors, different walks of life, different places, different times, different moods, different continents, three languages, writing on hundreds of controversial subjects and yet when they are brought together, there is absolute harmony from beginning to end . . . There is no other book in history to even compare to the uniqueness of this continuity.

QUESTIONS

1. **What kinds of people did God pick to write the Bible?**

2. **How do their different circumstances point to the divine inspiration of the Bible?**

3. **What is unique about the Bible's circulation?**

4. Can you think of any places around the world today where people make the same mistake as Diocletian?

5. According to Josh McDowell, what is the one unfolding story throughout the Bible?

PREACHER'S PROGRESS

Ben Lyon: "The Bible has mistakes in it."

Christian: "Where?"

Ben Lyon: "In Genesis. There are two creations."

Christian: "It's one creation, with the second account giving details."

Ben Lyon: "Okay, then...how about the death of Judas? There are two different accounts."

Christian: "True, but they don't contradict each other."

Ben Lyon: "Yes, they do. One says that Judas hanged himself. The other says that he fell headlong and all his bowels gushed out."

Christian: "Doesn't the second account sound strange to you?"

Ben Lyon: "It sure does, and it shows the Bible has mistakes."

Christian: "No, it doesn't. What would make someone's 'bowels gush out'?"

Ben Lyon: "I haven't the foggiest idea."

Christian: "I have. If a body is left hanging, it won't be long until it decomposes, falls headlong, and the bowels gush out. There's no mistake."

Ben Lyon: "Okay. There are plenty of other mistakes."

Christian: "Name them."

Ben Lyon: "I can't think of any at the moment."

Christian: "Have you ever read the Bible?"

Ben Lyon: "I've read it through four or five times."

Christian: "Really?"

Ben Lyon: "Yes."

Christian: "That's quite a claim. The Bible is a huge collection of sixty-six books. What is the Book of Zephaniah about?"

Ben Lyon: "I can't remember."

Christian: "Can you name the Ten Commandments?"

Ben Lyon: "Yes. You shall not lie. You shall not steal...kill...commit adultery..."

Christian: "Have you ever lied or stolen?"

Ben Lyon: "Never."

Christian: "Are you perfect in thought, word, and deed?"

Ben Lyon: "Yes."

Christian: "Okay. If that's true, you have nothing at all to fear on Judgment Day. Thanks for listening to me."

FEATHERS FOR ARROWS

Great Leaders Speak About the Bible

"The best religion the world has ever known is the religion of the Bible. It builds up all that is good." *Rutherford B. Hayes*

"Here is a Book worth more than all the other books which were ever printed." *Patrick Henry*

"That book, Sir, is the Rock upon which our republic rests." *Andrew Jackson*

"The more profoundly we study this wonderful Book, and the more closely we observe its divine precepts, the better citizens we will become and the higher will be our destiny as a nation." *William McKinley*

"There are a good many problems before the American people today, and before me as President, but I expect to find the solution of those problems just in the proportion that I am faithful in the study of the Word of God." *Woodrow Wilson*

"The whole inspiration of our civilization springs from the teachings of Christ and the lessons of the prophets. To read the Bible for these fundamentals is a necessity of American life." *Herbert Hoover*

"We cannot read the history of our rise and development as a nation, without reckoning the place the Bible has occupied in shaping the advances of the Republic." *Franklin D. Roosevelt*

Last Words

Edgar Allen Poe (1809–1849), American author and poet, was credited with having pioneered the detective story. It is recorded that as he died he uttered the brief word:

"Rest, shore, no more."

Memory Verse

"With my whole heart have I sought you: O let me not wander from your commandments. Your word have I hid in my heart, that I might not sin against you."
PSALM 119:10,11

LESSON 54

The Bible, Part 3

"Given the large portion of the New Testament written by him, it's extremely significant that Luke has been established to be a scrupulously accurate historian, even in the smallest details. One prominent archaeologist carefully examined Luke's references to thirty-two countries, fifty-four cities, and nine islands, finding not a single mistake."

JOHN MCRAY

Kirk's Comment The Bible is God's Word. It is trustworthy, powerful, and effective. It cuts through self-righteousness and leads men to faith in Jesus Christ—the antidote for death. The facts in this lesson lay a good foundation for your trust in God's Word.

QUESTIONS & OBJECTIONS

"Christians can't use 'circular reasoning' by trying to prove the Bible by quoting from the Bible!"

The "circular reasoning" argument is absurd. That's like saying you can't prove that the President lives in the White House by looking into the White House. It is looking into the White House that will provide the necessary proof. The fulfilled prophecies, the amazing consistency, and the many scientific statements of the Bible prove it to be the Word of God. They provide evidence that it is supernatural in origin.

Archaeology and History Attest to the Reliability of the Bible

By Richard M. Fales, Ph.D.

N o other ancient book is questioned or maligned like the Bible. Critics looking for the flyspeck in the masterpiece allege that there was a long span between the time the events in the New Testament occurred and when they were recorded. They claim another gap exists archaeologically between the earliest copies made and the autographs of the New Testament. In reality, the alleged spaces and so-called gaps exist only in the minds of the critics.

Manuscript Evidence. Aristotle's *Ode to Poetics* was written between 384 and 322 B.C. The earliest copy of this work is dated A.D. 1100, and there are only forty-nine extant manuscripts. The gap between the original writing and the earliest copy is 1,400 years. There are only seven extant manuscripts of Plato's Tetralogies, written 427–347 B.C. The earliest copy is A.D. 900—a gap of over 1,200 years.

What about the New Testament? Jesus was crucified in A.D. 30. The New Testament was written between A.D. 48 and 95. The oldest manuscripts date to the last quarter of the first century, and the second oldest A.D. 125. This gives us a narrow gap of thirty-five to forty years from the originals written by the apostles.

From the early centuries, we have some 5,300 Greek manuscripts of the New Testament. Altogether, including Syriac, Latin, Coptic, and Aramaic, we have a whopping 24,633 texts of the ancient New Testament to confirm the wording of the Scriptures. So the bottom line is, there was no great period between the events of the New Testament and the New Testament writings. Nor is there a great time lapse between the original writings and the oldest copies. With the great body of manuscript evidence, it can be proved, beyond a doubt, that the New Testament says exactly the same things today as it originally did nearly 2,000 years ago.

Corroborating Writings. Critics also charge that there are no ancient writings about Jesus outside the New Testament. This is another ridiculous claim. Writings confirming His birth, ministry, death, and resurrection include Flavius Josephus (A.D. 93), the Babylonian Talmud (A.D. 70–200), Pliny the Younger's letter to the Emperor Trajan (approx. A.D.

100), the Annals of Tacitus (A.D. 115–117), Mara Bar Serapion (sometime after A.D. 73), and Suetonius' *Life of Claudius* and *Life of Nero* (A.D. 120).

Another point of contention arises when Bible critics have knowingly or unknowingly misled people by implying that Old and New Testament books were either excluded from or added into the canon of Scripture at the great ecumenical councils of A.D. 336, 382, 397, and 419. In fact, one result of these gatherings was to confirm the church's belief that the books already in the Bible were divinely inspired. Therefore, the church, at these meetings, neither added to nor took away from the books of the Bible. At that time, the thirty-nine Old Testament books had already been accepted, and the New Testament, as it was written, simply grew up with the ancient church. Each document, being accepted as it was penned in the first century, was then passed on to Christians of the next century. So, this foolishness about the Roman Emperor Constantine dropping books from the Bible is simply uneducated rumor.

Fulfilled Prophecies. Prophecies from the Old and New Testaments that have been fulfilled also add credibility to the Bible. The Scriptures predicted the rise and fall of great empires like Greece and Rome (Daniel 2:39,40), and foretold the destruction of cities like Tyre and Sidon (Isaiah 23). Tyre's demise is recorded by ancient historians, who tell how Alexander the Great lay siege to the city for seven months. King Nebuchadnezzar of Babylon had failed in a 13-year attempt to capture the seacoast city and completely destroy its inhabitants. During the siege of 573 B.C., much of the population of Tyre moved to its new island home half a mile from the land city. Here it remained surrounded by walls as high as 150 feet until judgment fell in 332 B.C. with the arrival of Alexander the Great. In the seven-month siege, he fulfilled the remainder of the prophecies (Zechariah 9:4; Ezekiel 26:12) concerning the city at sea by completely destroying Tyre, killing 8,000 of its inhabitants and selling 30,000 of its population into slavery. To reach the island, he scraped up the dust and rubble of the old land city of Tyre, just like the Bible predicted, and cast them into the sea, building a 200-foot-wide causeway out to the island.

Alexander's death and the murder of his two sons was also foretold in the Scripture. Another startling prophecy was Jesus' detailed prediction of

Jerusalem's destruction, and the further spreading of the Jewish diaspora throughout the world, which is recorded in Luke 21. In A.D. 70, not only was Jerusalem destroyed by Titus, the future emperor of Rome, but another prediction of Jesus Christ in Matthew 24:1,2 came to pass—the complete destruction of the temple of God.

Messianic Prophecies. In the Book of Daniel, the Bible prophesied the coming of the one and only Jewish Messiah prior to the temple's demise. The Old Testament prophets declared He would be born in Bethlehem (Micah 5:2) to a virgin (Isaiah 7:14), be betrayed for thirty pieces of silver (Zechariah 11:12,13), die by crucifixion (Psalm 22), and be buried in a rich man's tomb (Isaiah 53:9). There was only one person who fits all of the messianic prophecies of the Old Testament who lived before A.D. 70: Jesus of Nazareth, the Son of Mary.

Because fulfilled prophecies are so beneficial in showing the supernatural origin of the Bible, and are lacking in other religions, we will look in depth at prophecies in upcoming lessons.

Yes, the Bible is an amazing book.

QUESTIONS

1. **In your opinion, what is the motivation for critics who claim there are gaps between when New Testament events occurred and were recorded, and between the original writing and the existing copies?**

2. **How does the Bible compare to other ancient writings in the number of early manuscripts?**

3. How does the Bible compare to other ancient writings in the age of early manuscripts?

4. Where can some of the extra-biblical references to Jesus be found?

5. Which books of the Bible were excluded from the canon of Scripture at the early church councils?

FEATHERS FOR ARROWS

Great Leaders Speak About the Bible

"I say to you, search the Scriptures! The Bible is the book of all others, to be read at all ages, and in all conditions of human life; not to be read once or twice or thrice through, and then laid aside, but to be read in small portions of one or two chapters every day, and never to be intermitted, unless by some overruling necessity." *John Quincy Adams*

"Within the covers of the Bible are all the answers for all the problems men face. The Bible can touch hearts, order minds and refresh souls." *Ronald Reagan*

"In all my perplexities and distresses, the Bible has never failed to give me light and strength." *Robert E. Lee*

"I have read the Bible through many times, and now make it a practice to read it through once every year. It is a book of all others for lawyers, as well as divines; and I pity the man who cannot find in it a rich supply of thought and of rules for conduct. It fits a man for life—it prepares him for death." *Daniel Webster*

"It is impossible to rightly govern the world without God or the Bible." *George Washington*

"A thorough knowledge of the Bible is worth more than a college education." *Teddy Roosevelt*

"The Bible is the sheet anchor of our liberties. Write its principles upon your heart and practice them in your lives." *Ulysses S. Grant*

Last Words

George Herbert (1593–1633), English poet, said to friends gathered around his bed:

> **"I shall be free from sin and all the temptations and anxieties that attend it: and this being fact, I shall dwell with men made perfect— dwell where these eyes shall see my Master and Saviour."**

Memory Verse

"Give me understanding, and I shall keep your law; yes, I shall observe it with my whole heart. Make me to go in the path of your commandments; for therein do I delight."
PSALM 119:34,35

LESSON 55

The Bible, Part 4

"We account the Scriptures of God to be the most sublime philosophy. I find more sure marks of authenticity in the Bible than in any profane history whatsoever."

SIR ISAAC NEWTON

Kirk's Comment The Dead Sea Scrolls are a wonderful archeological discovery. They show quite clearly that the Bible we have today has not changed over the centuries.

QUESTIONS & OBJECTIONS

"I've tried to read the Bible, but I can't understand it."

The Scriptures tells us that the "natural man" cannot understand the things of the Spirit of God. Most Americans would find it difficult to understand the Chinese language. However, a child who is *born* into a Chinese family can understand every word. That's why you must be born again with God's Spirit living within you to give you understanding (John 3:3). The moment you become part of God's family, the Bible will begin to make sense.

The Dead Sea Scrolls: "The greatest manuscript discovery of all times"

By William F. Albright

The discovery of the Dead Sea Scrolls (DSS) at Qumran in 1949 had significant effects in corroborating evidence for the Scriptures. The ancient texts, found hidden in pots in cliff-top caves by a monastic religious community, confirm the reliability of the Old Testament text. These texts, which were copied and studied by the Essenes, include one complete Old Testament book (Isaiah) and thousands of fragments, representing every Old Testament book except Esther.

The manuscripts date from the third century B.C. to the first century A.D. and give the earliest window found so far into the texts of the Old Testament books and their predictive prophecies. The Qumran texts have become an important witness for the divine origin of the Bible, providing further evidence against the criticism of such crucial books as Daniel and Isaiah.

Dating the Manuscripts. Carbon-14 dating is a reliable form of scientific dating when applied to uncontaminated material several thousand years old. Results indicated an age of 1917 years with a 200-year (10 percent) variant.

Paleography (ancient writing forms) and orthography (spelling) indicated that some manuscripts were inscribed before 100 B.C. Albright set the date of the complete Isaiah scroll to around 100 B.C.—"there can happily not be the slightest doubt in the world about the genuineness of the manuscript."

Archaeological Dating. Collaborative evidence for an early date came from archaeology. Pottery accompanying the manuscripts was late Hellenistic (c. 150–63 B.C.) and Early Roman (c. 63 B.C. to A.D. 100). Coins found in the monastery ruins proved by their inscriptions to have been minted between 135 B.C. and A.D. 135. The weave and pattern of the cloth supported an early date. There is no reasonable doubt that the Qumran manuscripts came from the century before Christ and the first century A.D.

Significance of the Dating. Previous to the DSS, the earliest known manuscript of the Old Testament was the Masoretic Text (A.D. 900) and two others (dating about A.D. 1000) from which, for example, the King James version of the Old Testament derived its translation. Perhaps most would have considered the Masoretic text as a very late text and therefore questioned the reliability of the Old Testament wholesale. The Dead Sea Scrolls eclipse these texts by 1,000 years and provide little reason to question their reliability, and further, present only confidence for the text. The beauty of the Dead Sea Scrolls lies in the close match they have with the Masoretic text—demonstrable evidence of reliability and preservation of the authentic text through the centuries. So the discovery of the DSS provides evidence for the following:

1. Confirmation of the Hebrew Text

2. Support for the Masoretic Text

3. Support for the Greek translation of the Hebrew Text (the Septuagint). Since the New Testament often quotes from the Greek Old Testament, the DSS furnish the reader with further confidence for the Masoretic texts in this area where it can be tested.

(Adapted from Norman Geisler, "Dead Sea Scrolls," *Baker Encyclopedia of Christian Apologetics.*)

Archaeology Confirms the Bible

In his article "Is the Bible True?" (*Reader's Digest*, June 2000), Jeffery L. Sheler reports how archaeological finds confirm the Bible: During the past four decades, spectacular discoveries have produced data corroborating the historical backdrop of the Gospels. In 1968, for example, the skeletal remains of a crucified man were found in a burial cave in northern Jerusalem . . . There was evidence that his wrists may have been pierced with nails. The knees had been doubled up and turned sideways and an iron nail (still lodged in the heel bone of one foot) driven through both heels. The shinbones appeared to have been broken, perhaps corroborating the Gospel of John.

A hidden burial chamber, dating to the first century, was discovered in 1990 two miles from the Temple Mount. One bore the bones of a man in his 60s, with the inscription "Yehosef bar Qayafa" —meaning "Joseph, son of Caiaphas." Experts believe this was Caiaphas, the high priest of Jerusalem, who was involved in the arrest of Jesus, interrogated Him, and handed Him over to Pontius Pilate for execution.

A few decades earlier, excavations at Caesarea Maritama, the ancient seat of Roman government in Judea, uncovered a stone slab whose complete inscription may have read: "Pontius Pilate, the prefect of Judea, has dedicated to the people of Caesarea a temple in honor of Tiberius."

The discovery is truly significant, establishing that the man depicted in the Gospels as Judea's Roman governor had the authority ascribed to him by the Gospel writers. Sheler writes, "In extraordinary ways, modern archeology is affirming the historical core of the Old and New Testaments, supporting key portions of crucial biblical stories."

Following the 1993 discovery in Israel of a stone containing the inscriptions "House of David" and "King of Israel," *Time* magazine (December 18, 1995) reported, "This writing—dated to the 9th century B.C., only a century after David's reign—described a victory by a neighboring king over the Israelites...The skeptics' claim that David never existed is now hard to defend."

According to Dr. Nelson Glueck, "It may be stated categorically that no archaeological discovery has ever controverted a Biblical reference. Scores of archaeological findings have been made which confirm in clear outline or exact detail historical statements in the Bible. And, by the same token, proper evaluation of Biblical descriptions has often led to amazing discoveries."

For example, the Scriptures make more than 40 references to the great Hittite Empire. However, until one hundred years ago there was no archaeological evidence to substantiate the biblical claim that the Hittites existed. Skeptics claimed that the Bible was in error, until their mouths were suddenly stopped. In 1906, Hugo Winckler uncovered a huge library of 10,000 clay tablets, which completely documented the lost Hittite Empire. We now know that at its height, the Hittite civilization rivaled Egypt and Assyria in its glory and power.

Dr. Joseph P. Free stated, "Archaeology has confirmed countless passages which have been rejected by critics as unhistorical or contradictory to known facts...Yet archaeological discoveries have shown that these critical charges...are wrong and that the Bible is trustworthy in the very statements which have been set aside as untrustworthy...We do not know of any cases where the Bible has been proved wrong."

QUESTIONS

1. What are the Dead Sea Scrolls?

2. What portions of Scripture do the Dead Sea Scrolls contain?

3. How much older are the Dead Sea Scrolls than the previous copies of Scripture?

4. Why are the Dead Sea Scrolls important?

5. How has archaeology helped to validate the accuracy of the Bible?

6. How has this information inspired you to speak confidently to the lost about the Bible's reliability?

PREACHER'S PROGRESS

Lotsa Faithinman: "There is no evidence that Jesus Christ even existed."

Christian: "Have you looked at the date on your newspaper lately?"

Lotsa Faithinman: "What do you mean?"

Christian: "What's the year on your newspaper?"

Lotsa Faithinman: "2003."

Christian: "Since when?"

Lotsa Faithinman: "Since…"

Christian: "Since Jesus Christ. He left such an impact on the world that He split time in two. History is *His story*."

Lotsa Faithinman: "Well, the Bible can't be trusted. Besides that, there have been plenty of people in history who said things about loving your neighbor and doing to others as you would have them do to you."

Christian: "Who?"

Lotsa Faithinman: "Plenty. Historians tells us they existed."

Christian: "Why do you have faith in history books—the words of men—but doubt the Bible—the Word of God?"

Lotsa Faithinman: "I just do."

Christian: "Have you ever considered why you feel like that?"

Lotsa Faithinman: "No."

Christian: "A wise man once said that if you meet someone who is against the things of God, follow him home and you will probably find out why. If you became a Christian today, what do you think you would have to give up?"

Lotsa Faithinman: "Things."

Christian: "What things?"

Lotsa Faithinman: "Smoking."

Christian: "No. You can smoke and be a Christian. Plenty of people come to Christ and struggle with smoking for some time before they let it go. God doesn't reject them because they smoke. What is it that you would have to give up right away? Do you look at pornography?"

Lotsa Faithinman: "Sometimes."

Christian: "Do you lie?"

Lotsa Faithinman: "Yes."

Christian: "Can't you see that it's your love for sin that makes you feel the way you do about God? You refuse to trust Him because of your guilt. You are like a criminal who cowers in the darkness because he is afraid of the police. If you come to the light—if you repent of those things you know are wrong, and put your faith in Jesus Christ—God will forgive you and change your desires. He will also save you from hell and grant you the gift of everlasting life. Good deal, huh?"

Lotsa Faithinman: "I guess it is."

Memory Verse

"For the word of God is quick, and powerful, and sharper than any two-edged sword, piercing even to the dividing asunder of soul and spirit, and of the joints and marrow, and is a discerner of the thoughts and intents of the heart."

HEBREWS 4:12

Last Words

John Locke (1632–1709), English philosopher, being read to out of Psalms by Lady Masham, exclaimed:

"Oh the depth of the riches of the goodness and knowledge of God. Cease now."

Contradictions in the Bible

"Every man must do two things alone; he must do his own believing, and he must do his own dying."

MARTIN LUTHER

> **Kirk's Comment** Many of us are intimidated about witnessing because we're afraid someone will point out an error in the Bible that we can't explain. Are there contradictions in the Bible, or do they just seem like contradictions? We'll look at a few of these together.

QUESTIONS & OBJECTIONS

"There are contradictions in the resurrection accounts. Did Christ appear first to the women or to His disciples?"

Both Matthew and Mark list women as the first to see the resurrected Christ. Mark says, "He appeared first to Mary Magdalene" (16:9). But Paul lists Peter (Cephas) as the first one to see Christ after His resurrection (1 Corinthians 15:5).

Jesus appeared first to Mary Magdalene, then to the other women, and then to Peter. Paul was not giving a complete list, but only the important one for his purpose. Since only men's testimony was considered legal or official in the first century, it is understandable that the apostle would not list the women as witnesses in his defense of the resurrection.

The order of Christ's resurrection appearances is as follows:

Appeared to:	References:
1. Mary Magdalene	John 20:10–18
2. Mary and women	Matthew 28:1–10
3. Peter	1 Corinthians 15:5
4. Two disciples	Luke 24:13–35
5. Ten apostles	Luke 24:36–49; John 20:19–23
6. Eleven apostles	John 20:24–31
7. Seven apostles	John 21
8. All apostles	Matthew 28:16–20; Mark 16:14–18
9. 500 brethren	1 Corinthians 15:6
10. James	1 Corinthians 15:7
11. All apostles	Acts 1:4–8
12. Paul	Acts 9:1–9; 1 Corinthians 15:8

The Bible has many *seeming* contradictions within its pages. A contradiction is an inconsistency or discrepancy, which may give the appearance of an error. The four Gospels, for example, give four differing accounts as to what was written on the sign that hung on the cross. Matthew said, "This is Jesus the King of the Jews" (27:37). However, Mark contradicts that with "The King of the Jews" (15:26). Luke says something different: "This is the King of the Jews" (23:38), and John maintains that the sign read "Jesus of Nazareth the King of the Jews" (19:19). Those who are *looking* for contradictions may therefore say, "See—the Bible is *full* of mistakes!" and choose to reject it entirely as being untrustworthy. However, those who trust God have no problem harmonizing the Gospels. There is no contradiction if the sign simply read "This is Jesus of Nazareth the King of the Jews."

The godly base their confidence on two truths: 1) "all Scripture is given by inspiration of God" (2 Timothy 3:16); and 2) an elementary rule of Scripture is that God has deliberately included *seeming* contradictions in His Word to "snare" the proud. He has "hidden" things from the "wise and prudent" and "revealed them to babes" (Luke 10:21), purposely choosing foolish things to confound the wise (1 Corinthians 1:27). If an ungodly man refuses to humble himself and obey the gospel, and instead desires to build a case against the Bible, God gives him enough material to build his own gallows.

This incredible principle is clearly illustrated in the account of the capture of Zedekiah, king of Judah. Jeremiah the prophet told Zedekiah that God would judge him. He was informed that he would be "delivered into the hand of the king of Babylon" (Jeremiah 32:4). This is confirmed in Jeremiah 39:5–7 where we are told that he was captured and brought to King Nebuchadnezzar, then they "bound him with chains, to carry him to Babylon." However, in Ezekiel 12:13, God Himself warned, "I will bring him to Babylon... *yet he shall not see it*, though he shall die there" (emphasis added). Here is material to build a case against the Bible! It is an *obvious* mistake. Three Bible verses say that the king would go to Babylon, and yet the Bible in another place says that he would not see Babylon. How can someone be taken somewhere and not see it? It makes no sense at all—unless Zedekiah was *blinded*. And that is precisely what happened. Zedekiah saw Nebuchadnezzar face to face, saw his sons killed before his eyes, then "the king of Babylon... put out Zedekiah's eyes" before taking him to Babylon (Jeremiah 39:6,7).

This is the underlying principle behind the many "contradictions" of Holy Scripture (such as how many horses David had, who was the first to arrive at the tomb after the resurrection of Jesus, etc.). God has turned the tables on proud, arrogant, self-righteous man. When he proudly stands outside of the kingdom of God, seeking to justify his sinfulness through evidence that he thinks discredits the Bible, he doesn't realize that God has simply lowered the door of life, so that only those who are prepared to exercise faith and bow in humility may enter.

Since every word of the Lord is pure, any seeming "mistakes" are there because God has put them there, and they are therefore not mistakes. In time, we will find that the "mistakes" are actually ours. Therefore, never have fear if someone points out a "contradiction" in the Bible that you can't answer. Simply ask for the person's phone number, e-mail, or mailing address so you can get back to him with a solid answer. If he doesn't take you up on it, it proves that he really wasn't interested in an answer but rather used the "contradiction" as a smoke screen to hide behind.

It's also interesting to note that the *seeming* contradictions in the Gospels attest to the fact that there was no corroboration between the writers.

QUESTIONS

1. **How would you define a contradiction?**

2. **On what should the godly base their confidence when it comes to seeming contradictions?**

3. **What is the underlying principle behind the "contradictions" in Scripture?**

4. **Do you get worried when someone mentions a "contradiction" in the Bible?**

5. If you don't know the answer to a "contradiction," what should you say?

6. Why are the seeming contradictions in the Gospels a benefit?

FEATHERS FOR ARROWS

A new convert was reading his Bible when he called out, "Wow! Praise the Lord!"

A liberal minister heard him, and asked him what the noise was about. The young Christian replied with great enthusiasm, "This is incredible. It says here that God performed a miracle of deliverance by opening up the Red Sea for the Jews to march through!"

The minister replied, "Owing to tidal patterns around that time of year, the Red Sea was a swamp that was only three inches deep."

Somewhat subdued, the young man continued reading, but soon exclaimed, "Wow! Praise the Lord!"

"What's the matter now?" asked the minister. The Christian replied, "God has just drowned the whole Egyptian army in three inches of water!"

Over 3,000 times, the Bible speaks of its inspiration by God. His Word is true, and you can believe every word of it.

PREACHER'S PROGRESS

Ima Knowitall: "I've studied fundamentalism. You guys are strange."

Christian: "What do you mean by 'fundamentalism'?"

Ima Knowitall: "Someone who takes the Bible literally."

Christian: "I don't believe that everything in the Bible is to be taken literally. When Jesus said, 'I am the door,' I don't think it means He's a literal door, with hinges."

Ima Knowitall: "Okay, so some things are obviously metaphoric. But you do believe in a literal Adam and Eve, Noah's ark, Jonah and the whale, Joshua and the walls of Jericho, Samson and his long hair. You do believe in Daniel and the lion's den, and Moses and the Red Sea. Admit it—you think all those fairy tales really happened, don't you?"

Christian: "Of course. I believe that they were literal people and those things literally happened."

Ima Knowitall: "I can't believe that you believe them. That's so stupid. They were obviously mythical figures. Your presuppositions are fallacious. Why don't you read a few books? Broaden your horizons, open your mind by studying some of the great thinkers of the past, like Freud, Kant, or D'Arville. There's a world out there. Get your small mind out of that book."

Christian: "So you would consider yourself to be a broadminded, educated person?"

Ima Knowitall: "Absolutely. Among other things, I have a master's degree in human psychology."

Christian: "Do you know everything?"

Ima Knowitall: "Almost."

Christian: "May I ask you an important question?"

Ima Knowitall: "Sure."

Christian: "What is the purpose for man's existence?"

Ima Knowitall: "Mankind is on earth to enjoy himself."

Christian: "No. I didn't ask what we are to do while we are here. I'm asking why we are here."

Ima Knowitall: "Um...the reason we...the purpose for...ah...I don't know."

Christian: "Doesn't it concern you that we can place a man on the moon and yet we haven't the foggiest idea what we are doing on earth?"

Ima Knowitall: "It is kind of strange."

Christian: "You are obviously an open-minded person. May I explain why I believe all those 'fairy tales'?"

Ima Knowitall: "Go ahead."

Christian: "It's because God has deliberately chosen seemingly foolish things of this world to confound those who think they are wise, those who are puffed up with pride. But before I explain that, let me ask you a question. Do you consider yourself to be a morally upright person?"

Ima Knowitall: "Definitely."

Christian: "Let's see if you are, by looking for a few moments at the Ten Commandments..."

Last Words

Wolfgang Amadeus Mozart (1756–1791), the famous Austrian composer, is best remembered for his great operas *The Marriage of Figaro* and *Don Giovanni*. At the end, his dear partner was at his side offering him refreshment for his parched lips. His last words were:

> **"You spoke of refreshment, my Emilie. Take my last notes, sit down to my piano here and sing them to the hymn of your sainted mother. Did I not tell you that it was for myself—I composed this death chant."**

Memory Verse

"But God has chosen the foolish things of the world to confound the wise; and God has chosen the weak things of the world to confound the things which are mighty."

1 CORINTHIANS 1:27

LESSON 57

Prophecy

"God's Word is our primary weapon in evangelism. It is not designed to destroy life, but to give it. It is not to be used to harm but, like a surgeon's scalpel, to save. Just as a builder knows his tools and an artist knows his brushes and pens, we need to know the Bible."

GREG LAURIE

Kirk's Comment Many people believe that Jesus was a good man, but either He was more than a good man (He was God) or He shouldn't be listened to at all. Messianic prophecy provides the evidence to prove that Jesus was God in human flesh.

QUESTIONS & OBJECTIONS

"The Bible calls God 'the God of peace' who tells men to 'beat their swords into plowshares' (Romans 15:33; Isaiah 2:4). It also calls Him 'a man of war' who says to 'beat your plowshares into swords' (Exodus 15:3; Joel 3:9,10). Which is correct?"

There is peace inside of God's kingdom. He desires His enemies to be reconciled to Him so they have peace with Him. But if they refuse, then they are subject to His judgment. The passage from Joel is referring to Judgment Day. Note Joel 3:12, which says, "Let the heathen be wakened, and come up to the valley of Jehoshaphat: for there will I sit to judge all the

372

heathen round about." Isaiah is referring to the millennial kingdom, where there will be no more war.

ω ο τ m ω ο τ m ω ο τ m ω ο τ m ω ο τ m ω ο τ m ω ο τ m ω ο τ m ω ο τ m ω ο τ m ω ο τ m

There are about 3,856 verses directly or indirectly concerned with prophecy in Scripture. God's challenge to the world is, "Prove me now...I the Lord have spoken it: it shall come to pass" (see Malachi 3:10; Ezekiel 24:14). The destruction of Tyre, the invasion of Jerusalem, the fall of Babylon and Rome—each event was accurately predicted in the Bible and later fulfilled to the smallest detail.

Some people argue that prophecies are not unique to the Bible, but are found in other holy books. Hence, prophecy has no value in proving the truth of Christianity over other religions. This is similar to the argument that miraculous events are claimed by all religions; hence, alleged miracles cannot be used to establish the truth of any one religion over another. This objection is subject to the same criticism.

First, it is not true that other religions have specific, repeated, and unfailing fulfillment of predictions many years in advance of events over which the predictor had no control. Mormons, Buddhists, and Muslims have their own sacred writings, but the element of proven prophecy is absent in them.

These kinds of predictions are unique to the Bible. The prophecies made by Muhammad in the Quran, the Bible's closest competitor, show the inequality between the two books.

R. S. Foster says of other holy books and the writings of pagan religions, "No well-accredited prophecy is found in any other book or even oral tradition now extant, or that has ever been extant in the world. The oracles of heathenism are not to be classed as exceptions. There is not a single one of them that meets the tests required to prove supernatural agency, which every Scripture prophecy evinces."

After making a careful examination of Hebrew and pagan prophets, Calvin Stow concluded that there were no credible prophecies in other writings, but that each "is just what we would expect from men of this world, who have no faith in another."

Psychics Have Made Predictions Like the Bible

Contemporary critics of biblical prophecy nominate psychic predictions for equality with Scripture. However, this is another quantum leap between every psychic and the unerring prophets of Scripture.

One test of a prophet was whether he ever uttered predictions that did not come to pass (Deuteronomy 18:22). Those who had even one prophecy fail were put to death (18:20), a practice that no doubt gave pause to any who were not absolutely sure whether their messages were from God. Amid hundreds of prophecies, biblical prophets are not known to have made a single error.

A study of prophecies made by psychics in 1975 and observed until 1981 showed that of the seventy-two predictions, only six were fulfilled in any way. Two of these were vague and two others were hardly surprising: the U.S. and Russia would remain leading powers and there would be no world wars.

In 1993 the psychics missed every major unexpected news story, including Michael Jordan's retirement, the Midwest flooding, and the Israel-PLO peace treaty. Among their false prophecies were that the Queen of England would become a nun, and Kathy Lee Gifford would replace Jay Leno as host of "The Tonight Show" (*Charlotte Observer*, Dec. 30, 1993).

Likewise, the highly reputed "predictions" of Nostradamus were not amazing at all. Contrary to popular belief, he never predicted either the place or the year of a great California earthquake, New York being attacked, or the assassination of John F. Kennedy. Only those who are ignorant of Bible prophecy will be impressed with Nostradamus. He read the Bible in secret, stole its prophecies, and claimed them as his own.

The majority of his "famous" predictions, such as the rise of Hitler, were vague. Like other psychics, he was frequently wrong, and would be considered a false prophet by biblical standards. (For more information, see my book *Nostradamus: The Attack on New York...and Other Incredible Prophecies* and video *The Secrets of Nostradamus Exposed*, available at www.livingwaters.com.)

When Were Biblical Prophecies Made?

Critics dismiss all biblical prophecies that are specific enough to be unexplainable by claiming that they were made after the events. Supposedly, Daniel's amazing statements were made quite late, and Isaiah's predictions about Cyrus were edited in after he arrived on the scene. They were therefore recording history, not uttering prophecies.

Neither these nor other charges of post-dated prophecies have any foundation in fact. Many fulfillments have occurred long after the writings are known to have existed.

Alleged Fulfillments Misinterpret the Texts

Critics also argue that the alleged fulfillments of Old Testament predictions are frequently misinterpretations of the Old Testament text. For example, Matthew repeatedly says "that it might be fulfilled." However, when the Old Testament passage is examined in context, they claim, it turns out that it was not a real prediction of the event to which Matthew applied it.

A case in point is Matthew 2:15, which says, "And so was fulfilled what the Lord had said through the prophet: 'Out of Egypt I called my Son.'"

When the Old Testament passage, Hosea 1:11, is examined, it is discovered that this is not a predictive prophecy about Jesus coming out of Egypt when He was a child, but a statement about the children of Israel coming out of Egypt at the exodus.

It is readily admitted that many "prophecies" are not solely predictive and that the New Testament applied certain Old Testament passages to Christ that were not directly predictive of Him. Many scholars speak of these Old Testament texts being "topologically fulfilled" in Christ; that is, some truth in the passage is appropriately applied to Christ, even though it was not directly predictive of Him.

Others speak of a generic meaning in the Old Testament passage, which applies both to its Old Testament reference (Israel) and the New Testament reference (Christ), both of whom were God's "Son." Some scholars describe this as a double-reference view of prophecy.

Numerous Old Testament passages, however, are not merely typological but are manifestly predictive, such as the time and place of Christ's birth and death.

In summary, the Bible is filled with specific predictive prophecies that have been literally fulfilled. In *The Encyclopedia of Biblical Prophecies*, J. Barton Payne calculated that 27 percent of the entire Bible contains predictive prophecy. This is true of no other book in the world. And it is a sure sign of its divine origin.

QUESTIONS

1. **What other books, besides the Bible, contain precise prophecies that have come to pass?**

2. **If a prophet was truly from the Lord, how many of his prophecies would come to pass according to Deuteronomy 18?**

3. **What percentage of the Bible contains predictive prophecy?**

4. **Did Nostradamus ever predict the attack on New York?**

5. **Why is prophecy a good tool to use in evangelism?**

WORDS OF COMFORT

One thing that amazes me is the timing of Murphy's Law. Take for instance the time Sue and I were mailing hundreds of copies of a newspaper we published. The only way we could transport such a large number was in two large trash bags. It was a holiday. No one was around, so it didn't matter if we used trash bags to transport them.

As we took handfuls of the papers out of the bags and stuffed them into the Post Office mailbox, a parade of local veterans turned a corner and marched by. It must have looked like we had found a quick and easy was to get rid of our trash.

On another well-timed occasion, I had just tried out a lawn mower that one of our neighbors loaned us. If we thought the mower did a good job on our front lawn, they would sell it to us at a reasonable price.

I wasn't too impressed with its performance. It was large and heavy. Sue could see that I was having difficulty with the huge machine. Thinking that perhaps there was a knack to handling it, she asked if she could try it for a moment.

I gave my petite 4'11" spouse the reigns and stood back on the sidewalk to see how the lawn looked so far. At that very moment, a woman from our church walked by. She smiled awkwardly as she glanced at my laboring wife, then back at me as I casually stood on the sidewalk and watched her work.

Memory Verse

"But there were false prophets also among the people, even as there shall be false teachers among you, who privately shall bring in damnable heresies, even denying the Lord that bought them, and bring upon themselves swift destruction."

2 PETER 2:1

Last Words

George Whitefield (1714–1770), whose name will live forever in the annals of evangelism, was a co-worker of the Wesleys before he settled in America. His name still stands as a synonym for the most marvelous exhibitions of pulpit eloquence. Dying the death of a righteous man, Whitefield uttered this prayer:

> **"Lord Jesus, I am weary in Thy work, but not of Thy work. If I have not yet finished my course, let me go and speak for Thee once more in the fields, seal the truth, and come home to die."**

58
Messianic Prophecies, Part 1

"I marvel that where the ambitious dreams of myself and of Alexander and of Caesar should have vanished into thin air, a Judean peasant—Jesus—should be able to stretch out his hands across the centuries, and control the destinies of men and nations."

NAPOLEON BONAPARTE

Kirk's Comment If Jesus is God, we should worship and obey Him. If Jesus is not God, then according to His own claims of His identity, we must dismiss Him as a liar or a crazy man.

QUESTIONS & OBJECTIONS

"On the cross, Jesus cried, 'My God, why have You forsaken Me?' This proves He was a fake. God forsook Him."

Jesus' words recorded in Matthew 27:46 and Mark 15:34 were the fulfillment of David's prophecy in Psalm 22:1. Verse 3 of this psalm then gives us insight into why God forsook Jesus on the cross: "But You are holy..." A holy Creator cannot have fellowship with sin. When Jesus was on the cross, the sin of the entire world was laid upon Him (Isaiah 53:6; 2 Corinthians 5:21), but Scripture says God is "of purer eyes than to behold evil, and cannot look on iniquity" (Habakkuk 1:13).

Messianic Prophecies

Unlike any other book, the Bible offers a multitude of specific predictions —some thousands of years in advance—that either have been literally fulfilled or point to a definite future time when they will come true. Fulfilled prophecies argue for omniscience—only one who is omniscient can accurately predict details of events thousands of years in the future. Limited human beings know the future only if it is told to them by an omniscient Being.

There are two categories of biblical prophecy: messianic (those that speak of the coming Messiah) and non-messianic. In his comprehensive catalogue of prophecies, *The Encyclopedia of Biblical Prophecies*, J. Barton Payne lists 191 prophecies concerning the anticipated Jewish Messiah and Savior. Each was literally fulfilled in the life, death, resurrection, and ascension of Jesus of Nazareth. A sampling of these prophecies follows.

Messiah's Birth

Isaiah predicted that one called Immanuel ("God with us") would be born of a virgin: "Therefore the Lord himself will give you a sign: The virgin will be with child and will give birth to a son, and will call him Immanuel" (7:14). This prediction was made over 700 years in advance.

The New Testament affirms that Jesus fulfilled this prediction, saying, "All this took place to fulfill what the Lord had said through the prophet: 'The virgin will be with child and will give birth to a son, and they will call him Immanuel'—which means, 'God with us'" (Matthew 1:22,23).

Micah made the unambiguous prophecy, "But you, Bethlehem Ephrathah, though you are small among the clans of Judah, out of you will come for me one who will be ruler over Israel, whose origins are from of old, from ancient times" (Micah 5:2). Even the unbelieving Jewish scribes identified this as a prediction of the Messiah and directed the inquiring magi to Bethlehem:

> After Jesus was born in Bethlehem in Judea, during the time of King Herod, Magi from the east came to Jerusalem and asked, "Where is the one who has been born king of the Jews? We saw his star in the

east and have come to worship him." When King Herod heard this he was disturbed, and all Jerusalem with him. When he had called together all the people's chief priests and teachers of the law, he asked them where the Christ was to be born. "In Bethlehem in Judea," they replied, "for this is what the prophet has written: 'But you, Bethlehem, in the land of Judah, are by no means least among the rulers of Judah; for out of you will come a ruler who will be the shepherd of my people Israel'" (Matthew 2:1–6).

Messiah's Ancestry

God declared in Genesis that the messianic blessing for all the world would come from the offspring of Abraham: "I will make you into a great nation and I will bless you; I will make your name great, and you will be a blessing. I will bless those who bless you, and whoever curses you I will curse; and all peoples on earth will be blessed through you" (Genesis 12:2,3; cf. 22:18).

Jesus Christ was indeed the seed of Abraham. Matthew's Gospel begins, "A record of the genealogy of Jesus Christ the son of David, the son of Abraham" (1:1). Paul adds, "The promises were spoken to Abraham and to his seed. The Scripture does not say 'and to seeds,' meaning many people, but 'and to your seed,' meaning one person, who is Christ" (Galatians 3:16).

The Redeemer would come through the tribe of Judah: "The scepter will not depart from Judah, nor the ruler's staff from between his feet, until he comes to whom it belongs and the obedience of the nations is his" (Genesis 49:10).

According to the New Testament genealogies, this was Jesus' ancestry:

> Now Jesus himself was about thirty years old when he began his ministry. He was the son, so it was thought, of Joseph, the son of Heli ... the son of Judah, the son of Jacob, the son of Isaac, the son of Abraham (Luke 3:23,33,34; cf. Matthew 1:1–3).

> For it is clear that our Lord descended from Judah (Hebrews 7:14).

The books of Samuel record the prediction that the Messiah would be of the house of David. God said to David: "When your days are over and you rest with your fathers, I will raise up your offspring to succeed you, who will come from your own body, and I will establish his kingdom. He is the one who will build a house for my Name, and I will establish the throne of his kingdom forever. I will be his father, and he shall be my son" (2 Samuel 7:13,14).

The New Testament repeatedly affirms that Jesus Christ was "the son of David" (Matthew 1:1). Jesus Himself claimed to be "the son of David" (Matthew 22:42–45). The Palm Sunday crowd also hailed Jesus as "the son of David" (Matthew 21:9). Luke 1:32,33 says of Jesus: "He will be great and will be called the Son of the Most High. The Lord God will give him the throne of his father David, and he will reign over the house of Jacob forever; his kingdom will never end."

Herald of Messiah's Coming

Isaiah predicted that the Messiah would be heralded by a messenger of the Lord who would be "a voice of one calling: 'In the desert prepare the way for the LORD; make straight in the wilderness a highway for our God'" (40:3).

This prediction was literally fulfilled in the ministry of John the Baptist. Matthew records: "In those days John the Baptist came, preaching in the Desert of Judea and saying, 'Repent, for the kingdom of heaven is near.' This is he who was spoken of through the prophet Isaiah: 'A voice of one calling in the desert, "Prepare the way for the Lord, make straight paths for him"'" (3:1–3).

Isaiah 11:2 foretold that the Messiah would be anointed by the Holy Spirit for His ministry: "The Spirit of the LORD will rest on him—the Spirit of wisdom and of understanding, the Spirit of counsel and of power, the Spirit of knowledge and of the fear of the LORD."

This literally happened to Jesus at His baptism. Matthew 3:16,17 says, "As soon as Jesus was baptized, he went up out of the water. At that moment heaven was opened, and he saw the Spirit of God descending like a dove and lighting on him. And a voice from heaven said, This is my Son, whom I love; with him I am well pleased."

Isaiah 61 said that the Messiah would preach the gospel to the poor and brokenhearted. Jesus pointed out His fulfillment of this ministry in the Nazareth synagogue:

> The scroll of the prophet Isaiah was handed to him. Unrolling it, he found the place where it is written: "The Spirit of the Lord is on me, because he has anointed me to preach good news to the poor. He has sent me to proclaim freedom for the prisoners and recovery of sight for the blind, to release the oppressed, to proclaim the year of the Lord's favor" (Luke 4:17–19).

Jesus carefully cut off his reading in the middle of a sentence, failing to add the next phrase, "and the day of vengeance of our God." That refers to His second coming; it was not fulfilled that day in their hearing, as was the rest of the prophecy.

Isaiah 35:5,6 declared that the Messiah would perform miracles to confirm His ministry, asserting: "Then will the eyes of the blind be opened and the ears of the deaf unstopped."

The Gospel record is filled with Jesus' miracles. For example: "Jesus went through all the towns and villages, teaching in their synagogues, preaching the good news of the kingdom and healing every disease and sickness" (Matthew 9:35). Jesus even cited these very things for John the Baptist as His messianic calling card: "Go back and report to John what you hear and see: The blind receive sight, the lame walk, those who have leprosy are cured, the deaf hear, the dead are raised, and the good news is preached to the poor" (Matthew 11:4,5).

Messiah's Work

Among many psalms applicable to the ministry of Jesus is 118:22, which foretells Messiah's rejection by His people: "The stone the builders rejected has become the capstone."

This very verse is cited repeatedly in the New Testament. For example, Peter wrote, "Now to you who believe, this stone is precious. But to those who do not believe, 'The stone the builders rejected has become the capstone'" (1 Peter 2:7; cf. Matthew 21:42; Mark 12:10; Luke 20:17; Acts 4:11).

QUESTIONS

1. Why is the Bible like no other book?

2. Why do fulfilled prophecies argue for omniscience?

3. What are the two categories of biblical prophecy?

4. How many years in advance had Isaiah predicted that Jesus would be born of a virgin?

5. Could you prove Jesus is the Messiah by using just the Old Testament?

WORDS OF COMFORT

I was speaking at a church in Houston, Texas, and was very conscious of scorpions. The previous week, a number of the little beasts had been found in the house where I was staying.

While I was in the pulpit that Sunday, I saw one crawl across the floor in front of me, so I called out "Scorpion!" Much to the amusement of the congregation, it turned out to be a large grasshopper.

During the same sermon, I spied a large black spider heading for my hand as I leaned on the pulpit. I screamed, "Tarantula!", picked up a glass of water that was on the pulpit and dumped it on the brute. That delighted the congregation even more.

I was wrong again. It wasn't a tarantula, it was merely an oversized black widow—America's deadliest spider.

Memory Verse

"But now a righteousness of God without the law is manifested, being witnessed by the Law and the prophets; even the righteousness of God which is by faith of Jesus Christ to all and upon all them that believe."
ROMANS 3:21,22

Last Words

Michelangelo (1475–1564), the Italian artist and sculptor, was one of the greatest sculptors the world has ever known. His remarkable paintings in the Sistine Chapel at Rome made him famous. God-fearing, his brief will contained the statement: "I commit my soul to God, my body to the earth, my possessions to my nearest relatives. I die in the faith of Jesus Christ and in the firm hope of a better life." His last word was an exhortation to those at his bedside:

"Through life remember the suffering of Jesus."

LESSON 59

Messianic Prophecies, Part 2

"God proved His love on the cross. When Christ hung, and bled, and died, it was God saying to the world, 'I love you.'"

BILLY GRAHAM

QUESTIONS & OBJECTIONS

"When Jesus died on the cross, did the centurion say that Jesus was innocent, or that He was the Son of God?"

Matthew (27:54) and Mark (15:39) agree that the centurion exclaimed that Jesus "was the Son of God!" Luke, however, mentions that the centurion refers to Jesus as "a righteous man" (23:47). Is it hard to believe that the centurion said both? Nowhere in any of the Gospel narratives do the writers claim that was all the centurion had to say.

Matthew and Mark were more interested by the declaration of divinity used by the centurion, whereas Luke is interested in the humanity of Jesus, one of the main themes of his Gospel. Thus he refers to the corresponding statement made by the centurion.

The Suffering and Death of Christ

One of the most amazing predictions about Christ in all of Scripture is that of Isaiah 53:2–12. This precise description predicts twelve aspects of the Messiah's sufferings and death, all of which were literally fulfilled (see Matthew 26—27; Mark 15—16; Luke 22—23; John 18—19). Jesus...

1. Was rejected

2. Was a man of sorrow

3. Lived a life of suffering

4. Was despised by others

5. Carried our sorrow

6. Was smitten and afflicted by God

7. Was pierced for our transgressions

8. Was wounded for our sins

9. Suffered like a lamb

10. Died with the wicked

11. Was sinless

12. Prayed for others

Further confirmation of the predictive nature of Isaiah 53 is that it was common for Jewish interpreters before the time of Christ to teach that Isaiah here spoke of the Jewish Messiah. Only after early Christians began using the text apologetically with great force did it become in rabbinical teaching an expression of the suffering Jewish nation. This view is implausible in the context of Isaiah's standard references to the Jewish people in the first-person plural whereas he always refers to the Messiah in third-person singular, as in Isaiah 53 ("he," "his," and "him").

Predictions elsewhere about Christ's death include:

- The piercing of His hands and feet (Psalm 22:16; cf. Luke 23:33)

- The piercing of His side (Zechariah 12:10; cf. John 19:34)

- The casting of lots for His garments (Psalm 22:18; cf. John 19:23,24)

While it wasn't recognized until after the fact, one of the most precise predictions in Scripture gives the very year in which the Christ would die.

Daniel was speaking of both the exile of Israel and the atonement for sin when he recorded a prayer of confession for the sins of his people and a vision that the angel Gabriel gave him:

> Seventy "sevens" are decreed for your people and your holy city to finish transgression, to put an end to sin, to atone for wickedness, to bring in everlasting righteousness, to seal up vision and prophecy and to anoint the most holy. Know and understand this: From the issuing of the decree to restore and rebuild Jerusalem until the Anointed One [Messiah], the ruler, comes, there will be seven "sevens," and sixty-two "sevens"…After the sixty-two "sevens," the Anointed One will be cut off… (9:24–26).

The context indicates that Daniel knew Gabriel was speaking of years, since he was meditating on the "number of years" God had revealed to Jeremiah that Jerusalem would lay waste, namely "seventy years" (v. 2).

God told Daniel that it would be seven "sevens" plus sixty-two "sevens" (years) after the decree to rebuild before the Messiah would come and be cut off (die). In other words, it would be $69 \times 7 = 483$ years to the time of Christ's death. Artaxerxes ordered Nehemiah "to restore and rebuild Jerusalem" (Daniel 9:25; cf. Nehemiah 2) in 445/444 B.C. Adding the widely accepted date of A.D. 33 for the crucifixion would be $444 + 33 = 477$.

Add six years to compensate for the five days in our solar year that are not in the lunar year followed by Israel ($5 \times 477 = 2,385$ days or 6+ years): $477 + 6 = 483$ years. Daniel's prediction takes us to the very time of Christ.

Christ's Resurrection

The Old Testament also foretold the resurrection of the Messiah from the dead. In Psalm 16:10 David declares, "You will not abandon me to the grave, nor will you let your Holy One see decay."

This passage is cited in the New Testament as predictive of the resurrection of Christ. Peter said explicitly of David's prophecy, "But he was a prophet and knew that God had promised him on oath that he would place one of his descendants on his throne. Seeing what was ahead, he spoke of the resurrection of the Christ, that he was not abandoned to the grave, nor did his body see decay" (Acts 2:30,31).

Indeed, using passages such as this, "Paul went into the synagogue, and on three Sabbath days he reasoned with them from the Scriptures, explaining and proving that the Christ had to suffer and rise from the dead. 'This Jesus I am proclaiming to you is the Christ,' he said" (Acts 17:2,3).

This would scarcely have been possible unless his skeptical Jewish audience did not recognize the predictive nature of passages such as Psalm 16.

The Ascension of Christ

In Psalm 110:1, David even predicted the ascension of Christ, writing, "The LORD says to my Lord: 'Sit at my right hand until I make your enemies a footstool for your feet.'"

In Matthew 22:43,44, Jesus applied this passage to Himself. Peter also applied it to the ascension of Christ: "For David did not ascend to heaven, and yet he said, 'The Lord said to my Lord: "Sit at my right hand until I make your enemies a footstool for your feet"'" (Acts 2:34,35).

PROPHECY AND THE MESSIAH

It is important to note the unique aspect of biblical prophecies. Unlike many psychic predictions, many of these were *very specific*, giving, for example, the very name of the tribe, city, and time of Christ's coming. Unlike forecasts found in tabloids at the supermarket checkout counter, *none of these predictions failed.*

Since the 191 prophecies of the Messiah were written hundreds of years before Christ was born, the prophets could not have been reading the trends of the times or making intelligent guesses. Many predictions were beyond human ability to fake a fulfillment.

If Christ were a mere human being...

- He would have had no control over when (Daniel 9:24–27), where (Micah 5:2), or how He would be born (Isaiah 7:14).

- He would have had no control over how He would die (Psalm 22; Isaiah 53).

- He would not have been able to do miracles (Isaiah 35:5,6).

- He would not have been able to rise from the dead (Psalms 2, 16).

It is statistically impossible that all these events would have converged randomly in the life of one man. Mathematicians have calculated the probability of just sixteen predictions being fulfilled in one person at 1 in 10^{45}. For forty-eight predictions to meet in one person, the probability is 1 in 10^{157}. It is almost impossible to even conceive of a number that large.

But it is not just a statistical impossibility that rules out the theory that Jesus engineered His prophecy fulfillments; it is morally implausible that an all-powerful and all-knowing God would allow His plans for prophetic fulfillment to be ruined by someone who just happened to be in the right place at the right time. God cannot lie (Hebrews 6:18), nor can He break a promise (Joshua 23:14). So we must conclude that He did not allow His prophetic promises to be thwarted by chance.

All the evidence points to Jesus as the divinely appointed fulfillment of the messianic prophecies. He was God's man, confirmed by God's signs (Acts 2:22).

QUESTIONS

1. **Name three of the twelve aspects of the suffering of the Messiah that Isaiah mentions in chapter 53 of his book.**

2. **Why is Daniel 9 considered to be such an amazing prophecy?**

3. Where in the Old Testament is the resurrection of Jesus prophesied?

4. How is biblical prophecy unlike psychic predictions?

5. Why were many Bible predictions beyond human ability to fake a fulfillment?

6. How could you explain to someone the mathematical impossibility of Jesus fulfilling all 191 messianic prophecies?

Feathers for Arrows

Imagine that you tried to describe the workings of a television to someone who had never seen a TV set. You show him one and say, "This is a television set. When you press this button, a man comes on and reads the up-to-date news to you." Your skeptical friend says, "How does he get into the box?" You reply, "He's not actually in the box." He says, "Is he in there or isn't he?" You answer, "Well, his image is sent via invisible television waves through the air, to an antenna, down a wire, up a cord, and into the box." Your friend becomes a little impatient and says, "So this newsreader of yours floats invisibly through the air, slides down an antenna, crawls up a cord, into your set? What kind of simpleton do you think I am?"

Your confidence isn't shaken because you can prove your claim, fantastic though it may sound. You pass him the remote control and say, "Push the button and see for yourself."

The claim of the Christian faith is fantastic in the truest sense of the word—repent and trust in Jesus Christ, and the invisible God of creation will reveal Himself to you (John 14:21). Our confidence isn't shaken in the face of a skeptical world, simply because the claim can be proven. Any skeptic who will push the button of repentance toward God and faith toward the Lord Jesus Christ will experience the miracle of conversion.

Last Words

Christopher Columbus (1451–1506) made several voyages westward and is credited with the discovery of the West Indies. When he died, the parting message from his lips was:

"Lord, into Thy hands I commit my spirit."

Memory Verse

"This is what is written: The Christ will suffer and rise from the dead on the third day, and repentance and forgiveness of sins will be preached in his name to all nations, beginning at Jerusalem. You are witnesses of these things."
LUKE 24:46–48

Non-Messianic Prophecies

"But from whence shall I fetch my argument? With what shall I win them? Oh, that I could tell! I would write to them in tears, I would weep out every argument, I would empty my veins for ink, I would petition them on my knees. Oh, how thankful I would be if they would be prevailed with to repent and turn!"

JOSEPH ALLEINE

Kirk's Comment When God predicts something, He is always 100 percent accurate. If there were even one prophecy that was wrong, that would discredit the entire Bible and its claim to be the inerrant Word of God.

QUESTIONS & OBJECTIONS

"God said He would blot out all remembrance of Amalek. The Bible itself disproves this statement by mentioning Amalek to this day."

In Exodus 17:14, God told Moses to "write this for a memorial in a book." Moses did that and God preserved the Book for 5,000 years so skeptics would know that God keeps every promise He makes. The phrase "I will utterly put out the remembrance of Amalek from under heaven" means that He will blot them out as a nation from the earth. There are no descendants of the Amalekites on the earth. They don't exist.

Succession of Great World Kingdoms

An amazing prediction in the Bible is the succession of the world empires of Babylon, Medo-Persia, Greece, and Rome, which God told to Daniel. Interpreting the metallic man in the dream of King Nebuchadnezzar of Babylon, Daniel told the king:

> You, O king, are the king of kings... You are that head of gold. After you, another kingdom will rise, inferior to yours. Next, a third kingdom, one of bronze, will rule over the whole earth. Finally, there will be a fourth kingdom, strong as iron—for iron breaks and smashes everything—and as iron breaks things to pieces, so it will crush and break all the others (Daniel 2:38–40).

So precise and accurate is this prophecy that even critics agree that Daniel spoke in order of Babylon, Medo-Persia, Greece, and Rome. Critics try to avoid the supernatural nature of the prophecy by claiming that these words were written after the fact, in about 165 B.C., but there is no real substantiation for this claim.

King Cyrus of Persia

One of the most specific Old Testament predictions identifies Cyrus of Persia before he was even born. Isaiah 44:28—45:1 says,

> The LORD... who says of Cyrus, "He is my shepherd and will accomplish all that I please; he will say of Jerusalem, 'Let it be rebuilt,' and of the temple, 'Let its foundations be laid.'" This is what the LORD says to his anointed, to Cyrus, whose right hand I take hold of to subdue nations before him and to strip kings of their armor, to open doors before him so that gates will not be shut.

This prediction was made some 150 years before Cyrus was even born. Since Isaiah lived between about 740 and 690 B.C. (2 Kings 25—21) and Cyrus did not make his proclamation for Israel to return from exile until about 536 B.C. (Ezra 1), there would have been no human way for Isaiah to know what Cyrus would be named or do.

The attempt of critics to divide Isaiah and postdate the prophecy is without foundation and is a backhanded compliment to the detail and accuracy of the prediction.

The Return of Israel to Their Homeland

Given their long exile of some nineteen centuries and the animosity of the occupants of Palestine against them, any prediction of the return, restoration, and rebuilding of the nation of Israel was extremely unlikely. Yet predictions made centuries in advance about the restoration of the Jews to their homeland, and predictions made over two and a half millennia in advance about their restoration as a nation, have been literally fulfilled.

The first return was under Ezra and Nehemiah in the sixth century B.C. But Israel was sent again into exile in A.D. 70 when the Roman armies destroyed Jerusalem and leveled the temple. For nearly 2,000 years the Jewish people remained in exile and the nation did not exist. Then, just as the Bible foretold, millions of Jews returned to their country and were reestablished after World War II following a bitter struggle with the Arab Palestinians.

In 700 B.C. the prophet Isaiah predicted, "In that day the Lord will reach out his hand a second time to reclaim the remnant that is left of his people from Assyria, from Lower Egypt, from Upper Egypt, from Cush, from Elam, from Babylonia, from Hamath and from the islands of the sea" (11:11). In Isaiah 66:7,8, he gives a strange prophecy: "Before she travailed, she brought forth; before her pain came, she was delivered of a man child. Who has heard such a thing? Who has seen such things? Shall the earth be made to bring forth in one day? Or shall a nation be born at once? For as soon as Zion travailed, she brought forth her children."

In 1922 the League of Nations gave Great Britain the mandate (political authority) over Palestine. On May 14, 1948, Britain withdrew her mandate, and the nation of Israel was "born in a day." No other nation in history has managed so successfully to keep a culture, identity, and language intact over hundreds of years, let alone against the genocidal hatred repeatedly encountered by the Jews. This Bible prediction is incredible evidence of the supernatural origin of the Scriptures.

There are more than 25 Bible prophecies concerning Palestine that have been literally fulfilled. Probability estimations conclude that the chances of these being accidentally fulfilled are less than one in 33 million.

The Closing of the Golden Gate

The Golden Gate is the eastern gate of Jerusalem, through which Christ made His triumphal entry on Palm Sunday before His crucifixion (Matthew 21). Ezekiel 44:2 predicted that it would be closed one day, and not reopened until the Messiah returned:

> The LORD said to me, "This gate is to remain shut. It must not be opened; no one may enter through it. It is to remain shut because the LORD, the God of Israel, has entered through it."

In 1543 Sultan Suleiman the Magnificent closed the gate and walled it up as Ezekiel had predicted. He had no idea he was fulfilling prophecy. He simply sealed it because the road leading to it was no longer used for traffic. It remains sealed to this day exactly as the Bible predicted, waiting to be reopened when the King returns.

The Doom of Edom (Petra)

Unlike many Old Testament predictions of doom, Edom was not promised any restoration, only "perpetual desolation" (Jeremiah 25:12). Jeremiah wrote in 49:16,17:

> "The terror you inspire and the pride of your heart has deceived you, you who live in the clefts of the rocks, who occupy the heights of the hill. Though you build your nest as high as the eagle's, from there I will bring you down," declares the Lord. "Edom will become an object of horror; all who pass by will be appalled and will scoff because of all its wounds."

Given the virtually impregnable nature of the ancient city carved out of rock and protected by a narrow passageway, this was an incredible prediction. Yet, in A.D. 636 it was conquered by Muslims and today stands deserted but for tourists and passersby.

Flourishing of the Desert in Palestine

For centuries Palestine lay wasted and desolate. These conditions extended throughout the land. But Ezekiel 36:33–35 predicted,

> This is what the Sovereign LORD says: On the day I cleanse you from your sins, I will resettle your towns, and the ruins will be rebuilt. The desolate land will be cultivated instead of lying desolate in the sight of all who pass through it. They will say, "This land that was laid waste has become like the garden of Eden; the cities that were lying in ruins, desolate and destroyed, are now fortified and inhabited."

Today roads have been built, the land is being cultivated, and Israel's agriculture is flourishing. This renovation began before the turn of the twentieth century and continues a century later. Agricultural crops, including a large orange harvest, are part of the restoration—just as Ezekiel had predicted.

Conclusion

A fact often overlooked by critics is that only one real case of fulfilled prophecy is needed to establish Scripture's supernatural origin. Even if most biblical predictions could be explained naturally, even one clear case establishes the rest and confirms the prophetic event. Thus, if the critic is to make the case against prophecy, then *all* instances must be naturally explainable.

QUESTIONS

1. **Which book of the Bible gives the amazing prediction of a succession of world empires?**

2. Which book of the Bible identifies Cyrus of Persia before he was born?

3. Which prophet predicted that the Eastern gate in Jerusalem would be closed and not re-opened?

4. What is unique about the Jews' return to their homeland?

5. Which prophet predicted "perpetual desolation" for Edom (Petra)?

6. Who predicted that Palestine, after lying desolate for centuries, would once again flourish?

PREACHER'S PROGRESS

Ima Pewsitter: "I go to church every week."

Christian: "Have you been born again? Are you familiar with that term?"

Ima Pewsitter: "Yes."

Christian: "Have you?"

Ima Pewsitter: "No, I'm not a 'born-again,' if that's what you are asking."

Christian: "No, I'm not asking that. In John chapter 3, Jesus said, 'You must be born again.' That's how you become a Christian—by being born again."

Ima Pewsitter: "I've always been a Christian."

Christian: "You mean, you've always believed in God."

Ima Pewsitter: "And Jesus. I was also baptized as a baby."

Christian: "The difference between 'believing' and being born again is like the difference between believing in a parachute and actually putting it on."

Ima Pewsitter: "What do you mean?"

Christian: "If someone sits on a plane and believes in a parachute, but doesn't put it on, he will see his big mistake when he jumps. The Bible says to 'put on the Lord Jesus Christ.' That happens when you are born again. If someone merely believes in Jesus, but doesn't put Him on, he will see his tragic mistake when he passes through the door of death."

Ima Pewsitter: "That's scary."

Christian: "It is, and the church is filled with people who have never been born again. Do you consider yourself to be a good person?"

Ima Pewsitter: "Yes."

Christian: "May I ask you a few questions to see if you measure up to God's standard of goodness?"

Ima Pewsitter: "Sure."

Christian: "Hold on, because His standard is pretty high. Have you ever told a lie?" Etc.

Last Words

Jonathan Edwards, Jr., son of the eminent American preacher who was greatly used in revivals, died at 55—the same age as his father. His last words were:

"Trust in God and you shall have nothing to fear."

Scientific Facts in the Bible, Part 1

"The nearer I approach the end of my pilgrimage, the clearer is the evidence of the divine origin of the Bible. The grandeur and sublimity of God's remedy for fallen man are more appreciated and the future is illuminated with hope and joy."

SAMUEL MORSE (inventor of the telegraph)

Kirk's Comment The evidence for the existence of God is truly overwhelming—something of which many people are completely unaware. The laws of natural science, archeology, astronomy, biology, and prophecy all point to an infinitely intelligent Creator, as the next few lessons show.

QUESTIONS & OBJECTIONS

"If God is perfect, why did He make an imperfect creation?"

The Bible tells us that the Genesis creation was "good." There was no sin and therefore no suffering or death. Why then did God give Adam and Eve the ability to sin, knowing full well that they would sin and bring death and pain to the human race? Some believe that if Adam had been created without the ability to choose, then he would have been a "robot." A father *cannot* make his children love him. They choose to love him because they have a free will. Others point out that humanity would never have seen the depth of the love of God, as displayed in the cross, unless Adam had sinned, and that fact could be one reason why God allowed sin to enter the world.

w o t m w o t m w o t m w o t m w o t m w o t m w o t m w o t m w o t m w o t m

M any people view the Bible with a great deal of skepticism—and they should. It's always wise to consider the evidence before deciding whether something is true. In the following three lessons you will find valuable information you can share with the lost—compelling evidence that the Bible is no ordinary book. God has revealed numerous scientific and medical facts in the Bible, thousands of years before scientists "discovered" them. As Hank Hanegraaff said, "Faith in Christ is not some blind leap into a dark chasm, but a faith based on established evidence."

Science expresses the universe in five terms: time, space, matter, power, and motion. Genesis 1:1,2 revealed such truths to the Hebrews in 1450 B.C.: "In the beginning [*time*] God created [*power*] the heaven [*space*] and the earth [*matter*] ... And the Spirit of God moved [*motion*] upon the face of the waters." The first thing God tells man is that He controls of all aspects of the universe.

Only in recent years has science discovered that everything we see is composed of invisible atoms. Scripture tells us in Hebrews 11:3 that the "things which are seen were not made of things which do appear."

It is also interesting to note that scientists now understand the universe is expanding or stretching out. Nine times in Scripture we are told that God *stretches* out the heavens like a curtain (e.g., Psalm 104:2).

At a time when it was believed that the earth sat on a large animal or a giant (1500 B.C.), the Bible spoke of the earth's free float in space: "He ...hangs the earth upon nothing" (Job 26:7).

The prophet Isaiah also tells us that the earth is round: "It is he that sits upon the circle of the earth" (Isaiah 40:22). This is not a reference to a flat disk, as some skeptics maintain, but to a sphere. Secular man discovered this 2,400 years later. At a time when science believed that the earth was flat, it was the Scriptures that inspired Christopher Columbus to sail around the world.

For ages, scientists believed in a geocentric view of the universe. The differences between night and day were believed to be caused by the sun revolving around the earth. Today, we know that the earth's rotation on its axis is responsible for the sun's rising and setting. But 4,000 or more years ago, it was written, "Have you commanded the morning since your days; and caused the day spring [dawn] to know his place? ... It [the earth] is turned as clay to the seal" (Job 38:12,14). The picture here is of a clay vessel being turned or rotated upon the potter's wheel—an accurate analogy of the earth's rotation.

Luke 17:34–36 says the Second Coming of Jesus Christ will occur while some are asleep at night and others are working at daytime activities in the field. This is another clear indication of a revolving earth, with day and night occurring at the same time.

In speaking of the sun, the psalmist says that "his going forth is from the end of the heaven, and his circuit unto the ends of it: and there is nothing hid from the heat thereof" (Psalm 19:5,6). For many years critics scoffed at these verses, thinking that the sun was stationary. Then it was discovered in recent years that the sun is in fact moving through space at approximately 600,000 miles per hour. It is traveling through the heavens and has a "circuit" just as the Bible says. Its circuit is so large that it would take approximately 200 million years to complete one orbit.

The Scriptures say, "Thus the heavens and the earth were finished, and all the host of them" (Genesis 2:1). The original Hebrew uses the past definite tense for the verb "finished," indicating an action completed in the past, never again to occur. The creation was "finished"—once and for all. That is exactly what the First Law of Thermodynamics says. This law (often referred to as the Law of the Conservation of Energy and/or Mass) states that neither matter nor energy can be either created or destroyed. It was because of this Law that Sir Fred Hoyle's "Steady-State" (or "Continuous Creation") Theory was discarded. Hoyle stated that at points in the universe called "irtrons," matter (or energy) was constantly being created. But the First Law states just the opposite. Indeed, there is no "creation" ongoing today. It is "finished" exactly as the Bible states.

Three places in the Bible (Isaiah 51:6; Psalm 102:25,26; Hebrews 1:11) indicate that the earth is wearing out. This is what the Second Law of Thermodynamics (Law of Increasing Entropy) states: in all physical processes, every ordered system over time tends to become more disordered. Everything is running down and wearing out as energy is becoming less available for use. That means the universe will eventually "wear out" so that (theoretically speaking) there will be a "heat death" and therefore no more energy available for use. This wasn't discovered by man until fairly recently, but the Bible states it in clear, succinct terms.

God told Job in 1500 B.C.: "Can you send lightnings, that they may go, and say to you, Here we are?" (Job 38:35). The Bible here is making what appears to be a scientifically ludicrous statement—that light can be *sent*, and then manifest itself in speech. But did you know that radio waves travel at the speed of light? This is why you can have *instantaneous* wireless communication with someone on the other side of the earth. Science didn't discover this until 1864 when "British scientist James Clerk Maxwell suggested that electricity and light waves were two forms of the same thing" (*Modern Century Illustrated Encyclopedia*).

Job 38:19 asks, "Where is the way where light dwells?" Modern man has only recently discovered that light (electromagnetic radiation) has a "way," traveling at 186,000 miles per second.

Science has discovered that stars emit radio waves, which are received on earth as a high pitch. God mentioned this in Job 38:7: "When the morning stars sang together..."

With all these truths revealed in Scripture, how could a thinking person deny that the Bible is supernatural in origin? There is no other book in any of the world's religions (Vedas, Bhagavad-Gita, Koran, Book of Mormon, etc.) that contains scientific truth. In fact, they contain statements that are clearly unscientific.

QUESTIONS

1. **What are the five aspects of the universe, which God mentions in Genesis 1:1,2?**

2. Scientists now understand that the universe is expanding or stretching out. Where does the Bible tells us this well-known fact?

3. Skeptics still sometimes claim that the Bible states the earth is flat. What does the Bible really say about the earth?

4. How does Scripture confirm the First Law of Thermodynamics?

5. Identify a verse in Scripture that confirms the Second Law of Thermodynamics.

PREACHER'S PROGRESS

Alec Tricity: "Wassup? Hey, Christian man, I don't believe there's any proof that Jesus is the Son of God."

Christian: "Then who do you think He was?"

Alec Tricity: "He was just a man."

Christian: "The Bible says that God became a Man in Jesus Christ."

Alec Tricity: "Are you sure?"

Christian: "That's what the Bible teaches. Here's how you can know whether it's true. I believed in Jesus before I became a Christian."

Alec Tricity: "Huh?"

Christian: "True. Let me explain what I mean. A little kid was looking at an electric heater. His dad came in and said, 'Son, that heater is hot. Don't touch it.' The kid said, 'Okay. I believe that the heater is hot.' At that point the kid believed the heater was hot. He had an intellectual assent. Do you see that?"

Alec Tricity: "I see what you're saying."

Christian: "His dad leaves the room. The kid says, 'I wonder if it really is hot.' So he reaches out and touches the heater. The second his flesh burns, he stops *believing* that the heater's hot. He now..."

Alec Tricity: "...*knows* it's hot!"

Christian: "Right. He's moved out of the realm of belief and into the realm of experience. Know what I'm saying?"

Alec Tricity: "I know what you're saying. He now knows!"

Christian: "Before I was born again, I believed in God and I believed that Jesus was the Son of God. But when I turned from my sin and called on the name of the Lord, I reached out and touched the heater bar of God's love and forgiveness. I moved out of the realm of belief and into the realm of experience. I now know Him! Get it?"

Alec Tricity: "That's cool. I see what you're saying, man."

Christian: "Look at this. It's John 14:21 in the Bible. It says that if you obey the Lord, Jesus and His Father will reveal themselves to you. That's either true or it isn't. Let's now look at the Ten Commandments for a moment. Okay?"

Alec Tricity: "Sure."

Memory Verse

"Then said Jesus to those Jews which believed on him, If you continue in my word, then are you my disciples indeed; and you shall know the truth, and the truth shall make you free."

JOHN 8:31,32

Last Words

Andrew Jackson (1767–1845), seventh President of the U.S., exhorted his family with his last breath:

"Oh, do not cry. Be good children, and we will all meet in heaven."

Scientific Facts in the Bible, Part 2

"I do not feel obliged to believe that the same God who has endowed us with sense, reason, and intellect has intended us to forgo their use."

GALILEO GALILEI

Kirk's Comment   Did you know that many disciplines of modern science were founded by men who had a solid belief in the existence of God? True science is discovering and explaining what God has set into motion.

QUESTIONS & OBJECTIONS

"What if I don't feel that I have enough faith?"

It is not the *amount* of faith that saves you—it is *in whom* you place your faith. The question is: "Is the Savior strong enough and dependable enough to save me when I ask?"

Picture a two-story building that's on fire. You happen to be on the top floor. The fire is coming up from the bottom and there is no escape. You run to the roof and see a fire truck pull up to the front. Five big firemen get out and unfold a great big net. They look up at you and yell, "Jump!"

Your first thought is, "You've got to be kidding! I'm two stories up. I can't jump."

But the firemen say, "Don't you have faith? We'll catch you."

Now, you don't have a lot of faith, but with fear and trembling, you jump off the roof. As a result, the firemen catch you. It's not your faith that saved you, it was the firemen. But they couldn't save you until you jumped.

Now, let's change the story a little bit. Picture another person on the roof with the fire coming toward him. This man sees the firemen. And unlike you, he has a lot of faith. He confidently jumps off the roof, only to discover halfway down that the firemen have no net; they are just standing around holding hands. How much will the man's faith save him then? You'd better have real firemen holding a real net, or your faith won't save you.

In salvation, it's not how much faith you have or how sincere you are; rather, everything depends on the object of your faith. Have you placed your faith in a real Savior? It's not your faith that saves you, it's Jesus who saves you. You just need to step off and place yourself in His hands.

The more deeply we believe that Christ did all that is necessary in providing our salvation, the greater our assurance will be when we place our trust in Him. We might begin with a small faith (Christ said that faith the size of a mustard seed is all that is required), but know that in time our faith will grow. But whether our faith is little or much, it must be directed to Christ alone, for God accepts only those who accept His Son (1 John 2:23).

wotmwotmwotmwotmwotmwotmwotmwotmwotmwotmwotmwotm

Scientists Who Believe

In their book *What is Creation Science?* Henry M. Morris and Gary E. Parker wrote that most of the great scientists of the past who founded and developed the key disciplines of science were creationists. Note the following sampling:

Physics: Newton, Faraday, Maxwell, Kelvin

Chemistry: Boyle, Dalton, Pascal, Ramsay

Biology: Ray, Linnaeus, Mendel, Pasteur

Geology: Steno, Woodward, Brewster, Agassiz

Astronomy: Kepler, Galileo, Herschel, Maunder

These men, as well as scores of others who could be mentioned, were creationists, not evolutionists, and their names are practically synonymous with the rise of modern science. To them, the scientific enterprise was a high calling, one dedicated to "thinking God's thoughts after Him."

Johannes Kepler declared, "The chief aim of all investigation of the external world should be to discover the rational order and harmony which has been imposed on it by God." Kepler was prepared to put aside the plans he had made for his life, and to humbly follow God's leading. As a result, he was able to say in later life, "I had the intention of becoming a theologian...but now I see how God is, by my endeavors, also glorified in astronomy, for 'the heavens declare the glory of God.'"

Arthur H. Compton, winner of the Nobel Prize in Physics, stated, "Science is the glimpse of God's purpose in nature. The very existence of the amazing world of the atom and radiation points to a purposeful creation, to the idea that there is a God and an intelligent purpose back of everything...An orderly universe testifies to the greatest statement ever uttered: 'In the beginning, God...'"

Many of the greatest scientists clearly see God's hand in creation:

- *Lord Kelvin:* "With regard to the origin of life, science...positively affirms creative power."

- *Louis Pasteur:* "The more I study nature, the more I stand amazed at the work of the Creator."

- *Sir Isaac Newton:* "All material things seem to have been composed of the hard and solid particles abovementioned, variously associated in the first creation by the counsel of an intelligent Agent. For it became Him who created them to set them in order. And if he did so, it's unphilosophical to seek for any other origin of the world, or to pretend that it might arise out of a chaos by the mere laws of nature."

- *Albert Einstein:* "Science can only be created by those who are thoroughly imbued with the aspiration toward truth and understanding. This source of feeling, however, springs from the sphere of religion. To this there also belongs the faith in the possibility that the regulations valid for the world of existence are rational, that is, comprehensible to reason. I cannot conceive of a genuine scientist without that profound faith."

In *What if Jesus Had Never Been Born?* D. James Kennedy and Jerry Newcombe explained, "Calvin said that the Bible—God's special revelation—was spectacles that we must put on if we are to correctly read the book of nature—God's revelation in creation. Unfortunately, between the beginning of science and our day, many scientists have discarded these glasses, and many distortions have followed."

Richard Wurmbrand wrote, "In antiquity and in what is called the Dark Ages, men did not know what they now know about humanity and the cosmos. They did not know the lock but they possessed the key, which is God. Now many have excellent descriptions of the lock, but they have lost the key. The proper solution is union between religion and science. We should be owners of the lock *and* the key. The fact is that as science advances, it discovers what was said thousands of years ago in the Bible" (*Proofs of God's Existence*).

Religion and science are not at odds, as many claim; in fact, true science is rooted in the truths of God's Word. Sir John Frederick Herschel, an English astronomer who discovered over 500 stars, stated: "All human discoveries seem to be made only for the purpose of confirming more and more strongly the truths that come from on high and are contained in the Sacred Writings." His father, Sir William Herschel, also a renowned astronomer, insisted, "The undevout astronomer must be mad."

One of the scientific truths contained in the Bible is that God created the "lights" in the heavens "for signs, and for seasons, and for days and years" (Genesis 1:14). Through the marvels of astronomy we now understand that a year is the time required for the earth to travel once around the sun. The seasons are caused by the changing position of the earth in relation to the sun—"astronomers can tell exactly from the earth's motion around the sun when one season ends and the next one begins" (*Worldbook Multimedia Encyclopedia*). We also now understand that a "month [is] the time of one revolution of the moon around the earth with respect to the sun" (*Encyclopedia Britannica*). How could Moses (the accepted author of Genesis) have known 3,500 years ago that the "lights" of the sun and moon were the actual determining factors of the seasons, days, and years, unless God inspired his words?

QUESTIONS

1. Name at least two founders of the key disciplines of science who were creationists.

2. What might account for their success in the scientific enterprise?

3. According to Richard Wurmbrand, what is the proper relation between religion and science? Why?

4. Based on John Frederick Herschel's comment, why might God be behind scientific discoveries?

5. How could Moses have known 3,500 years ago that the "lights" of the sun and moon were the determining factors of the seasons, days, and years?

FEATHERS FOR ARROWS

Memory Verse

"For by him were all things created, that are in heaven, and that are in earth, visible and invisible, whether they be thrones, or dominions, or principalities, or powers: all things were created by him, and for him."

COLOSSIANS 1:16

"Many people think they can break the Ten Commandments right and left and get by with it. That reminds me of the whimsical story of the man who jumped off the Empire State Building in New York City. As he went sailing by the fiftieth floor, a man looked out the window and said to him, 'Well, how is it?' The falling man replied, 'So far, so good.' That is not where the law of gravity enforces itself. Fifty more floors down and the man will find out, 'So far, not so good.' The interesting thing is that a law must be enforced to be a law and therefore God says in Ezekiel 18:4, 'The soul that sins, it shall die.' The Law must be enforced and the breaker of the Law must pay the penalty." —*J. Vernon McGee*

Last Words

Louis XVIII, King of France, died 1824:

"A king should die standing."

LESSON 63

Scientific Facts in the Bible, Part 3

"The study of the Book of Job and its comparison with the latest scientific discoveries has brought me to the matured conviction that the Bible is an inspired book and was written by the One who made the stars."

CHARLES BURCKHALTER, Chabot Observatory

Kirk's Comment While scientific evidence can persuade the mind, the conscience persuades the heart. If we are successful in convincing the mind, but fail to turn the heart, all is still lost for the now intellectually convinced sinner. Facts open the mind, while the Ten Commandments prepare the soil of the heart, both working together to prepare the way for the gospel.

QUESTIONS & OBJECTIONS

"Did Jesus bear His own cross or not?"

John 19:17 states that He went out carrying His own cross to the place of the skull. Matthew 27:31,32 tells us that He was led out to be crucified and that it was only as they were going out to Golgotha that Simon was forced to carry the cross.

Mark 15:20,21 agrees with Matthew and gives us the additional information that Jesus started out from inside the palace (Praetorium). As Simon was on his way in from the country, it is clear that he was passing by in the street. This implies that Jesus carried His cross for some distance, from the palace into the street. Weak from his floggings and torture, it is likely that He either collapsed under the weight of the cross or was going very slowly. In any case, the soldiers forced Simon to carry the cross for Him. Luke 23:26 is in agreement, stating that Simon was seized as they led Jesus away.

Thus the contradiction vanishes. Jesus started out carrying the cross and Simon took over at some point during the journey.

w o t m w o t m w o t m w o t m w o t m w o t m w o t m w o t m w o t m w o t m w o t m

The Scriptures inform us, "All the rivers run into the sea; yet the sea is not full; unto the place from where the rivers come, there they return again" (Ecclesiastes 1:7). This statement alone may not seem profound. But when considered with other biblical passages, it becomes all the more remarkable. For example, the Mississippi River dumps approximately 6 million gallons of water per second into the Gulf of Mexico. Where does all that water go? And that's just one of thousands of rivers. The answer lies in the hydrologic cycle, so well brought out in the Bible.

Ecclesiastes 11:3 states that "if the clouds be full of rain, they empty themselves upon the earth." Amos 9:6 tells us, "He...calls for the waters of the sea, and pours them out upon the face of the earth." Job stated, "[God] made a decree for the rain, and a way for the lightning of the thunder" (Job 28:26). Centuries later, scientists began to discern the "decrees [rules] for the rain." Rainfall is part of a process called the "water cycle." The sun evaporates water from the ocean. The water vapor then rises and becomes clouds. This water in the clouds falls back to earth as rain, collects in streams and rivers, and then makes its way back to the ocean. That process repeats itself again and again. The idea of a complete water cycle was not fully understood until the seventeenth century. However, more than 2,000 years prior to the discoveries of Pierre Perrault, Edme Mariotte, Edmund Halley, and others, the Scriptures clearly spoke of a water cycle.

Solomon described a "cycle" of air currents 2,000 years before scientists "discovered" them. "The wind goes toward the south, and turns about to the north; it whirls about continually, and the wind returns again according to his circuits" (Ecclesiastes 1:6).

The Bible speaks of "the fish of the sea, and whatsoever passes through the paths of the seas" (Psalm 8:8). What does the Bible mean by "paths of the seas"? Man discovered the existence of ocean currents in the 1850s, but the Bible declared the science of oceanography 2,800 years ago. Matthew Maury (1806–1873), considered the father of oceanography, noticed the expression "paths of the sea" in Psalm 8:8. "If God said there are paths in the sea," Maury stated, "I am going to find them." Maury took God at His Word and went looking for these paths. We are indebted to his discovery of the warm and cold continental currents. His book on oceanography remains a basic text on the subject and is still used in universities. Maury used the Bible as a guide to a scientific discovery; if only more would use the Bible as a guide in their personal lives.

Only in recent years has man discovered that there are mountains on the ocean floor. This was revealed in the Bible thousands of years ago. While deep in the ocean, Jonah cried, "I went down to the bottoms of the mountains..." (Jonah 2:6). The reason the Bible and true science harmonize is that they have the same author.

The Bible speaks not just about the physical qualities of our universe, but about our bodies as well. Genesis 3:15 reveals that a female possesses a "seed" for childbearing. This was not common knowledge until a few centuries ago. It was widely believed that only the male possessed the "seed of life" and that the woman was nothing more than a "glorified incubator."

The great biological truth concerning the importance of blood in our body's mechanism has been fully comprehended only in recent years. Until 120 years ago, sick people were "bled," and many died because of the practice. If you lose your blood, you lose your life. Yet Leviticus 17:11, written 3,000 years ago, declared that blood is the source of life: "For the life of the flesh is in the blood."

Medical science has only recently discovered that blood clotting in a newborn reaches its peak on the eighth day, then drops. The Bible consistently says that a baby must be circumcised on the eighth day—the day that the coagulating factor in the blood, prothrombin, is the highest.

Encyclopedia Britannica documents that in 1845, a young doctor in Vienna named Dr. Ignaz Semmelweis was horrified at the terrible death rate of women who gave birth in hospitals. As many as 30 percent died after giving birth. Semmelweis noted that doctors would examine the bodies of patients who died, then, without washing their hands, go straight to the next ward and examine expectant mothers. This was their normal practice, because the presence of microscopic diseases was unknown. Dr. Semmelweis insisted that doctors wash their hands before examinations, and the death rate immediately dropped to 2 percent.

Look at the specific instructions God gave His people for when they encounter disease: "And when he that has an issue is cleansed of his issue; then he shall number to himself seven days for his cleansing, and wash his clothes, and bathe his flesh in running water, and shall be clean" (Leviticus 15:13). Until recent years, doctors washed their hands in a bowl of water, leaving invisible germs on their hands. However, the Bible says specifically to wash under "running water."

Grant R. Jeffery stated in *The Signature of God*, "During the devastating Black Death of the fourteenth century, patients who were sick or dead were kept in the same rooms as the rest of the family. People often wondered why the disease was affecting so many people at one time. They attributed these epidemics to 'bad air' or 'evil spirits.' However, careful attention to the medical commands of God as revealed in Leviticus would have saved untold millions of lives. Arturo Castiglione wrote about the overwhelming importance of this biblical medical law: 'The laws against leprosy in Leviticus 13 may be regarded as the first model of sanitary legislation' (*A History of Medicine*)."

QUESTIONS

1. **Which passages in the Bible describe the water cycle, over 2,000 years before "modern man" discovered it?**

2. Which book of the Bible mentioned a "cycle" of air currents centuries before scientists discovered it?

3. Cite an example where the Bible served as a catalyst for a scientific discovery.

4. Why is it that the Bible and true science do not contradict each other?

5. Why did God specify that circumcision be done on the eighth day?

6. What life-saving medical advice can be found in Leviticus?

PREACHER'S PROGRESS

Harry Diculous: "Does the Bible say that you can't smoke?"

Christian: "No."

Harry Diculous: "So I can smoke then?"

Christian: "If you want to."

Harry Diculous: "Good. Thank God for cigarettes."

Christian: "You can eat sand if you want."

Harry Diculous: "Huh?"

Christian: "God created sand. Eat it if you want. But don't complain if you get a bellyache. Smoke cigarettes if you want, but don't complain when your eyes bulge with terror as you slowly suffocate to death with emphysema. Do you know what happens when you smoke?"

Harry Diculous: "Never really thought about it. I just like it."

Christian: "The smoke doesn't just go into a 'bag' called your lungs. It takes seven seconds for the smoke to enter your brain. Then it goes into your blood stream. Do you drink alcohol?"

Harry Diculous: "Yep. Love it!"

Christian: "Did you know that it's a poison?"

Harry Diculous: "I've never really thought about it."

Christian: "Any chemist will tell you that it's a poison. People who smoke and drink do so because they think that they are free to do so. In truth, they are slaves."

Harry Diculous: No, I'm not!"

Christian: "Try to give up your cigarettes, then. You're like a man in a prison who thinks he's free to do what he wants. He is—until he tries to leave. It's the same with sin. Jesus said, 'He that serves sin is a slave to sin.'"

Harry Diculous: "I don't believe that."

Christian: "Okay, then, try to get away from it. Stop lusting—just for a day. It's only when you try to get away that you will realize the hold that it has on you."

Harry Diculous: "There's nothing wrong with lust."

Christian: "Maybe you don't think there is, but it brings forth sin, and sin when it's conceived brings forth death. If there was an answer to your problem of death, would you be interested?"

Harry Diculous: "I guess so..."

Christian: "Do you consider yourself to be a good person?" Etc.

FEATHERS FOR ARROWS

Just as the eighth day was the God-given timing for circumcision (Genesis 17:12), there is a God-given timing for every person who is "circumcised with the circumcision made without hands" (Colossians 2:11). Jesus appeared to Thomas on the eighth day. What Thomas saw cut away the flesh of his unbelieving heart. He became a Jew inwardly as his circumcision became "that of the heart, in the spirit, and not in the letter" (Romans 2:29). Thomas bowed his heart to Jesus of Nazareth as his Lord and his God. He needed a miracle, and God graciously gave it to him. Each of us is dealt with individually by God; some get incredible spiritual manifestations at conversion. Others quietly trust the promises of God, and God reveals Himself to them through faith rather than feelings of great joy. What matters is not *how* each of us came to Christ, but that we became new creatures in Christ, because that is the *real* miracle that proves the reality of salvation.

This is what Paul meant when he wrote, "For in Christ Jesus neither circumcision avails anything, nor uncircumcision, but a new creature" (Galatians 6:15).

Memory Verse

"I am he that lives, and was dead; and, behold, I am alive for evermore, Amen; and have the keys of hell and of death."
REVELATION 1:18

Last Words

Louis XIV (1638–1715), King of France:

"Why do you weep? Did you think I was immortal?"

417

64

Evolution, Part 1

"This most beautiful system of the sun, planets, and comets could only proceed from the counsel and dominion of an intelligent and powerful Being."

SIR ISAAC NEWTON

Kirk's Comment   Evolution is a religion that is believed by men and women, boys and girls, intellectuals and fools. I was one of them until I was willing to investigate the facts.

QUESTIONS & OBJECTIONS

"Doesn't the Big Bang theory disprove the Genesis account of creation?"

Try to think of any explosion that has produced order. Does a terrorist bomb create harmony? Big bangs cause chaos. How could a Big Bang produce a rose, apple trees, fish, sunsets, the seasons, hummingbirds, polar bears—thousands of birds and animals, each with its own eyes, nose, and mouth? A *child* can see that there is "grand design" in creation.

Here is an interesting experiment: Empty your garage of every piece of metal, wood, paint, rubber, and plastic. *Make sure there is nothing there.* Nothing. Then wait for ten years and see if a Mercedes evolves. If it doesn't appear, leave it for 20 years. If that doesn't work, try it for 100 years. Then try leaving it for 10,000 years.

Here's what will produce the necessary blind faith to make the evolutionary process believable: leave it for 250 million years.

What evolutionists attribute to a Big Bang, where the universe simply "exploded" into existence, is actually the work of God who merely spoke and the universe came into being. Jim Holt, science writer for the *Wall Street Journal*, wrote that "the universe suddenly exploded into being," yet he admitted, "The big bang bears an uncanny resemblance to the Genesis command." *Time* magazine reported, "Most cosmologists (scientists who study the structures and evolution of the universe) agree that the Genesis account of creation, in imagining an initial void, may be uncannily close to the truth" (Dec. 1976).

An article in *U.S. News & World Report* stated, "New scientific revelations about supernovas, black holes, quarks, and the big bang even suggest to some scientists that there is a 'grand design' in the universe" (March 31, 1997).

Ask an evolutionist who believes in the Big Bang, "Where did space for the universe come from? Where did the initial material come from? What sparked the explosion?" In order to have an explosion, there must be something there to explode, and there must be a catalyst to cause the explosion. You cannot create something out of nothing. Simply put, this destroys the Big Bang theory because there is nothing to go *boom*.

The Book of Genesis tells us that God created *everything*—nothing "evolved." Every creature was given the ability to reproduce *after its own kind* as is stated ten times in Genesis 1. Dogs do not produce cats. Neither do cats and dogs have a common ancestry. Dogs began as dogs and are still dogs. They vary in species from Chihuahuas to Saint Bernards, but you will not find a "dat" or a "cog" (part cat/dog) throughout God's creation. Frogs don't reproduce oysters, cows don't have lambs, and pregnant pigs don't give birth to rabbits. God made monkeys as monkeys, and man as man.

According to evolutionist Stephen J. Gould, professor of geology and paleontology at Harvard University, "This notion of species as 'natural kinds' fits splendidly with creationist tenets of a pre-Darwinian age. Louis Agassiz even argued that species are God's individual thoughts, made incarnate so that we might perceive both His majesty and His message. Species, Agassiz wrote, are 'instituted by the Divine Intelligence as the categories of his mode of thinking.' But how could a division of the organic world into discrete entities be justified by an evolutionary theory that proclaimed ceaseless change as the fundamental fact of nature?"

Each creature brings forth after its own kind. That's no theory; that's a fact. Why then should we believe that man came from another species? If evolution were true, it would prove that the Bible is false. However, the whole of creation stands in contradiction to the theory of evolution. Evolution is science fiction.

While we *do* see what's called "microevolution"—variations within species (such as different types of dogs)—we *don't* see any evidence of "macroevolution"—one species evolving into another species. Microevolution is observable, while macroevolution takes a tremendous leap of faith. If Christians had as much faith in God as atheists have in the theory of evolution, we would see revival. Like little children, atheists believe without a shred of evidence. In *The Answers Book*, Ken Ham writes:

> Adaptation and natural selection are biological facts; amoeba-to-man evolution is not. Natural selection can only work on the genetic information present in a population of organisms—it cannot create new information. For example, since no known reptiles have genes for feathers, no amount of selection will produce a feathered reptile. Mutations in genes can only modify or eliminate existing structures, not create new ones.

Evolutionists also claim that the human body has "vestigial organs"— worthless leftovers from evolution—such as the appendix and tailbone. The truth is that these do have a purpose: the appendix is part of the human immune system, and the "tailbone" actually supports muscles that are necessary for daily bodily functions.

The Peppered Moth: Evolution Comes Unglued

According to Mark Varney, "Almost all textbooks on evolution include the peppered moth as *the* classic example of evolution by natural selection. There are two types of peppered moths: a light-colored speckled variety and a dark variety. Most peppered moths in England were the light variety, which were camouflaged as they rested on tree trunks. The black variety stood out against the light bark and were easily seen and eaten by birds. But as the industrial revolution created pollution that covered tree trunks with soot, the dark variety was camouflaged better, so birds ate more of the light moths.

"The peppered moth story has been trumpeted since the 1950s as proof positive that evolution by natural selection is true. In 1978, one famous geneticist called the peppered moth 'the clearest case in which a conspicuous evolutionary process has actually been observed.'

"However, this 'clearest case' of purported Darwinian evolution by natural selection is not true! The nocturnal peppered moth does not rest on the trunks of trees during the day. In fact, despite over 40 years of intense field study, only two peppered moths have ever been seen naturally resting on tree trunks!

"So where did all the evolution textbook pictures of peppered moths on different colored tree trunks come from? They were all staged. The moths were glued, pinned, or placed onto tree trunks and their pictures taken. The scientists who used these pictures in their books to prove evolution *all* conveniently forgot to tell their readers this fact. If the *best* example of evolution is not true, how about all their other supposed examples? It makes you wonder, doesn't it?"

Aside from the pictures being staged, consider what is actually occurring in this "conspicuous evolutionary process": Before the moth's environment changed, some of the moths were mostly white, and some were mostly black. After their environment changed, some were mostly white, and some were mostly black. No new color or variety came into being, yet we have supposedly just witnessed evolution. Even if the "evidence" had not been faked, it still does not show anything evolving—except the evolutionary tale.

Evolutionist John Reader (*Missing Links*) explains this biased interpretation: "Ever since Darwin's work…preconceptions have led evidence by the nose." Harvard professor and evolutionist Steven Jay Gould admits this scientific bias: "Facts do not 'speak for themselves'; they are read in light of theory."

Even Charles Darwin concedes, "Alas, how frequent, how almost universal it is in an author to persuade himself of the truth of his own dogmas." When scientists proclaim the theory of evolution as "fact," keep in mind that they are not unbiased observers who are simply reporting the evidence. Men devised the theory of evolution precisely because it eliminates the need for God. If mankind has no Creator to whom he is accountable, each man can do what is right in his own eyes.

H. S. Lipson, professor of physics at the University of Manchester, UK, stated, "In fact, evolution became in a sense a scientific religion; almost all scientists have accepted it and many are prepared to 'bend' their observations to fit in with it."

In the Foreword to *Origin of Species* (100th edition), Sir Arthur Keith admitted, "Evolution is unproved and unprovable. We believe it only because the only alternative is special creation, and that is unthinkable."

QUESTIONS

1. Does an explosion create beauty and order, or chaos and disorder?

2. Define microevolution and macroevolution. Which one is not scientific?

3. In natural selection, can an organism create new genetic information?

4. What are some of the problems with the peppered moth story, supposedly "proof positive" of evolution by natural selection?

5. **How would you counter the argument that scientists are unbiased observers who are simply reporting the evidence?**

6. **Why is it a good idea to go through God's Law with an evolutionist?**

PREACHER'S PROGRESS

Miss Guided: "I believe that man evolved from apes."

Christian: "The Bible says that God made man is His image. So you think that God is an ape? That's blasphemous."

Miss Guided: "No! I'm not saying that."

Christian: "Then what are you saying?"

Miss Guided: "I'm saying that science has proved that we came from apes."

Christian: "So you are saying that the Bible is wrong."

Miss Guided: "I believe both."

Christian: "Evolution and the Bible are not compatible. The Scriptures tell us that every animal brings forth after its own kind. Dogs don't have kittens. Neither do horses have cows. It also says that there is one kind of flesh of the beasts and one kind of flesh of man. If evolution is true, then the Bible is wrong."

Miss Guided: "Well, the Bible must be wrong, because, like I said, science has proved evolution to be true."

Christian: "When?"

Miss Guided: "Fossils."

Christian: "What fossils?"

Miss Guided: "I don't know. They have found fossils."

Christian: "Who have found fossils?"

Miss Guided: "Scientists."

Christian: "Proving what?"

Miss Guided: "Evolution."

Christian: "You mean there are fossils that show man evolved from apes?"

Miss Guided: "Yes."

Christian: "Name one fossil that does that."

Miss Guided: "I can't, offhand."

Christian: "Do you think you are a good person?" *

Miss Guided: "What do you mean?"

Christian: "Do you think you are a good person?"

Miss Guided: "Sure."

Christian: "May I ask you three questions to see if you are?"

Miss Guided: "Okay."

Christian: "Have you ever told a lie?" Etc.

* Don't spend too much time on the subject of evolution. It is the gospel that is the power of God to salvation, so it's important to swing from apologetics (which address the intellect) to the Moral Law (which addresses the conscience) as quickly as is comfortably possible.

FEATHERS FOR ARROWS

A magnificent doe stands with its foal and drinks cool water from a mountain stream. The sun sparkles off the dew on deep green leaves of native tree branches. The mother gently caresses her offspring as it begins to drink from the brook. The scene is one of incredible serenity…the picture of innocence. What more could optimize the beauty of God's creation?

Suddenly a mountain lion leaps from a tree and digs its sharp claws deep into the mother's neck, dragging the helpless creature to the ground. As it holds its terrified prey in a death grip, its powerful jaws bite into the jugular vein, turning the mountain stream crimson with the creature's blood.

It is a strong consolation to know that this isn't the way God planned it in the beginning. Animals were not created to devour each other; they were created to be vegetarian (Genesis 1:29,30). The original creation was "good" and was not filled with violence and bloodshed. We live in a fallen creation (Romans 8:20–23). As a result of Adam's sin, the perfect creation was cursed and death was introduced into the world (Romans 5:12). The day will come when the entire creation will be delivered from the "bondage of corruption" and there will be no more curse. In the new heaven and new earth, "the wolf and the lamb shall feed together, and the lion shall eat straw like the bullock...They shall not hurt nor destroy in all my holy mountain" (Isaiah 65:25; see also Isaiah 11:6–9).

WORDS OF COMFORT

I once helped a middle-aged man get into his vehicle. The poor man was from out of state and had locked his keys in his truck. As I was walking by, he approached me and asked if I had any wire. When I found out what the problem was, I rushed home and grabbed a thin wire coat hanger. With a little twisting, he fashioned it into a tool, maneuvered it through his window, and opened the door.

It worked so well, as I walked away I thought, *That was great. I would be a fool not to keep a wire coat hanger in my van* (in case I ever locked myself out). That was intelligent. Think about it.

Memory Verse

"But we are all as an unclean thing, and all our righteousnesses are as filthy rags; and we all do fade as a leaf; and our iniquities, like the wind, have taken us away."

ISAIAH 64:6

Last Words

Mary, Queen of Scots (1542–1587) prayed fervently for peace in the world and for cruel Queen Elizabeth. Before the death stroke beheaded her, she exclaimed:

"Like as Thy arms, Lord Jesus Christ, were stretched out upon the cross, even so receive me with the outstretched arms of Thy mercy."

LESSON 65

Evolution, Part 2

"Evolution is a fairy tale for grown-ups. This theory has helped nothing in the progress of science. It is useless."
PROFESSOR LOUIS BOUNOURE,
Director, National Center of Scientific Research

Kirk's Comment As you will see in this lesson, it actually takes more faith to believe in Darwinian evolution than it does to believe in God. This information will help you intelligently refute evolution.

QUESTIONS & OBJECTIONS

"Where did Cain get his wife?"

Many ask this question thinking they've found a "mistake" in the Bible—that there must have been other people besides Adam and Eve. However, Scripture tells us that Adam is "the first man" (1 Corinthians 15:45); that there were no other humans when he was created, because God said, "It is not good that the man should be alone" (Genesis 2:18); and that Eve is "the mother of all living" (Genesis 3:20). Cain and Abel, then, must have married their sisters. All of the first-generation siblings married each other in order to populate the earth. At that time there was no law against incest. But as the population grew large enough, and as the risk of genetic problems increased due to sin's curse, God outlawed marriage between immediate family members.

Man's Dominion

The Bible tells us that animals are created "without understanding" (Psalm 32:9), and that human beings are different from animals. We are made in God's "image." As human beings, we are aware of our "being." God is "I AM," and we know that "we are." We have understanding that we exist.

Among other unique characteristics, we have an innate ability to appreciate God's creation. What animal gazes with awe at a sunset, or at the magnificence of the Grand Canyon? What animal obtains joy from the sounds of music or takes the time to form itself into an orchestra to create music? What animal among the beasts sets up court systems and apportions justice to its fellow creatures? We are moral beings.

While birds and other creatures have instincts to create (nests, etc.), we have the ability to uncover the hidden laws of electricity. We can utilize the law of aerodynamics to transport ourselves around the globe. We also have the God-given ability to appreciate the value of creation. We unearth the hidden treasures of gold, silver, diamonds, and oil and make use of them for our own benefit. Only humans have the unique ability to appreciate God for this incredible creation and to respond to His love.

No, man is not just an animal on the evolutionary food chain. God has given him dominion (authority) over all the animals (Genesis 1:28). Man is intellectually superior to them and has *priority* over them—every animal is "under his feet" and may be brought into submission by him (James 3:7). Birds (parrots) can be taught to speak. With a crack of a whip, lions will do what he says. Even killer whales obey his voice.

Man's dominion is obvious. Cows yield milk for his cereal, cheese for his hamburger, butter for his bread, yogurt to keep him healthy, and ice cream to delight his taste buds on hot days. The same cow gives him meat to keep him strong and leather to keep him warm. Sheep and goats also yield many of these same products. The chicken makes eggs for his breakfast and provides finger-licking meat for his dinner. The sea overflows with an incredible variety of fish for him to catch and eat. Dogs protect his property and herd his sheep. Elephants lift great weights for him.

Camels carry him across deserts. The horse is perfectly designed to be ridden by him.

Man is the pinnacle of God's earthly creation. He is not a mere part of the evolutionary process having to yield to the rights of animals. Jesus said that mankind is "much better" than birds and sheep (Matthew 12:12). He is to subdue the earth and bring its vast resources into submission. All were created for him by the infinite genius and loving hand of Almighty God.

Even evolutionist Stephen Hawking, considered the best-known scientist since Albert Einstein, acknowledges, "The universe and the laws of physics seem to have been specifically designed for us. If any one of about 40 physical qualities had more than slightly different values, life as we know it could not exist: Either atoms would not be stable, or they wouldn't combine into molecules, or the stars wouldn't form the heavier elements, or the universe would collapse before life could develop, and so on" (*Austin American-Statesman*, October 19, 1997). In *A Brief History of Time*, Hawking wrote, "It would be very difficult to explain why the universe should have begun in just this way, except as the act of a God who intended to create beings like us."

John Wheeler, Princeton University professor of physics, agrees: "Slight variations in physical laws such as gravity or electromagnetism would make life impossible... The necessity to produce life lies at the center of the universe's whole machinery and design" (*Reader's Digest*, Sept. 1986).

Law of Probabilities Refutes Evolution

Evolutionists have been unable to answer the question of how life spontaneously arose from dead matter. Sir Fred Hoyle, professor of astronomy at Cambridge University, said of evolution, "The chance that higher life forms might have emerged in this way is comparable to the chance that a tornado sweeping through a junkyard might assemble a Boeing 747 from the materials therein."

This famous statistician puts it in perspective for us: "The likelihood of the formation of life from inanimate matter is one out of $10^{40,000}$... It is big enough to bury Darwin and the whole theory of evolution. There was no primeval soup, neither on this planet nor on any other, and if the beginnings of life were not random, they must therefore have been the product of purposeful intelligence" (*Evolution from Space*).

Despite being a supporter of evolution, biochemistry professor Michael J. Behe confesses its improbability: "I believe that Darwin's mechanism for evolution doesn't explain much of what is seen under a microscope. Cells are simply too complex to have evolved randomly. Intelligence was required to produce them."

Earth's Population Refutes Evolution

Grant R. Jeffery writes in *The Signature of God:* "The evolutionary scientists who believe that man existed for over a million years have an almost insurmountable problem. Using the assumption of forty-three years for an average human generation, the population growth over a million years would produce 23,256 consecutive generations. We calculate the expected population by starting with one couple one million years ago and use the same assumptions of a forty-three-year generation and 2.5 children per family...The evolutionary theory of a million years of growth would produce trillions × trillions × trillions × trillions of people that should be alive today on our planet. To put this in perspective, this number is vastly greater than the total number of atoms in our vast universe. If mankind had lived on earth for a million years, we would all be standing on enormously high mountains of bones from the trillions of skeletons of those who had died in past generations. However, despite the tremendous archeological and scientific investigation in the last two centuries, the scientists have not found a fraction of the trillions of skeletons predicted by the theory of evolutionary scientists."

QUESTIONS

1. **Would you be able to explain to someone where Cain got his wife?**

2. **What are some of the ways man is superior to animals?**

3. **How could you argue that God designed the universe for mankind?**

4. **How does the law of probabilities disprove evolution's claim that life arose spontaneously?**

5. **What does the microscopic cell tell us about evolution?**

PREACHER'S PROGRESS

Christian: "Hi, guys. How are you doing?"

Tim Burr & Teresa Green: "We're fine."

Christian: "What are you doing here?"

Tim Burr & Teresa Green: "Looking at trees. We love them."

Christian: "Who doesn't? They look good, and they are so useful."

Tim Burr & Teresa Green: "We're here representing the eastside branch of TWIG."

Christian: "What's TWIG?"

Tim Burr & Teresa Green: "Trees Wherever I Go. It's an organization in which we promise to take care of trees wherever we go."

Christian: "That's commendable."

Tim Burr & Teresa Green: "Thanks. We're putting down roots in this area."

Christian: "I agree, we should take care of trees and use them for the purpose for which they were intended."

Tim Burr & Teresa Green: "Right."

Christian: "Do you know what God made them for?"

Tim Burr & Teresa Green: "We wouldn't actually say that God made trees. They evolved . . . over millions of years."

Christian: "Well, it seems kind of nice that we can use them to provide wood for housing and furniture, make maple syrup for pancakes, rubber for tires, etc., as well as turn the pulp into paper for books, etc. It's also a blessing that evolution thought of using trees to turn our carbon dioxide back into life-giving oxygen. We couldn't live without them."

Tim Burr & Teresa Green: "Whatever. But that's our point. If we keep cutting down trees, there won't be any to give the air its oxygen. Trees are the lungs of the earth! It's an environmental crisis. We have to prevent logging companies from cutting down the rain forests, or any trees for that matter!"

Christian: "I wouldn't be too concerned about that. Evolution will work something out if all the trees go. So you want to protect trees. That's nice. How do you feel about abortion?"

Tim Burr & Teresa Green: "It's a woman's right to do what she wants with her own body!"

Christian: "I have a question for you. Do you know what is the number one killer of drivers in the United States?"

Tim Burr & Teresa Green: "Drunk driving?"

Christian: "No. Trees." *

* Lining the highways of America are millions of trees. When a car goes off a road and hits a tree, the tree doesn't move, the driver does—into eternity.

WORDS OF COMFORT

Memory Verse

"For thus says the high and lofty One that inhabits eternity, whose name is Holy: I dwell in the high and holy place, with him also that is of a contrite and humble spirit, to revive the spirit of the humble, and to revive the heart of the contrite ones."

ISAIAH 57:15

I couldn't believe it—a prestigious Dallas Bible school had me picked up from the airport in a limo. As I sat in the back, I decided to call Sue on the car phone and tell her that I was riding through the streets of Dallas in the back seat of a black limousine. After bragging for some time, I hung up and began to give a presidential wave to the crowds in the street, but for some reason, no one waved back at me. When we arrived at our destination, I stepped out of the limo and realized why the crowds didn't return my wave—the windows were tinted and they couldn't see who I was! Then I went into my room, fixed myself some corn flakes, and decided to call Sue and brag again. As I lifted the phone to my ear, I accidentally knocked my bowl of corn flakes and poured half a cup of milk and cereal into my shirt pocket.

Last Words

Robert Burns (1759–1796), the Scottish poet, ranks as one of the two greatest figures in Scottish literature. That he appreciated, but failed to experience, the power of the Christian faith is apparent in his works. To his attendant, he said:

> **"Be a good man; be virtuous, be religious; nothing else will give you any comfort when you come to be here."**

66

Evolution, Part 3

"An increasing number of scientists, most particularly a growing number of evolutionists ... argue that Darwinian evolutionary theory is no genuine scientific theory at all ... Many of the critics have the highest intellectual credentials."

MICHAEL RUSE,
"Darwin's Theory: An Exercise in Science," *New Scientist*

Kirk's Comment   The earth is a masterpiece of God's design and creativity. Even scientists stand in awe and wonder of this beautiful display of God's handiwork.

QUESTIONS & OBJECTIONS

"Adam was a mythical figure who never really lived."

Adam is a key figure in Scripture. He is described as the "first Adam," the one who brought sin into the world (1 Corinthians 15:22). He made it necessary for Jesus, the "last Adam" (1 Corinthians 15:45), to atone for all humans, and then rise from the grave with the promise of complete redemption for fallen man and fallen creation. If Adam were just a myth, we would not be able to fully understand the work of Jesus. If Adam and Eve were not real, then we ought to doubt whether their children were real too, and their children … and then we ought to doubt the first eleven chapters of Genesis, and so on. All the genealogies accept Adam as being a literal person, so their children Cain and Abel (Genesis 4:9,10; Luke 11:50,51) must therefore be real too. The Bible tells us that Jesus was descended from Adam (Luke 3:38), and it is impossible to be descended from a myth.

w o t m w o t m w o t m w o t m w o t m w o t m w o t m w o t m w o t m w o t m

Rejection of the Bible's account of creation as given in the Book of Genesis could rightly be called "Genecide," because it eradicated man's purpose of existence and left a whole generation with no certainty as to its beginning. Consequently, theories and tales of our origin have crept like primeval slime from the minds of those who don't know God. This intellectual genocide has given the godless a temporary license to labor to the extremes of their imagination, giving birth to painful conjecture about our human beginnings. They speak in speculation, the uncertain language of those who drift aimlessly across the endless sea of secular philosophy.

The Scriptures, on the other hand, deal only with truth and certainty. They talk of fact, reality, and purpose for man's existence. The darkness of the raging sea of futility retreats where the lighthouse of Genesis begins. Genesis explains the origins of sin, the curse, death, marriage, the family, government, and so on.

In teaching about the significance of marriage (Mark 10:6–9), Jesus confirmed that the creation of Adam and Eve was a real historical event when He quoted Genesis 1:27 and 2:24. In quoting from both chapters 1 and 2 of Genesis, He showed that these chapters are not contradictory as some claim. Chapter 2 merely gives the details of chapter 1. A sports commentator is not in error when (after a game) he gives an in-depth analysis and fails to repeat every detail in chronological order. He is merely reviewing the completed game by mentioning the highlights. In all, Genesis is quoted more than sixty times in seventeen books of the New Testament. It is foundational to understanding the gospel.

Creation in Six Days

Most theologians throughout church history agree that in using the phrase "the evening and the morning were the first day," the Scriptures are speaking of a literal 24-hour day, rather than a period of years.

In *The Answers Book*, Ken Ham (et al.) writes: "To understand the meaning of 'day' in Genesis 1, we need to determine how the Hebrew word for 'day,' *yom*, is used in the context of Scripture...A number, and the phrase 'evening and morning,' are used for each of the six days of creation (Genesis 1:5,8,13,19,23,31). Outside Genesis 1, *yom* is used with a number 410 times, and each time it means an ordinary day—why would Genesis 1 be the exception? Outside Genesis 1, *yom* is used with the word 'evening' or 'morning' 23 times. 'Evening' and 'morning' appear in association, but without *yom*, 38 times. All 61 times the text refers to an ordinary day—why would Genesis 1 be the exception? In Genesis 1:5, *yom* occurs in context with the word 'night.' Outside of Genesis 1, 'night' is used with *yom* 53 times—and each time it means an ordinary day. Why would Genesis 1 be the exception? Even the usage of the word 'light' with *yom* in this passage determines the meaning as an ordinary day."

As a professor of Hebrew at Oxford University, Dr. James Barr stated, "So far as I know, there is no professor of Hebrew or Old Testament at any world-class university who does not believe that the writer(s) of Genesis 1–11 intended to convey to their readers the idea that (a) creation took place in a series of six days which were the same as the days of 24 hours we now experience; (b) the figures contained in the Genesis genealogies provided by simple addition a chronology from the beginning of the world up to later stages in the biblical story; (c) Noah's Flood was understood to be worldwide and extinguish all human and animal life except for those in the ark."

Points to Ponder About the Flood and Noah's Ark

By Dr. Kent Hovind

Second Peter 3:3–8 tells us that people who scoff at the Bible are "willingly ignorant" of the Creation and the Flood. In order to understand science and the Bible, we must not be ignorant of those two great events in the Earth's history.

1. Over 500 Flood legends from all parts of the world have been found. Most have similarities to the Genesis account.

2. Noah's ark was built only to float, not to sail anywhere. Many ark scholars believe that the ark was a "barge" shape, not a pointed "boat" shape. This would greatly increase the cargo capacity. Scoffers have pointed out that the largest sailing ships were less than 300 feet because of the problem of twisting and flexing the boat. These ships had giant masts and sails to catch the wind. Noah's ark needed neither of those and therefore had far less torsional stress.

3. Even using the small 18-inch cubit (my height is 6'1" and I have a 21-inch cubit), the ark was large enough to hold all the required animals, people, and food with room to spare.

4. The length-to-width ratio of 6 to 1 is what shipbuilders today often use. This is the best ratio for stability in stormy weather.

5. The ark may have had a "moon-pool" in the center. The larger ships would have a hole in the center of the bottom of the boat with walls extending up into the ship. There are several reasons for this feature:

    a) It allowed water to go up into the hole as the ship crested waves. This would be needed to relieve strain on longer ships.

    b) The rising and lowering water acted as a piston to pump fresh air in and out of the ship. This would prevent the buildup of dangerous gasses from all the animals on board.

    c) The hole was a great place to dump waste into the ocean without going outside.

6. The ark may have had large drogue (anchor) stones suspended over the sides to keep it more stable in rough weather. Many of these stones have been found in the region where the ark landed.

7. Noah lived for 950 years. Many Bible scholars believe the pre-Flood people were much larger than modern man. Skeletons over 11 feet tall have been found. If Noah were taller, his cubit (elbow to finger-

tip) would have been much larger also. This would make the ark larger by the same ratio.

8. God told Noah to bring two of each kind (seven of some), not of each species or variety. Noah had only two of the dog kind, which would include the wolves, coyotes, foxes, mutts, etc. The "kind" grouping is probably closer to our modern family division in taxonomy, and would greatly reduce the number of animals on the ark. Animals have diversified into many varieties in the last 4,400 years since the Flood. This diversification is not anything similar to great claims that the evolutionists teach.

9. Noah did not have to get the animals. God brought them to him ("shall come to thee," Genesis 6:20).

10. Only land-dwelling, air-breathing animals had to be included on the ark ("in which is the breath of life," Genesis 7:15,22).

11. Many animals sleep, hibernate, or become very inactive during bad weather.

12. All animals and people were vegetarian before and during the Flood (Genesis 1:20–30; 9:3).

13. The pre-Flood people were probably much smarter and more advanced than people today. The longer life spans, Adam's direct contact with God, and the fact that they could glean the wisdom of many generations that were still alive would greatly expand their knowledge base.

14. The Bible says that the highest mountains were covered by 15 cubits [20 feet] of water (Genesis 7:20). This is half the height of the ark. The ark was safe from scraping bottom at all times.

15. The large mountains, as we have them today, did not exist until after the Flood when "the mountains arose and the valleys sank down" (Psalm 104:5–9; Genesis 8:3–8).

16. There is enough water in the oceans right now to cover the earth 8,000 feet deep if the surface of the earth were smooth.

17. Many claim to have seen the ark in recent times in the area in which the Bible says it landed. There are two primary schools of thought about the actual site of the ark. Much energy and time have been expended to prove both views. Some believe the ark is on Mt. Ararat, covered by snow (CBS showed a one-hour special in 1993 about this site). Others believe the ark is seventeen miles south of Mt. Ararat in a valley called "the valley of eight" (eight souls on the ark). The Bible says the ark landed in the "mountains" of Ararat, not necessarily on the mountain itself.

18. The continents were not separated until 100–300 years after the Flood (Genesis 10:25). The people and animals had time to migrate anywhere on earth by then.

19. The top 3,000 feet of Mt. Everest (26,000–29,000 feet) is made up of sedimentary rock packed with seashells and other ocean-dwelling animals.

20. Sedimentary rock is found all over the world. Sedimentary rock is formed in water.

21. Petrified clams in the closed position (found all over the world, even on top of Mount Everest) testify to their rapid burial while they were still alive.

22. Bent rock layers, fossil graveyards, and polystrata fossils are best explained by a Flood.

23. People choose to not believe in the Flood because it speaks of the judgment of God on sin (2 Peter 3:3–8).

One Common Ancestor

Science is finding evidence that what the Bible tells us is true: all of mankind is descended from one ancestor. In addition to being descendants of Noah after the Flood, we are all offspring of Adam. An article in *U.S. News & World Report* stated, "Researchers suggest that virtually all modern men—99% of them, says one scientist—are closely related genetically and share genes with one male ancestor, dubbed 'Y-chromosome Adam.'

We are finding that humans have very, very shallow genetic roots which go back very recently to one ancestor...That indicates that there was an origin in a specific location on the globe, and then it spread out from there" (December 4, 1995).

QUESTIONS

1. What biblical proof is there that Adam was a literal person?

2. What genetic proof is there that Adam was a literal person?

3. Why is it necessary to believe the creation account given in Genesis?

4. What is the biblical justification for believing the creation days are ordinary 24-hour days?

5. According to 2 Peter 3:3–8, why are people who scoff at the Bible "willingly ignorant" of the Creation and the Flood?

PREACHER'S PROGRESS

Noah Conscience: "There is no such thing as guilt."

Christian: "Why do you believe that?"

Noah Conscience: "I don't 'believe' it. I know it. Guilt is something that has been pushed on humanity by religion."

Christian: "So you never feel guilty."

Noah Conscience: "I don't feel guilty about anything. Ever."

Christian: "Do you have a conscience?"

Noah Conscience: "No."

Christian: "So you don't know right from wrong."

Noah Conscience: "I know right from wrong. I just don't feel guilt."

Christian: "So you do have a conscience, but you have hardened it."

Noah Conscience: "Whatever…"

Christian: "Have you always been like this?"

Noah Conscience: "No. Church used to make me feel guilty. Not anymore."

Christian: "So you have felt guilt in the past—for lying and stuff like that?

Noah Conscience: "Yep."

Christian: "But now you've managed to shake it off."

Noah Conscience: "That's right. No guilt."

Christian: "Do you have a sister?"

Noah Conscience: "Yeah."

Christian: "Do you care about her?"

Noah Conscience: "I suppose so. Never really thought about it."

Christian: "If someone raped her, then cut her throat, do you think that he should be punished?"

Noah Conscience: "Of course."

Christian: "Let's say the murderer doesn't feel guilty about what he did. Should he still be punished?"

Noah Conscience: "Even more so. He *should* feel guilty."

Christian: "That's what will happen to you on Judgment Day if you refuse to repent. Your lack of sorrow for your sins makes you even more guilty. Does that make sense?"

Noah Conscience: "I guess so. I'm starting to feel guilty."

Last Words

Joseph Addison, English writer, died June 17, 1719:

"See in what peace a Christian can die."

Memory Verse

"Wherefore, as by one man sin entered into the world, and death by sin; and so death passed upon all men, for that all have sinned."

ROMANS 5:12

LESSON 67

Evolution, Part 4

"Scientists who go about teaching that evolution is a fact of life are great con-men, and the story they are telling may be the greatest hoax ever. In explaining evolution, we do not have one iota of fact."

DR. T. N. TAHMISIAN, Atomic Energy Commission

Kirk's Comment I was talking with a Christian friend who happens to be a top brain surgeon at Cedar Sinai Hospital in Los Angeles, CA. As he was explaining the intricate design of the human brain and its functions, he pointed out the fact that even the most gifted scientists and doctors, with the knowledge of all the revealing, new biomedical discoveries, cannot find any reason why we should be able to hold simple conversations. The complexity of the human body's design is beyond science's ability to comprehend.

QUESTIONS & OBJECTIONS

"How does the young-earth theory explain that we can see stars millions of light-years away? How would the light have reached us?"

Since God made the sun, moon, and stars "to give light upon the earth" (Genesis 1:14–18), those lights would be immediately visible on earth. They fulfilled their purpose on the day God spoke them into being, because He "saw that it was good." No doubt God also made Adam as a fully grown man—perhaps with the appearance of being 30 years old, even though he was only minutes old. Likewise, herbs and trees were already mature and fruit-bearing, to provide a ready supply of food. That would be the case with all of His creation.

We Are Wonderfully Made

In his book *Darwin's Black Box*, biochemistry professor Michael J. Behe, an evolutionist, acknowledges a "powerful challenge to Darwinian evolution"—something he refers to as "irreducible complexity." He gives a simple example: the humble mousetrap. The mousetrap has five major components that make it functional. If any one of these components is missing, it will not function. It becomes worthless as a mousetrap.

If we consider the human eye, just one small part of an incredibly complex creation, we will see this same principle of irreducible complexity. The eye cannot be reduced to anything less than what it is. It has thousands of co-equal functions that make it work. If we take away just one of those functions, the rest of the eye is worthless as an eye. How then did the eye evolve when all functions had to be present at once to give it any worth?

Charles Darwin wrote in *The Origin of Species*, "To suppose that the eye, with all its inimitable contrivances for adjusting the focus to different distances, for admitting different amounts of light, and for the correction of spherical and chromatic aberration, could have been formed by natural selection, seems, I freely confess, absurd in the highest degree." (No wonder—the focusing muscles in the eye move an estimated 100,000 times each day. The retina contains 137 million light-sensitive cells.) Darwin admitted, "If it could be demonstrated that any complex organ existed which could not possibly have been formed by numerous, successive, slight modifications, my theory would absolutely break down" (*The Origin of Species*). Thus, even the "father of evolution" himself concedes that evolution cannot be true. We are indeed fearfully and wonderfully made.

Evolution and Blood

Another example of irreducible complexity is our blood platelets, which play an important role in preventing blood loss. As blood begins to flow from a cut or scratch, platelets respond to help the blood clot so the bleeding stops quickly.

Platelets promote the clotting process by clumping together and forming a plug at the site of a wound and then releasing proteins called "clotting factors." These proteins start a series of chemical reactions that are extremely complicated. Every step of the clotting must go smoothly if a clot is to form. If one of the clotting factors is missing or defective, the clotting process does not work. A serious genetic disorder known as hemophilia results from a defect in one of the clotting factor genes. Because hemophilia sufferers lack one of the clotting factors, they may bleed uncontrollably from even small cuts or scrapes.

To form a blood clot there must be twelve specific individual chemical reactions in our blood. If evolution were true, and if this twelve-step process didn't happen in the first generation (i.e., if any one of these specific reactions failed to operate in their exact reaction and order), no creatures would have survived. They all would have bled to death!

God Made Them Male and Female

Almost all forms of complex life have both male and female—horses, dogs, humans, moths, monkeys, fish, elephants, birds, etc. The male needs the female to reproduce, and the female needs the male to reproduce. One cannot carry on life without the other. Which then came first according to the evolutionary theory? If a male came into being before a female, how did the male of each species reproduce without females? How is it possible that a male and a female each spontaneously came into being, yet they have complex, complementary reproductive systems? If each sex was able to reproduce without the other, why (and how) would they have developed a reproductive system that requires both sexes in order for the species to survive?

If every creature "evolved" with no Creator, there are numerous other problems. Take for instance the first bird. Did the bird breathe? Did it breathe before it evolved lungs? How did it do this? Why did it evolve lungs if it was happily surviving without them?

Did the bird have a mouth? How did it eat before it had evolved a mouth? Where did the mouth send the food before a stomach evolved?

How did the bird have energy if it didn't eat (because it didn't yet have a mouth and complete digestive system)? How did the bird see what there was to eat before its eyes evolved?

Evolution is intellectual suicide. It is an embarrassment. (See Romans 1:21,22.)

Questions for Evolutionists

According to Dr. Kent Hovind, the test of any theory is whether or not it provides answers to basic questions. Some well-meaning but misguided people think evolution is a reasonable theory to explain man's questions about the universe. Evolution is not a good theory—it is just a pagan religion masquerading as science. Following are some of the basic questions that Dr. Hovind asks.

1. Where did the space for the universe come from?

2. Where did matter come from?

3. Where did the laws of the universe come from (gravity, inertia, etc.)?

4. How did matter get so perfectly organized?

5. Where did the energy come from to do all the organizing?

6. When, where, why, and how did life come from dead matter?

7. When, where, why, and how did life learn to reproduce itself?

8. With what did the first cell capable of sexual reproduction reproduce?

9. Why would any plant or animal want to reproduce more of its kind since this would only make more mouths to feed and decrease the chances of survival? (Does the individual, or the species, have a drive to survive? How do you explain this?)

10. How can mutations (recombining of the genetic code) create any new, improved varieties? (Recombining English letters will never produce Chinese books.)

11. Is it possible that similarities in design between different animals prove a common Creator instead of a common ancestor?

12. Natural selection works only with the genetic information available and tends only to keep a species stable. How would you explain the increasing complexity in the genetic code that must have occurred if evolution were true?

13. When, where, why, and how did:

    a) Single-celled plants become multi-celled? (Where are the two- and three-celled intermediates?)

    b) Single-celled organisms evolve?

    c) Fish change to amphibians?

    d) Amphibians change to reptiles?

    e) Reptiles change to birds? (The lungs, bones, eyes, reproductive organs, heart, method of locomotion, body covering, etc., are all very different!) How did the intermediate forms live?

14. When, where, why, how, and from what did:

    a) Whales evolve?

    b) Sea horses evolve?

    c) Bats evolve?

    d) Eyes evolve?

    e) Ears evolve?

    f) Hair, skin, feathers, scales, nails, claws, etc., evolve?

15. Which evolved first (how, and how long, did it work without the others)?

    a) The digestive system, the food to be digested, the appetite, the ability to find and eat the food, the digestive juices, or the body's resistance to its own digestive juice (stomach, intestines, etc.)?

    b) The drive to reproduce or the ability to reproduce?

    c) The lungs, the mucus lining to protect them, the throat, or the perfect mixture of gases to be breathed into the lungs?

d) DNA or RNA to carry the DNA message to cell parts?

e) The termite or the flagella in its intestines that actually digest the cellulose it consumes?

f) The plants or the insects that live on and pollinate the plants?

g) The bones, ligaments, tendons, blood supply, or muscles to move the bones?

h) The nervous system, repair system, or hormone system?

i) The immune system or the need for it?

Dr. Hovind has a standing offer of $250,000 to "anyone who can give any empirical evidence (scientific proof) for evolution." His website is www.drdino.com.

Evolution Should Not Be Taught

Dr. Colin Patterson, senior paleontologist at the British Museum of Natural History, gave a keynote address at the American Museum of Natural History, New York City, in 1981. In it he explained his sudden "anti-evolutionary" view: "One morning I woke up and...it struck me that I had been working on this stuff for twenty years and there was not one thing I knew about it. That's quite a shock to learn that one can be misled so long...I've tried putting a simple question to various people: 'Can you tell me anything you know about evolution, any one thing, any one thing that is true?' I tried that question on the geology staff at the Field Museum of Natural History and the only answer I got was silence. I tried it on the members of the Evolutionary Morphology Seminar in the University of Chicago, a very prestigious body of evolutionists, and all I got there was silence for a long time and eventually one person said, 'I do know one thing—it ought not to be taught in high school.'"

British journalist and philosopher Malcolm Muggeridge stated, "I myself am convinced that the theory of evolution, especially the extent to which it has been applied, will be one of the great jokes in the history books of the future. Posterity will marvel that so flimsy and dubious an hypothesis could be accepted with the incredible credulity that it has."

QUESTIONS

1. What is irreducible complexity?

2. Give an example of irreducible complexity.

3. According to Darwin, how does irreducible complexity impact his theory?

4. What questions can you ask (e.g., about the reproductive system or digestive system) to help people consider the absurdity of evolution?

5. In asking his eminent colleagues about evolution, what did Dr. Colin Patterson learn that was true?

WORDS OF COMFORT

Almost every weekend I travel around the country teaching people how to inoffensively share their faith. My expertise is to give instruction on how they can do this without people feeling threatened.

A friend and I had gone out in his car, "cruising" for someone to speak to. I had seen three prospects and called "Stop!" but we were driving in the wrong lane and couldn't pull over in time.

A few minutes later when I called, "There's two!", my friend swung the car around the next corner and screeched to a halt. He felt bad that he had missed my previous call, so he made sure he got this one.

The two individuals I had my eye on were walking away from us, so I unfastened my seat belt and, with the enthusiasm of a religious zealot, jumped out of the car and called them back. They immediately did what I said. I had two of our new "optical illusion" tracts in my pocket, so I pulled them out. These gospel tracts are "incredible" in the truest sense of the word. You hold the pink card in your right hand and the blue one in the left. The one in the right looks much longer than the one in the left. When you change the cards and hold the pink one in the left hand and the blue one in the right, the blue one suddenly looks longer. People can't believe their eyes!

Neither could the two wide-eyed men believe their eyes when they saw the tracts. One of them immediately offered the fact that the bottles they had in brown paper bags were non-alcoholic. They told us later that they were terrified when I first approached them. They thought they were being busted by plain-clothed police officers, and that the optical illusion tracts were some sort of new sobriety test.

Memory Verse

"The heavens declare the glory of God; and the firmament shows his handiwork."
PSALM 19:1

Last Words

Lady Nancy Astor, when she woke briefly during her last illness and found all her family around her bedside, inquired:

"Am I dying or is this my birthday?"

LESSON 68

Evolution, Part 5

"The evolutionists seem to know everything about the missing link except the fact that it is missing."

G. K. CHESTERTON

Kirk's Comment An evolutionist once asked why God would try to confuse us with the fossil record. But God is not trying to confuse anyone. The fossil record does not support Darwinian evolution. Rather, it casts serious doubt on the theory. The fossil record clearly indicates that there were no transitional forms between species. Even Charles Darwin himself stated in his writings that if the fossil record did not demonstrate the necessary transitional forms, his theory should be discarded.

QUESTIONS & OBJECTIONS

"Where do all the races come from?"

Some have wondered, if we are all descendants of Adam and Eve, why are there so many races? The Bible informed us 2,000 years ago that God has made all nations from "one blood" (Acts 17:26). We are all of the same race—the "human race," descendants of Adam and Eve, something science is slowly coming to realize.

Reuters news service reported the following article by Maggie Fox:

Science may have caught up with the Bible, which says that Adam and Eve are the ancestors of all humans alive today.

Peter Underhill of Stanford University in California remarked on findings published in the November 2000 issue of the journal *Nature Genetics*... Geneticists have long agreed there is no genetic basis to race—only to ethnic and geographic groups. "People look at a very conspicuous trait like skin color and they say, 'Well, this person's so different'... but that's only skin deep," Underhill said. "When you look at the level of the Y chromosome you find that, gee, there is very little difference between them. And skin color differences are strictly a consequence of climate."

"Missing Link" Still Missing

In *U.S. News & World Report* (February 14, 2000), a writer asks: "Did dinos soar? Imaginations certainly took flight over *Archaeoraptor Liaoningensis*, a birdlike fossil with a meat-eater's tail that was spirited out of northeastern China, 'discovered' at a Tucson, Arizona, gem and mineral show last year, and displayed at the National Geographic Society in Washington, D.C. Some 110,000 visitors saw the exhibit, which closed January 17; millions more read about the find in November's *National Geographic*. Now, paleontologists are eating crow. Instead of 'a true missing link' connecting dinosaurs to birds, the specimen appears to be a composite, its unusual appendage likely tacked on by a Chinese farmer, not evolution.

"*Archaeoraptor* is hardly the first 'missing link' to snap under scrutiny. In 1912, fossil remains of an ancient hominid were found in England's Piltdown quarries and quickly dubbed man's ape-like ancestor. It took decades to reveal the hoax."

Charles Darwin acknowledged that his theory of evolution was dependent on these "missing links": "As by this theory innumerable transitional forms must have existed, why do we not find them embedded in countless numbers in the crust of the earth? The number of intermediate links between all living and extinct species must have been inconceivably great!"

In *The Signature of God*, Grant R. Jeffery wrote, "Darwin admitted that millions of 'missing links,' transitional life forms, would have to be discovered in the fossil record to prove the accuracy of his theory that all species had gradually evolved by chance mutation into new species. Unfortunately for his theory, despite hundreds of millions spent on searching for fossils worldwide for more than a century, the scientists have failed to locate *a single missing link* out of the millions that must exist if their theory of evolution is to be vindicated."

Time magazine reported, "Scientists concede that their most cherished theories are based on embarrassingly few fossil fragments and that huge gaps exist in the fossil record" (Nov. 7, 1977). According to David Berlinsky, "There are gaps in the fossil graveyard, places where there should be intermediate forms, but where there is nothing whatsoever instead. No paleontologist...denies that this is so. It is simply a fact. Darwin's theory and the fossil record are in conflict."

While the fossil evidence does not support evolution, it does point to creation. Biochemist D. B. Gower said, "The creation account in Genesis and the theory of evolution could not be reconciled. One must be right and the other wrong. The story of the fossils agrees with the account of Genesis. In the oldest rocks we did not find a series of fossils covering the gradual changes from the most primitive creatures to developed forms but rather, in the oldest rocks, developed species suddenly appeared. Between every species there was a complete absence of intermediate fossils" ("Scientist Rejects Evolution," *Kentish Times*).

Evolutionary Fraud

Our Times: The Illustrated History of the 20th Century details the fraud of an evolutionary "find": "Charles Dawson, a British lawyer and amateur geologist, announced in 1912 his discovery of pieces of a human skull and an apelike jaw in a gravel pit near the town of Piltdown, England...Dawson's announcement stopped the scorn cold. Experts instantly declared Piltdown Man (estimated to be 300,000 to one million years old) the evolutionary find of the century. Darwin's missing link had been identified.

"Or so it seemed for the next 40 or so years. Then, in the early fifties ...scientists began to suspect misattribution. In 1953, that suspicion gave way to a full-blown scandal: Piltdown Man was a hoax. Radiocarbon tests proved that its skull belonged to a 600-year-old woman, and its jaw to a 500-year-old orangutan from the East Indies."

The Piltdown Man fraud wasn't an isolated incident. The famed Nebraska Man was derived from a single tooth, which was later found to be from an extinct pig. Java Man, found in the early 20th century, was nothing more than a piece of skull, a fragment of a thigh bone, and three molar teeth. The rest came from the deeply fertile imaginations of plaster of Paris workers. Java Man is now regarded as fully human. Heidelberg Man came from a jawbone, a large chin section, and a few teeth. Most scientists reject the jawbone because it's similar to that of modern man.

Still, many evolutionists believe that he's 250,000 years old. No doubt they pinpointed his birthday with carbon dating. However, *Time* magazine (June 11, 1990) published a science article subtitled, "Geologists show that carbon dating can be way off." (For example, *Science* magazine [vol. 224, 1984] reported, "Shells from *living* snails were carbon dated as being 27,000 years old.") And don't look to Neanderthal Man for any evidence of evolution. He died of exposure. His skull was exposed as being fully human, not ape. Not only was his stooped posture found to be caused by disease, but he also spoke and was artistic and religious.

Evolution's Circular Reasoning

According to Dr. Kent Hovind, "At least six different radiometric dating methods are available. *The assumed age of the sample will dictate which dating method is used because each will give a different result.*

"For example, when dinosaur bones containing carbon are found, they are *not* carbon dated because the result would be only a few thousand years. Because this would not match the assumed age based on the geologic column, scientists use another method of dating to give an age closer to the desired result. All radiometric results that do not match the pre-assigned ages of the geologic column are discarded."

Ronald R. West, Ph.D., stated, "Contrary to what most scientists write, the fossil record does not support the Darwinian theory of evolution because it is this theory (there are several) which we use to interpret the fossil record. By doing so we are guilty of circular reasoning if we then say the fossil record supports this theory."

Life's Origins: The Ever-changing Mind of Science

According to an NBC News report in August 1999, there was a "remarkable" discovery in Australia. They reported that, according to the *Journal of Science,* scientists had found what they considered to be proof that life appeared on earth 2.7 billion years ago—a billion years earlier than previously thought. They now admit that they were wrong in their first estimate (a mere 1,000,000,000 years off), but with this discovery they are now sure that they have the truth…until their next discovery. CBS News reported in October 1999 that discoveries were made of the bones of an unknown animal in Asia that may be as much as 40 million years old. This changed scientific minds as to *where* man first originated. Scientists once believed that primates evolved in Africa, but now they think they may be wrong, and that man's ancestors may have originated in Asia. So they believe…until the next discovery.

USA Today (March 21, 2001) reported, "Paleontologists have discovered a new skeleton in the closet of human ancestry that is likely to force science to revise, if not scrap, current theories of human origins." Reuters reported that the discovery left "scientists of human evolution…*confused,*" saying, "Lucy may not even be a direct human ancestor after all."

Charles Spurgeon addressed this fallibility (and folly) of science: "We are invited, brethren, most earnestly to go away from the old-fashioned belief of our forefathers because of the supposed discoveries of science. What is science? The method by which man tries to hide his ignorance. It should not be so, but so it is. You are not to be dogmatical in theology, my brethren, it is wicked; but for scientific men it is the correct thing. You are never to assert anything very strongly; but scientists may boldly assert what they cannot prove, and may demand a faith far more credulous than any we possess. Forsooth, you and I are to take our Bibles and shape and mould our belief according to the ever-shifting teachings of so-called scientific men. What folly is this! Why, the march of science, falsely so called, through the world may be traced by exploded fallacies and abandoned theories. Former explorers once adored are now ridiculed; the continual wreckings of false hypotheses is a matter of universal notoriety. You may tell where the supposed learned have encamped by the debris left behind of suppositions and theories as plentiful as broken bottles."

Arthur N. Field concluded, "What is [evolution] based upon? Upon nothing whatever but faith, upon belief in the reality of the unseen—

belief in the fossils that cannot be produced, belief in the embryological experiments that refuse to come off. It is faith unjustified by works."

QUESTIONS

1. Could you explain where all the races come from?

2. How do transitional life forms prove or disprove the theory of evolution?

3. How does the fossil evidence point to creation?

4. Name some of the "missing links" between ape and man that have been proved fraudulent.

5. How reliable is carbon dating in establishing the age of fossils?

Preacher's Progress

Christian: "Did you get one of these? It's about the theory of evolution. It shows it to be false."

Eva Lution: "That's ridiculous! Evolution is a proven scientific fact."

Christian: "Scientific proof? What do you have?"

Eva Lution: "The appendix."

Christian: "How's that?"

Eva Lution: "The appendix! It has no purpose. It's an obvious 'leftover' from evolution."

Christian: "Is that scientific proof for the theory of evolution?"

Eva Lution: "Absolutely."

Christian: "Ear lobes don't have any real 'purpose,' but that doesn't prove anything. Actually the appendix does have a purpose. It is a part in the immune system."

Eva Lution: "I don't believe that. I'm an atheist and there's no way you can convince me that God exists. There is no scientific evidence for His existence. If I could see Him, then I would believe."

Christian: "Do you realize what you are saying? Look at the sun for ten seconds and it will blind you for life; and yet the sun is only a small part of the creation of Almighty God. No one can see God and live. How long have you been an atheist?"

Eva Lution: "Three years. I used to be a Christian . . . until I saw the light. Christians are naïve simpletons who live on blind faith."

Christian: "You knew the Lord?"

Eva Lution: "Yes . . . um . . . I mean . . . no . . . well, I thought I did."

Christian: "So you didn't know the Lord. You were only faking it? How long did that last?"

Eva Lution: "Um…about four years. I was in a youth group—took communion and all that."

Christian: "So, you proved to be a false convert. In a time of tribulation, temptation, and persecution, you fell away. Do you consider yourself to be a good person?"

Eva Lution: "Of course."

Christian: "Have you ever told a lie?" (Etc.)

WORDS OF COMFORT

I liked Benson. He was a native Micronesian who was now a full-time missionary. He was one of those powerfully built men who looked like a grizzly bear but proved to be more cuddly than grizzly. In fact, Benson would laugh at almost everything I said.

It was good to see him again. I was the guest speaker at a camp, and I happened to be in the same tent as giggly Benson.

A short time after the light was turned out, Benson went outside the tent. During the night, I saw the shadow of a figure sit up, as though he were about to say something. So, with the usual tongue-in-cheek humor he seemed to appreciate so much, I said, "Shut up and go to sleep!" That normally would have made him chuckle, but instead, he immediately lay down and I never heard another sound from him.

In the morning, I learned to my horror that it wasn't Benson who had been there, but another young man I had never seen before. The first words he heard from the guest speaker were, "Shut up and go to sleep!"

Memory Verse

"Because that, when they knew God, they glorified him not as God, neither were thankful; but became vain in their imaginations, and their foolish heart was darkened. Professing themselves to be wise, they became fools."
ROMANS 1:21,22

Last Words

Charles Darwin (1809–1882), English naturalist and father of the "Evolutionary Theory":

"I am not the least afraid to die."

LESSON 69

Atheism

"When a man calls himself an atheist, he is not attacking God; he is attacking his own conscience."

MICHAEL PEARL

Kirk's Comment   I denied the existence of God for many years. I later realized that my beliefs were not founded on truth, but on a love for my ungodly lifestyle and an unwillingness to investigate the facts.

QUESTIONS & OBJECTIONS

"I don't believe that God is knowable."

Amazingly, it is human nature to assume that our believing or not believing something makes it true. Some people may not believe in the law of gravity, and may feel they have "evidence" to back up their belief. However, gravity exists whether they believe in it or not. The truth is, God is knowable. Jesus testified, "And this is life eternal, that they might know you the only true God, and Jesus Christ, whom you have sent" (John 17:3). We not only have the testimony of Scripture to tell us this, but we have the testimony of multitudes of Christians who know the Lord personally. It is more truthful to say, "I don't *want* to know God." Sinful man runs from Him as did Adam in the Garden of Eden.

I don't believe in atheists. This isn't because I haven't met anyone who claimed the title, but because such a person cannot exist. If you encounter someone who claims to be an atheist, ask him these two questions: First, "Do you know the combined weight of all the sand on all the beaches of Hawaii?" We can safely assume that he doesn't. This brings us to the second question: "Do you know how many hairs are on the back of a full-grown male Tibetan yak?" Probably not. Therefore, it is reasonable to conclude that there are some things he doesn't know. It is important to ask these questions because some people think they know everything.

Let's say that the professing atheist knows an incredible 1 percent of all the knowledge in the universe. To know 100 percent, he would have to know absolutely everything. There wouldn't be a rock in the universe that he would not be intimately familiar with, or a grain of sand that he would not be aware of. He would know everything that has happened in history, from that which is common knowledge to the minor details of the secret love life of Napoleon's great-grandmother's black cat's fleas. He would know every hair of every head, and every thought of every heart. All history would be laid out before him, because he would be omniscient (all-knowing).

Bear in mind that one of the greatest scientists who ever lived, Thomas Edison, said, "We do not know a millionth of one percent about anything." Again, let's say that the atheist has an incredible *1 percent* of all the knowledge in the universe. Would it be possible, in the 99 percent of the knowledge that he hasn't yet come across, that there might be ample evidence to prove the existence of God? One who is reasonable will be forced to admit that it is possible. Somewhere, in the vast knowledge that he hasn't yet discovered, there could be enough proof that God does exist.

Let's look at the same thought from another angle. If I were to make an absolute statement such as, "There is no gold in China," what is necessary for that statement to be proved true? I would need absolute or total knowledge. I must know that there is no gold in any rock, in any river, in the ground, in any store, in any ring, or in any filling in any mouth in China. If there is one speck of gold in China, then my statement is false and I have no basis for it. I need absolute knowledge before I can make an

459

absolute statement. Conversely, for me to say, "There *is* gold in China," I don't need to have all knowledge. If there is even one speck of gold in the country, the statement is then true.

To say categorically, "There is no God," is to make an absolute statement. For the statement to be true, a person must know for certain that there is no God in the entire universe. No human being has all knowledge. Therefore, none of us is able to truthfully make this assertion.

One who insists upon disbelief in God must say, "Having the limited knowledge that I have at present, I *believe* that there is no God." Owing to a lack of knowledge on his part, he doesn't *know* if God exists. So, in the strict sense of the word, one cannot be an atheist. The only true qualifier for the title is the One who has absolute knowledge, and why on earth would God want to deny His own existence?

The professing atheist is actually what is commonly known as an "agnostic"—one who claims he "doesn't know" if God exists, or "one who professes ignorance." The Bible tells us that this ignorance is willful: "The wicked in his proud countenance does not seek God; God is in none of his thoughts" (Psalm 10:4). It's not that a person *can't* find God, but that he *won't*. It has been rightly said that the "atheist" can't find God for the same reason a thief can't find a policeman. He knows that if he acknowledges there is a God, he is admitting that he is ultimately accountable to Him. This is not a pleasant thought for some.

It is said that the Italian dictator Mussolini once stood on a pinnacle and cried, "God, if You are there, strike me dead!" When God didn't immediately bow to his dictates, Mussolini concluded that there was no God. However, his prayer *was* answered sometime later.

QUESTIONS

1. **What word is used to describe someone who knows all things?**

2. What did Thomas Edison say about our knowledge?

3. Give an example of an absolute statement.

4. What must you have to make an absolute statement that is true?

5. Do you need absolute knowledge to say that there is gold in China?

6. Why is there no such thing as an atheist?

7. The professing atheist is actually an "agnostic." What does the word mean?

8. **What does the Bible tell us about this ignorance?**

FEATHERS FOR ARROWS

Imagine for a moment that you are standing on the seashore gazing at a large ocean liner. The sun is shining. There is no wind and the sea is calm. To your amazement, about thirty people suddenly dive off the end of the ship and cling to a lifeboat.

You shake your head in disbelief at their foolishness. Then without warning, the great ocean liner strikes an iceberg and suddenly sinks, taking all onboard with it.

Those who looked like fools in abandoning the ship were actually wise, and those who seemed wise by staying onboard were, in truth, fools.

The world scoffs at those who abandon the ship of this world and cling to the lifeboat of the Savior. But Christians know that this great pleasure-cruiser will eventually come into contact with the immovable iceberg of the Law of God and sink into hell, taking all those onboard with it.

WORDS OF COMFORT

I had been left in charge of a megaphone that our church had rented for a picnic. I returned from the Sunday night meeting to find Sue still awake, well after 11 p.m., which was unusual. Sue explained that she had been trying to get to sleep for some time, but had been kept awake by a number of children playing on a neighbor's front lawn. I hit the sack, but was also hindered from stacking Z's by those little night owls, hooting and hollering into the night.

As I lay in bed, I suddenly remembered the weapon of warfare in the trunk of my car. I quickly slipped out to the garage, grabbed the megaphone, crept across the road onto the neighbor's lawn and up to the fence. Then, with the megaphone switched on full volume, I boldly said, *"You kids get to bed!"* I have never seen children move so fast. I was feeling quite happy with myself until the next day, when one of my boys shared some information that brought a hot flush to my face. One of our female neighbors also couldn't sleep because of the noise that night, and in the darkness of her kitchen was having a glass of milk. As she gazed out her window, she saw a sight that she said she would never forget. A grown man dressed in short pajamas crept across her lawn, squatted in her garden, yelled through a megaphone, then ran like an exuberant little child who just did something he shouldn't have, but loved it.

Memory Verse

"The fool has said in his heart, There is no God. They are corrupt, they have done abominable works, there is none that does good."

PSALM 14:1

Last Words

St. Francis of Assisi (1182–1226), founder of the Franciscan order of monks:

> "Farewell, my children; remain always in the fear of the Lord. That temptation and tribulation which is to come is now at hand and happy shall they be who persevere in the good they have begun. I hasten to go to our Lord, to whose grace I recommend you."

How to Prove the Existence of God

"It takes no brains to be an atheist. Any stupid person can deny the existence of a supernatural power because man's physical senses cannot detect it. But there cannot be ignored the influence of conscience, the respect we feel for the Moral Law, the mystery of first life . . . or the marvelous order in which the universe moves about us on this earth. All these evidence the handiwork of the beneficent Deity . . . That Deity is the God of the Bible and Jesus Christ, His Son."

DWIGHT EISENHOWER

Kirk's Comment   Proving God's existence is not difficult. But as it has been said, many atheists don't want to be "confused by the facts." Our job is to demonstrate Truth. The Holy Spirit is the One who can open an unbeliever's heart to receive that Truth.

QUESTIONS & OBJECTIONS

"Who made God?"

To one who examines the evidence, there can be no doubt that God exists. The fact of the existence of the Creator is axiomatic (self-evident). That's why the Bible says, "The fool has said in his heart, There is no God" (Psalm 14:1). The professing atheist denies the common sense given to him by

God, and defends his belief by thinking that the question "Who made God?" can't be answered. This, he thinks, gives him license to deny the existence of God.

The question of who made God can be answered by simply looking at space and asking, "Does space have an end?" Obviously, it doesn't. If there is a brick wall with "The End" written on it, the question arises, "What is behind the brick wall?" Strain the mind though it may, we have to believe (have faith) that space has no beginning and no end. The same applies with God. He has no beginning and no end. He is eternal.

The Bible also informs us that time is a dimension that God created, into which man was subjected. It even tells us that one day time will no longer exist. That will be called "eternity." God Himself dwells outside of the dimension He created (2 Timothy 1:9; Titus 1:2); He dwells in eternity and is not subject to time. God spoke history before it came into being. He can move through time as a man flips through a history book. Because we live in the dimension of time, logic and reason demand that everything must have a beginning and an end. We can understand the concept of God's eternal nature the same way we understand the concept of space having no beginning or end—by faith. We simply have to believe they are so, even though such thoughts put a strain on our distinctly insufficient cerebrum.

wotmwotmwotmwotmwotmwotmwotmwotmwotmwotmwotm

There are many who say, "You can't prove or disprove God. It's all a matter of faith." However, the existence of God has nothing to do with "faith." This is why.

When we look at a building, how do we know that there was a builder? We can't see him, hear him, touch, taste, or smell him. Of course, the building is proof that there was a builder. In fact, we couldn't want better evidence that there was a builder than to have the building in front of us. We don't need "faith" to know that there was a builder—all we need are eyes that can see and a brain that works.

This same profound, intellectual principle applies to paintings and painters. When we look at a painting, how can we know that there was a painter? Why, the painting is perfectly positive proof that there was a painter. In fact, we couldn't want better evidence that there was a painter than to have the painting in front of us. Isn't it true? (Pause for a moment and visualize a painting.) We don't need "faith" to believe in a painter—all we need are eyes that can see and a brain that works. This is so simple that a child can understand it. The only ones who have trouble with its simplicity are those who profess to be intellectuals. No wonder man is searching for intelligent life in the universe.

Everything on this earth that was "made" has a maker. The same principle of building/builder, painting/painter applies with the existence of God. When we look at creation, how can we know that there was a Creator? We can't see Him, hear Him, touch Him, taste Him, or smell Him. How can we know that He exists? Why, creation proves, beyond the shadow of the smallest doubt, that there is a Creator. You *cannot* have a "creation" without a Creator. (Webster's dictionary defines "creation" as "the act of creating; especially the act of bringing the world into ordered existence.") We couldn't want better proof that a Creator exists than to have creation in front of us. We don't need "faith" to believe in a Creator —all we need are eyes that can see and a brain that works.

The Bible tells us, "For the invisible things of him from the creation of the world are clearly seen [by the eyes that can see], being understood [by a brain that works] by the things that are made, even his eternal power and Godhead; so that they are without excuse" (Romans 1:20).

If, however, we want the builder to do something for us, then we need to have faith in him. This is where "faith" enters, in the form of "trust":

> Without faith it is impossible to please him: for he that comes to God must believe that he is, and that he is a rewarder of them that diligently seek him (Hebrews 11:6).

Let's put it another way: Only without doubt it is possible to please Him, for he who comes to God must not believe that He doesn't exist.

QUESTIONS

1. When we look at a building, how do we know that there was a builder?

2. When we look at a painting, how can we know that there was a painter?

3. When we look at creation, how can we know that there was a Creator?

4. What does someone need to be able to figure this out?

5. Do we need "faith" to believe in a Creator?

6. According to Romans 1:20, why does humanity have no excuse for not recognizing God?

7. **Could you explain who made God?**

PREACHER'S PROGRESS

Ken Outwitgod: "I've looked at women with lust, but I enjoy it."

Christian: "There's no argument there. The Bible acknowledges that sin has pleasure, but it's only for a season."

Ken Outwitgod: "What I want to know is, how much can I sin and still make it to heaven?"

Christian: "Don't you have any fear of God?"

Ken Outwitgod: "No. I will repent just before I die. The thief on the cross did."

Christian: "So you know about the cross?"

Ken Outwitgod: "Yes. I used to go to Sunday school."

Christian: "Do you know what your problem is?"

Ken Outwitgod: "What?"

Christian: "Idolatry."

Ken Outwitgod: "What's that?"

Christian: "You have the concept of a god that you think can be fooled; your god isn't too bright. In doing so, you have made a god to suit yourself. That's called 'idolatry,' and it's a transgression of the Second of the Ten Commandments."

Ken Outwitgod: "I didn't know that."

Christian: "What you are saying is that you think your Creator will let you do things that greatly offend Him, and then allow you to repent at the last minute. However, He may just kill you before you repent, and then you will end up in hell…for eternity."

Ken Outwitgod: "God doesn't kill people."

Christian: "Your non-existent god doesn't, but the God of the Bible does, and He's the God you must face on Judgment Day. Didn't they tell you that in Sunday school?"

Ken Outwitgod: "No."

Christian: "He killed a man in Genesis 38, because He didn't like what he did sexually. He also killed a man and his wife in the Book of Acts, because they told one lie."

Ken Outwitgod: "I didn't know that."

Christian: "You do now. There is no way you can fool God, Ken. He has seen every sin you have ever committed. He has even seen your thought-life. He's been patient with you up until now by not treating you according to your sins. Isn't that true?"

Ken Outwitgod: "I guess He has."

FEATHERS FOR ARROWS

Many years ago, I ran a children's club. At the end of the club I told about one hundred kids to line up for some candy. There was an immediate rush, and the line sorted itself into what I saw as a line of greed. The bigger, selfish kids were at the front, and the small and timid ones were at the back. So I did something that gave me great satisfaction. I instructed them to do an about-face and to stay where they were. I then took great delight in going to the other end of the line and giving the candy to the smaller, timid kids first.

In a world where the rich get richer and the poor get stomped on, we are informed that God has gone to the other end of the line with the message of everlasting life. How has He done that? Simply by choosing that which is weak, base, and despised. You can see this by asking a skeptic, "Do you believe that the following biblical accounts actually happened?"

Adam and Eve, Noah's ark, Jonah and the whale, Joshua and the walls of Jericho, Samson and his long hair, Daniel and the lion's den, Moses and the Red Sea

Of course he doesn't. To say that he believed such fantastic stories would mean that he would have to surrender his intellectual dignity. Who in his right mind would ever do that? The answer is simply *those who understand that God has chosen foolish, weak, base, and despised things of the world to confound those who think they are wise.*

Last Words

Perigood-Talleyrand (1754–1838), the renowned French statesman best remembered as Foreign Minister under Napoleon and later Foreign Minister to Louis XVIII, was likewise known for his infidel leanings. At his deathbed, King Louis asked Talleyrand how he felt. He replied:

"I am suffering, Sire, the pangs of the damned."

LESSON 71

Atheist Obstacles

"We must thrust the Sword of the Spirit into the hearts of men."
CHARLES SPURGEON

Kirk's Comment It is quite simple to prove that an atheist doesn't exist, while disproving God's existence is impossible. This lesson explains why.

QUESTIONS & OBJECTIONS

"I will believe if God will appear to me."

A proud and ignorant sinner who says this has no understanding of the nature of His Creator. No man has ever seen the essence of God. (When God "appeared" to certain men in the Old Testament, He manifested Himself in other forms, such as a burning bush or "the Angel of the Lord.") When Moses asked to see God's glory, God told him, "I will make all my goodness pass before you, . . . [but] you cannot see my face: for there shall no man see me, and live" (Exodus 33:18–23). If all of God's "goodness" were shown to a sinner, he would instantly die. God's "goodness" would just spill wrath upon evil man.

However, the Lord told Moses, "It shall come to pass, while my glory passes by, that I will put you in a cleft of the rock, and will cover you with my hand while I pass by." The only way a sinner can live in the presence of a holy God is to be hidden in the Rock of Jesus Christ (1 Corinthians 10:4).

A favorite argument of the atheist is that God's existence cannot be *disproved*. This is true. As mentioned earlier, one must be omniscient to disprove God's existence. However, one should also be *omnipresent* (dwelling everywhere at once) to be absolutely sure that God doesn't exist (although it could be argued that one who is totally omniscient wouldn't have to be omnipresent).

It is because the atheist is neither omniscient nor omnipresent that he then takes an illogical leap by concluding that there is no God, *because it cannot be proved that He doesn't exist.* Such reasoning is absurd. Why would anyone try to prove that God *doesn't* exist when it can be proved that He *does*? Creation proves scientifically and absolutely to any sane mind that there is a Creator. His existence is axiomatic.

The atheist also has a problem with both answered and unanswered prayer. Here's a scenario that no doubt happens daily somewhere in the world. A young boy becomes deathly ill. The entire family gathers for prayer. However, despite earnest and sincere prayer, the child tragically dies. The family's explanation for the death is that God took the child to heaven because He wanted him there. The atheist views that as "unanswered prayer." Or, if the child miraculously recovers, the family hails it as an evident miracle. God obviously answered the family's prayers by saving the child from death. The atheist maintains that it wasn't answered prayer but that the child recovered because his body healed itself.

Was the recovery a miracle? Perhaps. Then again, perhaps it wasn't. Only God knows. The fact is that we have no idea what happened. However, one thing we do know is that answered or unanswered prayer has nothing to do with God's existence. Let me explain. Let's say my vehicle has a mechanical problem. What would be my intellectual capacity if I concluded that it had no manufacturer simply because I couldn't contact them about the dilemma? The fact of their existence has nothing to do with whether or not they return my calls.

Neither does God's existence have anything to do with the fact that some have experienced miracles, seen visions, or supposedly heard His voice. The sun doesn't exist because we see its light, or because we feel its warmth. Its existence has nothing to do with any human testimony. Nor does it cease to exist because a blind man is not aware of its reality, or because it becomes cloudy, or the night falls. The sun exists, period.

God's existence isn't dependent on the Bible or its authenticity, the existence of the church, the prophets, or even creation. God existed before the Scriptures were penned, and before creation came into existence. Even if the Bible were proved to be fraudulent, God would still exist.

Adamant atheist April Pedersen writes, "The human trait of seeking comfort through prayer is a strong one." This is true. However, April fails to see that human nature itself is very predictable. If men will not embrace the biblical revelation of God, their nature is to predictably go into idolatry. "Idolatry" is the act of creating a god in our image, whether it is shaped with human hands (a physical "idol"), or shaped in the human mind through the imagination. Those who create their own god then use it as a "good-luck charm" to do their bidding. The idolater calls on his god to win a football game, a boxing match, the lottery, and, of course, to win a war. Idolatry is as predictable as it is illogical.

Idolaters (of which there are billions throughout the world) are deceived into thinking that their imaginary god really does exist. They assume that Almighty God changes like pliable putty to whatever they visualize Him to be. Such a thought is ludicrous. It is like standing before an oncoming steam roller and imagining it to be cotton candy. Our imaginings don't change reality. God doesn't change just because we change our perception of Him. The Bible says, "I am the LORD, I change not" (Malachi 3:6). However, there is something even more ludicrous than the imaginings of idolaters. It is that trait of human nature that is just as predictable —the intellectual suicide of the atheist.

By the way, I sent April Pedersen "Atheist's Obstacles" for her thoughts. This was her reply: "Thank you for sending this! It's worded with impeccable logic...It's nearly impossible to find holes in your premise that in order to claim there is no God, one must be omniscient. It's impossible for anyone to be omniscient. And you addressed the issue of "unanswered" prayers well too, where God exists independently regardless of our views of prayers, and is independent of the Bible as well...So *that* explains what people are praying to when they pray at ball games and the like...

They have created a false god as they want to see him, without even knowing they have fallen into this self-centered trap...an idol..."

QUESTIONS

1. **What does one need in order to prove that God doesn't exist?**

2. **Why is it that "miracles" and answered or unanswered prayer have no bearing on the existence of God?**

3. **What is "idolatry"?**

4. **What is the great deception of the idolater?**

5. **What Bible verse speaks of God's unchanging nature?**

FEATHERS FOR ARROWS

One moonless night, unbeknown to the passengers of a plane, hijackers broke into the cockpit. They took over the controls, contacted the control tower, and demanded that the White House release a large number of political prisoners. When authorities refused to comply with the demands, the terrorists threatened to fire on the passengers and force them out of an open door at 20,000 feet.

During negotiations, the captain was able to scribble a note on official paper warning of the hijackers' threat and telling passengers to reach under their seats. There they would find a parachute, which they were instructed to put on immediately.

As the note was passed among the passengers, there were different reactions. Some saw the note as obviously authentic because it was written on official paper. Besides, they remembered the strange jolt when the hijackers violently took control of the plane. They immediately put the parachute on realizing that they had nothing to lose but their pride if the note was fraudulent, and everything to gain if it was true.

Some passengers refused to believe the note because they thought there was no way that there could be a parachute beneath the seat. They were so sure that they didn't even check.

A couple rejected the note because they noticed a passenger who had only pretended to put on the parachute. They could see that he hadn't bothered to tighten the straps.

Others laughed at the note as though it were some joke, while others didn't bother reading it because they were watching an onboard movie.

Some passengers even ignored the evidence of the official paper and the jolt of the plane and instead maintained that the plane didn't even have a pilot and that there was no aircraft maker. As far as they were concerned it came together by accident, taking millions of years, and could fly itself.

Suddenly, the hijackers burst into the darkened cabin, thrust open the exit doors, and began firing automatic weapons over the terrified passengers' heads, forcing them to jump 20,000 feet into the blackness. Most fell to their deaths. However, those who had had the good sense to believe and obey the captain were saved from such a horrible demise.

There is nothing wrong with sinners questioning the mystery of prayer, the authenticity of the Bible, the existence of God, and the fact of hypocrisy. However, it is wise for them to put on the "parachute" first. They could be made to jump through the door of death into a black and horrifying eternity at any moment. There is a merciless Law awaiting them —a Law far harsher than the law of gravity. They desperately need the Savior. Encourage them to do what the "Note" says—reach under their seat and "Put on the Lord Jesus Christ" (Romans 13:14). After they have secured their own eternal salvation, they can worry about the fate of the pretender. If they think it's important, they can then try to figure out the age of the earth, etc.

Memory Verse

"He that believes on him is not condemned: but he that believes not is condemned already, because he has not believed in the name of the only begotten Son of God. And this is the condemnation, that light is come into the world, and men loved darkness rather than light, because their deeds were evil."

JOHN 3:18,19

Last Words

William Carey (1761–1834), known as "The Father of Modern Missions," developed remarkable gifts as a linguist. Sent out by the Baptist Missionary Society, he became the first missionary to India. His motto was, "Expect great things from God. Attempt great things for God." On his deathbed he said to a friend:

> **"When I am gone, say nothing about Dr. Carey; speak about Dr. Carey's Saviour."**

72 Atheists' Questions, Part 1

*"I believe in Christianity as I believe that the sun has risen:
not only because I see it, but because by it I see everything else."*

C. S. LEWIS

Kirk's Comment Read this atheist group's questionnaire. It is really insightful and wonderful material to have ready for your next encounter with an atheist.

QUESTIONS & OBJECTIONS

"Man is the master of his own destiny!"

If man is in total control of his future, then he should at least be in control of his own body. Instead, he is subject to involuntary yawning, sneezing, breathing, swallowing, sleeping, salivating, dreaming, blinking, and thinking. He can't even control hair and nail growth. He automatically does these things, irrespective of his will. God has set his body in motion and there is little he can do about it. He also has minimal control over his daily bodily functions. His kidneys, bladder, intestines, heart, liver, lungs, etc., work independently of his will. It is ludicrous to say that man controls his future when he has trouble predicting the stock market, political outcomes, earthquakes, and even the weather, let alone having control over these things.

The following questions are taken from the web site of a Hollywood atheist organization. As they have stated, this information is useful for those who "haven't thought much about religion since childhood and want to test their faith with adult questions... These questions are worthwhile only to those who think reason is the most valid tool in forming opinions."

I have given answers to their difficulties. Perhaps you can share these answers with others who have questions about Christianity.

1) How would you define God, and why are you so convinced that there is one?

God is the Creator, Upholder, and the Sustainer of the universe. He revealed Himself to Moses as the one and only true God.

2) If everything needs a creator, then who or what created God?

No person or thing created God. He created "time," and because we dwell in the dimension of time, *reason* demands that all things have a beginning and an end. God, however, dwells outside of the dimension of time. He moves through time as we flip through the pages of a history book; this can be proved by simple study of the prophecies of Matthew 24, Luke 21, and 2 Timothy 3. He dwells in "eternity," having no beginning or end. This is a dimension in which all humanity will dwell when God withdraws time.

3) How can something that cannot be described be said to exist?

The color blue cannot be accurately described to a man who was born blind. Just because it cannot be described doesn't mean that it doesn't exist. There is plant life on the bottom of the deepest oceans that has never been seen by man, let alone described by him. Despite this, it still exists. Does the (unseen) far side of a planet fail to exist merely because man cannot describe it?

4) Since countless religions in the world today claim to be the one true religion, *why do you think yours is* truer *than theirs?*

No religion is "truer" than another. "Religion" is man's futile effort to try to find peace with God. The Christian doesn't strive to have peace with his Creator. It was given to him in the person of the Savior. The uniqueness of Jesus of Nazareth is His statement, "The Son of Man has power on earth to forgive sins." No religion of man can do that. Christianity is not a manmade "religion," but a personal relationship with the one true God.

5) Can more than one of these religions be right?

In one sweeping statement, Jesus discards all other religions as a means of finding forgiveness of sins. Jesus, who claimed to be God, said, "I am the way, the truth, and the life. No one comes to the Father except through me" (John 14:6). The Bible says about Jesus, "There is one God and one Mediator between God and men, the Man Christ Jesus" (1 Timothy 2:5) and, "Nor is there salvation in any other, for there is no other name under heaven given among men by which we must be saved" (Acts 4:12). See also Answer #4.

6) If you feel in your heart that your religion is the right one, how do you answer those of other faiths who claim the same thing?

Christians don't base their faith on feelings; their feelings are irrelevant to truth. If I am flying from Los Angeles to New York, my feelings about whether I am going in the right direction have nothing to do with that fact. We can *know* with our intellect that Christianity is true, regardless of our feelings. The Bible's thousands of fulfilled prophecies, historical accuracy, and many infallible proofs attest to its reliability.

7) How do you settle the debate and find out which of these religions, if any, is the right one?

Jesus promises that He and the Father will reveal themselves to all who love and obey Him. This is the ultimate challenge to any skeptic. If you repent and place your faith in Jesus Christ, He will give you eternal life and you can *know* that your eternity is secure.

8) Why does God allow all these false religions to exist?

Because God wants mankind to worship and love Him, He gave Adam and Eve the free will to choose whether to obey or disobey Him. People have chosen to reject God's way and instead seek to establish their own righteousness through works-based religions.

God allows these false religions and atheism to exist for the same reason He allows sinful humans to exist. The Bible tells us that God is not willing that any should perish (regardless of whether they are religious or profess atheism), but that they all come to repentance.

9) Is the bloody history of Christianity consistent with what is supposed to be a religion of love, or does it simply illustrate the consequences of abandoning reason for faith?

The Bible commands Christians to love their enemies and do good to those who spitefully use them. The terrorists in the World Trade Center tragedy carried out their agenda in the name of Allah (their god). This is nothing new. The Crusaders and others who have committed atrocities in the name of Christianity were also evil men who were carrying out their depraved agendas. A thinking person can distinguish between those who use the Christian faith for their own political or "religious" ends and those who are true followers of Jesus. In other words, just because someone claims to be a Christian doesn't mean that he is. He could be what is commonly known as a hypocrite, or an impostor.

10) If everything is the product of a "grand design" by an omniscient, benevolent designer, why is the history of life a record of horrible suffering, blundering waste, and miserable failures? Why does this God go through billions of years of such carnage without yet arriving at His goal?

God's original creation was "good," but because of mankind's sin we now live in a "fallen" creation. Before sin entered the world there was no suffering, disease, decay, or death. The Bible's explanation of suffering actually substantiates the truth of Scripture.

11) Why did God intervene so many times in human affairs during antiquity (according to the Bible) and yet not do anything during the Holocaust of the Second World War?

No human can claim to know whether or not God intervened in the affairs of humanity at any time between 1939 and 1945. However, the Old

Testament makes it very clear that there were times when God didn't intervene in the affairs of His people. He purposefully allowed their enemies to overpower them so that they would turn back to Him.

12) Why should one's inner convictions about the existence of God indicate that He/She/They/It exists outside of that person's mind?

The Bible says that God has placed eternity in the hearts of men and given all people everywhere an awareness of Him so that they are without excuse. He created us to know Him. Throughout history and throughout the world, all cultures acknowledge the existence of God.

Besides, why should one's inner convictions about the non-existence of God indicate that He doesn't exist outside of that person's mind? Our personal convictions and beliefs do not affect reality. God simply is.

13) Can a God who would abandon His children when they needed Him the most still be considered "all good"?

One of humanity's great errors is to misunderstand the meaning of "good." A "good" judge will pronounce a stiff sentence on a vicious murderer. A "loving" judge who dismisses a case against a vicious killer because he loves him is not a good judge. Justice and goodness are inseparable. Many times God chastened Israel (gave them their just dessert) *because* of His goodness. He wanted them to turn back to Him for their own good.

14) If the God of the Bible is "all good," why does He Himself say that He created evil (Isaiah 45:7)?

The word translated "evil" in that verse ("I make peace, and create evil") means "calamity" or "suffering"—God uses both good and bad events in our lives to bring us into a right relationship with Him. However, because God is sovereign over all events, He did allow evil to come into being.

God gave mankind a choice to have a loving relationship with Him. The original sin was when Adam and Eve chose to eat from the tree of knowledge of good and evil. Once man knew both good and evil, he had to choose between the two. Because God wants people to worship Him freely out of love and enjoy His incredible blessings, He tells each one of us: "See, I have set before you today life and good, death and evil..., therefore choose life, that both you and your descendants may live" (Deuteronomy 30:15,19).

15) If something is not rational, should it be believed anyway?

At one time, the concept of a thousand-ton aircraft flying through the air seemed irrational and absurd. But after man studied the laws of physics, it was discovered to be quite rational and believable. If one studies God's Word and understands His Law, Christianity is seen to be infinitely rational and believable. Atheism, on the other hand, rejects logic and evidence and is the epitome of irrationalism. It should be abandoned by any rational person as being foolishness.

16) Is there a better way than reason to acquire knowledge and truth?

No. That's why the Bible says, "'Come now, and let us reason together,' says the LORD." That's why when the apostle Paul spoke "the words of truth and reason," King Agrippa said, "You almost persuade me to become a Christian." That's why Paul "reasoned" with Felix (the governor) about "righteousness, self-control, and judgment to come." And that's why Felix "was afraid."

17) If you would answer #16 with "faith," then why are there so many contradictory faiths in the world?

There are many faiths because all nations recognize that there is a Creator. However, in their ignorance they worship the moon, the sun, or an idol. No one has ever found an atheistic tribe, because people are not that ignorant. God has given light to every man.

18) Is comfort more important to you than intellectual integrity?

No, it's not. That's why I am a Christian.

QUESTIONS

1. Why is Christianity the one true religion? (See #4.)

2. According to the Bible, can more than one religion be true? (See #5.)

3. How can we know that Christianity is true? (See #6 & #7.)

4. Why does God allow other religions to exist? (See #8.)

5. How do you account for Christianity's bloody history? (See #9.)

6. Isn't Christianity irrational? (See #15 & #16.)

FEATHERS FOR ARROWS

Memory Verse

"The times of this ignorance God winked at; but now commands all men every where to repent: because he has appointed a day, in the which he will judge the world in righteousness..."

ACTS 17:30,31

A child finds that he has an insatiable appetite for chocolate. At the same time he notices that his face has broken out with ugly sores. Every time he looks in the mirror he sees a sight that makes him depressed. However, instead of giving up his beloved chocolate, he consoles himself by stuffing more into his mouth. Yet, the source of his pleasure is actually the *cause* of his suffering.

The whole face of the earth reveals the ugly sores of suffering. Everywhere we look we see unspeakable pain. But instead of believing God's explanation and asking Him to forgive us and change our appetite, we run deeper into sin's sweet embrace. There we find solace in its temporal pleasures, thus intensifying our pain, both in this life and in the life to come.

Last Words

David Livingstone (1813–1873), a Scottish missionary who spent over thirty years in Africa, mostly in unexplored country, was the one who discovered the Victoria Falls. Shortly before he died, he said to his servants:

"Build me a hut to die in. I'm going home."

He died as he knelt at his bedside. His heart was removed and buried in the Africa he gave his life for, and his body was preserved in salt and carried by affectionate natives to the coast over one thousand miles away and ultimately buried with honors in Westminster Abbey.

LESSON 73 Atheists' Questions, Part 2

"To convince the world of the truth of Christianity, it must first be convinced of sin. It is only sin that renders Christ intelligible."

ANDREW MURRAY

Kirk's Comment Atheism may seem intellectual, but intelligent people should also be reasonable and honest about the facts. If you've ever felt nervous about discussing the facts for the existence of God, don't be. The evidence is on the side of God. After reading this lesson, you'll be better equipped to talk with skeptics.

QUESTIONS & OBJECTIONS

"When you're dead, you're dead."

What if you are wrong? What if God, Jesus, the prophets, the Jews, and Christians are right and you are wrong? If there is no afterlife, no Judgment Day, no heaven, and no hell, then God is unjust and each of the above is guilty of being a false witness. It means that Almighty God couldn't care less about the fact that a man rapes a woman, then cuts her throat and is never brought to justice. If you are right, and there is no ultimate justice, you won't even have the joy of saying, "I told you so." However, if you are wrong, you will lose your soul and end up eternally damned. You are playing Russian roulette with a fully loaded gun.

This lesson is a continuation of the list of questions from a Hollywood atheist organization web site, along with my answers. These answers are not definitive, but will help you think through each question so you'll be ready with your own answers as you witness.

19) If you believe, as many do, that all religions worship the same God under different names, how do you explain the existence of religions which have more than one god, or Buddhism, which, in its pure form, has no god?

All religions do not worship the same God. People who reject the one true God of the Bible can find any number of gods, of any type, to suit their tastes. They may choose to worship a small wooden god that asks only for shelf space, one that promises paradise in exchange for a certain number of daily prayers, or one that demands specific offerings or good deeds. People who reject the one true God have always been able to devise a replacement.

20) What would it take to convince you that you are wrong?

I have already been convinced that I was wrong. I was wrong for my 22 years of unconverted life. Conversion to Christianity is when a fallible human being admits that he is wrong and that the infallible Creator is right.

21) If nothing can convince you that you are wrong, then why should your faith be considered anything other than a cult?

A cult is defined as "a system of religious worship and ritual," which would seem to describe every manmade religion. Christianity, on the other hand, is not a strict adherence to ritual, but a personal relationship with a living God. When a person repents of his sin and places his trust in Jesus, God fills him with His Spirit—the person becomes spiritually alive. He has moved out of the realm of *belief* into the realm of *experience*. Once he knows the truth, nothing can convince him otherwise.

Besides, why should adherence to the truth be a determining factor in whether a belief is valid? I believe in gravity and nothing can convince me that I am wrong—but my belief is still true.

22) If an atheist lives a decent, moral life, why should a loving, compassionate God care whether or not we believe in Him/Her/It?

No matter how decent and moral we think we are, we have all sinned by violating God's holy Laws. To see how you fare against God's standard, review the Ten Commandments (given in Exodus chapter 20). God's concern isn't whether or not we *believe* in Him; the Bible says that even the demons believe—and tremble. God commands that we repent of our sins and trust Jesus Christ alone for our salvation. If we refuse do that, we will be given justice on the Day of Judgment and we will perish.

23) Should any religion that demands we elevate faith over reason be trusted?

Never elevate faith over reason. Exercise faith *because* of reason. A man who has to jump 25,000 feet out of a plane exercises faith in a parachute because he reasons that he will perish without it.

24) How can the same God who, according to the Old Testament, killed everybody on Earth except for eight people be considered as anything other than evil?

Look at the lifestyle of those people—they deserved death because of their evil actions. That's what happens when men reject God. We will all die because God, the Judge of the universe, has pronounced the death sentence upon us: "The soul who sins shall die." Criminals rarely speak well of the judge. To them, he is "evil."

25) Must we hate our families and ourselves in order to be good Christians (Luke 14:26)?

No. Luke 14:26 is what is known as "hyperbole"—a statement of extremes, contrasting love with hate for the sake of emphasis. Jesus tells us that the first and greatest Commandment is to love God with all of our heart, soul, and mind (Matthew 22:37,38). As much as we treasure our spouse and family, and even our own life, there should be no one whom we love and value more than God, no one who takes precedence in our life. To place love for another (including ourself) above God is idolatry.

26) Since the ancient world abounded with tales of resurrected Savior-Gods that were supposed to have returned from the dead to save humanity, why is the Jesus myth any more reliable than all the others?

I have never heard of any such "tales of resurrected Savior-Gods." Any myths there have been have died out for lack of proof. The "Jesus myth," however, has endured through the ages in cultures all around the world because it is true and provable. Simply read John 14:21 and then try it ...if you dare. If you place your trust in Jesus Christ for your salvation, He will come into your life and reveal Himself to you.

27) If the Bible is the inerrant word of God, why does it contain so many factual errors, such as the two contradictory accounts of creation in Genesis?

There are not two accounts of creation in Genesis. Chapter 1 gives the account of creation; chapter 2 gives *details* of the same creation. I have been reading the Bible every day for thirty years (without fail) and I am not aware of any "factual errors."

28) Why isn't the Bible written in a straightforward way that leaves no doubt about what it means?

The Bible is very clear to those who obey God. It says of itself that it is spiritually understood, and that the "natural" man cannot receive the things of God. To someone who hasn't been born spiritually, "they are foolishness to him; nor can he know them, because they are spiritually discerned" (1 Corinthians 2:14). However, we can all understand enough to realize that we have sinned against a holy God and need to repent. Once we do that, God gives us the ability to understand His Word.

29) The last time Christianity attained total power, it resulted in the Dark Ages, so why should we expect anything different from Christian fundamentalists today?

It was not Christianity but the Roman Catholic church that had power during the Dark Ages. The doctrines of the Roman Catholic church and the Bible are opposed to one another. It was the Roman Catholic church that opposed Galileo, was responsible for the Inquisition, and refused the common people access to the Bible during the Dark Ages. The Christian Church isn't seeking "total power." Its agenda is not political.

30) Has anyone ever been killed in the name of atheism?

Yes. Atheistic Communist regimes have slaughtered 100 million people. In China an incredible 72 million were murdered, in the Soviet Union 20 million, Cambodia 2.3 million, North Korea 2 million, Africa 1.7 million, Afghanistan 1.5 million, Vietnam 1 million, Eastern Europe 1 million, Latin America 150,000.

However, the full implications of atheism won't be seen until the Day of Judgment, when those who profess to be atheists and therefore ignore God's mercy will lose their most precious possession, their very life.

QUESTIONS

1. **What would it take to convince a Christian that he's wrong? (See #20 & 21.)**

2. **Why is Christianity not a cult? (See #21.)**

3. **If an atheist lives a moral life, why would God care whether the person believes in Him? (See #22.)**

4. **With other tales of resurrected Savior-Gods, why is the story of Jesus' resurrection reliable? (See #26.)**

5. **Why isn't the Bible written clearly? (See #28.)**

FEATHERS FOR ARROWS

UPI, *Toronto* — Police reported that a lawyer demonstrating the safety of windows in a downtown Toronto skyscraper crashed through a pane with his shoulder and plunged 24 floors to his death. A police spokesman said that Garry Hoy, 39, fell into the courtyard of the Toronto Dominion Bank Tower early Friday evening as he was explaining the strength of the building's windows to visiting law students. Hoy previously had conducted demonstrations of window strength, according to police reports. Peter Lauwers, managing partner of the firm Holden Day Wilson, told the *Toronto Sun* newspaper that Hoy was one of the best and brightest in the 200-member association.

This tragic incident is an excellent illustration of how people will trust their lives to something that often proves untrustworthy.

Last Words

John Bunyan, author of *The Pilgrim's Progress*, died in the service of His Master. In 1628 a father and son became alienated, and Bunyan went to London on a mission of reconciliation. On the way home, he was caught in a violent storm and contracted a mysterious sickness; he died ten days later. His last words had a ring of triumph as he said to those at his deathbed:

> "Weep not for me, but for yourselves. I go to the Father of our Lord Jesus Christ; who will, no doubt, through the mediation of His Blessed Son, receive me, though a sinner: when I hope we shall ere long meet to sing the new song, and remain everlastingly happy, world without end. Amen!"

LESSON 74

Relativism, Part 1

"Tolerance is a virtue for those who have no convictions."
G. K. Chesterton

Kirk's Comment "Relativism" is just a fancy word for believing that "truth is what feels right for you." Or, "there is no real right and wrong, just whatever you personally feel is best." While this may seem ridiculous, many people embrace it because it gives them license to act any way they want.

Questions & Objections

"There is no absolute truth. You can't be sure of anything!"

Those who say that there are no absolutes are often very adamant about their belief. If they say that they are absolutely sure, then they are wrong because their own statement is an absolute. If they are not 100 percent sure, then there is a chance that they are wrong and they are risking their eternal salvation by trusting in a wrong belief. God tells us that there is an objective, absolute truth that is not subject to man's interpretations or whims, on which we can base our eternity. That truth is the Word of God (John 17:7).

Relativism

By Matthew J. Slick

Relativism is the philosophical position that all points of view are equally valid and that all truth is relative to the individual. This means that all moral positions, all religious systems, all art forms, all political movements, etc., are "truths" that are relative to the individual. Under the umbrella of relativism, whole groups of perspectives are categorized:

- **Cognitive relativism:** Cognitive relativism affirms that all truth is relative. This would mean that no system of truth is more valid than another one and that there is no objective standard of truth.

- **Moral/ethical relativism:** All morals are relative to the social group within which they are constructed.

- **Situational relativism:** Ethics (right and wrong) are dependent upon the situation.

Unfortunately, the philosophy of relativism is pervasive in our culture today. With the rejection of God, and of Christianity in particular, absolute truth is being abandoned. Our pluralistic society wants to avoid the idea that there really is a right and wrong. This is evidenced in our deteriorating judicial system which has more and more trouble punishing criminals, in our entertainment media which continues to push the envelop of morality and decency, in our schools which teach evolution and "social tolerance," etc. In addition, the plague of moral relativism is encouraging everyone to accept homosexuality, pornography on TV, fornication, and a host of other "sins" that were once considered wrong, but are now being accepted and even promoted in society. It is becoming so pervasive that if you speak out against moral relativism and its "anything goes" philosophy, you're labeled as an intolerant bigot. Of course, this is incredibly hypocritical of those who profess that all points of view are true, yet reject those who hold the view that there are absolutes in morality. It seems that what is really meant by the moral relativists is that all points of view are true *except* for the views that teach moral absolutes, or an absolute God, or absolute right and wrong.

Some typical expressions that reveal an underlying presupposition of relativism are comments such as "That is your truth, not mine," "It is true for you, but not for me," and "There are no absolute truths." Of course, these statements are illogical. Relativism is invading our society, our economy, our schools, and our homes. Society cannot flourish nor survive in an environment where everyone does what is right in his own eyes, where the situation determines actions and if the situation changes, lying or cheating is acceptable—as long as you're not caught. Without a common foundation of truth and absolutes, our culture will become weak and fragmented.

I must admit, however, that there is validity to some aspects of relativism. For example, what one society considers right (driving on the left side of the road) another considers wrong. These are customs to which a "right and wrong" are attached, but they are purely relativistic and not universal because they are culturally based. Childrearing principles vary in different societies as do burial practices and wedding ceremonies. These "right and wrong ways" are not cosmically set in stone nor are they derived from some absolute rule of conduct by some unknown god. They are relative and rightly so. But, their relativism is properly asserted as such. It doesn't matter which side of the road we drive on as long as we all do it the same way.

Likewise, there are experiences that are valid only for individuals. I might be irritated by a certain sound, where another person will not. In this sense, what is true for me is not necessarily true for someone else. It is not an absolute truth that the identical sound causes irritation to all people. This is one way of showing that certain aspects of relativism are true. But, is it valid to say that because there is a type of personal relativism that we can then apply that principle to all areas of experience and knowledge and say that they too are relative? No, it is not a valid assumption. First of all, to do so would be an absolute assessment, which contradicts relativism.

Furthermore, if all things are relative, then there cannot be anything that is absolutely true between individuals. In other words, if all people deny absolute truth and establish relative truth only from their experiences, then everything is relative to the individual. How then can there be a common ground from which to judge right and wrong or truth? It would seem that there cannot be.

Of course, the issue that is important here is whether or not there are absolute truths. Also, can there be different kinds of absolute truths if indeed there are absolute truths? We might ask, is it always wrong to lie? Or, does 1 + 1 always equal 2? Is it always true that something cannot be both in existence and not in existence at the same time? Is it always true that something cannot bring itself into existence if it first does not exist? If any of these questions can be answered in the affirmative, then relativism is refuted—at least to some degree.

Ethical Relativism

With ethical relativism, truth, right and wrong, and justice are all relative. If all moral views are equally valid, then do we have the right to punish anyone? In order to say that something is wrong, we must first have a standard by which we weigh right and wrong in order to make a judgment. If that standard of right and wrong is based on relativism, then it is not a standard at all. In relativism, standards of right and wrong are derived from social norms. Since society changes, the norms would change and so would right and wrong. If right and wrong change, then how can anyone be rightly judged for something he did wrong if that wrong might become right in the future?

Just because a group of people thinks that something is right does not make so. Slavery is a good example of this. Two hundred years ago in America, slavery was the norm and morally acceptable. Now it is not. Of course, a society involved in constant moral conflict would not be able to survive for very long. Morality is the glue that holds society together. There must be a consensus of right and wrong for a society to function well. Ethical relativism undermines that glue.

Relativism also does not allow for the existence of an absolute set of ethics. Logically, if there are no absolute ethics, then there can be no Absolute Ethics Giver, which can easily be extrapolated as being God. Therefore, ethical relativism would not support the idea of an absolute God and it would exclude religious systems based upon absolute morals; that is, it would be absolute in its condemnation of absolute ethics. In this, relativism would be inconsistent since it would deny beliefs of absolute values.

However, I do not believe that the best ethical patterns by which societies operate (honesty, fidelity, truth, no theft, no murder, etc.) are the product of our biological makeup or trial and error. As a Christian, I see them as a reflection of God's very character. They are a discovery of the rules God has established by which people best interact with people because He knows how He has designed them. The Ten Commandments are a perfect example of moral absolutes and have yet to be improved upon. They are transcendent; that is, they transcend social norms and are always true.

I was once challenged to prove that there were moral absolutes. I asked the gentleman whether or not there were logical absolutes—for example, whether it was a logical absolute that something could exist and also not exist at the same time. He said that it was not possible, so he agreed that there were indeed logical absolutes. I then asked him to explain how logical absolutes can exist if there is no God. I questioned him further by asking him to tell me how in a purely physical universe, logical absolutes, which are conceptual, can exist . . . without a God. He could not answer me. I then went on to say that these conceptual absolutes logically must exist in the mind of an absolute God because they cannot merely reside in the properties of matter in a purely naturalistic universe. And since logical absolutes are true everywhere all the time and they are conceptual, it would seem logical that they exist within a transcendent, omnipresent Being. If there is an absolute God with an absolute mind, then He is the standard of all things—as well as morals. Therefore, there would be moral absolutes. To this argument the gentleman chuckled, said he had never heard it before, and conceded that it may be possible for moral absolutes to exist.

Of course, as a Christian, as one who believes in the authority and inspiration of the Bible, I consider moral absolutes to be very real because they come from God and not because they somehow reside in a naturalistic universe.

Adapted from an article by the Christian Apologetics and Research Ministry (www.carm.org).

QUESTIONS

1. Define relativism.

2. What is cognitive relativism?

3. What is moral/ethical relativism?

4. What is situational relativism?

5. What is an example of a valid aspect of relativism?

6. If relativism were always true—if each individual established truth from his perspective—what problems would result?

FEATHERS FOR ARROWS

The thought may enter the mind of the sinner that perhaps God will overlook his sins. Perhaps God, in His mercy, could just look the other way. If He does so, then He is unjust. Think of it in connection with civil law. Can a judge look the other way when a criminal is obviously guilty, and be true to what is right? Even if the judge feels sorry for the criminal, he must stay true to the law. Justice must be done. In the ten years between 1980 and 1990, in the United States alone, there were more than 60,000 murderers who were never caught. At least 60,000 murders were committed, and the murderers got away totally free. No doubt the figure is higher as many "accidents and suicides" are actually murders in disguise. These are people who have raped, tortured, and strangled helpless victims. Their victims' bodies have been cut in pieces, dissolved in acid, or burned in flames. Police have no body...just evidence of a missing person. Should God overlook their crimes on Judgment Day? Should He turn a blind eye? Should He compromise Eternal Justice?

Last Words

Jane Seymour, the third consort of Henry VIII, stated:

"No, my head never committed any treason: but, if you want it, you can take it."

Memory Verse

"For God sent not his Son into the world to condemn the world; but that the world through him might be saved. He that believes on him is not condemned: but he that believes not is condemned already, because he has not believed in the name of the only begotten Son of God."

JOHN 3:17,18

Relativism, Part 2

"Love will find a way. Indifference will find an excuse."

UNKNOWN

Kirk's Comment This lesson explains why the concept of relativism has taken root in our society, and provides several ways you can easily counter its claims. Truth really *is* logical, so don't be intimidated by the arguments presented in this lesson; they're simple and effective in helping people see the illogic of their beliefs. You can then appeal to their conscience using the Ten Commandments.

QUESTIONS & OBJECTIONS

"I am too big a sinner."

Nobody is too big a sinner. The love of God and the sacrifice of Jesus are capable of cleansing the worst of all sin. Even Hitler could have been saved if he would have turned to Christ. Your sins are not too big for God to wipe away. Sin has no power over God, only over you.

Do you think murder and adultery are serious sins? David, who God called "a man after His own heart" (Acts 13:22), was a murderer and an adulterer. He even tried to hide his sin from everyone. But God knew his sins and exposed them. David repented and threw himself on the mercy of the Lord, and God forgave him. God will forgive you too if you put your trust in Jesus Christ and ask Him to forgive you of your sins (Romans 10:9,10).

wotmwotmwotmwotmwotmwotmwotmwotmwotmwotmwotm

Cognitive Relativism

By Matthew J. Slick

Cognitive relativism, which affirms that all truth is relative, would mean that there is no objective standard of truth to be found or claimed. It would, naturally, deny that there is a God of absolute truth. It would also deny the belief that rational thought can discover and verify truth.

Many believe that this relativism is self-contradictory. But, why has relativism gained a foothold in modern society? I think there are several factors contributing to its acceptance.

First, the success of science has increasingly promoted the idea that true answers are found within science. Many people believe whatever scientists tell them is factual. When science cannot answer something, it simply states that the truth will become known later. With this, people have faith in science and the only absolute is that what we know now may not be true later. Thereby, it can undermine absolute truth.

Second, with the broad acceptance of the evolutionary theory, God is pushed more and more out of the picture. Without God as a determiner of what is true and not true, we are left to do and believe "what is right in our own eyes."

Third, we are encountering more and more diverse cultures in the world. This tends to make us more comfortable with the idea that there is more than one way to do something, more than one way for a culture to operate, more than one way for something to be true or right. This isn't necessarily wrong, but it does contribute to a denial of absolutes.

Fourth, increasingly, the content of film, academia, and literature is moving away from the notion of the absolute and toward relativism. These media help shape our culture.

Fifth, there has been an increase in relativistic philosophies, particularly those found in the New Age movement, which teaches that there is no absolute truth and that each person can create his own reality. Though this movement is part of the relativistic "problem," it is well permeated into society.

Sixth, past philosophers such as Wittgenstein, Khuh, Kant, Marx, and Nietzsche have influenced the thinking of many with their relativistic principles and attacks on absolute truths.

The problem I see with cognitive relativism is that it denies the possibility of absolute truth. Furthermore, I believe cognitive relativism is easily refutable with the following example of a logical absolute: Something cannot bring itself into existence.

My proposed logical absolute is indeed logical and always true. For something to bring itself into existence, it must first exist. If it first existed, then it cannot bring itself into existence because it already is existing. Likewise, if something does not exist, then it is not possible for it to bring itself into existence since it isn't there to do anything.

This is an absolute truth and it is knowable. Since it is absolutely true, cognitive relativism, which states that all truth is relative, is false. What if relativism were true?

Relativism is the position that all points of view are as valid as any other points of view and that the individual is the measure of what is true for that person. I see a big problem with this. Following is an illustration to demonstrate it.

The setting: A thief is casing a jewelry store so he can rob it. He has entered it to check out any visible alarm settings, locks, layout, etc. In the process, he has unexpectedly gotten involved in a discussion with the owner of the jewelry store whose hobby is the study of philosophy and believes that truth and morals are relative.

"So," says the owner, "everything is relative. That is why I believe that all morals are not absolute and that right and wrong is up to the individual to determine within the confines of society. But there is no absolute right and wrong."

"That is a very interesting perspective," says the thief. "I was brought up believing that there was a God and that there was right and wrong. But I abandoned all of that and I agree with you that there is no absolute right and wrong and that we are free to do what we want."

The thief leaves the store and returns that evening and breaks in. He has disabled all the alarms and is in the process of robbing the store. That is when the owner of the store enters through a side door. The thief pulls out a gun. The owner cannot see the man's face because he is wearing a ski mask.

"Don't shoot me," says the owner. "Please take whatever you want and leave me alone."

"That is exactly what I plan to do," says the thief.

"Wait a minute. I know you. You are the man who was in the store earlier today. I recognize your voice."

"That is very unfortunate for you," says the thief. "Because now you also know what I look like. And since I do not want to go to jail, I am forced to kill you."

"You can't do that," says the owner.

"Why not?"

"Because it isn't right," pleads the desperate man.

"But did you not tell me today that there is no right and wrong?"

"But I have a family, and children who need me, and a wife."

"So? I am sure that you are insured and that they will get a lot of money. But since there is no right and wrong, it makes no difference whether or not I kill you. And if I let you live, you will turn me in and I will go to prison. Sorry, but that will not do."

"But it is a crime against society to kill me. It is wrong because society says so."

"As you can see, I don't recognize society's claim to impose morals on me. It's all relative, remember?"

"Please do not shoot me, I beg you. I promise not to tell anyone what you look like. I swear it!"

"I do not believe you and I cannot take that chance."

"But it is true! I swear I'll tell no one."

"Sorry, but it cannot be true because there is no absolute truth, no right and wrong, remember? If I let you live and then I left, you will break your so-called promise. There is no way I could trust you. Our conversation this morning convinced me that you believe everything is relative. Because of that, I cannot believe you will keep your word."

"But it is wrong to kill me. It isn't right!"

"It is neither right nor wrong for me to kill you. Since truth is relative to the individual, if I kill you, that is my truth. And, it is obviously true that if I let you live I will go to prison. Sorry, but you have killed yourself."

"No. Please do not shoot me. I beg you."

"Begging makes no difference."

Bang.

If relativism is true, then was it wrong to pull the trigger? Perhaps someone might say that it is wrong to take another life needlessly. But why is that wrong, if there is no standard of right or wrong? Others have said that it is a crime against society. But, so what? If what is true for you is simply true, then what is wrong with killing someone to protect yourself after you have robbed him? If it is true for you that to protect yourself you must kill, then who cares what society says? Why is anyone obligated to conform to social norms? Doing so is a personal decision.

Though not all relativists will behave in an unethical manner, I see relativism as a contributor to overall anarchy. Why? Because it is a justification to do whatever you want.

Refuting Relativism

The proposition of relativism, that all points of view are equally valid and that all truth is relative to the individual, is not logical. In fact, it is self-refuting.

- **All truth is relative.** If all truth is relative, then the statement "All truth is relative" would be absolutely true. If it is absolutely true, then not all things are relative and the statement that "All truth is relative" is false.

- **There are no absolute truths.** The statement "There are no absolute truths" is an absolute statement, which is supposed to be true. Therefore, it is an absolute truth and "There are no absolute truths" is false. If there are no absolute truths, then you cannot believe anything absolutely at all, including that there are no absolute truths. Therefore, nothing could be really true for you—including relativism.

- **What is true for you is not true for me.** If what is true for me is that relativism is false, then is it true that relativism is false? If you say no, then what is true for me is not true and relativism is false. If you say yes, then relativism is false. If you say that it is true only for me that relativism is false, then I am believing something other than relativism; namely, that relativism is false. If that is true, then how can relativism be true?

- **No one can know anything for sure.** If that is true, then we can know that we cannot know anything for sure, which is self-defeating.

- **That is your reality, not mine.** Is my reality really real? If my reality is different from yours, how can my reality contradict your reality? If yours and mine are equally real, how can two opposite realities that exclude each other really exist at the same time?

What Is Truth?

"What is truth?" is a very simple question. We can offer definitions like "Truth is that which conforms to reality, fact, or actuality." If there is such a thing as truth, then we should be able to find it. If truth cannot be known, then it probably doesn't exist. But, it does exist. For example, we know it is true that you are reading this. Is there such a thing as something that is always true all the time? Yes, there is. For example, "Something cannot bring itself into existence" is an absolute truth.

If we are to ever hope to determine if there is such a thing as truth apart from cultural and personal preferences, we must acknowledge that we are then aiming to discover something greater than ourselves, something that transcends culture and individual inclinations. To do this is to look beyond ourselves and outside of ourselves. In essence, it means that we are looking for God. God would be truth, the absolute and true essence of being and reality who is the author of all truth. If you are interested in truth beyond yourself, then you must look to God.

For the Christian, the ultimate expression of truth is found in the Bible, in Jesus who said, "I am the way, the truth, and the life" (John 14:6). Of course, most philosophers and skeptics will dismiss His claim, but for the Christian, He is the mainstay of hope, security, and guidance. Jesus, who walked on water, claimed to be divine, and rose from the dead, said that He was the truth and the originator of truth. If Jesus is wrong, then we should ignore Him. But, if He is right, then it is true that we should listen to Him.

The eyewitnesses recorded what they saw. They were with Him. They watched Him perform many miracles, heal the sick, calm a storm with a command, and even rise from the dead. You either believe or dismiss these claims. If you dismiss them, that is your prerogative. But, if you accept them, then you are faced with decisions to make about Jesus. What will you believe about Him? What will you decide about Him? Is He true? Is what He said true?

Truth conforms to reality. The reality is that Jesus performed many miracles and rose from the dead.

Adapted from an article by the Christian Apologetics and Research Ministry (www.carm.org).

QUESTIONS

1. **How has science played a role in promoting relativism?**

2. **How has the evolutionary theory contributed to relativism?**

3. **How has multiculturalism encouraged relativism?**

4. **What is an easy way to refute cognitive relativism?**

5. **What is the only source of transcendent truth?**

PREACHER'S PROGRESS

Christian: "I don't believe that all points of view are equally valid."

Rel A. Tivist: "Why not?"

Christian: "Because it doesn't make sense that everything is relative. That wouldn't be logical."

Rel A. Tivist: "Ah, you see? That is your problem. You are using logic to refute relativism and you cannot do that. Relativism isn't based upon logic. It isn't the same thing. So you can't use logic to refute relativism."

Christian: "If you say I cannot use logic to refute relativism, then you are using logic to say this since you give me the logical statement and conclusion that I cannot use logic to refute relativism because relativism isn't based on logic. I hope you can see that you made a logical case here for not using logic. If that is so, then your complaint is self-contradictory and invalid. Would you want me to follow a system of thought that is self-contradictory?"

Rel A. Tivist: "I can see why they call you slick. But, the point is that relativism is true within itself and logic is not a necessary property of relativism. It can be used within relativism, but it is not superior to relativism."

Christian: "To say that relativism is true within itself is an absolute statement. Don't you see that you can't do that if relativism is true? You would have to say something like, 'Relativism is true some of the time.'"

Rel A. Tivist: "You are playing word games here."

Christian: "I do not see how. I am simply responding to what you said. I think what you are doing is simply making assertions without proof. You are saying that it is true because it is true. In essence, you are telling me an absolute truth that relativism is its own self-existing truth. This is an absolute statement which again refutes the notion that relativism is true. Furthermore, if relativism is true then relativism itself is relative. In other words, if relativism is true, then relativism may or may not be true in and of itself. If that is true, then relativism can be false. If relativism can be false, then relativism can't be true."

Rel A. Tivist: "There you go using logic again. Logic is not the whole means by which truth is determined. Relativism goes beyond logic to truths that logic cannot prove."

Christian: Okay, then without using logic, can you tell me why relativism is true?"

Rel A. Tivist: "It is true because it is true that people believe different things and that people have different perceptions of reality and what is right for them."

Christian: "I agree that people believe different things, but does believing different things make them true because they are believed?"

Rel A. Tivist: "No, of course not. But you must understand that we perceive things differently, and that these different perceptions are true for different people."

Christian: "I can agree with that, but I am not speaking about things that really are relative, like which side of the bed you should get out of in the morning. I'm talking about things like lying, cheating, stealing, etc. If relativism is true and all points of view are equally valid, then someone's view that it is okay to steal is valid."

Rel A. Tivist: "Technically, it would be, depending on the circumstances. For example, if it meant feeding your family or helping someone."

Christian: "I see. Okay, give me your money right now. I want to steal it from you. If I had a gun, I'd point it at you and rob you. Is that okay?"

Rel A. Tivist: "Of course not."

Christian: "Why not? My view is that in order to win the argument, I must rob from you to demonstrate the absurdity of your position. Therefore, it is right for me. You should approve.

Rel A. Tivist: "But I cannot, because it isn't right for me that you steal from me."

Christian: Oh, so relativism has boundaries? It is true only for the individual, no one else?"

Rel A. Tivist: "In that case, yes."

Christian: "Then relativism isn't a universal truth, is it? If it is only true for individuals on an individual basis, it may or may not be true or false or right or wrong or whatever. It is just a kind of 'whatever you want to do' philosophy."

Rel A. Tivist: "Sort of, but you can't harm anyone else."

Christian: "Are you saying that it is an absolute that you are not to harm anyone else?"

Rel A. Tivist: "There you go again turning this into an argument on absolutes."

Christian: "But I am only following your lead. You're the one who said that relativism is true because it is true. Correct?"

Rel A. Tivist: "Yes, I said that, but you have to understand that it is relative to the individual."

Christian: "If relativism is true because it is true, then can I say that it is false because it is false?"

Rel A. Tivist: "You could if you wanted to."

Christian: "Then would it be false or not?"

Rel A. Tivist: "It would be false for you."

Christian: "But that isn't what I said. I said it was false 'because it is false.' I didn't say it was false for me. I said that it is by nature false. Don't you see? You said it was true 'because it is true.' You spoke of it as being true 'by nature.' You implied an absolute quality to relativism as a real truth. If I can do the same thing in the opposite direction, then how does my assertion become different in nature than yours? In other words, 'by nature' it is true and 'by nature' it is false. Both cannot be true. Therefore relativism doesn't work."

Rel A. Tivist: "What you are doing is using logic again. Relativism and logic are different things. You cannot use one thing to judge another."

Christian: "But you just did. You made a statement and drew a conclusion. You said that relativism and logic are different. Then you said that I cannot use one to judge the other. In other words, you made a statement and drew a logical conclusion. Look, if you want to validate relativism using relativism, then why do you keep using logic to do it?"

Rel A. Tivist: "You keep going back to these logic games. You have to understand that they are simply different."

Christian: "So then, what you are saying is that I am not allowed to examine relativism in a logical manner. Correct?"

Rel A. Tivist: "Correct."

Christian: "You want truth, right?"

Rel A. Tivist: "Of course."

Christian: "But, if I must accept that relativism is simply true, how can I possibly know if it is ever false? What you are saying is that it is never false. If it is never false, then it is always true. If it is always true, then it isn't relative, is it?"

Rel A. Tivist: "There you go using logic again."

Christian: "I'm trying to ask questions. But, it seems that you want me to avoid thinking and just accept relativism as true. If I were to say that relativism is true, then it is absolutely true that relativism is true, which would mean that the opposing view that relativism is false could not be true... which would mean that relativism is not true since it states that all views are true. It seems to me that the only way relativism is true is if you stop thinking logically and just accept it on blind faith that it is true."

Rel A. Tivist: "This is the problem with the Western, Aristotelian logic system. It teaches you that there are absolutes when there are not."

Christian: "But to say there are not absolutes is an absolute statement, which is self-refuting. Again, it seems that the only way to accept relativism is to not think logically. You have to believe it on faith."

Rel A. Tivist: "The nature of relativism is that it is not subject to logic. No logical reasons are necessary to establish this. Relativism, by its nature, is not of logic, but beyond logic. The essence of relativism is that relativism itself is true."

Christian: "Then you are simply stating that relativism is true without proving it. In other words, you can't prove it. You just say it is true and that's it."

Rel A. Tivist: "We are getting nowhere."

Christian: "I disagree. I think we are making great progress."

Rel A. Tivist: "See? It is how you perceive it, isn't it?"

Christian: "Then, is it valid that we have made progress? After all, relativism says that all points of view are equally valid."

Rel A. Tivist: "It's valid for you, not for me."

Christian: "I have a different type of question for you. Have you ever told a lie?"

Rel A. Tivist: "Yes."

Christian: "What does that make you?" (Etc.)

> ## Memory Verse
>
> *"And I will pray the Father, and he shall give you another Comforter, that he may abide with you for ever; even the Spirit of truth; whom the world cannot receive, because it sees him not, neither knows him: but you know him; for he dwells with you, and shall be in you."*
>
> **JOHN 14:16,17**

Last Words

Princess Amelia, daughter of George III:

"I could not wish for a better trust than in the merits of the Redeemer."

LESSON 76

Reincarnation

*"The Christian world is in a deep sleep; nothing but
a loud shout can awaken them out of it!"*
GEORGE WHITEFIELD

Kirk's Comment   It amazes me that so many believe in the lie of reincarnation. While there are many religious philosophies that appeal to our senses, we must always go back to what God has said on the subject. And He has said, "It is appointed to men *once* to die, but after this the judgment" (Hebrews 9:27). That means there will be no second chance to reverse our karma through reincarnation, but rather we must each give an account of our life to God and receive the gift of heaven or the punishment of eternal hell.

QUESTIONS AND OBJECTIONS

"Hell isn't a place. This life is hell."

Skeptics who say this are trying to dismiss the reality of hell. They might like to think that life as we know it couldn't get any worse, but the sufferings in this life will be heaven compared to the suffering in the next life—for those who die in their sins. This life is the closest thing to hell that Christians will ever know, and the closest thing to heaven that sinners will ever know.

One of the most popular beliefs in the world concerning death is the transmigration or reincarnation of the soul. This belief is the main competitor today to the Christian concept of heaven and hell.

Hollywood stars such as Shirley Maclaine have given reincarnation great popularity. There are increasing references to it in TV shows and movies, and the supermarket tabloids run sensational stories "proving" it every week. What is reincarnation all about and how should Christians respond to it?

The orthodox Hindu idea of reincarnation teaches that when you die, your soul does not go to heaven or hell. Instead, your soul goes into some other kind of body here on earth. This body can be an insect, fish, animal, or human body. This is why Hindus practice vegetarianism and will not even kill the pests that destroy their harvests.

When occultists such as Edgar Cayce realized that the thought of reincarnating into animal and insect bodies would not be attractive to Westerners, they decided to alter the concept.

Using the Western concepts of evolution and progress, they taught that through reincarnation the soul always progressively evolves up the scale of being. Thus you cannot regress back into an insect or animal body once you have reached the human stage. You are either born into another human body or you are absorbed back into oneness, depending on your karma.

In Hindu theology, there is no personal God who hands out rewards and punishments like in the Bible. Instead, the non-personal principle of karma determines, based on the good and evil you have done in this life, whether you will be reborn as rich or poor, healthy or handicapped, slave or master, etc.

Karma teaches that your suffering or prospering in your present life is due to the evil or good you did in a previous life. If you are born as a poor "crack" baby in Harlem with terrible physical and mental sufferings, you are only getting what you deserve. You must have done some very evil things in a past life to have such "bad" karma. But if you are born into a rich family with health and wealth all your days, then you too are only getting what you deserve. You must have done some very good things in a past life to have such "good" karma.

The Arguments for Reincarnation

Believers in reincarnation offer the following arguments as proof of its validity:

- *It solves the problem of evil karmic reincarnation by viewing it in terms of punishment and reward. People suffer or prosper based on their actions in a past life, so everyone is only getting what they deserve.*

  Karmic reincarnation does not solve the problem of evil. There is ultimately a "first" life in which there was no previous life to explain the evil in it. Otherwise, evil is eternal, which only extends the problem, not solves it.

- *Reincarnational recall proves it. In addition to déjà vu, recall types can be spontaneous, hypnotic, or psychic.*

  These arguments are erroneous. The dictionary defines déjà vu as "the illusion of having already experienced something actually being experienced for the first time." Déjà vu can be "felt" with things built in your lifetime such as a house or a city as well as with people.

  Spontaneous recall never happens under scientific conditions; thus it is worthless as evidence. Hypnotic recall is highly unreliable (as in the example of Bridey Murphy), and psychic recall is plagued with the problem of fraud. How can you tell if the psychic really knows who you were in a past life?

  Besides, why are recalls usually of important people? And why is it that all recall experiences teach Hindu doctrine? In the hundreds of cases I have researched, I did not find a single instance where orthodox Christians were recalled. Where are the recalls of Spurgeon, Calvin, Edwards, etc.? Also, logically speaking, when more than one person at the same time claims to be the present reincarnation of Jesus, Buddha, Elvis, etc., either one is right and the others are liars or they are all liars. But they can't all be right.

- *The Bible teaches it. John the Baptist was a reincarnation of Elijah, and Jesus told us we must be "born again" into a new body at death.*

  Matthew 11:14 is often used to justify belief in reincarnation by claiming that Elijah was reincarnated as John the Baptist. But John merely came "in the spirit and power of Elijah" (Luke 1:17). And, since Elijah never died (he was taken up to heaven in a whirlwind; 2 Kings 2:11), he cannot be reincarnated. The "new birth" that Jesus spoke of has to do with spiritual regeneration in this life (John 3:5,6; Romans 8:9–11; 1 Peter 1:23).

• *Christianity once taught it, but it was later removed by church councils.* What council? When? Where? There is no evidence of this in church history. The early church fathers all wrote against it.

The Christian's response to reincarnation is twofold: the atonement of Christ makes reincarnation unnecessary, and the resurrection of the body makes reincarnation impossible. As Hebrews 9:27 shows, there is no such thing as reincarnation. It is merely wishful thinking for guilty sinners. They like to think that if they don't "get it right" in this lifetime, they'll have multiple opportunities in future lives. That people don't need to trust in Jesus before they die is one of Satan's greatest lies.

Adapted from "The Riddle of Reincarnation" by Dr. Robert A. Morey.

QUESTIONS

1. **Why is reincarnation an attractive alternative to the Christian faith?**

2. **Name an actress who helped to popularize reincarnation.**

3. **According to orthodox Hinduism, what happens at death?**

4. **How is the Western concept of reincarnation different?**

5. **What is the theory of karma?**

6. **How would you answer the argument that the Bible says John the Baptist was a reincarnation of Elijah?**

PREACHER'S PROGRESS

Ray N. Carnation: "I believe that we are reincarnated."

Christian: "Why?"

Ray N. Carnation: "It just seems to make sense."

Christian: "What do you think you were in past lives?"

Ray N. Carnation: "I think I was Napoleon."

Christian: "Bonaparte?"

Ray N. Carnation: "Yes."

Christian: "And before that?"

Ray N. Carnation: "I'm not sure."

Christian: "What happens if you live an evil life?"

Ray N. Carnation: "You come back as a fly or a spider."

Christian: "What did you do in a previous life to come back as a human?"

Ray N. Carnation: "What do you mean?"

Christian: "If you did evil, you would be a fly. So to be a human, you must have done something good—that is, if you believe that the human being is higher on the life chain than a fly."

Ray N. Carnation: "Yes, I do. I don't know what I did."

Christian: "Do you think you will come back as a fly or a human in the next life?"

Ray N. Carnation: "A human."

Christian: "Why?"

Ray N. Carnation: "Because I have lived a good life."

Christian: "Do you want to do a check?"

Ray N. Carnation: "Sure."

Christian: "Okay, we will go through a few of the Ten Commandments to see if you deserve to come back as a human or a fly. Have you ever told a lie?" Etc.

Ray N. Carnation: "Okay, so I'm a lying, thieving, adulterer-at-heart, and will come back as a fly. So what?"

Christian: "Reincarnation is not the exciting mysticism it's made out to be. It's actually a hopelessly spiraling Hindu doctrine, and there is no truth to it. The Bible says, 'It is appointed to men once to die, but after this the judgment.' So there is no second chance. If God treats you according to your sins, you won't even make it as a fly. You will be damned in hell forever. Pretty scary thought, huh?"

Memory Verse

"It is appointed to men once to die, but after this the judgment."

HEBREWS 9:27

Last Words

The **Duke of Hamilton**, as he was dying, was visited by his old tutor. As they were talking about astronomy, the Duke said:

> **"Within a little while, sir, I will know more about the stars than all of you put together."**

Islam, Part 1

"God, send me anywhere, only go with me. Lay any burden on me, only sustain me. And sever any tie in my heart except the tie that binds my heart to Yours."

DAVID LIVINGSTONE

Kirk's Comment Islam is a religion with millions of followers. Study this lesson to absorb as much as you can in order to help your Muslim friends see their need for the only Savior, Jesus Christ.

QUESTIONS & OBJECTIONS

"Religion has caused more wars than anything else in history."

It is true that man has used religion for political gain. The Nazis had *"God mitt uns"* (God with us) engraved on their belt buckles. America said, "Praise the Lord and pass the ammunition." The law may even allow you to start the Christian Nazi Party, if you so desire. You can become a "reverend" for a few dollars through the tabloid classifieds and then further your political agenda with the world's blessing, no matter how much it smears the name of Christ.

Jesus tells us in John 16:2,3 that there will be some who, in their error, commit atrocities and murder in the name of God: "The time is coming that whosoever kills you will think that he does God service." However,

He informs us that these are not true believers: "And these things will they do to you, because they have not known the Father, nor me." (See also 1 John 3:15.)

Jesus told His followers to love their enemies. So if a man puts a knife into someone's back in the name of Christianity, something obviously isn't right. If we human beings can detect it, how much more will God? He will deal with it on Judgment Day.

Abraham Lincoln stated, "I know that the Lord is always on the side of right. But it is my constant anxiety and prayer that I—and this nation—should be on the Lord's side."

w o t m w o t m w o t m w o t m w o t m w o t m w o t m w o t m w o t m w o t m w o t m

Islam is the world's second largest religion, behind only Christianity. The following information will give you an overview of Islam, how its doctrines contrast with Christianity, and questions and answers to use when witnessing.

Official Name: Islam

Key Figure in History: Muhammad (A.D. 570–632)

Date of Establishment: A.D. 622

Adherents: Worldwide: Estimated 800 million to 1 billion; 58 percent live in South and Southeast Asia; 28 percent in Africa; 9 percent in Near and Middle East; 5 percent other

U.S.: Estimated 6.5 to 8 million

What Is Islam?

Islam is the world's youngest major world religion. It claims to be the restoration of original monotheism and truth and thus supersedes both Judaism and Christianity. It stresses submission to *Allah*, the Arabic name for God, and conformity to the "five pillars" or disciplines of that religion as essential for salvation. From its inception, Islam was an aggressively missionary-oriented religion. Within one century of its formation, and often using military force, Islam had spread across the Middle East, most of North Africa, and as far east as India. While God is, in the understanding of most Muslims, unknowable personally, His will is believed to be perfectly revealed in the holy book, the *Qur'an*. The Qur'an is to be followed completely and its teaching forms a complete guide for life and society.

Who Was Muhammad?

Muhammad is believed by Muslims to be the last and greatest prophet of God—"the seal of the prophets." It was through him that the Qur'an was dictated, thus according him the supreme place among the seers of God. A native of Mecca, Muhammad was forced to flee that city in A.D. 622 after preaching vigorously against the paganism of the city. Having secured his leadership in Medina, and with several military victories to his credit, Muhammad returned in triumph to Mecca in A.D. 630. There he established Islam as the religion of all Arabia.

What Is the Qur'an?

The Qur'an is the sacred book of Islam and the perfect word of God for the Muslim. It is claimed that the Qur'an was dictated in Arabic by the angel Gabriel to Muhammad and were God's precise words. As such, it had preexisted from eternity in heaven with God as the "Mother of the Book" and was in that form uncreated and co-eternal with God. Islam teaches that it contains the total and perfect revelation and will of God. The Qur'an is about four-fifths the length of the New Testament and is divided into 114 *surahs* or chapters. While Islam respects the Torah, the psalms of David, and the four Gospels, the Qur'an stands alone in its authority and absoluteness. It is believed to be most perfectly understood in Arabic and it is a religious obligation to seek to read and quote it in the original language.

What Are the "Five Pillars"?

The five pillars are the framework for the Muslims' life and discipline. Successful and satisfactory adherence to the pillars satisfies the will of Allah. They form the basis for the Muslim's hope for salvation along with faith and belief in Allah's existence, the authority of Muhammad as a prophet, and the finality and perfection of the Qur'an.

The five pillars are:

1. **The Confession of Faith or *Shahada:*** It is the declaration that there is no god but Allah and Muhammad is his prophet. Sincerity in the voicing of the confession is necessary for it to be valid. It must be held until death; repudiation of the *Shahada* nullifies hope for salvation.

2. **Prayer of *Salat:*** Five times a day, preceded by ceremonial washing, the Muslim is required to pray facing Mecca. Specific formulas recited from the Qur'an (in Arabic), along with prostrations, are included. Prayer is, in this sense, an expression of submission to the will of Allah. While most of Islam has no hierarchical priesthood, prayers are led in mosques by respected lay leaders. The five times of prayer are before sunrise, noon, midafternoon, sunset, and prior to sleep.

3. **Almsgiving or *Zakat:*** The Qur'an teaches the giving of two-and-a-half percent of one's capital wealth to the poor and/or for the propagation of Islam. By doing so, the Muslim's remaining wealth is purified.

4. **The Fast or *Sawm:*** During the lunar month of Ramadan, a fast is to be observed by every Muslim from sunrise to sunset. Nothing is to pass over the lips during this time, and they should refrain from sexual relations. After sunset, feasting and other celebrations often occur. The daylight hours are set aside for self-purification. The month is used to remember the giving of the Qur'an to Muhammad.

5. **Pilgrimage or *Hajj:*** All Muslims who are economically and physically able are required to journey to Mecca at least once in their lifetime. The required simple pilgrim's dress stresses the notion of equality before God. Another element of the Hajj is the mandatory walk of each pilgrim seven times around the *Kaabah*—the shrine of the black rock, the holiest site of Islam. Muhammad taught that the Kaabah was the original place of worship for Adam and later for Abraham. The Kaabah is thus venerated as the site of true religion, the absolute monotheism of Islam.

The Doctrines of Islam

God: He is numerically and absolutely one. Allah is beyond the understanding of man so that only his will may be revealed and known. He is confessed as the "merciful and compassionate one."

Sin: The most serious sin that can be ascribed to people is that of *shirk* or considering god as more than one. Original sin is viewed as a "lapse" by Adam. Humankind is considered weak and forgetful but not as fallen.

Angels: Islam affirms the reality of angels as messengers and agents of god. Evil spirits or *Jinn* also exist. Satan is a fallen angel. Angels perform important functions for Allah both now and at the end of time.

Final Judgment: Allah will judge the world at the end of time. The good deeds and obedience of all people to the five pillars and the Qur'an will serve as the basis of judgment.

Salvation: It is determined by faith, as defined by Islam, as well as by compiling good deeds primarily in conformity to the five pillars.

Marriage: Muslims uphold marriage as honorable and condemn adultery. While many Muslim marriages are monogamous, Islamic states allow as many as four wives. Men consider a woman as less than an equal, and while a man has the right to divorce his wife, the wife has no similar power (see Surah 2:228; 4:34). Nonetheless, the female has a right to own and dispose of property. Modesty in dress is encouraged for both men and women.

War: The term *jihad* or "struggle" is often considered as both external and internal, both a physical and a spiritual struggle. The enemies of Islam or "idolaters," states the Qur'an, may be slain "wherever you find them" (Surah 9:5; Surah 47:4). Paradise is promised for those who die fighting in the cause of Islam (see Surah 3:195; 2:224). Moderate Muslims emphasize the spiritual dimension of *jihad* and not its political element.

Answering Muslim Objections to Christianity

Christians and Jews are acknowledged as "people of the book," although their failure to conform to the confession of Islam labels them as unbelievers. Following are several questions that Muslims have about Christianity.

Is the Trinity a belief in three Gods?

Christians are monotheistic and believe that God is one. But both in His work in accomplishing salvation through the person of Jesus Christ and through biblical study it has become clear that His oneness in fact comprises three persons—Father, Son (Jesus Christ), and the third person of the Godhead, the Holy Spirit. Mary is not part of the Godhead. The notion of God, who is three-in-one, is part of both the mystery and greatness of God. God is in essence one while in persons three. This truth helps us understand God as truly personal and having the capacity to relate to other persons. As well, Christians confirm the holiness, sovereignty, and greatness of God.

How can Jesus be the Son of God?

Scripture affirms that Jesus was conceived supernaturally by the Holy Spirit and was born of the virgin Mary. It does not in any way claim that Jesus was directly God the Father's biological and physical son. It rejects the notion of the Arabic word for son, *walad*, meaning physical son, for the word *ibin*, which is the title of relationship. Jesus is the Son in a symbolic manner designating that He was God the Word who became man in order to save humankind from its sin. The virgin birth was supernatural as God the Holy Spirit conceived in Mary, without physical relations, Jesus the Messiah. In this manner even the Qur'an affirms the miraculous birth of Christ (see Surah 19:16–21). Jesus was in this sense "God's unique Son." During His earthly ministry He carried out the will of the Father. Notably the Qur'an affirms Jesus' supernatural birth, life of miracles, His compassion, and ascension to heaven (see Surah 19:16–21,29–31; 3:37–47; 5:110).

How could Jesus have died on the cross especially if He's God's Son?

The testimony of history and the *Injil*, or the four Gospels, is that Jesus died on the cross. If it is understood that God is loving, and that humankind is lost in sin, then is it not likely that God would have provided a sacrifice for sin? Jesus is God's sacrifice for all the sins of the world and is a bridge from a holy God to fallen and sinful humans. This truth is revealed in the Injil, John 3:16. Even the Qur'an states in Surah 3:55 that "Allah said: O Isa [Jesus], I am going to terminate [to put to death] the period of your stay (on earth) and cause you to ascend unto Me." What other way could this concept have any meaning apart from Jesus' death for sin and His subsequent resurrection? Muslims believe that God took Jesus from the cross and substituted Judas in His place, or at least someone who looked like Jesus. He was then taken to heaven where He is alive and from where one day He will return.

Answering Muslims' Questions to Christians About Islam

What do you think about the prophet Muhammad?
Muhammad was apparently a well-meaning man who sought to oppose paganism and evil in his day. While he succeeded in uniting the Arabian Peninsula and upheld several important virtues, we do not believe he received a fresh revelation from God. Jesus Christ fulfilled not only the final prophetic role from God, but He is the Savior of the world and God the Son. While Islam believes that some Bible passages refer to Muhammad (see Deut. 18:18,19; John 14:16; 15:26; 16:7), that is clearly not the meaning of the texts. Other passages may help in understanding and interpreting the previous texts (see Matthew 21:11; Luke 24:19; John 6:14; 7:40; Acts 1:8–16; 7:37).

What is your opinion of the Qur'an?
It is a greatly valued book for the Muslim. It is not received or believed to be a divine book by the Christian. The statements of the Qur'an are accepted only where they agree with the Bible.

What is your opinion about the five pillars?
Salvation is from God and comes only through the saving work of Jesus Christ. When we put our faith in Him, we are saved (see John 3:16–21, 31–36).

Witnessing to Muslims

- Be courteous and loving. Reflect interest in their beliefs. Allow them time to articulate their views.

- Be acquainted with their basic beliefs. Be willing to examine passages of the Qur'an concerning their beliefs.

- Stick to the cardinal doctrines of the Christian faith but also take time to respond to all sincere questions.

- Point out the centrality of the person and work of Jesus Christ for salvation. Stress that because of Jesus, His cross, and His resurrection, one may have the full assurance of salvation, both now and for eternity (see 1 John 5:13).

- Share the plan of salvation with the Muslim. Point out that salvation is a gift and is not to be earned.

- Pray for the fullness of the Holy Spirit. Trust Him to provide wisdom and grace.

- Be willing to become a friend and a personal evangelist to Muslims.

Phil Roberts, © 1996 North American Mission Board of the Southern Baptist Convention, Alpharetta, Georgia. All rights reserved. Reprinted with permission.

QUESTIONS

1. **What is the origin of the Qur'an?**

2. **On what do Muslims base their hope of salvation?**

3. Describe the "five pillars."

4. How might Muslims' understanding of God (Allah) affect their reaction to the Christian God?

5. Muslims think Christians believe that Jesus is the physical son of God, a concept they find offensive. How could you use the Bible to correct their thinking?

6. Muslims believe that Muhammad is a greater prophet than Jesus. What could you say to convince them that Jesus is truly God?

FEATHERS FOR ARROWS

If I offered you a fistful of diamonds or a bucket of cold water, which would you take? The diamonds, of course; who in his right mind wouldn't? But if you were crawling through a desert with blistered lips and a swollen tongue, dying of thirst, and I offered you a fistful of diamonds or a bucket of cool water, you would despise the diamonds and cry, "Give me water—or I'll die!" That is called "circumstantial priorities." Your priorities change according to your circumstances.

Christianity demands a choice between the sparkling diamonds of sin and the cool, clear waters of everlasting life. Most people prefer the diamonds of sin, something quite normal for sin-loving humanity. But on Judgment Day their circumstances will radically change. They will find themselves in the desert of God's Judgment, upon their faces, about to perish under the burning heat of a Creator who warns us that He is a "consuming fire." They despised the Water of Life when it was offered to them in Christ. Now they must face eternal consequences. Those sparkling diamonds they so dearly clutch will suddenly be the glaring evidence for their condemnation.

Last Words

Louis B. Mayer, film producer, died October 29, 1957:

> **"Nothing matters. Nothing matters."**

Memory Verse

"For God so loved the world, that he gave his only begotten Son, that whosoever believes in him should not perish, but have everlasting life. For God sent not his Son into the world to condemn the world; but that the world through him might be saved."

JOHN 3:16,17

Islam, Part 2

"We cannot come to Christ to be justified until we have first been to Moses to be condemned. But once we have gone to Moses and acknowledged our sin, guilt and condemnation, we must not stay there."

JOHN R. W. STOTT

Kirk's Comment Someone once said, "Know the truth so well that you can spot a lie the moment it appears on the horizon." Knowing the truth in this lesson will help you as you witness to Muslims.

QUESTIONS & OBJECTIONS

"Why is there suffering? That proves there is no 'loving' God."

Sadly, many use the issue of suffering as an excuse to reject any thought of God, when its existence is the *very reason* we should accept Him. Suffering stands as terrible testimony to the truth of the explanation given by the Word of God. But how can we know that the Bible is true? By studying the prophecies of Matthew 24, Luke 21, and 2 Timothy 3. A few minutes of open-hearted inspection will convince any honest skeptic that this is no ordinary book. It is the supernatural testament of our Creator about why there is suffering... and what we can do about it.

The Bible tells us that God cursed the earth because of Adam's transgression. Weeds are a curse. So is disease. Sin and suffering cannot be separated. The Scriptures inform us that we live in a *fallen* creation. In the beginning, God created man perfect, and he lived in a perfect world without suffering. *It was heaven on earth.* When sin came into the world, death and misery came with it. Those who understand the message of Holy Scripture eagerly await a new heaven and a new earth "wherein dwells righteousness" (2 Peter 3:13).

In that coming kingdom there will be no more pain, suffering, disease, or death. We are told that no eye has ever seen, nor has any ear heard, neither has any man's mind ever imagined the wonderful things that God has in store for those who love Him.

w o t m w o t m w o t m w o t m w o t m w o t m w o t m w o t m w o t m w o t m w o t m

How to Witness to Muslims

In Acts 17:22–31, the apostle Paul built on areas of "common ground" as he prepared his listeners for the good news of the gospel. Even though he was addressing Gentiles whose beliefs were erroneous, he didn't rebuke them for having a doctrine of devils—"the things which the Gentiles sacrifice, they sacrifice to devils, and not to God" (1 Corinthians 10:20). Neither did he present the great truth that Jesus of Nazareth was Almighty God manifest in human form. This may have initially offended his hearers and closed the door to the particular knowledge he wanted to convey. Instead, he built on what they already knew. He first established that there is a Creator who made all things. He then exposed their sin of transgression of the First and Second Commandments. Then he preached future punishment for sin.

There are three main areas of common ground upon which Christians may stand with Muslims. First, that there is one God—the Creator of all things. The second area is the fact that Jesus of Nazareth was a prophet of God. The Bible makes this clear: "And he shall send Jesus Christ,...For Moses truly said to the fathers, A prophet shall the Lord your God raise up to you of your brethren, like to me; him shall you hear in all things whatsoever he shall say to you" (Acts 3:20–22).

The Qur'an says: "Behold! The angel said 'O Mary! Allah giveth you Glad Tidings of a word from Him. His name will be (Christ Jesus) the son of Mary, held in honor in this world and the hereafter and of (the company of) those nearest to Allah'" (Surah 3:45). In Surah 19:19, the angel said to Mary, "I am only a messenger of thy Lord to announce to you a gift of a holy son." Surah 3:55 says, "Allah said: 'O Jesus! I will take you and raise you to Myself.'"

It is because of these and other references to Jesus in the Qur'an that a Muslim will not object when you establish that Jesus was a prophet from God.

This brings us to the third area of common ground. Muslims also respect Moses as a prophet of God. Therefore, there should be little contention when Christians speak of God as Creator, Jesus the prophet, and the Law of the prophet Moses.

Most Muslims do have some knowledge of their sinfulness, but few see sin in its true light. It is therefore essential to take them through the spiritual nature of the Ten Commandments. While it is true that the Law of Moses begins with, "I am the LORD your God, you shall have no other gods before me," it may be unwise to tell a Muslim, at that point, that Allah is a false god. Such talk may close the door before you are able to speak to his conscience. It is wise rather to present the Law in a similar order in which Jesus gave it in Luke 18:20. He addressed the man's sins of the flesh. He spoke directly to sins that have to do with his fellow man. Therefore, ask your hearer if he has ever told a lie. When he admits that he has, ask him what that makes him. Don't call him a liar. Instead, gently press him to tell you what someone is called who has lied. Try to get him to say that he is a "liar."

Then ask him if he has ever stolen something, even if it's small. If he has, ask what that makes him (a thief). Then quote from the prophet Jesus: "Whosoever looks on a woman to lust after her has committed adultery with her already in his heart" (Matthew 5:28). Ask if he has ever looked at a woman with lust. If he is reasonable, he will admit that he has sinned in that area. Then gently tell him that, *by his own admission*, he is a "lying, thieving, adulterer-at-heart." Say, "If God judges you by the Law of Moses on Judgment Day, will you be innocent or guilty?"

He may say he will be innocent, because he confesses his sins to God. However, the Qur'an says: "Every soul that has sinned, if it possessed all that is on earth, would fain give it in ransom" (Surah 10:54). In other words, if he possessed the whole world and offered it to God as a sacrifice for his sins, it wouldn't be enough to provide atonement for his sins.

Imagine that a criminal is facing a $50,000 fine. He is penniless, so he sincerely tells the judge that he is sorry for a crime and vows never to do it again. The judge won't let him go on the basis of his sorrow, or his vow never to commit the crime again. Of course, he should be sorry for what he has done, and of course, he shouldn't break the law again. The judge will, however, let him go if someone else pays the fine for him.

Now tell him that Moses gave instructions to Israel to shed the blood of a spotless lamb to provide a temporary atonement for their sin; and that Jesus was the Lamb that God provided to make atonement for the sins of the world. Through faith in Jesus, he can have atonement with God. All his sins can be washed away—once and for all. God can grant him the gift of everlasting life through faith in Jesus Christ on the basis of His death and resurrection.

The uniqueness of Jesus of Nazareth was that He claimed He had power on earth to forgive sins (Matthew 9:2–7). No other prophet of any of the great religions made this claim. Only Jesus can provide peace with God. This is why He said, "I am the way, the truth, and the life: no man comes to the Father, but by me" (John 14:6). God commands sinners to repent and trust in Jesus as Lord and Savior, or they will perish.

To try to justify himself, your listener may say something like, "The Bible has changed. It has been altered. There are many different versions, but the Qur'an has never changed." Explain to him that there are many different versions, printed in different languages and in modern English, to help people understand the Bible, but the content of the Scriptures remains the same. The Dead Sea Scrolls prove that God has preserved the Scriptures. Tell him that the 100% accurate prophecies of Matthew 24, Luke 21, and 2 Timothy 3 prove that this is the Book of the Creator.

Your task is to present the truth of the gospel. It is God who makes it come alive (1 Corinthians 3:6,7). It is God who brings conviction of sin (John 16:7,8). It is God who reveals who Jesus is (Matthew 16:16,17). All God requires is your faithful presentation of the truth (Matthew 25:21).

QUESTIONS

1. How we can follow Paul's example when witnessing to Muslims?

2. What three areas of common ground do Christians have with Muslims?

3. How can we use the Law in a way Muslims will more readily accept?

4. How does the Qur'an corroborate Psalm 49:7,8?

5. What claim of Jesus makes Him unique among prophets?

WORDS OF COMFORT

I was in Southern California passing out gospel tracts to people who had stopped to see our "Light Show." Things were going well. Hundreds of people had been taking our tracts. Suddenly I looked up and saw a woman heading toward me in a wheel chair. It must have been running on electricity, because she passed by quietly and very quickly. My heart went out to her when I saw that some terrible disease had twisted her hands. It was because of the speed and her twisted hands that I wasn't able to get a tract to her. She was gone in a matter of seconds.

About ten minutes later, I saw her again. This time someone was pushing her chair toward me. She was moving much slower, so I reached out to put the tract into her hand. She reached back toward me to take it, and almost violently thrust her hand at it (I realized later that the disease had left her without the ability to speak). My heart again went out to this poor woman, who was desperately trying to take my gospel tract, but because of muscle spasms, couldn't grip it. I began to walk alongside her wheel-chair and again she tried her best to take the tract. Each time the disease stopped her controlling her movements. Her hand violently thrust back and forth. I could see that the woman was becoming very frustrated. That made me determine even more to give her the tract. I tried to put it between her fingers. That didn't help. The horrible disease made her thrust her contorted hand about even more violently.

After two or three attempts to get the tract in between her fingers, and each time seeing the hand violently thrust back and forth, I heard her friend say, "Leave her alone! Can't you see . . . she doesn't want it!" Oh dear.

Memory Verse

"He that believes on the Son of God has the witness in himself: he that believes not God has made him a liar; because he believes not the record that God gave of his Son."
1 JOHN 5:10

Last Words

Alexander Pope, writer, died May 30, 1744:

> "Here am I, dying of a hundred good symptoms."

531

LESSON 79

Hinduism

"Even if I were utterly selfish and had no care for anything but my own happiness, I would choose, if God allowed, to be a soul winner, for never did I know perfect, overflowing, unutterable happiness of the purest and most ennobling order till I first heard of one who had sought and found a Savior through my means."

CHARLES SPURGEON

Kirk's Comment Religious people think their own good works will earn them a place in heaven. Christians know they will never earn heaven, but in fact deserve hell. They turn from sin and trust solely in God's mercy. Christians are motivated to do good works, not by personal ambition, but out of gratitude for the cross. This, of course, is in stark contrast to Hinduism.

QUESTIONS & OBJECTIONS

"I prefer to remain open-minded."

Open-mindedness means looking at everything honestly. Are you willing to do that with Christianity? Do you want to see what Jesus has said and learn about what He can offer you?

If you say you are going to remain open-minded and not accept Christianity, then in reality you are being very closed-minded. Maybe Christianity is true. Your open-mindedness could keep you from discovering it.

Hinduism is the world's third largest religion, yet it leaves close to a billion people in spiritual darkness. Mahatma Ghandi acknowledged the inability of his religion to atone for sin. Despite his moral lifestyle and good works, he admitted, "It is a constant torture to me that I am still so far from Him whom I know to be my very life and being. I know it is my own wretchedness and wickedness that keeps me from Him." All works-based religions lead to futility and death. It is only in Jesus Christ that sinners can find forgiveness for their sins and deliverance from death and hell.

The following information will give you a brief overview of Hinduism, how its main beliefs contrast with Christianity, and thoughts to keep in mind when witnessing.

Origin: India, about 1500 B.C. to 2500 B.C.

Founder: No single person.

Adherents: 1998 worldwide: 825–850 million; India 780 million; Bangladesh 20 million; Nepal 20 million; Indonesia 7 million; Sri Lanka 3 million; Pakistan 2 million. In Fiji, Guyana, Mauritius, Surinam, and Trinidad and Tobago, over 20 percent of their people practice Hinduism. A considerable number of Hindus live in Africa, Myanmar, and the United Kingdom.

U.S.: Estimated 1.5 to 2 million.

Scriptures: *Vedas, Upanishads, epics, Puranas,* and the *Bhagavad Gita* explain the essence of Hinduism. Hinduism is the world's oldest surviving organized religion. It is a complex family of sects whose copious scriptures, written over a period of almost 2,000 years (1500 B.C.–A.D. 250), allow a diverse belief system. Hinduism has no single creed and recognizes no final truth. At its core, Hinduism has a pagan background in which the forces of nature and human heroes are personified as gods and goddesses. They are worshiped with prayers and offerings. Hinduism can be divided into *Popular Hinduism,* characterized by the worship of gods through offerings, rituals, and prayers; and *Philosophical Hinduism,* the complex belief system understood by those who can study ancient texts, meditate, and practice yoga.

GOD: God (*Brahman*) is the one impersonal, ultimate, but unknowable, spiritual Reality. Sectarian Hinduism personalizes Brahman as *Brahma* (Creator, with four heads symbolizing creative energy), *Vishnu* (Preserver, the god of stability and control), and *Shiva* (Destroyer, god of endings). Most Hindus worship two of Vishnu's ten mythical incarnations: Krishna and Rama. On special occasions, Hindus may worship other gods, as well as family and individual deities. Hindus claim that there are 330 million gods. In Hinduism, belief in astrology, evil spirits, and curses also prevails.

Christian Response: If God (Ultimate Reality) is impersonal, then the impersonal must be greater than the personal. However, our life experiences reveal that the personal is of more value than the impersonal. Even Hindus treat their children as having more value than a rock in a field. The Bible teaches that God is personal and describes Him as having personal attributes. The Bible regularly describes God in ways used to describe human personality. God talks, rebukes, feels, becomes angry, is jealous, laughs, loves, and even has a personal name (Gen. 1:3; 6:6,12; Ex. 3:15; 16:12; 20:5; Lev. 20:23; Deut. 5:9; 1 Sam. 26:19; Ps. 2:4; 59:9; Hos. 1:8,9; Amos 9:4; Zeph. 3:17). The Bible also warns Christians to avoid all forms of idolatry (Gen. 35:2; Ex. 23:13; Josh. 23:7; Ezek. 20:7; 1 Cor. 10:20). No idol or pagan deity is a representation of the true God. They are all false deities and must be rejected.

CREATION: Hindus accept various forms of pantheism and reject the Christian doctrine of creation. According to Hinduism, Brahman alone exists; everything is ultimately an illusion (*maya*). God emanated itself to cause the illusion of creation. There is no beginning or conclusion to creation, only endless repetitions or cycles of creation and destruction. History has little value since it is based on an illusion.

Christian Response: Christianity affirms the reality of the material world and the genuineness of God's creation. The Bible declares that all is not God. God is present in His creation but He is not to be confused with it. The Bible teaches that in the beginning God created that which was not God (Gen. 1:1ff; Heb. 11:3). The Bible contradicts pantheism by teaching creation rather than pantheistic emanation. The Bible issues strong warnings to those who confuse God with His creation (Rom. 1:22,23). God created the world at a definite time and will consummate His creation (2 Pet. 2:12,13). Christianity is founded upon the historical event of God's incarnation in Jesus Christ (John 1:1–14).

MAN: The eternal soul (*atman*) of man is a manifestation or "spark" of Brahman mysteriously trapped in the physical body. *Samsara*, repeated lives or reincarnations, are required before the soul can be liberated (*moksha*) from the body. An individual's present life is determined by the law of *karma* (actions, words, and thoughts in previous lifetimes). The physical body is ultimately an illusion (*maya*) with little inherent or permanent worth. Bodies generally are cremated, and the eternal soul goes to an intermediate state of punishment or reward before rebirth in another body. Rebirths are experienced until karma has been removed to allow the soul's reabsorption into Brahman.

 Christian Response: People are created in God's image (Gen. 12:7). The body's physical resurrection and eternal worth are emphasized in John 2:18–22 and 1 Corinthians 15. The Bible declares, "And as it is appointed unto men once to die, but after this the judgment: so Christ was once offered to bear the sins of many" (Heb. 9:27,28, KJV). Since we die only once, reincarnation cannot be true. Instead of reincarnation, the Bible teaches resurrection (John 5:25). At death, Christians enjoy a state of conscious fellowship with Christ (Matt. 22:32; 2 Cor. 5:8; Phil. 1:23) to await the resurrection and heavenly reward. A person's eternal destiny is determined by his or her acceptance or rejection of Jesus Christ as Savior and Lord (John 3:36; Rom. 10:9–10).

SIN: Hindus have no concept of rebellion against a holy God. Ignorance of unity with Brahman, desire, and violation of *dharma* (one's social duty) are humanity's problems.

 Christian Response: Sin is not ignorance of unity with Brahman, but is rather a willful act of rebellion against God and His commandments (Eccl. 7:20; Rom. 1:28–32; 2:1–16; 3:9,19; 11:32; Gal. 3:22; 1 John 1:8–10). The Bible declares, "All have sinned and fall short of the glory of God" (Rom. 3:23, NIV).

SALVATION: There is no clear concept of salvation in Hinduism. *Moksha* (freedom from infinite being and self-hood and final self-realization of the truth) is the goal of existence. *Yoga* and meditation (especially *raja-yoga*) taught by a *guru* (religious teacher) is one way to attain *moksha*. The other valid paths for *moksha* are: the way of works (*karma marga*), the way of knowledge (*jnana marga*), and the way of love and devotion (*bhakti marga*). Hindus hope to eventually get off the cycle of reincarnation. They believe the illusion of personal existence will end and they will become one with the impersonal God.

Christian Response: Salvation is a gift from God through faith in Jesus Christ (Eph. 2:8–10). Belief in reincarnation opposes the teaching of the Bible (Heb. 9:27). The Christian hope of eternal life means that all true believers in Christ will not only have personal existence but personal fellowship with God. It is impossible to earn one's salvation by good works (Titus 3:1–7). Religious deeds and exercises cannot save (Matt. 7:22,23; Rom. 9:32; Gal. 2:16; Eph. 2:8,9).

WORSHIP: Hindu worship has an almost endless variety with color symbolism, offerings, fasting, and dance as integral parts. Most Hindus daily worship an image of their chosen deity, with chants (*mantras*), flowers, and incense. Worship, whether in a home or temple, is primarily individualistic rather than congregational.

Hindus in the United States

- Traditional movements include the Ramakrishna Mission and Vedanta Societies, Sri Aurobindo Society, Satya Sai Baba Movement, Self-Realization Fellowship, and International Sivananda Yoga Society.

- Hindu-based sects include the International Society for Krishna Consciousness (Hare Krishna), Transcendental Meditation, Vedanta Society, Self-Realization Fellowship, Theosophy, and Eckankar.

- Sects that have "Americanized" Hindu concepts include Church of Christ, Scientists (Christian Science); Unity School of Christianity; and several groups within the New Age Movement.

Witnessing to Hindus

- Pray and trust the Holy Spirit to use the gospel message to reach the heart and mind of your Hindu friend.

- Share your personal faith in Jesus Christ as your Lord and Savior. Keep your testimony short.

- Stress the uniqueness of Jesus Christ as God's revelation of Himself.

- Stress the necessity of following Jesus to the exclusion of all other deities.

- Keep the gospel presentation Christ-centered.

- Share the assurance of salvation that God's grace gives you and about your hope in the resurrection. Make sure you communicate that your assurance is derived from God's grace and not from your good works or your ability to be spiritual (1 John 5:13).

- Give a copy of the New Testament. If a Hindu desires to study the Bible, begin with the Gospel of John. Point out passages that explain salvation.

N.S.R.K. Ravi, © 1999 North American Mission Board of the Southern Baptist Convention, Alpharetta, Georgia. All rights reserved. Reprinted with permission.

QUESTIONS

1. **Who founded Hinduism?**

2. **What are the names of the Hindu scriptures?**

3. **How do Hindus view God?**

4. **What does Hindu worship consist of?**

5. **How does this religion's concept of sin differ from the biblical view?**

6. **According to this religion, what must adherents do to achieve salvation?**

WORDS OF COMFORT

When I was speaking in San Francisco, some of the meetings were being held in a Russian church building, which was kindly loaned to the missionary organization hosting the convention.

I had been using sleight-of-hand during one of the meetings to show how easily we are fooled. I also had another trick that is totally mind-boggling. Through sleight-of-hand, I could turn nickels into pennies, then back again. I also had a wonderful trick using three cards and dice. The leader of the missionary organization hadn't seen these, so I decided to show them to him during a lunch break.

There was a shortage of chairs in the room, so he was sitting on the floor. I joined him and showed him the tricks, and he was predictably impressed with what he saw.

Suddenly, the door opened and one of the Russian church leaders walked through the office. To do so, he had to step over the cards, the money, and the dice.

I put my hand over the dice, thinking, *This must look like the leaders of the missionaries are gambling—what else would we be doing with cards, money, and dice!* To add to the dilemma, the man didn't speak a word of English, so we just sat in dumb silence as he walked through. I felt sick.

That night I saw the man, so I approached him and slowly mouthed the words, "Sleight-of-hand..." This was dumber than dumb because he didn't speak a word of English. In controlled panic, I took the three cards out of my top pocket to try to illustrate that they were merely tricks. He must have thought I was wanting him to place a bet, because he gave me a blank look and walked off!

Last Words

Leonardo da Vinci, artist, died 1519:

> **"I have offended God and mankind because my work did not reach the quality it should have."**

Memory Verse

"For the wages of sin is death; but the gift of God is eternal life through Jesus Christ our Lord."
ROMANS 6:23

LESSON 80

Buddhism, Part 1

"Nothing can damn a man but his own righteousness;
nothing can save him but the righteousness of Christ."

CHARLES SPURGEON

Kirk's Comment The world's religions are a vain attempt to reach God and make people feel good about themselves by doing good works. Christianity is unique in that it strips us of our self-righteousness by exposing our thoroughly sinful nature, and causes us to see that our only hope is for God to reach down to us in mercy.

QUESTIONS & OBJECTIONS

"Why do I need a Savior?"

If you were to place a dried-out leaf in the presence of fire, you would see that the fire would not hesitate to consume the leaf in a matter of seconds. The fire must consume the leaf because of its very nature. Even if the fire didn't want to dispose of the leaf, it wouldn't matter; it still must consume it because their very natures are diametrically opposed.

Deuteronomy 4:24 and Hebrews 12:29 describe God as a consuming fire. By His very nature, God must consume anything and everything that opposes His nature. We must put on the Lord Jesus Christ, or we will be consumed by the ever-pure, burning holiness of the King of kings.

Buddhism is the world's fourth largest religion. The following information will give you a brief overview of Buddhism, how its main beliefs contrast with Christianity, and bridges to use when evangelizing.

Founder: Siddhartha Gautama, a prince from northern India near modern Nepal who lived about 563–483 B.C.

Scriptures: Various, but the oldest and most authoritative are compiled in the Pali Canon.

Adherents: 613 million worldwide; 1 million in the United States.

General Description: Buddhism is the belief system of those who follow the Buddha, the Enlightened One, a title given to its founder. The religion has evolved into three main schools:

1. *Theravada* or the Doctrine of the Elders (38%) is followed in Sri Lanka (Ceylon), Myanmar (Burma), Thailand, Cambodia (Kampuchea), and Vietnam.

2. *Mahayana,* the Greater Vehicle (56%), is strong in China, Korea, and Japan.

3. *Vajrayana,* also called Tantrism or Lamaism, (6%) is rooted in Tibet, Nepal, and Mongolia.

Theravada is closest to the original doctrines. It does not treat the Buddha as deity and regards the faith as a worldview—not a type of worship. *Mahayana* has accommodated many different beliefs and worships the Buddha as a god. *Vajrayana* has added elements of shamanism and the occult and includes taboo breaking (intentional immorality) as a means of spiritual enlightenment.

Growth in the United States: Buddhists regard the United States as a prime mission field, and the number of Buddhists in this country is growing rapidly due to surges in Asian immigration, endorsement by celebrities such as Tina Turner and Richard Gere, and positive exposure in major movies such as *Siddhartha, The Little Buddha,* and *What's Love Got to Do with It?* Buddhism is closely related to the New Age Movement and may to some extent be driving it. Certainly Buddhist growth is benefiting from the influence of New Age thought on American life.

Historic Background: Buddhism was founded as a form of atheism that rejected more ancient beliefs in a permanent, personal, creator God (*Ishvara*) who controlled the eternal destiny of human souls. Siddhartha Gautama rejected more ancient theistic beliefs because of difficulty he had over reconciling the reality of suffering, judgment, and evil with the existence of a good and holy God.

Core Beliefs: Buddhism is an impersonal religion of self-perfection, the end of which is death (extinction)—not life. The essential elements of the Buddhist belief system are summarized in the Four Noble Truths, the Noble Eightfold Path, and several additional key doctrines. The Four Noble Truths affirm that (1) life is full of suffering (*dukkha*); (2) suffering is caused by craving (*samudaya*); (3) suffering will cease only when craving ceases (*nirodha*); and (4) this can be achieved by following the Noble Eightfold Path consisting of right views, right aspiration, right speech, right conduct, right livelihood, right effort, right mindfulness, and right contemplation. Other key doctrines include belief that nothing in life is permanent (*anicca*), that individual selves do not truly exist (*anatta*), that all is determined by an impersonal law of moral causation (*karma*), that reincarnation is an endless cycle of continuous suffering, and that the goal of life is to break out of this cycle by finally extinguishing the flame of life and entering a permanent state of pure nonexistence (*nirvana*).

Bridges for Evangelizing Buddhists

The gospel can be appealing to Buddhists if witnessing focuses on areas of personal need where the Buddhist belief system is weak. Some major areas include:

Suffering: Buddhists are deeply concerned with overcoming suffering but must deny that suffering is real. Christ faced the reality of suffering and overcame it by solving the problem of sin, which is the real source of suffering. Now, those who trust in Christ can rise above suffering in this life because they have hope of a future life free of suffering. "We fix our eyes not on what is seen [suffering], but on what is unseen [eternal life free of suffering]. For what is seen [suffering] is temporary, but what is unseen [future good life with Christ] is eternal" (2 Cor. 4:18, NIV).

Meaningful Self: Buddhists must work to convince themselves they have no personal significance, even though they live daily as though they do. Jesus taught that each person has real significance. Each person is made in God's image with an immortal soul and an eternal destiny. Jesus demonstrated the value of people by loving us so much that He sacrificed His life in order to offer eternal future good life to anyone who trusts Him. "God demonstrates his own love for us in this: While we were still sinners, Christ died for us" (Rom. 5:8, NIV).

Future Hope: The hope of nirvana is no hope at all—only death and extinction. The hope of those who put their trust in Christ is eternal good life in a "new heaven and new earth" in which God "will wipe every tear from their eyes. There will be no more death or mourning or crying or pain, for the old order of things [suffering] has passed [will pass] away" (Rev. 21:4, NIV).

Moral Law: Because karma, the Buddhist law of moral cause and effect, is completely rigid and impersonal, life for a Buddhist is very oppressive. Under karma, there can be no appeal, no mercy, and no escape except through unceasing effort at self-perfection. Christians understand that the moral force governing the universe is a personal God who listens to those who pray, who has mercy on those who repent, and who with love personally controls for good the lives of those who follow Christ. "In all things God works for the good of those who love him" (Rom. 8:28, NIV).

Merit: Buddhists constantly struggle to earn merit by doing good deeds, hoping to collect enough to break free from the life of suffering. They also believe saints can transfer surplus merit to the undeserving. Jesus taught that no one can ever collect enough merit on his own to earn everlasting freedom from suffering. Instead, Jesus Christ, who has unlimited merit (righteousness) by virtue of His sinless life, meritorious death, and resurrection, now offers His unlimited merit as a free gift to anyone who will become His disciple. "For it is by grace you have been saved, through faith—and this not from yourselves, it is the gift of God—not by works, so that no one can boast" (Eph. 2:8,9, NIV).

Desire: Buddhists live a contradiction—they seek to overcome suffering by rooting out desire, but at the same time they cultivate desire for self-control, meritorious life, and nirvana. Christians are consistent—we seek to reject evil desires and cultivate good desires according to the standard of Christ. "Flee the evil desires of youth and pursue righteousness, faith, love and peace, along with those who call on the Lord out of a pure heart" (2 Tim. 2:22, NIV).

Jesus and the Eightfold Path

Because Buddhists think a good life consists of following the Eightfold Path, the stages of the path can be used to introduce them to Christ as follows:

Right views: Jesus is the way, the truth, and the life (John 14:6), and there is salvation in no one else (Acts 4:12).

Right aspiration: Fights and quarrels come from selfish desires and wrong motives (Jas. 4:1–3); right desires and motives honor God (1 Cor. 10:31).

Right speech: A day of judgment is coming when God will hold men accountable for every careless word they have spoken (Matt. 12:36).

Right conduct: The one who loves Jesus must obey Him (John 14:21), and those who live by God's wisdom will produce good acts/fruit (Jas. 3:17).

Right livelihood: God will care for those who put Him first (Matt. 6:31, 33), and all work must be done for God's approval (2 Tim. 2:15).

Right effort: Like runners in a race, followers of Christ must throw off every hindrance in order to give Him their best efforts (Heb. 12:1,2).

Right mindfulness: The sinful mind cannot submit to God's law (Rom. 8:7), and disciples of Jesus must orient their minds as He did (Phil. 2:5).

Right contemplation: The secret of true success, inner peace, self-control, and lasting salvation is submission to Jesus Christ as Savior and Lord and setting your heart and mind on things above where He now sits in glory waiting to bring the present order of sin and suffering to an end (Col. 3:1–4).

When Witnessing to Buddhists

- Avoid terms such as "new birth," "rebirth," "regeneration," or "born again." Use alternatives such as "endless freedom from suffering, guilt, and sin," "new power for living a holy life," "promise of eternal good life without suffering," or "gift of unlimited merit."

- Emphasize the uniqueness of Jesus Christ.

- Focus on the gospel message and do not get distracted by details of Buddhist doctrine.

- Understand Buddhist beliefs enough to discern weaknesses that can be used to make the gospel appealing ("Bridges for Evangelizing Buddhists" and "Jesus and the Eightfold Path").

- While using bridge concepts (see "Bridges for Evangelizing Buddhists"), be careful not to reduce Christian truth to a form of Buddhism. Buddhism has been good at accommodating other religions. Do not say, "Buddhism is good, but Christianity is easier."

- Share your own testimony, especially your freedom from guilt, assurance of heaven (no more pain), and personal relationship with Jesus Christ.

- Prepare with prayer. Do not witness in your own strength.

Daniel R. Heimbach, © 1996 North American Mission Board of the Southern Baptist Convention, Alpharetta, Georgia. All rights reserved. Reprinted with permission.

QUESTIONS

1. Who is the founder of Buddhism? Why did he found it?

2. What does "Buddha" mean?

3. In what are the essential elements of Buddhism summarized?

4. How does their belief about suffering differ from the biblical view?

5. In what ways are their key doctrines similar to the beliefs of Hindus?

6. What are some of the ways you can use the Noble Eightfold Path to talk about Jesus?

PREACHER'S PROGRESS

Iva Loginmyeye: "God's a hypocrite."

Christian: "Why do you say that?"

Iva Loginmyeye: "Because He forbids us to do things He does Himself."

Christian: "Where did you hear that?"

Iva Loginmyeye: "It's in the Bible. God told Joshua to kill every man, woman, and child. That makes me sick. Who does He think He is? If that's your 'God of love,' I don't want to have anything to do with Him!"

Christian: "He's God and He can do what He wants."

Iva Loginmyeye: "Okay. I will therefore do anything I want to do!"

Christian: "You can if you want, but you will have to answer to God for your actions."

Iva Loginmyeye: "I don't believe that."

Christian: "That doesn't matter. You will still have to face Him on Judgment Day."

Iva Loginmyeye: "I live a good life, so Judgment Day doesn't worry me."

Christian: "Are you perfect?"

Iva Loginmyeye: "Of course not."

Christian: "Have you ever lied?"

Iva Loginmyeye: "Yes."

Christian: "Stolen?"

Iva Loginmyeye: "Yes."

Christian: "Jesus said that if you look with lust, you have committed adultery already in your heart. Have you ever looked with lust?"

Iva Loginmyeye: "Plenty of times."

Memory Verse

"He that believes on the Son of God has the witness in himself: he that believes not God has made him a liar; because he believes not the record that God gave of his Son. And this is the record, that God has given to us eternal life, and this life is in his Son. He that has the Son has life; and he that has not the Son of God has not life."
1 JOHN 5:10–12

Christian: "So Iva, by your own admission, you are a lying, thieving, adulterer-at-heart...yet you stand in judgment of God's moral character and proclaim Him guilty? Jesus told us to remove the log from our own eye first, so that we can see all things clearly. Then we will be able to make right judgments."

Last Words

Jerome, who was burned at the stake, said while the fire was being kindled:

"Bring hither the torch; bring thy torch before my face. Had I feared death, I might have avoided it."

Buddhism, Part 2

"It is easier to denature plutonium, than to denature the evil spirit of man."

ALBERT EINSTEIN

Kirk's Comment Buddhism is an interesting religion, in that its founder didn't claim to be God or even believe in God.

QUESTIONS & OBJECTIONS

"Why are there so many different religions?"

It has been well said that "religion" is man's way of trying to deal with his guilt. Different religions have different ways for their adherents to attempt to rid themselves of sin and its consequences. They fast, pray, deny themselves legitimate pleasures, or chasten themselves, often to a point of inflicting pain. They do this because they have an erroneous concept of what God (or "the gods") is like, so they seek to establish their own righteousness, being "ignorant of God's righteousness."

The Good News of the Christian faith is that no one need suffer the pains of religious works. Christ's blood can cleanse our conscience from the "dead works" of religion (Hebrews 9:14). Jesus took our punishment upon Himself, and He is the only One who can save us from sin and death (see Acts 4:12 and John 14:6).

By Dr. Robert Morey

Buddhism is an Eastern religion that has gained many followers in the West, especially among movie stars. It is only appropriate that we examine the origin of this ancient pagan religion.

The Buddha

Buddhism is supposedly built upon the teachings and example of a Hindu guru who was called the "Buddha," i.e., Enlightened One. The problem is that this guru did not write down any of his teachings; neither did any of his early disciples. A few manuscripts appear four to five hundred years after his death, but most of the manuscripts do not appear until nearly 1,000 years after his death! This gives plenty of time for legends and myths to arise that falsify the life and teachings of the guru.

This problem is further complicated by the development of two contradictory literary traditions: Pali and Sanskrit. These divergent literary traditions produced hundreds of Buddhist sects, which disagree with each other on many major points.

No Primary Sources

Because of the lack of primary source materials for the history of Buddhism, modern scholars seriously doubt the reliability of the traditional legends about the Buddha. In fact, if he were alive today he would not recognize the religion that bears his name! Since Buddhists themselves disagree on the "facts" of the life and teachings of their guru, there is more than adequate reason to cast doubt on the entire history of the "Buddha."

What We Know

There are only a few facts about this Hindu guru that are agreed upon by most scholars. He was born around 563 B.C. in what is now called Nepal. His exact name and its spelling are not known for certain. One variation, Siddhartha Gautama, is doubted by many scholars, but we will use it for lack of a better alternative.

It is universally agreed that Siddhartha did not intend to start a new religion. He was born a Hindu, he lived as a Hindu, and he died a Hindu in 483 B.C. The myths and legends that gradually built up around him over the centuries are no safe guide to what he really believed or practiced.

As Buddhism evolved over the centuries, many different authors from varying cultures set forth their own ideas in the name of the Buddha. As a result, Buddhism developed inherent contradictions. When this was realized, Buddhism embraced these contradictions as a badge of honor. Thus the making of self-contradictory statements has become one of the pronounced features of Zen and other esoteric forms of Buddhism.

The Myths

The many conflicting and fascinating legends about his early life, marriage, wanderings, and enlightenment are unreliable. Siddhartha was supposedly born into a wealthy family and grew up very isolated from the poverty and suffering in the surrounding culture. Some legends exaggerate the wealth of his family and even make them into royalty. But these legends are obvious embellishments and there is no historical evidence to back them up.

He was married and had one infant child by the age of 29. Disobeying his father's wishes, he went out into the world and for the first time saw the pain and suffering of the unwashed poor and the untouchables. Their suffering made him feel guilty over his life of ease and luxury.

As he became psychologically obsessed with guilt, instead of doing something positive to alleviate human suffering, like setting up a hospital or giving food to the hungry, Siddhartha decided to increase human suffering by abandoning his family and taking up the life of a Hindu beggar/monk. By making his family suffer as well as himself, he only added to human suffering. This is one of the great defects of both Hinduism and Buddhism: they increase human suffering with their belief systems.

For six years Siddhartha wandered around the countryside begging and abusing his body in an attempt to purify his soul. But his suffering did not profit anything for anyone including himself. The legends state that he was sitting under a fig tree when it dawned on him that the source of all his suffering was his failure to find a Middle Way between pleasure and pain, wealth and poverty, etc. He had gone from one extreme to another and both experiences had left him dissatisfied with life.

Then a new idea came into his mind. His real problem was that he had *desires*. When his desires were not met, he became dissatisfied. Thus the way to avoid frustration and the suffering it caused is to arrive at the place where he had no desires for anything, good or evil. For example, he should have no desire to see his wife or child or to help the poor and needy. Desire itself must be eradicated.

With these insights, Siddhartha was proclaimed a "Buddha"—an Enlightened One. Did this mean he went back to his family and fulfilled his moral obligation to his wife and child? No, his wife and child remained abandoned. Siddhartha's "enlightenment" was intensely self-centered and inherently selfish. This is still one of the main problems of Buddhism.

Now that he was a "Buddha," he should not have any desires to be or do anything. We would therefore expect him to withdraw to a cave and die in isolation. But his desire to preach sermons and make converts was apparently alive and well. He set forth preaching his new message to all who would hear him.

According to the legends, from his enlightened lips came the Four Noble Truths, the Eightfold Path, the Ten Perfections, and many other sophisticated teachings. But Siddhartha never really taught any of these things. They were developed many centuries after his death and his name was invoked in order to give them the air of authority.

No God

Siddhartha never taught that he was a god or that he should be worshiped as a god. He did not even claim to be a saint or an avatar (an incarnation of a god). As a Hindu, he believed in millions of finite gods and goddesses. But being finite deities, they were of little consequence and could be ignored except when you needed their assistance. Thus, most Buddhists call upon the gods only when they need something.

Christianity and Buddhism

Buddhism is inferior to Christianity in many ways.

1. "Southern" Buddhism is polytheistic, involving the worship of idols including the Buddha (a huge, fat, smiling, pot-bellied man sitting in

the lotus position). Some rub his stomach for good luck. Sacrifices are presented to him. The Old Testament prophets pointed out the defects of polytheism and the folly of worshiping what we make with our own hands.

2. "Northern" Buddhism is more atheistic than polytheistic. If any god is acknowledged, it is the "god" within us. Buddhists deny the existence of the infinite, personal Maker of heaven and earth. They are atheistic in this sense.

3. Having no infinite, personal Creator, Buddhism cannot provide any basis for truth, justice, meaning, morals, or beauty. It cannot answer the riddles of the origin or goal of life.

4. Its inward orientation made the development of science impossible.

5. Its concept of suffering prevented them from alleviating human suffering.

6. Their concept of karma and reincarnation compounded the problem of evil by adding more suffering to it.

7. Because Buddhism teaches that man's problem is primarily ignorance, it never developed a way to gain forgiveness for sin.

8. Because it strives only for enlightenment, Buddhism offers no plan of salvation.

9. Its goal is not to glorify God or to make a positive contribution to humanity, but the extinction of individual consciousness in the ocean of nothingness called *nirvana*. Its failure to find a purpose and meaning for life that is greater than life itself is one of its greatest defects.

10. Because of its narcissistic and self-centered nature, Buddhism appeals to those who seek justification for living a selfish life style. This is why Hollywood movie stars are drawn to it.

11. Buddhism fails the test of history by being based on groundless myths and legends. It thus has no basis in history and it is built on lies and deceptions set forth in Buddha's name.

The Answer to Buddhism

1. *The Biblical Doctrine of Creation*: The universe is not eternal as Buddhism teaches. It had a beginning and will have an end. Man is created in the image of an infinite, personal Creator. God created matter as well as mind and both are good. Buddhism fails the test of science with its idea of an eternal universe.

2. *The Biblical Doctrine of the Fall:* Man's problem is moral and not metaphysical. He has sinned against God's Law by violating its commands and failing to live up to it standards. Our problem is not that we have a body or that we are conscious of our individual existence. Our problem is that we are sinners in need of salvation. Buddhism fails the test of morals because it neglects to address the sin problem.

3. *The Biblical Doctrine of Redemption:* We broke God's divine Law (Ten Commandments) and are worthy of hell. God so loved us that He sent His Son to die for our sins on the cross. His atoning work renders karma and reincarnation unnecessary. The goal is to retain our individual consciousness for all eternity in service to God and others. Buddhism fails the test of salvation because it provides none.

Buddhism is legendary while Christianity is historical. Buddhism is irrational and attempts to escape logic and reason. But Christianity is the very essence of logic and reason. Buddhism is a death-wish philosophy and is not mentally healthy. It does not really enable people to cope with the real world but tries to escape reality and live according to illusion and fantasy. In every respect it fails the tests of truth. Jesus Christ alone is the way, the truth, and the life. We cannot get to the Father without Him.

QUESTIONS

1. How does the existence of early manuscripts about the teachings of Buddha compare to those about Jesus?

2. How did Siddhartha's response to suffering differ from the Christian response?

3. After experiencing both extremes—wealth and poverty—how did Siddhartha's reaction differ from that given in Proverbs 30:8?

4. Why do you think someone would choose to believe in a religious system in which the individual ceases to exist?

5. Explain why Buddhism is a narcissistic belief system.

6. Why is Buddhism not mentally healthy?

WORDS OF COMFORT

Something within me said that it wasn't a wise move. I had told my 22-year-old daughter that I would go shopping with her. I would take my credit card, and she could pick out some clothes for her birthday.

I, like most men, am not the best company in malls. I like to drive to the mall, go to a store, buy what I want, and go home. Women aren't like men, and my daughter is a woman. After wandering around the store while she looked for what she wanted, I decided to tell her that it was time to leave. I had viewed every item in the store, and had spoken to several people. Besides, I had to record a program for a radio station that afternoon.

After looking across the store, I couldn't locate my daughter, so I decided to use our "family whistle." That never fails.

I walked around, quietly whistling the family whistle as I went. I went up and down racks of clothes, whistling slightly louder as I did so. Still no sign of my daughter. I walked around the entire store, whistling louder than when I started. The practice was making me bolder. Finally, after checking the whole store, I felt frustrated. I stood at one end and quietly hollered, "Rachel!"

Still no daughter. Why would she leave the store? Perhaps she hadn't been able to find me and had gone outside looking for me. It was while I was gazing out through the front doors that a frustrated-looking daughter, laden with clothes, approached me. She quietly informed me that she had been in the fitting room (which was situated in the middle of the store), and had heard every whisper, whistle, and the Jericho shout as I circled the fitting room.

Memory Verse

"Jesus said to him, I am the way, the truth, and the life: no man comes to the Father, but by me."

JOHN 14:6

Last Words

Rudolph Valentino, actor, died August 23, 1926:

"Don't worry, chief, it will be all right."

What Makes a Group Non-Christian?

"It comes down to a question of truth. Every false religious expression is a religion of darkness. That doesn't mean there are no good things in that faith. It's not an effort to fail to notice the value of these things. But if Jesus is to be taken seriously when he says, 'No one comes to the Father but through me,' every other proposal is one of darkness."

PAIGE PATTERSON

Kirk's Comment This lesson is about how to know whether or not a particular group is truly Christian. Many claim to be Christians, but their views on essential doctrines will show that they are not.

QUESTIONS & OBJECTIONS

"What gives you the right to judge me?"

To pronounce another religious group to be false can seem a pompous undertaking, especially in a culture that preaches tolerance for everything from homosexuality to a mother's "right" to kill her unborn child. Tolerance is the banner that unites much of our culture, and anyone who points a judging finger at someone or something is often ridiculed.

But Christians are told in the Bible to separate themselves from the sinful practices of man and to expose error. God's Word tells us to examine all things and hold fast to that which is true (1 Thessalonians 5:21). So we do.

What does it mean to examine if we do not judge what is right and wrong? Jesus judged the Pharisees as hypocrites. Peter judged Ananias and Sapphira as liars (Acts 5:3,4). Paul judged the Galatians as fools (Galatians 3:1).

Something can be said to be right or wrong because the Bible has laid out before us a moral and doctrinal standard that is clear. It is wrong to lie, so we are able to say to someone who lies, "What you are doing is wrong." That is making a judgment.

Likewise, with the cults, as Christians we are commanded to be able to give answers to everyone (1 Peter 3:15) and to contend for the faith that was delivered to the saints (Jude 3). If we do not fight for the faith, the faith will be lost. If we do not expose the errors of the cults, then the cults will move unchecked in the world and lead even more people into eternal destruction.

To make a judgment means we must recognize that there are absolutes. In a world that worships relativism, absolutes are not welcome and the cults that espouse their demonic doctrines beg tolerance.

The true Church stands for the truth of God's Word, not a compromising collection of beliefs that changes as people's whims change. The cults are cults because they deny the true God, add works to salvation, and corrupt a multitude of biblical truths. Their end and the end of all who follow them is damnation. To do anything other than warn people about them would be unloving.

wotmwotmwotmwotmwotmwotmwotmwotmwotmwotmwotm

By Matthew J. Slick

There are many non-Christian religions and cults in America: Mormonism, Jehovah's Witnesses, Christian Science, Unity, The Way International, Unitarianism, etc. All claim special revelation and privilege. The dictionary defines a cult as "a system of religious worship or ritual; devoted attachment to, or extravagant admiration for, a person, principle, etc.; a group of followers." This is a typical secular definition and by it, any believer in any god is a cultist, even atheists since they have an admiration for a principle and are a group of followers of the philosophy of atheism.

The definition I use for "non-Christian cult" or "non-Christian religion" encompasses groups that may or may not include the Bible in their set of authoritative scriptures. If a group does include the Bible, it distorts the true biblical doctrines that effect salvation sufficiently so as to void salvation. If it doesn't use the Bible, it is a non-Christian religion and does not participate in the benefit of divine revelation.

The term "cult" can range from any group of worshipers of any god who pay no attention to the Bible, to a small, highly paranoid, apocalyptic people who gather around a charismatic leader who uses the Bible to control them. Groups like the Mormons and Jehovah's Witnesses object to the label "cult" because it often gets an emotional reaction and is a label they want to avoid.

Most Christian bookstores have "cult" sections that include Mormons, Jehovah's Witnesses, etc., so I am not alone in describing what a non-Christian, Bible-based cult is. Nevertheless, a group is non-Christian when it denies the essential doctrines of the Bible:

- The deity of Christ, which involves the Trinity
- The resurrection of Jesus
- Salvation by grace alone

All of the cults add to the finished work of Jesus on the cross. Some cult groups even add to the Bible, e.g., Mormonism has the Book of Mormon, Doctrine and Covenants, and *The Pearl of Great Price*. Christian Science has added *Science and Health with Key to the Scriptures*. The Jehovah's Witnesses, however, have actually changed the text of the Bible to make it fit what they want it to.

Cults add their own efforts, their own works of righteousness to the finished work of salvation accomplished by Jesus on the cross. All cults say that Jesus' sacrifice is sufficient, yet our works must be "mixed with" or "added to" His in order to prove that we are saved and worthy of salvation. They say one thing but believe another. They maintain that they must try their best to please God and prove to Him that they are sincere, have worked hard, and are then worthy to be with Him. In other words, they do their best and God takes care of the rest.

This is absolutely wrong. The Bible says that we are saved by grace, not by works: "For by grace you have been saved through faith...not as a result of works, that no one should boast (Ephesians 2:8,9, NASB); we are not saved by anything we do: "For we maintain that a man is justified by faith apart from works of the Law" (Romans 3:28, NASB). Because if there was anything that we could do to merit the forgiveness of our sins, then Jesus died needlessly: "nevertheless knowing that a man is not justified by the works of the Law but through faith in Christ Jesus, even we have believed in Christ Jesus, that we may be justified by faith in Christ, and not by the works of the Law; since by the works of the Law shall no flesh be justified...I do not nullify the grace of God; for if righteousness comes through the Law, then Christ died needlessly" (Galatians 2:16,21, NASB).

People in cults will often cite James 2:26, which says that faith without works is dead, in an attempt to demonstrate that works are part of becoming saved. While it is true that faith without works is dead, it isn't the works that save us. James is saying that if you have real and true faith, it will result in real and true works of Christianity. In other words, you do good works *because* you are saved, not to get saved. He isn't saying that our works are what saves us, or that they, in combination with the finished work of Christ, save us. This agrees with Paul who tells us that faith is what saves us: "Therefore having been justified by faith, we have peace with God through our Lord Jesus Christ" (Romans 5:1). This faith is real faith, or true saving faith, not just an empty mental acknowledgment of God's existence, which is what those who "say" they have faith but show no corresponding godliness are guilty of. Incidentally, you should realize that faith is only as good as the object in which you place it. Just having faith in something doesn't mean you're saved. That is why it is important to have the true Jesus, because if you have great faith but it is in the wrong Jesus, then your faith is useless.

In Mormonism, Jesus is the brother of the devil begotten through sexual intercourse with a god who came from another planet. In Jehovah's

Witnesses, he is Michael the Archangel who became a man. In the New Age Movement, he is a man in tune with the divine consciousness. Which is true? The only true Jesus is the one of the Bible, the one who is prayed to (1 Corinthians 1:1,2; Acts 7:55–60); worshiped (Matthew 2:2–11; 14:33, John 9:35–38; Hebrews 1:8), and called God (John 20:28; Colossians 2:9). The Jesus of the cults is not prayed to, worshiped, or called God. And since the Jesus of the Bible is the only one who reveals the Father (Luke 10:22) so that you may have eternal life (John 17:3), you must have the true Jesus who alone is the way, the truth, and the life (John 14:6).

Another common denominator among cults is their methods of twisting Scripture. Some of the errors they commit in interpreting Scripture are: 1) taking Scripture out of context; 2) reading into the Scriptures information that is not there; 3) picking and choosing only Scriptures that suit their needs; 4) ignoring other explanations; 5) combining Scriptures that don't have anything to do with each other; 5) quoting a verse without giving its location; 6) incorrect definitions of key words; and 7) mistranslations. These are only a few of the many ways cults misuse Scripture.

If you want to be able to witness well to a person in a cult, you need to understand their doctrines as well as your own. It would be a good idea to study Christian doctrine regarding the Bible, God, Jesus, the Holy Spirit, salvation, creation, man, etc., to become better equipped. Through study you will be able to answer questions that often come up in witnessing encounters. A Christian should know his doctrine well enough to be able to recognize not only what is true, but also what is false in a religious system (1 Peter 3:15; 2 Timothy 2:15).

Jesus warned us that in the last days false Christs and false prophets would arise and deceive many (Matthew 24:24). The Lord knew that there would be a rise of the spirit of antichrist (1 John 4:1–3) in the last days. Its manifestation is here in the forms of Mormonism, Jehovah's Witnesses, and the New Age Movement, among others.

Adapted from an article by the Christian Apologetics and Research Ministry (www.carm.org).

QUESTIONS

1. Give three examples of a cult.

2. What determines if a group is a non-Christian religion or cult?

3. What essential biblical doctrines do cults deny?

4. How have cults distorted the doctrine of salvation?

5. How have cults distorted the deity of Jesus?

6. What are some of the errors that cultists commit when interpreting Scripture?

FEATHERS FOR ARROWS

An African chief got wind of a mutiny being planned in his tribe. In an effort to quash the revolt, he called the tribe together and said that *anyone* caught in rebellion would be given one hundred lashes, *without mercy.*

A short time later, to the chief's dismay, he found that his own brother was behind the revolt. He was trying to overthrow him so that he could be head of the tribe. Everyone thought the chief would break his word. But being a just man, he had his brother tied to a tree. Then he had himself tied next to him, and he took those one hundred lashes across his own bare flesh in his brother's place. In doing so, he not only kept his word (justice was done), but he also demonstrated his great love and forgiveness toward his brother.

Last Words

Prince Henry of Wales gave utterance to these lines:

> "Tie a rope round my body, pull me out of bed, and lay me in ashes, that I may die with repentant prayers to an offended God. Oh! Tom! I in vain wish for that time I lost with thee and others in vain recreations."

Memory Verse

"Beloved, believe not every spirit, but try the spirits whether they are of God: because many false prophets are gone out into the world. Hereby know you the Spirit of God: Every spirit that confesses that Jesus Christ is come in the flesh is of God: and every spirit that confesses not that Jesus Christ is come in the flesh is not of God."

1 JOHN 4:1–3

83

Unitarianism

"Our God is a consuming fire, and we try to reduce Him to something we can handle or are comfortable with ... We are religious consumers. We want our religion to be convenient. It's the perpetual job of writers, preachers, the church and the gospel to help people respond to God as He reveals Himself."

EUGENE PETERSON

Kirk's Comment   The Unitarian philosophy is more common than we may think. It would be good to become familiar with this belief system so you will know how it differs from the teaching of Scripture.

QUESTIONS & OBJECTIONS

"Religion is whatever you feel is right."

How do you know that what you feel is right? Haven't your feelings ever turned out to be wrong? If you are saying that what you feel determines truth, then you are putting yourself in the place of God and looking to yourself for what you "feel" is right. And what if someone felt that something was right and another person felt it was wrong? Would they both be right? I've never known truth to contradict itself. How could there be a contradiction like that if feelings determined truth?

If your statement is true and religion is whatever you feel is right, then that could lead to chaos. What if some people had a religion where they felt it was acceptable to steal, lie, and cheat? After all, Hitler felt killing Jews was right. He was wrong. The Bible says that the heart is deceitful and untrustworthy (Jeremiah 17:9). If you could come to know truth by what you felt, then the Bible, which is the revelation of God, didn't need to be written. But, it has been written and it has revealed that only God is the Source of truth, not your feelings.

wotmwotmwotmwotmwotmwotmwotmwotmwotmwotmwotm

By Matthew J. Slick

Unitarianism is the belief that God exists in one person, not three. It is a denial of the doctrine of the Trinity as well as the full divinity of Jesus. Therefore, it is not Christian. Several groups fall under this umbrella, including Jehovah's Witnesses, Christadelphianism, and The Way International. Another term for this type of belief is "monarchianism." Unitarians have no dogma and hold to a common system of believing as you will about God, salvation, sin, etc. They also hold to the universal redemption of all mankind.

In the context of universalism, the Unitarianism discussed here is the belief that denies the Trinity, the deity of Christ, the personhood of the Holy Spirit, eternal punishment, and the vicarious atonement of Jesus. Unitarian Universalists use many biblical concepts and terms but with non-biblical meanings. Unitarianism is not Christian.

There is a group known as the Unitarian Universalists Association, which was formed in 1961 when the American Unitarian Association and the Universalist Church of America merged. Its membership is around 175,000.

The General Convention of the Unitarian Universalists formulated the five principles of the Universalist Faith in 1899:

- The Universal Fatherhood of God

- The spiritual authority and leadership of His Son Jesus Christ

- The trustworthiness of the Bible as containing a revelation from God

- The certainty of just retribution for sin

- The final harmony of all souls with God

Additional beliefs generally held by Unitarian Universalists are:

- Jesus became the Son of God at His baptism.

- The Holy Spirit is not a person, does not have a will, etc.

- There will be rewards and punishments according to one's actions, but this does not include the traditional doctrine of hell.

- Human reason and experience should be the final authority in determining spiritual truth.

This last point, "Human reason and experience should be the final authority in determining spiritual truth," is perhaps the most revealing of Unitarian Universalists. They believe, "In the end religious authority lies not in a book or person or institution, but in ourselves. We are a 'non-creedal' religion: we do not ask anyone to subscribe to a creed." Instead of God and His Word being the final authority on truth and error, right and wrong, Unitarian Universalists subject God and His Word to their understanding, feeling, and reason. This is exemplified in the following quotes from the official Unitarian Universalist website (www.uua.org):

- "I want a religion that respects the differences between people and affirms every person as an individual."

- "I want a church that values children, that welcomes them on their own terms—a church they are eager to attend on Sunday morning."

- "I want a congregation that cherishes freedom and encourages open dialogue on questions of faith, one in which it is okay to change your mind."

- "I want a religious community that affirms spiritual exploration and reason as ways of finding truth."

- "I want a church that acts locally and thinks globally on the great issues of our time—world peace; women's rights; racial justice; homelessness; gay, lesbian, bisexual, and transgender rights; and protection of the environment."

Notice that each of the five statements begins with "I want..." This is not the humble attitude of one indwelt by the Holy Spirit of God. It is not the attitude of one who wants to put God first.

It can plainly be seen that this is a religion based on personal hopes and desires and not on the Bible.

I cannot help thinking of the five "I will's" listed in Isaiah 14:13,14:

> But you said in your heart,
> "*I will* ascend to heaven;
> *I will* raise my throne above the stars of God,
> *I will* sit on the mount of assembly in the recesses of the north.
> *I will* ascend above the heights of the clouds;
> *I will* make myself like the Most High."

Many commentators believe that these five "I wills" were uttered by Satan as he sought to be exalted and equal to God. They reflect the arrogance of the evil one as his heart was filled with pride and he put his own will before God's. He placed his desires before God's.

But notice what Isaiah says in the next verse: "Nevertheless you will be thrust down to Sheol, to the recesses of the pit."

Jesus said, "Out of the abundance of the heart, the mouth speaks" (Matthew 12:34). We can see that the Unitarian Universalists speak first from their own desires, according to their own wisdom, and not according to the wisdom of God. What does God say about this?

"For the wisdom of this world is foolishness before God" (1 Corinthians 3:19).

Adapted from an article by the Christian Apologetics and Research Ministry (www.carm.org).

QUESTIONS

1. **Do Unitarians hold to the doctrine of the Trinity?**

2. **What do Unitarians believe should be the final authority in determining spiritual truth?**

3. **According to Unitarianism, when did Jesus become the Son of God?**

4. **What do Unitarians believe about the Holy Spirit?**

PREACHER'S PROGRESS

Miss Tolerant: "I think it's wrong to say that Jesus is the only way to God."

Christian: "But if I told you that there were other ways, I would be lying to you."

Miss Tolerant: "You are full of hatred. You've got no respect for other religions. What about Hinduism, Islam, Buddhism, etc.—don't you care about them?"

Christian: "The Bible says, 'Neither is there salvation in any other. There is no other name under heaven given among men, whereby we must be saved.'"

Miss Tolerant: "But those people are sincere."

Christian: "What if I sincerely believed that I was on a plane flying to Hawaii, but in truth I was heading for Afghanistan? You are forgetting that someone can be sincerely wrong."

Miss Tolerant: "Are you saying all those people will go to hell just because they are not Christians?"

Christian: "I never said that. I am saying that the only way to God is through Jesus Christ. There is one Mediator between man and God, the Man Christ Jesus. Here's the big difference between Christianity and other religions: Jesus said, 'The Son of Man has power on earth to forgive sins.' No religion can forgive sin—only Jesus . . . because of the cross."

Miss Tolerant: "Will they go to hell?"

Christian: "Only if they have broken the Commandments. If they are perfect in thought, word, and deed on the Day of Judgment, they will be fine. If they have lied, stolen, lusted, fornicated, etc., they will be in big trouble—no matter how religious they are. The Bible says, 'Whoever transgresses, and abides not in the doctrine of Christ, has not God.'"

Miss Tolerant: "I think you are deranged!"

Christian: "Do you think that I should be more tolerant toward other religions?"

Miss Tolerant: "Yes."

Christian: "Are you tolerant of other religions?"

Miss Tolerant: "Yes."

Christian: "How about Christianity? Are you tolerant of the claims of Christianity—that Jesus is the only way to God?"

Miss Tolerant: "No."

Christian: "So you are saying that we should be tolerant of every religion except Christianity. You need to practice what you preach."

WORDS OF COMFORT

It's amazing how many people love their animals. I have watched individuals who look and act like statesmen suddenly become like little boys when they are with their dogs.

A true dog-lover lets his dog lick his mouth. I'm not a "true" dog-lover. It's a dog-sniff-dog world, and after watching dogs in action, I have trained our dogs to keep their tongues off my face. However, I am not embarrassed to admit that I hug my dogs. I also give the occasional kiss—not on the lips as the true dog-lover, but on the head. But lately, I have abandoned the practice of dog-kissing. This is because one time when I grabbed one of the animals and gave it a big smooch, there was an unusual aroma. I pulled back and saw that the animal's ear had flipped back and my pursed lips had gone deep into the cave of a hot inner ear!

Memory Verse

"O generation of vipers, how can you, being evil, speak good things? for out of the abundance of the heart the mouth speaks."

MATTHEW 12:34

Last Words

Robert Cecil (1563–1612), who became Earl of Salisbury, said:

"Ease and pleasure quake to hear of death; but my life full of cares and miseries, desireth to be dissolved."

LESSON 84

Mormonism, Part 1

"I can tell you that there is no greater joy than leading someone to faith in Jesus Christ. Even if they reject your message, it still feels great to obey Christ. Yet regardless of how we feel, we need to remember this is what He has commanded."

D. JAMES KENNEDY

Kirk's Comment Are Mormons Christians? Many Mormons use words and phrases that are similar to Christian terminology, but whose meanings are drastically different. "The skin of the truth stuffed with a lie" is an appropriate description for Mormonism.

QUESTIONS & OBJECTIONS

"I tried Christianity once."

The Bible says that once you are saved, you are never the same again; you are a new creature (2 Corinthians 5:17). If you have gone back to your old ways, then most probably you were never saved. If, however, you were saved, then God won't let you stay in rebellion for long. He will deal with you in whatever way is necessary to bring you back into fellowship with Him.

Did you "try" Christianity by going to church or by asking Jesus to forgive you of your sins? The latter makes you a Christian; the former doesn't.

The following information will give you a brief overview of Mormonism, how its main beliefs contrast with Christianity, and thoughts to keep in mind when witnessing.

Official Name: Church of Jesus Christ of Latter-day Saints (LDS, Mormons)

Founder: Joseph Smith Jr., on April 6, 1830

Current Leader: Gordon B. Hinckley (b. 1910)

Headquarters: Salt Lake City, Utah

Membership (1998): Worldwide: 10.3 million in 28,670 wards and branches in 162 countries; United States: 5.1 million in all 50 states and D.C.; Canada: 152,000

Missionaries (1998): 58,700

The Church of Jesus Christ of Latter-day Saints was founded by Joseph F. Smith Jr. (1805–1844). Smith claimed to have had a visitation from God in 1820 in which God directed him to establish the true church. Consequently, he organized the Mormon church on April 6, 1830, with six original members. Beginning with a few hundred followers, the church moved to Ohio, Missouri, and Illinois before Smith's death at the hands of a mob at the Carthage, Ill., jail.

Smith had been arrested for encouraging the destruction of the *Expositor*, a Nauvoo, Ill., newspaper. After Smith's death, Brigham Young was affirmed as president of the church by a majority of the church's leaders and led several thousand followers to Utah where they established Salt Lake City in 1847. Joseph Smith's widow, Emma, resided in Independence, Mo. Those who affirmed her son, Joseph Smith, as the true successor of his father and as prophet of the church helped found the Reorganized Church of Jesus Christ of Latter Day Saints, now headquartered in Independence, Mo., in 1852.

Major Beliefs of Mormons

One True Church: The Mormon church claims to be the only true church. In God's supposed revelation to Joseph Smith, Jesus Christ told him to join no other church for "they were all wrong…their creeds were an abomination…those professors [members] were all corrupt" (*The Pearl of Great Price*, Joseph Smith History—1:19). Mormons teach that after the New Testament, all churches became heretical and no true saints existed until the "Church of the Latter-day Saints" was organized, hence their name. Non-Mormons are thus called "Gentiles." The new revelations given to Smith, the institution of the prophet and apostles in the church, the restoration of the divine priesthoods, and the temple ceremonies make the church authentic. True and full salvation or exaltation is found only in the LDS church.

Biblical Response: The true Church of Jesus Christ has had an ongoing presence and witness in the world since Pentecost. Jesus Christ promised that His Church, *true* baptized and regenerate believers, would not fail (Matt. 16:17,18). The marks of a true church include faithfulness to the teaching of the first apostles (Acts 2:42)—not the creation of new doctrines.

Authority of the Prophet: The *president* or *prophet* of the church is thought to be the sole spokesman and revelator of God. Joseph Smith was the initial prophet, but each successive president holds that position. Through him God's will can be made known to the church. All revelations are made scripture and no Mormon can attain godhood without accepting Joseph Smith as a true prophet. The Mormon scriptures state that Latter-day Saints "shalt give heed unto all his [the prophet's] words and commandments…For his word ye shall receive as if from mine [God's] own mouth" (*Doctrine and Covenants* 21:4–5).

Biblical Response: Old and New Testament prophets were God's spokesmen. Their words were always consistent with the Bible and pointed to God's Son, Jesus Christ. A test of genuineness for prophets was that any prediction they proclaimed would come true (Deut. 18:20–22).

For example, Joseph Smith predicted that the temple of the church would be built in Independence, Mo., within his lifetime (*Doctrine and Covenants* 84:2–5). No temple has yet been built there. New Testament prophets spoke, along with teachers, pastors, and evangelists, in evangelizing with and edifying the church (Eph. 4:11–13).

Mormon Scripture: Mormons accept four books as scripture and the word of God. The King James Version of the Bible is one of them, but only "as far as it is translated correctly"—seemingly allowing for possible questions about its authority. Joseph Smith made over 600 corrections to its text. Other "standard works" are the Book of Mormon, *Doctrine and Covenants*, and *The Pearl of Great Price*. The Bible is missing "plain and precious parts" according to the Book of Mormon (1 Nephi 13:26), which the other three volumes complete. The Book of Mormon has the "fullness of the gospel" and tells the story of a supposed migration of Israelites in 600 B.C. to the American continent.

These Israelites subsequently lapsed into apostasy although their story was preserved on golden plates written in "Reformed Egyptian." Joseph Smith, it is said, translated the plates by the "gift and power of God" (*Doctrine and Covenants* 135:3). Reformed Egyptian does not exist as a language. The golden plates were returned to the angel Moroni after they were transcribed and Moroni returned them to heaven. The Book of Mormon does not contain explicit Mormon doctrine. *Doctrine and Covenants* contains the revelations of the Mormon prophets—138 in number along with two "declarations." Here most of Mormon doctrine can be found including the priesthood, baptism for the dead, godhood, and polygamy. *The Pearl of Great Price* contains Smith's religious history, the Articles of Faith, the Book of Abraham, and the Book of Moses.

Biblical Response: The Bible explicitly warns against adding to or detracting from its teaching (Rev. 22:18; Deut. 4:2). The New Testament contains the inspired and totally accurate witness of contemporary disciples and followers of Jesus. It alone claims to be fully inspired by God and usable for the establishment of doctrine (2 Tim. 3:15–17; 2 Pet. 1:19–21).

Establishment of Temples: The first Mormon temple was constructed in Kirtland, Ohio, in 1836. A temple was constructed in Nauvoo, Ill., in 1846. Presently there are at least 53 operating temples throughout the world including the one finished in Salt Lake City in 1893. The purpose and function of temples is for the practice of eternal ordinances, including primarily baptism for the dead, endowments, and celestial marriages. Baptism in the Mormon church, for both the living and the dead, is essential for the fullness of salvation. The dead often are baptized by proxy, which affords them after death the opportunity to become Mormons. Celestial marriage for "time and eternity" is also a temple ordinance. It is necessary for godhood and seals the marriage forever. Temples form an essential part of Mormon salvation. Only Mormons in possession of a "temple recommend" by their bishop may enter a temple.

Biblical Response: The Temple of the Old Testament was a place of symbolic sacrifice fore-figuring the sacrifice of Christ. Worship in the Jewish temple in Jerusalem was a practice of early Jewish believers (Acts 2:46). Otherwise there is no mention of any such practice in the New Testament. Never was the Jewish temple used for baptism for the dead, marriage, or other secret ceremonies. It was the place in the Old Testament where the glory of God occasionally dwelt. Today the individual believer is God's dwelling place and not a physical building (1 Cor. 3:16).

God Is an Exalted Man: Elohim, the god of this universe, was previously a man in a prior existence. As a result of having kept the requirements of Mormonism, he was exalted to godhood and inherited his own universe. God is confined to a "body of flesh and bones" (*Doctrine and Covenants* 130:22) and yet is thought to be omniscient and omnipotent. He obviously cannot be omnipresent. There are an infinite number of gods with their own worlds—these too were previously men. The Holy Ghost, Jesus Christ, and "Heavenly Father" comprise three separate and distinct gods. Heavenly Father sires spiritual children in heaven destined for human life on earth. All humans, as well as Jesus Christ and Lucifer, are god's heavenly children. (See *Doctrine and Covenants* 130:22; God, Jesus, and the Spirit thus had beginnings.)

Biblical Response: God is Spirit and is not confined to a physical body (John 4:24). Jesus Christ was incarnated through a miraculous and nonphysical conception through the Virgin Mary. He was fully God from the beginning (John 1:1). Together with the person of the Holy Spirit, they form the triune (three-in-one) eternal God.

Jesus Is God's "Son": Jesus was Heavenly Father's firstborn spirit child in heaven. He was begotten by God through Mary in a "literal, full and complete sense" in the same "sense in which he is the son of Mary" (Bruce McConkie, *A New Witness for the Articles of Faith* [Salt Lake City: Deseret

Book Co., 1993], 67). These two elements of Jesus being literally God's son form his uniqueness in Mormon theology. In the Garden of Gethsemane as well as on the cross, Jesus atoned for Adam's sin and guaranteed all humankind resurrection and immortality. Jesus visited the Israelites or Indians of North America after his resurrection and established the true church among them. We are the spiritual, but literal, younger brothers and sisters of Christ. Some Mormon documents claim that Jesus was married at Cana in Galilee (Mark 2) and had children himself.

Biblical Response: Jesus is viewed as God, the Word or Son, eternally existent with the Father and worthy of identity as God (John 1:1–14). He was born of the Virgin Mary who had conceived him supernaturally by the Holy Spirit. He lived a perfect life, died on the cross for the sins of the world, and was raised from the dead. He will come again and reign as Lord of lords.

Humans Are Gods in Embryo: Every human being has the potential of becoming a god by keeping the requirements of Mormonism. A well-known statement within Mormonism is, "As man is god once was, as god is man may become." From a prior spirit existence in heaven, humans may be born on earth in order to exercise freedom to choose good or evil and to have a body for the resurrection. Basically humans are good, but they will be punished for their sin. By keeping Mormon teaching and obeying the church and the Prophet, after the resurrection worthy Mormon males may pass the celestial guards, bring their wives with them, and achieve a status similar to Elohim—the god of this world. The consequences of their sin are erased by their allegiance to the tenets of Mormonism. In resurrection faithful Mormons receive exaltation to godhood and will exercise dominion over their world.

Biblical Response: Human beings are God's special creation. There is no evidence from Scripture of preexistence; rather, God states that it was in the womb of our mothers that He formed us (Isaiah 44:2). A sinful nature is part of humanity's experience. Liberation from the power and presence of sin is experienced as a result of faith in Christ. At that point God's image is begun to be remade in every Christian. Although the believer is being transformed to Christlikeness, the Bible does not teach literal godhood as the inheritance of the saints (Rom. 8:29; Rev. 1:5,6).

Mormon Plan of Salvation: The Mormon plan of salvation is built on the idea that all people have eternal life, but only the most faithful Mormons have godhood or enter the celestial Kingdom. In order to obtain this ultimate step, Mormons must exercise faith in the God of Mormonism, its Christ, and the Church of Jesus Christ of Latter-day Saints; exercise repentance; and be baptized in the LDS church. Additionally, Mormons must keep the "Word of Wisdom" by abstaining from alcohol, tobacco, and caffeine; tithe to the church; attend weekly sacrament meetings; support the Mormon prophet; do temple works; and be active in their support of the church.

Biblical Response: Salvation, according to the Bible, is due to God's grace and love. He provided Jesus as the sacrifice for the sins of the world. It is through faith in the crucified and risen Jesus that we may be saved. Works are excluded (John 1:12; 3:16; Rom. 10:9–13; Eph. 2:8,9).

Evangelizing Mormons

- Know clearly the Christian faith and the gospel. Be aware of the unique Mormon doctrines. Remember, Mormons use Christian vocabulary (gospel, atonement, god) but radically redefine their meanings. Define clearly what you mean when you use biblical words.

- Present a clear testimony of your faith in Christ alone for your salvation. Show your Mormon friend that the Bible teaches salvation alone through the cross of Jesus Christ (John 3:16; Rom. 10:4,10–13; Eph. 2:8,9). Emphasize that salvation is a gift to be received, not a merit to be earned.

- Warn the Mormon about trusting in feelings (i.e., the burning in the bosom) for a validation of Mormonism's truth claim. Without historical, objective verification, feelings are useless.

- When Mormons use a Bible verse, read carefully the verses before and afterward to make clear the exact meaning and purpose of the passage. Don't let them take Bible verses out of context. Read carefully the full reference in the Bible before deciding what any one verse means.

- Keep the central doctrines of the faith as the focus of your discussion.

- Do the basics: pray, trust the Holy Spirit, and be loving, patient, and steadfast.

QUESTIONS

1. **How did the Mormon church originate?**

2. **What is a simple biblical response to the Mormon's claim that Joseph Smith was a prophet of God?**

3. **What is the Mormon view of the Trinity?**

4. **How does their concept of Jesus differ from the biblical teaching?**

5. **What is the goal of "salvation" for Mormons?**

6. How do they hope to achieve salvation?

7. Little about the Mormon faith can be verified historically to validate its claims. What evidence can you give, from history, archaeology, fulfilled prophecies, etc., to verify the accuracy of Christianity?

PREACHER'S PROGRESS

Ernest Fingerpointer: "The reason I'm not a Christian is that there are so many hypocrites."

Christian: "The hypocrite is like a man in a plane who pretends to be wearing a parachute when he's not. When he jumps, who do you think will be the big loser? Him, or the other passengers who have their parachutes on?"

Ernest Fingerpointer: "He will."

Christian: "When the hypocrite passes through the door of death, he will face a Law harsher than the law of gravity. He hasn't fooled God. He probably hasn't fooled his friends. The only one he has deceived is himself."

Ernest Fingerpointer: "I see what you are saying."

Christian: "So, the hypocrite—the person who pretends to be a Christian—will have to give an answer for himself, as will every person, including you."

Memory Verse

"Neither is there salvation in any other: for there is no other name under heaven given among men, whereby we must be saved."

ACTS 4:12

Last Words

François Rabelais, writer, died 1553:

"**I owe much; I have nothing; the rest I leave to the poor.**"

LESSON 85

Mormonism, Part 2

"We may deceive all the people sometimes; we may deceive some of the people all the time, but not all the people all the time, and not God at any time."

ABRAHAM LINCOLN

Kirk's Comment I used to avoid difficult conversations with Mormons because I didn't feel equipped to debate them. This lesson will help you focus on the essentials and learn how to compassionately lead Mormons to the cross.

QUESTIONS & OBJECTIONS

"It must be possible for us to reach perfection, because the Bible tells us to be perfect."

Some believe Jesus didn't really mean "perfect" in Matthew 5:48, because that would require that we be "without defect, flawless." Instead, they think He was telling us to be "mature." If that were true, then He would be saying, "Be therefore mature, even as your Father which is in heaven is mature." However, calling God "mature" implies that He was once immature. Such a thought is contrary to Scripture. God never changes (Malachi 3:6); He has always been perfect and doesn't need to mature.

Throughout the Sermon on the Mount Jesus expounded the perfect Law of a perfect Creator. God's work is perfect (Deuteronomy 32:4), His way is perfect (Psalm 18:30), and His Law is perfect (Psalm 19:7; James

1:25). Jesus then climaxes His exposition with the demand of the Law—perfection in thought, word, and deed.

In magnifying the Law and making it honorable, He put righteousness beyond the reach of sinful humanity. He destroyed the vain hope that we can get right with a perfect Creator by our own imperfect efforts, i.e., by the works of the Law.

Instead, we must seek righteousness by another means—through faith alone in the Savior (Romans 3:21,22). In doing so, Jesus was showing us the right use of the Law—as a "schoolmaster to bring us to Christ" (Galatians 3:24). This is what Jesus did with the rich young ruler. The young man asked, "Good Master, what good thing shall I do, that I may have eternal life?" (Matthew 19:16). Jesus corrected his misuse of the word "good," gave him five of the Ten Commandments, and then said, "If you will be perfect..." The young man's hope of "doing" something to be saved was dashed and he went away sorrowful. However, this is not a negative incident; it is positive when a sinner's vain hope is dashed. If he cannot find salvation "by the works of the Law," he may just seek it "by the hearing of faith" (Galatians 3:2). This is why we should use the Law when reasoning with the lost and press home its requirement of absolute perfection. (See James 2:10,11.) On hearing the demands of a perfect Law, it is not uncommon to hear a guilty sinner say, "Wow! Nobody's perfect." That's the point of the Law.

Our mission is to preach Christ and to warn sinners, "that we may present every man perfect in Christ Jesus" (Colossians 1:28).

w o t m w o t m w o t m w o t m w o t m w o t m w o t m w o t m w o t m w o t m w o t m

There are at least two approaches to use in witnessing to Mormons. We can either debate the doctrines of Mormonism (baptism for the dead, "burning" in the bosom, Joseph Smith as a prophet of God, the validity of the Book of Mormon, the Trinity, "God was once a man," "protective" underwear, etc.), or we can present the gospel biblically. One creates an atmosphere of contention and often leaves the Christian feeling frustrated, while the other creates an atmosphere of concern for the eternal welfare of the Mormon. Our goal should be to win a soul to Christ rather than merely win a doctrinal argument.

One point of frustration for the Christian is that Mormons often agree when they hear words such as "salvation," or Jesus as "Savior." The problem is that *their* understanding of the words differs from the biblical revelation of the words. "Salvation" for a Mormon can mean the salvation of all humanity—when the "Savior" will eventually raise everyone from the dead. Rather than speak of "going to heaven," the Christian should ask what the Mormon has to do to be at peace with the "heavenly Father." This is language they can understand, and will reveal the basis for their salvation. Are they trusting in self-righteousness, or solely in the righteousness of Christ?

Mark J. Cares writes: "Although Mormons commonly appear self-assured and self-righteous, many are undergoing great stress. This is because Mormonism holds up perfection as an attainable goal. The one Bible passage the Mormon church constantly holds up before its membership is Matthew 5:48: 'Be ye therefore perfect, even as your Father which is in heaven is perfect.' They then expound on it with numerous exhortations to strive for perfection. Spencer W. Kimball, for example, wrote: 'Being perfect means to triumph over sin. This is a mandate from the Lord. He is just and wise and kind. He would never require anything from his children which was not for their benefit and which was not attainable. Perfection therefore is an achievable goal' (*Life and Teachings of Jesus and His Apostles*, Church of Jesus Christ of Latter-day Saints).

"This emphasis on perfection permeates every aspect of a Mormon's life. Its most common form is the unending demand on them to be 'worthy.' Every privilege in Mormonism is conditioned on a person's worthiness. Kimball wrote: 'All blessings are conditional. I know of none that are not' (*Remember Me*, Church of Jesus Christ of Latter-day Saints).

"Christians need to recognize that this constant striving for perfection—and the resultant stress it produces—offers an excellent opening to talk to Mormons about Jesus and the imputed perfection that we receive through Him. Average hard-working Mormons view this striving for perfection as a heavy but manageable burden. They can cultivate illusions of perfection because the Mormon church has greatly watered down the concept of sin. Consequently, the Christian witness needs to show Mormons both the severity of their predicament and the impossibility of their becoming perfect. In other words, they need to have a face-to-face confrontation with the stern message of God's Law, because 'through the Law we become conscious of sin' (Romans 3:21).

"The Law must first convince Mormons of the severity of their predicament. The best way to accomplish this is to tell them, lovingly but firmly, that they are going to 'outer darkness.' (Outer darkness is the closest concept in Mormonism to an eternal hell.) Most Mormons have never been told this, nor have they ever considered that possibility for themselves, since Mormonism teaches that nearly everyone will enter one of Mormonism's three kingdoms of heaven. Therefore, until you introduce the thought of eternal suffering, they will not feel any real urgency to take your witness to heart. On the contrary, most, if they are willing to talk at all, will view any religious conversation as nothing more than an interesting intellectual discussion.

"Christians often hesitate to be this blunt. They feel that if anything will turn Mormons off, telling them that they are going to outer darkness surely will. I shared that fear when I began using this approach. To my amazement, however, rejection wasn't the reaction I received. Most have been shocked, but they were also eager to know why I would say such a thing. The key is to speak this truth *with love*, in such a way that our concern for their souls is readily apparent.

"Alerting Mormons to the very real danger of their going to outer darkness opens the door to telling them the *basis* for that judgment—which is, they are not meeting God's requirement for living with Him (they are not *presently* perfect). The key to explaining this is the present imperative, *be perfect*, in Matthew 5:48."

QUESTIONS

1. How can we avoid one point of frustration in witnessing to Mormons?

2. How can you use "perfection" as an opening to talk about Jesus?

3. How can the Law be used to help Mormons see their need for a Savior?

4. What do Mormons believe about heaven and hell?

5. Why should we not hesitate to speak about hell, or outer darkness, with Mormons?

PREACHER'S PROGRESS

Faye Kinnitt: "Hey, I'm a Christian."

Christian: "Really?"

Faye Kinnitt: "Yep. I gave my heart to the Lord a few years ago."

Christian: "Why are your friends laughing?"

Faye Kinnitt: "I dunno. I carry a Bible with me all the time. Here it is in my bag. I've had it for years."

Christian: "It looks new. Do you read it much?"

Faye Kinnitt: "Once or twice. My boyfriend and I have read it first thing in the morning."

Christian: "Do you live with him?"

Faye Kinnitt: "Yes. But we don't do anything."

Christian: "Your friends are laughing again."

Faye Kinnitt: "I don't care what they think. Sex is okay if you love someone, and I love my boyfriend."

Christian: "So you were lying to me when you said that you don't do anything."

Faye Kinnitt: "Just a small lie."

Christian: "Do you think you will go to heaven when you die?"

Faye Kinnitt: "Yes."

Christian: "Why?"

Faye Kinnitt: "Because I'm a good person."

Christian: "No, you're not. You have told me that you are a liar and a fornicator, and the Bible says that liars and fornicators will not enter the kingdom of God. It says, 'All liars will have their part in the lake of fire.'"

Faye Kinnitt: "You're trying to scare me."

Christian: "I'm only telling you the truth because I care about you. I don't want you to go to hell; neither does God. Why would I say these things if they weren't true?"

Faye Kinnitt: "I guess you wouldn't..."

Christian: "Do you know that you're a hypocrite? That's why your friends laugh at you when you say you are a Christian. If you can't fool them, you surely can't fool God. I think you need to truly repent—that means to turn from all sin—sex before marriage, lying, hypocrisy. What do you think?"

Faye Kinnitt: "I think you're right."

Words of Comfort

Memory Verse

"He was wounded for our transgressions, He was bruised for our iniquities; the chastisement for our peace was upon Him, and by His stripes we are healed. All we like sheep have gone astray; we have turned, every one, to his own way; and the Lord has laid on Him the iniquity of us all."

ISAIAH 53:5,6

The South Island of New Zealand doesn't have crows or mocking birds. For the first year or so in the U.S., we were fascinated by the different birdcalls we heard in California. One day, while out in the yard digging a hole, I stopped to listen to the variety of songs. One in particular gripped my ears. It sounded very similar to a phone ringing. I stood there captivated by the sound. It was so close to the sound of a telephone ringing that I said to myself, "I bet Californians call it a phone bird. Listen to it. It sounds exactly like a phone ringing." Suddenly it dawned on me—it *was* the phone! I missed the caller.

Last Words

Pancho Villa, Mexican revolutionary, died 1923:

> **"Don't let it end like this. Tell them I said something."**

Jehovah's Witnesses, Part 1

"Some evangelists are prepared to be anything to anybody as long as they get somebody at the altar for something."

LEONARD RAVENHILL

Kirk's Comment There are many cults that profess to be Christian, but upon closer examination, they are not in line with God's Word at all. They may initially sound good, but that's always how Satan disguises his lies. A solid knowledge of the truth is the best tool to identify lies.

QUESTIONS & OBJECTIONS

"How can you know that you are saved?"

Christians believed in God's existence before their conversion. However, when they obeyed the Word of God, turned from their sins, and embraced Jesus Christ, they stopped merely believing. In that moment, they moved out of the realm of belief into the realm of experience. This experience is so radical, Jesus referred to it as being "born again."

The Bible says that those who don't know God are spiritually dead (Ephesians 2:1; 4:18). We are born with physical life, but not spiritual life. Picture unbelievers as corpses walking around who, by repenting and placing their faith in Christ, receive His very life. There is a radical difference between a corpse and a living, breathing human, just as there is when sinners pass from spiritual death to life. The apostle Paul said if you are "in Christ," you are a brand new creature (2 Corinthians 5:17).

Those who now have God's Spirit living in them will love what He loves and desire to do His will; they will have a hunger for His Word, a love for other believers, and a burden for the lost. The Holy Spirit also confirms in their spirit that they are now children of God (Romans 8:16). Those who believe on the name of the Son of God can know that they have eternal life (1 John 5:12,13).

wotmwotmwotmwotmwotmwotmwotmwotmwotmwotmwotm

Speaking the Truth in Love to Jehovah's Witnesses

By Clint DeBoer

You've almost certainly had Jehovah's Witnesses come knocking on your door on a Saturday afternoon and you may have even engaged a Jehovah's Witness in a theological discussion. In talking to other Christians, I find that when presented with a face-to-face encounter with a Jehovah's Witness, there are usually two responses:

- A "frontal assault" via debate or heated discussion; or

- A polite "no thanks, I'm already a Christian" followed by an all too abrupt closing of the door. For the mature Christian, what's usually missing is the realization that this is a true witnessing opportunity—one that has arrived right at your doorstep.

In my earliest attempts at grabbing the proverbial bull by the horns, I tried engaging them in direct debates, often quoting from several texts I had studied regarding the cultic practices of the Jehovah's Witnesses. After several failed "conversion" attempts, often ending with thoroughly frustrated Jehovah's Witnesses unwilling to ever return to my residence, I arrived at a startling realization: Jehovah's Witnesses are real people, with real needs and real feelings. They can feel frustration, anger, fear, and confusion. I then realized that the reason my frontal assaults on the Jehovah's Witnesses never seemed to work was because I had not put myself in their place and taken their feelings into account. A wise man once said, "When you want to get someone's attention, you don't shine a flashlight in his eyes." In presenting my arguments and facts without giving them time to prepare, I had forgotten that they were human beings searching for the truth. I had not been speaking this truth in love.

Months later, when I was again presented with an opportunity to speak with Jehovah's Witnesses at my door, I engaged them in conversation, and agreed to do a weekly Bible study with them in order to further discuss what exactly they believed. They agreed, with the understanding that along the way I would ask questions whenever we arrived at a topic or subject that I disagreed with or failed to understand. The amazing difference was that instead of blindsiding them with questions and points of contention, I was giving them an opportunity to prepare themselves for a topic of discussion. More importantly, though, I began to care about them personally and yearn for their salvation. In this way, I am able to meet with Witnesses on a weekly basis and take them off the streets, focusing on critical topics such as the requirement that one be born again to enter the kingdom of God, the unbiblical theology of a two-class system of believers, and the true identity of Jesus Christ.

Jehovah's Witnesses: Witnessing Tips

By David A. Reed, Ex-Jehovah's Witness elder

Encounters between Christians and Jehovah's Witnesses (JWs) typically revolve around a discussion of deity. The reason for this is twofold. First, this is the area where Watchtower theology deviates most dramatically from orthodox Christianity. In contrast to the Trinitarian concept of one God in three Persons—Father, Son, and Holy Spirit—the JWs have been taught to believe that God the Father alone is "Jehovah," the only true God; that Jesus Christ is Michael the archangel, the first angelic being created by God; and that the Holy Spirit is neither God nor a person, but rather God's impersonal "active force."

Second, the subject of deity is a frequent confrontational focus because *both* Jehovah's Witnesses and Christians (at least those who like to witness to JWs) feel confident and well-prepared to defend their stand and attack the opposing viewpoint. Due to the profound theological differences, such discussions often take the form of spiritual trench warfare—a long series of arguments and counterarguments, getting nowhere and ending in mutual frustration. But this need not be the case, especially if the Christian will "become all things to all men" by taking a moment to put himself in the Witness's shoes, so to speak (see 1 Corinthians 9:22). In the JW's mind he himself is a worshiper of the true God of the Bible, while you are a lost soul who has been misled by the devil into worshiping a pagan three-headed deity. He is, no doubt, quite sincere in these beliefs and feels both threatened and offended by the doctrine of the Trinity. To give any serious consideration to your arguments in support of the Trinity is simply unthinkable to the JW; he would be sinning against Jehovah God to entertain such a thought. So, to make any headway with the Witness, it is necessary to bridge the gap—to find common ground that will enable him to rethink his theology.

Rather than plunging into a defense of "the doctrine of the Trinity," which can be mind-boggling even to a Christian, take things one step at a time. A good first step would be to consider the question, "Is Jesus Christ really an angel?" It will be frightening to the Jehovah's Witness to open this cherished belief of his to critical reexamination, but not nearly as frightening as to start off discussing evidence that God is triune. Since the Watchtower Society speaks of "Jesus Christ, whom we understand from the Scriptures to be Michael the archangel" (*The Watchtower*, February 15, 1979, p. 31), put the JW on the spot and ask him to show you "the Scriptures" that say Jesus is Michael. There are none.

The Watchtower Society *New World Translation* (NWT) mentions Michael five times as: 1) "one of the foremost princes" (Daniel 10:13); 2) "the prince of [Daniel's] people" (Daniel 10:21); 3) "the great prince who is standing in behalf of the sons of [Daniel's] people" (Daniel 12:1); 4) "the archangel" who "had a difference with the devil and was disputing about Moses' body" but "did not dare to bring a judgment against him in abusive terms" (Jude 9); and 5) a participant in heavenly conflict when "Michael and his angels battled with the dragon" (Revelation 12:7).

Ask the Jehovah's Witness which one of these verses says that Michael is Jesus Christ. Help him to see that it is necessary to read Scripture *plus* a complicated Watchtower argument to reach that conclusion. Rather than being merely "*one of* the foremost princes," Jesus Christ is "Lord of lords and King of kings" (Revelation 17:14, NWT) and is "far above every government and authority and power and lordship and every name named, not only in this system of things, but also in that to come" (Ephesians 1:21, NWT). And, unlike "Michael who did not dare condemn the Devil with insulting words, but said, 'The Lord rebuke you!'" (Jude 9, *Today's English Version*), Jesus Christ displayed His authority over the devil when He freely commanded him, "Go away, Satan!" (Matthew 4:10, NWT).

In arguing that Jesus is Michael the archangel, the Watchtower Society also points to another verse that does not use the name Michael but says that "the Lord himself will descend from heaven with a commanding call, with an archangel's voice and with God's trumpet..." (1 Thessalonians 4:16, NWT). However, the expression "with an archangel's voice" simply means that the archangel, like God's trumpet, will herald the coming of the Lord, not that the Lord is an archangel.

Point out to the JW that none of the verses he has attempted to use as proof-texts even comes close to stating that Jesus Christ is Michael the archangel. In fact, Scripture clearly teaches the opposite: namely, that the Son of God is *superior* to the angels. The entire first chapter of Hebrews is devoted to this theme. Have the Witness read Hebrews chapter 1 aloud with you, and, as you do so, interrupt to point out the sharp contrast between angels and the Son of God. "For to what angel did God ever say, 'Thou are my Son...?' And again, when he brings the first-born into the world, he says, 'Let all God's angels worship him'" (vv. 5,6, *Revised Standard Version*). Remind the JW that angels consistently refuse worship ("Be careful! Do not do that!... Worship God," Revelation 22:8,9, NWT), but the Father's command concerning the Son is, "Let all God's angels worship him" (Hebrews 1:6). That is how the Watchtower's own *New World Translation* read for some 20 years until, in 1970, the Society changed it to read "do obeisance to him" instead of "worship him"—part of their consistent campaign to eliminate from their Bible all references to the deity of Christ.

True, you have not yet proved the "doctrine of the Trinity" in this discussion. But you have laid a good foundation by giving the Jehovah's Witness convincing evidence that Jesus Christ is not an angel (he is now faced with the question of who Jesus really is), and you have shown that the Watchtower Society has misled him, even resorting to altering Scripture to do so. Now you are in a much better position to go on to present the gospel.

QUESTIONS

1. If Jehovah's Witnesses come to your door, how will you respond?

2. Why is having a weekly Bible study with JWs a better idea than arguing at the door?

3. How do JWs view Christians?

4. How does the JW concept of God differ from the biblical teaching?

5. What verses could you use to show Jesus' superiority to the angels?

6. What can be gained by showing that Jesus is not Michael the archangel?

WORDS OF COMFORT

Sue was out for an hour or so, so I decided to bake a chocolate cake as a surprise. Wisely, I was very careful to put in the right amount of ingredients. I did, however, add an extra half teaspoon of baking powder. That makes it rise just a little bit more.

I didn't burn the cake, and it rose to my expectations. Sometimes it's hard to stay humble. Even the frosting went on smoothly. It looked as good as a store-bought cake. However, it did smell a little strange.

When Sue arrived home, she didn't notice the smell. She was very impressed with how good it looked. I cut a slice for her and watched her face as she tasted it. Joy. It's more blessed to bake than to eat. Suddenly, she squirmed, then wanted a drink of milk real quick! She mumbled something about getting the "bitter taste" out of her mouth.

I had put baking soda in the cake, instead of baking powder.

Memory Verse

"He that believes on the Son has everlasting life: and he that believes not the Son shall not see life; but the wrath of God abides on him."

JOHN 3:36

Last Words

Dylan Thomas, poet, died 1953:

"I've had eighteen straight whiskies. I think that's the record..."

Jehovah's Witnesses, Part 2

*"Why does the Church stay indoors? They have a theology that
has dwindled into a philosophy, in which there is no thrill of faith,
no terror of doom, and no concern for souls. Unbelief has put out
the fires of passion, and worldliness garlands the altar of
sacrifice with the tawdry glitter of unreality."*

SAMUEL CHADWICK

Kirk's Comment I spoke with a Jehovah's Witness on a plane, and she
had as little knowledge of the Bible as I did before I became a Christian. She
prided herself on "knowledge," and told me that once I had more knowledge,
I'd see her point of view. Ironically, she was void of biblical understanding
and her mind was filled with the twisted teaching of this cult. Study this lesson to understand the JW's errors.

QUESTIONS & OBJECTIONS

"The Bible was written so that it would only look like Jesus fulfilled prophecy."

This would mean that the New Testament writers lied about Jesus—He
really didn't rise from the dead and all those miracles about Him are really false.

If that were the case, how would you account for the writers of the New Testament teaching about truth, love, honesty, giving, etc., all based on lies? Why would they suffer hardships like beatings, starvation, shipwreck, imprisonments, and finally execution for nothing but lies? This claim doesn't make any sense and raises more questions than it answers.

While many cult members (Muslims, Mormons, Jehovah's Witnesses) will die for their faith as well, they die for something they *believe* in, not that they have seen. But the New Testament believers died for what they *saw* and believed, not for what they believed only. That is a big difference. The NT writers died claiming that they had *seen* the risen Lord. The cult members die for what they believe, and we know that believing something doesn't make it true.

The only logical explanation is that the fulfilled prophecies really did happen. Jesus actually rose from the dead. He performed miracles and He forgave sins. He can still forgive sins now just as He did then. My sins are forgiven; are yours?

wotmwotmwotmwotmwotmwotmwotmwotmwotmwotmwotm

This lesson presents the basic doctrines of the Jehovah's Witnesses, and provides a biblical analysis and response.

Official Names: Watchtower Bible and Tract Society of New York, Inc., International Bible Students Association, Watchtower Bible and Tract Society of Pennsylvania

Founder: Charles Taze Russell (1852–1916)

Present Leader: Milton G. Henschel (b. 1918)

World and USA Headquarters: "Bethel," Brooklyn, New York

Active Participants ("Publishers"), 1999 Worldwide: 5.9 million in 234 countries; U.S.: 990,340; Canada: 111,032

Key Publications: Periodicals: *The Watchtower* (16.5 million in 120 languages), *Awake!* (16 million in 78 languages); Bible Translations: *The Kingdom Interlinear Translation of the Greek Scriptures*—1964, *The New World Translation of the Holy Scriptures* (NWT)—1984

Doctrinal Beliefs

The Bible: The Bible is considered the divinely inspired and infallible Word of God. *The New World Translation of the Holy Scriptures* (NWT) is the English Bible Version published by the Watchtower Bible and Tract Society (WBTS). The translation committee members remain anonymous. Jehovah's Witnesses regard it as the best translation because "the translators held so closely to what is in the original Bible languages" (*Reasoning*, p. 279).

    Biblical Response: The Bible is indeed the inspired, inerrant, and infallible Word of God (see 2 Tim. 3:16,17; 2 Pet. 1:20,21). The NWT, however, reflects WBTS theology, especially its bias against the deity of Jesus Christ and the historic doctrine of the Trinity. For example, John 1:1 reads "and the Word was a god" in the NWT. Nearly all other standard English Bible translations say "and the Word was God."

Jehovah Is God: The true God is not a nameless God. His name is Jehovah (Deut. 6:4; Ps. 83:18). His principal attributes are love, wisdom, justice, and power. God is a "spirit-being," invisible and eternal, but has a spiritual body and is not omnipresent (*Insight*, vol. 1, pp. 969–970). The historic Christian doctrine of the Trinity is denied. "The dogma of the Trinity is not found in the Bible, nor is it in harmony with what the Bible teaches. It grossly misrepresents the true God" (*Reasoning*, p. 424).

    Biblical Response: The Bible teaches there is only one God. He was called by several names in the Scripture. Christians acknowledge that the term "Trinity" is not found in the Bible; nonetheless, the doctrine is clearly taught in Scripture. The Bible teaches that the One God exists in the three persons of the Father, Son, and Holy Spirit (see Matt. 28:19; 1 Cor. 8:6; 12:4–6; 2 Cor. 1:21,22; 13:14; 1 Pet. 1:2).

Jesus Christ—Jehovah's First Created Being: Jesus had three periods of existence. In his pre-human existence he was called "God's 'only-begotten Son' because Jehovah created him directly. As the 'first-born of all creation,' Jesus was used by God to create all other things (Colossians 1:15; Revelation 3:14) . . . After Jehovah brought him into existence, the Word [Jesus] spent ages with God in heaven before becoming a man on earth"

(*Knowledge*, p. 39). "John 1:1 says that 'the Word' (Jesus in his pre-human existence) was with God 'in the beginning.' So the word was with Jehovah when 'the heavens and earth' were created" (*Knowledge*, p. 39). He also had the personal name Michael (the archangel) (*Insight*, vol. 2, p. 394).

"The Second Stage of Jesus' life course was here on earth. He willingly submitted as God transferred his life from heaven to the womb of a faithful Jewish virgin named Mary" (*Knowledge*, p. 40). He became the Messiah at his baptism, who was executed on a torture stake, and rose again spiritually. "Though the Bible reports on Jesus' death, he is now alive! He is a mighty reigning King! And very soon now, he will manifest his rulership over our troubled earth" (*Knowledge*, p. 41).

Biblical Response: The Bible teaches that Jesus was not created but was deity from all eternity and coequal with the Father. He came to earth in bodily form to reveal God's nature and character to mankind. He now reigns with the Father in heaven and will return some day to close the age and judge all people. The Jehovah's Witnesses NWT translation of John 1:1, Colossians 1:15, and Revelation 3:14 are biased against Jesus' deity. There is no biblical basis for identifying Jesus with Michael the archangel (see John 1:1–14; 5:17,18; 8:56–59; 10:30–33; Col. 1:15–20; 2:9).

Holy Spirit—God's Active Force: The personality and deity of the Holy Spirit is denied. Holy Spirit is not capitalized in the NWT. "With this viewpoint, it is logical to conclude that the holy spirit is the active force of God. It is not a person but is a powerful force that God causes to emanate from himself to accomplish his holy will" (*Reasoning*, p. 381).

Biblical Response: The personality of the Holy Spirit is evidenced in numerous New Testament Scriptures (see Luke 12:12; John 15:26; Acts 5:3–10; 13:2–4; 1 Cor. 12:11; Eph. 4:30; Heb. 3:7). His deity is demonstrated by His divine attributes as revealed in Scripture. The Holy Spirit convicts the lost of sin and He indwells believers at conversion and empowers them to live the Christian life (see Matt. 12:31,32; 28:19; Mark 3:29; John 14—16; Rom. 8:4,26,27; 1 Cor. 12; Eph. 2:18,19; 5:14–33).

Mankind's Sin Brought Death: God created man in his own image, but Adam and Eve willfully and deliberately disobeyed God. "In the day that our first parents ate from the tree of the knowledge of good and bad, they were sentenced by God and died from his standpoint. Then they were expelled from Paradise and began their descent into physical death" (*Knowledge*, p. 58). The spirit, or lifeforce, that God gives us at our birth departs at death. There is no conscious existence at death. "Where do the dead go? To Sheol, the common grave of mankind. Our dead loved ones are not conscious of anything. They are not suffering, and they cannot affect us in any way" (*Knowledge*, p. 83).

Biblical Response: Adam and Eve's sin indeed brought evil and death into the world. Thus, we are dead spiritually and separated from God. However, at death, believers in Christ maintain a conscious relationship with Him while awaiting the resurrection (see Matt. 22:32; Luke 16:22,23; 23:43; John 11:26; 2 Cor. 5:8; 12:2–4; Phil. 1:23,24; 1 Thes. 4:14—5:10; 2 Pet. 2:9).

Jesus Paid a Ransom Sacrifice: Due to Adam's sin, it was necessary that an atonement be made to restore what he had lost. "Only a man with perfect human life could offer up the equivalent of what Adam lost. After Adam, the only perfect man born on earth was Jesus Christ" (*Knowledge*, p. 65). "The Roman governor Pontius Pilate sentenced him to death on a torture stake. He was nailed to a wooden pole and hung there upright ...Thus, it was on Nisan 14, 33 C.E. [A.D.], that Jesus gave his life as a 'ransom in exchange for many'" (*Knowledge*, p. 66). "He slept in death for parts of three days, and then Jehovah God resurrected him to life as a mighty spirit being" (*Knowledge*, p. 68).

Biblical Response: Jesus was not just a perfect man, but also God incarnate (see Col. 2:9). Thus, His death on a Roman cross was the self-sacrificial atonement of God Himself for mankind's sin (see 1 Cor. 1:17–24; 2:2; 15:3,4). He rose again from the dead physically, not just spiritually (see Luke 24:14–39; John 2:19–21; 20:26–29; 1 Cor. 15:18).

Salvation—Faith and Obedience: "Therefore, let us show our gratitude for the love displayed by God and Christ by exercising faith in Jesus' ransom sacrifice" (*Knowledge*, p. 69). Requirements for salvation, in addition to faith, include baptism by immersion, active association with the WBTS, righteous conduct, and absolute loyalty to Jehovah. There is no assurance of salvation, only hope for a resurrection. Those who fail to live up to the above requirements or who are disfellowshiped by the WBTS have no hope of salvation.

Biblical Response: Salvation is "by grace through faith" in Jesus Christ alone. No amount of works or membership in any organization guarantees salvation. It is totally through faith in Christ (see Rom. 4:4,5; Eph. 2:8,9; Titus 3:5). Good works are the natural response to salvation already received, not its cause (see Eph. 2:10). Salvation is eternally assured for those who have accepted Christ as Lord and Savior (see John 1:12; 5:24; 1 John 5:13).

Two Classes of Saved People: Only 144,000 faithful elect Jehovah's Witnesses, known as the "Anointed Class," will go to heaven at death to rule with Jesus. Only those born since 33 C.E. (A.D.) can be part of that number (based on Rev. 14:1–3). Most Jehovah's Witnesses hope to be among the "other sheep" or "great crowd" who will not go to heaven, but, after Armageddon and the millennium, will live forever in Paradise on Earth (based on John 10:16; Rev. 7:9).

Biblical Response: The WBTS' doctrine of a duality of saved people is not supported by a careful study of the Scriptures. The Bible makes no distinction of two classes of saved people (see Matt. 5:12; Phil. 3:20). In Revelation 7 and 14, both the 144,000 and the "great crowd" or "multitude" are "before the throne" in heaven. All born-again Christians will live forever in heaven (see John 3:16; 14:3).

Final Judgment and Paradise on Earth: After the millennium, Satan and his allies will be destroyed. Faithful Jehovah's Witnesses will inherit everlasting life on perfect Paradise Earth. Those who have disobeyed Jehovah and his law will be annihilated out of existence with Satan and his demons. This is the "second death." Hell is the grave and not a place of eternal punishment. The doctrine of eternal hell is regarded as unscriptural, unreasonable, contrary to God's love, and unjust.

Biblical Response: All people will face the final judgment of God. The doctrine of eternal hell is based on a number of biblical texts and the teachings of Jesus Himself. He taught that righteous saved people will have eternal life in heaven but the wicked lost will suffer eternal punishment in hell (see Matt. 18:8,9; 25:41–46; Mark 9:43–48; 2 Thes. 1:9).

Witnessing to Jehovah's Witnesses

- Have a clear understanding of your faith and the Bible.

- Make a definite plan for the witnessing encounter and keep the initiative.

- Be prepared to cite and explain specific biblical passages supporting Christian doctrines.

- Define your terms clearly and ask the Jehovah's Witness to do so also.

- Focus the discussion on the primary issue of the person and work of Christ. Stress the need for a personal relationship with Him.

- Share your personal testimony of God's grace and your faith in Jesus as Savior and Lord.

- Present the basic plan of salvation and encourage the Jehovah's Witness to make a decision.

- Pray and trust the Holy Spirit to lead you.

Tal Davis, © 1998 North American Mission Board of the Southern Baptist Convention, Alpharetta, Ga. All rights reserved.

QUESTIONS

1. **How does the Jehovah's Witnesses' official Bible translation affect their beliefs about God?**

2. **What is their belief about God?**

3. Explain what JWs view as Jesus' three periods of existence.

4. How does the JW's concept of what happens at death contrast with the biblical view?

5. According to JWs, what are the requirements for salvation?

Memory Verse

"Marvel not at this: for the hour is coming, in the which all that are in the graves shall hear his voice, and shall come forth; they that have done good, to the resurrection of life; and they that have done evil, to the resurrection of damnation."
JOHN 5:28,29

WORDS OF COMFORT

Sometimes it's not easy to know how to do good within a society. I remember seeing a sexually explicit magazine cover in a store right at the eye-level of children, so I decided to show my protest by turning the publication over. It would prevent it from being seen by kids, and would send a message to the management that some people don't like sexually explicit pictures displayed in public. I would have to be quick, though. If someone saw me touching it and knew I was a Christian, it would look bad. So, with great speed, I grabbed the filthy magazine and turned it over.

As I went to make a quick exit, I looked back and saw to my horror that the back cover was far worse than the front!

I crept back, turned it over, and made a quick and heated exit.

Last Words

Sir Walter Raleigh, at his execution:

"So the heart be right, it is no matter which way the head lieth."

LESSON 88

Catholicism

"If your sorrow is because of certain consequences which have come on your family because of your sin, this is remorse, not true repentance. If, on the other hand, you are grieved because you also sinned against God and His holy laws, then you are on the right road."

BILLY GRAHAM

Kirk's Comment   Catholicism is tricky; it sounds so similar to Christianity, but it is not. Many Catholics don't understand why they are not Christians because they have not taken the time to understand what God's Word says. Study this lesson carefully and remember to always season your evangelistic words with grace and compassion.

QUESTIONS & OBJECTIONS

"How should I witness to someone who belongs to a denomination, who I suspect isn't trusting the Savior?"

The most effective way to speak about the issues of eternity to a religious person is not to get sidetracked from the essentials of salvation. Upon hearing a person's background, we may feel an obligation to speak to issues such as infant baptism, transubstantiation, etc. However, it is wise rather to build on the points of agreement between the Bible and the person's denomination, such as the virgin birth, the cross, and so on.

One point of agreement will almost certainly be the Ten Commandments. They are the key to bringing any religious person to a saving knowledge of the gospel. After someone is converted to Jesus Christ, the Bible will come alive and he will be led into all truth by the indwelling Holy Spirit. God's Word will then give him light, and he will forsake religious tradition as he is led by God.

While there are strong biblical arguments that may convince unregenerate people that their church's traditions contradict Holy Scripture, there is a difficulty. Some religious people hold the teachings of their church to be on a par with, or of greater authority than, Holy Scripture. It is therefore often futile to try to convince them intellectually that their trust should be in the person of Jesus Christ, rather than in their own righteousness or in their church traditions. For this reason we should aim at the conscience, rather than the intellect. Take sinners through the Law of God (the Commandments) to show them that they are condemned despite their works, and strongly emphasize that we are saved by grace, and grace alone, rather than by trusting in our own righteousness or religious traditions.

If they are open to the gospel, and are interested in what God's Word says in reference to their church's teachings, they will listen to Scripture. For example, in Matthew 8:14 we see that Peter (whom the Roman Catholic church maintains was the first pope) was married, as were many of the other apostles (see 1 Corinthians 9:5).

wotmwotmwotmwotmwotmwotmwotmwotmwotmwotmwotm

Earning Your Justification

By Matthew J. Slick

Justification is a divine act where God declares the sinner to be innocent of his sins. It is a legal action in that God declares the sinner righteous—as though he has satisfied the Law of God. This justification is based entirely on the sacrifice of Christ by His shed blood: "...having now been justified by His blood..." (Rom. 5:9). Justification is a gift of grace (Rom. 3:24; Titus 3:7) that comes through faith (Rom. 3:28; 5:1). Christians receive Jesus (John 1:12) and put their faith-filled trust in what

Jesus did on the cross (Isaiah 53:12; 1 Pet. 2:24), and in so doing are justified by God. The Bible states that justification is not by works (Rom. 3:20, 28; 4:5; Eph. 2:8,9) because our righteous deeds are filthy rags before God (Isaiah 64:6). Therefore, we are saved by grace alone, through faith alone, in Christ alone.

Those who are justified are saved and salvation is a free gift (Rom. 6:23), something we cannot earn (Eph. 2:1–10). However, Roman Catholic doctrine denies justification by faith alone and says: "If any one saith, that by faith alone the impious is justified; in such wise as to mean, that nothing else is required to co-operate in order to the obtaining the grace of Justification, and that it is not in any way necessary, that he be prepared and disposed by the movement of his own will; let him be anathema" (Council of Trent, *Canons on Justification*, Canon 9).

Anathema, according to Catholic theology, means excommunication, "the exclusion of a sinner from the society of the faithful." Roman Catholic theology therefore pronounces a curse of excommunication, of being outside the camp of Christ, if you believe that you are saved by grace through faith alone in Jesus.

Does the Roman Catholic church specifically state that we are "saved by grace and works"? Not that I am aware of. But, when the Roman Catholic church negates justification by faith alone, it necessarily implies that we must do something for justification, for if it is not by faith alone, then it must be by faith and something.

At this point many Catholics appeal to James 2:24, which says, "You see that a man is justified by works, and not by faith alone." But the context of James is speaking of dead faith as opposed to living, saving faith. James states that if you "say" you have faith but have no works (James 2:14), that faith cannot save you because it is a dead faith (v. 17). In other words, mere intellectual acknowledgment of Christ is a dead faith that produces no regeneration and no change in a person's life. This faith does not justify. Rather, it is only that real and believing faith in Christ that results in justification. Someone who is truly justified is saved and regenerated, and the results of true saving faith are manifested in the changed life of the one justified by faith alone. Real faith produces good works, but it isn't these works that save you. Good works are the *effect* of salvation, not the cause of it in any way and they certainly do not help anyone keep their salvation.

The Bible maintains that justification is not by works in any way but is by grace through faith in Christ and His sacrifice alone. The Bible says, "If you confess with your mouth Jesus as Lord, and believe in your heart that God raised Him from the dead, you shall be saved" (Rom. 10:9). Furthermore, the Bible states explicitly: "For by grace are you saved through faith; and that not of yourselves: it is the gift of God: Not of works, lest any man should boast" (Eph. 2:8,9).

Catholicism teaches that certain things must be done by people in order to be justified and to keep that justification. Of these acts, baptism is the first requirement. Consider these quotes:

> Baptism is the first and chief sacrament of forgiveness of sins because it unites us with Christ, who died for our sins and rose for our justification, so that "we too might walk in newness of life" (*Catechism of the Catholic Church*, par. 977).

> Justification has been merited for us by the Passion of Christ. It is granted to us through Baptism. It conforms us to the righteousness of God, who justifies us. It has for its goal the glory of God and of Christ, and the gift of eternal life. It is the most excellent work of God's mercy (*CCC*, par. 2020).

I do not see the Bible saying anywhere that we are justified by baptism. This would contradict the clear teaching of Rom. 3:20,28; 4:3; 5:1; and Eph. 2:8, which says salvation is by grace through faith, not grace through faith and baptism. However, according to Roman Catholicism, baptism is only the *first* sacrament of forgiveness. Good works, according to Roman Catholicism, are also required and are rewarded with going to heaven:

> We can therefore hope in the glory of heaven promised by God to those who love him and do his will. In every circumstance, each one of us should hope, with the grace of God, to persevere 'to the end' and to obtain the joy of heaven, as God's eternal reward for the good works accomplished with the grace of Christ (*CCC*, par. 1821).

The above quote clearly states that heaven is the "eternal reward for the good works accomplished with the grace of Christ." Catholic theology asserts that works are a predecessor to justification in direct contradiction to God's Word which states that "a man is justified by faith without the deeds of the law" (Rom. 3:28). What are the deeds of the Law? Anything we do in hopes of getting or maintaining our righteousness before God.

In the *CCC*, par. 2010, it says, "Moved by the Holy Spirit and by charity, we can then merit for ourselves and for others the graces needed for our sanctification." How does anyone merit for himself the undeserved kindness of God's grace? Grace is by definition unmerited favor. This is an utterly false teaching. So how does the Catholic church get around this apparent dilemma that grace is unmerited but it is obtained through our merits? It states, "Sanctifying grace is the gratuitous gift of his life that God makes to us; it is infused by the Holy Spirit into the soul to heal it of sin and to sanctify it" (*CCC*, par. 2023).

This is the crux of the problem. Roman Catholic theology asserts that God's grace is granted through baptism and infused into a person by the Holy Spirit. This then enables him or her to do good works which then are rewarded with heaven. Basically, this is no different from the theology of the cults which maintain that justification is by grace through faith and your works, whether it be baptism, going to "the true church," keeping certain laws, receiving the sacraments, or anything else you are required to do. In response, I turn to God's Word at Galatians 3:1–3:

> You foolish Galatians, who has bewitched you, before whose eyes Jesus Christ was publicly portrayed as crucified? This is the only thing I want to find out from you: did you receive the Spirit by the works of the Law, or by hearing with faith? Are you so foolish? Having begun by the Spirit, are you now being perfected by the flesh?

Does not the above Scripture clearly state that receiving God's Spirit is by faith and not by what we do? Does it not teach us that we cannot perfect our salvation by the works we do in the flesh? To receive Jesus (John 1:12) means to become the temple of the Holy Spirit (1 Cor. 6:19), which means a person is saved, justified. Is this salvation something we attained through our effort? Of course not! Is it something we maintain through our effort? Not at all. It is given to Christians by God and assured by God because it rests in what God has done and not in anything we have done—that is why salvation is by faith and not works. If it did rest in any way in our works, then our salvation could not be secure and we would end up trying to be good enough to get to heaven. That only leads to bondage to the Law and the result is a lack of assurance of salvation, a constant worry of not being good enough, and a repeated subjection to the church's teachings and requirements about what one must do to be saved. The only natural effect of such a teaching would be that you can lose your salvation over and over again and that you must perform the necessary requirements of the Catholic church to stay saved.

Maintaining Your Justification

Because the Catholic view of justification is a cooperative effort between God and man, this justification can be lost by man's failure to maintain sufficient grace through meritorious works. Roman Catholicism teaches that works are necessary for "re-attainment" of justification. According to Catholic theology, penance is a sacrament where a person, through a Catholic priest (*CCC*, par. 987), receives forgiveness of the sins committed after baptism. The penitent person must confess his sins to a priest. The priest pronounces absolution and imposes acts of penance to be performed.

> Christ instituted the sacrament of Penance for all sinful members of his Church: above all for those who, since Baptism, have fallen into grave sin, and have thus lost their baptismal grace and wounded ecclesial communion. It is to them that the sacrament of Penance offers a new possibility to convert and to recover the grace of justification. The Fathers of the Church present this sacrament as 'the second plank (of salvation) after the shipwreck which is the loss of grace' (*CCC*, par. 1446).

Acts of penance vary, but some of them are prayer, saying the rosary, reading the Scripture, saying a number of "Our Father" or "Hail Mary" prayers, doing good works, fasting, and other such things. Is it by doing these acts of penance that the Catholic is able to regain his justified state before God? In essence it is earning one's salvation. Think about it. If you do not have it and you get it by saying prayers, fasting, and/or doing good works, then you are guilty of works righteousness salvation, which is condemned by the Bible.

I confess my sins to God. He forgives me (1 John 1:9). I do not need a Catholic priest to be my mediator of forgiveness. I need the true High Priest, Jesus, who alone is my Mediator (1 Tim. 2:5). He has all authority in heaven and earth (Matt. 28:18) to forgive my sins and intercede for me. He finished the work on the cross (John 19:30) so that I do not need to perform any work in order to gain, maintain, or regain my salvation. That is why the Bible teaches that we are justified by faith (Rom. 5:1) apart from works (Rom. 3:28).

To say that we can add to the finished work of Christ on the cross is to say that what He did was not sufficient to save us. May this never be! We are saved by grace through faith, not grace through faith and our works: "But if it is by grace, it is no longer on the basis of works, otherwise grace is no longer grace" (Rom. 11:6).

God desires fellowship with His people (1 Cor. 1:9), not rituals and works righteousness that cannot save us. May God receive all the glory due Him because of His grace.

Adapted from an article by the Christian Apologetics and Research Ministry (www.carm.org).

QUESTIONS

1. **What is the biblical definition of justification?**

2. According to the Bible, how is justification accomplished?

3. How does the Roman Catholic teaching differ from the biblical view?

4. On what is the Catholic's hope of heaven based?

5. What is the result of trying to earn salvation by works?

6. Is there any biblical basis for the concept of penance?

PREACHER'S PROGRESS

Christian: "How are you doing?"

Dale E. Bread: "Good."

Christian: "Did you get one of these?"

Dale E. Bread: "One of what?"

Christian: "It's a gospel tract."

Dale E. Bread: "I'm only worried about this life—not some pie in the sky stuff."

Christian: "Don't you ever think about death and what happens after you die?"

Dale E. Bread: "I've given it some thought. I've come to the conclusion that when you're dead, you're dead. So all that really concerns me is this day."

Christian: "You really believe that there's no afterlife?"

Dale E. Bread: "I do."

Christian: "If I could give you some evidence to prove otherwise, would you be interested?"

Dale E. Bread: "I guess so. I'm not closed-minded about the subject."

Christian: "Do you believe God exists?"

Dale E. Bread: "Of course."

Christian: "Do you think that He has a sense of right and wrong?"

Dale E. Bread: "Definitely."

Christian: "Let's consider the life of Adolph Hitler. Do you think God should punish him for taking the lives of six million Jews?"

Dale E. Bread: "It would only be right that such a man was punished."

Christian: "Well, God's place of punishment for the wicked is called hell."

Dale E. Bread: "Okay, so evil people are punished. What happens to the rest of us? Like I said, I believe that when you're dead, you're dead."

Christian: "So you concede that evil people will stand before God on Judgment Day and receive what they justly deserve, while good people stay dead."

Dale E. Bread: "That makes sense to me . . . I guess."

Christian: "Which category do you think you are in—good or evil?"

Dale E. Bread: "Good, of course."

Christian: "What's your definition of 'good'?"

Dale E. Bread: "Always doing what's right, I suppose."

Christian: "So you always do what's right."

Dale E. Bread: "Yes."

Christian: "Have you ever told a lie?" (Etc.)

Last Words

Lord George Lyttleton, who died in 1773, was a British statesman who was not ashamed to own his Savior's name and define His cause:

"The evidence of Christianity, studied with attention, made me a firm believer of the Christian religion. I have erred and sinned, but have repented."

Memory Verse

"Therefore being justified by faith, we have peace with God through our Lord Jesus Christ: by whom also we have access by faith into this grace wherein we stand, and rejoice in hope of the glory of God."

ROMANS 5:1,2

89

Oneness Pentecostals

"The gospel has not been clearly preached if the hearer doesn't know that not to make a decision is a decision."

DAN ARNOLD

Kirk's Comment Again, the more you know the truth, the easier it is to spot a lie. If you've ever dealt with Oneness Pentecostals, this lesson will be very helpful.

QUESTIONS & OBJECTIONS

"Why are there so many denominations?"

In the early 1500s, a German monk named Martin Luther was so conscious of his sins that he spent up to six hours in the confessional. Through study of the Scriptures he found that salvation didn't come through anything he did, but simply through trusting in the finished work of the cross of Jesus Christ. He listed the contradictions between what the Scriptures said and what his church taught, and nailed his "95 Theses" to the church door in Wittenberg, Germany.

Martin Luther became the first to "protest" against the Roman church, and thus he became the father of the Protestant church. Since that split, there have been many disagreements about how much water one should baptize with, how to sing what and why, who should govern who, etc., causing thousands of splinter groups. Many of these groups are convinced that they are the only ones who are right. These groups have become known as Protestant "denominations." Despite the confusion, these churches subscribe to certain foundational beliefs such as the deity, death, burial, and resurrection of Jesus Christ. The Bible says, "The foundation of God stands sure, having this seal, The Lord knows them that are his" (2 Timothy 2:19).

wotmwotmwotmwotmwotmwotmwotmwotmwotmwotmwotm

By Gregory A. Boyd

The most problematic aspect of my theology when I was a Oneness Pentecostal was the belief that no one other than us Oneness Pentecostals was going to heaven. Trinitarian Christians simply were not saved! So every time I met Trinitarian Christians who clearly reflected the loving presence of Jesus in their lives by the way they related to me, I confronted more strong evidence that my theology could not be true.

A second vitally important component of witnessing to Oneness Pentecostals is to confront their misunderstandings of what Trinitarians believe. Like most Oneness Pentecostals, I was firmly convinced that Trinitarians worshiped three separate gods and that they didn't "really" believe that Jesus Christ was Himself the Lord God Almighty. This is how Oneness Pentecostals are indoctrinated to perceive Trinitarians. Hence, when dialoguing with Oneness Pentecostals, it is vitally important to be utterly emphatic about your own belief that there is *only one God*—not three—and that Jesus Christ is *the incarnation of this one God!*

If need be, explain to them that the Trinitarian creedal language about God existing in "three persons" does not literally mean that there are three "people" who are God. Rather, it is simply a shorthand way of saying that God eternally exists in three personally distinct ways. (Who would deny that God is *capable* of that?)

Most importantly, emphasize as strongly as possible that Jesus Christ is the very center of your faith and life. Oneness Pentecostals honestly believe that *they* are the only ones for whom this is true. When I was a Oneness Pentecostal and was first confronted by some informed Trinitarians who successfully conveyed this to me, it effectively loosened the grip that my elitist theology had on me.

The third important ingredient in a witness to Oneness Pentecostals is confronting their theology on its weakest points. Like other authoritarian doctrinal systems, Oneness Pentecostal theology pretty much stands or falls as a whole in the minds of its followers. If you can show it to be in error at all, even on a peripheral point, you have gone a long way toward undermining their trust in the entire doctrinal system, which holds them in bondage.

Among the erroneous beliefs that Oneness Pentecostals hold, four are especially weak and open to effective refutation: 1) their belief that tongues is the necessary sign of salvation; 2) their denial of the pre-existence of Christ; 3) their belief that Jesus was Himself the Father; and 4) their belief that baptism "in Jesus' name" is necessary for salvation.

Oneness Pentecostals believe that unless one has spoken in tongues, one does not *have* the Holy Spirit (not just the *fullness* of the Holy Spirit, as certain other Pentecostals hold). And, since a person cannot be saved without the Holy Spirit (Rom. 8:9), it follows that only those who have spoken in tongues are truly saved. This belief is (loosely) based on the fact that speaking in tongues is mentioned in three of the four accounts of people receiving the Holy Spirit in the Book of Acts (2:4; 10:46; 19:6). What follows are some of the considerations which were most effective in changing my views on this matter and which I have in turn found effective in helping other Oneness Pentecostals out of their misguided theology.

1. The Oneness Pentecostal position frequently results in sincere believers "seeking for the Holy Ghost" for days, weeks, and even years (I've seen some die yet seeking!). These poor souls are literally begging God to save them. The reason they do not receive the Holy Spirit, and hence salvation, is presumably because they lack sufficient faith, or they have unacknowledged sin in their lives. In a loving way, ask Oneness Pentecostals if they have ever wondered why there is no biblical precedent for this sad phenomenon. (I assure you, they have!)

Why is salvation so "easy" in the Bible? And if sinners must first believe "sufficiently" and cleanse themselves "sufficiently" in order to receive (as a reward?) the Holy Spirit, why does the New Testament portray faith and sanctification as the *result*, not the basis, of receiving the Holy Spirit (1 Cor. 12:3; Rom. 15:16; 2 Thes. 2:13)?

2. The "tongues" doctrine of Oneness Pentecostalism is a doctrine based entirely on a historical record, not on an explicit teaching. Explain to your Oneness friend that by all recognized scholarly standards, this constitutes very unsound hermeneutics (Bible interpretation). One can no more base a doctrine about the necessity of tongues on a historical report about tongues than one can base a doctrine about the necessity of communal sharing of property in the church on Luke's historical report about it in the early church (Acts 4:32–37). To say *that* something occurred is very different from saying that this something *should always* occur. Luke tells us the former but not the latter. His purpose is simply to provide an "orderly account" of what happened in the early church so that Theophilus, his reader, will be convinced of the truth of the Gospel message (Luke 1:1–4). This is very different from teaching doctrine.

Ask the Oneness Pentecostal why—if it is in fact so clearly taught in the Bible that salvation itself hangs on believing it—no one throughout church history has ever arrived at the Oneness Pentecostal position on tongues until the twentieth century?

3. If your Oneness Pentecostal friend maintains that Acts is a blueprint for all church history, ask him to show you where in Acts does one find *individuals seeking* for the Holy Spirit and *expecting to receive tongues* as the sign that He's come? This is the standard way the "baptism of the Spirit" occurs among Oneness Pentecostals, but it has no parallel in Acts. In Acts, the Holy Spirit always falls on entire groups who are not expecting tongues (or any other sign). So the Oneness Pentecostals do not even follow their own (misguided) hermeneutic. This insight was a wound to my pride as a Oneness Pentecostal, for the belief that "we alone do it *just like the Bible says*" is the essence of the Oneness Pentecostal position.

Unlike orthodox Christianity, members of the United Pentecostal Church and other Oneness groups do not believe that Jesus existed as the Son of God from all eternity. Since they deny that there are three eternal persons in the Godhead, the only sense in which Jesus could have existed prior to His human birth in Bethlehem is either as God the Father or as an idea in the Father's mind (as an aspect of God's foreknowledge).

This position is central to Oneness theology, but it is easily refuted by pointing out to Oneness believers that there are many places in Scripture that clearly speak of Jesus as existing *with* (not *as*) God the Father prior to His earthly existence, and *not* as a mere idea in God's mind! For example, John 1:1 explicitly identifies "the Word" (Jesus Christ, v. 14) who is God and who from eternity was *with* God. This could not refer to a mere idea in God's mind since the Word *is* God (and God is certainly no mere idea). Moreover, the same one who was "in the beginning" and who is Creator (can a mere idea create?) is said to have come to His own world and to have been rejected by it—an unambiguous reference to the *real* Jesus Christ (vv. 10–14).

In this same context we find John the Baptist referring to Christ's real preexistence (John 1:15,31), as well as Jesus Himself making reference to the same thing. Jesus notes how He shall ascend to the Father where He was "before" (6:62). He says, numerous times, that He has "come forth" from the Father, is "going back" to the Father, has "come down from heaven" and "come into the world"—all statements that clearly presuppose He *really* existed with the Father prior to His earthly birth (John 1:15,31; 3:13,31; 6:33,38,41,46,51,57,58,62; 8:42; 13:3; 16:27,28).

In conjunction with these verses, one should lead the Oneness believer through a careful reading of such passages as Colossians 1:16,17, 1 Corinthians 8:6, and Hebrews 1:2–10, which clearly speak of Jesus as the Son of God creating the world. From my own experience as a Oneness believer, I can assure you that these verses are extremely troublesome to the Oneness position.

The most forceful response to the Oneness claim that Jesus is the Father as well as the Son is to simply point out how contrary this belief is to the general teaching of the New Testament. Help your Oneness friend to see that, while Jesus is never once explicitly called "Father" in the New Testament, He is explicitly referred to as "the Son" (of God, of man, etc.) over 200 times. What is more, the Father is referred to as distinct from Jesus the Son throughout the New Testament over 200 times. And over 50 times, Jesus the Son and the Father are put side by side within the same verse. Ask your Oneness friend why there is this overwhelming (indeed, unanimous) emphasis on Jesus being the Son of God and being distinct from the Father if in fact Scripture also wants to teach us that Jesus is *Himself* the Father? Why is Scripture so clear on the first point and yet so silent on the second?

It is also helpful to point out to a Oneness believer why the arguments they have for the "Fatherhood" of Jesus simply do not hold water. Oneness believers have splendid arguments for the deity of Christ, and this they believe also proves that Jesus is the Father. Reassure your Oneness friends that you fully accept the position that Jesus is Himself God Almighty, but remind them that this does not itself prove that He is therefore God the Father. What is more, the verses that Oneness believers misuse to demonstrate that Christ is the Father simply speak either of His parental ("fatherly") love (Isa. 9:6; John 14:18), or of Christ's unity with the Father, not His identity as the Father (e.g., John 10:30; 14:7–9).

4. The Oneness belief that baptism must be "in Jesus' name for the remission of sins" can be refuted by four brief considerations. First, at least 60 times the New Testament speaks of salvation by faith alone without mentioning baptism. If baptism is in fact necessary for salvation, why is there this emphasis on faith for salvation but not on baptism in Scripture? Second, the phrase "for the remission of sins," used by Peter in Acts 2:38, is also used to describe John the Baptist's baptism (Luke 3:3; Mark 1:4), but no one supposes that his baptism literally washed away people's sins. (Why would they need to later be rebaptized? Cf. Acts 19:1–6.) The word "for" in the Greek (*eis*) need only mean "with a view toward," for we know that the Jews baptized people "for" such things as "freedom," "God's justice," etc.

Third, the Oneness insistence that the words "in Jesus' name" have to be said over a person while he or she is being baptized is also without scriptural justification. When this phrase is used in Acts (e.g., 10:45–48), it only means "in the authority of" or "for the sake of." It is not a formula (which is why it never occurs the exact same way twice in Acts). We are commanded to do all things "in the name of Jesus," but this obviously does not mean we have to say "in Jesus' name" before we do anything (Col. 3:17). Again, the Jews baptized people "in the name of" many things (Mt. Gerizim, a rabbi, etc.), but they placed no significance on saying these words while performing the ceremony.

Finally, Jesus tells us to baptize "in the name of the Father, and of the Son, and of the Holy Spirit" (Matt. 28:19), and there is simply no reason to think that Jesus was here cryptically referring to Himself. The fact that next to no one throughout history has understood Jesus to be doing this itself shows that either the Oneness interpretation is wrong, or Jesus is a very poor communicator (and on a point which supposedly affects our salvation!).

It was arguments such as these that led me out of Oneness Pentecostalism, and—when combined with a loving, nondefensive approach—I have found them to be very effective in helping other Oneness believers as well.

For more information on Oneness Pentecostals contact Christian Research Institute (CRI), P.O. Box 7000, Rancho Santa Margarita, CA 92688; www.equip.org; (949) 858-6100.

QUESTIONS

1. **How do Oneness Pentecostals view Trinitarian Christians?**

2. **What Scripture supports the Oneness Pentecostals' belief that one must speak in tongues to be truly saved?**

3. **Identify at least one verse that clearly teaches that Jesus preexisted with the Father from all eternity.**

4. **What forceful response could you give to the claim that Jesus is the Father as well as the Son?**

5. **What is the biblical argument against baptism "in Jesus' name" as a requirement for salvation?**

WORDS OF COMFORT

We were meeting my daughter and her husband for dinner at an outdoor restaurant. They had already arrived and were sitting at their table. I noticed them over a flower-covered fence, and saw that my son-in-law had his back to me. Suddenly I did something very out-of-character for me. I picked up a small pebble and gently tossed it over the fence. It would softly land on him, he would swing around and see me, and perhaps give me a friendly smile. Men often show their affection with a punch to the shoulder, a slap on the back, . . . a rock on the head, etc.

As life goes on, I find that my throwing arm lacks the strength it once had. It also lacks the accuracy. I threw the stone too high and it landed on a large patio umbrella, rolled down, and landed on a middle-aged couple's table, then (according to my embarrassed daughter, who looked the other way), it fell into the man's lap.

My son thinks I should wear a wrist-leash.

Last Words

William Ceiller, eminent British physician and medical lecturer, said as he died:

> **"I wish I had the power of writing; I would describe how pleasant it is to die."**

LESSON 90

International Church of Christ

"The number one reason people don't share their faith is that their walk doesn't match their talk."

MARK CAHILL

Kirk's Comment I find it confusing and frustrating when trying to unravel the lies of some cults. An honest study of this particular cult will be beneficial. As always, remember to use the Word of God as your standard of truth when you speak to a cult member.

QUESTIONS & OBJECTIONS

"How should I witness to my coworkers?"

When we interact with people on a daily basis, we have many opportunities for sharing our faith.

First, be sure you are respectful to your employer and set a good example in your work ethic by working "as to the Lord" (Colossians 3:23). When others around you grumble and complain, if you have a calm, forgiving, steadfast spirit, it will make an impression. As you respond in a Christlike way to angry coworkers and stressful circumstances, people will see a difference in your life.

Always be friendly and courteous, and show genuine interest in your coworkers' lives. Invite them out to lunch to get better acquainted. Share their joys and sorrows by congratulating them in their good times and offering to pray for them in their bad times. Be sure you do pray for them, then follow up by asking them about the situation you prayed for. They will be moved by your concern.

If coworkers are discussing what they did during the previous weekend, you can share your excitement about attending church services or a special church event. Ask others if they have any plans for celebrating Easter or Christmas; be nonjudgmental of their answer, but be ready (if asked) to explain why you celebrate as you do. Displaying a favorite Scripture or a devotional calendar, or reading your Bible during lunchtime, may prompt others to inquire about your faith.

Bringing home-baked goods or leaving a small gift with a note on a coworker's desk can sometimes have a greater impact than a thousand eloquent sermons. We can show our faith by our works. Others may not like a tree of righteousness, but they cannot help but like its fruit. Pray for opportunities to share the gospel, being careful not to infringe on your employer's time.

w o t m w o t m w o t m w o t m w o t m w o t m w o t m w o t m w o t m w o t m

Witnessing to Disciples of the International Churches of Christ

By Joanne Ruhland

Initially, members of the International Churches of Christ (ICC; also known as the Boston movement, the Boston Church of Christ, etc.) might resemble Christians who are excited about serving the Lord. They sound evangelical and they claim the Bible is their only source for doctrine. Such similarities are superficial. ICC disciples (their terminology) are members of one of the fastest growing heretical movements in the world.

Why classify this seemingly Bible-based organization as heretical? To warrant this designation, a sect must deny one or more of the cardinal tenets of the historic Christian faith. Among ICC's doctrinal deviations are a works-oriented plan of salvation that is related to a faulty understanding of grace and the rejection of the doctrine of original sin.

While purporting to believe in salvation by grace through faith (Eph. 2:8,9) in Jesus Christ, in actuality, certain sequential acts have been added as prerequisites for salvation. One must become a disciple, which by ICC definition includes changing one's lifestyle to conform with the movement's standards for Christians, and be baptized. With these additions ICC departs from the gospel of grace, which is the sufficiency of Christ's redemptive work for all who believe (1 Cor. 15:1–4; John 3:16; Eph. 2:8,9), and enters the realm of the cults.

Kip McKean, the leader of the movement, explains ICC's beliefs regarding salvation: "When you preach who is really saved—that you gotta have faith, you gotta repent, you gotta become a *true disciple* of Jesus, and then you gotta be water immersed for the forgiveness of sins received through the Holy Spirit—that excludes all other denominations...everybody else that's out there." The first two requirements are orthodox. The latter two, as *conditions* of salvation rather than as *results* of it, are works.

ICC's aberration from orthodoxy in its distinctive doctrine of salvation is emphasized by Nick Young, lead evangelist for the ICC congregation in Dallas-Ft. Worth:

> Once you become a disciple, then you can be baptized, but you cannot be baptized until you become a disciple. And that's where, as far as I know, the rest of the entire religious world got it all messed up. I don't know of any religious group in this world that teaches you gotta be a disciple to be baptized, and yet that is what Jesus said two thousand years ago. And it's as clear as any verse in the Bible. That's as clear as John 3:16. That's as clear as Acts 2:38. That's as clear as any verse you're gonna read, and yet I don't know of any other religious group that teaches you gotta be a *totally committed disciple* of Jesus to get baptized into Christ (emphasis added).

To become a disciple, the prospective convert must complete some or all of a series of studies with one or more ICC members, agree to attend all services, promise to read the Bible daily, begin recruiting others, agree to obey the church leaders, and give tithes weekly. Also, the individual must list all the sins he or she has ever committed, confess these sins to one or more members, and be "cut to the heart" by the severity of Christ's death on the cross as atonement for our sins.

After meeting all prerequisites, the prospective member's eligibility for salvation then depends on the leadership determining if the candidate is ready for baptism. Ultimately, then, receiving God's grace in ICC depends on faith plus the completion of works, the presumptuousness of the leaders judging another's heart, and water baptism.

Other problematic areas in ICC include inadequate views of the perfection of God and Christ, exclusivity, an unbiblical form of authority, and elevation of certain historical biblical occurrences to the level of normative doctrine (e.g., "one church to one city," based on universalizing Rev. 2—3).

Preparing to Witness. In principle, preparation for witnessing to disciples is similar to the preparation necessary for reaching members of other cults. Besides knowing their doctrinal errors, it is valuable to understand their worldview, methodology, terminology, and the degree to which the individual understands and follows the movement's teachings.

Inherent in disciples' thinking is the belief that theirs is the only true church and the movement of God. Any criticism of ICC is viewed as persecution. As do members of other cults, ICC disciples interpret this so-called "persecution" as proving theirs is God's true church. Most members fervently believe there is no valid reason to leave their church. Leaving it would be tantamount to forsaking God. They readily dismiss doctrinal and leadership errors with this rationale: "We don't say we can't make mistakes. If we make one, we admit it and correct it." Obviously, then, trust in ICC as the movement of God becomes a powerful obstacle to the disciples' believing anyone who would present material contrary to the group's teachings.

Beginning the Dialogue. Fortunately, the desire to know and serve God and a commitment to the Bible as the Word of God provide a foundation for dialogue. An effective witnessing approach incorporates affirming the disciple's zeal for God with proving that ICC is not the true church by demonstrating that it promotes a false gospel—salvation based on works. Establishing an agreement on the criteria for evaluating the gospel ICC promotes is the next step in exposing the works-based gospel of this movement. A conversation might begin something like this:

Christian: I understand your church teaches that it alone is the movement of God.

Disciple: We believe we're following God. We only teach what the Bible teaches. There may be others out there who have come to the truth that only baptized disciples are saved. If they are really good-hearted, they will want to be with true disciples.

Christian: Do you believe a Christian church must present the gospel without adding or subtracting anything?

Disciple: Yes. That's what we do!

Christian: Would you examine the gospel with me?

Disciple: Sure. I'd be glad to study the Bible with you. Why don't we meet tonight at your house? I'd like to bring a friend too.

Christian: That sounds fine, except I prefer not to meet with anyone else yet. Maybe another time.

Disciple: I'll see you tonight!

Certain comments made by the disciple should be noted. "Study the Bible" is another way of saying "We'll use our 'Bible' studies." The disciple might attempt to introduce a segment from their proselytizing studies, *First Principles*. The "Discipleship" segment is skillfully designed to lead the potential convert to one conclusion—he is not a Christian! Unless the Christian is careful, he could lose control of the conversation. "I'd like to bring a friend," is an attempt to establish a numerical advantage.

The Second Meeting: How Can You Baptize a Nation? Essential to this movement's existence is its teaching concerning discipleship and making disciples. Matthew 28:18–20 is the primary passage cited as proof that Jesus established an unchangeable order of steps required for salvation: "Therefore go and make disciples of all nations, baptizing them in the name of the Father and of the Son and of the Holy Spirit, and teaching them to obey everything I have commanded you…" The ICC teaches that the first step indicated in this passage is to become a *disciple* (according to their definition); the second is baptism. Only *baptized disciples* are saved.

To demonstrate the untenableness of this interpretation, it is important to have several reference works available: an NIV Bible (ICC's preferred version), an exhaustive concordance, and an expository dictionary of New Testament words (e.g., V*ine's*). Spatial constraints limit this discussion to the *disciple* aspect of their salvation formula.

The following conversation demonstrates an approach to refuting one of their departures from this gospel of grace—becoming a disciple as a prerequisite to salvation.

Christian: *Christian* appears three times in the New Testament, and *disciple* occurs more than 250 times. To whom does *disciple* refer?

Disciple: Christians. Disciples were first called Christians in Antioch (Acts 11:26,27).

Christian: Doesn't your church teach "disciple=Christian=saved"?

Disciple: That's what the Bible teaches.

Christian: If *disciple*, *Christian*, and *saved* are synonymous, they can be used interchangeably for *disciples* in Matthew 28:19,20: "Therefore go and make *Christians* of all nations, baptizing them in the name of the Father and of the Son and of the Holy Spirit, and teaching them to obey everything I have commanded you..." (or) "Therefore go and make *saved* of all nations, baptizing them..." With these substitutions applied, is Jesus actually commanding a person to be a baptized disciple to be saved?

Disciple: Well, maybe not, but Jesus commanded us to be disciples to be saved.

Christian: Let's study this further. Who's speaking in this passage?

Disciple: Jesus.

Christian: Do you believe Jesus, God the Son, could make a mistake when He spoke?

Disciple: No.

Christian: Can we agree that Matthew was inspired by the Holy Spirit, and that the Bible is inerrant?

Disciple: Yes.

Christian: Then, if Jesus wanted to convey a different meaning, this passage would be worded differently. In verse 19, He says to baptize "them." *Them* is a pronoun. In Greek and English, a pronoun must refer to a noun, not a verb. In Greek, *make disciples* is a verb. (Have the member look this up in an expository dictionary.) Thus, the pronoun *them* must refer to the noun *nations*. According to this grammatical rule, we must conclude Jesus cannot be teaching that a person must be a disciple before he is baptized or saved.

Disciple: But if *them* refers to *nations*, how can you baptize a nation?

Christian: Baptizing a whole nation would be tough. However, *baptizing* and *teaching* are participles. As participles, they must refer to the verb, *make disciples*. They describe how a disciple is made, by being baptized and taught. They are not commands that you must do certain things to be a disciple, and then be baptized to be saved. To make disciples, and then baptize them, is not what Jesus commanded.

Disciple: What about the nations?

Christian: The Greek word for *nations* is *ethnos*. (Have the disciple locate *nation* in an expository dictionary.) To whom is Jesus speaking?

Disciple: The disciples.

Christian: Right. Of what race were they?

Disciple: They were Hebrews.

Christian: Exactly. Did they believe the Messiah was to come for the Jews, or for the whole world?

Disciple: They believed Jesus came for the Jews.

Christian: What new teaching was Jesus conveying to the disciples?

Disciple: Oh, I see. They were to begin preaching to all people, not just to the Jews.

Christian: Yes. Before Christ's crucifixion and resurrection, His followers did not preach the gospel to other ethnic groups. Afterward, Jesus commanded them to go to all nations. Did you need to know Greek to study as we just did?

Disciple: No.

Christian: Could there be any reason your leaders, some of whom have seminary training, or anyone else, could not study this passage just as you have?

Disciple: No.

Christian: Your leaders assert they have "rediscovered" a so-called lost biblical doctrine that actually never existed. Instead, they added to the passage, and included the work of being a disciple as a requirement for salvation. Would you read Proverbs 30:5,6 with me? ("Every word of God is flawless; . . . Do not add to his words, or he will rebuke you and prove you a liar.") Now, let's read what Paul wrote in Galatians 1:8,9. ("But even if we or an angel from heaven should preach a gospel other than the one we preached to you, let him be eternally condemned!") Would these warnings apply to ICC's misinterpretation of Matthew 28:18–20?

Disciple: Well, uh, I don't know.

Christian: If ICC were really God's true church, it would not promote this false gospel.

Disciple: Maybe we made a mistake here. We don't claim to be perfect. But Jesus still said we have to be His disciples, so what difference does it make?

Christian: You are right. We are to be His disciples. Disciple is another word for follower, and all people who know Christ as Savior are His followers. But to live as a disciple before being saved is not something we can do, nor would Jesus require us to do so. In fact, we cannot live the regenerate life of a disciple until after salvation, when the Holy Spirit indwells and empowers us, and changes us from within. To expect people to change and live a godly life by themselves, instead of by the power of God, is expecting the impossible. Adding requirements to the gospel of salvation makes a mockery of His grace.

Disciple: Okay, I understand. This may be wrong. But can you show me any other examples of where we're not following the Bible?

Next, the discussion should explore ICC's other works-oriented teachings on salvation contrasted with salvation by grace, as well as the movement's denial of man's sin nature, its unscriptural views on authority, and the belief that Revelation 2—3 commands only one church to each city. Above all, do these things in love, with patience, gentleness, and respect.

Joanne Ruhland is in countercult ministry, specializing in the International Churches of Christ. She can be reached c/o Here's Life, San Antonio, P.O. Box 12472, San Antonio, TX, 78212.

QUESTIONS

1. **What does the International Church of Christ (ICC) teach about salvation?**

2. **What do they require before an individual can be baptized?**

3. **What is the prerequisite for baptism according to Acts 8:36,37?**

4. **What new teaching was Jesus trying to convey to the disciples in Matthew 28:18–20?**

5. What is the primary reason that one need not be a committed disciple before being saved?

FEATHERS FOR ARROWS

The BBC once broadcast a documentary about a man who played castanets to his tomatoes. The gentleman placed earphones on his tomatoes and played classical music for them—in stereo, of course. This man was obviously a nut. However, the program then revealed that the man's name was in *The Guinness Book of World Records* for having the world's largest tomato: four-and-a-half pounds. The valuable lesson learned is that we should never knock something until we see its results.

The next time you see a caterpillar on a leaf, study it for a while. You will notice that it twists and turns until it has wound itself into a web, finally encasing itself into a cocoon. We don't knock what it's doing because we know that a metamorphosis is taking place within the cocoon. A miracle of nature is happening. In time, a beautiful butterfly will appear.

To those who don't understand, Christians are doing no more than wrapping themselves with rules and regulations, hiding from the real world in the cocoon of Christianity. But wait. Don't knock it until you see the results. When you look at the Church today, you're looking at the grub. Granted, we do seem to lack in so many areas. But the One who created the process of metamorphosis is at work in the hearts of those who love Him, and the day will come when the butterfly will emerge.

Memory Verse

"Every word of God is pure: he is a shield unto them that put their trust in him. Add not unto his words, lest he reprove you, and you be found a liar."
PROVERBS 30:5,6

Last Words

David M. Moir, Scottish physician and poet who died in 1851, was a sincere believer and said on his deathbed:

> **"May the Lord my God not separate between my soul and body until He has made a final separation between my soul and sin, for the sake of my Redeemer."**

Seventh-Day Adventists

"Preach earnestly the love of God in Christ Jesus, and magnify the abounding mercy of the Lord; but always preach it in connection with His justice."

CHARLES SPURGEON

Kirk's Comment Are Seventh-day Adventists just Christians who worship on a different day? Again, being familiar with other beliefs will help you know how to share the biblical truths with those you encounter.

QUESTIONS & OBJECTIONS

"All religions are different paths to the same place."

If all religions are different paths to the same place, then why do the paths contradict each other? Let's review the teachings of just three religions: Buddhism is pantheistic and says there is no personal God and everyone can reach godlikeness on his own. Islam says that Jesus was just a prophet and not the only way to God. Christianity says that there is a personal God and that the only way to Him is through Jesus (John 14:6). If these three religions are, as you say, different paths to the same place, then why do they contradict each other? Does truth contradict itself?

By Dr. James Bjornstad

Seventh-day Adventism originated during the great "Second Advent" wakening of the 19th century. In 1818 William Miller, a Baptist minister, read Daniel 8:14 and predicted Christ's return in twenty-five years—between March 21, 1843, and March 21, 1844 [2300 years from 457 B.C.]. Later his associates set the date for October 22, 1844. During the following years, from 1844–1847, three groups came together to form Seventh-day Adventism:

- Hiram Edson provided the doctrine of the Sanctuary and Christ's final ministry in the Holy of Holies (the Investigative Judgment). On October 23, 1844, "Suddenly there burst upon his mind the thought that there were two phases to Christ's ministry in the Heaven of Heavens, just as in the earthly sanctuary of old. Instead of our high priest coming out of the most holy of the heavenly sanctuary to come to this earth on the tenth day of the seventh month at the end of the twenty-three hundred days, He for the first time entered on that day the second apartment of that sanctuary, and that He had a work to perform in the most holy before coming to this earth."

- Joseph Bates provided the doctrine of seventh-day worship, the Sabbath.

- Ellen G. Harmon (White) provided the doctrine of the "Spirit of Prophecy." Her visions and prophecies brought together the theological notions above to form a unique religious system.

Theology

Seventh-day Adventists are in basic agreement with historic, biblical Christianity in many areas: the inspiration and inerrancy of the Bible; the Trinitarian nature of the Godhead (the Fatherhood of God, the deity of Jesus Christ, and the person and deity of the Holy Spirit); and that man was created in the image of God, but is in a fallen state of sin and in need of redemption. They teach that Jesus Christ was virgin-born; lived a sinless life; was crucified, dead, and buried; and rose bodily from the grave.

On the other hand, Seventh-day Adventists also have a number of distinctive doctrines that are not in accord with historic Christianity.

The Role of Ellen G. White

Seventh-day Adventists claim that Ellen G. White "performed the work of a true prophet during the seventy years of her public ministry. As Samuel was a prophet, as Jeremiah was a prophet, as John the Baptist, we believe that Mrs. White was a prophet to the Church of Christ today" (*The Advent*). *The Seventh-day Adventist Church Manual* states: "As the Lord's messenger, her writings are a continuing and authoritative source of truth which provide for the church comfort, guidance, instruction, and correction." Mrs. White herself claimed, "When I send you a testimony of warning and reproof, many of you declare it to be merely the opinion of Sister White. You have thereby insulted the Spirit of God."

However, there are some problems with Mrs. White's "gift of prophecy." Walter Rea, in his book *The White Lie*, documents extensive plagiarism. She was also frequently in error, as she herself admitted.

The Person of Jesus Christ

Seventh-day Adventism differs from historic Christian doctrine in some of its teachings regarding the person of Jesus Christ, such as the following:

- Some early Seventh-day Adventists contended that the Son was not fully equal to the Father, and that the former must have had a beginning in the remote past.

- The name Michael is applied not to a created angel but to the Son of God in His pre-incarnate state.

- When Christ became a man, He took upon Himself human flesh and a human nature, but no human soul as a distinct immaterial substance.

The Sleep of the Soul and the Destruction of the Wicked

In contrast to historic Christian teaching, Seventh-day Adventism holds that the soul represents the whole man and the whole man (the body) remains in the tomb until the resurrection morning. The soul cannot exist apart from the body, and there is no conscious existence after death. The righteous will be resurrected and caught up to meet the Lord at His return; the unrighteous will be resurrected after the millennium and then cast into the lake of fire where they will be annihilated.

The Sabbath and the Mark of the Beast

Seventh-day Adventists teach that the Seventh-day Sabbath (Friday evening until Saturday evening) was instituted by God, and that observance of this day is a test of one's loyalty to Christ. A counterfeit Sabbath will be proclaimed during the Tribulation period. Those who worship on that day will receive the mark of the beast; those who remain faithful to God will continue to worship on the Sabbath.

The Heavenly Sanctuary, the Investigative Judgment, and the Scapegoat

Once again, we see a contrast to historic Christian doctrine in Seventh-day Adventist teachings:

- Jesus entered into the heavenly sanctuary in 1844 to begin a second phase of His ministry.

- The sins of believers have been transferred to, deposited or recorded in the Heavenly Sanctuary, and are now being dealt with in the Investigative Judgment. Those who have died are examined to determine if they are worthy of being part of the first resurrection. The living are also examined to determine those who are abiding and keeping God's commandments. When the cases of all the righteous have been decided (the standard being the Ten Commandments), their sins will be blotted out and Jesus will return to this earth in all His glory.

- Azazel (the goat the high priest sent out into the wilderness on the Day of Atonement) designates Satan, and "Satan will ultimately have to bear the retributive punishment for his responsibility in the sins of all men, both righteous and wicked."

Law, Grace, and Salvation

Finally, we see a difference in doctrine when we examine two perspectives of law, grace, and salvation. On the one hand we see justification by faith alone. Opposed to that we find justification by faith which is demonstrated by obedience to God's commandments. This view strongly advocates Sabbath-keeping and the Old Testament dietary laws, which is difficult to harmonize with Seventh-day Adventists' assurance that salvation is by grace through faith and not of works. For example, in *Just What Do You Believe About Your Church*, Fordyce Detamore wrote:

> The best summary of the requirements for salvation is found in the counsel Jesus gave the rich young nobleman (Mt. 19:16–22), "If thou wilt enter into life, (1) keep the commandments...and (2) follow me." There is no other hope of salvation. By the standard of God's holy law we shall be judged in the day of reckoning. (pp. 32–34)
>
> As long as Isaiah 66:15–17 is in this book, how dare I tell you it doesn't make any difference whether or not you eat swine's flesh and other unclean foods?...It would be much easier for me to say, "Go ahead and eat as you please; you needn't worry about those things anymore." But God says those who are eating unclean things when He comes will be destroyed. Wouldn't you rather I put it plainly so that you'll not be deceived and be destroyed at our Lord's coming? (pp. 22,23)

Sharing the Truth with Seventh-day Adventists

Our concern is to be sure that individual Adventists are confronted with the one true gospel. If an Adventist will admit that Mrs. White was fallible, that no record in heaven could possibly bring a believer into condemnation, and that the works of the Law such as Sabbath-keeping are not necessary conditions of salvation, then other things being equal, he should be acknowledged as an evangelical.

On the other hand, if the Adventist persists in defending Mrs. White's infallibility, the Investigative Judgment, and the Old Testament dietary laws, he places himself under the curse of the Law (Galatians 3:10) and is preaching another gospel (Galatians 1:8,9). In response, to those who believe faith must be demonstrated by obedience to God's commandments:

1. Stress the biblical teaching that a man is justified by faith in Jesus apart from the deeds of the Law (Romans 3:28; 4:6; Galatians 2:16; 3:10–14).

2. Point out that the Law of Moses (the ceremonial and moral aspects) has been fulfilled in Jesus Christ. By His perfect life He met all the requirements of the moral aspect of the Law; by His death He fulfilled all the ceremonial ordinances which prefigured His incarnation and sacrifice (Romans 5:10; Colossians 2:16,17).

3. The law or commandment that Christians are called upon to follow is the law of love (e.g., Matthew 22:37–40; Romans 13:8–10).

To those who believe the Sabbath is binding on the Christian, you might point out that:

1. Constantine did not, as Adventists claim, change the day of worship from Saturday to Sunday. He enacted that the first day of the week should be a public holiday, but centuries before Constantine, Christians gathered together for worship on the first day of the week. Reference to worship on the first day of the week can be found in Acts 2:41; 20:6,7; 1 Corinthians 16:2; Revelation 1:10, etc. (Also, both the *Didache* and Ignatius refer to Sunday as the "Lord's Day" ["*Kuriake*"].)

   In addition, references to worship on the first day of the week can be found in the writings of the early church fathers: Ignatius (110 A.D.); Justin Martyr (100–165 A.D.); Barnabas (120–150 A.D.); Irenaeus (178 A.D.); Bardaisan (154 A.D.); Tertullian (200 A.D.); Origen (225 A.D.); Cyprian (200–258 A.D.); Peter of Alexandria (300 A.D.); and Eusebius (315 A.D.).

2. There is no indication in the New Testament that the observance of the Sabbath was binding on Gentile believers. On the contrary, we find such words as these: "One man regards one day above another, another regards every day alike. Let each man be fully convinced in his own mind. He who observes the day, observes it for the Lord" (Romans 14:5,6). "Therefore let no one act as your judge in regard to . . . a Sabbath day" (Colossians 2:16).

Adapted from an article by the Ankerberg Theological Research Institute (www.johnankerberg.org).

QUESTIONS

1. How have false prophets played a role in the SDA church?

2. How does the SDA teaching about Jesus differ from Christian doctrine?

3. What do Seventh-Day Adventists believe happens after death?

4. How does the SDA teaching about receiving the mark of the beast differ from the biblical teaching?

5. On what do Seventh-Day Adventists base their salvation?

WORDS OF COMFORT

One thing I like about my life is that it is free from stress. Because I'm my own boss, I plan my life so that it is devoid of pressure.

Something went a little awry, though, when I was in Salt Lake City in September 1995. I had arrived at a hotel in plenty of time for the pastor to pick me up for a meeting. I had about 40 minutes to relax and unwind after an afternoon of travel. It was around that time that Sue called to tell me that she had forgotten to put a tie in my bag (the first slip up in hundreds of trips). No problem. Someone had mentioned that there was a mall "across the street from the hotel," so I assured Sue that everything was under control.

"Across the street" turned out to be over a highway, across some grass, up an off-ramp, over two busy freeways, through some eye-level-high grass, over a head-height wire fence, and through a large parking lot. I finally arrived at the mall, found a tie, then rushed back through the parking lot, over the fence, through the grass, across two busy freeways, down an off-ramp, across some grass, over a highway, and back to my hotel room.

It was around ninety degrees and very humid, so I ripped off my wet shirt and stood in the cool of an air-conditioned room. Everything was under control. No stress. I had plenty of time to get it together before the meeting. It was then that the pastor called, and told me that he had made a mistake in the meeting time. It was actually 30 minutes earlier, and he was on his way to pick me up.

One good thing about the weekend was that I ended up with a nice new tie. The day after I got back, one of our dogs went upstairs, into our closet, and from all my ties, picked my new one and dragged it downstairs to chew on!

Memory Verse

"In whom we have redemption through his blood, the forgiveness of sins, according to the riches of his grace."

EPHESIANS 1:7

Last Words

Leon Trotsky, Russian revolutionary, died 1940:

"I feel here that this time they have succeeded."

92 New Age Movement

"The greatest fault is to be conscious of none."
THOMAS CARLYLE

Kirk's Comment The New Age Movement is seductive and enticing to many. It is man-centered and almost had me in its grip before I was saved. You'll find this philosophy everywhere.

QUESTIONS & OBJECTIONS

"Did John the Baptist recognize Jesus before His baptism, or not?"

By his statement "I did not know Him" (John 1:31,33), John the Baptist is conveying that he did not have a personal knowledge of Jesus before He came to be baptized. At that time, the Holy Spirit revealed to John the identity of the One he had been sent to proclaim. As John saw Jesus approaching, he declared, "Behold the Lamb of God..." (John 1:29).

John was filled with the Holy Spirit from before his birth (Luke 1:15), and amazingly recognized the presence of Jesus even while both were still in their mothers' wombs (Luke 1:41–44). In light of this witness of the Holy Spirit within John, the sign of the Holy Spirit resting on Jesus was simply a confirmation of what he already knew. God removed any doubt so John could be sure that it was not his imagination or someone else's mistake.

By Matthew J. Slick

The New Age Movement (NAM) has many subdivisions, but it is generally a collection of Eastern-influenced metaphysical thought systems, a conglomeration of theologies, hopes, and expectations held together with an eclectic teaching of salvation, of "correct thinking," and "correct knowledge." It is a theology of "feel-goodism," universal tolerance, and moral relativism.

The NAM is difficult to define because there is no hierarchy, dogma, doctrine, collection plate, or membership. It is an assortment of different theologies with the common threads of toleration and divergence weaving through its tapestry of "universal truth."

The term "New Age" refers to the "Aquarian Age" which, according to New Age followers, is dawning. It is supposed to bring in peace and enlightenment and reunite man with God. Man is presently considered separated from God not because of sin (Isaiah 59:2), but because of lack of understanding and knowledge concerning the true nature of God and reality.

New Age Beliefs

In the New Age Movement, man is central. He is viewed as divine, as co-creator, as the hope for future peace and harmony. A representative quote might be: "I am affected only by my thoughts. It needs but this to let salvation come to all the world. For in this single thought is everyone released at last from fear" (*A Course in Miracles*, Huntington Station, NY: The Foundation for Inner Peace, p. 461).

Unfortunately for New Agers, the fear they want to be released from might very well be the fear of damnation, of conviction of sin, and sometimes even the fear of Christianity and Christians. Though the NAM is tolerant of almost any theological position, it is opposed to Christianity's "narrow-mindedness" that there are moral absolutes and that Jesus is the only way. Following are their views on the main tenets of Christianity:

- God is not a personal heavenly Father but an impersonal force. God is all and all is God. God is not the "wholly other" Creator of all, but part of all that exists. There is nothing that is not God. (This is pantheism, an eastern mystical belief system that has crept into mainstream America.)

- There is no sin, only incorrect understanding of truth. Since the NAM doesn't acknowledge sin or sinfulness, there is no need for a Redeemer like Jesus.

- Salvation, in the New Age sense, is self-achieved through understanding your natural godlikeness and goodness, combined with proper knowledge. It means to be in tune with the divine consciousness, in harmony with reality and whatever is perceived to be true. Because salvation is a form of knowledge, of achieving correct thought—the realization of our divine nature—we need to be saved from ignorance, not sin. Therefore knowledge is what saves, not Jesus.

- Jesus was just one of many teachers of divine truth. He exemplified the "Christ consciousness" probably better than anyone else. Christ is a consciousness, a form of the higher self. It is possessed by all because everyone is divine.

- Hell is not a place but an experience here on Earth; it is a state of mind.

- After death, most New Agers believe that the soul is reincarnated. Many even believe the Bible was changed to remove any verses that taught reincarnation, but the Bible, of course, never contained any references supporting the concept. Reincarnation opposes the Word of God, which says that it is appointed for man to die once, and then face judgment (Heb. 9:27). Reincarnation is appealing to New Agers because with it there is no judgment, and there is a second chance, a third chance, a fourth, etc.

The New Age Movement is a religious system with two basic beliefs: evolutionary godhood and global unity.

Evolutionary Godhood

Since all is God, and man is part of all, then man is God. Therefore, man has infinite potential. In evolutionary godhood, mankind will soon see itself as god, as the "Christ principle." For the most part, the NAM espouses evolution of both body and spirit, and views this as the next step in humanity's evolution. Man is developing and will soon leap forward into new spiritual horizons.

The NAM teaches that man's basic nature is good and divine. This opposes God's Word which says that we are sinners (Rom. 5:12) and that our nature is corrupt (Eph. 2:3). It teaches that since man is divine by nature, he then has divine qualities. This is an important aspect of NAM thinking. Because the average New Ager believes himself to be divine, he can create his own reality. If, for example, a person believes that reincarnation is true, that's fine because that is his reality. If someone else doesn't believe in it, that is all right too because that is his reality. They can each have a reality for themselves that "follows a different path."

New Agers who believe in their own divinity and ability to create usurp the authority and position of God. Their arrogant conclusion, based on concepts of grandiose self-worth, is a deceptive, self-satisfying indulgence into pride. As Satan wanted to be like God (Isaiah 14:12–17) and encouraged Adam and Eve to be like God also (Gen. 3:1–5), the New Ager listens to the echo of that Edenic lie and yields to it willingly.

Global Unity

The second major element of the New Age Movement is global unity, which consists of three major divisions: man with man; man with nature; and man with God.

Man with man: The NAM teaches that we will all learn our proper divine relationship with one another and achieve harmony, mutual love, and acceptance through the realization and acceptance of this divine proper knowledge.

The New Age Movement attempts to absorb all religions, cultures, and governments. It seeks to unify all systems into one spiritual, socioeconomic unity. The average New Ager is looking for a single world leader who, with New Age principles, will guide the world into a single harmonious economic whole. It is also hoped that this leader will unite the world into a spiritual unity; that is, one world religion. The New Age hope is reminiscent of the Scriptures that speak of the coming Antichrist (2 Thes. 2:3,4; Rev. 13:17; 14:9,11; 16:2; 19:20).

Man with nature: Since the NAM says that God is all, and all is God, then nature is also part of God. Man is also one with the universe. Man must then get in tune with nature and learn to nurture it and be nurtured by it. In this, all people can unite. American Indian philosophies are popular among New Agers because they focus on the earth and nature, and on man's relationship to them.

New Age philosophy generally seeks to merge with those philosophies that put man and nature on an equal level. We are no more or less important or no different than our cousins the animals, birds, and fish. We must live in harmony with them, understand them, and learn from them. This is opposed to the Scriptural teaching of man's superiority over animals (Gen. 1:26,27; 2:19). This does not mean that man may abuse them, but he is given the responsibility of caring for and being a steward of God's creation (Gen. 2:15). God will hold Christians responsible for the stewardship that has been entrusted to them.

The New Agers have a name for the earth: Gaia. Gaia is to be revered and respected. Some New Agers even worship the earth and nature. This opposes the Scripture that says we are not to have any other gods before God (Ex. 20:3).

Man with God: Since the NAM teaches that man is divine by nature, all people, once they see themselves as such, will be helped in their unity of purpose, love, and development. The goal is to fully realize our own goodness. It is obvious that this contradicts Scripture, such as in Rom. 3:10–12.

Because the New Ager seeks to elevate himself to godhood, he must lower the majesty and personhood of the true God. In other words, the universe isn't big enough for one true God, but it is big enough for a bunch of little ones. New Agers view God as impersonal, omnipresent, and benevolent, therefore he (it) won't condemn anyone. An impersonal God will not reveal himself nor will he have specific requirements regarding morality, belief, and behavior.

As such, there are no moral absolutes in the New Age. Instead, they claim to have a spiritual tolerance for all "truth systems," which they call "harmonization." There is an obvious problem here. To say that there are no moral absolutes is an absolute in itself, which is self-contradictory.

Also, if morality is relative, then stealing may be right sometimes, along with lying, adultery, cheating, etc. Living in a world of moral relativism would not bring a promising future.

It would follow that if reality is relative and truth is too, then driving a car would be difficult. After all, if one New Ager thinks the light is red and another thinks it is green, when they collide, their different realities will come crashing down on them. That is something most interesting about New Agers: they don't live what they believe. That is because, in reality, New Age thinking doesn't work.

The New Age movement *does* espouse honesty, integrity, love, peace, etc.—just without the true God. New Agers want to live not on His terms, but on their own.

New Age Terminology

The New Age Movement has its own vocabulary, including such words as: holistic, holographic, synergistic, unity, oneness, harmony, at-one-ment, awakening, networking, energy, consciousness, transformation, personal growth, and human potential. These words are prevalent in New Age conversations and writings. In fact, if you were to scan the titles in a New Age bookstore, you would see that a disproportionate number contain the word "self."

New Age Practices

Many New Age practices are designed to push New Agers into the new spiritual horizons of evolutionary godhood. These practices include astral projection, which is training your soul to leave your body and travel around; contacting spirits so they may speak through you or guide you; using crystals to purify the energy systems of your body and mind; and visualization, where you use mental imagery to imagine yourself as an animal, in the presence of a divine being, being healed of sickness, etc.

New Agers use various means to have mystical experiences with God and/or nature and/or self. Some of the methods were described in the Dec. 1988 *Omni* magazine in an article entitled "How to Have a Mystical Experience": *imagining*, where you are told to imagine your own reality;

transcendence, going beyond the limits of time; *sleep deprivation,* with the purpose of inducing a mystical experience; *focusing,* "to experience all of reality as unified and not as a collection of disparate objects"; *avoidance,* where communication with the outside world is stopped in order to reinterpret the world without its influence on you; *identification,* "To trade places mentally with a dog or a cat, canary, or animal in the zoo"; *reflection,* an exercise designed to help you to view the year to come, differently; and *star-gazing,* "to induce a sense of objectivity about your life and a feeling of connectedness to the rest of cosmos" (pp. 137–145).

As you can see, the New Age Movement is a false religious system that contradicts Christianity in almost all of its main tenets. As Christians, we should be watchful to recognize what is false and teach what is true. We should be wary because the Edenic lie still rings strong in the hearts of the deceived—and they want us to believe as they.

Witnessing to New Agers

1. **Ask questions.** For example, ask them how, if we are divine, our mere ignorant self could so easily override our divine goodness. Also ask if truth contradicts itself. It does not. If we each have our own truth, these different truths can't ultimately contradict each other—or they wouldn't be true. The NAM says that Jesus is only one of many ways to God; but Jesus said He is the only way to God (John 14:6). They can't both be right; therefore, the NAM teaching that we can create our own truths cannot be true.

2. **Don't let them use Christian words out of the context of biblical meaning.** New Agers recognize the tremendous influence and spotless reputation of Jesus. They want Him to be associated with their beliefs. As a result, you might find yourself facing New Agers who use Christian words—but with non-Christian definitions. Listen carefully, and question the terms they use. Make sure that what they mean by Christian terms is the same thing that you mean by them.

3. **Listen for internal contradictions.** Listen to what New Agers are saying and you will hear inconsistencies arise, usually when discussing the relationship between reality and belief. For example, a New Ager

might say that you can create your own reality. You might reply, "Good. Then if I believe red lights are really green, would you want to go driving with me?"

QUESTIONS

1. **Why is the NAM difficult to define?**

2. **How is man viewed in the New Age Movement?**

3. **How does the New Age Movement view God?**

4. **Does the NAM believe that people can sin?**

5. **What is salvation according to the NAM?**

6. **The New Age Movement is a religious system with two basic beliefs. What are they?**

Memory Verse

"Thus says the LORD, your redeemer, and he that formed you from the womb, I am the LORD that makes all things; that stretches forth the heavens alone; that spreads abroad the earth by myself."

ISAIAH 44:24

FEATHERS FOR ARROWS

There was once a portion of road on which there were continual fatalities. Drivers, despite warning signs, would speed around a corner and be killed. Finally, one of the local councilmen had a bright idea. He suggested putting a flock of chickens on the side of the road. This was done, and fatalities dramatically dropped. The drivers slowed down for the sake of the chickens.

It would seem that the speedsters saw the danger of speed for chickens, but not for themselves. Why? Because inherent within each of us is this senseless idea that "it will never happen to me." It's always the other guy who gets killed; it's always the other guy who gets cancer. You can be sure that every person who died before us had the "I never thought it would happen to me" attitude.

Last Words

Sir Thomas Smith, Secretary of State to Queen Elizabeth I (died 1577):

"It is a matter of lamentation that men know not for what end they were born into the world until they are ready to go out of it."

The Will of God

"She is a traitor to the Master who sent her if she is so beguiled by the beauties of taste and art as to forget that to 'preach Christ... and Him crucified' is the only object for which she exists among the sons of men. The business of the Church is salvation of souls."

CHARLES SPURGEON

Kirk's Comment In frustration over wanting to know God's specific plans for my life, I've even asked Him to kindly send me a brief e-mail, detailing His instructions. This lesson is better than e-mail; it put me on the right track and engaged my ability to further trust in God.

QUESTIONS & OBJECTIONS

"How can people be happy in heaven, knowing that their unsaved loved ones are suffering in hell?"

A person asking this question falls into the category of those who asked Jesus a similar question. The Pharisees said that a certain woman had seven consecutive husbands, so whose wife will she be in heaven (Mark 12:23)? Jesus answered by saying that they knew neither the Scriptures nor the power of God. The unregenerate mind has no concept of God's mind or His infinite power. If God can speak the sun into existence; if He can see every thought of every human heart at the same time; if He can

647

create the human eye with its 137,000,000 light-sensitive cells, then He can handle the minor details of our eternal salvation.

John writes that in heaven "we shall be like him; for we shall see him as he is" (1 John 3:2), so perhaps we will be fully satisfied that God is perfectly just and merciful. Because He has given light to every man (John 1:9), and His will is that none should perish but that all should come to repentance (2 Peter 3:9), we can trust that He gave every individual the opportunity to accept or reject Him. However He works it out, God promises that there will not be sorrow or crying in heaven. Our focus in heaven won't be on our loss, but on our gain.

wotmwotmwotmwotmwotmwotmwotmwotmwotmwotmwotm

When things don't work out as we think they should, we often quote Isaiah 55:8: "For my thoughts are not your thoughts, neither are your ways my ways, says the LORD." God's ways are higher than our ways, and often we have no idea why He allows certain things to happen. But the Scripture we so frequently lean on for consolation is not directed at the godly. Here it is in context:

> Seek the LORD while he may be found, call upon him while he is near: let the wicked forsake his way, and the unrighteous man his thoughts... For my thoughts are not your thoughts, neither are your ways my ways, says the LORD (Isaiah 55:6–8).

God is directing this to the wicked and unrighteous man. He is speaking to the unregenerate, those whose "carnal mind is enmity against God" (Romans 8:7), who "walk in the vanity of their mind, having the understanding darkened" (Ephesians 4:17,18). Before we trust in the Savior, we are enemies of God in our minds through wicked works, and even our thoughts are an abomination to the Lord (Proverbs 15:26). Like lost sheep, we have all "gone astray; we have turned every one to his own way" (Isaiah 53:6), and our way is an abomination to the Lord (Proverbs 15:9).

Once, our lives were dead in trespasses, governed by sin, selfishness, Satan, and our senses. Upon our conversion, God puts His Law into our minds (Hebrews 8:10), gives us the "mind of Christ" (1 Corinthians 2:16), and renews us in the "spirit of our mind" (Ephesians 4:23). Now God's ways are our ways and His thoughts become our thoughts. We are led by the Spirit, walking "in His ways" (Psalm 119:3).

If we are walking in the Spirit, with our sinful nature crucified, we can be assured that the desires we now have are in line with God's desires. For example, before I was a Christian, it never entered my mind to publish a paper about Jesus, or get a bus and put Bible verses all around it; that would have been the last thing I would have been interested in. Now my desires are radically different.

I'm sure few of us have failed to underline Psalm 37:4 in our Bibles: "Delight yourself also in the LORD: and he shall give you the desires of your heart." But what are our desires? What do we want most in life? Do we desire above all things to have a better paying job, a bigger house, thicker carpet, a superior car, and more money? Are we controlled by the lust of the flesh, the lust of the eyes, and the pride of life? Or have we been transformed from the way of this world by "the renewing of [our] mind" (Romans 12:2), that we may prove what is that good, and acceptable, and perfect will of God? Are our desires now in line with God's desires? Are we above all things "not willing that any should perish, but that all should come to repentance" (2 Peter 3:9)? If that is our testimony, it is because we have the same Spirit in us as the apostle Paul, who said, "For it is God who works in me both to will and to do of His good pleasure" (Philippians 2:13). Look at this verse in the *Amplified Bible*:

> (Not in your own strength) for it is God Who is all the while effectually at work in you—energizing and creating in you the power and desire—both to will and to work for His good pleasure and satisfaction and delight.

Scripture tells me that the reason I have desires to do exploits for God is that He is in me "energizing and creating in [me] the power and desire ...to work for His good pleasure." When I get aspirations to do things to reach the unsaved, it is because His desires have become my desires. I can pursue these aspirations, trusting that they are in the will of God, and therefore I can confidently expect Him to grant them. Remember, this is not presumption, "an arrogant taking for granted," but a pure, unadulterated desire to do the right thing by reaching out to the lost.

Read the following verses and see if you can detect whose idea it was for Peter to walk on water:

> In the fourth watch of the night Jesus went to them, walking on the sea. And when the disciples saw him walking on the sea, they were troubled, saying, It is a spirit; and they cried out for fear. But straightway Jesus spoke to them, saying, Be of good cheer; it is I; be not afraid. And Peter answered him and said, Lord, if it be you, bid me come to you on the water. And he said, Come. And when Peter was come down out of the ship, he walked on the water, to go to Jesus (Matthew 14:25–29).

Peter said, "Lord, if it be you, bid me come to you on the water." Peter had the concept, and Jesus put His blessing on Peter's idea. Peter knew Jesus intimately—he knew the mind of the Master. He knew that his desire wasn't an impertinent presumption, but just a longing to follow the Lord into the realm of the supernatural. Jesus said, "If any man serve me, let him follow me; and where I am, there shall also my servant be: if any man serve me, him will my Father honor" (John 12:26).

This is why, when you and I do godly exploits, we can trust that we are in the will of God and that He will honor them. This is the thought behind Jesus' words in Mark 11:24: "What things soever you desire, when you pray, believe that you receive them, and you shall have them." The same applies to John 15:7: "If you abide in me, and my words abide in you, you shall ask what you will, and it shall be done to you."

Does this mean that we need merely speak the words, "Mercedes Benz, diamond rings, fur coats," into the air in believing prayer, and God will give them to us? Not according to Scripture. If our covetous heart has been crucified with Christ, our desire won't be for material things, but that none would perish. When we seek first the kingdom of God and His righteousness, God promises to meet our true needs—food, drink, clothing, etc. (Luke 12:31). Scripture actually warns that a covetous prayer will not be answered: "You ask, and receive not, because you ask amiss, that you may consume it upon your lusts" (James 4:3).

Instead, if we follow the advice of Psalm 37:4 and delight ourselves in the Lord, the desires of our heart will match His—and those are the desires He will grant.

QUESTIONS

1. Upon conversion, what does God do to our minds?

2. If we are walking in the Spirit, what should we have assurance of regarding our desires?

3. According to Psalm 37:4, what should be our desires?

4. What can we learn from the reaction of Jesus to Peter's idea to walk on the water?

FEATHERS FOR ARROWS

"Read and read again, and do not despair of help to understand the will and mind of God though you think they are fast locked up from you. Neither trouble your heads though you have not commentaries and ex-position. Pray and read, read and pray; for a little from God is better than a great deal from men. Also, what is from men is uncertain, and is often lost and tumbled over by men; but what is from God is fixed as a nail in a sure place. There is nothing that so abides with us as what we receive from God; and the reason why the Christians in this day are at such a loss as to some things is that they are contented with what comes from men's mouths, without searching and kneeling before God to know of Him the truth of things." —*John Bunyan*

WORDS OF COMFORT

I had a can of Diet Cherry Coke in hand. As I poured the foaming syrup into a plate on the ground, I mumbled, "A dog's life is too short; they need to have some pleasure in life." Then I switched from benefactor into more of an analyst. The older dog turned her nose up at the drink, while the younger one lapped it up. I thought it must be that the older dog discerned all the chemicals in the drink.

This was interesting to an inquiring mind, so I called my daughter and said, "Look at this. The older dog hates this drink, but the younger one loves it!" Then I said, "I had better put this away before your mother sees it. She would be upset that I was giving this stuff to the dogs." A minute later, all the evidence was gone. The incident optimized my kind heart... kind of like a dog Santa Claus.

About five minutes later I heard my wife, Sue, yell, "Yuk! The dog's thrown up!"

Memory Verse

"Not everyone who says to Me, 'Lord, Lord,' shall enter the kingdom of heaven, but he who does the will of My Father in heaven."

MATTHEW 7:21

Last Words

Voltaire, the noted French infidel, used his pen to try to retard Christianity. He once boasted, "In twenty years Christianity will be no more. My single hand shall destroy the edifice it took twelve apostles to rear." Shortly after his death, his house became the depot of the Geneva Bible Society. The nurse who attended Voltaire said, "For all the wealth in Europe I would not see another infidel die." His physician said that Voltaire cried out most desperately:

"I am abandoned by God and man! I will give you half of what I am worth if you will give me six months' life. Then I shall go to hell; and you will go with me. O Christ! O Jesus Christ!"

LESSON 94

Our Most Valuable Commodity

"God has placed you where He has placed no one else. No one else in the world has the same relationships you have. No one will stand in the same grocery store line at exactly the same moment you do. No one else will come across a hungering diplomat in the desert at exactly the same time you do. God hasn't put you in those places merely to model the truth. Listen for the voice of the Spirit to whisper in your ear. Watch for the stranger on the road. And be aware of your opportunities to go where He would send you."

CHUCK SWINDOLL

Kirk's Comment It's been said that a person's priorities can be determined by looking at his calendar and his checkbook. This lesson made me examine my own heart and rethink how I spend the time and resources that God has given me.

QUESTIONS & OBJECTIONS

"I have things I need to do before I become a Christian."

Your statement implies that you believe following God will mean you won't be able to do the things you want to do. If that is true, then that means the things you intend to do would displease God. Are you saying you prefer to do something God wouldn't want you to do? If so, you are willfully sinning against God and putting yourself in a dangerous situation. That is all the more reason you need His forgiveness.

If the things you want to do are good, why can't you become a Christian and then do them? Nothing you can do could be more important than your relationship with God. To put Him off is unwise. What if you die before you become a Christian? Then you would be eternally without hope.

w o t m w o t m w o t m w o t m w o t m w o t m w o t m w o t m w o t m w o t m w o t m

Imagine there is a bank that credits your account each morning with $86,400. It carries over no balance from day to day—every evening it erases whatever part of the balance you failed to use during the day. What would you do? Draw out every cent, of course.

Each of us has such a bank. Its name is "time." Every morning it credits you with 86,400 seconds and every night it writes off as lost whatever portion of this you have failed to invest to good purpose. It carries over no balance; it allows no overdrafts. Each day it opens a new account for you; each night it burns the remains of the day. If you fail to use the day's deposits, the loss is yours. There is no going back, no drawing against the "tomorrow." You must live in the present on today's deposits. Invest it so as to get from it the utmost in God's will. The clock is running; make the most of today.

To realize the value of one year, ask the student who failed a grade; one month, ask the mother who gave birth to a premature baby; one week, ask the editor of a weekly newspaper; one hour, ask the lovers who are waiting to meet; one minute, ask the person who just missed a train; one second, ask the person who just avoided an accident; one millisecond, ask the silver medal winner in the Olympics.

In the following letter from an atheist, even he can see how the Christian should best spend his time:

> You are really convinced that you've got all the answers. You've really got yourself tricked into believing that you're 100% right. Well, let me tell you just one thing. Do you consider yourself to be compassionate of other humans? If you're right about God, as you say you are, and you believe that, then how can you sleep at night? When

you speak with me, you are speaking with someone who you believe is walking directly into eternal damnation, into an endless onslaught of horrendous pain, which your "loving" god created, yet you stand by and do nothing. *If you believed one bit that thousands every day were falling into an eternal and unchangeable fate, you should be running the streets mad with rage at their blindness.* That's equivalent to standing on a street corner and watching every person that passes you walk blindly directly into the path of a bus and die, yet you stand idly by and do nothing. You're just twiddling your thumbs, happy in the knowledge that one day that "walk" signal will shine your way across the road. Think about it. Imagine the horrors hell must have in store if the Bible is true. You're just going to allow that to happen and not care about saving anyone but yourself? If you're right, then you're an uncaring, unemotional and purely selfish (expletive) that has no right to talk about subjects such as love and caring.

Consider these probing questions about how you spend your time: Do you read you Bible every day without fail? Do you find time to eat food each day? Which comes first in your life—your Bible or your belly? Do you ever weep for the unsaved? Have you shared your faith verbally with more than 12 people in the last 12 months? Do you pray for laborers as Jesus commanded us to (see Luke 10:2)? If you were to be given $1,000 for every person you witnessed to, could you deal with your "fear of man" problem? Can you say that you love your neighbor as much as you love yourself? Have you made it a habit to always carry gospel tracts with you?

Yesterday is history, tomorrow a mystery. Today is a gift. That is why it is called the present. Be wise, and remember to "redeem the time, because the days are evil" (Ephesians 5:15).

QUESTIONS

1. **How are you investing your time wisely for God's kingdom?**

2. **How did the letter from the atheist make you feel?**

3. **What do your priorities say about your commitment to Christ?**

PREACHER'S PROGRESS

Christian: "Do you know if there are any good churches around here?"

Nick O'Deamus: "No, not really. I haven't been to church for a while."

Christian: "Do you have a Christian background?"

Nick O'Deamus: "Yes. I'm a Roman Catholic . . . born in Ireland."

Christian: "Have you been born again?"

Nick O'Deamus: "Yes. I was baptized as a child."

Christian: "No. I'm not talking about being baptized. This is something different. It's when you are born again. It's in the Catholic Bible, in John chapter 3."

Nick O'Deamus: "I've never heard of that. How can you be born again?"

Christian: "The difference between believing in God and being born again is like the difference between believing in a parachute and actually putting one on. There's a big difference when you jump. Does that make sense?"

Nick O'Deamus: "Yes, it does."

Christian: "Do you know what made me see that I had to be born again?"

Nick O'Deamus: "No, what?"

Christian: "It was the Ten Commandments. Do you think you have keep them?"

Nick O'Deamus: "No."

Christian: "So you see yourself as a sinner."

Nick O'Deamus: "Oh, yes. Definitely."

Christian: "If you died tonight, where do you think you would go?"

Nick O'Deamus: "Probably Purgatory."

Christian: "There's no such place. If you die in your sins, the Bible makes it clear that you will go to hell. Did you know that Jesus said if you even look with lust, you have committed adultery in your heart?"

Nick O'Deamus: "No, I didn't know that. I've done that many times."

Christian: "So where would you go if you died tonight?"

Nick O'Deamus: "I would go to hell."

Christian: "Do you know what God did for you so that you wouldn't have to go to hell?"

Nick O'Deamus: "He died on the cross."

Christian: "That's right. Jesus, once and for all, took your punishment upon Himself, then He rose from the dead. Now God will give you the gift of everlasting life if you repent—that is, confess your sins not to a priest, but to God, and then forsake them—and put your trust in Jesus Christ. Then you will be born again, with a new heart and new desires. Do you think you are ready to do that?"

Nick O'Deamus: "I am."

Christian: "Then quietly confess your sins to God—ask for His forgiveness and tell Him that you are going to trust Jesus. Then I will pray for you, and show you some incredible promises in the Bible. Okay?"

Nick O'Deamus: "Okay."

Memory Verse

"See then that you walk circumspectly, not as fools, but as wise, redeeming the time, because the days are evil."
EPHESIANS 5:15,16

Last Words

Grover Cleveland (1837–1908), 22nd and 24th President of the U.S.:

"I have tried so hard to do the right."

95 Consolation for the Average Christian

"Never be afraid to try something new. Remember, amateurs built the ark; professionals built the Titanic."

UNKNOWN

Kirk's Comment   Most of the heroes of the Bible were average people you might never have picked out of a crowd. God uses the normal, average Christian to accomplish supernatural, extraordinary things for His glory. We just need to determine to trust and obey.

QUESTIONS & OBJECTIONS

"Should we ever swear an oath?"

Numbers 30:2 says, "If a man vow a vow to the LORD, or swear an oath . . . he shall not break his word." But in James 5:12 we are told, "Swear not, neither by heaven, neither by the earth, neither by any other oath: but let your yes be yes; and your no, no; lest you fall into condemnation."

   The first verse pertains to swearing to the Lord; the second verse deals with the issue of swearing *by* something. It is vain to swear by something over which we have no control. The only legitimate application would be to swear by our own integrity, but that is implied when we swear an oath. God swears by Himself because He has control over Himself (Hebrews 6:13). But to swear on our mother's grave or something similar is simply vain. It's meaningless, and such a person would be falsely implying that he has control over such things, which is where sin comes into play.

wotmwotmwotmwotmwotmwotmwotmwotmwotmwotmwotm

In August 1992, *Reader's Digest* published an article entitled "How 'Average' People Excel." It related how "fast-trackers," people who succeed in school, often fizzle in the real world. Their main problem is that they are driven by their own inflated ego, and they set goals too high for themselves. They, more than anybody, understand how clever they are, so they are never happy with playing second fiddle to anyone. In other words, their pride is their downfall. The article, written from a purely secular viewpoint, had some very relevant thoughts that we may apply to the kingdom of God. Here are the keys to success found by a corporate consultant, after interviewing more than 190 "ordinary" individuals who had achieved secular success:

- **Learn self-discipline.** This is the key to being successful as a Christian. Of course, we don't measure success in dollars as the world does; we measure it in terms of our lifestyles being pleasing to God. Self-discipline means that we read the Word daily and obey what it says. It means listening to the voice of our conscience and the voice of the Spirit. Self-discipline means self-denial. Consider Jesus in this respect. His ministry was a complete denial of self, from the temptation in the wilderness, to Calvary's terrible cross. He denied His own will, and disciplined Himself to follow the will of the Father, for the sake of the kingdom of God.

- **Bring out the best in people.** There is nothing more pathetic than a selfish person. The Christian has crucified selfishness, and now lives to love his neighbor as much as he loves himself. The dividends are rich. He who loves others will be loved himself, and he who brings out the best in others will bring out the best in himself. Jesus lived and died for others. This is the key to successful relationships and especially to a good marriage.

- **Build a knowledge base.** Think of Jesus when He sat as a twelve-year-old at the feet of those who could give Him understanding of the Scriptures. He grew in grace and knowledge of the things of the kingdom of God. We are commanded to give all diligence to "add to your faith virtue, and to virtue knowledge..." (2 Peter 1:5). To do so is to enrich the Christian life.

- **Develop special skills.** Our skills are not in the natural realm. We seek skills that will save sinners from everlasting damnation. We long to rightly divide the Word of truth as a skillful worker who need not be ashamed. We develop dexterity so that we might be sensitive to the voice of the Spirit, and so that we might speak a word in season to those who are weary.

- **Keep promises.** A Christian always keeps his word even when it hurts him (see Psalm 15:4). His "Yes" will be yes, and his "No," no. If he says he will do something, he will do it if it is at all possible. In this way, he is following after righteousness, and simply doing what is upright.

- **Bounce back from defeat.** I have had many failures. I have begun writing books that I have abandoned. I have printed tracts that I have thrown into the trash. I have floundered while witnessing. I have wasted money on projects that have failed. I have preached dry sermons, prayed pathetic prayers, and made just about every blunder one can make. When our ministry first started in 1974, we published a Christian paper called "Living Waters." On the back I ran a large advertisement with the words "Problems? Just call this number. You don't have to say a word...just listen." The number was for a local Dial-a-sermon, and I thought it would be a blessing to those who found themselves needing comfort. Unfortunately, I forgot to include the area code and some poor woman in another part of the country began getting calls with heavy breathing on the line. People with problems called her and they didn't say a word. They just listened.

Most of us could write a book on flops, washouts, mess-ups, blunders, botches, duds, bungles, and failures, but who hasn't blown something in his life? Those who blunder the least are usually those who attempt the least. Steven Pile, the head of the "Not Terribly Good Club" of Great Britain, was forced to resign from his position when a book he wrote, *The Book of Heroic Failures*, became a bestseller. He couldn't even succeed in his position as president! Albert Einstein said, "Anyone who has never made a mistake has never tried anything new." Don't let the past limit you. With God all things are possible...so strive to do what others think is impossible. Donald Trump said, "As long as you're going to be thinking anyway, THINK BIG."

QUESTIONS

1. **Why do some people do well at school but afterwards fizzle?**

2. **What is the first key to being successful as a Christian?**

3. **What does self-discipline involve for a Christian?**

4. **What are some things you can do to bring out the best in others?**

5. **According to the Bible, how important is it to keep our promises?**

PREACHER'S PROGRESS

Ima B. Leever: "I have broken the Commandments. I've lied and stolen, etc., but I believe in God."

Christian: "Everyone does. For instance, did you know that Hitler believed in God?"

Ima B. Leever: "I didn't know that."

Christian: "The Bible says that even the demons believe in God—and they tremble."

Ima B. Leever: "So what are you saying?"

Christian: "I'm saying that God doesn't want your belief. He wants your obedience. Have you obeyed the gospel?"

Ima B. Leever: "Yes. I was baptized as a child and I confess my sins to the priest."

Christian: "That won't help you. Would you like to know why?"

Ima B. Leever: "Yes."

Christian: "A criminal has been given a $50,000 fine for a very serious crime. He stands in front of the judge and confesses his crime to him, saying that he is truly sorry. Then he says that he will never commit the offense again. Will the judge just let him go?"

Ima B. Leever: "No. He has a fine to pay."

Christian: "That's right. The criminal should be sorry for what he's done. And of course he should not commit the crime again. The judge won't let him go on the basis that he is sorry, or that he won't break the law again. However, he will let him go if someone pays his fine."

Ima B. Leever: "That makes sense."

Christian: "Two thousand years ago, Someone paid your fine. Jesus took your punishment, once and for all, upon Himself. So when the Bible speaks of 'believing' in Jesus, it means 'trusting' Him—the same way you would trust a parachute to save you. What would you think of a man who 'believed' in a parachute, but jumped without putting it on?"

Ima B. Leever: "He'd be a nut."

Christian: "So, don't just believe in the Savior—'put on the Lord Jesus Christ.'"

FEATHERS FOR ARROWS

In 1950, a woman said of her first husband, "I love him better every day." She divorced him and in 1952 said of her second husband, "I just want to be with him, to be his wife." That marriage ended in divorce. In 1959 she predicted that she would be with husband number four for "thirty or forty years." That also ended in divorce. In 1964 she said of her next husband, "This marriage will last forever." After divorcing him and then re-marrying him in 1975 she said, "We are stuck together like chicken feathers to tar." After divorcing him in 1976 she married a senator and said, "I have never been so happy." She divorced him also, and as she married Larry Fortensky in 1991, she said, "This is it, forever." Their divorce was in 1995. Who is this woman? Elizabeth Taylor.

Last Words

William Pope, who died in 1797, was the leader of a company of infidels who ridiculed everything religious. One of their exercises was to kick the Bible around the floor or tear it up. Friends present in his death-chamber spoke of it as a scene of terror as he died crying:

"I have no contrition. I cannot repent. God will damn me. I know the day of grace is past...You see one who is damned forever...Oh, Eternity! Eternity! Nothing for me but hell. Come eternal torments... I hate everything God has made, only I have no hatred for the devil— I wish to be with him. I long to be in hell. Do you not see? Do you not see him?"

Memory Verse

"Whosoever will come after me, let him deny himself, and take up his cross, and follow me. For whosoever will save his life shall lose it; but whosoever shall lose his life for my sake and the gospel's, the same shall save it."

MARK 8:34,35

LESSON 96

When You've Been Wronged

"I was honored today with having a few stones, dirt, rotten eggs, and pieces of dead cats thrown at me."

GEORGE WHITEFIELD

Kirk's Comment   This lesson requires us to swallow our pride. If we are going to walk like Jesus walked, we must learn how to lay down our pride and love those who hurt us.

QUESTIONS & OBJECTIONS

"I knew some Christians once and they wronged me."

Christians aren't perfect. They make mistakes like anyone else. I hope you can find it in your heart to forgive them. I think that is what they would do for you.

Maybe they didn't know they wronged you. Was it something really bad or was it just a mistake? Have you gone to them and spoken to them about it? Maybe if you were to forgive them you would begin to understand the forgiveness God has for you. We all need to be forgiven, don't you agree?

Pride is a subtle thing. I remember many years ago stepping forward to take a closer look at a sofa in a shop display. Suddenly I came to an abrupt halt. I had walked straight into a plate glass door. Did I give thought to the pain coming from a flattened nose? No. My first thought was, *Who saw me?* When I realized that no one had seen the incident, I proceeded to give comfort to my nose.

I once saw a woman walk behind me while I was preaching outdoors. As she did so, she stumbled and twisted her ankle. It apparently didn't hurt at all. With the utmost composure, she graciously walked across in front of the crowd as though nothing had happened. Yet from my viewpoint, I saw that when she got around the corner, she doubled up with pain.

The Bible says God hates pride. It is a sin that will stop multitudes from entering the kingdom of heaven. Pride destroys families. It keeps spouses from admitting that they are wrong. They would rather break up a family and keep their pride, than humble themselves and be reconciled, even for the sake of the children.

When I went to give blood at the local Red Cross, I had to spend quite some time filling out a form about my background. The AIDS virus had left blood banks justifiably paranoid. Ordinary banks are worried about bad withdrawals; blood banks are worried about bad deposits. The list of questions seemed endless: did I have HIV, heart disease, fainting spells, etc. I looked down the long list, then across to the boxes on the right side of the form. It was simple. All they contained were "Yes" or "No," so I went down the boxes and did what all good people from Down-Under do—I crossed out the non-applicable ones. Did I have HIV? I crossed out the "Yes" in the box, leaving a clear "No" for the person reviewing the form. It made sense to me.

I then took the form to the nurse and sat beside her. She stared at it for about three seconds, and then looked at me in horror. My answers indicated that I had HIV, hepatitis, typhoid, malaria, cancer, heart disease, lumps under my arms, skin rashes, fainting spells, and that I'd had diarrhea for over a month—among a number of other distasteful things.

Her facial expression changed when I told her that New Zealanders walk around upside-down, drive on the other side of the road, and fill out forms differently.

In one sense, you have (by way of your commitment to Christ) moved into a radically different culture. You are now living in a kingdom which has rules that are revolutionary. You have bowed your knee to the sovereignty of the King of kings. As author Larry Tomczak explained, "Coming under the loving Lordship of Jesus Christ means an end to our 'rights' as well as to our wrongs. It means the end of life on our own terms." Now you owe your allegiance to Him above all else—and His ways are certainly different. Never a man spoke like this Man. Jesus said to bless those who curse you, do good to those who hate you, and pray for those who spitefully use you (Matthew 5:44).

Many have missed the point of why the Christian should let another person stomp on him. The reason is not that the Christian is a wimp, but that he has surrendered the job of vengeance to the Lord. If someone does me wrong, I am not to take the law into my own hands. Instead, I give it all to God in prayer, and if (in His perfect judgment) He sees fit to do so, He will stomp on the person who stomped on me; and He has a righteous (and bigger) stomp.

Let me give you some examples of how this works. Sue and I used to let people have our books and tapes on a credit system. After a seminar, if people didn't have any money at the time, we would let them take what they wanted, and we would send them a bill. It was a good system, except that after awhile we discovered we had $3,000 worth of unpaid bills. Professing Christians were taking our property and not paying for it.

We sent reminders. That didn't produce any response at all. So we decided we would get radical and do it God's way. We mailed a gift of ten dollars to each of those who had stolen books and tapes from us, based on the fact that Jesus said to do good to those who hate you and pray for those who spitefully use you. He said that if someone wants to take your coat, you should give the person your cloak also (see Matthew 5:40). What we were saying was, "God, we give it all to You. We want You to be our financial Adviser. If You see fit to stomp on these people, that's up to You. You know their circumstances. Perhaps they are in financial difficulty. In the meantime, we will love our neighbors as ourselves and do them good."

The following weekend I did a series of meetings for a church, and the honorarium they gave me was ten times the normal amount! We like the way God works, so now we do things His way.

This wasn't just an isolated incident. I once sent fourteen boxes of books to South Africa. When they arrived, the person who ordered them called me and said they were all damaged. We were 4,000 miles apart, so all I could do was to ask him to claim the insurance. For some reason, he refused. A friend told me to instigate court proceedings, but I felt led to draw on the wisdom of my Business Adviser. Instead I gave the whole thing to God in prayer and wrote it off. The next weekend at a Christian camp, we sold more than seven times as many books and tapes as we usually sell.

A close friend of mine was a partner in a Christian T-shirt company. One of their shirts had a particular word on it that was used by a well-known apparel company. Not long after the shirt was released, the apparel company threatened to sue my friend's company for using the word unless they came up with a quick $10,000. Even though their lawyers felt there was no way they could lose the case in court, he prayed about it and felt led to obey the Scriptures. Because Jesus said that if someone sues you for your coat, you should give him your cloak also, he gave them a number of checks (over a short period) totaling $10,000, then an extra $1,000 check.

What he did didn't make much sense. Yet within one month, God had so blessed the T-shirt company that they expanded from eight employees to forty-two. In fact, within three years of business, they sold over one million T-shirts.

You may not be involved in book or T-shirt sales, but you can put these same principles into practice. If someone does you wrong, don't let pride rear its ugly head. Stop for a minute and consider, "What would man have me do, and what would Jesus have me do?" Man's way is for you to stick up for your rights. That will be a way that feels good to your natural mind, a way that seems right—but I encourage you to give it all to God in prayer, then do it His way. If someone wrongs you at your place of work, buy him a gift. Do the person good, and then pray that through God's love his heart will be open to the claims of the gospel. Such a radical action in the mind of a hard heart is worth a thousand eloquent sermons.

QUESTIONS

1. **Why does God hate pride?**

2. **How would you explain the "Lordship" of Christ?**

3. **Why are we not to seek vengeance on our own?**

4. **Have you ever been seriously wronged? Did you react God's way or man's way?**

5. **Were you blessed or depressed by your reaction to the wrong?**

6. How did Jesus react when He was wronged? (See 1 Peter 2:23.)

FEATHERS FOR ARROWS

The life and death of Jesus Christ is a standing rebuke to every form of pride of which men are capable:

- *Pride of birth and rank:* "Is not this the carpenter's son?" (Matthew 13:55)

- *Pride of wealth:* "The Son of man has no where to lay his head." (Matthew 8:20)

- *Pride of personal appearance:* "There is no beauty that we should desire him." (Isaiah 53:2)

- *Pride of reputation:* "A friend of publicans and sinners." (Matthew 11:19)

- *Pride of learning:* "How does this Man know letters, having never studied?" (John 7:15)

- *Pride of superiority:* "I am among you as he that serves." (Luke 22:27)

- *Pride of success:* "He was despised and rejected of men." (Isaiah 53:3)

- *Pride of ability:* "I can of my own self do nothing." (John 5:30)

- *Pride of intellect:* "As my Father has taught me, I speak these things." (John 8:28)

- *Pride of self-will:* "I seek not my own will, but the will of the Father who has sent me." (John 5:30)

- *Pride in death:* "He became obedient unto death, even the death of the cross." (Philippians 2:8)

Words of Comfort

We faced some relatively minor adjustments when we moved from New Zealand to the United States in 1989. Down-Under, light switches are "up" for off, and "down" for on. The water goes down the drain the opposite way. The sun goes across on the other side of the sky. We drive on the other side of the road. When it's summer here, it's winter there. The accent is different. Also, Down-Under, a "fag" is a cigarette butt, not a homosexual. This last colloquialism is minor until one uses the word while preaching. I was preaching open-air in Hawaii when a heckler began yelling at me. He called himself a Christian, even though he was drunk and had a cigarette hanging from his mouth. After a brief exchange, much to my consternation he began to leave, so I called, "Going off for another fag, huh?" The crowd roared, and I was left bewildered. I was later filled in about why I had received that response.

Last Words

Matthew Henry (1662–1774) was the eminent theologian whose devotional commentary still holds a foremost place in its field. He died a week after settling in London as pastor of a church in Hackney, but his end was full of confidence in the Savior's grace. Among his last words were:

> "A life spent in the service of God, and in communion with Him, is the most comfortable life that anyone can lead in this present world."

The Source of Revival

> *"Have you noticed how much praying for revival has been going on of late—and how little revival has resulted? I believe the problem is that we have been trying to substitute praying for obeying, and it simply will not work. To pray for revival while ignoring the plain precept laid down in Scripture is to waste a lot of words and get nothing for our trouble. Prayer will become effective when we stop using it as a substitute for obedience."*

A. W. TOZER

Kirk's Comment This lesson makes me consider how much I actually love people. If I'm really concerned about their eternal salvation, I ought to be wrestling in prayer day and night, talking with the unsaved as often as possible, and begging God for a mighty move of His Spirit.

QUESTIONS & OBJECTIONS

"How should I witness to a Jew?"

Sadly, many of today's Jews profess godliness but don't embrace the Scriptures as we presume they do. Therefore, it is often difficult to reason with them about Jesus being the Messiah. This is why it is imperative to ask a Jew if he has kept the Law of Moses—to "shut" him up under the Law

(Galatians 3:23) and strip him of his self-righteousness. The Law will show him his need of a Savior and become a "schoolmaster" to bring him to Christ (Galatians 3:24), as happened to Paul, Nicodemus, and Nathaniel. It was the Law that brought 3,000 Jews to the foot of the cross on the Day of Pentecost. Without it they would not have known that they had sinned (Romans 7:7), and therefore would not have seen their need of the Savior.

wotmwotmwotmwotmwotmwotmwotmwotmwotmwotmwotm

Prayer was the ignition to every revival fire in history, and the key to the doorway of ministry for every preacher used by God in the past. It is evident that God is calling His Church to prayer, the kind of prayer that will storm the very gates of hell. We need a worldwide revival in the Church that will boil over into the world! We need to seek God daily to break the hard hearts of hell-bound sinners. And we need such an anointing on our preaching that men will weep from a sense of their own sinfulness. That can come only through prayer.

God is not willing that any perish; He wants *all* to "come to the knowledge of the truth" (2 Timothy 3:7). Therefore we can confidently pursue God for men—then, in urgent zeal, pursue men for God.

Look at the burden on the heart of Oswald J. Smith as he speaks about the type of prayer that moves Heaven's Hand:

> Can we travail for a drowning child, but not for a perishing soul? It is not hard to weep when we realize that our little one is sinking below the surface for the last time. Anguish is spontaneous then. Nor is it hard to agonize when we see the casket containing all that we love on earth borne out of the home. Ah, tears are natural at such a time. But oh, to realize and know that souls, precious, never dying souls, are perishing all around us, going out into the blackness of darkness and despair, eternally lost, and yet to feel no anguish, shed no tears, know no travail! How cold are our hearts! How little we know of the compassion of Jesus! And yet God can give us this, and the fault is ours if we do not have it. Jacob, you remember, travailed until he prevailed. But oh, who is doing it today? Who is really travailing in prayer? How many, even of your most spiritual Christian

leaders, are content to spend half an hour a day on their knees and then pride themselves on the time they have given to God!

If you are a normal human being, you will find it hard to pray. The flesh resists the thought of travailing prayer. Other things in our busy life will want to have priority. However, being a Christian means being a disciplined person. It means setting aside time to deny ourselves and pray. Here are some practical things you can do in the battle to pray:

1. Find yourself a regular "closet." This is a place of secret prayer. It may be a spare room, an attic, a basement, or even a physical closet. This means that you will not only be free from distractions, but you will have no one to impress with "eloquent" prayers. It will be just you and your Creator.

2. Kneel down. Humble yourself in both body and soul.

3. Put a pen and pad beside you, and write down thoughts and verses that may come to you in prayer.

4. Confess any sins to God. Pour out your heart to Him. Ask for forgiveness for that second look, that failure to share your faith, selfishness you exhibited, or some harsh words spoken during the day.

5. Ask the Holy Spirit to help you pray, then begin crying out for lost souls. Think of their eternal destiny in hell. Pray for laborers to reach them. Offer to be one of those laborers. Ask God to open doors for you. Ask Him to help you overcome your fears, your pride, your self-indulgence. Pray for great wisdom. Name unsaved loved ones, friends, coworkers, and strangers. Pray for our leaders. Pray for nations. Think big. Believe big—because nothing is too hard for God.

Look again at Oswald J. Smith's passion to reach the lost:

We expect extraordinary results, and extraordinary results are quite possible; signs and wonders will follow, but only through extraordinary efforts in the spiritual realm. Hence, nothing short of continuous, agonizing pleading for souls, hours upon hours, days and nights of prayer, will ever avail. Therefore, 'gird yourselves, and lament, ye priests; howl, ye ministers of the altar: come, lie all night in sackcloth, ye ministers of my God. Sanctify ye a fast, call a solemn assembly, gather the elders and all the inhabitants of the land unto the house of the LORD your God, and cry unto the LORD' (Joel 1:13,14). Ah, yes, Joel knew the secret. Let us then lay aside everything else and 'cry unto the Lord.'

We read in the biographies of your forefathers, who were most successful in winning souls, that they prayed for hours in private. The question therefore arises, can we get the same results without following their example? If we can, then let us prove to the world that we have found a better way, but if not, then in God's name let us begin to follow those who through faith and patience obtained the promise. Our forefathers wept and prayed and agonized before the Lord for sinners to be saved, and would not rest until they were slain by the Sword of the Word of God. That was the secret of their mighty success; when things were slack and would not move, they wrestled in prayer till God poured out His Spirit upon the people and sinners were converted.

Beware, however, of the subtlety of passive prayer. Many Christians are praying for revival—that God would pour out His Spirit and save this world—but it is made blatantly evident by statistics that few actually share their faith. They are substituting prayer for a move of God, for obedience to the Word of God.

True prayer is a travail of the soul. It is a groaning empathy. However, it does more than groan outside the grave of Lazarus. It tells him to "Come forth." To travail in prayer for revival, but to fail to speak to those who are dead in trespasses and sins, is to have a Gethsemane without a Calvary. It is to stay in the Upper Room and worship the One who commanded us to move out and preach the gospel to every creature. A. W. Pink said, "It is true that [many] are praying for worldwide revival. But it would be more timely, and more scriptural, for prayer to be made to the Lord of the harvest, that He would raise up and thrust forth laborers who would fearlessly and faithfully preach those truths which are calculated to bring about a revival."

In Ephesians 6:11, we are told to put on the whole armor of God. Many Christians are truthful; they have their heart free of sin, are sure of their salvation, and rightly use the Word of God. But they are shoeless—they are not prepared to share the "gospel of peace" (v. 15). Those who do not advance the cause of the gospel are stationary soldiers; any evangelistic movement is too painful for them. If they are not seeking to save the lost, they are not taking ground for the kingdom of God. Paul climaxed his admonition to the Ephesians by highlighting what the battle is for. He pleads with them to pray for him to have boldness to reach out to the unsaved, citing his moral responsibility (v. 20).

Make sure you don't pacify a guilty conscience by simply praying for the salvation of the lost, but not preaching to them. It is the *gospel* that is the power of God unto salvation. How shall they hear without a preacher (Romans 10:14)?

QUESTIONS

1. **What has been the ignition to every revival fire in history?**

2. **Would you be anguished to see a child drown? Are you as anguished about the unsaved? If not, what does this tell you about yourself?**

3. **What can you do to right this situation?**

4. What are some of the reasons we find it hard to pray?

5. What are many Christians doing to promote revival?

6. What is "true prayer"?

WORDS OF COMFORT

No one likes bad drivers. They fail to signal. They tailgate. They drive too fast, or they drive too slow. Some even read maps while driving. They shouldn't be allowed on the road. I thank God that I am not like them.

Don't get me wrong—I do have one small driving flaw. I tend to get lost very easily. In fact, I have the sense of direction of a blind ostrich on a moonless night.

I was aware of this minor fault when I planned to drive about 15 miles down a Los Angeles freeway to a business that sold magnets. I have always had an attraction to magnets, and these folks made what was supposed to be the world's strongest.

I wisely printed out a map with driving directions, grabbed it as it came out of my printer, and ran out the door. Sue was a little worried that I would get lost, but I assured her that with the map in hand I would have no trouble at all. In fact, I called her on my cell phone when I was halfway there, just to let her know that getting lost was a thing of the past.

I exited the freeway and confidently lifted the full-color map, being careful to slow down as I approached the lights. Unfortunately, I had run out of my office before the *second* page of the map had printed out, and (unbeknown to me) my directions finished at the point of telling me where to exit the freeway.

As I looked at the map, my van accidentally drove onto the island in the middle of the road (just for a few feet). I skillfully pulled the vehicle back onto the road and followed the turn lane left onto a side street. I then picked up the map again, wondering why it didn't give me any directions when I needed them. This time I wisely slowed down to about 3 mph. It was then that I heard a *honk*, and noticed that a truck was tailgating me. I quickly sped up and pulled into a driveway, both to let the truck pass me and to look again at the driving directions.

As I sat in the driveway, I heard another *honk*. It was the tailgating truck. I had pulled into his driveway. I drove forward, did a U-turn, and parked the van. I then called Sue (who wasn't surprised to hear from me) and had her guide me step-by-step to my destination.

Memory Verse

"How, then, can they call on the one they have not believed in? And how can they believe in the one of whom they have not heard? And how can they hear without someone preaching to them?"

ROMANS 10:14

Last Words

Queen Jane of Navarre (1572), sometimes referred to as Jeanne D'Albrets, died saying:

"Weep not for me, I pray you. God by this sickness calls me hence to enjoy a better life; and now I shall enter into the desired haven toward which this frail vessel of mine has been a long time steering."

Hindrances to Revival

"I have no confidence at all in polished speech or brilliant literary effort to bring about a revival, but I have all the confidence in the world in the poor saint who would weep her eyes out because people are living in sin."

CHARLES SPURGEON

Kirk's Comment   I believe revival would be the most wonderful thing I could ever see in this lifetime. Clean hands, a pure heart, and an obedient life is what I want to offer the Lord. Let this lesson help you search your heart for anything keeping you from fully serving God.

QUESTIONS & OBJECTIONS

"The Bible says, 'Judge not lest you be judged.' You therefore have no right to judge me when it comes to my sins!"

The lost often take this verse out of context and use it to accuse Christians of being "judgmental" when they speak of sin. In the context of the verse, Jesus is telling His disciples not to judge one another, something the Bible condemns (Romans 14:10; James 4:11). In Luke 6:41,42 He speaks of seeing a speck in a *brother's* eye. In John 7:24 He said, "Judge not according to the appearance, but judge righteous judgment." If someone steals, lies, commits adultery or murder, etc., the Christian can make a (righteous) moral judgment and say that the actions were morally wrong, and that these sins will have eternal consequences. Chuck Colson said, "True tolerance is not a total lack of judgment. It's knowing what should be tolerated —and refusing to tolerate that which shouldn't."

w o t m w o t m w o t m w o t m w o t m w o t m w o t m w o t m w o t m w o t m w o t m

While it may appear controversial to some to say that sin on our part could hinder a revival, it is both a biblical and a historical fact that when God's people sanctified themselves, it preceded a move of God's Spirit. Therefore, if we are serious about reaching this sinful world with the message of salvation, it is wise to search our hearts under the spotlight of a tender conscience to see if we harbor any secret sin. The content of this lesson comes from Oswald J. Smith's book *The Revival We Need*. In it he wrote:

It is a common experience to find souls kneeling at the altar and calling upon God with apparent great anguish of heart, who fail to receive anything. And it is just as common for groups of people to gather together for nights of prayer for a revival and yet never have their prayers answered. What is the trouble? Let the Word of God answer: "Your iniquities have separated between you and your God and your sins have hid His face from you, that He will not hear" (Isaiah 59:2). Hence, let us uncover our sin first of all; let us make straight the crooked ways, let us gather out the stones, and then we may ask in faith and expectancy for showers of blessing.

Let us take our sins one by one and deal with each transgression separately. And let us ask ourselves the following questions. It may be we are guilty and God will speak to us:

1. Have we forgiven everyone? Is there any malice, spite, hatred or enmity in our hearts? Do we cherish grudges; and have we refused to be reconciled?

2. Do we get angry? Are there any uprisings within? Is it true that we still lose our tempers? Does wrath hold us at times in its grip?

3. Is there any feeling of jealousy? When another is preferred before us, does it make us envious and uncomfortable? Do we get jealous of those who can pray, speak and do things better than we can?

4. Do we get impatient and irritated? Do little things vex and annoy, or, are we sweet, calm and unruffled under all circumstances?

5. Are we offended easily? When people fail to notice us and pass by without speaking, does it hurt? If others are made much of and we are neglected, how do we feel about it?

6. Is there any pride in our hearts? Are we puffed up, do we think a great deal of our own position and attainments?

7. Have we been dishonest? Is our business open and above reproach? Do we give a yard for a yard and a pound for a pound? Are we honest in our statements, or do we exaggerate and convey false impressions?

8. Have we been gossiping about people? Do we slander the character of others? Are we talebearers and busybodies?

9. Do we criticize unlovingly, harshly, severely? Are we always finding fault and looking for the flaws in others?

10. Do we rob God? Have we stolen time that belongs to Him? Has our money been withheld?

11. Are we guilty of the sin of unbelief? In spite of all He has done for us, do we still refuse to believe the promises of His Word?

12. Have we committed the sin of prayerlessness? Are we intercessors? Do we pray? How much time are we spending on our knees? Have we crowded prayer out of our lives?

13. Are we neglecting God's Word? How many chapters do we read each day? Are we Bible students? Do we draw our source of supply from the Scriptures?

14. Are we burdened for the salvation of souls? Have we a love for the lost? Is there any compassion in our hearts for those who are perishing?

15. Have we failed to confess Christ openly? Are we ashamed of Jesus? Do we keep our mouths closed when we are surrounded by worldly people? Are we witnessing daily?

16. Are our lives filled with lightness and frivolity? Is our conduct unseemly? Would the world by our actions consider us on its side?

17. Have we wronged anyone and failed to make restitution? Or, has the spirit of Zacchaeus possessed us? Have we restored the many little things that God has shown us?

18. Are we worried or anxious? Do we fail to trust God for our temporal and spiritual needs? Are we continually crossing bridges before we come to them?

19. Are we guilty of lustful thoughts? Do we allow our minds to harbor impure and unholy imaginations?

QUESTIONS

1. What is often the catalyst for revival?

2. Why do you think our sin could hinder revival?

3. Why are our prayers sometimes "unanswered"?

4. What must we do to receive "showers of blessing"?

5. **Of which of the listed transgressions are you guilty?**

FEATHERS FOR ARROWS

Many years ago, a young man purchased two Java sparrows for his bird aviary. They were attractive little birds, with smooth gray feathers and brightly colored beaks. As usual, the pet store had placed them in a brown paper bag and stapled the top. It was a workday and some time before he went home, so he cut a small opening in the side of the bag as an air hole and placed the bag on his office desk.

As the day passed, he was amazed at the pattern of human reaction. Most who stepped into his office wondered why on earth he had a moving paper bag on his desk. When he told them it was a bag of birds, they would pick it up, put their eye to the hole and say, "Wow! What sort of birds are they?" It was at that moment that he would mumble, "Mexican eye-peckers." It was amazing to see how quickly a bag could be pulled from the eye.

If we are so quick to care for the eye, how much more should we care for the soul, the very life that looks through the eye?

Imagine if you picked up a newspaper and noticed the following advertisement: "Wanted: eyes—must be fresh. Transplant doctor offering $500,000 for one eye; $1,000,000 for a matching pair." All you have to do is go in and let them painlessly remove both of your eyes and a million dollars is yours! Now you can see the world! No, you can't. If you sell your eyes, you will sit in darkness until the day of your death. Think about it. How much would you sell your eyes for? I am sure that you wouldn't think of it; they are priceless. Yet they are just the windows of your soul. If the eyes are priceless, how much must your soul be worth? The Bible says it is without price.

Of all the things that should be supremely important to you, it's not your eyes (or your health) that you should be most concerned about—it is the eternal salvation of your soul.

WORDS OF COMFORT

When we returned home after three weeks of ministry in Hawaii, we found everything in order, except that the greenhouse door was opened slightly. It was a good greenhouse. I had made it myself, and hardly spilled a pint of blood in doing so. It had a strong wooden frame with a thick plastic covering. I was pleased that, even under the hot penetrating sun, it had lasted three years. There wasn't a single hole in it.

I was always very careful if I carried a rake or sharp garden tool inside. One dumb move and there would be an irreparable tear. So I was a little concerned to find that the greenhouse door wasn't closed all the way.

As I gently pushed it open, I saw a black cat on the far side of the greenhouse. It glared at me, aware that it shouldn't be in my precious greenhouse. Sometimes animals, especially cats, panic if they can't find a way out. It was important that I didn't alarm the animal and cause it to damage my tomato plants. All I had to do was to gently coax it out the door. I smiled and gingerly whispered, "Here, kitty...it's all right. You come out the way you came in... over here, kitty, kitty." The petrified animal glanced at me, then looked up at the wall of the greenhouse. I yelled, "No!" That was all it needed. It went vertical, up the plastic wall with its sharp penetrating claws, making holes in the plastic with every terrified step. Then it darted past me and disappeared out the door.

Memory Verse

"If my people, which are called by my name, shall humble themselves, and pray, and seek my face, and turn from their wicked ways; then will I hear from heaven, and will forgive their sin, and heal their land."

2 CHRONICLES 7:14

Last Words

Edward VI (1537–1553), King of England:

"Lord God, deliver me from this miserable, wretched life, and receive me among Thy chosen. Oh, Lord God, defend this realm and maintain Thy true religion. Lord, have mercy upon me and receive my spirit."

99

How to Maintain Zeal

> *"No man who preaches the gospel without zeal is sent from God to preach at all."*
>
> **CHARLES SPURGEON**

Kirk's Comment Oh, how I long to be interested not in what people think of me, but only in who God wants me to be and what He wants me to do. I must live for an audience of One or I'm wasting so much precious time.

QUESTIONS & OBJECTIONS

"How can I witness to family members?"

This advice may save you a great deal of grief. As a new Christian, I did almost irreparable damage by acting like a wild bull in a crystal showroom. I bullied my mom, my dad, and many of my friends into making a "decision for Christ." I was sincere, zealous, loving, kind, and stupid. I didn't understand that salvation doesn't come through making a "decision," but through repentance, and repentance is God-given (2 Timothy 2:25). The Bible teaches that no one can come to the Son unless the Father "draws" him (John 6:44). If you are able to get a "decision" but the person has no conviction of sin, you will almost certainly end up with a stillborn on your hands.

In my "zeal without knowledge" I actually inoculated the very ones I was so desperately trying to reach. There is nothing more important to you than the salvation of your loved ones, and you don't want to blow it. If you do, you may find that you don't have a second chance. Fervently pray for them, asking God for their salvation. Let them see your faith. Let them feel your kindness, your genuine love, and your gentleness. Buy gifts for no reason. Do chores when you are not asked to. Go the extra mile. Put yourself in their position. You know that you have found everlasting life—*death has lost its sting!* Your joy is unspeakable. But as far as they are concerned, you've been brainwashed and have become part of a weird sect. So your loving actions will speak more loudly than ten thousand eloquent sermons.

For this reason you should avoid verbal confrontation until you have knowledge that will guide your zeal. Pray for wisdom and sensitivity to God's timing. You may have only one shot, so make it count. Keep your cool. If you don't, you may end up with a lifetime of regret. Believe me. It is better to hear a loved one or a close friend say, "Tell me about your faith in Jesus Christ," rather than you saying, "Sit down. I want to talk to you." Continue to persevere in prayer for them, that God would open their eyes to the truth.

w o t m w o t m w o t m w o t m w o t m w o t m w o t m w o t m w o t m w o t m w o t m

A zeal for God should be the norm in the Christian life. As Charles Spurgeon stated, "If you never have sleepless hours, if you never have weeping eyes, if your hearts never swell as if they would burst, you need not anticipate that you will be called zealous. You do not know the beginning of true zeal, for the foundation of Christian zeal lies in the heart. The heart must be heavy with grief and yet must beat high with holy ardor. The heart must be vehement in desire, panting continually for God's glory, or else we shall never attain to anything like the zeal which God would have us know."

Where does this zeal come from? In Acts 20:22–24 the apostle Paul, who was the picture of zeal, reveals that he was warned about what God had in store for him. This is what he said:

> And now, behold, I go bound in the spirit to Jerusalem, not know-
> ing the things that shall befall me there: save that the Holy Spirit wit-
> nesses in every city, saying that bonds and afflictions abide me. But
> none of these things move me, neither count I my life dear to myself,
> so that I might finish my course with joy, and the ministry, which I
> have received of the Lord Jesus, to testify the gospel of the grace of
> God.

He was told his future held nothing but "bonds and afflictions." Yet
Paul responded with a courageous attitude of joyful resignation to the
will of God. How could Paul despise the suffering that he was about to
face? It would seem that he did so in light of the cross of Calvary. He said,
"God forbid that I should glory, save in the cross of our Lord Jesus Christ,
by whom the world is crucified to me, and I to the world" (Galatians
6:14). As far as Paul was concerned, he was already dead to the world and
all its pleasures. He lived only for the will of the One who laid down His
life for him. Paul had sat at the feet of Gamaliel (the great teacher of the
Law), and had seen the depth of his own sinful heart in light of the Law
of a holy God. He had caught a glimpse of the exceedingly sinful nature
of sin, and in doing so, he also glimpsed the depth of the love of God.

There is an amazing irony in the Christian faith. The more we see
ourselves as hell-deserving sinners, the more we appreciate the fact that
we are heading for an undeserved heaven. Few know that there is a gold-
mine of joy at the foot of the cross, and it is the Law that unearths that
great treasure. From the lowly position of a humble heart, an enlightened
sinner can see nothing but love in the blood-sodden soil of Calvary. From
such a position comes an explosion of returned love, gratitude, and zeal
for God that has the potential to swallow our fears. That was the apostle
Paul's wonderful key.

Love toward God for the cross unlocks the prison of fear. Instead of
being concerned about what man may do, it frees Christians to be concerned about what God wants us to do. We love Him because He first
loved us, and 1 John 4:18 tells us, "There is no fear in love; but perfect
love casts out fear: because fear has torment. He that fears is not made
perfect in love."

All fear is vanquished by *perfect* love, which is a "mature" love for God. Such love is as deep as the ocean and can swallow fear when it rains on the Christian.

Have you seen your sin in light of the Law of God? Do you understand in your heart of hearts that if every secret sin is manifest on the Day of Wrath and if justice had its way, you would fall like lightning into hell? Have you fallen prostrate in the blood-soaked earth at the foot of the cross? Have you pictured Jesus Christ crucified? Have you seen the precious blood pouring from His hands and His feet, and cried, "For me He dies"?

If you have, horror mingled with unspeakable gratitude will drive you to your knees, and you will whisper, "Oh, God, because You did that for me, I will do anything for You!" This zeal for God will produce in you a zeal for the lost. Remember that whispered prayer of surrender the next time you fear hollers at you as you hand someone a tract.

QUESTIONS

1. **How did Charles Spurgeon describe zeal?**

2. **What awaited Paul in every city he was about to visit?**

3. **How would this make you feel if that were God's plan for your life?**

4. What was Paul's attitude toward what he was about to face?

5. Do you count your life dear to you? (Give this deep thought before you answer.)

6. How can we develop a zeal for God?

WORDS OF COMFORT

I have no trouble believing the teaching of the Bible that we live in a *fallen* creation. This has not only been confirmed in my mind, when a piglike snort has woken me from a deep sleep and I was the only one in the room, but it has been corroborated by life's experience.

When I was a child, I remember finding that my guinea pigs had gone stiff in a heavy frost. It was either the freezing cold, or the rhubarb leaves I fed them the night before that caused their demise (rhubarb leaves, I learned, are poisonous). My dog was killed on the road, our cat and another dog vanished into thin air, and my frog croaked.

When Sue and I were first married, I purchased a goat that I named "Abraham." I thought he would keep the grass down. Its name should have been "Skunk." We kept it for only a day.

Later on in life, I bought two white mice for our children. One day Sue found only one, rather fat mouse in the cage. All that was left of the other was a tail with a little blood on one end. It seemed that one mouse fancied the other for lunch. We threw the cannibal over the fence into an empty lot.

When a lovable little duckling that waddled into our yard was apparently handled too much by our kids, it went to that great lake in the sky. One of our hens followed hard on its heels, after nearly turning itself inside out while straining to lay an egg.

Around that time, I visited a bird aviary and found to my horror that the owner was about to have a mass execution. There were three birds on death row, and their only crimes were that one was too fat, one was blind, and the other had only one leg.

I successfully obtained a stay of execution, gained custody, and found myself with an aviary that depicted the kingdom of God, containing the rejects of society: the oppressed, the lame, and the blind. We named the birds Big Bird, Peg-leg, and Bartimaeus.

However, it wasn't long until I found the sorry sight of Peg-leg lying on his back with his one and only leg reaching for the sky. Big Bird soon followed. Bartimaeus turned a blind eye to the goings-on and laid an egg, which meant that "he" had a quick name change to Bartimaette.

A father parakeet viciously pecked his six offspring to death, which put us off parakeets, so we turned our energies to canaries. Things were humming for a time, especially when a number of our canary moms laid and hatched eggs—twenty-six of them.

Twenty-three of the chicks died. The mothers for some reason gave up feeding their babies just as they were beginning to mature. They would fly to the other side of the cage, ignore their parental responsibilities, and sit in the sun and preen.

I fostered the offspring and tried feeding them with an eyedropper, but somehow air would get in and explode mushy food onto the chicks. Sadly, a number of birds left the land of the living stiffly encased in concrete bird food. It got to a point where I would tell Sue that another egg had hatched and she would say, "Okay…I'll dig another hole."

Memory Verse

"Have mercy upon me, O God, according to your loving-kindness: according unto the multitude of your tender mercies blot out my transgressions. Wash me thoroughly from my iniquity, and cleanse me from my sin."

PSALM 51:1,2

Last Words

Louis XVII (1795) left this last word:

"I have something to tell you."

Ten Ways to Raise Laborers in Your Church

"You must have, more or less, a distinct sense of the dreadful wrath of God and of the terrors of the judgment to come, or you will lack energy in your work and so lack one of the essentials of success."

CHARLES SPURGEON

Kirk's Comment This lesson contains the mandate I want to live by. It is my highest calling, my greatest honor, and my personal responsibility. Read it carefully and enlist in God's army.

QUESTIONS & OBJECTIONS

"If God is all-knowing and He knows our future, then how is that free will?"

God knows the future of what the free-will creatures choose. Free will does not stop becoming free just because God knows what will happen. For example, I know that my child will choose to eat chocolate cake over cauliflower. If I were to set them both before her and turned to my wife and knowingly said, "We know which one she will choose, don't we?" this is not taking away the freedom of my child. Likewise, for God to know what a person will choose does not mean that the person has no freedom to make the choice. It simply means that God knows what the person will choose. This is necessarily so since God knows all things (1 John 3:20).

Christian pollster George Barna may have put his finger on the problem in many of our churches when it comes to witnessing. He said, "It occurred to me that in our work with secular organizations, the leader shapes the heart and passion of the corporate entity. In our work with non-profit organizations, we have found the same principle to be operative. If this is true, and most churches seem to lack the fervor and focus for evangelism, is it reasonable to conclude that it may be because of the lack of zeal most pastors have for identifying, befriending, loving and evangelizing non-Christian people?"

I pray that this is not the case with you or your church. Here's how to avoid becoming complacent in your Christian walk and how to faithfully, fearlessly share the gospel with the lost.

1) Pray the Prayer.

In Luke 10:2 Jesus said, "The harvest truly is great, but the laborers are few: pray therefore the Lord of the harvest, that he would send forth laborers into his harvest." It has been 2,000 years since Jesus told His disciples to seek God in prayer for laborers, and it seems that we still have the same dilemma. In his book *The Coming Revival*, Bill Bright reports that "only two percent of believers in America regularly share their faith in Christ with others" (NewLife Publications, p. 65).

One would therefore suspect that Luke 10:2 is probably the most neglected exhortation to prayer in the Bible. What church is going to feel comfortable praying for laborers if it is not laboring in the harvest fields itself? It will instead pray for a *sovereign* revival, for a "move of God," for a manifestation of His power…anything *but* for laborers. In doing so they hand the job of evangelism back to heaven. In essence they are saying, "We know you have commanded us to preach the *gospel* to every creature; but we will stay here and pray. Your Word says, 'How will they hear without a preacher?' but we will stay here and pray. You have told us that the gospel is the power of God to salvation, but we will stay here and pray; because it sure is easier to *talk to God about men, than to talk to men about God.*" Luke 10:2 should be boldly stamped on the forefront of every praying mind, and on the front of every Christ-centered pulpit. If we love Him we will keep His commandments, and this commandment is to pray for laborers.

2) Use the Law.

Experience has shown that those who know what they have been saved *from* know what they have been saved *for*. The Law reveals that sin is exceedingly sinful (Romans 7:13), and therefore it makes grace abound in the hearts of those who come to Christ (Romans 5:20). If this is your experience (you find that gratitude for God's mercy continually feeds your zeal to do His will), then seek to bring others through the same door. Christians must be taught that the Law prepares the way for the gospel to do its work (Galatians 3:24). It is the solid soil from which Calvary's cross arises. This is the foundation for biblical evangelism.

3) Stir the Lukewarm.

Gently confront those who don't share their faith. They need to be reminded of the sobering words of Jesus in Matthew 7:21–23 and Revelation 3:16. Those verses should cause to tremble all who name the name of Christ yet lack a concern for the unsaved. Some who sit within the church are false converts and need to be awakened by the Law; others are Christians who have not been taught the biblical priority of the church —that they have a moral responsibility to reach out to the lost. There are masses within the Body of Christ who have never once identified with Paul's "Woe is to me if I preach not the gospel," and as long as they remain in that state we will lack laborers.

4) Use Tracts.

God has saved multitudes through tracts, so encourage Christians to always carry some with them. Let them know that literature can be used as a conversation opener ("Did you get one of these?"), a conversation closer ("Here's something further for you to read"), and can also be left in places without the daunting thought of human confrontation. Many Christians, like four-days-dead Lazarus, have nothing to do with the outside world. They have been scared to death by the very thought of evangelism. They sit paralyzed on the pew, wrapped in the shroud of the fear of man. Therefore, groan in prayer for them, then lift up your voice and call the dead church to come out of the grave. There is great joy among laborers when a cold and lifeless corpse comes out of the tomb of inactivity, to be a living witness of Him who is the resurrection and the life.

5) Preach the Fear of God.

In Romans 3:10–18, the apostle Paul gives a stinging indictment of the moral state of humanity. He says that we are corrupt, ignorant, rebellious, and violent. Then he puts his finger on the cause of such a sinful state. He says, "There is no fear of God before their eyes," and immediately swings the subject to God's Law—the cure to the moral dilemma. Psalm 111:10 informs us, "The fear of the LORD is the beginning of wisdom: a good understanding have all they that do his commandments." Therefore *preach* that which is the beginning of wisdom. Teach the true character of our Creator using the Law to show His perfect righteousness. A failure to use the Law lawfully has left few in the world (or even in the church) ever hearing that sinners are enemies of God in their minds through wicked works (Colossians 1:21). They are by nature children of wrath (Ephesians 2:3). His wrath abides on them (John 3:36). Our God is a consuming fire, and it is a fearful thing to fall into His holy hands. Eyes should be plucked out, and hands severed at the thought of sinning against Him. We should fear Him who has power to cast the body and soul into hell. It is when we see Him in truth that we will say with Paul, "Knowing therefore the terror of the Lord, we persuade men" (2 Corinthians 5:11). Those who don't persuade men don't know the terror of the Lord, so let His terror be known among your brethren.

Notice that Psalm 111:10 also links the "commandments" with the fear of the Lord. After speaking of the fear of the Lord the psalmist tells us "a good understanding have all they that do his commandments." It is the Commandments that make sinners and saints tremble. The Law puts the fear of God in their hearts. Sinners tremble when they have an understanding that the wrath of the Law calls for their blood (Romans 4:15). Saints tremble at the foot of a bloodied cross, because it was the Law that called for their blood (1 Peter 1:17–19) but instead shed the precious blood of the Savior. Always remember that it is the fear of the Lord that makes men depart from sin (Proverbs 16:6), both before and after the cross. The fear of the Lord doesn't disappear when we come to know His love. It remains and continues to do its most necessary work: "The fear of the LORD tends to life: and he that has it shall abide satisfied; he shall not be visited with evil" (Proverbs 19:23). Memorize that verse—and live by it.

Scripture likens sin to leprosy, a disease characterized by spots on the flesh. When we reach out to sinners we are exhorted to "hate even the garment *spotted* by the flesh" (Jude 23), and to keep ourselves "*unspotted* from the world" (James 1:27). A symptom of leprosy is that the victim loses any sense of pain. Mild pain prompts us to move around when we sit or lie down for too long in one position. This allows blood to flow freely throughout our body, and our blood is the life of our flesh. If there is no pain, there is no movement, and the flesh therefore rots. Sin dulls the pains of an accusing conscience, so that there is no movement away from it (repentance). It causes the soul to rot ("fleshly lusts, which war against the soul," 1 Peter 2:11). Jesus is coming for a spotless Church—for a "glorious church, not having spot, or wrinkle"—so we need to therefore continually wash ourselves in the water of the Word, scrub the walls of our minds, and burn anything that may be contaminated by the defilement of this evil world. The fear of the Lord will give us motivation to do so. See Psalm 37:30,31.

6) Preach Future Punishment.

It's not enough to preach the Ten Commandments, or even to open up the spiritual nature of the Law. We must couple that with the truths of Judgment Day and of the horrifying reality of hell. Without the threat of punishment, no one will flee from the wrath to come. The very thought of the existence of hell will be scorned by the world if the Law *and the consequences of its transgression* are not preached. Great damage has been done for the cause of the gospel by "hell-fire" preaching (the preaching of hell without the "reasoning" of the Law). Great damage has also been done by swinging the pendulum the other way, with many in the church (out of a fear of man) adopting worthless clichés such as a "Christless eternity" and "eternal separation from God." These soften the thought of

God's wrath, and at the same time defuse our evangelism of a sense urgency. The true and faithful witness will make sure the evangelistic pendulum remains where it should.

7) Break Out of the Comfort Zone.

Many Christians live in monasteries without walls. They fellowship in the holy huddle and cozy comfort of the Saved. Excommunicate yourself from the monastery. Show by example that we are called to be in, but not of the world: "That you may be blameless and harmless, the sons of God, without rebuke, in the midst of a crooked and perverse nation, among whom you shine as lights in the world" (Philippians 2:15). We should be *in the midst, among, in the world.* We should be accused (like Jesus) of being a friend of sinners, and our mingling with them should be motivated solely by a deep concern for their eternal welfare. Have you ever heard a clap of thunder that was so loud it seemed to make the heavens tremble? Did its noise terrify you for a moment? It will be but a tiny whisper compared to the "great noise" and "flaming fire" that will be revealed when Almighty God rips apart the sky at the Second Coming. In that "great and terrible Day of the Lord," the elements "shall melt with fervent heat, the earth also and the works that are therein shall be burned up" (2 Peter 3:10).

Is there any fear when we read these words: "Whose voice then shook the earth: but now he has promised, saying, Yet once more I shake not the earth only, but also heaven" (Hebrews 12:26)? Where is our horror at the fate of the lost? Where is our concern for them? We must be the most hard-hearted generation since Adam. We have so much light and yet we keep it to ourselves. We say that we are rich, and yet compared to the church of the Book of Acts, we are poor, blind, wretched, miserable, and naked. We have become so introverted, we have forgotten the meaning of the word "compassion." Once the walls of the monastery mindset have been broken down, prohibit any "vows of silence." Monks in monasteries and vows of silence are for the religious, not for the Christian. We have something to shout from the housetops. We are called to lift up our voices like a trumpet, not silence them, and we will not do that unless we go *into* the world and reach out in our personal spheres of influence.

8) Feed on the Word.

If we want to see laborers raised up and witness the miracle of a world-wide revival, we would be wise to fulfill the requirements of Psalm 1. If we meditate on the Law of God both day and night (and like Job we say, "I have esteemed the words of His mouth more than my necessary food"), then we will be as a tree planted by rivers of water. We will bring forth fruit in season. Our leaf will not wither... and "whatever" we do will then "prosper." That includes our evangelistic efforts.

9) Meditate on the Destiny of the Ungodly.

Meditate on and remind Christians of the fate of the ungodly. Pray for a tender heart that will weigh heavy if we meet an unsaved person, or even walk past them without reaching out to them either verbally or with a tract. May we weep over Jerusalem and may our tender hearts shame the hard hearts within the church. It seems that most of us can weep at every human tragedy, except the ultimate tragedy of hell. Our dry eyes reveal a hard heart. We either don't believe the horror that "whosoever was not found written in the book of life was cast into the lake of fire" (Revelation 20:15) or we don't care. Both are sin.

10) Redeem the Time.

Teach folks to make the best use of every moment. This life is like a burning desert, and time is like water cupped in our hands. An ignorant man will let its precious drops fall through his fingers, not realizing that it is his very life. We must treat every valuable minute as though it was our last drop of time, because one day it will be. Remind yourself of that fact at the beginning of every day. Spurgeon said that men have been taught to live by remembering that they have to die. So use your time very wisely, and the wisest thing you can do with that most precious of commodities is to seek and save that which is lost.

QUESTIONS

1. Why do individuals and churches often neglect this exhortation to prayer?

2. Do you regularly obey the command of Luke 10:2?

3. Why should we use the Law when witnessing?

4. Why should we encourage the preaching of future punishment?

5. What Bible verse tells us how Christians are to relate to the world?

FEATHERS FOR ARROWS

A little boy once said to his mom, "I am sick of the food you keep giving me—potatoes, carrots, and spinach. From now on I choose my own diet. I am having nothing but chocolate candy bars for breakfast, lunch, and dinner." Imagine what the child would look like if he were allowed to eat what he wanted. His face would break into pimples. He may become very sick and even die because of a lack of proper food. His facial condition would be an evident token that he was on the wrong diet—even though it tastes good to him, it's not good *for* him.

Man's attitude is, "God, from now on, I don't want your diet—I want mine." He chooses sin rather than righteousness. He wants what tastes good rather than what is good. As a direct result of humanity's sinful diet, painful pimples have broken out over the whole face of the earth. There are diseases, floods, earthquakes, starvation, endless suffering, and death. All these things should show us that something is radically wrong with our diet. Instead of using the sufferings of humanity as an excuse to re-

> ### Last Words
>
> **Joshua Reynolds** (1723–1792) was a British poet who achieved great fame for his portrait painting. He was one of the founders and first president of the Royal Academy. The last word he was heard to say was:
>
> **"I know that all things must have an end."**

ject God, see them as stark evidences to accept Him and the explanations given in His Word. They are very real reminders that what God says is true.

The Christian's Prayer

"Each person we meet on a daily basis who does not know Christ is hell-bound. That may make some folks bristle—but it's a fact. When we refuse to warn people that their actions and lifestyles have eternal consequences, we're not doing them any favors. If everybody feels good about his or her sin, why would anyone repent?"

FRANKLIN GRAHAM

Kirk's Comment This moving prayer was eye-opening for me. The response to the prayer really made me think of the biblical way to present the gospel to the unsaved. Ponder this lesson carefully, and it will change your prayer life.

QUESTIONS & OBJECTIONS

"I don't want to give up what I like doing."

If you become a Christian, are you saying that you must stop doing what you're doing now? That means you know it is wrong. Let me ask you something. If you were to become a Christian and God were to live in your heart and you looked back on your life now, would you say to yourself, "I did a lot of things I wish I hadn't done"? Probably so. The Bible speaks about just such a thing. Romans 6:21 says, "What fruit had you

699

then in those things whereof you are now ashamed? For the end of those things is death." What you are saying is that God will require you to give up certain things that you like to do. Since God only wants what is good and right, and you don't want to give up what you are doing, then you want what is wrong.

Will you let your pleasures get in the way of salvation? Is your life of sin worth an eternity of pain? Jesus said, "For what shall it profit a man, if he shall gain the whole world, and lose his own soul?" (Mark 8:36).

by Matthew Slick (www.carm.org)

w o t m w o t m w o t m w o t m w o t m w o t m w o t m w o t m w o t m w o t m w o t m

The Christian's Prayer

"Father, I have a problem. It's weighing heavy on me. It's all I can think about, night and day.

"But before I bring it to you in prayer, I suppose I should pray for those who are less fortunate than me—those in this world who have hardly enough food for this day, and those who don't have a roof over their heads at night. I also pray for families who have lost loved ones in sudden death, for parents whose children have leukemia, for the many people who are dying of brain tumors, for the hundreds of thousands who are laid waste with other terrible cancers, for people whose bodies have been suddenly shattered in car wrecks, for those who are lying in hospitals with agonizing burns over their bodies, whose faces have been burned beyond recognition.

"I pray for people with emphysema, whose eyes fill with terror as they struggle for every breath merely to live, for those who are tormented beyond words by irrational fears, for the elderly who are wracked with the pains of aging, whose only 'escape' is death.

"I pray for people who are watching their loved ones fade before their eyes through the grief of Alzheimer's disease, for the many thousands who are suffering the agony of AIDS, for those who are in such despair that they are about to commit suicide, for people who are tormented by the demons of alcoholism and drug addiction.

"I pray for children who have been abandoned by their parents, for those who are sexually abused, for wives held in quiet despair, beaten and abused by cruel and drunken husbands, for people whose minds have been destroyed by mental disorders, for those who have lost everything in floods, tornadoes, hurricanes, and earthquakes.

"I pray for the blind, who never see the faces of the ones they love or the beauty of a sunrise, for those whose bodies are horribly deformed by painful arthritis, for the many whose lives will be taken from them today by murderers, for those wasting away on their deathbeds in hospitals.

"Most of all, I cry out for the millions who don't know the forgiveness that is in Jesus Christ...for those who in a moment of time will be swept into hell by the cold hand of death, and find to their utter horror the unspeakable vengeance of eternal fire. They will be eternally damned to everlasting punishment. O God, I pray for them.

"Now, for my problem...Strange. I can't seem to remember what it was.

"In Jesus' name I pray. Amen."

A Response We Received to the Prayer

"I was really tracking with the prayer until you got to the horribly cruel notion that people can be won to the loving kingdom of God by sharing with them the darkness and torment of HELL. How could you possibly end such a beautiful prayer, full of compassion and grace, with such horribly twisted thoughts of eternal damnation and doom? Is this the picture that our Lord Jesus Christ, in all His love and mercy, would have us share? I'm sorry, if this is the Christ you serve, then I must pass on the invitation. The world I live in is often a living hell without someone painting an even more depressing image of an eternal hell as a means to show me the love, mercy, and grace of Christ.

"Please prayerfully rethink the ending of this prayer. Please seek to draw those who are in despair and those who do not know the Christ by painting an image of a loving God who cares enough to give all that heaven had to offer—Himself! Thank you for the effort. I wish it would have ended differently. Your brother in Christ..."

My friend, I stand in judgment now,
And feel that you're to blame somehow.
On earth I walked with you by day,
And never did you show the way.

You knew the Savior in truth and glory,
But never did you tell the story.
My knowledge then was very dim.
You could have led me safe to Him.

Though we lived together, here on earth,
You never told me of the second birth.
And now I stand before eternal hell,
Because of heaven's glory you did not tell!

— *Anonymous*

QUESTIONS

1. **What impact did the "Christian's Prayer" have on your problems?**

2. **Give your thoughts on the "Response to the Prayer."**

3. **Put in your own words what Jesus was saying in Mark 9:47,48.**

PREACHER'S PROGRESS

Christian: "Excuse me. Do you have the time?"

Ben Thair: "Yes. It's 3:31."

Christian: "Thanks."

Ben Thair: "You're welcome."

Christian: "Do you know if there are any good churches around here?"

Ben Thair: "None, as far as I know."

Christian: "Have you had a Christian background?"

Ben Thair: "Yes. My parents go to church."

Christian: "Do you ever go?"

Ben Thair: "No."

Christian: "Any reason why not?"

Ben Thair: "Yeah. Been there, done that. I think it's boring."

Christian: "I can understand why you don't go if you think it's boring.

Ben Thair: "No one at that church can answer this question: Why doesn't God stop evil? That's another reason I don't go."

Christian: "What sort of evil do you think He should stop?"

Ben Thair: "Murderers, for a start."

Christian: "What should He do to them?"

Ben Thair: "He should kill them. They took someone's life, so they should pay for it with their own life."

Christian: "How thorough do you think God should be in punishing evil?"

Ben Thair: "Obviously He should punish all of it."

Christian: "How about rape?"

Ben Thair: "Yes, of course. I said all of it."

Christian: "How about adultery, theft, and lying?"

Ben Thair: "Um...maybe theft. Major theft."

Christian: "Why not adultery? Is it right or wrong for someone to commit adultery?"

Ben Thair: "I don't consider it to be too serious."

Christian: "Why do you feel like that?"

Ben Thair: "I just do."

Christian: "Have you ever lied or stolen?"

Ben Thair: "Er...I may have sometime in the past."

Christian: "Have you ever committed adultery?"

Ben Thair: "That's my business. I'd rather not talk about this any longer, if you don't mind."

Christian: "I don't mind. I appreciate you listening to me as much as you have."

FEATHERS FOR ARROWS

The story of the *Titanic* has incredibly close parallels to the biblical plan of salvation. Just as the great pleasure ship struck an iceberg and sank, this great world—with all its inhabitants—is slowly sinking into the cold grip of death. As with the *Titanic*, where only those passengers who believed that they were in impending danger looked to the lifeboats, so only those who believe that they are in mortal danger will look to the Lifeboat of the Savior, Jesus Christ. The great "iceberg" that will take the world to an icy grave is the Moral Law—the Ten Commandments.

Here is the evidence that we are sinking: Jesus said that if we look with lust, we commit adultery in our heart. No one who has had sex outside of marriage, or any liar, or any thief will enter heaven. The Bible says that if we hate someone, we are guilty of murder. We fail to put God first. We make a god in our image. We break all the Commandments. If we stay with the "ship," we will perish on the Day of Judgment, when all of our sins come out as evidence of our guilt. God, however, is rich in mercy and doesn't want anyone to go to hell. He made a way for us to be saved. Jesus Christ, the One whom the Bible calls the "Captain of our salvation," gave His life so that we could have a place in the lifeboat. He took our punishment upon Himself, suffering on the cross for us. We broke God's Law, but He paid our fine. Then He rose from the dead, defeating death. The moment we repent and trust in Him alone for our eternal salvation, God will forgive us and grant us the gift of eternal life.

Don't hesitate. You may wait until it's too late! It was reported that some of the lifeboats that left the *Titanic* early were only half full. Many more on board could have been saved, but they refused to believe that the great "unsinkable" ship was sinking. They perished because their faith was misguided. Don't be like them. Believe the gospel. Repent and trust Jesus Christ today…and God will never let you down.

Last Words

Elizabeth Barrett Browning, poet, died June 28, 1861. Her last word was in reply to her husband who had asked how she felt:

"Beautiful."

Memory Verse

"I am the door: by me if any man enter in, he shall be saved, and shall go in and out, and find pasture. The thief comes not, but for to steal, and to kill, and to destroy: I am come that they might have life, and that they might have it more abundantly."

JOHN 10:9,10

Answers

Answers

T he letters "S/A" indicates that the question is to be self-answered; these are questions where there is no right or wrong answer, or where an opinion is requested.

LESSON 1

1. Paul sought to persuade his hearers about Jesus using both the Law of Moses and the prophets. He did this because fulfilled prophecy, which proves the inspiration of the Scriptures, appeals to the intellect, while the Law appeals to the conscience. Prophecy produces faith in God's Word, and the Law produces knowledge of sin.

2. The Law of the Lord is perfect converting the soul.

3. The preaching of the cross seems like foolishness because it will not make any sense without the sinner knowing what he has done wrong. It is offensive because it insinuates that the person has broken God's Law when he doesn't think he has.

4. Before someone is told the good news he should be taken through God's Moral Law, the Ten Commandments, to show him that he has offended a holy God. He must first understand precisely how he has violated God's Law and be convinced that he is a transgressor. Then the good news will make sense.

5. God's Law stops sinners from justifying themselves by thinking that they're not really a bad person or they're not as bad as other people. The Law shows them their own sin according to the holy Standard and leaves them guilty before God.

6. The four functions of God's Law for humanity are as follows: It stops sinners from justifying themselves; helps the whole world realize that they are guilty; brings the knowledge of sin; and acts as a schoolmaster to bring them to Christ.

7. The biblical definition of sin is transgression of the Law.

LESSON 2

1. Grace can be defined as "unmerited favor to the infinitely ill-deserving," or as "God's Richest At Christ's Expense."

2. The Christian should be concerned about how to make grace amazing to the world because a passion for the lost should be our primary concern in life. We should earnestly study how we may be most effective in reaching the lost.

3. It is sin that makes grace abound, according to Romans 5:20, and it is the Law that makes sin abound.

4. It was the law that showed the speedster the seriousness of his transgression. It didn't matter that others were doing the same thing; the law showed him that he *personally* was guilty and responsible for his offense.

5. Charles Spurgeon said that the Law serves "a most necessary purpose" and that sinners "will *never* accept grace, until they tremble before a just and holy Law."

6. The prostitute's tears were an emotional response to the need for a father's love. They had nothing to do with contrition.

7. John Newton, who wrote "Amazing Grace," said that a wrong understanding of the harmony between Law and grace would produce "error on the left and the right hand."

LESSON 3

1. Between 80 and 90 percent of those making decisions for Christ fall away from the faith.

2. Around the turn of the century, modern evangelism stopped using the Law to convert souls and drive sinners to Christ, and instead chose to attract sinners by using "benefits." Life enhancement is now the typical drawing card to bring someone to Christ.

3. He was promised the parachute would improve the flight and all he got was embarrassment and humiliation. He became disillusioned and bitter toward the person who gave him the parachute, because he was told to put it on for the wrong reason.

4. Because the second passenger knew the parachute would save his life, he didn't notice its weight on his shoulders or the fact that he couldn't sit upright. He was able to withstand the mockery of the other passengers because he didn't put the parachute on for a better flight, but to escape the jump to come. Everything paled in comparison to the horrific thought of having to jump without the parachute. He had gratitude toward those who gave him the parachute.

5. We should be telling people that they have an appointment with death that they will not miss. They have broken God's Law and will face Him on Judgment Day. Unless they repent and put on the Lord Jesus Christ, they will be under God's wrath.

6. According to Proverbs 11:4, riches will not help us on the Day of Wrath; the only thing that can deliver us from death is righteousness.

7. Christians have joy and peace in believing because we know that the righteousness of Christ will deliver us from the wrath to come.

8. If we have "put on the Lord Jesus Christ" for the right motive (to avoid the wrath to come), tribulation won't make us lose our joy and peace. In fact, it should cause us to cling even tighter to the Savior.

LESSON 4

1. Their idea of "wonderful" will be different from ours. They think of a "wonderful plan" as having a problem-free life. But God's Word promises us trials, tribulations, and suffering in this life (although He will see us through them). If people come to Christ for the wrong reason, without repentance, they will not be saved.

2. In Luke 18:18, the rich, young ruler came to Jesus asking how he could get everlasting life. Jesus pointed him to the Law by giving him five "horizontal" Commandments having to do with his fellow man. When he said he's kept those Commandments, Jesus used the essence of the First Commandment to show the man that his god was his money.

3. God's love should be mentioned only in the context of the cross. The biblical way to express God's love to a sinner is to use the Law to show

him how great his sin is, and then tell him of the incredible grace of God in Christ.

4. David realized that he had sinned against God when Nathan began by talking about something in the natural realm, got David to admit the wrongness of the act according to the Law, then confronted David about his *personal* transgression.

5. Simply telling a sinner that *all* have sinned will not bring about an awareness of his *personal* transgression against a holy God and will not produce godly sorrow, which is necessary for repentance. He needs to be able to cry out, "I have sinned against the Lord."

Lesson 5

1. The First Commandment is, "You shall have no other gods before me" (Exodus 20:3).

2. Humanity has such a shallow understanding of what God requires of them because the god of this world has blinded their minds.

3. If the first and greatest Commandment is to love God with all of our heart, soul, mind, and strength, then the greatest sin is failure to do so.

4. S/A.

5. In Psalm 14 and Romans 3:10–18, the characteristics of human nature include: unbelief, being corrupt, doing abominable works, failing to do good, not understanding, not seeking God, going astray, becoming filthy; none are righteous, all are unprofitable, they practice deceit, are full of cursing and bitterness, are swift to shed blood, spread destruction and misery, don't know peace, and have no fear of God.

6. Jesus demonstrated that He kept this Commandment by always doing those things that pleased the Father. Obeying the Father's will was His utmost concern. He ultimately proved this by giving Himself on the cross out of an obedient heart.

7. We should put God first because it is our reasonable service to yield our all to Him because He gave us life itself.

Lesson 6

1. Idolatry is perhaps the greatest sin because it opens the door to unrestrained evil; it allows people not only to tolerate sin but to sanction it.

2. Idolatry appeals to the secular mind because an idol has no moral dictates. An idolater can make a god to suit himself, and his god will remain silent while he sins his heart out.

3. S/A.

4. S/A.

5. The Catholic version of the Ten Commandments deleted this as the Second Commandment, and divided the Tenth Commandment to keep the total at ten. They therefore do not have this prohibition against worshiping idols.

LESSON 7

1. Using God's name to express revulsion shows man's contempt toward his Creator, revealing that unregenerate man hates God and His Law.

2. Idolaters will contest that they don't hate God because they have created a concept of God (an idol) that they're comfortable with.

3. God's name is synonymous with His glory and His goodness. If man saw God in all of His glory, he would die. When blasphemers stand before God to give an account for every idle word, God's goodness will ensure that His justice is carried out.

4. In dismissing their blasphemy by saying that God's name is "just a word," they are showing their disdain and disrespect for Him.

5. Rather than saying that we're offended by his blasphemy, we should greet the person, talk about something in the natural realm, and try to witness to him.

LESSON 8

1. The Fourth Commandment says to *rest* on the Sabbath—to work six days and rest on the seventh.

2. The Sabbath was given as a perpetual sign to the children of Israel (Exodus 31:13–17) to separate them from the world. Thousands of years later, the Jews continue to keep the Sabbath holy. Nowhere is it given as a sign to the church.

3. Paul went to the synagogue every Sabbath, not to keep the Law, but to reason with the Jews so he could win them to Christ.

4. The Christian is free from the Law because the demands of the Law have been satisfied in Christ. The Christian is under no obligation to keep the Sabbath holy. Salvation is by grace, through faith—not of works.

LESSON 9

1. To honor your parents means to treat them in a way that is pleasing in the sight of God. It means to esteem and respect them, and submit to their authority.

2. Yes, someone should honor his mother even if she's a prostitute. All parents are imperfect and none are "worthy" of honor. We are to honor our parents not because they deserve honor, but because God commands us to.

3. If a child will not submit to the authority of his parents, who are God's agents to train and discipline him, it is very unlikely that he will submit to God's authority and obey God's Laws.

4. It's important to go through the Commandments that deal with the sins of the flesh before mentioning this one because some people will claim to have kept this Commandment. However, if the person has lied and stolen, he will see that he has dishonored his parents' name by being a lying thief.

LESSON 10

1. Civil law can't see everything that a man does or know what he thinks.

2. Explain that Jesus said we don't have to actually kill someone to be found guilty of breaking this Commandment; those who even hate without cause are equally guilty. The Bible also says in 1 John 3:15 that if we hate someone, we are murderers.

3. Some people who hate would actually commit murder if they had opportunity and knew they would never be brought to justice by God or man. God also considers it murder if we refuse to give someone we hate the words of life, thereby indicating our desire for their eternal death.

4. S/A.

5. S/A.

6. No, the Bible does not equate capital punishment with murder. In fact, in Genesis 9:6 and Numbers 35:30,31, God commands us to put to death

the person who deliberately takes a human life. God made man in His image, and this shows the value that God places on human life.

LESSON 11

1. The Messiah made the Law "honorable" by explaining that God requires more than an outward show of piety. He judges even the thought-life.

2. Some of the sins that accompany lust are fornication, adultery, perversion, rape, and even murder.

3. What lust really wants from you is your death.

4. S/A.

5. If you have a problem with lust, it shows that you are struggling with it rather than yielding to it. This problem reveals that the conscience is still alive.

6. Viewing pornography, lusting after someone in the heart, is considered committing adultery. It is a sin, and is so serious that Jesus said it would be better to be blind and go to heaven than for your eye to cause you to sin and end up in hell.

7. We can learn from Proverbs 2:1–5 that if we treasure God's commands, incline our ear to wisdom, apply our heart to understanding, cry out for knowledge and discernment, seek it as we would for silver or hidden treasures, then we will understand the fear of the Lord and find the knowledge of God.

LESSON 12

1. If someone takes just a dollar out of your wallet, it is still stealing. Theft is theft regardless of the value of the item stolen.

2. That someone returning a lost wallet is newsworthy reveals that the world doesn't think much of the character of human nature. It is "news" when a human being exhibits honesty. This is a testimony to the fact that our spiritual father is a thief and we do his will.

3. Yes, stealing is stealing even when a man steals because he is hungry. It is still wrong. The person should instead humble himself and beg before he breaks the Law of God.

4. S/A.

5. S/A.

6. It's not enough for a thief to reform his ways because God still sees him as a thief even though he has decided not to steal any longer. A murderer is still a murderer, even though he decides not to kill anymore.

LESSON 13

1. The dictionary definition of a lie is a false statement deliberately presented as being true; a falsehood; something intended to deceive or give a wrong impression.

2. Discretion is showing wise self-restraint in speech, often in order not to hurt someone's feelings. Lying is intentionally being deceitful, usually in order to harm someone or to avoid bearing the consequences of our behavior.

3. S/A.

4. There is *no* difference between an exaggeration, white lie, half-truth, and a fib. They are all lies in the sight of God.

5. Telling just one lie will make someone a liar.

6. All liars will have their part in the Lake of Fire, which is the second death.

LESSON 14

1. To covet means to jealously desire something, to long for anything that belongs to another—house, car, income, lifestyle, etc.

2. Coveting often leads to other sins: before a man steals, he covets; before he rapes or commits adultery, he covets. Covetousness is the spark that sets off the fuse of sin, and is the bedfellow of jealousy, greed, and lust.

3. The opposite of coveting—wanting something that we don't have—is contentment—being satisfied with whatever we already have.

4. According to Psalm 23, if the Lord is our shepherd, we will not "want." If He is guiding our thoughts and desires, we will be content with what He has given us.

5. S/A.

6. We live in a prosperous nation in a very materialistic age. Advertising bombards us with things we "must" have, and credit cards help to fuel our greed.

LESSON 15

1. "Conscience" means "with knowledge." According to the dictionary, it is "the human faculty that enables one to decide between right and wrong acts or behavior, especially in regard to one's own conduct."

2. The function of the conscience is to give "light" to every man so that whenever we sin, we do so "with knowledge" that what we're doing is wrong. As Oswald Chambers said, "Conscience is the internal perception of God's Moral Law."

3. Sinners dull the voice of their conscience, ignoring its warning, by thinking that God won't punish sin. They snuff out the light and abandon themselves to the dark world of sin.

4. When we shine the light of the Law, the Holy Spirit awakens the conscience and affirms the truth of the Commandments. The conscience bears witness that the Law is written on the sinner's heart.

5. According to John Wesley, "It is the ordinary method of the Spirit of God to convict sinners by the Law."

6. Some phrases you can use when addressing the conscience are: "God gave you a conscience, so you know right from wrong." "Listen to the voice of your conscience. Let it remind you of the sins of your youth."

LESSON 16

1. It would be easier to tell sinners to "believe" than to repent because the word "repentance" carries connotations of sin, judgment, and condemnation. It implies that the sinner is guilty of doing something wrong. However, the word "believe" carries less reproach and is therefore less likely to produce persecution.

2. The old soldier summed up repentance by saying, "God said, 'Attention! About turn! Quick march!'"

3. Because God is holy, wicked men cannot have fellowship with Him unless they repent of their sins. We are dead in our trespasses and sins and must repent before we can be made alive in Christ. If God is truly drawing someone to Him, He would also be drawing the person away from his sin.

4. God commands all men everywhere to repent.

5. Jesus commanded that "repentance and remission of sins should be preached in his name among all nations" (Luke 24:47). He sent out His disciples to preach that "men should repent" (Mark 6:12).

LESSON 17

1. The four principles of evangelism are Relate, Create, Convict, and Reveal (RCCR).

2. S/A.

3. As long as it's asked in a spirit of love and gentleness, there won't be any offense because the "work of the Law [is] written in their hearts" and their conscience will also bear "witness" (Romans 2:15).

4. Our unbelief will not negate reality because truth can never be altered. You can stand on the freeway and say you don't believe in trucks, but that won't change the reality that you would become "road kill" if you tried. Whether someone believes in hell or not, he will still have to face God on Judgment Day.

5. Sinners may think that God is good so He will not send them to hell; but because God is a good and just Judge, He must by nature punish all wrongdoers.

6. We should tell the sinner about the Savior once he has been humbled by the Law and is ready for grace. Unless the person is convinced that he has the disease of sin, he will not embrace the cure of the gospel.

LESSON 18

1. When someone is "born of God," we just need to make sure that the person *understands* what he is doing, like Philip asked the Ethiopian eunuch if he understood what he read.

2. In the parable of the sower, the only true convert (the "good soil" hearer) is the one who hears "and understands." Someone can say a prayer, but if he doesn't fully understand salvation and is not repentant, he will be a false convert—a stillborn.

3. This understanding comes only by the Law in the hand of the Spirit, who will "convict the world of sin, and of righteousness, and of judgment."

4. God just looks at the heart; as long as there is godly sorrow, the words don't matter.

5. S/A.

LESSON 19

1. Jesus told His disciples, "Do you not know [understand] this parable? and how then will you know [understand] all parables?" (Mark 4:13). In other words, the Parable of the Sower is the key to unlocking the mysteries of all the other parables.

2. Some of Jesus' parables about true and false conversions are: the Wheat and Tares (true and false), the Good Fish and Bad Fish (true and false), the Wise Virgins and the Foolish (true and false), and the Sheep and Goats (true and false).

3. False converts will be exposed on Judgment Day when the wheat and the tares, etc., will be separated.

4. A Christian who doesn't understand the possibility of a false conversion can cause devastating damage. If we aren't aware that those who fail to repent are strangers to conversion, we are liable to think that simply "praying a sinner's prayer" or responding to an altar call will save someone.

5. We can ensure that we are not bringing false converts into the church by preaching biblically. That means using the Law to bring the knowledge of sin. It means mentioning Judgment Day, not casually, but impressing upon the mind of the sinner that he must face a holy God and answer for every sin he has committed against Him. It also means preaching the cross and the necessity of repentance. We should avoid modern methods where emotions are stirred in an effort to get decisions. We may rejoice over "decisions," but heaven reserves its rejoicing for repentance.

LESSON 20

1. Those who bring up this argument usually do so because of sin in their own lives, and they're trying to find an excuse for themselves on Judgment Day.

2. Hypocrisy is "the practice of professing beliefs, feelings, or virtues that one does not hold."

3. There are no hypocrites in the Church because the world mistakenly thinks that the Church is the building, and that those who sit within its confines are Christians. However, the Church is the Body of Christ, which

consists only of true believers; hypocrites are "pretenders" who sit among God's people.

4. All hypocrites—those merely pretending to be Christians—will end up in hell.

5. The root of hypocrisy is idolatry. The false convert has created a god of whom he has no fear. If his concept of God were according to Scripture, he would rid himself of any pretense.

6. We should examine ourselves to ensure that we are in the faith, that Jesus Christ lives in us, so that we can first make sure we are Christians. If we are, we should live holy, blameless lives so that we don't cause anyone to stumble because of what they perceive as hypocrisy in our lives.

LESSON 21

1. John the Baptist was imprisoned because he preached the Law of God, coupled with the judgment of God.

2. Hananiah prophesied that Judah would have a future of peace, not of judgment.

3. Such a message is rebellious because when the preaching of a coming judgment is neglected, there are no consequences for sin, and people will therefore see no reason to repent.

4. When we tell people only of God's love and neglect to warn them of His wrath and justice, they will see no need to repent. When a coming judgment is not explained, they will not understand the consequences for sin.

5. Judah sinned against God by transgressing the First, Second, Sixth, Seventh, Eighth, and Ninth Commandments.

6. S/A.

7. God showed both His retribution and His compassion in the gospel—the good news that Jesus died for us on the cross. God must punish sin because He is just, but because of His great compassion He offers us forgiveness through the Savior.

LESSON 22

1. Sinners should rightly fear God because they have sinned against Him and are therefore "children of wrath"; they are commanded to repent.

2. If we don't tell sinners of the coming judgment as the reason for them to repent, they will be passive about responding to the Savior and will be false converts who only believe but do not repent. They won't fear God enough to obey Him.

3. Preaching about judgment and hell without referring to the Law, to show sinners *why* God is angry with them, will leave them bewildered and angry because the punishment will seem unreasonable. Without the Law, a sinner cannot comprehend that God would send anyone to hell, because he is deceived into thinking that God's standard of righteousness is the same as his own. The damage is done when a sinner concludes that hell is unreasonable and he therefore doesn't need a Savior.

4. The Law appeals to the "reason" of sinners and helps them see that judgment is reasonable.

5. According to R. C. Sproul, there's probably no concept in theology more repugnant to modern America than the idea of divine wrath.

6. That God would punish sin with eternal punishment shows His absolute and uncompromising holiness, and how serious sin really is in His eyes.

LESSON 23

1. If hell didn't exist, it would mean that the Bible's authors were wrong and the Bible is therefore a hoax; Jesus is a liar; and God is unjust.

2. Some picture hell as an enjoyable place to be with their friends; as a fun-filled place to enjoy hedonistic pleasures; as the grave, where conscious existence ceases (annihilation); or even as a place of punishment for other people.

3. The Bible describes hell as a place of eternal, conscious punishment, where there is unquenchable fire, blackness, weeping, gnashing of teeth, anguish, shame, everlasting contempt, and no rest from the torment day or night.

4. We instinctively desire that justice be done when someone is wronged, but with the concept of annihilation there is no justice. People can commit the most heinous crimes and they will face no punishment for them, but at death will simply cease to have a conscious existence.

5. God's Moral Law will help people see that they have sinned against a holy God and that His wrath abides on them.

LESSON 24

1. "Original sin" refers both to the first sin of Adam, and to the sinful nature possessed by every person since Adam.

2. The sinful nature is called "depravity."

3. Every individual at birth is "depraved" in these four ways:

   1) They have no original righteousness.

   2) They have no affection toward God.

   3) The things inside them defile them.

   4) They have a continual bias toward evil.

4. All people can certainly have some qualities that are pleasing; their condition of depravity, however, means that they are basically self-centered instead of God-centered. They cannot love God with all their heart, soul, and strength, as the Law requires.

5. The greatest defense against sin is to be shocked at it.

6. S/A.

LESSON 25

1. The lighthouse keeper neglected his primary responsibility—to keep the light shining.

2. The lighthouse keeper's misguided priorities resulted in the tragic death of human beings. The judge had to punish him because he had done wrong, and also as a sober warning to other lighthouse keepers who might be tempted to neglect their responsibility.

3. The primary responsibility of the Church is to obey the Great Commission by warning sinners of danger. We must shine the light of the gospel so that sinners can avoid God's wrath and escape eternal damnation.

4. Smith said that we are loaded down with church activities while we're neglecting the real work of the Church: evangelism.

5. S/A.

6. If we neglect our primary responsibility to warn sinners, we are impostors. If we don't have love and concern for others, then we don't know God. If we have no wish for others to be saved, then we are not saved ourselves.

LESSON 26

1. Paul experienced "weakness, fear, and much trembling."

2. Fear makes us rely on God. It makes us aware of our weaknesses and insufficiency, and causes us to rely on God's strength and ability.

3. We can put our fears in perspective by realizing that we're not being forced to preach to a crowd, and we're not risking jail for witnessing. All we have to do is hand one tract to one person.

4. The recruits were to learn how to take control of situations, including controlling their fears.

5. We should quote Scripture in the face of fear because it is more than mere words. When the light of the Word is spoken, the darkness of the enemy must vanish.

6. According to William Gurnall, we fear man so much because we fear God so little. We can overcome our fear of man by turning our thoughts to the wrath of God.

LESSON 27

1. God gave His Spirit to the Church so that believers would have the power to witness.

2. When the disciples received the Holy Spirit, they went out into the world and became fearless witnesses of Jesus Christ.

3. Dr. Bright said, "Only two percent of believers in America regularly share their faith in Christ with others."

4. Perhaps the reason why so many don't share their faith is that they have not been genuinely converted, they are not filled with (controlled by) the Holy Spirit, or they have never been instructed that evangelizing the world is the Church's number one priority.

5. One way to be filled with the Holy Spirit is to go somewhere quiet (a "closet"), confess all known sin, and turn control of your daily life over to God. Ask God to fill you to overflowing.

LESSON 28

1. An often-overlooked tool for reaching the lost is their fear of death, also called "the will to live."

2. Hebrews 2:15 tells us that all human beings fear death: "And deliver them who through fear of death were all their lifetime subject to bondage."

3. "Years" makes death sound too far into the distance, whereas we can better relate to the "weekends" that we spend.

4. It should shake us enough to ask what we're doing with our life and consider whether we're obediently reaching the lost.

5. We should be concerned for the ungodly because their end will be eternal torment in hell. This should horrify us, and drive us to pray for and reach out to them with the gospel. Everything else should pale in importance.

6. Charles Spurgeon said, "Men have been helped to live by remembering that they must die."

Lesson 29

1. George Whitefield, a diver, and the great missionary Hudson Taylor were all saved through a gospel tract.

2. Tracts can provide an opening for us to share our faith. They can do the witnessing for us. They speak to the individuals when they are ready. They can find their way into people's homes when we can't. They don't get into arguments; they just state their case.

3. Greet people warmly then ask, "Did you get one of these?" It makes them feel as though they are missing out on something—and they are.

4. We may have a fear of rejection, or a fear of looking foolish, which is a form of pride. Also, the devil tries to paralyze us with fear.

5. We can conquer fear by asking God to give us compassion for the lost, by meditating on the fate of the ungodly in hell, and confronting our fears.

6. Spurgeon's advice is to always have a tract ready for when preaching and private talk are not available, and to get good tracts and never go out without them.

Lesson 30

1. Fifty-three percent of all who come to Christ worldwide come through the use of printed gospel literature.

2. Tracts are useful for people who feel they have little power or ability to preach the gospel, but who want to do something for Christ. They may not be eloquent, but they can be diligent to distribute thousands of tracts.

3. Spurgeon called gospel tracts "silent preachers."

4. S/A.

5. S/A.

LESSON 31

1. We should begin in the natural realm because Jesus did, to establish a connection with the person and show that we care.

2. The woman at the well was able to persuade others because of her personal experience: she had met the Savior. She had heard His voice. She knew the Lord.

3. In essence, she said that God is omniscient and sees our sin, and she pointed to Jesus as the Christ (Messiah).

4. We should include the spiritual nature of the Ten Commandments so the person knows what sin is. We should emphasize that God sees our sins—He knows everything we do, think, and say—and that we will have to give an account of ourselves on the Day of Judgment.

5. Our testimony should lead from sin and judgment to the cross of Christ, because our salvation centers on the cross.

6. Because the Bible tells us that we should always be ready to share our testimony: "Be ready always to give an answer to every man that asks you a reason of the hope that is in you with meekness and fear" (1 Peter 3:15).

7. We know that we know Him if we keep His commandments.

LESSON 32

1. Giving money helps establish credibility with listeners because people rarely get something for nothing. People are astounded that you give them a dollar for merely answering a question.

2. Asking questions gives you a chance to interact with people, and perhaps laugh with them. Once you've established a rapport, they're more willing to listen to you.

3. Scripture should be quoted because the Word of God is quick and powerful, sharper than a two-edged sword, and it cannot return void. (See Hebrews 4:12; Isaiah 55:11.)

4. The job of the Holy Spirit is to draw the sinner, and to convict him of sin, righteousness, and judgment.

5. Our job as Christians is to faithfully plant the seed of God's Word in the heart of the sinner.

LESSON 33

1. S/A.

2. S/A.

3. Although the unsaved are concerned about having their immediate pain relieved, it is only temporary. The most serious wound is the sin issue—which will lead to their death and eternal damnation.

4. When speaking with someone who has lost a loved one, we must remember to show a deep empathy for the person, express sorrow about his loss, and show genuine sensitivity.

5. We should avoid any talk about the salvation of a deceased loved one, because it may cause an offense that will hinder the salvation of the one we are trying to reach.

LESSON 34

1. John the Baptist, Jesus, Peter, and Paul all preached open-air where sinners gather. Also, a good open-air preacher can reach more sinners in thirty minutes than the average church does in twelve months.

2. Realize that you are qualified for the job. God works through "nobodies" who are submitted to Him for His use. According to His power working in us, He promises to do abundantly more than we can imagine.

3. You can get people to stop by asking interesting, humorous questions, and promising a dollar to whoever has the right answer. Once you have the crowd's attention, lead into the gospel by asking if anyone considers himself a good person.

4. Other Christians with you should form an audience and listen to you, because a crowd draws a crowd. They should also face you, not talk with each other, and not argue with hecklers.

5. Being elevated when you preach will give people a reason to stop and listen. It will give you protection as well as authority.

LESSON 35

1. A good heckler can quickly increase a crowd. The situation gives people a reason to stop and listen.

2. Remember the attributes of 2 Timothy 2:23–26: be patient, gentle, humble, etc. Show him genuine respect and honor; don't offend him unnecessarily; bless him if he curses you.

3. If a "mumbling heckler" won't speak up, ignore him and keep talking. If he gets angry enough to speak up, it will draw hearers.

4. If you are "reviled" for the name of Jesus, "rejoice, and be exceeding glad." Cling to the promise of Matthew 5:10–12.

5. We are instructed to teach sinners, to bring them to a point of understanding their need before God. They will not flee from God's wrath unless they understand that they are under His condemnation.

6. The Law brings the knowledge of sin, so the sinner understands that he is under God's wrath, and reveals God's will—if the sinner is "instructed out of the Law" (Romans 2:18).

LESSON 36

1. We should not be discouraged by an angry reaction to our message because anger is a thousand times better than apathy. Anger is a sign of conviction. We've hit a nerve in the heart of the sinner.

2. John Wesley told his evangelist trainees that when they preached, people should either get angry or get converted.

3. While apologetics are legitimate in evangelism, they should merely be "bait," with the Law of God being the "hook" that brings the conviction of sin.

4. "Decisions for Christ" (which can be obtained through the manipulative methods of modern evangelism) are meaningless unless there is a God-given repentance. If there is no repentance, there is no salvation.

5. The modern concept of success in evangelism is to relate how many people were "saved" (that is, how many prayed the "sinner's prayer"). This produces a "no decisions, no success" mentality. Success should be based on faithfully planting the seed of the Word of God in the hearts of sinners.

6. According to 2 Timothy 2:24–26, we are to not strive, be gentle, be able to teach, be patient and meek.

LESSON 37

1. According to Hebrews 11:1, "Faith is the substance of things hoped for, the evidence of things not seen."

2. Faith in general is being fully persuaded of something, having a confident belief or conviction that something is true. Its primary idea is trust. When you believe with certainty that a thing is true, it is therefore worthy of trust.

3. The young man was offended because my lack of faith in him implied that I thought he wasn't trustworthy—that he was a liar trying to deceive me.

4. Some of the things in which people have faith are the weather forecast, daily newspapers, and airline pilots. They trust their car's brakes, history books, medical journals, and elevators.

5. Someone who finds it hard to have faith in God is implying that God is not trustworthy—that He is a liar and a deceiver.

6. The Bible draws on the strength of the word "impossible" to show that it against God's holy nature to deceive.

7. S/A.

LESSON 38

1. The name of the giant in Doubting Castle is Giant Despair. His name is applicable because those who doubt God's promises are thrown into hopeless despair.

2. Going through tribulation tests the depth of our faith in God. The amount of joy we retain in our trials reveals the amount of faith that we actually have in God.

3. The reason any of us would lose faith in the promises of God is that we lose sight of His faithfulness.

4. Nehemiah 8:10 tell us that "the joy of the Lord is your strength."

5. Someone in Scripture who slept when others would have been fearful is Peter. He slept while awaiting execution in Herod's prison.

LESSON 39

1. The moment we repent and trust the Savior, we step into a battle with three enemies: the world, the flesh, and the devil.

2. The way to overcome the devil is to be outfitted with the spiritual armor of God, including the sword of the Spirit (the Word of God).

3. The only access the enemy has to cause us to sin is through the flesh.

4. Sin takes the "edge" off our prayer life by bringing with it guilt and removing our bold confidence before God.

5. Most of our fear about witnessing comes from our Adamic (fleshly) nature, which prefers the praise of men to the praise of God. It is proud and more concerned with self than with the eternal welfare of sinners.

6. In order to stop the enemy's access, we must consider the old nature dead to sin. Rather than obeying its lusts, we must yield ourselves fully to God and offer our bodies to Him as instruments of righteousness.

LESSON 40

1. If a Christian does not have a battle with lust, it may be that he isn't fighting. He may have surrendered to the enemy.

2. The sex drive is from God, and can find satisfaction in marriage. Lust is an overwhelming desire that draws us like a moth to a flame, leading us to sin.

3. Deceitfulness exemplifies sin. Sin can deceive and delude people into thinking something bad is actually good.

4. People who are sinful are not always miserable. Sin can be enjoyable, fun, and pleasurable—that's why we're drawn to it.

5. We are always susceptible in the battle against "the lust of the flesh, the lust of the eyes, and the pride of life," but we become a target for the enemy especially when we desire to share our faith.

6. One great tool that the enemy likes to exploit is an idle hand.

7. Guard our minds, have a fear of God so we will not choose to indulge in sin, make a covenant with our eyes not to look with lust, keep busy by abounding in the labor of the Lord.

LESSON 41

1. As soldiers in God's army, each of us is called by God to become personally involved in the battle to win the world for Christ.

2. According to Billy Graham, mass crusades will never finish the job. We must reach the lost by sharing our faith one on one.

3. If we're not fishing for men, we may be following Jesus at too great a distance. We can't see Jesus' example or hear His voice.

4. Satan may attack us through the most unexpected source: through another Christian or someone close to us. The person may try to discourage us from doing God's will—seeking the lost.

5. Satan often withholds an attack until we are vulnerable. He will not strike when we are full of faith and power, but when we are tired, fasting, or carrying a problem on our shoulders.

6. The children of Israel were not allowed to speak as they walked around Jericho.

7. With their shields of faith, Christians should deflect the subtle words of discouragement from the enemy.

LESSON 42

1. The god of this world, Satan, has blinded the minds of unbelievers.

2. The unbeliever's understanding is darkened because he is alienated from the life of God due to his ignorance and the blindness of his heart.

3. Satan is a counterfeiter who can transform himself into an angel of light.

4. Satan is also called the god and prince of this world, the ruler of darkness, our adversary, a devourer, a liar, the father of lies, and a murderer.

5. Satan hates for Christians to use the Law because that's what the Holy Spirit uses to convince and convict men of their sin. It enables sinners to have a clear understanding of sin and salvation.

6. If preaching fails to present the standard of the Law, there might be a spurious conversion, or the sinner might lack gratitude because his decision was based solely on fear.

7. Satan has created a massive religious system—filled with false apostles, deceitful workers, and false ministers of righteousness—that masquerades as God's representative on earth.

LESSON 43

1. Prayer is our lifeline, our line of communication with God. It is our weapon in the spiritual battle.

2. Four Bible references tell us to pray continually: Romans 12:12—"Continuing instant [steadfast] in prayer"; Ephesians 6:18—"Praying always"; Colossians 4:2—"Continue in prayer"; and 1 Thessalonians 5:17—"Pray without ceasing."

3. Prayerlessness reflects idolatry—a trust in substitutes for God. It says that we don't need God, short-circuits His working through our lives, and is sinful.

4. According to Proverbs 15:8, our prayers delight God.

5. For our prayers to be heard, we need to pray with faith, pray with clean hands and a pure heart, pray genuine heartfelt prayers (not vain repetitions), and be sure to pray to the God revealed in Scripture.

6. S/A.

LESSON 44

1. S/A.

2. Second Peter 1:3 says that God's divine power has given us all things that pertain to life and godliness—we have been given everything we need to live a life pleasing to Him.

3. Knowing God more intimately strengthens our faith, and reading His Word acts as a mirror to help us recognize our sin and cultivate a tender conscience.

4. The psalmist rejoiced over God's Word because of the wealth it contains.

5. Paul exercised self-discipline so he wouldn't be disqualified (declared unfit) when he preached.

6. S/A.

LESSON 45

1. Today "holiness" may mean sitting half-naked with your legs crossed and getting paid to bless people; sitting on poles for twenty years; cutting yourself off from any contact with sinners in holier-than-thou legalism; or living in a monastery with a vow of silence.

2. The church has become a "monastery without walls"—living with little contact with the world and in a "vow of silence" by not talking to sinners —because it has lost sight of its mandate: to reach out to the lost.

3. "True holiness" is separation from sin.

4. Jesus was a "friend of sinners" because He loved them. He came to save sinners.

5. We should have no fellowship with hypocrites.

6. We can cultivate holiness by reading God's Word daily, keeping a tender conscience, having an obedient heart, and living in the fear of God.

LESSON 46

1. Two verses where Jesus mentioned water baptism are Matthew 28:19 and Mark 16:16.

2. The Greek word *baptizo* means "immersion."

3. Jesus taught in Matthew 28:19 that believers should be baptized "in the name of the Father, and of the Son, and of the Holy Spirit."

4. It is true that baptism is an outward sign of an inward work.

5. S/A.

LESSON 47

1. Adding any other requirement to salvation besides grace becomes "works" in disguise.

2. Ephesians 2:8,9 tells us that salvation is by grace alone, and not by works.

3. Acts of obedience that are important but not essential to salvation include water baptism, prayer, good works, fellowship, witnessing, etc.—all of which issue from our faith in Christ.

4. According to Mark 16:16, it is unbelief that brings damnation.

5. The thief on the cross was never baptized, yet he received salvation.

6. In 1 Corinthians 1:17 Paul said, "Christ sent me not to baptize, but to preach the gospel." He made a distinction between the gospel and being baptized.

LESSON 48

1. The word "Trinity" does not occur anywhere in the Bible, although God's triune nature is clearly described.

2. The doctrine of the Trinity says that there is one God who exists eternally as three distinct persons: the Father, the Son, and the Holy Spirit.

3. According to Ephesians 1, the Father chooses those in Christ to be saved (verse 4); the Son redeems them (verse 7); and the Holy Spirit seals them (verse 13).

4. Instead of recognizing God as three separate, equal, eternal persons—the Father, the Son, and the Holy Spirit—the Jehovah's Witnesses view God as only one person, the Father, with Jesus as a created being and the Holy Spirit as merely a force.

5. S/A.

LESSON 49

1. Although we can tell people about Jesus, according to Matthew 13:14–17 the Father must open their eyes and reveal who Jesus truly is.

2. S/A.

3. S/A.

4. If Jesus were merely a good man, He would not have allowed people to worship Him. Because only God is to be worshiped, accepting worship would have been a sin, which would mean Jesus wasn't a good man.

5. S/A.

6. Man can only refashion or reform something using materials that already exist, but God can truly create something out of nothing.

LESSON 50

1. The four main things that the Holy Spirit does for sinners are to draw them, convict them, give birth to them, and keep them.

2. Billy Graham stated that the Holy Spirit convicts us by showing us the Ten Commandments.

3. According to Paris Reidhead, when the Law is not used in witnessing, the Holy Spirit is deprived of the only instrument He has to prepare sinners for grace.

4. The Holy Spirit is the Creator (gives us life), can be blasphemed, and calls men to ministry.

5. S/A.

6. S/A.

LESSON 51

1. Of the variety of evidence we have available, none is more compelling than the fact that over five hundred individuals saw Jesus (1 Corinthians 15:6) during a 40-day period following His death and burial (Acts 1:3).

2. We know that the Romans had no motive for stealing Christ's body because the last thing they wanted was any turmoil that was sure to follow such an event.

3. The Jewish religious leaders would have had no intentions of stealing the body since that would only stir up the very movement they tried to crush.

4. The disciples would not have stolen the body; after all, would anyone suffer and die for a cause that they knew to be a lie?

5. After Jesus endured several trials, a crown of thorns, scourging, crucifixion, a spear in His side, the loss of blood, three days without medical attention or food, it's ridiculous in the extreme to think He pushed a two-ton stone away from the tomb entrance and overpowered an armed Roman guard while walking on pierced feet.

6. Within five weeks of Jesus' death, more than 10,000 Jewish believers suddenly altered or abandoned their important religious rituals (offering sacrifices, obeying the Mosaic law, keeping the Sabbath), and began the sacraments of communion and baptism.

LESSON 52

1. The word "Bible" simply means "book."

2. There are 66 books in the Bible: 39 in the Old Testament and 27 in the New Testament.

3. The Old Testament was written from approximately 1400 B.C. to 400 B.C., and the New Testament was written from approximately A.D. 50 to A.D. 90.

4. The Bible tells us about the nature of God, the purpose of mankind, and the purpose of history, and served as the basis of science and law.

5. If we had only an oral communication from God, the message could be changed and misinterpreted when repeatedly told. A written revelation solves doctrinal controversies, can be studied as an authoritative source, and can be translated into different languages.

6. The central verse in the Bible says, "It is better to trust in the Lord than to put confidence in man" (Psalm 118:8).

LESSON 53

1. To write the Bible, God picked 40 writers from all walks of life—fishermen, politicians, generals, kings, shepherds, and historians—from three different continents, in three different languages, over approximately 1,500 years.

2. Even 10 people from the same time and place couldn't all agree on one controversial topic. But these 40, from various times, places, and backgrounds, wrote on hundreds of controversial subjects with agreement and harmony.

3. The Bible was not only the first book printed on a printing press, it is the most printed and most read book in history.

4. S/A.

5. The Bible's one unfolding story is the redemption of mankind through the Messiah—the Old Testament tells of the coming Messiah; the New Testament tells of the Messiah who has come. Genesis describes how paradise was lost, and Revelation describes the paradise gained.

LESSON 54

1. S/A.

2. Works by Aristotle and Plato have only 49 and 7 existing manuscripts, respectively. The New Testament has over 24,000 ancient copies to confirm its wording.

3. In the works by Aristotle and Plato, there are gaps of 1,200 to 1,400 years between the time of writing and the earliest copies. The oldest manuscripts of the New Testament date to within 35 years of their writing.

4. Other ancient sources that verify Jesus' existence—His birth, ministry, death, and resurrection—include the Babylonian Talmud, the Annals of Tacitus, Mara Bar Serapion, and writings by Josephus, Pliny the Younger, and Suetonius.

5. No books were excluded from the Bible by the early church councils; in fact, the councils confirmed the divine inspiration of the books already accepted as Scripture.

LESSON 55

1. The Dead Sea Scrolls are ancient texts that were discovered at Qumran in 1949, hidden in pots in cliff-top caves. They are portions of Scripture that were copied and studied by the Essenes.

2. The Dead Sea Scrolls comprise thousands of fragments of every Old Testament book except Esther, and include the complete book of Isaiah.

3. Previously, the earliest known manuscript of the Old Testament was the Masoretic Text dated A.D. 900. The Dead Sea Scrolls are 1,000 years older.

4. The Qumran texts confirm the reliability of the Old Testament text and have become an important witness for the divine origin of the Bible. The close match they have with the Masoretic text demonstrates the reliability and preservation of the authentic text through the centuries.

5. Archaeological finds have affirmed the historical core of the Bible, proving the existence of key Bible characters and substantiating its claims. No archaeological discovery has ever controverted a biblical reference, showing that the Bible is trustworthy.

6. S/A.

LESSON 56

1. A contradiction is an inconsistency or discrepancy, which may give the appearance of an error.

2. The godly can base their confidence on the fact that all Scripture is inspired by God, and that God has deliberately included *seeming* contradictions in His Word to "snare" the proud.

3. God has purposely chosen the foolish things to confound the "wise." A proud, self-righteous man attempts to justify himself by discrediting the Bible, not realizing that God allows only those who exercise faith and humility to enter the door of life.

4. S/A.

5. Ask for the person's phone number, e-mail, or address so you can get back to him with a solid answer. If the person doesn't agree, he really

wasn't interested in an answer but just used the "contradiction" as a smoke screen.

6. The *seeming* contradictions in the four Gospels attest to the fact that there was no corroboration between the writers.

LESSON 57

1. There is no other book, other than the Bible, that contains precise prophecies that have come to pass.

2. If a prophet was truly from the Lord, 100 percent of his prophecies would come to pass. If even one fails, he is a false prophet.

3. Close to 30 percent of the Bible contains predictive prophecy.

4. Contrary to popular opinion, Nostradamus never predicted the attack on New York.

5. Prophecy is a good tool to use in evangelism because no other religion can use it to authenticate its writings as supernatural in origin. God alone can see tomorrow as clearly as we see yesterday.

LESSON 58

1. Unlike any other book, the Bible offers a multitude of specific predictions—some thousands of years in advance—that either have been literally fulfilled or point to a definite future time when they will come true.

2. Fulfilled prophecies argue for omniscience because only one who is omniscient can accurately predict details of events thousands of years in the future.

3. The two categories of biblical prophecy are messianic and non-messianic.

4. Isaiah's prediction about Jesus being born of a virgin was made over 700 years in advance.

5. S/A.

LESSON 59

1. Jesus was rejected, was a man of sorrow, lived a life of suffering, was despised by others, carried our sorrow, was smitten and afflicted by God, was pierced for our transgressions, was wounded for our sins, suffered like a lamb, died with the wicked, was sinless, and prayed for others.

2. Daniel 9 is considered to be such an amazing prophecy because it gives the very year in which the Christ would die.

3. Psalm 16:10 foretold the resurrection of the Messiah from the dead.

4. Unlike many psychic predictions, many of the biblical prophecies were *very specific*, giving, for example, the very name of the tribe, city, and time of Christ's coming.

5. Many predictions were beyond human ability to fake a fulfillment because if Jesus had been a mere human being, He would have had no control over when, where, or how He would be born, or how He would die; He would not have been able to do miracles or rise from the dead.

6. For just sixteen predictions to be fulfilled in one person, the probability is 1 in 10^{45}. For forty-eight predictions to meet in one person, the probability is 1 in 10^{157}—mathematically impossible.

LESSON 60

1. Daniel gives the amazing prediction of the succession of the world empires of Babylon, Medo-Persia, Greece, and Rome.

2. Isaiah identifies Cyrus of Persia before he was even born.

3. Ezekiel predicted that the Eastern gate in Jerusalem would be closed one day, and not reopened until the Messiah returned.

4. Despite 2,000 years during which their nation did not exist, the Jews managed to keep a culture, identity, and language intact and were reestablished as a nation when Israel was "born in a day."

5. The prophet Jeremiah predicted that Edom would experience only "perpetual desolation."

6. Ezekiel predicted that after lying in waste and desolate for centuries Palestine would one day return to a place of flourishing.

LESSON 61

1. Science expresses the universe in five terms: time, space, matter, power, and motion, all of which God mentioned in Genesis 1:1, 2.

2. Nine times in Scripture we are told that God stretches out the heavens like a curtain (e.g., Psalm 104:2).

3. The Bible tells us that the earth is round (Isaiah 40:22). In fact, the Scriptures inspired Columbus to sail around the world.

4. Genesis 2:1 says that "the heavens and the earth were finished"—the creation was "finished," once and for all. The First Law of Thermodynamics states that neither matter nor energy can be either created or destroyed. Creation is "finished" exactly as the Bible states.

5. The Second Law of Thermodynamics states that every ordered system over time tends to become more disordered. Everything is running down and wearing out as less energy becomes available for use. That means the universe will eventually "wear out." Isaiah 51:6, Psalm 102:25,26, and Hebrews 1:11 all indicate that the earth is wearing out.

LESSON 62

1. Newton, Faraday, Maxwell, Kelvin, Boyle, Dalton, Pascal, Ramsay, Ray, Linnaeus, Mendel, Pasteur, Steno, Woodward, Brewster, Agassiz, Kepler, Galileo, Herschel, and Maunder are all great scientists who were creationists.

2. They expected our God of order to impose rational order and harmony in His creation, so they considered science to be dedicated to "thinking God's thoughts after Him."

3. There should be a union between religion and science. We should be the owners of the lock (humanity and the cosmos) *and* the key (God). This is because as science advances, it discovers what was said thousands of years ago in the Bible.

4. Perhaps God is behind scientific discoveries because they seem to be "made only for the purpose of confirming more and more strongly the truths that…are contained in the Sacred Writings." God is giving mankind more proofs for the truth of His Word.

5. Moses knew 3,500 years ago that the "lights" of the sun and moon determined the seasons, days, and years because God inspired his words.

LESSON 63

1. The Bible describes the water cycle in Ecclesiastes 1:7, Ecclesiastes 11:3, and Amos 9:6.

2. Solomon described a "cycle" of air currents in Ecclesiastes 1:6.

3. After reading Psalm 8:8, Matthew Maury said, "If God said there are paths in the sea, I am going to find them." Based on God's Word, he went looking for these paths and found them.

4. The Bible and true science harmonize because they have the same author.

5. The eighth day is when prothrombin, which coagulates the blood, is the highest. Blood clotting peaks on that day, then drops.

6. Leviticus 15:13 says to wash under running water, which will remove invisible germs. Leviticus 13 advises quarantine for those with an infectious disease.

LESSON 64

1. An explosion will always create chaos and disorder. This is a basic law.

2. Microevolution is variations within species, and is scientifically observable. Macroevolution is one species evolving into another species; there is no evidence for macroevolution.

3. Natural selection can only work on the genetic information present in a population of organisms—it cannot create new information. For example, a reptile will never produce feathers. Mutations in genes can only modify or eliminate existing structures, not create new ones.

4. Peppered moths are nocturnal and don't rest on tree trunks during the day, so they couldn't have been seen and eaten by birds as claimed; the photos showing evidence of the moths "evolving" were all faked; and nothing changed anyway. No new color or variety came into being, so nothing actually "evolved"!

5. S/A.

6. It's always a good idea to go through the Law as soon as possible so you don't waste valuable time on unnecessary rabbit trails. It does no good to win an argument, but not win the soul. Tickle the person's intellect only as long as necessary, then swing over to his conscience and allow the Holy Spirit to convict him of sin, righteousness, and judgment.

LESSON 65

1. S/A.

2. Man was made in God's image, has self-awareness, has artistic appreciation, is moral, can relate to God, is intellectually superior, and has God-

given dominion over animals. Jesus Himself said man is much more valuable than animals.

3. If any one of about 40 physical qualities had more than slightly different values, life as we know it could not exist. Even well-known scientist Stephen Hawking, an evolutionist, admitted, "It would be very difficult to explain why the universe should have begun in just this way, except as the act of a God who intended to create beings like us."

4. Hoyle, the famous statistician, determined that the likelihood of life forming from inanimate matter is 1 in $10^{40,000}$—statistically impossible. He compared it to the chance that "a tornado sweeping through a junkyard would assemble a Boeing 747 from the materials therein."

5. According to biochemistry professor and evolutionist Michael J. Behe, Darwin's theory of evolution can't explain what is seen under a microscope. Even a single cell is too complex to have evolved randomly, and intelligence was required for it to be produced.

LESSON 66

1. All the genealogies accept Adam as being a literal person; the Bible says that Jesus was descended from Adam; and Jesus confirmed that the creation of Adam and Eve was a real historical event. It's necessary to believe the first Adam is real in order to understand the work of the "last Adam," Jesus.

2. According to *U.S. News & World Report*, researchers suggest that virtually all modern men share genes with one male ancestor; they even call this common ancestor "Y-chromosome Adam." They've found that our genetic roots are very, very shallow and go back very recently to one ancestor.

3. Rejecting the Bible's account of creation as given in Genesis eradicates the purpose for man's existence. The Book of Genesis explains the origins of sin, the curse, death, marriage, the family, government, and so on. It is foundational to understanding the gospel. Genesis is quoted more than sixty times in seventeen books of the New Testament.

4. According to Ken Ham, outside of Genesis 1, *yom* (the Hebrew word for "day") is used with a number 410 times, and each time it means an ordinary day. All 61 times "evening" or "morning" occurs outside of Genesis, it refers to an ordinary day. Outside of Genesis 1, each of the 53 times "night" is used with *yom* it means an ordinary day. Using the word "light"

with *yom* also indicates an ordinary day. Why would Genesis 1 be the exception to all these?

5. People choose to not believe in the Flood because it speaks of the judgment of God on sin.

LESSON 67

1. Something is incredibly complex when it requires several components to make it functional. If any one of these components is missing, it will not function and becomes worthless.

2. The eye cannot be reduced to anything less than what it is. It has thousands of co-equal functions to make it work. If we take away just one of those functions, the rest of the eye is worthless as an eye. Another example is the blood clotting process, which requires twelve specific individual chemical reactions in our blood. All twelve steps must occur in the right order or the person would bleed to death.

3. Darwin conceded the failure of his theory, admitting, "If it could be demonstrated that any complex organ existed which could not possibly have been formed by numerous, successive, slight modifications, my theory would absolutely break down."

4. S/A.

5. The prestigious body of evolutionists couldn't identify anything that they knew to be true about evolution, and in fact stated that it shouldn't be taught in high school.

LESSON 68

1. S/A.

2. The lack of intermediate life forms disproves the theory of evolution. If evolution were true, there should be millions of transitional life forms discovered in the fossil record. But despite spending hundreds of millions of dollars and more than a hundred years searching for fossils worldwide, scientists have failed to locate even one "missing link." Darwin's theory and the fossil record are in conflict.

3. The fossil record agrees with the Genesis account. Rather than the oldest rocks showing a gradual transition from primitive creatures to developed

forms, the oldest rocks show developed species suddenly appearing. There is a complete absence of intermediate fossils between species.

4. Piltdown Man, Nebraska Man, Java Man, Heidelberg Man, and Neanderthal Man have all been shown to be fully human or fully ape, and all involved either error or intentional fraud.

5. According to Dr. Kent Hovind, at least six different radiometric dating methods are used, depending on the assumed age of the sample. Scientists choose the method of dating that will give an age close to the desired result, and discard all results that do not match the assumed age.

LESSON 69

1. Someone who knows all things is "omniscient."

2. Thomas Edison said, "We do not know a millionth of one percent about anything."

3. An example of an absolute statement is, "There is no gold in China."

4. To make an absolute statement that is proven true, you would need to have absolute or total knowledge.

5. You don't need to have all knowledge to say, "There *is* gold in China." If there is even a speck of gold in the country, the statement is true.

6. "There is no God" is an absolute statement, which can be truthfully asserted only by one who has absolute knowledge. Only God is omniscient and therefore qualified to make such a statement.

7. An "agnostic" is one who claims to not know if God exists, or "one who professes ignorance."

8. Psalm 10:4 says that this ignorance is willful: "The wicked in his proud countenance does not seek God; God is in none of his thoughts."

LESSON 70

1. We know that there was a builder by the building itself. The building is proof that there was a builder. In fact, we couldn't want better evidence that there was a builder than to have the building in front of us.

2. The painting is perfectly positive proof that there was a painter. In fact, we couldn't want better evidence that there was a painter than to have the painting in front of us.

3. Since everything that was made has a maker, the creation itself proves, beyond the shadow of the smallest doubt, that there is a Creator.

4. All that is needed to figure this out are eyes that can see and a brain that works. Faith is not necessary.

5. We can recognize the existence of a Creator without having "faith" in Him, but we must exercise faith when we "come to God" (see Hebrews 11:6).

6. According to Romans 1:20, evidence of God—His eternal power and Godhead—is clearly seen in creation and is understood by the things that are made, so men are without excuse.

7. S/A.

LESSON 71

1. One must be omnipresent (dwelling everywhere at once) or omniscient to prove that God doesn't exist.

2. Whether "miracles" exist and whether prayers are answered or unanswered have no bearing on the existence of God because His existence is not dependent on any human testimony. God exists regardless of whether He chooses to move or not move in the way we desire.

3. "Idolatry" is the act of creating a god in our image, whether it is shaped with human hands (a physical "idol"), or shaped in the human mind through the imagination. Those who create their own god then use it as a "good-luck charm" to do their bidding.

4. The great deception of the idolater is thinking that their imaginary god really exists, and that Almighty God changes like pliable putty to whatever they visualize Him to be. However, our imaginings don't change reality. God doesn't change just because we change our perception of Him.

5. Malachi 3:6 says, "I am the LORD, I change not."

LESSON 72

1. Christianity is not a manmade "religion" in which man futilely tries to find peace with God; it is a personal relationship with the one true God. The Christian doesn't strive to have peace with his Creator, but received it in the Savior who forgave his sins.

2. According to Jesus, who is God, no other religion provides forgiveness of sins. Jesus said, "I am the way, the truth, and the life. No one comes to the

Father except through me" (John 14:6). The Bible says about Jesus, "There is one God and one Mediator between God and men, the Man Christ Jesus" (1 Timothy 2:5) and, "Nor is there salvation in any other, for there is no other name under heaven given among men by which we must be saved" (Acts 4:12).

3. We can know with our intellect that Christianity is true, regardless of our feelings, because the Bible's thousands of fulfilled prophecies, historical accuracy, and many infallible proofs attest to its reliability. In addition, if we repent and place our faith in Jesus Christ, Jesus promises that He and the Father will reveal themselves to all who love and obey Him.

4. God gave mankind the free will to choose whether to love and obey Him. He allows false religions and atheism to exist for the same reason He allows sinful humans to exist. God is not willing that any should perish, but wants all to come to repentance.

5. Since the Bible commands Christians to love their enemies and do good to those who spitefully use them, those who use Christianity for their own ends are not true followers of Jesus.

6. If one studies God's Word and understands His Law, Christianity is seen to be infinitely rational and believable, whereas atheism rejects logic and evidence. That's why God invites us, "Come now, and let us reason together," and why Paul spoke "words of truth and reason" when trying to persuade others to become Christians.

LESSON 73

1. A Christian has already been convinced that he was wrong, before his conversion. Conversion to Christianity is when a fallible human being admits that he is wrong and that the infallible Creator is right. When a person repents of his sin and places his trust in Jesus, he becomes spiritually alive; he has moved out of the realm of belief into the realm of experience. Once he knows the truth, nothing can convince him otherwise.

2. A cult is "a system of religious worship and ritual," which describes every manmade religion. Christianity, on the other hand, is not a strict adherence to ritual, but a personal relationship with a living God.

3. God's concern isn't whether people believe in Him; even the demons believe—and tremble. Even "moral" people have sinned by violating God's

holy Laws, and must repent and trust Jesus Christ for their salvation. All who refuse to do so will be given justice on Judgment Day.

4. If there were any such myths, they have died out for lack of proof. The story of Jesus' resurrection has endured through the ages in cultures all around the world because it is true and provable.

5. Although the "natural" man cannot understand the things of God, the Bible is very clear to those who obey Him. We can all understand enough to realize that we have sinned against a holy God and need to repent. Once we do that, God gives us the ability to understand His Word.

LESSON 74

1. Relativism is the philosophical position that all points of view are equally valid and that all truth is relative to the individual.

2. Cognitive relativism affirms that all truth is relative. No system of truth is more valid than any other and there is no objective standard of truth.

3. In moral or ethical relativism, all morals are relative to the social group in which they are constructed.

4. In situational relativism, or situational ethics, ethics (right and wrong) are dependent upon the situation.

5. Valid aspects of relativism include culturally based considerations such as which side of the road to drive on, how to rear children, and how to conduct burials and weddings. They are not universally right or wrong but are what that society determines.

6. There would be no common ground from which to judge what is right and wrong, or truth. If all moral views are equally valid, a society cannot determine right from wrong and establish punishment for wrongdoers.

LESSON 75

1. Science promotes the idea that it alone has the true answers. Many people have faith in science even when it cannot answer questions and when the "truths" of today change tomorrow. It thereby undermines absolute truth.

2. When the theory of evolution is believed, God becomes unnecessary. Without God to determine what is true and not true, we are free to do "what is right in our own eyes."

3. Encountering diverse cultures makes us more comfortable with the idea that there is more than one way to do something, more than one way for a culture to operate, more than one way for something to be true or right.

4. Cognitive relativism can easily be refuted by the absolute truth "Something cannot bring itself into existence." For something to bring itself into existence, it must first exist. If it first existed, then it cannot bring itself into existence because it already is existing. Likewise, if something does not exist, then it is not possible for it to bring itself into existence since it isn't there to do anything.

5. In order for something to be absolutely true, for everyone at all times, it must come from a source greater than ourselves. For truth beyond ourselves, we must look to God, the author of all truth.

LESSON 76

1. Reincarnation is attractive because it negates the concept of hell, so guilty sinners don't need to trust in Jesus. Also, individuals who don't "get it right" in this life can have multiple opportunities in future lives.

2. Actress Shirley Maclaine helped popularize reincarnation.

3. Orthodox Hinduism teaches that at death the soul goes into some other kind of body here on earth. This body can be an insect, fish, animal, or human body.

4. In the Western concept of reincarnation, the soul always progressively evolves up the scale of being, so humans can't regress back into an insect or animal body.

5. Karma is the principle that determines, on the basis of the good and evil you have done in previous lives, whether you will be reborn as rich or poor, healthy or handicapped, slave or master, etc. Eventually, with enough good karma, the individual progresses enough to be absorbed back into oneness.

6. The Bible doesn't teach that John the Baptist is a reincarnation of Elijah, but that John merely came "in the spirit and power of Elijah" (Luke 1:17). Also, since Elijah never died, he cannot be reincarnated.

LESSON 77

1. The Qur'an was supposedly dictated to Muhammad in Arabic by the angel Gabriel. It is considered God's precise words, and preexisted in heaven with God.

2. Muslims must abide by the "five pillars," and must believe in Allah, Muhammad's authority as a prophet, and the perfection of the Qur'an.

3. The "five pillars" require Muslims to do the following: declare that there is no God but Allah and Muhammad is his prophet; pray five times a day facing Mecca; give alms of 2.5%; fast during the month of Ramadan; and make at least one lifetime journey to Mecca.

4. They believe Allah is only one, and that the most serious sin is to consider god as more than one. They would therefore be very unreceptive to our belief in the Trinity—that God is three persons in one.

5. S/A.

6. S/A.

LESSON 78

1. Like Paul did with the men of Athens on Mars Hill, we can find common ground with Muslims to springboard into the gospel, rather than telling them where they are in error.

2. We agree that there is one God who is the Creator of all things; that Jesus of Nazareth was a prophet of God; and that Moses was a prophet of God.

3. We can identify it as the Law of the prophet Moses, quote how the prophet Jesus magnified the Law, and cite the Law of Moses as the standard by which they will be judged.

4. According to Psalm 49:7,8 and Surah 10:54 of the Qur'an, no amount of money is ever enough to pay the ransom to redeem a soul.

5. Only Jesus claimed that He had power on earth to forgive sins; no other prophet of any great religion—including Muhammad—ever made this claim. Only Jesus can provide peace with God.

LESSON 79

1. Hinduism was not founded by a single individual.

2. The Hindu scriptures are the Vedas, Upanishads, epics, Puranas, and the Bhagavad Gita.

3. Hindus view God as an impersonal and unknowable Ultimate Reality called Brahman, which some personalize as Brahma, Vishnu, and Shiva (Creator, Preserver, and Destroyer). They also personify the forces of nature (pantheism) and recognize 330 million gods.

4. They worship primarily as individuals, through a variety of means such as prayers, offerings, rituals, meditation, yoga, color symbolism, fasting, dance, chants, flowers, and incense.

5. Hindus don't believe that humanity's problem is sin, but is its ignorance about unity with the impersonal Ultimate Reality, the presence of desires, and avoidance of social duty. Christianity declares that sin is a willful rebellion against God and His Law.

6. Hindus believe that they will endure a cycle of reincarnations until they eventually end the illusion of personal existence and become one with the impersonal Ultimate Reality (Brahman).

LESSON 80

1. Siddhartha Gautama founded Buddhism because he couldn't reconcile the reality of suffering, judgment, and evil with the existence of a good and holy God. He therefore rejected the concept of a personal God.

2. "Buddha" means "the Enlightened One," and is a title given to Buddhism's founder.

3. The essential elements of Buddhism are summarized in the Four Noble Truths and the Noble Eightfold Path.

4. They believe that suffering is caused by craving, and that suffering will cease only when craving ceases, which they try to accomplish by following the Noble Eightfold Path. In the Bible God tells us that suffering is a result of man's sin, and that all suffering will cease in heaven for those who place their trust in Christ.

5. Their views are similar to the Hindus' in that individual selves do not truly exist (they're an illusion), they believe in karma and reincarnation, and the goal of life is eventually extinguishing personal existence.

6. S/A.

LESSON 81

1. Most of the manuscripts about the teachings of Buddha did not appear until nearly 1,000 years after his death, whereas the New Testament was written within 18 to 65 years of Jesus' death (see Lesson 47).

2. The Christian response to suffering is to take action to alleviate it, such as establish a hospital or give food to the hungry, whereas Siddhartha's response was to increase suffering by abandoning his wife and child.

3. The writer of this proverb wanted "neither poverty nor riches," but to rely on God to meet his needs and to be satisfied with whatever God gave him. When Siddhartha's desires were not met by either wealth or poverty, he became dissatisfied and looked not to God but to himself. He concluded that he should have no desires for himself, for his family, or for others.

4. S/A.

5. S/A.

6. Buddhism has a death-wish philosophy, does not enable people to cope with the real world, and encourages them to escape reality and live according to illusion.

LESSON 82

1. Mormonism, Jehovah's Witnesses, Christian Science, Unity, The Way International, and Unitarianism are all examples of cults.

2. A group is a non-Christian religion or cult if it either doesn't include the Bible in its set of authoritative scriptures, or it includes the Bible but distorts the key biblical doctrines.

3. An organization is a cult when it denies the essential doctrines of the Bible, such as the deity of Christ (which involves the Trinity), the resurrection of Jesus, and salvation by grace alone.

4. All cults believe that they must add their own works of righteousness to Jesus' sacrifice on the cross in order to be worthy of salvation.

5. Mormons believe that Jesus is the brother of the devil, begotten through sexual intercourse with a god from another planet. In Jehovah's Witnesses, He is Michael the Archangel who became a man. In the New Age Movement, Jesus is a man in tune with the divine consciousness.

6. Some of the errors cultists commit in interpreting Scripture are: 1) taking Scripture out of context; 2) reading into the Scriptures information that is not there; 3) picking and choosing only the Scriptures that suit their needs; 4) ignoring other explanations; 5) combining Scriptures that don't have anything to do with each other; 5) quoting a verse without giving its location; 6) incorrect definitions of key words; and 7) mistranslations.

LESSON 83

1. Unitarianism is the belief that God exists in one person, not three. It is a denial of the doctrine of the Trinity as well as the full divinity of Jesus.

2. Unitarians believe that human reason and experience should be the final authority in determining spiritual truth.

3. According to Unitarianism, Jesus *became* the Son of God at His baptism.

4. Unitarians believe that the Holy Spirit is not a person, and that He does not have a will.

LESSON 84

1. The Mormon church was founded by Joseph Smith after he claimed God visited him and directed him to establish the true church. Supposedly, all other churches were an abomination and corrupt.

2. The Bible says that if a prophet has even one prophecy fail, he is not a true prophet from God. Joseph Smith falsely predicted that a temple would be built in Independence, Mo., within his lifetime; therefore, he is a false prophet.

3. Mormons believe that the Holy Ghost, Jesus Christ, and "Heavenly Father" comprise three separate and distinct gods.

4. Rather than viewing Jesus as God, who is Spirit and was incarnated in a physical body through a virgin birth, they view him as a God's literal, physical son. They believe His death guaranteed immortality to everyone, whereas the Bible says that only those who repent and place their trust in Him will be saved.

5. Faithful Mormons will achieve the status of Elohim, will be exalted to godhood, and will be given their own world over which they will exercise dominion.

6. Mormons hope to achieve their salvation through faith in the God of Mormonism and the LDS church, plus a variety of works: baptism; abstaining from alcohol, tobacco, and caffeine; tithing; attending weekly sacrament meetings; supporting the Mormon prophet; doing temple works; and actively supporting the church.

7. S/A.

LESSON 85

1. Be aware that Mormons will often agree when we use words such as "salvation," "Savior," or "going to heaven," but their understanding of the words differs from the biblical meaning. We should be careful to use language that they can understand, and that will reveal the basis for their salvation.

2. Many Mormons are under great stress because they're taught that perfection is an attainable goal. We can talk about the imputed perfection we have received through Jesus.

3. Because the Mormon church has greatly watered down the concept of sin, God's Holy Law will enable them to become conscious of their sin. It will help them see the impossibility of their becoming perfect and the severity of their predicament.

4. Mormons believe that almost everyone will go to one of three kingdoms of heaven; they are not taught the concept of eternal suffering in hell.

5. Since Mormons assume they will go to heaven, it's eye-opening to them when we lovingly but firmly say that they will go to "outer darkness" because of their sins. They are often shocked, but eager to know why we would say such a thing.

LESSON 86

1. S/A.

2. Arguing about beliefs will likely only frustrate them, whereas studying the Bible together allows everyone to prepare, ask questions, and discuss calmly. It also helps develop a caring, personal relationship.

3. JWs view Christians as lost souls who have been misled by the devil into worshiping a pagan three-headed deity.

4. Rather than believing in one God who exists in three Persons—Father, Son, and Holy Spirit—JWs believe that only God the Father is "Jehovah"; that Jesus Christ is Michael the archangel, a created being; and that the Holy Spirit is merely God's impersonal "active force."

5. S/A.

6. Once the JW realizes that the Watchtower Society has misled him, he will be open to listen to you share the truth, and once he knows who Jesus isn't, he will then be at a point to consider who Jesus really is.

LESSON 87

1. Their Bible, the *New World Translation*, has been revised to reflect their theology, and is biased against the deity of Jesus. Those who think they are reading the true Word of God will be deceived about who God is.

2. They believe God's only name is Jehovah, He has a spiritual body, and He is therefore not omnipresent. They deny the Trinity.

3. According to JWs, Jesus was a created being who existed in heaven with God (Jehovah); He was incarnated on earth then rose spiritually after His death; and He will come again to reign over the earth (not to judge it).

4. JWs believe that the dead go to Sheol, the grave of all mankind, and that the consciousness ends at death. Faithful JWs will inherit eternal life in heaven or on Paradise Earth; the disobedient will be annihilated. The Bible teaches that all souls are eternal, and will spend eternity either in heaven with God or in conscious torment in hell.

5. In order to be saved, JWs must have faith plus works: they must be baptized by immersion, be an active member of the WBTS, have righteous conduct, and be absolutely loyal to Jehovah. Even then, there is no assurance of salvation, only hope for a resurrection.

LESSON 88

1. Justification is a divine act where God declares the sinner to be innocent of his sins. It is a legal action in that God declares the sinner righteous— as though he has satisfied the Law of God.

2. Justification is accomplished entirely by Christ's shed blood and is a gift of grace that comes through faith. When we trust in Jesus' sacrifice for us on the cross, we are declared justified by God. The Bible states that justi-

fication is not by works, but by grace alone, through faith alone, in Christ alone.

3. Roman Catholic doctrine not only denies justification by faith alone but pronounces a curse of excommunication, of being outside the camp of Christ, on those who believe in salvation by grace through faith in Jesus alone.

4. Catholics hope to gain heaven as an eternal reward for their good works.

5. Those who try to earn salvation by their works will be in bondage to the Law and have a lack of assurance of salvation, will constantly worry about not being good enough, and will continually be in subjection to the church's teachings about what one must do to be saved.

6. Trying to earn forgiveness through practices such as empty repetition of words or "good" works is not only not endorsed anywhere in Scripture, it is condemned by the Bible.

LESSON 89

1. Oneness Pentecostals think Trinitarian Christians worship three separate gods, don't believe that Jesus was truly God, and therefore are not saved.

2. There is not a single verse in the Bible that states that one must speak in tongues to be saved.

3. Verses clearly teaching that Jesus did in fact exist before time began include John 1:15,31; 3:13,31; 6:33,38,41,46,51,57,58,62; 8:42; 13:3; and 16:27,28.

4. Jesus is referred to as "the Son" over 200 times; the Father is referred to as distinct from Jesus the Son over 200 times; and Jesus the Son and the Father are put side by side in the same verse over 50 times.

5. The New Testament mentions salvation by faith alone at least 60 times, without mentioning baptism as a requirement. Jesus Himself tells us to baptize "in the name of the Father, and of the Son, and of the Holy Spirit" (Matthew 28:19), which simply means "in the authority of."

LESSON 90

1. The ICC teaches that, in addition to having faith and repenting, salvation is achieved after becoming a "true" disciple, conforming one's lifestyle to their standards, and being baptized.

2. A prospective convert must be a "totally committed disciple" by completing ICC studies; agreeing to attend all services; promising to read the Bible daily; beginning to recruit others; agreeing to obey church leaders; giving tithes weekly; listing all sins ever committed and confessing them to a member; being "cut to the heart" by Christ's death for us; and being judged eligible by the leadership—*then* the individual can be "baptized into Christ."

3. According to Acts 8:36,37, if you believe with all your heart that Jesus Christ is the Son of God, you may be baptized.

4. Jesus' point in Matthew 28:18–20 was that the disciples were to preach the gospel to *all* nations—all other ethnic groups.

5. Unregenerate people cannot live the godly life of a disciple until after salvation, when the Holy Spirit comes to live within them and change them. Not only is it impossible, but it makes a mockery of God's grace.

LESSON 91

1. Jesus didn't return when William Miller predicted, so Hiram Edson had the thought that on that date something *did* happen—but instead of coming to earth, Jesus entered into the heavenly sanctuary to begin a second phase of His ministry. Ellen White, considered a prophet of God on a par with Samuel and Jeremiah, provides an "authoritative source of truth," yet plagiarizes and is frequently in error.

2. Seventh-Day Adventists believe that before Jesus came to earth, He was Michael the archangel. Some early SDAs claimed Jesus was not equal with the Father and has not always existed.

3. They believe in "soul sleep"—that there is no conscious existence after death. When Christ returns, the righteous will be resurrected and receive eternal life; after the millennium, the unrighteous will be resurrected and cast into the lake of fire where they will be annihilated.

4. The Bible consistently says that the mark of the beast will be given to those "who worship the beast and his image"—not to those who worship God on a particular day, as the SDAs teach.

5. They state that salvation is by faith, yet they advocate obeying the Old Testament laws such as keeping the Sabbath and abiding by dietary laws —faith plus works.

LESSON 92

1. The New Age Movement is difficult to define because there is no hierarchy, dogma, doctrine, collection plate, or membership. It is an assortment of different theologies with the common threads of toleration and divergence weaving through its tapestry of "universal truth."

2. In the New Age Movement, man is central. He is viewed as divine, as co-creator, as the hope for future peace and harmony. Man's nature is good and divine.

3. God is not a personal heavenly Father but an impersonal force. God is all and all is God. God is not separate from the creation, but part of everything that exists.

4. NAM states that there is no sin, only incorrect understanding of truth. Knowledge is what saves, not Jesus.

5. Salvation in the NAM means to be in tune with the divine consciousness, in harmony with reality and whatever is perceived to be true. It is self-achieved through understanding your natural godlikeness and goodness, combined with proper knowledge.

6. Two basic beliefs of the NAM are evolutionary godhood and global unity.

LESSON 93

1. Upon conversion, God puts His Law into our minds, gives us the "mind of Christ," and renews us in the "spirit of our mind."

2. If we are walking in the Spirit, with our sinful nature crucified, we can be assured that the desires we now have are in line with God's desires.

3. According to Psalm 37:4, if we delight ourselves in the Lord, the desires of our heart should be in line with God's desires—primarily to seek and save that which is lost.

4. We can learn that God will honor our desire to follow Jesus, even if it means walking on water to get to Him.

LESSON 94

1. S/A.

2. S/A.

3. S/A.

LESSON 95

1. Some people who do well at school but then fizzle have an inflated ego, and are not happy playing second fiddle to anyone. Their pride leads to their downfall.

2. The first key to being a successful Christian is to learn self-discipline.

3. Self-discipline for a Christian involves daily reading and obeying of the Bible, listening to the guidance of our conscience and God's Spirit, and self-denial—submitting our will to God's.

4. S/A.

5. According to James 5:12 and Psalm 15:4, we should always follow through with what we said we would do and keep our word even when it may seem to hurt us.

LESSON 96

1. Pride is a sin that will keep multitudes from repenting so they may enter the kingdom of heaven. It also keeps spouses from admitting that they are wrong, so they would rather destroy their family than humble themselves.

2. The Lordship of Christ means we give up our "rights"; we live life on His terms, not ours, and we give our allegiance to Him alone. We do things His way.

3. When we surrender our lives to the Lord, we also surrender the job of vengeance to Him. We are not to take matters into our own hands when we are wronged, but are to give it all to God in prayer and let Him in His perfect judgment decide what to do.

4. S/A.

5. S/A.

6. When Jesus was wronged, He committed Himself to Him who judges righteously (the Father).

LESSON 97

1. Prayer has ignited every revival fire in history.

2. S/A.

3. S/A.

4. Our flesh resists travailing prayer. We're too busy; we give other things higher priority. We're undisciplined.

5. Many are praying for revival, but not sharing their faith. They are substituting prayer for a move of God, for obedience to the Word of God.

6. True prayer is a travail of the soul, a groaning empathy. But then it tells the dead to "Come forth."

LESSON 98

1. When God's people sanctified themselves, when they searched their hearts with a tender conscience to see if they harbored any secret sin, it preceded a move of God's Spirit.

2. S/A.

3. If we are calling upon God even with great anguish, yet fail to receive anything, it might be that our prayers are unanswered because of sin. The Bible says that our iniquities will keep God from hearing us.

4. We can ask in faith and expect answers if we uncover our sin, make straight the crooked ways, and gather out the stones in our hearts.

5. S/A.

LESSON 99

1. Spurgeon described zeal as having sleepless hours, weeping eyes, and bursting hearts for the lost. The heart is heavy with grief and vehement in desire, yet beats with holy ardor and pants for God's glory.

2. Awaiting Paul in every city he was about to visit were bonds and afflictions.

3. S/A.

4. Paul had a courageous, joyful resignation to the will of God. Because he was crucified to the world and its pleasures, he didn't count his life dear to himself, but joyfully finished the course God set for him.

5. S/A.

6. When we see ourselves as hell-deserving sinners and appreciate the fact that we are heading for an undeserved heaven, we will be bursting with love, gratitude, and zeal for God.

LESSON 100

1. If they are not laboring in the harvest fields themselves, they will feel guilty or uncomfortable praying for laborers. Instead, they will pray for God to move so they won't have to. They find it easier to talk to God about men than to talk to men about God.

2. S/A.

3. Those who have a thorough understanding of what they have been saved *from* will know what they are saved *for*. The Law makes grace abound in the heart and feeds a zeal to do God's will.

4. We should encourage the preaching of future punishment because without the threat of Judgment Day and the horrifying reality of hell, no one will flee from the wrath to come.

5. Philippians 2:15 instructs Christians to be in, but not of the world: "That you may be blameless and harmless, the sons of God, without rebuke, in the midst of a crooked and perverse nation, among whom you shine as lights in the world." We should be friends of sinners so we can lead them to the Savior.

LESSON 101

1. S/A.

2. S/A.

3. S/A.

Recommended Resources

I f you would like more information to help you better defend the Christian faith, understand other religions, and know your rights in the public square, consult any of the following resources.

Books

Christian Apologetics

Armstrong, John, ed. *Roman Catholicism: Evangelical Protestants Analyze What Divides and Unites Us.* Moody Publishers, 1999.

Craig, William Lane. *Reasonable Faith: Christian Truth and Apologetics.* Crossway Books, 1994.

Geisler, Norman L. *Baker Encyclopedia of Christian Apologetics.* Baker Book House, 1999.

Geisler, Norman L., and Ralph E. MacKenzie. *Roman Catholics and Evangelicals: Agreements and Differences.* Baker Book House, 1995.

Geisler, Norman L., and Ronald M. Brooks. *When Skeptics Ask.* Chariot Victor Books, 1990.

Lochaas, Philip H. *How to Respond to Secular Humanism.* Concordia Publishing House, 1991.

Martin, Walter. *Kingdom of the Cults.* Bethany House, 2002.

McDowell, Josh. *Evidence That Demands a Verdict.* Thomas Nelson, 1999.

———. *He Walked Among Us: Evidence for the Historical Jesus.* Thomas Nelson, 1993.

———. *The Resurrection Factor.* Thomas Nelson, 1993.

Montgomery, John Warwick, ed. *Evidence for Faith.* Probe Books, 1991.

Moreland, J. P. *Scaling the Secular City: A Defense of Christianity.* Baker Book House, 1987.

Rhodes, Ron. *Reasoning from the Scriptures with the Jehovah's Witnesses.* Harvest House Publishers, 1993.

Sproul, R. C. *Reason to Believe.* Zondervan, 1982.

Van Til, Cornelius. *Christian Apologetics.* P & R Press, 2003.

———. *The Defense of the Faith.* P & R Press, 1980.

Vos, Howard F. *Can I Really Believe?* World Publications Inc., 1995.

Zacharias, Ravi. *A Shattered Visage: The Real Face of Atheism.* Baker Book House, 1993.

———. *Can Man Live Without God?* Word Publishing, 1996.

Evangelism

Comfort, Ray. *Hell's Best Kept Secret.* Whitaker House, 1989.

———. *How to Win Souls and Influence People.* Bridge-Logos Publishers, 2000.

———. *The Evidence Bible.* Bridge-Logos Publishers, 2001.

———. *The Way of the Master.* Tyndale, 2004.

The Trinity

McGrath, Alister E. *Understanding Jesus.* Zondervan, 1990.

———. *Understanding the Trinity.* Zondervan, 1990.

Morey, Robert. *Trinity: Evidence and Issues.* Riverside World, 1996.

Doctrine of Scripture

Archer, Gleason L. *Encyclopedia of Bible Difficulties.* Zondervan, 1982.

Bruce, F. F. *The Canon of Scripture.* Intervarsity Press, 1988.

Geisler, Norman L., and Thomas Howe. *When Critics Ask: A Popular Handbook on Bible Difficulties.* Baker Book House, 1992.

Geisler, Norman L., and William E. Nix. *A General Introduction to the Bible.* Moody Press, 1986.

Doctrine of Salvation

Alleine, Joseph. *A Sure Guide to Heaven.* Banner of Truth, 1989.

Lloyd-Jones, D. Martyn. *The Plight of Man and the Power of God.* Baker Book House, 1982.

Piper, John. *Future Grace.* Multnomah Publishers, 1998.

Sproul, R. C. *Faith Alone: The Evangelical Doctrine of Justification.* Baker Book House, 1995.

Spurgeon, Charles H. *All of Grace.* Moody Publishers, 1984.

Watson, Thomas. *The Doctrine of Repentance.* Banner of Truth, 1988.

Whitefield, George. *The Lord Our Righteousness.* Evangelical Press, 1997.

Mormonism

McKeever, Bill. *Answering Mormons' Questions.* Bethany House, 1991.

Morey, Robert A. *How to Answer a Mormon.* Bethany House, 1983.

Reed, David A., and John R. Farkas. *Mormons: Answered Verse by Verse.* Baker Book House, 1992.

Rhodes, Ron. *Reasoning from the Scriptures with the Mormons.* Harvest House Publishers, 1995.

Islam

Geisler, Norman L., and Abdul Saleeb. *Answering Islam: The Crescent in Light of the Cross.* Baker Book House, 2002.

Morey, Dr. Robert. *The Islamic Invasion.* Harvest House Publishers, Inc., 1992.

WEBSITES

Cults and Apologetics

Christian Apologetics and Research Ministry: www.carm.org

Christian Research Institute: www.equip.org

Stand to Reason: www.str.org

Christian Answers: www.christiananswers.net

Ankerberg Theological Research Institute: www.johnankerberg.org

Archaeology

Bible Archaeology Search & Exploration Institute: www.baseinstitute.org

Scrolls from the Dead Sea: www.ibiblio.org/expo/deadsea.scrolls.exhibit/
intro.html

Evolution

Creation Science Evangelism: www.drdino.com

Answers in Genesis: www.answersingenesis.org

Institute for Creation Research: www.icr.org

The Biblical Creation Society: www.biblicalcreation.org.uk

The True Origin Archive: www.trueorigin.org

Legal Rights

American Center for Law and Justice: www.aclj.org

Christian Law Assocation: www.christianlaw.org

Jehovah's Witnesses

Watch the Tower: Official Website of Ex-Jehovah's Witnesses:
www.geocities.com/heartland/2919/main2.html

Mormonism

Mormonism Research Ministry: www.mrm.org

Why Are You LDS?: www.yrulds.com

Utah Lighthouse Ministry: www.utlm.org

Islam

Answering Islam: A Christian-Muslim Dialogue: www.answering-islam.org

The Good Way: www.the-good-way.com

Islam Review: www.islamreview.com

Memorizing and Remembering Scripture

I t's important for all Christians to have the Word of God hidden in their hearts. However, just as with witnessing, we all know we should do it, but we often don't know how. There are a number of ways to memorize the Word of God. The following is one suggestion, and is the method I use.

On a 3×5 index card, write out the memory verse. On the top left, write a topic to categorize the verse, and on the top right, record the verse reference. Place the reference again under the verse.

Read the verse two or three times out loud. Pay attention to the sound of the verse, and listen for any helpful memory aids, such as words in alphabetical order.

As you begin to memorize the verse, say the Topic > Reference > Verse > Reference, one portion at a time. Here's an example:

God's Love
Romans 5:8
"But God demonstrates His own love"
Romans 5:8

God's Love
Romans 5:8
"But God demonstrates His own love for us in this:"
Romans 5:8

God's Love
Romans 5:8
"But God demonstrates his own love for us in this: While we were still sinners"
Romans 5:8

God's Love
Romans 5:8
"But God demonstrates his own love for us in this: While we were still sinners, Christ died for us."
Romans 5:8

Repeat each phrase until you can correctly quote everything up to that point. Then repeat the whole thing a few more times to get it lodged in your memory. Quote it throughout the day:

God's Love
Romans 5:8
"But God demonstrates his own love for us in this: While we were still sinners, Christ died for us."
Romans 5:8

Think about it as you lay down at night, and when you wake up in the morning.

You may also find it helpful to record, on the reverse side of the card, what the verse means to you and your meditations on the verse.

The Most Important Step: Review

It's very easy to memorize Scripture. It's not quite as easy, however, to remember what you memorized last week...or even three days ago—not to mention what you memorized six months ago.

To help you recall them, you may want to carry about twenty verses with you. After you have begun memorizing each new verse, add it to a keyring. Review these verses daily during your quiet time, as well as when you stand in line, eat lunch, wait at a traffic light, etc.—anytime you have a free minute, you can quickly review one or two verses.

If you purchase an index card box and dividers, it will help you greatly (of course, you can make your own storage device if these are not available). Label the dividers as follows:

Sunday | Monday | Tuesday | Wednesday | Thursday | Friday | Saturday

Once you have about twenty cards on your keyring, remove the first one, which should now be well-memorized, and place it behind "Sunday." With the next verse you add to your keyring, remove the oldest, and place it behind "Monday." Do this with each new verse you add, removing the oldest, putting it in the next day of the week.

Now, every Sunday, take out the cards for "Sunday" and review them. On Monday, get the cards for "Monday." Each day of the week, you will now be reviewing the twenty verses that you carry with you, plus a new set of verses previously memorized. This will help the verses to become firmly lodged in your memory.

You may want to find a friend to help you practice reviewing your verses. As you recite each verse, your friend can make sure you say the complete verse and reference correctly.